Fixed-Income Securities

Wiley Finance Series

Fixed-Income Securities

Valuation, Risk Management and Portfolio Strategies

Lionel Martellini

Philippe Priaulet

and

Stéphane Priaulet

WILEY

Other Wiley Editorial Offices

John Wiley & Sons Inc., 111 River Street, Hoboken, NJ 07030, USA

Jossey-Bass, 989 Market Street, San Francisco, CA 94103-1741, USA

Wiley-VCH Verlag GmbH, Boschstr. 12, D-69469 Weinheim, Germany

John Wiley & Sons Australia Ltd, 33 Park Road, Milton, Queensland 4064, Australia

John Wiley & Sons (Asia) Pte Ltd, 2 Clementi Loop #02-01, Jin Xing Distripark, Singapore 129809

John Wiley & Sons Canada Ltd, 22 Worcester Road, Etobicoke, Ontario, Canada M9W 1L1

Wiley also publishes its books in a variety of electronic formats. Some content that appears
in print may not be available in electronic books.

The views, thoughts and opinions expressed in this book are those of the authors in their individual capacities and should
not in any way be attributed to Philippe Priaulet as a representative, officer or employee of HSBC-CCF.

The views, thoughts and opinions expressed in this book are those of the authors in their individual capacities and should
not in any way be attributed to Stéphane Priaulet as a representative, officer or employee of AXA.

Library of Congress Cataloging-in-Publication Data

Martellini, Lionel.
    Fixed-income securities : valuation, risk management, and portfolio strategies / Lionel
  Martellini, Philippe Priaulet, and Stéphane Priaulet
      p. cm.—(Wiley finance series)
  Includes bibliographical references and index.
  ISBN 0-470-85277-1 (pbk. : alk. paper)
  1. Fixed-income securities—Mathematical models. 2. Portfolio
  management—Mathematical models. 3. Bonds—Mathematical models. 4. Hedging
  (Finance)—Mathematical models. I. Priaulet, Philippe. II. Priaulet, Stéphane. III. Title. IV.
  Series.

  HG4650.M367 2003
  332.63′2044—dc21
                                      2003041167

British Library Cataloguing in Publication Data

A catalogue record for this book is available from the British Library

ISBN 978-0-470-85277-4

Typeset in 10/12.5pt Times by Laserwords Private Limited, Chennai, India

This book is printed on acid-free paper responsibly manufactured from sustainable forestry
in which at least two trees are planted for each one used for paper production.

To Adhara, Antonella, Calypso, Daphné, Isabelle and Manon

To our parents and families

To our friends

Contents

PART I
INVESTMENT ENVIRONMENT

PART II
TERM STRUCTURE OF INTEREST RATES

PART III
HEDGING INTEREST-RATE RISK

Contents

PART V
SWAPS AND FUTURES

PART VI
MODELING THE TERM STRUCTURE OF INTEREST RATES AND CREDIT SPREADS

PART VII

PLAIN VANILLA OPTIONS AND MORE EXOTIC DERIVATIVES

xiv

Contents

xvi

PART VIII
SECURITIZATION

About the Authors

Lionel Martellini is an Assistant Professor of Finance at the Marshall School of Business, University of Southern California, where he teaches "fixed-income securities" at the MBA level. He is also a research associate at the EDHEC Risk and Asset Management Research Center, and a member of the editorial boards of *The Journal of Bond Trading and Management* and *The Journal of Alternative Investments*. He holds master's degrees in business administration, economics, statistics and mathematics, as well as a Ph.D. in finance from the Haas School of Business, University of California at Berkeley. His expertise is in derivatives valuation and optimal portfolio strategies, and his research has been published in leading academic and practitioners' journals. He has also served as a consultant for various international institutions on these subjects.

Philippe Priaulet is a fixed-income strategist in charge of derivatives strategies for HSBC. His expertise is related to fixed-income asset management and derivatives pricing and hedging, and his research has been published in leading academic and practitioners' journals. Formerly, he was head of fixed-income research in the Research and Innovation Department of HSBC-CCF. He holds master's degrees in business administration and mathematics as well as a Ph.D. in financial economics from University Paris IX Dauphine. Member of the editorial board of *The Journal of Bond Trading and Management*, he is also an associate professor in the Department of Mathematics of the University of Evry Val d'Essonne and a lecturer at ENSAE, where he teaches "fixed-income securities" and "interest rate modeling".

Stéphane Priaulet is senior index portfolio manager in the Structured Asset Management Department at AXA Investment Managers. Previously, he was head of quantitative engineering in The Fixed Income Research Department at AXA Investment Managers. He also teaches "fixed-income securities" as a part-time lecturer at the University Paris Dauphine. He is a member of the editorial board of *The Journal of Bond Trading and Management*, where he has published several research papers. He holds a diploma from the HEC School of Management, with specialization in economics and finance, and has completed postgraduate studies in mathematics at the University Pierre et Marie Curie (Paris VI), with specialization in stochastic calculus.

Preface

Debt instruments have evolved beyond the straight bonds with simple cash-flow structures to securities with increasingly complex cash-flow structures that attract a wider range of investors and enable borrowers to reduce their costs of raising funds. In order to effectively employ portfolio strategies that may control interest-rate risk and/or enhance returns, investors must understand the forces that drive bond markets and the valuation of these complex securities and their derivative products.

What this Book is About

This book is about interest rates and risk management in bond markets. It develops insights into different bond portfolio strategies and illustrates how various types of derivative securities can be used to shift the risks associated with investing in fixed-income securities. It also provides extensive coverage on all sectors of the bond market and the techniques for valuing bonds.

While there certainly exists an impressive list of books that cover in some detail the issues related to bond and fixed-income derivative pricing and hedging, we just could not find, in existing textbooks, the same level of depth in the analysis of active and passive bond portfolio strategies. This is perhaps unfortunate because we have learnt a lot about active and passive bond portfolio strategies in the past thirty years or so. While no financial economist or practitioner in the industry would claim they have found a reliable model for the valuation of stocks, we indeed have reached a fairly high level of understanding on how, why and when to invest in bonds.

We have written this book in an attempt to achieve the following goal: provide the reader with a detailed exposure to modern state-of-the-art techniques for bond portfolio management. We cover not only traditional techniques used by mutual fund managers in the fixed-income area but also advanced techniques used by traders and hedge fund managers engaged in fixed-income or convertible arbitrage strategies.

More specifically, we attempt to achieve the following:

- *Describe important financial instruments that have market values that are sensitive to interest-rate movements. Specifically, the course will survey the following fixed-income assets and related securities: zero-coupon government bonds, coupon-bearing government bonds, corporate bonds, exchange-traded bond options, bonds with embedded options, floating-rate notes, caps, collars and floors, floating-rate notes with embedded options, forward contracts, interest-rate swaps, bond futures and options on bond futures, swaptions, credit derivatives, mortgage-backed securities, and so on.*

- *Develop tools to analyze interest-rate sensitivity and value fixed-income securities. Specifically, the course will survey the following tools for active and passive bond management:*

construction of discount functions, duration, convexity, and immunization; binomial trees for analysis of options; hedging with bond futures, using models of the term structure for pricing and hedging fixed-income securities; models for performance evaluation; systematic approach to timing; valuation of defaultable bonds; bonds with embedded options; interest-rate derivatives, and so on.

For the Reader

This book is original in that it aims at mixing theoretical and practical aspects of the question in a systematic way. This duality can be traced back to the professional orientations of the authors, who are active in both the academic and the industrial worlds. As such, this book can be of interest to both students and professionals from the banking industry. To reach the goal of providing the reader with a practical real-world approach to the subject, we have ensured that the book contains detailed presentations of each type of bond and includes a wide range of products. Extensive discussions include not only the instruments but also their investment characteristics, the state-of-the art technology for valuing them and portfolio strategies for using them. We make a systematic use of numerical examples to facilitate the understanding of these concepts.

The level of mathematical sophistication required for a good understanding of most of the material is relatively limited and essentially includes basic notions of calculus and statistics. When more sophisticated mathematical tools are needed, they are introduced in a progressive way and most really advanced material has been placed in dedicated appendices. As a result, the book is suited to students and professionals with various exposure to, or appetite for, a more quantitative treatment of financial concepts. Generally speaking, the material devoted to the modeling of the term structure and the pricing of interest-rate derivatives is more technical, even though we have consistently favored intuition and economic analysis over mathematical developments. Appendix 2 to Chapter 12, devoted to advanced mathematical tools for term-structure modeling, can be skipped by the nonquantitatively oriented reader without impeding his/her ability to understand the remaining six chapters.

For the Instructor

The book is complemented with a set of problems (more than 200 of them) and their solutions, posted on a dedicated website (www.wiley.co.uk/martellini), as well as a complete set of Excel illustrations and PowerPoint slides (more than 400 of them). This makes it ideally suited for a typical MBA audience, in the context of a basic or more advanced "Fixed-Income Security" course. It can also be used by undergraduate, graduate and doctoral students in finance.

The first nine chapters offer a detailed analysis of all issues related to bond markets, including institutional details, methods for constructing the yield curve and hedging interest-rate risk, as well as a detailed overview of active and passive bond portfolio strategies and performance evaluation. As such, they form a coherent whole that can be used for a shorter quarter course on the subject. Chapters 10 to 18 cover a whole range of fixed-income securities, including swaps, futures, options, and so on. This second half of the book provides a self-contained study of the modern approach for pricing and hedging fixed-income securities and interest-rate options. The text mostly focuses on the binomial approach to the pricing of fixed-income derivatives, providing cutting-edge theory and technique, but continuous-time models are also discussed and put in context. This material can be taught either in the context of an advanced fixed-income class or as the second half of a general semester course on fixed-income securities.

By the way, we are aware that "Martellini, Priaulet and Priaulet" is a long, funny-sounding reference name. Please feel free to refer our textbook to your students as MPP, or MP^2 (MP squared).

Acknowledgments

We would like to express our gratitude to a number of people who have provided invaluable feedback at different stages of the manuscript or helped in the publication process. We are particularly grateful to Noel Amenc, Tarek Amyuni, Yoann Bourgeois, Vicent Altur Brines, Moorad Choudhry, Christophe Huyghues-Despointes, Yonathan Ebguy, Rémy Lubeth, Victoria Moore, Moez Mrad, Daad Abou Saleh, Alexandre Van den Brande and Franck Viollet for their comments and suggestions.

Notation

This glossary contains some standard definitions and notations that are used throughout the book.

- α is the risk-adjusted expected return on a bond portfolio.

- β_0, β_1 and β_2 are the parameters measuring respectively the level, slope and curvature of the term structure in the Nelson and Siegel (1987) model.

- β_0, β_1, β_2 and β_3 are the parameters measuring respectively the level, slope and curvatures of the term structure in the Svensson (1994) model.

- Δ (delta) is a measure of the first-order sensitivity of an option price with respect to small changes in the value of the underlying rate or asset.

- γ (gamma) is a measure of the second-order sensitivity of an option price with respect to small changes in the value of the underlying rate or asset.

- $\gamma(t, T)$ is the volatility at date t of the instantaneous forward rate $f(t, T)$.

- $\sigma(t, T)$ is the volatility at date t of the zero-coupon bond $B(t, T)$.

- $\Phi(x)$ is the distribution function of a standardized Gaussian, that is, it is the probability that a normally distributed variable with a mean of zero and a standard deviation of 1 is less than x.

- $\Phi'(x)$ is the first derivative of Φ with respect to x.

- ν (vega) is a measure of the first-order sensitivity of an option price with respect to small changes in the volatility of the underlying rate or asset.

- ρ (rho) is a measure of the first-order sensitivity of an option price with respect to small changes in the interest rate.

- θ (theta) is a measure of the first-order sensitivity of an option price with respect to small changes in time to maturity.

- AC_t is the accrued interest on a bond at date t.

- BPV is the basis point value, which is the change in the bond (or bond portfolio) given a basis point change in the bond's (or bond portfolio) yield.

- $B(t, T)$ is the price at date t of a zero-coupon bond (also called a pure discount bond) maturing at time $T \geq t$, that is, the price of a bond paying \$1 at date T and nothing before (no intermediate coupon payment).

- c is the coupon rate.

- $c(n)$ is the par yield for maturity n, that is, the annual coupon rate that should be paying an n-year maturity fixed bond with a \$100 face value so that it quotes at par.

xxviii

- CF_t is the cash flow at date t on a fixed-income security.

- $\mathbb{C}ov(X, Y)$ is the covariance between the two stochastic variables X and Y.

- CPI_t is the Consumer Price Index on date t.

- $\$Conv$ is the dollar convexity of a bond or a bond portfolio; it is a measure of the second-order absolute sensitivity of a bond or bond portfolio with respect to small changes in the yield to maturity.

- D is the (Macaulay) duration of a bond or bond portfolio, that is, a measure of its weighted average maturity, where the weights are proportional to the size of the cash flows.

- $\$Dur$ is the dollar duration of a bond or a bond portfolio; it is a measure of the first-order absolute sensitivity of a bond or bond portfolio with respect to small changes in the yield to maturity.

- $\mathbb{E}(X)$ is the mean of the stochastic variable X.

- F_t is the price of a futures contract at date t.

- $f(t, s)$ is an instantaneous (continuously compounded) forward rate as seen from date t and starting at date s.

- $F(t, s, T - s)$ is a forward zero-coupon rate as seen from date t, starting at date s and with residual maturity $T - s$ (or equivalently with maturity date T).

- $F^c(t, s, T - s)$ is a continuously compounded forward zero-coupon rate as seen from date t, starting at date s and with residual maturity $T - s$ (or equivalently with maturity date T).

- FV is the face value of a bond.

- IP is the invoice price, that is, the price that the buyer of a futures contract must pay to the seller when a bond is delivered.

- $M^\top$ is the transpose of matrix M.

- M^{-1} is the inverse matrix of matrix M.

- MD is the modified duration of a bond or a bond portfolio; it is a measure of the relative first-order sensitivity of a bond or bond portfolio with respect to small changes in the yield to maturity.

- p_t is the instantaneous probability of default at date t on a corporate bond.

- P_t is the market price of a bond or bond portfolio at date t.

- $\hat{P}_t$ is the theoretical price of a bond or bond portfolio at date t, that is, the price that is obtained from a model of the term structure.

- r_t is a spot rate; it can be regarded as the continuously compounded internal rate of return on a zero-coupon bond with infinitesimal residual maturity.

- $R(t, \theta)$ is a zero-coupon rate (pure discount rate), starting at date t for a residual maturity of θ years (or equivalently maturing at date $t + \theta$).

- $R^c(t, \theta)$ *is a continuously compounded zero-coupon rate, starting at date t with residual maturity* θ *(or equivalently with maturity date* $t + \theta$ *).*

- *RC is the relative convexity of a bond or a bond portfolio; it is a measure of the relative second-order sensitivity of a bond or bond portfolio with respect to small changes in the yield to maturity.*

- *TE is the tracking error, that is, the standard deviation of the difference between the return on the portfolio and that of the benchmark; it is a measure of the quality of replication in the context of a bond indexing strategy.*

- $\mathbb{V}ar(X)$ *is the variance of the stochastic variable X.*

- $V(t, \theta)$ *is the volatility at date t of the zero-coupon rate with maturity* $t + \theta$.

- *W is a Brownian motion, a process with independent normally distributed increments.*

- $[X - K]^+ = Max[X - K; 0]$

- *y is the yield to maturity (YTM), that is, the single rate that sets the present value of the cash flows equal to the bond price.*

- y_c *is the current yield, that is, the coupon payment divided by the bond price.*

- y_d *is the yield on a discount basis.*

- y_m *is the yield on a money-market basis.*

Investment Environment

PART I

1 Bonds and Money-Market Instruments

Fixed-income markets are populated with a vast range of instruments. In the present chapter, we provide a typology of the most simple of these instruments, namely bonds and money-market instruments, and describe their general characteristics.

1.1 Bonds

1.1.1 General Characteristics of Bonds

Definition of a Standard Bond

A debt security, or a bond, is a financial claim by which the issuer, or the borrower, is committed to paying back to the bondholder, or the lender, the cash amount borrowed, called *principal*, plus periodic interests calculated on this amount during a given period of time. It can have either a standard or a nonstandard structure. A standard bond is a fixed-coupon bond without any embedded option, delivering its coupons on periodic dates and principal on the maturity date.

For example, a US Treasury bond with coupon 3.5%, maturity date 11/15/2006 and a nominal issued amount of $18.8 billion pays a semiannual interest of $329 million ($18.8 billion $\times$ 3.5%/2) every six months until 11/15/2006 included, as well as $18.8 billion on the maturity date. Another example would be a Euro Treasury bond with coupon 4%, maturity date 07/04/2009 and a nominal issued amount of Eur11 billion, which pays an annual interest of Eur440 million (Eur11 billion $\times$ 4%) every year until 07/04/2009 included, as well as Eur11 billion on the maturity date.

The purpose of a bond issuer (the Treasury Department, a government entity or a corporation) is to finance its budget or investment projects (construction of roads, schools, development of new products, new plants) at an interest rate that is expected to be lower than the return rate of investment (at least in the private sector). Through the issuance of bonds, it has a direct access to the market, and so avoids borrowing from investment banks at higher interest rates. In the context of financial disintermediation, this practice tends to increase rapidly. One point to underscore is that the bondholder has the status of a creditor, unlike the equity holder who has the status of an owner of the issuing corporation. This is by the way the reason why a bond is, generally speaking, less risky than an equity.

Terminology and Convention

A bond issue is characterized by the following components:

- **The issuer's name**   *For example, Bundesrepublik Deutschland for a Treasury bond issued in Germany.*
- **The issuer's type**   *This is mainly the sector it belongs to: for example, the oil sector, if Total Fina Elf is the bond issuer.*

- *The market in which the bond is issued*   *It can be the US domestic market, the Euro zone domestic market, the domestic market of any country, the eurodollar market, which corresponds to bonds denominated in USD and issued in any other country than the US.*

- *The issuer's domicile*

- *The bond's currency denomination*   *An example is US$ for a US Treasury bond.*

- *The method used for the calculation of the bond price/yield*   *The method depends on the bond category. For US Treasury bonds, the method used is the street convention, which is the standard calculation method used by the market.*

- *The type of guarantee*   *This is the type of underlying guarantee for the holder of the security. The guarantee type can be a mortgage, an automobile loan, a government guarantee...*

- *The maturity date*   *This is the date on which the principal amount is due.*

- *The coupon type*   *It can be fixed, floating, a multicoupon (a mix of fixed and floating or different fixed). For example, a step-up coupon bond is a kind of multicoupon bond with a coupon rate that increases at predetermined intervals.*

- *The coupon rate*   *It is expressed in percentage of the principal amount.*

- *The coupon frequency*   *The coupon frequency for Treasury bonds is semiannual in the United States, the United Kingdom and Japan, and annual in the Euro zone, except for Italy where it is semiannual.*

- *The day-count type*   *The most common types are Actual/Actual, Actual/365, Actual/360 and 30/360. Actual/Actual (Actual/365, Actual/360) means that the accrued interest between two given dates is calculated using the exact number of calendar days between the two dates divided by the exact number of calendar days of the ongoing year (365, 360). 30/360 means that the number of calendar days between the two dates is computed assuming that each month counts as 30 days. For example, using the 30/360 day-count basis, there are 84 days ($2 \times 30 + 24$) from 01/01/2001 to 03/25/2001 and 335 ($11 \times 30 + 5$) from 01/01/2001 to 12/06/2001. Using the Actual/Actual or Actual/365 day-count basis, there are 83 days from 01/01/2001 to 03/25/2001 and 339 days from 01/01/2001 to 12/06/2001. Using the Actual/Actual day-count basis, the period from 08/01/1999 to 09/03/2001 converted in years is $\frac{152}{365} + 1 + \frac{246}{365} = 2.0904$. Using the Actual/365 day-count basis, the period from 08/01/1999 to 09/03/2001 converted in years is $764/365 = 2.0931$. Using the Actual/360 day-count basis, the period from 08/01/1999 to 09/03/2001 converted in years is $764/360 = 2.1222$. Using the 30/360 day-count basis, the period from 08/01/1999 to 09/03/2001 converted in years is $752/360 = 2.0888$.*

- *The announcement date*   *This is the date on which the bond is announced and offered to the public.*

- *The interest accrual date*   *This is the date when interest begins to accrue.*

- *The settlement date*   *This is the date on which payment is due in exchange for the bond. It is generally equal to the trade date plus a number of working days. For example, in Japan, the settlement date for Treasury bonds and T-bills is equal to the trade date plus three working days. On the other hand, in the United States, the settlement date for Treasury bonds and T-bills is equal to the trade date plus one working day. In the United Kingdom, the settlement date for Treasury bonds and T-bills is equal to the trade date plus one and two working days, respectively. In the Euro zone, the settlement date for Treasury bonds is equal to the trade date plus three working days, as it can be one, two or three workings days for T-bills, depending on the country under consideration.*

- **The first coupon date**   This is the date of the first interest payment.

- **The issuance price**   This is the percentage price paid at issuance.

- **The spread at issuance**   This is the spread in basis points to the benchmark Treasury bond (see the next section called "Market Quotes").

- **The identifying code**   The most popular ones are the ISIN (International Securities Identification Number) and the CUSIP (Committee on Uniform Securities Identification Procedures) numbers.

- **The rating**   The task of rating agencies' consists in assessing the default probability of corporations through what is known as rating. A rating is a ranking of a bond's quality, based on criteria such as the issuer's reputation, management, balance sheet, and its record in paying interest and principal. The two major ones are Moody's and Standard and Poor's (S&P). Their rating scales are listed in Table 1.1. We get back to these issues in more details in Chapter 13.

Table 1.1   Moody's and S&P's Rating Scales.

Moody's	S&P	Definition
Investment Grade (High Creditworthiness)		
Aaa	AAA	Gilt-edged, best quality, extremely strong creditworthiness
Aa1	AA+	
Aa2	AA	Very high grade, high quality, very strong creditworthiness
Aa3	AA−	
A1	A+	
A2	A	Upper medium grade, strong creditworthiness
A3	A−	
Baa1	BBB+	
Baa2	BBB	Lower medium grade, adequate creditworthiness
Baa3	BBB−	
Speculative Grade (Low Creditworthiness)		
Ba1	BB+	
Ba2	BB	Low grade, speculative, vulnerable to nonpayment
Ba3	BB−	
B1	B+	
B2	B	Highly speculative, more vulnerable to nonpayment
B3	B−	
	CCC+	
Caa	CCC	Substantial risk, in poor standing, currently vulnerable to nonpayment
	CCC−	
Ca	CC	May be in default, extremely speculative, currently highly vulnerable to nonpayment
C	C	Even more speculative
	D	Default

Note: The modifiers 1, 2, 3 or +, − account for relative standing within the major rating categories.

- **The total issued amount** *It appears in thousands of the issuance currency on Bloomberg.*

- **The outstanding amount** *This is the amount of the issue still outstanding, which appears in thousands of the issuance currency on Bloomberg.*

- **The minimum amount and minimum increment that can be purchased** *The minimum increment is the smallest additional amount of a security that can be bought above the minimum amount.*

- **The par amount or nominal amount or principal amount** *This is the face value of the bond. Note that the nominal amount is used to calculate the coupon bond. For example, consider a bond with a fixed 5% coupon rate and a $1,000 nominal amount. The coupon is equal to $5\% \times \$1,000 = \$50$.*

- **The redemption value** *Expressed in percentage of the nominal amount, it is the price at which the bond is redeemed on the maturity date. In most cases, the redemption value is equal to 100% of the bond nominal amount.*

We give hereafter some examples of a Bloomberg bond description screen (DES function), for Treasury and corporate bonds.

Example 1.1   A US T-Bond Description on Bloomberg

The T-bond (Figure 1.1), with coupon rate 3.5% and maturity date 11/15/2006, bears a semiannual coupon with an Actual/Actual day-count basis. The issued amount is equal to $18.8 billion; so is the outstanding amount. The minimum amount that can be purchased is equal to $1,000. The T-bond was issued on 11/15/01 on the US market, and interests began to accrue from this date on. The price at issuance was 99.469. The first coupon date is 05/15/02, that is, 6 months after the interest accrual date (semiannual coupon). This bond has a AAA rating.

Example 1.2   A German Government Bond Description on Bloomberg

In comparison with the previous US T-bond, the German T-bond (called *Bund*) (Figure 1.2) with coupon rate 4% and maturity date 07/04/2009 has an annual coupon with an Actual/Actual day-count basis. It was issued on the market of the Euro zone, for an amount of Eur11 billion, on 03/26/1999. The price at issuance was 100.17. The minimum amount that can be purchased is equal to Eur0.01. The first coupon date was 07/04/2000. The minimum amount that can be purchased is equal to Eur0.01. This bond has a AAA rating.

Example 1.3   An Elf Aquitaine Corporate Bond Description on Bloomberg

In comparison with the two previous bonds, the Elf Aquitaine (now Total Fina Elf) bond (Figure 1.3) has a Aa2 Moody's rating. It belongs to the oil sector. The issued amount is

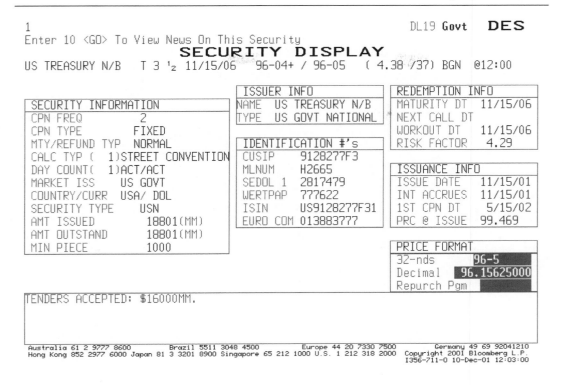

```
1                                                    DL19 Govt   DES
Enter 10 <GO> To View News On This Security
                    SECURITY DISPLAY
US TREASURY N/B   T 3 ½ 11/15/06   96-04+ / 96-05   ( 4.38 /37) BGN  @12:00

                     ┌─ISSUER INFO──────────┐ ┌─REDEMPTION INFO────────┐
┌─SECURITY INFORMATION──────┐│NAME  US TREASURY N/B  │ │MATURITY DT  11/15/06   │
│CPN FREQ         2          ││TYPE  US GOVT NATIONAL │ │NEXT CALL DT            │
│CPN TYPE       FIXED        │└──────────────────────┘ │WORKOUT DT   11/15/06   │
│MTY/REFUND TYP  NORMAL      │┌─IDENTIFICATION #'s────┐ │RISK FACTOR  4.29       │
│CALC TYP (  1)STREET CONVENTION│CUSIP     9128277F3  │ └────────────────────────┘
│DAY COUNT(  1)ACT/ACT       ││MLNUM     H2665        │ ┌─ISSUANCE INFO──────────┐
│MARKET ISS    US GOVT       ││SEDOL 1   2817479      │ │ISSUE DATE   11/15/01   │
│COUNTRY/CURR  USA/ DOL      ││WERTPAP   777622       │ │INT ACCRUES  11/15/01   │
│SECURITY TYPE   USN         ││ISIN      US9128277F31 │ │1ST CPN DT    5/15/02   │
│AMT ISSUED      18801(MM)   ││EURO COM  013883777    │ │PRC @ ISSUE   99.469    │
│AMT OUTSTAND    18801(MM)   │└──────────────────────┘ └────────────────────────┘
│MIN PIECE       1000        │                         ┌─PRICE FORMAT───────────┐
└───────────────────────────┘                         │32-nds        96-5      │
                                                       │Decimal   96.15625000   │
                                                       │Repurch Pgm             │
                                                       └────────────────────────┘
TENDERS ACCEPTED: $16000MM.

Australia 61 2 9777 8600        Brazil 5511 3048 4500    Europe 44 20 7330 7500      Germany 49 69 92041210
Hong Kong 852 2977 6000 Japan 81 3 3201 8900 Singapore 65 212 1000 U.S. 1 212 318 2000  Copyright 2001 Bloomberg L.P.
                                                                                     I356-711-0 10-Dec-01 12:03:00
```

Figure 1.1 © 2003 Bloomberg L.P. All rights reserved. Reprinted with permission.

Eur1 billion and the minimum purchasable amount is Eur1,000. The price at issuance was 98.666. It delivers an annual fixed 4.5% coupon rate. Its maturity date is 03/23/09. Its spread at issuance amounted to 39 basis points over the French T-bond (Obligation Assimilable du Trésor (OAT)) with coupon 4% and maturity date 04/25/2009.

Market Quotes

Bond securities are usually quoted in price, yield or spread over an underlying benchmark bond.

Bond Quoted Price   The quoted price (or market price) of a bond is usually its *clean price*, that is, its *gross price* minus the *accrued interest*. We give hereafter a definition of these words. Note first that the price of a bond is always expressed in percentage of its nominal amount.[1] When an investor purchases a bond, he is actually entitled to receive all the future cash flows of this bond, until he no longer owns it. If he buys the bond between two coupon payment dates, he logically must pay it at a price reflecting the fraction of the next coupon that the seller of the bond is entitled to receive for having held it until the sale. This price is called the *gross price* (or *dirty price* or

---

[1] When the bond price is given as a $ (or Eur or £ . . .) amount, it is directly the nominal amount of the bond multiplied by the price in % of the nominal amount.

```
1                                                    DL19 Corp   DES
SECURITY DESCRIPTION                       Page 1/ 1
DEUTSCHLAND REP   DBR 4 07/04/09      95.6300/95.6900   (4.70/4.69) BGN  @11:55
┌─ISSUER INFORMATION────────┐┌─IDENTIFIERS───────────┐ 1) Additional Sec Info
│Name BUNDESREPUB. DEUTSCHLAND││Common    009612181   │ 2) Identifiers
│Type Sovereign              ││ISIN      DE0001135119 │ 3) Ratings
│Market of Issue EURO-ZONE   ││Wertpap.  113511       │ 4) Fees/Restrictions
├─SECURITY INFORMATION───────┤├─RATINGS───────────────┤ 5) Custom Notes
│Country DE      Currency EUR││Moody's     Aaa        │ 6) Issuer Information
│Collateral Type BONDS       ││S&P         AAA        │ 7) ALLQ
│Calc Typ( 60)GERMAN BONDS   ││Composite   AAA        │ 8) Pricing Sources
│Maturity   7/ 4/2009 Series 99├─ISSUE SIZE───────────┤ 9) Related Securities
│NORMAL                      ││Amt Issued             │10) Executable Prices
│Coupon  4          FIXED    ││EUR 11,000,000   (M)   │
│ANNUAL       ACT/ACT        ││Amt Outstanding        │
│Announcement Dt   3/26/99   ││EUR 11,000,000   (M)   │
│Int. Accrual Dt   3/26/99   ││Min Piece/Increment    │
│1st Settle Date   3/26/99   ││        0.01/     0.01 │
│1st Coupon Date   7/ 4/00   ││Par Amount        0.01 │
│Iss Pr 100.1700             │├─BOOK RUNNER/EXCHANGE──┤
│                            ││                       │65) Old DES
│NO PROSPECTUS               ││ALL GERMAN SE          │66) Send as Attachment
└────────────────────────────┘└───────────────────────┘
€1.7211BLN RETAINED FOR MKT INTERVENTION. LONG 1ST CPN. ADD'L €5BLN ISS'D 4/99 @
101.11% & €1BLN ISS'D 6/99.
Australia 61 2 9777 8600        Brazil 5511 3048 4500        Europe 44 20 7330 7500      Germany 49 69 92041210
Hong Kong 852 2977 6000 Japan 81 3 3201 8900 Singapore 65 212 1000 U.S. 1 212 318 2000 Copyright 2001 Bloomberg L.P.
                                                                              I356-711-0 10-Dec-01 12:04:50
```

Figure 1.2   © 2003 Bloomberg L.P. All rights reserved. Reprinted with permission.

full price). It is computed as the sum of the clean price and the portion of the coupon that is due to the seller of the bond. This portion is called the *accrued interest*. Note that the accrued interest is computed from the settlement date on.

Example 1.4 An investor buys on 12/10/01 a given amount of the US Treasury bond with coupon 3.5% and maturity 11/15/2006. The current clean price is 96.15625. Hence the market value of $1 million face value of this bond is equal to 96.15625% × $1 million = $961,562.5. The accrued interest period is equal to 26 days. Indeed, this is the number of calendar days between the settlement date (12/11/2001) and the last coupon payment date (11/15/2001). Hence the accrued interest is equal to the last coupon payment (1.75, because the coupon frequency is semiannual) times 26 divided by the number of calendar days between the next coupon payment date (05/15/2002) and the last coupon payment date (11/15/2001). In this case, the accrued interest is equal to $1.75 \times (26/181) = 0.25138$. The gross price is then 96.40763. The investor will pay $964,076.3 (96.40763% × $1 million) to buy this bond.

Note that the *clean price* of a bond is equal to the gross price on each coupon payment date and that US bond prices are commonly quoted in /32ths.

1   DL19 Corp   **DES**

SECURITY DESCRIPTION   Page 1/ 1
ELF AQUITAINE   FPFP 4 ¹₂ 03/09   95.7440/96.2440   (5.21/5.13) BGN @12/07

ISSUER INFORMATION	IDENTIFIERS	1) Additional Sec Info
Name ELF AQUITAINE	Common 009552197	2) Identifiers
Type Oil Comp-Integrated	ISIN XS0095521976	3) Ratings
Market of Issue EURO-ZONE	French 049452	* 4) Fees/Restrictions
SECURITY INFORMATION	RATINGS	5) Sec. Specific News
Country FR Currency EUR	Moody's Aa2	6) Involved Parties
Collateral Type SR UNSUB	S&P NR	7) Custom Notes
Calc Typ(962)STREET CONVENTION	Composite AA2	8) Issuer Information
Maturity 3/23/2009 Series	ISSUE SIZE	9) ALLQ
NORMAL	Amt Issued	10) Pricing Sources
Coupon 4 ¹₂ FIXED	EUR 1,000,000 (M)	11) Related Securities
ANNUAL ACT/ACT	Amt Outstanding	12) Executable Prices
Announcement Dt 3/ 4/99	EUR 1,000,000 (M)	13) Issuer Web Page
Int. Accrual Dt 3/23/99	Min Piece/Increment	
1st Settle Date 3/23/99	1,000.00/ 1,000.00	
1st Coupon Date 3/23/00	Par Amount 1,000.00	
Iss Pr 98.6660 Reoffer 98.666	BOOK RUNNER/EXCHANGE	
SPR @ FPR 39.0 vs FRTR 4 04/09	BNP,GS	65) Old DES
NO PROSPECTUS	LONDON	66) Send as Attachment

UNSEC'D. SEASONED EFF 5/02/99.

Australia 61 2 9777 8600   Brazil 5511 3048 4500   Europe 44 20 7330 7500   Germany 49 69 92041210
Hong Kong 852 2977 6000 Japan 81 3 3201 8900 Singapore 65 212 1000 U.S. 1 212 318 2000 Copyright 2001 Bloomberg L.P.
                                                          I356-711-0 10-Dec-01 12:06:00

Figure 1.3   © 2003 Bloomberg L.P. All rights reserved. Reprinted with permission.

Example 1.5 A T-bond quoting a price of 98–28 has actually a price of $98 + 28/32 = 98.875$.

Bond Quoted Yield   The quoted yield of a bond is the discount yield that equalizes its gross price times its nominal amount to the sum of its discounted cash flows (see Chapter 2 for a mathematical definition of a bond yield and for calculations).

Example 1.6   Bond Yield Quotes on Bloomberg

In the previous example, the cash flow schedule of the bond with $1 million face value is the following:

Date	Cash flow	Date	Cash flow	Date	Cash flow	Date	Cash flow
05/15/02	17,500	11/15/03	17,500	05/15/05	17,500	05/15/06	17,500
11/15/02	17,500	05/15/04	17,500	11/15/05	17,500	11/15/06	1,017,500
05/15/03	17,500	11/15/04	17,500				

Fixed Income Securities

```
YA                                           DL19 Govt  YA
Enter all values and hit <GO>.
              YIELD  ANALYSIS        CUSIP     9128277F3
US TREASURY N/B   T 3 ½ 11/15/06  96-04+ / 96-05  ( 4.38 /37) BGN
                                                      @12:00
PRICE 96-5            SETTLEMENT DATE 12/11/2001
YIELD              MATURITY   CASHFLOW ANALYSIS
CALCULATIONS       11/15/2006 To 11/15/2006WORKOUT   1000M FACE
STREET CONVENTION        4.375    PAYMENT INVOICE
TREASURY CONVENTION      4.374  PRINCIPAL[RND(Y/N) N ]  961562.50
TRUE YIELD               4.375   26 DAYS ACCRUED INT     2513.81
EQUIVALENT  1 /YEAR COMPOUND 4.423 TOTAL               964076.31
JAPANESE YIELD (SIMPLE)  4.450       INCOME
PROCEEDS/MMKT EQUIVALENT        REDEMPTION VALUE      1000000.00
                                COUPON PAYMENT         175000.00
REPO EQUIVALENT          3.610  INTEREST @ 4.375 %      18270.91
EFFECTIVE @ 4.375 RATE(%) 4.375 TOTAL                 1193270.91
TAXED: INC 39.60 % CG 28.00 %  2.672      RETURN
*ISSUE PRICE = 99.469.  OID BOND WITH MARKET DISCOUNT.* GROSS PROFIT  229194.60
SENSITIVITY ANALYSIS            RETURN                   4.375
CNV DURATION(YEARS)      4.549
ADJ/MOD DURATION         4.452   FURTHER ANALYSIS
RISK                     4.292  HIT 1 <GO> COST OF CARRY
CONVEXITY                0.230  HIT 2 <GO> PRICE/YIELD TABLE
DOLLAR VALUE OF A  0.01  0.04292 HIT 3 <GO> TOTAL RETURN
YIELD VALUE OF A   0 3/2  0.00728
Australia 61 2 9777 8600     Brazil 5511 3048 4500   Europe 44 20 7330 7500    Germany 49 69 92041210
Hong Kong 852 2977 6000 Japan 81 3 3201 8900 Singapore 65 212 1000 U.S. 1 212 318 2000 Copyright 2001 Bloomberg L.P.
                                                               I356-711-0 10-Dec-01 12:09:13
```

Figure 1.4

The table hereafter shows the Bloomberg yield analysis screen (YA function) (Figure 1.4) associated with this bond. Its quoted yield is equal to 4.375% (see street convention). The equivalent 1-year compounded yield of this bond is equal to 4.423% (see Chapter 2 on this point).

Bond Quoted Spread   Corporate bonds are usually quoted in price and in spread over a given benchmark bond rather than in yield. So as to recover the corresponding yield, you simply have to add this spread to the yield of the underlying benchmark bond.

Example 1.7   The table hereafter gives an example of a bond yield and spread analysis as can be seen on a Bloomberg screen (Figure 1.5). The bond bears a spread of 156.4 basis points (see Interpolated Spread (ISPRD) function) over the interpolated US$ swap yield, whereas it bears a spread of 234 basis points over the interpolated US Treasury benchmark bond yield. Furthermore, its spread over the US Treasury benchmark bond with the nearest maturity amounts to 259.3 basis points (Spread (SPRD) function). It is 191 and 144 basis points over the 10-year Treasury benchmark bond and the 30-year Treasury benchmark bond, respectively.

```
YAS                                            DL19 Corp  YAS
Enter #<GO> for Detailed Analysis. Enter 99<GO> for Menu of Related Functions.
YIELD & SPREAD ANALYSIS              CUSIP345397GX  PCS BGN
FORD MOTOR CRED  F 6 ³₄ 08/15/08     98.1738/ 98.8405  (7.10/6.97) BGN MATRIX
    SETTLE 12/13/01    FACE AMT        1000 M  or PROCEEDS        1,010,529.66
1) YA        YIELDS        2) YASD  RISK &   F 6 ³₄ 08/15/08
PRICE 98.840466                      HEDGE     workout        HEDGE BOND
YIELD        6.968 Wst              RATIOS   8/15/08  OAS        OAS
 SPRD        259.30 bp  yld-decimals 3/3  Mod Dur  5.18   5.26      4.53
          versus                                   5.231  5.313     4.369
5yr  T 3 ¹₂ 11/15/06        BENCHMARK Convexity 0.33   0.34      0.24
    PRICE 96-5          Save  Delete   Workout HEDGE Amount:1,219 M
    YIELD      4.375 %     sd: 12/11/01  OAS HEDGE Amount:1,216 M
     Yields are: Semi-Annual
3) OAS         SPREADS       4) ASW  5) FPA        FINANCING
OAS: 241.0 CRV# CMT    VOL    Opt    Repo% 1.730  (360/365)360  Days  1
OAS: 160.5 CRV# I52                  Int Income   187.50      Carry P&L
ASSET SWAP: (A/A) 149.5  TED: -137.5  Fin Cost   -48.56        138.94
ISPRD 156.4 CRV# I52  US $ SWAP 30/360  Amortiz   -6.98<->     131.96
 Yield Curve: I25  US TREASURY ACTIVES  Forwrd Prc  98.826572
 + 234 v  6.7yr ( 4.625 %) INTERPOLATED  Prc Drop   0.013894
 + 259 v 5yr  ( 4.37) T 3 ¹₂ 11/15/06   Drop (bp)    0.25
 + 191 v 10yr ( 5.06) T 5 08/15/11  Accrued Interest  /100   2.212500
 + 144 v 30yr ( 5.52) T 5 ³₈ 02/15/31  Number Of Days Accrued  118
Australia 61 2 9777 8600      Brazil 5511 3048 4500    Europe 44 20 7330 7500    Germany 49 69 92041210
Hong Kong 852 2977 6000 Japan 81 3 3201 8900 Singapore 65 212 1000 U.S. 1 212 318 2000  Copyright 2001 Bloomberg L.P.
                                                                  I356-711-0 10-Dec-01 12:08:05
```

Figure 1.5 © 2003 Bloomberg L.P. All rights reserved. Reprinted with permission.

Note that this last way of quoting spreads over treasury bonds is fairly common on bond markets. Indeed, in this case the underlying treasury bond is clearly identified, whereas using an interpolation on the treasury bond curve may lead to different results depending on the two bonds as well as the kind of interpolation considered. To finish, it is worth mentioning that every traded bond has a bid as well as an ask quoted price. The bid price is the price at which an investor can sell a bond, whereas the ask price is the price at which he can buy it. The ask price is of course higher than the bid price, which means that the ask yield is lower than the bid yield. The difference between the two yields is known as the bid–ask spread. It is a kind of transaction cost. It is very small for liquid bonds such as US or Euro Treasury bonds and is large for fairly illiquid bonds. The bond's mid price is simply the average of its bid and ask prices. The same holds for the mid yield.

Example 1.8 Illustration of the Bid–Ask Price Spread on the US T-Bond Market

The following Bloomberg screen (Figure 1.6) provides the bid–ask spread price for some of the US T-bonds quoted on the market. In columns 2 and 3, you can see the coupon rate and the maturity of the instrument. The bid–ask spread appears in the next two columns. Note that prices are quoted in 32ths. The sixth column gives the yield to maturity (YTM) for each instrument (see Chapter 2 for large developments concerning the yield to maturity)

Fixed Income Securities

```
<HELP> for explanation.                              N200 Govt
ENTER # <GOVT> <GO> TO SELECT SECURITY
              GOVERNMENT    SECURITIES           Page 13of 14
          SECURITY                 BID     ASK    YTM    DUR   RISK PSRC
 1) US TREASURY N/B   8 7⁄8   11/15/98
 2) US TREASURY N/B   8 7⁄8    2/15/99
 3) US TREASURY N/B   8 7⁄8    5/15/00
 4) US TREASURY N/B   8 7⁄8    8/15/17   135-17  135-19  5.49   9.80  12.99 BGN
 5) US TREASURY N/B   8 7⁄8    2/15/19   137-2+  137-4+  5.53  10.34  13.85 BGN
 6) US TREASURY N/B   9         5/15/98
 7) US TREASURY N/B   9        11/15/18  138-8   138-10  5.52  10.06  13.82 BGN
 8) US TREASURY N/B   9 1⁄8    5/15/99
 9) US TREASURY N/B   9 1⁄8    5/15/09   112-5   112-6+  7.04   5.68   6.31 BGN
10) US TREASURY N/B   9 1⁄8    5/15/18   139-3+  139-5+  5.51   9.87  13.63 BGN
11) US TREASURY N/B   9 1⁄4    8/15/98
12) US TREASURY N/B   9 1⁄4    2/15/16   137-24+ 137-26+ 5.43   9.15  12.33 BGN
13) US TREASURY N/B   9 3⁄8    2/15/06   119-13  119-14  4.50   3.78   4.44 BGN
14) US TREASURY N/B   9 7⁄8   11/15/15   143-27  143-29  5.40   8.80  12.59 BGN
15) US TREASURY N/B  10         5/15/10  118-12  118-13+ 7.12   6.09   7.14 BGN
16) US TREASURY N/B  10 3⁄8   11/15/09   117-17  117-18+ 7.46   5.77   6.72 BGN
17) US TREASURY N/B  10 3⁄8   11/15/12   128-21  128-23  6.69   7.23   9.23 BGN
18) US TREASURY N/B  10 5⁄8    8/15/15   150-27  150-29  5.39   8.72  12.87 BGN
19) US TREASURY N/B  10 3⁄4    2/15/03   109-27  109-28  3.65   1.37   1.49 BGN
20) US TREASURY N/B  10 3⁄4    5/15/03   111-12+ 111-13+ 3.71   1.55   1.75 BGN
21) US TREASURY N/B  10 3⁄4    8/15/05   122-15  122-16  4.46   3.37   4.06 BGN
Australia 61 2 9277 8655      Brazil 5511 3048 4500     Europe 44 20 7330 7575      Germany 49 69 92041210
Hong Kong 852 2977 6200 Japan 81 3 3201 8880 Singapore 65 212 1234 U.S. 1 212 318 2000  Copyright 2001 Bloomberg L.P.
                                                                    I708-368-0 05-Sep-01 16:06:18
```

Figure 1.6

as the seventh column provides the duration (see Chapter 5). The pricing source is BGN (Bloomberg Generic Value). It is the average of the prices given by the five most active providers in the market.

Nonstandard Bonds

We discuss hereafter strips, floating-rate notes and inflation-indexed bonds. Convertible bonds and bonds with embedded options are discussed in depth in Chapter 14.

Strips   Strips (Separate Trading of Registered Interest and Principal) are zero-coupon bonds mainly created by stripping government bonds of the G7 countries.[2] The strips program was created in 1985 by the US Treasury Department in response to investment banks who, in the early 1980s, had been buying long-term Treasury bonds and then issuing their own zero-coupon bonds, collateralized by the payments on the underlying Treasury bonds. These so-called trademark zeros were a success, but because of the higher liquidity of strips, they were dominated by them.

The only cash flow distributed by strips is the principal on the maturity date.

---

[2]Strips are also traded in other countries and in New Zealand, in particular.

Example 1.9 An investor buys for $20,000 the Treasury strip bond with maturity 05/15/30 and nominal amount $100,000. As a bondholder, he is entitled to receive back $100,000 on 05/15/30, if he has of course not sold the bond meanwhile.

Such a bond that yields no coupon interest over the investment period may seem rather peculiar and unattractive. In fact, it typically bears interest on the maturity date as it is bought at a price that is lower than its maturity price. The investors who buy these bonds are usually long-term investors like pension funds and insurance companies, and have at least one main purpose, which is securing a return over their long-term investment horizon. To understand this point, consider an investor who is supposed to guarantee 6% per annum over 20 years on its liabilities. If he buys and holds a strip with a maturity equal to its investment horizon, that is 20 years, and a YTM of 6%, he perfectly meets his objective because he knows today the return per annum on that bond, which is 6%. In contrast, coupon-bearing bonds do not allow him to do so, because first they bear an interest reinvestment risk and second their duration hardly ever, if not never, reaches 20 years (see Chapter 5 on this point).

There exist two types of strips—coupon strips and principal strips. Coupon strips and principal strips are built by stripping the coupons and the principal of a coupon-bearing bond, respectively. The main candidates for stripping are government bonds (Treasury bonds and government agency bonds).

Strips are not as liquid as coupon-bearing bonds. Their bid–ask spread is usually higher.

Floating-Rate Notes

Definition and Characteristics Floating-Rate Notes (FRN) are bond securities that bear floating coupon rates. Actually, this generic denomination encompasses two categories of bonds:

- *Floating-rate bonds*
- *Variable-rate bonds or adjustable-rate bonds.*

The former category denotes bonds whose coupon rates are indexed on a short-term reference with a maturity inferior to 1 year, like the 3-month Libor, whereas the latter designates bonds whose coupon rates are indexed on a longer-term reference with a maturity superior to 1 year, like the 10-year Constant Maturity Treasury (CMT) bond yield (see the following example entitled "The French 10-Year CMT Bond Description on Bloomberg"). The coupons of floating-rate bonds are reset more than once a year. This is not necessarily the case for variable-rate bonds, which may have a reset frequency exceeding 1 year. Usually, the reset frequency is equal to the coupon payment frequency.

Furthermore, FRNs differ from each other as regards the nature of the coupon rate indexation. Coupon rates can be determined in three ways:

- *First, as the product of the last reference index value and a multiplicative margin.*
- *Second, as the sum of the last reference index value and an additive margin.*
- *Third, as a mix of the two previous methods.*

Note that when the sign of the multiplicative margin is negative, the bond is called *an inverse floater*. The coupon rate moves in the opposite direction to the reference index. So as to prevent it from becoming negative, a floor is determined that is usually equal to zero. Such bonds have become fairly popular under a context of decreasing interest rates. Let us now develop some examples.

Example 1.10   An investor buying a floating-rate bond whose coupon rate is equal to 3-month Libor+20 bp is entitled to receive, every period determined in the contract (usually every 3 months), a coupon payment inversely proportional to its annual frequency and principal payment on the maturity date. The coupon rate will be reset every 3 months in order to reflect the new level of the 3-month Libor.

Example 1.11   An investor buying an inverse floater whose coupon rate is equal to $16\% - 2x$, where x is the 2-year T-Bond yield, is entitled to receive, every period determined in the contract (usually every year), a coupon payment inversely proportional to its annual frequency and principal payment on the maturity date. The coupon rate will be reset every 2 years in order to reflect the new level of the 2-year bond yield.

Example 1.12   The French 10-Year CMT Bond Description on Bloomberg

The French 10-year CMT bond (Figure 1.7) with maturity date 10/25/2006 bears a quarterly floating coupon that is indexed on TEC 10. TEC 10 is a French 10-year Constant Maturity Treasury reference. It is determined on a daily basis as the 10-year interpolated yield between two active Treasury bond yields with very close maturity dates. The coupon rate is equal to TEC10 − 100 bp and entitles the bondholder to receive every quarter on January 25th, April 25th, July 25th and September 25th a coupon payment equal to $(1 + \text{TEC10} - 100\text{ bp})^{\frac{1}{4}} - 1$, and principal payment on 10/25/2006. Coupon rates are reset every quarter with an Actual/Actual day-count basis. For example, the coupon paid on April 25th is determined using the TEC 10 index five working days before January 25th. The issued amount is equal to Eur11.888 billion, like the outstanding amount. The minimum amount that can be purchased is equal to Eur1. The bond was issued in the Euro zone. It has a AAA rating. Its price at issuance was 101.55. The bid−ask prices on 12/13/01 were 99.504/99.5665.

Uses   When buying a FRN, an investor is typically hedged against parallel shifts of the interest-rate curve because the coupons of the bond reflect the new level of market interest rates on each reset date. So, FRNs usually outperform fixed-rate bonds with the same maturity when interest rates shift upwards and underperform them when interest rates shift downwards. Regarding inverse floaters, the issue is more complex because of the way they are structured. A decrease in interest rates will not necessarily result in the price appreciation of inverse floaters despite the increase in the coupon rate. Their performance depends actually on the evolution of the interest-rate curve shape.

1   DL19 Corp   **DES**

SECURITY DESCRIPTION   Redenominates on **1/ 1/99**
FRANCE O.A.T.   FRTR Float 10/06   99.5040/99.5665   BGN @12/12

ISSUER INFORMATION	IDENTIFIERS	1) Euro Redenomination
Name FRANCE (GOVT OF)	Common 008960194	2) Additional Sec Info
Type Sovereign	ISIN FR0000570541	3) Floating Rates
Market of Issue EURO-ZONE	French 057054	4) Identifiers
SECURITY INFORMATION	RATINGS	5) Ratings
Country FR Currency EUR	Moody's Aaa	6) Custom Notes
Collateral Type BONDS	S&P AAA	7) Issuer Information
Calc Typ(624)TEC10:FFR VAR NOTE	Composite AAA	8) ALLQ
Maturity 10/25/2006 Series TC10	ISSUE SIZE	9) Pricing Sources
NORMAL	Amt Issued	10) Related Securities
Coupon3.76 FLOATING QUARTLY	EUR 11,887,669 (M)	
TEC10 -100 ACT/ACT	Amt Outstanding	
Announcement Dt 4/12/96	EUR 11,887,669 (M)	
Int. Accrual Dt 4/25/96	Min Piece/Increment	
1st Settle Date 4/25/96	1.00/ 1.00	
1st Coupon Date 7/25/96	Par Amount 1.00	
Iss Pr 101.5500	BOOK RUNNER/EXCHANGE	
	BNP/CDC	65) Old DES
NO PROSPECTUS	EURONEXT-PARIS	66) Send as Attachment

CPN RATE=TEC10 -100BP. ORIG Ffr18BLN ISS'D 4/25/96. ADD'L Ffr8.155BLN ISS'D
5/24/96,Ffr7.146BLN 6/25/96,Ffr6.124BLN 7/96,Ffr8.916 9/96,Ffr8.264 10/96,Ffr8.32BLN

Australia 61 2 9777 8600   Brazil 5511 3048 4500   Europe 44 20 7330 7500   Germany 49 69 92041210
Hong Kong 852 2977 6000 Japan 81 3 3201 8900 Singapore 65 212 1000 U.S. 1 212 318 2000 Copyright 2001 Bloomberg L.P.
                                                                          I356-711-1 13-Dec-01 17:45:44

Figure 1.7 © 2003 Bloomberg L.P. All rights reserved. Reprinted with permission.

Inflation-Indexed Bonds

Definition and Characteristics   Inflation-indexed bonds deliver coupons and principal that are indexed on the future inflation rates. They are structured so as to protect and increase an investor's purchasing power. They are mainly issued by governments to make it clear that they are willing to maintain a low inflation level. They are more developed in the United Kingdom where they represent over 20% of outstanding treasury bonds. In the United States, they represented only 7% of the issued treasury debt in 1999. In France, there were only three inflation-indexed bonds (OATi) in December 2001.

The inflation rate between date t and date $t + 1$, denoted by $IR_{t,t+1}$, is defined as

$$IR_{t,t+1} = \frac{CPI_{t+1}}{CPI_t} - 1$$

where CPI_t is the consumer price index on date t.

The major characteristic of inflation-indexed bonds is that they deliver coupons and redemption values linked to the increase in the CPI index. We treat hereafter the case of French Treasury inflation-indexed bonds called *OATi*:

- *The daily inflation reference on date t, denoted by DIR_t, is computed by using a linear interpolation of two CPIs as follows:*

$$DIR_t = CPI_{m-3} + \frac{nt - 1}{ND_m} \times (CPI_{m-2} - CPI_{m-3})$$

where

CPI_m is the consumer price index of month m.

ND_m is the number of days of month m.

nt is the day of date t (for example, the day of 04/26/01 is 26).

- The coupon payment of an OATi received on date t, denoted by C_t, is

$$C_t = FV \times RC \times \left(\frac{DIR_t}{DIR_{initial}}\right)$$

where

FV is the face value

RC is the real coupon

$DIR_{initial}$ is the daily inflation reference on the initial date, which is a date varying with each OATi.

Example 1.13   The initial date of the OATi maturing on 07/25/29 is 07/25/99.

- The redemption value of an OATi received on date T, denoted by RV_T, is obtained using the following formula:

$$RV_T = FV \times \left(\frac{DIR_T}{DIR_{initial}}\right)$$

- The accrued interest of an OATi on date t, denoted by AC_t, is

$$AC_t = FV \times RC \times \frac{number\ of\ accrued\ days}{actual\ number\ of\ days\ of\ the\ coupon\ period} \times \left(\frac{DIR_t}{DIR_{initial}}\right)$$

Example 1.14   A French Inflation-Indexed Treasury Bond Description on Bloomberg

The OATi, with real coupon 3% and maturity date 07/25/2012, bears an annual coupon with an Actual/Actual day-count basis. The issued amount is equal to Eur6.5 billion, like the outstanding amount. The minimum amount that can be purchased is equal to Eur1. The first coupon date is 07/25/02. This bond has a AAA rating. The bid–ask price on 12/13/01 was 99.09/99.22 (Figure 1.8).

Uses   An inflation-indexed bond can be used to hedge a portfolio, to diversify a portfolio or to optimize asset–liability management.

- When buying an inflation-indexed bond, an investor is typically hedged against a rise in the inflation rate.

- This product presents a weak correlation with other assets such as stocks, fixed-coupon bonds and cash, which makes it an efficient asset to diversify a portfolio.

1   DL19 Corp   **DES**

```
SECURITY DESCRIPTION                    Page 1/ 1
FRANCE O.A.T.I/L FRTR 3 07/25/12    99.0900/99.2200    (3.10/3.09) BGN  @17:20
┌─────────────────────────────┬──────────────────────┬──────────────────────────┐
│ ISSUER INFORMATION          │ IDENTIFIERS          │ 1) Additional Sec Info   │
│ Name FRANCE (GOVT OF)       │ Common    013817669  │ 2) Identifiers           │
│ Type Sovereign              │ ISIN    FR0000188013 │ 3) Ratings               │
│ Market of Issue EURO-ZONE   │ French    018801     │ 4) Sec. Specific News    │
│ SECURITY INFORMATION        │ RATINGS              │ 5) Involved Parties      │
│ Country FR     Currency EUR │ Moody's    NA        │ 6) Custom Notes          │
│ Collateral Type DEBENTURES  │ S&P        NA        │ 7) Issuer Information     │
│ Calc Typ( 864)FRANCE I/L:STREET │ Fitch   NA        │ 8) ALLQ                  │
│ Maturity  7/25/2012 Series OATe │ ISSUE SIZE        │ 9) Pricing Sources       │
│ NORMAL                      │ Amt Issued           │ 10) Related Securities   │
│ Coupon  3          FIXED    │ EUR  6,500,000  (M)  │                          │
│ ANNUAL       ACT/ACT        │ Amt Outstanding      │                          │
│ Announcement Dt 10/23/01    │ EUR  6,500,000  (M)  │                          │
│ Int. Accrual Dt  7/25/01    │ Min Piece/Increment  │                          │
│ 1st Settle Date 10/31/01    │     1.00/    1.00    │                          │
│ 1st Coupon Date  7/25/02    │ Par Amount     1.00  │                          │
│ Iss Pr 100.1730             │ BOOK RUNNER/EXCHANGE │                          │
│                             │ BARCLY,DB,SG         │ 65) Old DES              │
│ NO PROSPECTUS               │ EURONEXT-PARIS       │ 66) Send as Attachment   │
└─────────────────────────────┴──────────────────────┴──────────────────────────┘
EURO-ZONE INFLATION INDEX LINKED BOND (INDEX LINKED TO CPXTEMU).

Australia 61 2 9777 8600      Brazil 5511 3048 4500      Europe 44 20 7330 7500      Germany 49 69 92041210
Hong Kong 852 2977 6000 Japan 81 3 3201 8900 Singapore 65 212 1000 U.S. 1 212 318 2000 Copyright 2001 Bloomberg L.P.
                                                                   I356-711-0 13-Dec-01 19:00:11
```

Figure 1.8 © 2003 Bloomberg L.P. All rights reserved. Reprinted with permission.

- *Insurance companies can use this product to hedge inflation risk between the time a sinister appears and the time it is paid to the client; some pension funds guarantee a performance indexed on inflation to their clients, and so buy inflation-indexed bonds to reduce the mismatch between assets and liabilities.*

1.1.2 Bonds by Issuers

Government and Municipal Bonds

Main Characteristics of the US Market

- *Government securities can be divided into two categories: Treasury securities and Federal Agency securities. We treat the US case below.*

  - *Treasury securities are issued by the US Department of the Treasury and backed by the full faith and credit of the US government. The Treasury market is the most active market in the world, thanks to the large volume of total debt and the large size of any single issue. The amount of outstanding marketable US Treasury securities is huge, with $3.0 trillion as of December 31, 2000. The Treasury market is the most liquid debt market, that is, the one where pricing and trading are most efficient. The bid–ask spread is by far lower than in the rest of the bond market. Recently issued Treasury securities are referred to as on-the-run securities, as opposed to off-the-run securities, which are old issued securities.*

Special mention must be made of benchmark securities, which are recognized as market indicators. There typically exists one such security on each of the following curve points: 2 years, 5 years, 10 years and 30 years. As they are overliquid, they trade richer than all their direct neighbors.

Example 1.15 On 12/07/2001, the 5-year US Treasury benchmark bond had a coupon of 3.5% and a maturity date equal to 11/15/2006. It had been issued on 11/15/2001. In contrast, a 5-year off-the-run US T-bond had a coupon of 7% and a maturity date equal to 07/15/2006. Its issuance date was 07/15/1996. Note the difference of coupon level between the two. There are two reasons for that: first, the 5-year off-the-run T-bond was originally a 10-year T-bond. Its coupon reflected the level of 10-year yields at that time. Second, the level of the US government yield curve on 07/15/96 was at least 200 basis points over the level of the US government yield curve on 11/15/2001. Furthermore, on 12/07/2001, the yield of the off-the-run bond was 4.48% as opposed to a yield of 4.45% for the benchmark bond, which illustrates the relative richness of the latter (see Chapter 2 for more details about the notion of bond yield).

- *Agency securities are issued by different organizations, seven of which dominate the market in terms of outstanding debt: the Federal National Mortgage Association (Fannie Mae), the Federal Home Loan Bank System (FHLBS), the Federal Home Loan Mortgage Corporation (Freddie Mac), the Farm Credit System (FCS), the Student Loan Marketing Association (Sallie Mae), the Resolution Funding Corporation (REFCO) and the Tennessee Valley Authority (TVA). Agencies have at least two common features. First, they were created to fulfill a public purpose. For example, Fannie Mae and Freddie Mac aim to provide liquidity for the residential mortgage market. The FCS aims at supporting agricultural and rural lending. REFCO aims to provide financing to resolve thrift crises. Second, the debt of most agencies is not guaranteed by the US government. Whereas federally sponsored agency securities (Fannie Mae, FHLBS, Freddie Mac, FCS, Sallie Mae, REFCO) are generally not backed by the full faith and credit of the US government, and so contain a credit premium, federally related institution securities (GNMA: Government National Mortgage Association) are generally backed by the full faith and credit of the US government, but as they are relatively small issues, they contain a liquidity premium. Agencies are differently organized. While Fannie Mae, Freddie Mac and Sallie Mae are owned by private-sector shareholders, the Farm Credit System and the Federal Home Loan Bank System are cooperatives owned by the members and borrowers. One sizeable agency, the Tennessee Valley Authority, is owned by the US government.*

- *Municipal securities constitute the municipal market, that is, the market where state and local governments, such as counties, special districts, cities and towns, raise funds in order to finance projects for the public good such as schools, highways, hospitals, bridges and airports. Typically, bonds issued in this sector are exempt from federal income taxes, which makes this sector referred to as the tax-exempt sector. There are two generic types of municipal bonds: general obligation bonds and revenue bonds. The former have principal and interest secured by the full faith and credit of the issuer and are usually supported by either the issuer's unlimited or limited taxing*

Table 1.2 Sector Breakdown of the US Broad Investment-Grade Index as of June 30, 2001.

	Market weight (%)
Treasury	**25.81**
Government sponsored	**12.06**
● Agency	11.06
● Supranational	1.00
Collateralized	**36.96**
● Mortgage	36.13
● Asset-backed	0.83
Credit	**25.16**
● AAA/AA	4.93
● A	11.48
● BBB	8.74

Source: Salomon Smith Barney.

power. The latter have principal and interest secured by the revenues generated by the operating projects financed with the proceeds of the bond issue. Many of these bonds are issued by special authorities created for the purpose.

We provide in Table 1.2 the sector breakdown of the US broad investment-grade index as of June 30, 2001.

Credit Risk

- *Treasury securities are considered to have no credit risk. The interest rates they bear are the key interest rates in the United States as well as in the international capital markets.*

- *Agency securities' debt is high-quality debt. As a matter of fact, all rated agency senior debt issues are triple-A rated by Moody's and Standard & Poor's. This rating most often reflects healthy financial fundamentals and sound management, but also and above all, the agencies' relationship to the US government. Among the numerous legal characteristics of the Government Agencies' debt, one can find that*

    - *agencies' directors are appointed by the President of the United States,*
    - *issuance is only upon approval by the US Treasury,*
    - *securities are issuable and payable through the Federal Reserve System,*
    - *securities are eligible collateral for Federal Reserve Bank advances and discounts,*
    - *securities are eligible for open market purchases.*

- *Municipal debt issues, when rated, carry ratings ranging from triple-A, for the best ones, to C or D, for the worst ones. Four basic criteria are used by rating agencies to assess municipal bond ratings:*

    - *the issuer's debt structure;*
    - *the issuer's ability and political discipline for maintaining sound budgetary operations;*
    - *the local tax and intergovernmental revenue sources of the issuer;*
    - *the issuer's overall socioeconomic environment.*

Other Characteristics Government and municipal securities can be distinguished by their cash flow type, their maturity level, their maturity type and their interest-rate type.

Regarding the cash flow type, there exist, on the one hand, discount securities and, on the other hand, fixed and floating coupon securities. As for maturity level, the 1-year maturity is the frontier separating money-market instruments (with maturity below it) from bond instruments (with maturity above it). For example, Treasury securities with original maturity equal or below 1 year are called *Treasury bills*; they are discount securities. Treasury securities with original maturity between 2 years and 10 years are called *Treasury notes*, and *Treasury securities* with original maturity over 10 years are called *Treasury bonds*; both are coupon securities, and some of them are stripped. According to the maturity type, the security can be retired or not prior to maturity. A security with a single maturity is called *a term security* while a security that can be retired prior to maturity is called *a callable security*. Although the US government no longer issues callable bonds, there are still outstanding issues with this provision. Apart from this, Treasury bonds are bullet bonds, meaning that they have no amortization payments. Concerning the interest-rate type, agency securities, municipal securities and most Treasury securities are nominal coupon-bearing securities. Only a few Treasury securities are inflation-linked, that is, they bear real coupons. They are called *TIPS* (Treasury Inflation Protected Securities).

Markets Treasury securities are traded on the following four markets: the primary market, the secondary market, the when-issued market and the repo market.

- *The primary market is the market where newly issued securities are first sold through an auction which is conducted on a competitive bid basis. The auction process happens between the Treasury and primary/nonprimary dealers according to regular cycles for securities with specific maturities. Auction cycles are as follows: 2-year notes are auctioned every month and settle on the 15th. Five-year notes are auctioned quarterly, in February, May, August and November of each year, and settle at the end of the month. Ten-year notes are auctioned quarterly, in February, May, August and November of each year, and settle on the 15th of the month. Thirty-year bonds are auctioned semiannually, in February and August of each year, and settle on the 15th of the month. Auction is announced by the Treasury one week in advance, the issuance date being set one to five days after the auction.*

- *The secondary market is the market where previously issued securities are bought and sold, a group of US government security dealers offering continuous bid and ask prices on specific outstanding Treasury securities. It is an over-the-counter market.*

- *The when-issued market is the market where Treasury securities are traded on a forward basis before they are issued by the Treasury.*

- *Finally, the repo market is the market where securities are used as collateral for loans. A distinction must be made between the general-collateral (GC) repo rate and the special repo rate. The GC repo rate applies to the major part of Treasury securities. Special repo rates are specific repo rates. They typically concern on-the-run and cheapest-to-deliver securities, which are very expensive. This is the reason why special repo rates are at a level below the GC repo rate. Indeed, as these securities are very much in demand, the borrowers of these securities on the repo market receive a relatively lower repo rate compared to normal Treasury securities.*

Table 1.3 JP Morgan Global Government Bond Index Country Weights as of June 1, 2001 and September 1, 1997.

	Market weights as of 06/01/01 (%)	Market weights as of 09/01/97 (%)	Weights' evolution between 09/97 and 06/01 (%)
Euroland*	33.24	30.94	+7.43
Japan	30.27	14.72	+105.67
US	25.37	39.84	−36.32
UK	5.80	6.73	−13.87
Canada	3.12	3.11	—
Denmark	1.14	1.80	—
Sweden	0.68	1.74	—
Australia	0.38	1.12	—

*Belgium, France, Germany, Italy, Netherlands, Spain.
Source: JP Morgan.

Main Issuers Overview   The four major government bond (government bond refers here to bond and note issued by the Treasury of each country) issuers in the world are Euroland, Japan, the United States and the United Kingdom. Table 1.3 gives a country percentage breakdown of the JP Morgan Global Government Bond Index, which is a benchmark index for developed government debt markets. Note that if we include the remaining EMU (European Monetary Union) countries, Euroland's weight is slightly higher.

It is worth noting that between 1997 and 2001 Japan's weight has more than doubled, whereas the US weight has decreased by approximately one-third and the UK weight has fallen by nearly 15%. Meanwhile, Euroland's weight has slightly increased. Typical reasons for this are the US budget surpluses and the Treasury buyback program, as well as the credit crunch situation in Japan, having led to tremendous JGBs (Japanese Government Bonds) issuance programs.

Corporate Bonds

Main Characteristics   Corporate bonds are issued by entities (firms, banks) belonging to the private sector. They represent what market participants call *the credit market*. They are far less liquid than government bonds: they bear higher bid–ask spreads.

Example 1.16   On 12/10/2001, the bid–ask price spread for the T-bond 6% 08/15/2009 amounted to 1.5 cents, whereas for the Ford corporate bond 7.375% 10/28/2009 it amounted to 60 cents. The pricing source that is used is the BGN, which is the average of the prices of the most active contributors. It is a market consensus price.

As is the case for government and municipal bonds, the issuer of a corporate bond has the obligation to honor his commitments to the bondholder.

A failure to pay back interests or principal according to the terms of the agreement constitutes what is known as default. Basically, there are two sources of default. First, the shareholders of a corporation can decide to break the debt contract. This comes from their limited liability status: they are liable of the corporation's losses only up to their investment in it. They do not have to pay back their creditors when it affects their personal wealth. Second, creditors can prompt bankruptcy when specific debt protective clauses, known as covenants, are infringed.

Corporate bonds are said to be affected by default or credit risk. Their yields contain a default premium over Treasury bonds, accounting for total default or credit risk, as well as over swaps,[3] accounting for specific default or credit risk. In case of default, there are typically three eventualities:

- *First, default can lead to immediate bankruptcy. Depending on their debt securities' seniority and face value, creditors are fully, partially or not paid back, thanks to the sale of the firm's assets. The percentage of the interests and principal they receive, according to seniority, is called recovery rate.*

- *Second, default can result in a reorganization of the firm within a formal legal framework. For example, under Chapter 11 of the American law, corporations that are in default are granted a deadline so as to overcome their financial difficulties. This depends on the country's legislation.*

- *Third, default can lead to an informal negotiation between shareholders and creditors. This results in an exchange offer through which shareholders propose to creditors the exchange of their old debt securities for a package of cash and newly issued securities.*

We now refer the reader to Chapter 13 "Modeling the Credit Spreads Dynamics" for more information on the assessment of default.

The Corporate Bond Market

The Market Size   In the context of a historically low level of interest rates, linked to a decreasing trend in inflation as well as in budget deficits, the corporate bond market is rapidly developing and growing. This strong tendency affects both supply and demand. While corporate supply is expanding, in relation with bank disintermediation, corporate demand is rising as more and more investors accustomed to dealing with only government bonds are including corporate bonds in their portfolios so as to capture spread and generate performance. Within the four major bond markets in the world, the US Dollar (USD) corporate market is the most mature, followed by the Sterling (GBP) market and the Euro (EUR) market, the growth of the latter being reinforced by the launching of the Euro. The Japanese Yen (JPY) market differentiates itself from the others, because of the credit crunch situation and economic difficulties it has been facing since the Asian crisis. Tables 1.4, 1.5, 1.6 and 1.7 hereafter give an appraisal of the corporate bond market size and weight for the four previous markets, as of September 2001 (source: Merrill Lynch, Master and Broad indices). The USD corporate bond market appears much bigger and also more diversified than the others: it is, for instance, more than twice as big as the Euro market, and low investment-grade ratings are much more represented (over 80%).

---

[3] Swap spread, which is the difference between swap yield and Treasury yield with same maturity, is regarded as systematic credit premium. The reason is that swap yields reflect bank risk with rating AA, which is the first rating grade below AAA, the rating for Treasury bonds.

Table 1.4   Market Weight of the US Corporate Bond Market as of September 2001.

Description	Par amount (in billion USD)	Weight (in %)
USD broad investment-grade bond market	6,110.51	100.00
USD govt./govt. sponsored	2,498.23	40.88
USD collateralized	2,216.73	36.28
USD corporate	1,395.56	22.84
USD corporate (large capitalizations)	869.96	14.24
USD corporate	1,395.56	100.00
AAA	35.33	2.53
AA	200.81	14.39
A	653.76	46.90
BBB	505.65	36.23

Table 1.5   Market Weight of the Euro Corporate Bond Market as of September 2001.

Description	Par amount (in billion USD)	Weight (in %)
EUR broad investment-grade bond market	3,740.77	100.00
EUR govt./govt. sponsored	2,455.24	65.63
EUR collateralized	685.78	18.33
EUR corporate	599.75	16.03
EUR corporate (large capitalizations)	416.96	11.15
EUR corporate	599.75	100.00
AAA	143.10	23.86
AA	151.55	25.27
A	220.36	36.74
BBB	84.74	14.13

Table 1.6   Market Weight of the UK Corporate Bond Market as of September 2001.

Description	Par amount (in billion USD)	Weight (in %)
GBP broad investment-grade bond market	529.84	100.00
GBP govt./govt. sponsored	359.58	67.87
GBP collateralized	1.41	0.27
GBP corporate	168.85	31.87
GBP corporate (large capitalizations)	83.49	15.76
GBP corporate	168.85	100.00
AAA	32.41	19.19
AA	45.29	26.82
A	65.36	38.71
BBB	25.79	15.27

Table 1.7   Market Weight of the Japan Corporate Bond Market as of September 2001.

Description	Par amount (in billion USD)	Weight (in %)
JPY broad investment-grade bond market	2,183.33	100.00
JPY govt./govt. sponsored	1,726.55	79.08
JPY collateralized	0.58	0.03
JPY corporate	456.20	20.89
JPY corporate (large capitalizations)	252.87	11.58
JPY corporate	456.20	100.00
AAA	7.27	1.59
AA	198.79	43.59
A	193.30	42.39
BBB	56.66	12.43

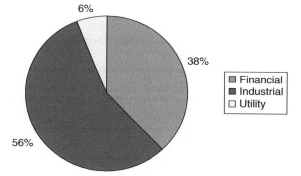

Figure 1.9

Sector breakdown of the US corporate bond market.

The Sector Breakdown   The corporate bond market can be divided into three main sectors: financial, industrial and utility. Figures 1.9, 1.10 and 1.11 hereafter show the breakdown of the US market into these sectors, and, furthermore, the breakdown of each sector into subsectors.[4] Sources come from Merrill Lynch (Broad corporate indices as of September 2001).

Note that apart from the USD market, the financial sector is overrepresented. It is another proof of the maturity of the USD market, where the industrial sector massively uses the market channel in order to finance investment projects. It is also worth noting that the sector composition in the USD market is far more homogeneous than in the other markets. For example, the banking sector is systematically predominant in the GBP, EUR and JPY financial markets (see the Appendix of this chapter), while the telecommunication sector exceeds one-third of the Euro industrial market. As a result, local credit portfolio diversification can be better achieved in the USD market than in the others.

---

[4]See the Appendix at the end of this chapter for the sector breakdown of the Euro, the UK and the Japan corporate bond markets.

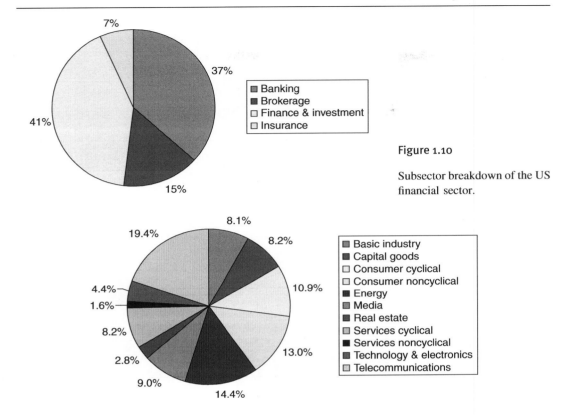

Figure 1.10

Subsector breakdown of the US financial sector.

Figure 1.11   Subsector breakdown of the US industrial sector.

1.2   Money-Market Instruments

1.2.1   Definition

Money-market instruments are short-term debt instruments with a maturity typically inferior or equal to 1 year. Some of these instruments such as certificates of deposit may have a maturity exceeding 1 year. These instruments are very sensitive to the Central Bank monetary policy. There are basically three categories of issuers on this market: government (at both the federal and local levels), banks and corporations. We will review the following instruments: *Treasury Bills, Certificates of Deposit, Bankers' acceptances* and *Commercial papers*. We will also have a close look at *interbank deposits* and *repo transactions*.

1.2.2   The Role of the Central Bank

Before we start describing money-market instruments, let us focus on the essential role of the Central Bank. Through its privileged triple status of government's banker, banks' banker and nation's banker, it literally steers the general level of interest rates. Indeed, as the government's banker, it finances budget deficits; as the banks' banker, it supervises and regulates the banking system; as the nation's banker, it conducts the monetary policy of the nation. All these tasks are guided by two objectives: first, the stability of prices, and second, the support of a sustainable economic growth. In order to meet these targets, the Central Bank has the responsibility of setting the official interest rate of the nation, through its open market operations, that is, the purchase and sale of government securities, which allows it to control money supply. This key interest rate is basically an interest rate at which banks can borrow. It is

- *either the overnight interest rate at which banks can borrow from the Central Bank (UK, Euro area) in exchange for eligible securities such as Treasury Bills. In this case, it is called a repo rate;*

Definition 1.1 Overnight means for one trading day.

- *or the overnight interest rate set in the Central Bank funds market, at which banks can borrow or lend Central Bank funds so as to meet their reserve requirements (US, Japan) with the Central Bank. It is called the Fed Funds rate in the United States and the unsecured overnight call rate in Japan.*

Remark 1.1 Central Bank funds are called *Fed funds* in the United States.

Remark 1.2 The Central Bank is called the *Federal Reserve* in the United States. It is called the *European Central Bank* in the Euro area.

Remark 1.3 Depository institutions (commercial banks and thrifts) are required to maintain a specific amount of reserves (what we call Fed Funds in the United States) at their Central Bank.

Note that these two types of interest rates, which both exist in each of the above-mentioned countries, are very close to one another, the repo rate being lower owing to the fact that the corresponding loan is collateralized by a security. This key interest rate then affects the whole spectrum of interest rates that commercial banks set for their customers (borrowers and savers), which in turn affects supply and demand in the economy, and finally the level of prices. The shorter the debt instrument, the greater its sensitivity to monetary policy action. Indeed, as shown in Chapter 3 devoted to the theories of the term structure of interest rates, medium-term and long-term debt instruments are more sensitive to the market expectations of future monetary policy actions than to the current Central Bank action itself.

1.2.3 T-Bills

Treasury Bills are Treasury securities with a maturity below or equal to 1 year. They entail no default risk because they are backed by the full faith and creditworthiness of the government. They bear no interest rate and are quoted using the yield on a discount basis or on a money-market basis depending on the country considered.

- *The yield on a discount basis denoted by y_d is computed as*

$$y_d = \frac{F - P}{F} \times \frac{B}{n}$$

where F is the face value (redemption value), P the price, B the year-basis (360 or 365) and n the number of calendar days remaining to maturity.

It is the yield calculation used in the Euro zone, in the United States and in the United Kingdom. The year-basis is 360 in the United States, 365 in the United Kingdom and can be 360 or 365 in the Euro zone depending on the country considered.

Example 1.17   Compute on a discount basis the yield on a 90-day US T-bill with price $P = \$9,800$, and face value $\$10,000$.

$$y_d = \frac{10,000 - 9,800}{10,000} \times \frac{360}{90} = 8\%$$

When you know the yield on a discount basis, you can retrieve the T-bill price using

$$P = F \times \left(1 - \frac{n \times y_d}{B}\right)$$

Example 1.18   The US T-bill with maturity 03/28/2002 and a discount yield of 1.64% as of 12/17/2001 has a price P equal to

$$P = 100 \times \left(1 - 1.64\% \times \frac{101}{360}\right) = 99.5399$$

Indeed, there are 101 calendar days between 12/17/2001 and 03/28/2002.

- *The yield on a money-market basis denoted by y_m is computed as*

$$y_m = \frac{B \times y_d}{B\text{-}n \times y_d}$$

It is the yield calculation used in Japan where the year-basis is 365.

Example 1.19   Compute the yield on a money-market basis on a 62-day Japan T-bill with price $P = 99$ yens and face value 100 yens. The yield on a discount basis is

$$y_d = \frac{100 - 99}{100} \times \frac{365}{62} = 5.887\%$$

The yield on a money-market basis is

$$y_m = \frac{365 \times 5.887\%}{365 - 62 \times 5.887\%} = 5.947\%$$

When you know the yield on a money-market basis, you can retrieve the T-bill price using

$$P = \frac{F}{\left(1 + \dfrac{n \times y_m}{B}\right)}$$

Example 1.20 The French T-bill (BTF) with maturity 03/07/2002 and a money-market yield of 3.172% as of 12/17/2001 has a price P equal to

$$P = \frac{100}{\left(1 + 3.172\% \times \dfrac{80}{360}\right)} = 99.30$$

Indeed, there are 80 calendar days between 12/17/2001 and 03/07/2002.

The liquidity of T-Bills may be biased by the so-called squeeze effect, which means that the supply for these instruments is much lower than the demand, because investors buy and hold them until maturity. This phenomenon is particularly observable in the Euro market.

1.2.4 Certificates of Deposit

Certificates of Deposit are debt instruments issued by banks in order to finance their lending activity. They entail the credit risk of the issuing bank. They bear an interest rate that can be fixed or floating, and that is paid either periodically or at maturity with principal. Their maturity typically ranges from a few weeks to three months, but it can reach several years. They trade on a money-market basis. The price is computed using the following equation

$$P = F \times \frac{\left(1 + c \times \dfrac{n_c}{B}\right)}{\left(1 + y_m \times \dfrac{n_m}{B}\right)}$$

where F is the face value, c the interest rate at issuance, n_c is the number of days between issue date and maturity date, B is the year-basis (360 or 365), y_m is the yield on a money-market basis, n_m is the number of days between settlement and maturity.

Example 1.21 The Certificate of Deposit issued by the French bank Credit Lyonnais on 07/27/2001, with maturity 04/29/2002, face value Eur80 million, an interest rate at issuance of 4.27% falling at maturity and a yield of 4.19% as of 08/13/2001, has a price P equal to

$$P = 100 \times \frac{\left(1 + 4.27\% \times \dfrac{276}{360}\right)}{\left(1 + 4.19\% \times \dfrac{259}{360}\right)} = 100.25$$

which corresponds to a market value of Eur80.201 million (80 million $\times$ 100.25%) on 08/13/2001.

Indeed, there are 276 calendar days between 07/27/2001 and 04/29/2002, and 259 calendar days between 08/13/2001 and 04/29/2002.

1.2.5 Bankers' Acceptances

Bankers' acceptances are drafts that are drawn and accepted, and therefore guaranteed by banks. These bills of exchange mainly guarantee foreign trade transactions: they often work as guarantees of business between a manufacturer and an importer. Typically, the importer, who cannot pay for the goods imported on the date set by the manufacturer, asks its bank to guarantee the payment. For this purpose, the bank issues a letter of credit according to which it agrees to pay to the holder of this letter the face value of the transaction at maturity. Bankers' acceptances are traded on a discount basis in the United States and a money-market basis in the Euro area. They bear no interest rate. So, the market price of a bankers' acceptance is calculated in the same manner as the price of a T-Bill. Its discount or money-market yield accounts for the credit risk that neither the importer nor the bank honor their commitment.

> **Example 1.22** An investor buying a banker's acceptance with maturity 04/10/2002 and a discount yield of 1.90% as of 12/14/2001 for a face value of $30 million will pay a price P equal to
>
> $$P = 100 \times \left(1 - 1.90\% \times \frac{117}{360}\right) = 99.3825$$
>
> that is, a market value of $29.815 million (30 million × 99.3825%). Indeed, there are 117 calendar days between 12/14/2001 and 04/10/2002.

1.2.6 Commercial Papers

Commercial papers are unsecured short-term debt securities issued by corporations including industrial and financial companies. Their maturity ranges from 2 to 270 days. They bear no interest rate and are traded on a discount basis in the United States and on a money-market basis in the Euro area. They entail the credit risk of the issuing entity. Note that they are slightly riskier than bankers' acceptances as the latter are guaranteed by the accepting bank beside the guarantee of the issuing company. Corporations typically use them either as a way of raising short-term funds or as interim loans to finance long-term projects while awaiting more attractive long-term capital market conditions, which is called *bridge financing*. Regarding short-term financing, commercial papers are simply rolled over by the issuing corporation until reaching its lending horizon.

> **Example 1.23** Consider the commercial paper issued by L'Oreal on 10/11/2001 and maturing on 01/15/2002. At issuance, its money-market yield amounts to 3.62%, its nominal value to Eur70 million. Its market value MV is equal to
>
> $$MV = \frac{70,000,000}{\left(1 + 3.62\% \times \frac{96}{360}\right)} = Eur69,330,727$$
>
> Indeed, there are 96 calendar days between 10/11/2001 and 01/15/2002.

1.2.7   Interbank Deposits

Interbank deposits are short-term deposits made between banks, which use them to place surplus funds. These instruments are also accessible to investors with large amounts of cash. They are traded over the counter, which means that the interest rate of the deposit depends on the counterparts that bid for and offer deposits to each other. The interbank bid rate (for example, Libid, Euribid) and the interbank offered rate (for example, Libor, Euribor) serve as reference rates for these transactions. These rates are fixed for maturities ranging basically from 1 day to 12 months.

> **Remark 1.4**   The interbank overnight rate is the 1-day interbank rate. For example, it is called the *Eonia* (Euro overnight index average deposit rate) in the Euro area and the *Sonia* (Sterling overnight index average deposit rate) in the United Kingdom. The equivalent rate in the United States is the *Fed Fund rate*, and in Japan *the unsecured overnight call rate*.

The fixing is the average of the rates quoted by the major banks of a market place. For example, the Libor and Libid rates are derived from the quotations of the major banks in London. The interbank bid rate is of course lower than the interbank offered rate, usually by 12.5 basis points. Interbank deposits entail the credit risk of the quoting banks, that is a AA credit risk. As these instruments are very closely associated with the money-market core institutions and the quotations of the reference rates are widely publicized, interbank rates are regarded as the main money-market benchmark rates. Interbank deposits bear a fixed interest rate paid on the deposit amount.

> **Remark 1.5**   The coupon interest rate is calculated on an Actual/360 daily basis in the United States, the Euro area and Japan, and on an Actual/365 daily basis in the United Kingdom, on the basis of the interbank fixing rate that prevailed 2 days before the coupon starting date in the United States, the Euro area and Japan, and that prevails on the coupon starting date in the United Kingdom.

> **Example 1.24**   Consider an investor who deposits $100 million on 12/14/2001 at an interest rate of 3.35% until 03/14/2002. At maturity, he receives the amount of its deposit plus the interest earned over the period, that is,
>
> $$\$100 \text{ million} \times \left(1 + 3.35\% \times \frac{90}{360}\right) = \$100.8375 \text{ million}$$

1.2.8   Repo and Reverse Repo Market Instruments

Repurchase (repo) and reverse repurchase (reverse repo) agreement transactions are commonly used by traders and portfolio managers to finance either long or short positions (usually in government securities).

A repo is for an investor a means to lend bonds in exchange for a loan of money, while a reverse repo is a means for an investor to lend money in exchange for a loan of securities. More precisely, a repo agreement is a commitment by the seller of a security to buy it back from the buyer at a specified price and at a given future date. It can be viewed as a collateralized loan, the collateral here being the security. A reverse repo agreement is the same transaction viewed from the buyer's perspective. The repo desk acts as the intermediary between the investors who want to borrow cash and lend securities and the investors who want to lend cash and borrow securities. The borrower of cash will pay the bid repo rate times the amount of cash borrowed, while the lender of cash will get the ask repo rate times the amount of cash lent. The repo desk gains the bid–ask spread on all the transactions that it makes. The repo rate is computed on an Actual/360 day-count basis. In the following examples, we do not take into account the bid–ask spreads. First, let us give an example of a repo transaction.

Example 1.25 An investor lends Eur1 million of the 10-year Bund benchmark bond (i.e., the Bund 5% 07/04/2011 with a quoted price of 104.11, on 10/29/2001) over 1 month at a repo rate of 4%. There is 117 days accrued interest as of the starting date of the transaction.

At the beginning of the transaction, the investor will receive an amount of cash equal to the gross price of the bond times the nominal of the loan, that is,

$$(104.11 + 5 \times 117/360)\% \times 1,000,000 = \text{Eur}1,057,350$$

At the end of the transaction, in order to repurchase the securities he will pay the amount of cash borrowed plus the repo interest due over the period, that is,

$$1,057,350 \times (1 + 4\% \times 30/360) = \text{Eur}1,060,875$$

We now describe two examples of financing a short position and a long position using repos.

Example 1.26

Financing a Long Position

An investor wants to finance a long position of Eur1 million Bund with coupon 5% and maturity date 07/04/2011.

He can purchase these securities and then lend them through a repo transaction, like the one that has just been described. He will use the resulting borrowed cash to pay for them. On the one hand, the investor will gain the coupon income times the nominal amount of the securities he owns, that is, he will gain $5\% \times 1,000,000/360 = \text{Eur } 138.89$ a day. On the other hand, he will lose the repo rate times the borrowed amount of cash, which is equal to the full price of the bond securities times the nominal amount, that is, he will lose $1,057,350 \times 4\%/360 = \text{Eur}117.48$ a day. His net gain per day equals $138.89 - 117.48 = \text{Eur}21.41$.

Financing a Short Position

An investor has to make delivery of Eur1 million Bund on his short sale position. He can borrow the securities through a reverse repo transaction and then lend the money resulting from the short sale to the repo desk as collateral. Suppose the reverse repo is 4%. On the one hand, the investor will gain the reverse repo rate times the lent amount of cash, which is equal to the full price of the bond securities times the nominal amount. On the other hand, he will lose the coupon income times the nominal amount of the securities sold. His net loss per day amounts to Eur 21.41.

Note that financing a long (short, respectively) position may result in either a net gain or a net loss, equal to the difference between the coupon income and the repo interest (the difference between the reverse repo interest and the coupon income, respectively).

When the maturity of the loan is 1 day, the repo is called an *overnight repo*. When the maturity exceeds 1 day, the repo is called a *term repo*.

From an investment point of view, the repo market offers several opportunities:

- *The opportunity of contracting less expensive loans than traditional bank loans (because repo loans are secured loans).*

- *The opportunity of investing in a very liquid short-term market.*

- *The opportunity of investing cash over tailor-made horizons, by rolling over either several overnight transactions or different repo transactions with various maturity horizons. This is particularly attractive for an investor who has a short-term undefined horizon. It allows him to avoid the price risk he would incur if he had chosen to invest in a money-market security.*

- *The opportunity for a buy-and-hold investor of putting idle money to work. Indeed, by lending the securities he owns in his portfolio, he receives some cash that he can invest in a money-market instrument. His gain will be the difference between the money-market income and the repo cost.*

- *The opportunity to take short positions that enable portfolio managers to construct alternative strategies by combining long and short positions (see Chapter 8 "Active Fixed-Income Portfolio Management" for some more details on these strategies).*

Lastly, note that for a short-term investor with an unknown investment horizon, the strategy of buying a money-market security and the strategy of rolling over cash on the repo market do not entail the same interest-rate risk. The former bears the risk that the security may be sold before its maturity date (price risk) at an unknown price, while the latter bears the risk that the cash may be reinvested at an unknown repo rate (reinvestment risk). We will come back to that issue in Chapters 2 and 5.

1.3 End of Chapter Summary

Fixed-income markets are populated with a vast range of instruments. In this chapter, we provide a typology of the most simple of these instruments, namely, bonds and money-market instruments, and describe their general characteristics.

A *bond* is a financial claim by which the issuer, or the borrower, is committed to paying back to the bondholder, or the lender, the cash amount borrowed (called *the principal*), plus periodic interests calculated on this amount during a given period of time. It can have either a standard or a nonstandard structure. A standard bond is a fixed-coupon bond without any embedded option, delivering its coupons on periodic dates and the principal on the maturity date. Nonstandard bonds such as strips, floating-rate notes and inflation-indexed bonds are also traded on bond markets. Other types of bonds exist that contain embedded options; they are discussed in Chapter 14. These bonds can be issued by government agencies, municipalities, or corporations. Bond quotes are usually expressed in terms of price, yield or spread over an underlying benchmark bond. The quoted price of a bond is usually its *clean price*, that is, its *gross price* minus the *accrued interest*. The quoted yield of a bond is the discount yield that equalizes its gross price times its nominal amount to the sum of its discounted cash flows. Corporate bonds are usually quoted in price and in spread over a given benchmark bond rather than in yield; to recover the corresponding yield, you simply have to add this spread to the yield of the underlying benchmark bond.

Money-market instruments are short-term debt instruments with a maturity typically inferior or equal to 1 year. These instruments are very sensitive to the Central Bank monetary policy. There are again three categories of issuers on this market: government (at both the federal and local levels), banks and corporations. Treasury bills, certificates of deposit, bankers' acceptances and commercial paper are common money-market instruments. We also discuss interbank deposits and repo transactions, which are over-the-counter transactions.

1.4 References and Further Reading

1.4.1 Books and Papers

Bennani, K., and J.C. Bertrand, 1998, *Les Obligations à Taux Variable*, Economica, Paris.
Choudhry, M., 2001, *Bond Market Securities*, Prentice Hall, New York.
Choudhry, M., 2001, *Bond and Money Markets: Strategy, Trading and Analysis*, Butterworth-Heinemann, Woburn, MA.
Choudhry, M., 2002, *The REPO Handbook*. Butterworth-Heinemann, Woburn, MA.
Deacon, M., and A. Derry, 1998, *Inflation-Indexed Securities*, Prentice Hall, New York.
Fabozzi, F.J., (Editor), 2000, *The Handbook of Fixed Income Securities*, 6th Edition, McGraw-Hill, New York.
Fabozzi, F.J., S.V. Mann, and M. Choudhry, 2002, *The Global Money Markets*, John Wiley & Sons, Chichester.
Youngdahl, J., B. Stone, and H. Boesky, 2001, "Implications of a Disappearing Treasury Debt Market", *Journal of Fixed Income*, **10** (4), 75–86.

1.4.2 Websites and Others

Websites of Treasury Bond Issuers and Central Banks

www.treas.gov

www.francetresor.gouv.fr

www.bankofengland.co.uk

www.publicdebt.treas.gov

www.federalreserve.gov

www.ecb.int

www.boj.or.jp

www.bankofcanada.ca

www.bis.org/cbanks.htm

Websites of Data and Information Providers

www.bloomberg.com

www.reuters.com

www.YieldCurve.com

www.bondsonline.com

www.bondtalk.com

www.bondsinasia.com

www.bondmarkets.com

www.investinginbonds.com

www.buybonds.com

www.YieldCurve.com

See HSBV, the Bloomberg site of the global fixed-income strategy of HSBC.

1.5 Problems

1.5.1 Problems on Bonds

Exercise 1.1   On 12/04/01 consider a fixed-coupon bond whose features are the following:

- face value: $1,000
- coupon rate: 8%
- coupon frequency: semiannual
- maturity: 05/06/04

What are the future cash flows delivered by this bond?

Exercise 1.2   Consider the same bond as in the previous exercise. We are still on 12/04/01.

1. Compute the accrued interest, taking into account the Actual/Actual day-count basis.
2. Same question if we are now on 09/06/02.

Exercise 1.3   An investor has a cash of $10,000,000 at disposal. He wants to invest in a bond with $1,000 nominal value and whose dirty price is equal to 107.457%.

1. What is the number of bonds he will buy?
2. Same question if the nominal value and the dirty price of the bond are respectively $100 and 98.453%.

Exercise 1.4   On 10/25/99 consider a fixed-coupon bond whose features are the following:

- face value: Eur100
- coupon rate: 10%
- coupon frequency: annual
- maturity: 04/15/08

Compute the accrued interest, taking into account the four different day-count bases: Actual/Actual, Actual/365, Actual/360 and 30/360.

Exercise 1.5   Some bonds have irregular first coupons.

- A long first coupon is paid on the second anniversary date of the bond and starts accruing on the issue date. So, the first coupon value is greater than the normal coupon rate.
- A long first coupon with regular value is paid on the second anniversary date of the bond and starts accruing on the first anniversary date. So, the first coupon value is equal to the normal coupon rate.
- A short first coupon is paid on the first anniversary date of the bond and starts accruing on the issue date. The first coupon value is smaller than the normal coupon rate.
- A short first coupon with regular value is paid on the first anniversary date of the bond and has a value equal to the normal coupon rate.

Consider the following four bonds with nominal value equal to Eur 1 million and annual coupon frequency:

- Bond 1: issue date 05/21/96, coupon 5%, maturity date 05/21/02, long first coupon, redemption value 100%;
- Bond 2: issue date 02/21/96, coupon 5%, maturity date 02/21/02, long first coupon with regular value, redemption value 99%;
- Bond 3: issue date 11/21/95, coupon 3%, maturity date 3 years and 2 months, short first coupon, redemption value 100%;
- Bond 4: issue date 08/21/95, coupon 4.5%, maturity date 08/21/00, short first coupon with regular value, redemption value 100%.

Compute the future cash flows of each of these bonds.

Exercise 1.6   The ex-dividend date is the date at which the gross price of a bond decreases by the present value of the next coupon. Some Treasury bonds trade ex-dividend. During this period (seven business days between the ex-dividend date and the next coupon date for UK Gilts), the accrued interest is negative. Explain why.

Exercise 1.7   What is a discount security? Give two examples.

Exercise 1.8   An investor wants to buy a standard bond of the automotive sector. He has two choices: either invest in a US corporate bond denominated in euros or in a French corporate bond with same maturity and coupon. Are the two bonds comparable?

Exercise 1.9 1. Consider the inverse floater with coupon $M - I_t$ (M being a constant rate, I_t a floating rate) and maturity n.
How can you replicate a long position in that bond? What is its price equal to?
2. Consider the inverse floater with coupon $M - k \times i_t$ and maturity n.
How can you replicate a long position in that bond? What is its price equal to?

Exercise 1.10 Some US government agency bonds, known as federally related institution bonds, like those of GNMA, are backed by the full faith and credit of the US government, which makes them as safe as Treasury bonds. Yet the yields on these securities trade at 20 to 50 basis points over Treasury bonds. Explain why.

Exercise 1.11 What does it mean when a Treasury bond trades "on special"? If you own such a bond, how can you profit from the fact that it is "on special"?

Exercise 1.12 Consider two US Treasury bonds with the same maturity date. One has a higher YTM than the other. Explain why.

1.5.2 Problems on Money-Market Instruments

Exercise 1.13 Treasury bills are quoted using the yield on a discount basis or on a money-market basis.

1. The yield on a discount basis denoted by y_d is computed as

$$y_d = \frac{F - P}{F} \times \frac{B}{n}$$

where F is the face value, P the price, B the year-basis (365 or 360) and n is the number of calendar days remaining to maturity.
    Prove in this case that the price of the T-bill is obtained using the following equation:

$$P = F\left(1 - \frac{n \times y_d}{B}\right)$$

2. The yield on a money-market basis denoted by y_m is computed as

$$y_m = \frac{B \times y_d}{B - n \times y_d}$$

Prove in this case that the price of the T-bill is obtained using the following equation:

$$P = \frac{F}{\left(1 + \dfrac{n \times y_m}{B}\right)}$$

3. Show that

$$y_d = \frac{B \times y_m}{B + n \times y_m}$$

Exercise 1.14   1. What is the yield on a discount basis of a bill whose face value F is 1,000, price P is 975 and n the number of calendar days remaining to maturity is 126? We assume that the year-basis is 360.
2. What is the yield on a money-market basis of the same bill?

Exercise 1.15   What is the price P of the certificate of deposit issued by bank X on 06/06/00, with maturity 08/25/00, face value $10,000,000, an interest rate at issuance of 5% falling at maturity and a yield of 4.5% as of 07/31/00?

Exercise 1.16   On 01/03/2002 an investor buys $1 million US T-Bill with maturity date 06/27/2002 and discount yield 1.76% on the settlement date.

1. What is the price of the T-Bill?
2. What is the equivalent money-market yield?

Exercise 1.17   On 01/03/2002 an investor buys Eur1 million BTF (French T-Bills) with maturity date 04/11/2002 and money-market yield 3.18% on the settlement date.

1. What is the price of the BTF?
2. What is the equivalent discount yield?

Exercise 1.18   Consider the following list of money-market instruments:

- Bankers' acceptances
- Treasury Bills
- Commercial papers

Order them from the least risky to the most risky and explain your choice.

Exercise 1.19   What is the difference between the Euro-Libor and the Euribor?

1.6   Appendix: Sector Breakdown of the Euro, the UK and the Japan Corporate Bond Markets

Table A1   Sector Breakdown of the European Corporate Bond Market.

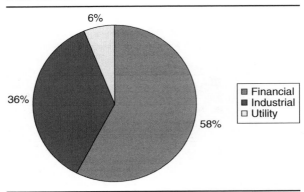

Table A2   Subsector Breakdown of the European Financial Sector.

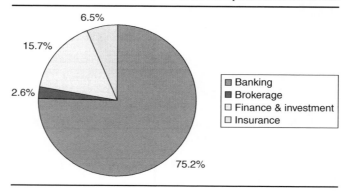

Table A3   Subsector Breakdown of the European Industrial Sector.

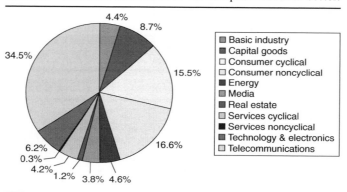

Table A4   Sector Breakdown of the UK Corporate Bond Market.

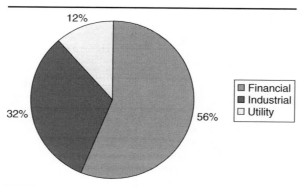

Table A5   Subsector Breakdown of the UK Financial Sector.

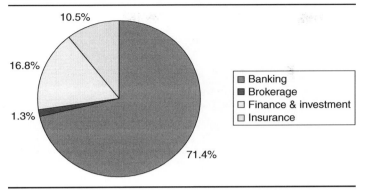

Table A6   Subsector Breakdown of the UK Industrial Sector.

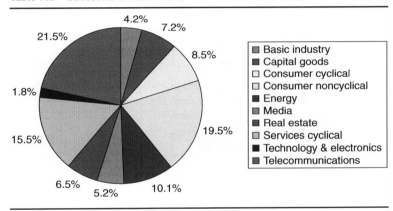

Table A7   Sector Breakdown of the Japan Corporate Bond Market.

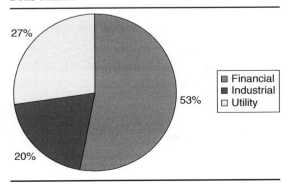

Fixed Income Securities

Table A8   Subsector Breakdown of the Japan Financial Sector.

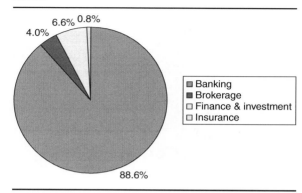

Table A9   Subsector Breakdown of the Japan Industrial Sector.

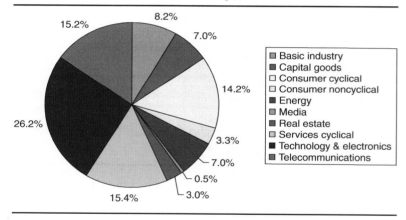

2 Bond Prices and Yields

Fixed income is a fascinating part of finance but it is fairly quantitative. The good news is, however, that most of it is not really technical. Pricing of bonds, for example, is straightforward, at least in principle.

2.1 Introduction to Bond Pricing

Bond pricing can be viewed as a three-step process.

- *Step 1: obtain the cash flows the bondholder is entitled to.*

- *Step 2: obtain the discount rates for the maturities corresponding to the cash flow dates.*

- *Step 3: obtain the bond price as the discounted value of the cash flows.*

First, one needs to obtain the cash flows on the bond to be priced. In particular, let us first assume that we are dealing with a straight default-free, fixed-coupon bond, so that the value of cash flows paid by the bond are known with certainty *ex ante*, that is, on the date when pricing is performed. In general, there are two parameters that are needed to fully describe the cash flows on a bond. The first is the maturity date of the bond, on which the principal or face amount of the bond is paid and the bond retired. The second parameter needed to describe a bond is the coupon rate.

Example 2.1 A Canadian Government bond issued in the domestic market pays one-half of its coupon rate times its principal value every 6 months up to and including the maturity date. Thus, a bond with an 8% coupon and $5,000 face value maturing on December 1, 2005, will make future coupon payments of 4% of principal value, that is, $200 on every June 1 and December 1 between the purchase (BTP) date and the maturity date.

Then, one needs to apply some kind of discounted value type of formula to obtain the current value of the bond. Given that the cash flows are known with certainty *ex ante*, only the time-value needs to be accounted for, using the present value rule, which can be written as the following relationship

$$PV(CF_t) = B(0, t)CF_t$$

where $PV(CF_t)$ is the present value of the cash flow CF_t received at date t and $B(0, t)$ is the price at date 0 (today) of $1 (or Eur1 or £1...) to be received on date t. $B(0, t)$ is known as the discount factor. You might be more familiar with an expression of the kind

$$PV(CF_t) = \frac{CF_t}{[1 + R(0, t)]^t}$$

where $R(0, t)$ is the annual *spot rate* (or *discount rate*) at date 0 for an investment up to date t. Actually, those two expressions are just two equivalent ways of expressing the same concept, and obviously nothing prevents us from setting $B(0, t) = \frac{1}{[1+R(0,t)]^t}$.

> **Example 2.2** A $R(0, 3) = 5\%$ annual 3-year interest rate corresponds to a discount factor $B(0, 3) = \frac{1}{(1+0.05)^3} = 0.863838$.

It is actually sometimes more convenient to think in terms of discount factors than in terms of rates. Besides, a simple additivity rule holds

$$PV \text{ (Bond)} = \sum_{t=1}^{T} \frac{CF_t}{[1 + R(0, t)]^t} = \sum_{t=1}^{T} B(0, t)CF_t \tag{2.1}$$

Note that it amounts to a very simple rule: you get a sum of different terms weighted by their prices, *like any other basket of goods*.

There are, however, a small number of important issues one needs to address in an attempt to turn this simple principle into sound practice.

- *Where do we get the discount factors $B(0, t)$ from?*

- *Do we use equation (2.1) to obtain bond prices or implied discount factors?*

- *Can we deviate from this simple rule? Why?*

The answer to the first question is: *any relevant information concerning the pricing of a security should be obtained from market sources.* More specifically, $B(t, T)$ is the price at date t of a unit pure discount bond (zero-coupon bond) paying \$1 at date T. If one could find zero-coupon bonds corresponding to all possible initial dates and maturities, it would be easy to obtain $B(t, T)$ and it would be fairly straightforward to price and hedge fixed-income securities. Unfortunately, no such abundance of zero-coupon bonds exists in the real world, since the vast majority of traded bonds are (nonzero) coupon bonds. Therefore, a robust methodology for extracting implied zero-coupon prices from the market prices is what we need for valuing and hedging nonrandom cash flows. Chapter 4 is entirely devoted to that question.

The answer to the "chicken-and-egg" second question is of course: *it depends on the situation.* Roughly speaking, one would like to use the price of primitive securities as given, and derive implied discount factors or discount rates from them. Then, one may use that information (more specifically the *term structure of discount rates*) to price any other security. This is known as *relative pricing*.

The answer to the third question is: *any deviation from the pricing rules would imply arbitrage opportunities.* Practical illustrations of that concept will be presented in what follows.

Everything we cover in this chapter and also in Chapter 4 can be regarded as some form of perspective on these issues.

2.2 Present Value Formula

If you were asked the question: "would you prefer to receive $1 now or $1 in a year from now?", chances are that you would go for money now. There may be different motivations behind that choice. First, you might have a consumption need sooner rather than later. In a world where fixed-income markets exist, this reason does not actually hold: if you are entitled to receive $1 in a year from now, you may as well borrow today against this future income, and consume now. In the presence of money market, the only reason one would prefer receiving $1 as opposed to $1 in a year from now is because of the *time-value of money*.

2.2.1 Time-Value of Money

Indeed, if you receive $1 today, you may as well invest it in the money market (say buy a 1-year T-Bill) and obtain some interest on it, so that you are finally left with strictly more than $1 in a year from now, as long as the interest rate $R(0, 1)$ is strictly positive. To see that, just check that you will be receiving $1 + \$R(0, 1) > \$1$ if $R(0, 1) > 0$. Since you are not willing to exchange $1 now for $1 in a year from now, it clearly means that the present value of $1 in a year from now is less than $1. Now, how much exactly is worth this $1 received in a year from now? Would you be willing to pay 90, 80, 20, 10 cents to acquire this dollar paid in a year from now? While it must sell at a discount with respect to the par value, it certainly cannot be obtained for free; that would be a clear arbitrage opportunity.

The answer to the question is simply $\frac{\$1}{1+R(0,1)}$. Indeed, note that if you start with $\frac{\$1}{1+R(0,1)}$ and invest it at the rate $R(0, 1)$, you will end up with $1 at the end of the period.

> **Example 2.3** The 1-year interest rate is 4%. The present value of $1 is $\frac{\$1}{1+0.04} = \$0.961538$. If you invest that amount for 1 year, you eventually obtain $0.961538 $(1 + 0.04) = \$1$.

Therefore, there is no difference between getting $\frac{\$1}{1+R(0,1)}$ today or $1 in a year from now, so you should be willing to exchange one for the other. In other words, the fair price of a contract that promises to pay $1 in 1 year from now is $\frac{\$1}{1+R(0,1)}$. It is the *present value* of $1.

Of course, one may extend the principle to obtain the present value of a series of cash flows, that is,

$$PV\left(\sum_{t=1}^{T} CF_t\right) = \sum_{t=1}^{T} \frac{CF_t}{[1 + R(0, t)]^t}$$

This formula is the very key to the valuation of bonds.

2.2.2 The Mathematics of Discounting

There is a very convenient formula that allows one to compute the present value of a series of cash flows when all cash flows and all discount rates across various maturities are identical and,

44

respectively, equal to CF and y. The formula is

$$P_0 = \sum_{t=1}^{T} \frac{CF}{(1+y)^t} = CF \times \frac{1}{y} \times \left(1 - \frac{1}{(1+y)^T}\right)$$

More generally, we have

$$P_0 = C \times \frac{1}{y} \times \left(1 - \frac{1}{(1+y)^T}\right) + \frac{N}{(1+y)^T} \tag{2.2}$$

where P_0 is the present value of the bond, T is the maturity of the bond, N is the nominal value of the bond, $C = c \times N$ is the coupon payment, c is the coupon rate and y is the discount rate.

Example 2.4 As an illustration, we consider the problem of valuing a series of cash flows promised by a bond with a 5% annual coupon rate, a 10-year maturity and a $1,000 face value. We also assume all discount rates equal to 6%. Before we compute the present value of this bond, denoted by P_0, we first identify the cash flows. We have $CF_1 = CF_2 = \cdots = CF_9 = 50$ and $CF_{10} = 1,050$. Therefore, the value of this bond is

$$P_0 = \sum_{t=1}^{9} \frac{50}{(1+6\%)^t} + \frac{1,050}{(1+6\%)^{10}}$$

$$= 50 \times \frac{1}{6\%} \times \left(1 - \frac{1}{(1+6\%)^{10}}\right) + \frac{1,000}{(1+6\%)^{10}} = \$926.3991$$

It is useful to note the following result. **When the discount rate is equal to the coupon rate, then bond value is equal to face value.** To see this, just use equation (2.2) with the assumption that $c = y$ or equivalently that $C = yN$

$$P_0 = yN \times \frac{1}{y} \times \left(1 - \frac{1}{(1+y)^T}\right) + \frac{N}{(1+y)^T}$$

$$= N - \frac{N}{(1+y)^T} + \frac{N}{(1+y)^T} = N$$

Example 2.5 If we replace the 6% discount rate assumption with a 5% discount rate assumption in the previous example, we obtain

$$P_0 = \sum_{t=1}^{10} \frac{50}{(1+5\%)^t} + \frac{1,000}{(1+5\%)^{10}}$$

$$= 50 \times \frac{1}{5\%} \times \left(1 - \frac{1}{(1+5\%)^{10}}\right) + \frac{1,000}{(1+5\%)^{10}} = \$1,000$$

One may also wonder what would be the price of a bond paying a given coupon amount every year over an unlimited horizon. Such a bond is known as a *perpetual bond*. We obtain

$$P_0 = \lim_{T \to \infty} \sum_{t=1}^{T} \frac{CF}{(1+y)^t} = \lim_{T \to \infty} CF \times \frac{1}{y} \times \left(1 - \frac{1}{(1+y)^T}\right) = \frac{CF}{y}$$

Example 2.6 How much money should you be willing to pay in order to buy a contract offering $100 per year for perpetuity? Assume the discount rate is 5%. The answer is

$$P_0 = \frac{\$100}{0.05} = \$2,000$$

Remark 2.1 In practice, it should be noted that most bonds pay either annual or semiannual coupons.

The price P_0 at date $t = 0$ of a bond **delivering coupons semiannually** is given by the following formula

$$P_0 = \sum_{i=1}^{2n} \frac{N \times c/2}{(1+y/2)^i} + \frac{N}{(1+y/2)^{2n}}$$

which simplifies into

$$P_0 = \frac{N \times c}{y} \left[1 - \frac{1}{(1+y/2)^{2n}}\right] + \frac{N}{(1+y/2)^{2n}}$$

where N, c, y and n are, respectively, the nominal value, the coupon rate, the yield to maturity (YTM) and the number of semiannual periods to maturity of the bond.

In particular, when c is equal to y, the bond value is equal to face value, as for bonds with annual coupons.

2.2.3 Nominal versus Real Interest Rates

In the previous reasoning, we have actually left aside the issue of inflation. Inflation is a concern, though. You might be able to buy a hamburger with $1 today, but you might not be able to do so in a year from now. The good news is, if one wants to include inflation in the reasoning, one just needs to think in terms of *real* interest rates and apply the previous formulas.

Indeed, most individuals derive utility from consumption of goods, rather than from dollar wealth (and the market acts as if this were the case). So, what we really care about is the real return on investments. Let us see what the real interest rate means: say 5 lbs of potatoes today cost $1. Next year, 5 lbs will cost $1.10. Also suppose that the nominal interest rate (the one the bank quotes to you) is 32%. This means you can invest $1 today and get back $1.32. With these proceeds you can buy 6-lb sacks of potatoes, so the real rate is $(6 - 5)/5 = 20\%$. Without worrying about dollars, this just means you should be able to give someone 5 lbs of potatoes today in exchange for 6 lbs of potatoes (fresh ones, not a year old!) next year. In general, the formula for the real interest rate is

$$1 + R_{\text{real}} = \frac{1 + R_{\text{nominal}}}{1 + i}$$

where i is the inflation rate. For low inflation rates, subtracting inflation from the nominal rate is actually a good proxy for the real rate

$$R_{\text{real}} \simeq R_{\text{nominal}} - i$$

Example 2.7 Let us assume that the nominal interest rate is 5% and the inflation rate is 2%. Then the real interest rate is equal to

$$R_{\text{real}} = \frac{1 + 5\%}{1 + 2\%} - 1 = 2.94118\% \simeq 3\%$$

Remark 2.2 When there is more than one good out there, "the inflation rate" is an elusive statistic. In the United States, one reported figure is the Consumer Price Index (CPI), a scaled price of a representative basket of goods, where the contents of the basket change slowly over time. Now, since individuals will generally substitute goods that have increased in relative cost with goods that have decreased in relative cost (i.e., if the price of Granny Smith apples rises much faster than that of Golden Delicious apples, I may start consuming more Golden Delicious), the CPI inflation rate will probably exceed the effective rate people face.

2.2.4   Time Basis and Compounding Frequency Conventions

Now, careful attention needs to be paid to the question of how an interest rate is defined. To apply present value formulas, one must have some information about both the time basis (usually interest rates are expressed on an annual basis) and the compounding frequency.

Example 2.8 If you invest $100 at a 6% 2-year annual rate with semiannual compounding, you would get $100 $\left(1 + \frac{6\%}{2}\right)$ after 6 months, $100 $\left(1 + \frac{6\%}{2}\right)^2$ after 1 year, $100 $\left(1 + \frac{6\%}{2}\right)^3$ after 1.5 year, and $100 $\left(1 + \frac{6\%}{2}\right)^4$ after 2 years.

Example 2.9 If you invest $100 at a 4% 3-year semiannual rate with semiannual compounding, you would get $100(1 + 4\%)$ after 6 months, $100(1 + 4\%)^2$ after 1 year, ..., $100(1 + 4\%)^6$ after 3 years.

Example 2.10 If you invest $100 at a 3% 1-year semiannual rate with monthly compounding, you would get $100 $\left(1 + \frac{3}{6}\%\right)$ after 1 month, $100 $\left(1 + \frac{3}{6}\%\right)^2$ after 2 months,

..., $100 \left(1 + \frac{3}{6}\%\right)^6$ after 6 months, $100 \left(1 + \frac{3}{6}\%\right)^{12} = \$106.1678$ after 1 year. A simpler way of expressing this would be to consider an equivalent 6.1678% annual rate with annual compounding.

More generally, we obtain the following formula. A x amount invested at the interest rate R_n expressed on an annual basis and compounded n times per year grows to the amount $x \left(1 + \frac{R_n}{n}\right)^{nT}$ after T years. The effective equivalent annual (i.e., compounded once a year) rate $R_1 = R$ is defined as the solution to

$$x \left(1 + \frac{R_n}{n}\right)^{nT} = x(1 + R)^T$$

or

$$R = \left(1 + \frac{R_n}{n}\right)^n - 1$$

For example, bond yields are often expressed on a yearly basis with semiannual compounding in the United States and in the United Kingdom, as they are expressed on a yearly basis with annual compounding in France or Germany. One can always turn a bond yield into an *effective annual yield* (EAY), that is, an interest rate expressed on a yearly basis with annual compounding.

Example 2.11 What is the effective annual yield of a bond with a $y_2 = 5.5\%$ semiannual compounded yield

$$EAY = \left(1 + \frac{y_2}{2}\right)^2 - 1 = \left(1 + \frac{0.055}{2}\right)^2 - 1 = 0.055756$$

These examples illustrate the relative difficulty in working with interest rates as opposed to discount factors. In practice, most interest rates are expressed on a same time basis, which is an annual basis. So that takes care of one dimension of the problem. Now, it seems desirable to have a homogeneous convention in terms of compounding frequency as well. This is where the concept of *continuous compounding* is useful.

2.2.5 Continuous Compounding

When there are n compounding periods per year, we see that the effective annual interest rate is equal to $R = \left(1 + \frac{R_n}{n}\right)^n - 1$. One natural question is: what happens if we let the compounding frequency increase without bound, so that we virtually perform a continuous compounding. The amount of money obtained per x invested after T years is

$$\lim_{n \to \infty} x \left(1 + \frac{R_n}{n}\right)^{nT} = xe^{R^c T}$$

where R^c expressed on an annual basis is a continuously compounded rate.

Proof If you are interested in a proof of that result, just note that

$$\ln\left(1 + \frac{R_n}{n}\right)^{nT} = nT \ln\left(1 + \frac{R_n}{n}\right) = R_n T \frac{\ln\left(1 + \dfrac{R_n}{n}\right)}{\dfrac{R_n}{n}} = R_n T \frac{\ln\left(1 + \dfrac{R_n}{n}\right) - \ln(1)}{\dfrac{R_n}{n}}$$

As n goes to infinity, $\frac{R_n}{n}$ goes to zero, so that we have

$$\ln\left(1 + \frac{R_n}{n}\right)^{nT} = R_n T \frac{f\left(1 + \dfrac{R_n}{n}\right) - f(1)}{\dfrac{R_n}{n}} \xrightarrow[n \to \infty]{} R^c T f'(1)$$

where f is defined by $f(x) = \ln(x)$. You may indeed recall from calculus that

$$f'(x) = \lim_{h \to 0} \frac{f(x + h) - f(x)}{h}$$

Given that $f'(x) = \frac{1}{x}$, we obtain $\ln\left(1 + \frac{R_n}{n}\right)^{nT} \xrightarrow[n \to \infty]{} R^c T$ or $\left(1 + \frac{R_n}{n}\right)^{nT} \xrightarrow[n \to \infty]{} e^{R^c T}$. ∎

This is convenient because it allows us to obtain a very easy derivation of the future or present value of any cash flow, using

$$FV_t(CF_0) = CF_0 e^{R^c t}$$

$$PV(CF_t) = CF_t e^{-R^c t}$$

where $FV_t(CF_0)$ is the future value at date t of a cash flow CF_0 invested at date 0 at a R^c continuously compounded rate, and $PV(CF_t)$ is the present value at date 0 of a cash flow CF_t received at date t.

Example 2.12 The future value of \$1 invested over 2.5 years, when the continuously compounded rate is 5.25% (expressed on an annual basis), is \$1 $\times$ e$^{2.5 \times 0.0525}$ = \$1.140253.

Example 2.13 The present value of \$100 received in 6.3 years, when the continuously compounded rate is 4.5% (expressed on an annual basis), is \$100 $\times$ e$^{-6.3 \times 0.045}$ = \$75.3143.

One may of course easily obtain the effective equivalent annual (i.e., compounded once a year) rate R as the solution to

$$xe^{R^c T} = x(1 + R)^T$$

or

$$R = e^{R^c} - 1$$

It should be noted that the difference $R - R^c$ is actually small when R is small. Indeed, we know from numerical analysis that

$$e^x = 1 + x + \frac{x^2}{2!} + \frac{x^3}{3!} + \cdots + \frac{x^j}{j!} + \cdots$$

so that $R \simeq R^c$ as a first-order approximation.

Example 2.14 The equivalent annual rate of a 6% continuously compounded interest rate is $R = e^{0.06} - 1 = 6.1837\%$.

Note that $R - R^c > 0$. That makes sense; it means that one should invest at a higher rate when compounding is less frequent to generate the same amount of cash at the end of a given period.

2.3 Taxonomy of Rates

There are a host of types of interest rates involved in the fixed-income jargon. It is very important that you obtain a good understanding of the meaning of each concept before you move further along.

2.3.1 Coupon Rate and Current Yield

The coupon rate is the stated interest rate on a security, referred to as an annual percentage of face value. It is commonly paid twice a year (in the United States, for example) or once a year (in France and Germany, for example). It is called the *coupon rate* because bearer bonds carry coupons for interest payments. Each coupon entitles the bearer to a payment when a set date has been reached. Today, most bonds are registered in holders' names, and interest payments are sent to the registered holder, but the term *coupon rate* is still widely used.

It is essentially used to obtain the cash flows and shall not be confused with the actual *current yield*. The current yield y_c is obtained using the following formula

$$y_c = \frac{cN}{P}$$

where c is the coupon rate, N is the nominal value and P is the current price.

Example 2.15 A $1,000 bond has an annual coupon rate of 7%, so it pays $70 a year. If you buy the bond for $900, your actual current yield is

$$7.78\% = \frac{\$70}{\$900}$$

If you buy the bond for $1,100, the current yield is

$$6.36\% = \frac{\$70}{\$1,100}$$

In any event, the 7% coupon rate does not change.

2.3.2 Yield to Maturity

The yield to maturity (YTM) is the single rate that sets the present value of the cash flows equal to the bond price. More precisely, the bond price P is found by discounting future cash flows back to their present value as indicated in the two following formulas depending on the coupon frequency:

- *When we assume that coupons are paid semiannually*

$$P = \sum_{t=1}^{2T} \frac{CF_t}{\left(1 + \frac{y_2}{2}\right)^t}$$

the yield denoted by y_2 is expressed on a yearly basis with semiannual compounding where $2T$ is the number of semiannual periods.

- *When we assume that coupons are paid annually*

$$P = \sum_{t=1}^{T} \frac{CF_t}{(1 + y)^t}$$

the yield denoted by y is expressed on a yearly basis with annual compounding where T is the number of annual periods.

In other words, the YTM is the internal rate of return (IRR) of the series of cash flows. Hence, each cash flow is discounted using the same rate. We implicitly assume that the yield curve is flat at a point in time. In brief, an IRR is an average discount rate assumed to be constant over the different maturities. It is equivalently the unique rate that would prevail if the yield curve happened to be flat at date t (which of course is not generally the case). It may be easily computed by trial and error (as well as by using built-in functions in spreadsheet software such as the IRR function in Microsoft's *Excel*).

Example 2.16 We consider a $1,000 nominal value 2-year bond with 8% coupon paid semiannually, which sells for 103–23. What is the yield to maturity of this bond? To answer this question, we first note that 103–23 corresponds to $\left(103 + \frac{23}{32}\right)\% = 103.72\%$ and obtain the following equation

$$1,037.2 = \frac{40}{1 + \frac{y_2}{2}} + \frac{40}{\left(1 + \frac{y_2}{2}\right)^2} + \frac{40}{\left(1 + \frac{y_2}{2}\right)^3} + \frac{1,040}{\left(1 + \frac{y_2}{2}\right)^4}$$

This equation can be solved by trial and error and we obtain $\frac{y_2}{2} = 3\%$ or $y_2 = 6\%$.

Example 2.17 We consider a $1,000 face value 3-year bond with 10% annual coupon, which sells for 101. The yield to maturity of this bond verifies the following equation

$$1,010 = \frac{100}{1 + y} + \frac{100}{(1 + y)^2} + \frac{1,100}{(1 + y)^3}$$

This equation can be solved by trial and error and we obtain $y = 9.601\%$.

A YTM can also be seen as a total return rate. This is the point of view of the following remark.

Remark 2.3   Yield to Maturity as a Total Return Rate

Today, we buy a bond with a 3-year maturity and a YTM of 10% for $87.57. The bond pays an annual coupon of $5 and a principal of $100 at maturity. We will receive $5 at the end of the first year, $5 at the end of the second year and $105 after 3 years. Assuming we reinvest the intermediate cash flows, that is, the coupons paid after 1 year and 2 years, at an annual rate of 10%, the total cash flows we receive at maturity are

$$5 \times (1.1)^2 + 5 \times (1.1) + 105 = \$116.55$$

Our investment therefore generates an annual total return rate y over the period, such that

$$(1 + y)^3 = \frac{116.55}{87.57}$$

$$y = 10\%$$

Under certain technical conditions, there exits a one-to-one correspondence between the price and the YTM of a bond. Therefore, giving a YTM for a bond is equivalent to giving a price for the bond. It should be noted that this is precisely what is actually done in the bond market, where bonds are often quoted in yield to maturity. It should, however, be emphasized that a bond YTM is not a very meaningful number. This is because there is no reason one should discount cash flows occurring on different dates with a unique discount rate. In other words, YTM is a complex average of pure discount rates that makes the present value of the bond's payments equal to its price. Unless the term structure of interest rates is flat, there is no reason one would consider the YTM on a 10-year bond as the relevant discount rate for a 10-year horizon. The relevant discount rate is the 10-year pure discount rate, which is discussed below. You may actually want to think about the YTM as just a convenient way of reexpressing the bond price.

2.3.3   Spot Zero-Coupon (or Discount) Rate

This is a very important concept. It is implicitly defined in the following way:

$$B(0, t) = \frac{1}{[1 + R(0, t)]^t}$$

where $B(0, t)$ is the market price at date 0 of a bond paying off $1 at date t. Note again that such an instrument may not exist in the market. For now, we shall assume that the instrument is traded, and we will see in Chapter 4 how to proceed in the absence of the unit zero-coupon bond with the desired maturity.

Note that the yield to maturity and the zero-coupon rate of a strip bond (i.e., a zero-coupon bond) are identical.

Example 2.18   Let us consider a 2-year zero-coupon bond that trades at $92. The 2-year zero-coupon rate $R(0, 2)$ is such that

$$92 = \frac{100}{[1 + R(0, 2)]^2}$$

$$R(0, 2) = 4.26\%$$

Note that the 2-year discount factor is simply 0.92.

In practice, when we know the spot zero-coupon yield curve $\theta \longmapsto R(0, \theta)$, we are able to obtain spot prices for all fixed-income securities with known future cash flows. Chapter 4 is entirely devoted to the very important question of deriving the zero-coupon yield curve.

Besides, zero-coupon rates make it possible to find other very useful forward rates and par yields.

2.3.4   Forward Rates

If $R(0, t)$ is the rate at which you can invest today in a t period bond, we can define an implied forward rate (sometimes called *forward zero-coupon rate*) between years x and y as

$$F(0, x, y - x) = \left[\frac{(1 + R(0, y))^y}{(1 + R(0, x))^x} \right]^{\frac{1}{y-x}} - 1 \qquad (2.3)$$

$F(0, x, y - x)$ is the forward rate as seen from date $t = 0$, starting at date $t = x$, and with residual maturity $y - x$. In practice, it is very common to draw the forward curve $\theta \longmapsto F(0, x, \theta)$ with rates starting at date x. $F^c(0, x, y - x)$ is the continuously compounded equivalent of $F(0, x, y - x)$.

Basically, $F(0, x, y - x)$ is the rate at which you could sign a contract today to borrow or lend between periods x and y, as is now explained in the following remark.

Remark 2.4   A Rate That Can Be Guaranteed

The forward rate is the rate that can be guaranteed now on a transaction occurring in the future. Take a simple example. We simultaneously borrow and lend $1 repayable at the end of 2 years and 1 year, respectively. The cash flows generated by this transaction are as follows:

	Today	In 1 year	In 2 years
Borrow	1		$-(1 + R(0, 2))^2$
Lend	-1	$1 + R(0, 1)$	
Total	0	$1 + R(0, 1)$	$-(1 + R(0, 2))^2$

This is equivalent to borrowing $1 + R(0, 1)$ in 1 year, repayable in 2 years at the amount of $(1 + R(0, 2))^2$. The implied rate on the loan is given by the following equation

$$\frac{(1 + R(0, 2))^2}{1 + R(0, 1)} - 1 = F(0, 1, 1)$$

$F(0, 1, 1)$ is therefore the rate that can be guaranteed now for a loan starting in 1 year and repayable after 2 years.

In particular, we have that

$$R(0, t) = [(1 + R(0, 1))(1 + F(0, 1, 1))(1 + F(0, 2, 1)) \cdots (1 + F(0, t-1, 1))]^{\frac{1}{t}} - 1$$

Besides, the forward rate may be seen as a break-even point that equalizes the rate of return on bonds across the entire maturity spectrum. This is the point of view developed in the following remark.

Remark 2.5   Forward Rate as a Break-Even Point

The forward rate can also be considered as the break-even point that equalizes the rates of return on bonds (which are homogeneous in terms of default risk) across the entire maturity spectrum. Assume a zero-coupon yield curve today from which we derive the forward yield curve starting in 1 year (see table below). The 1-year and 2-year zero-coupon rates are 4% and 4.5%, respectively. The rate of return for the coming year of the 1-year zero-coupon bond is of course 4%, while the return on the 2-year bond depends on the selling price of the bond in 1 year. What is the level of the 1-year zero-coupon rate in 1 year that would ensure that the 2-year bond also has a 4% rate of return? The answer is 5.002%. With this rate, the price of the 2-year bond will rise from the initial 91.573 ($100/1.045^2$) to 95.236 ($100/1.05002$) in 1 year, generating a return of 4% over the period. So the forward rate $F(0, 1, 1)$ at 5.002% is the future level of the 1-year zero-coupon rate that makes the investor indifferent between the 1-year and the 2-year bonds during the year ahead.

	Zero-coupon rate (%)		Forward rate starting in 1 year (%)
$R(0, 1)$	4.000	$F(0, 1, 1)$	5.002
$R(0, 2)$	4.500	$F(0, 1, 2)$	5.504
$R(0, 3)$	5.000	$F(0, 1, 3)$	5.670
$R(0, 4)$	5.250	$F(0, 1, 4)$	5.878
$R(0, 5)$	5.500	$F(0, 1, 5)$	6.104
$R(0, 6)$	5.750	$F(0, 1, 6)$	6.191
$R(0, 7)$	5.875	$F(0, 1, 7)$	6.289
$R(0, 8)$	6.000	$F(0, 1, 8)$	6.394
$R(0, 9)$	6.125	$F(0, 1, 9)$	6.503
$R(0, 10)$	6.250	—	—

If the forward rate $F(0, 1, 2)$ is 5.504%, a zero-coupon bond with a 3-year maturity also returns 4% for the coming year. Consequently, all the bonds have the same 4% return rate for the year ahead. Breakeven is therefore the future scenario that balances all bond investments.

There is a particular forward rate that is called the *instantaneous forward rate*. The instantaneous forward rate $f(t, s)$ is the forward rate seen at date t, starting at date s and maturing an infinitely small instant later on. It is a continuously compounded rate. The instantaneous forward rate is defined mathematically by the following equation

$$f(t, s) = \lim_{T-s \to 0} F^c(t, s, T - s) \tag{2.4}$$

Note that $f(t, t) = r(t)$ is the short-term interest rate at date t. Typically, this is the rate with a 1-day maturity in the market. By making s vary between 1 day and 30 years, it is possible to plot the level of instantaneous forward rates at dates that are staggered over time. This is what is called the *instantaneous forward yield curve*. In practice, the market treats the instantaneous forward rate as a forward rate with a maturity of between 1 day and 3 months. It is especially useful for modeling purposes. For example, the Heath–Jarrow–Morton model (1992), which will be studied in Chapter 12, begins by modeling the instantaneous forward yield curve.

2.3.5 Bond Par Yield

In practice, the YTM curve suffers from the coupon effect. Two bonds having the same maturity but different coupon rates do not necessarily have the same YTM. For example, in the case of an upward sloping curve, the bond that pays the highest coupon has the lowest YTM. To overcome this coupon effect, it is customary to plot the par yield curve. Recall that a par bond is a bond with a coupon identical to its yield to maturity. The bond's price is therefore equal to its principal. Then we define the par yield $c(n)$ so that a n-year maturity fixed bond paying annually a coupon rate of $c(n)$ with a \$100 face value quotes par

$$\frac{100 \times c(n)}{1 + R(0, 1)} + \frac{100 \times c(n)}{[1 + R(0, 2)]^2} + \cdots + \frac{100 + 100 \times c(n)}{[1 + R(0, n)]^n} = 100$$

We finally obtain

$$c(n) = \frac{1 - \dfrac{1}{(1 + R(0, n))^n}}{\displaystyle\sum_{i=1}^{n} \dfrac{1}{(1 + R(0, i))^i}} \tag{2.5}$$

Accordingly, we can extract the par yield curve $\theta \longmapsto c(\theta)$ when we know the zero-coupon rates $R(0, 1), R(0, 2), \ldots, R(0, \theta)$.

Typically, the par yield curve is used to determine the coupon level of a bond issued at par.

2.4   End of Chapter Summary

Bond pricing is typically performed by taking the discounted value of the bond cash flows. In this chapter, we review the basics of the mathematics of discounting, including time basis and compounding conventions. We also provide the reader with a definition of the various types of interest rates involved in the fixed-income jargon; in particular, we define the notions of coupon rate, current yield, yield to maturity, spot rate, forward rate and bond par yield.

2.5   References and Further Reading

Choudhry, M., 2001, *Bond Market Securities*, Prentice Hall, New York.
Fabozzi, F.J., 1996, *Fixed-Income Mathematics*, 3rd Edition, McGraw-Hill, New York.

Fabozzi, F.J., 1999, *Bond Markets: Analysis and Strategies*, 4th Edition, Prentice Hall, New York.

Florent, I., and P. Priaulet, 2001 Focus on Interest Rates: Comparing the Approaches of Portfolio Managers and Option Writers, Quants, HSBC-CCF, No. 39.

2.6 Problems

Exercise 2.1   Suppose the 1-year continuously compounded interest rate is 12%. What is the effective annual interest rate?

Exercise 2.2   If you deposit $2,500 in a bank account that earns 8% annually on a continuously compounded basis, what will be the account balance in 7.14 years?

Exercise 2.3   If an investment has a cumulative 63.45% rate of return over 3.78 years, what is the annual continuously compounded rate of return?

Exercise 2.4   How long does it take to double a $100 initial investment when investing at a 5% continuously compounded interest rate?

Exercise 2.5   A invests $1,000 at 5% per annum on a continuously compounded basis. B invests $200 at 20% per annum on a continuously compounded basis. Does B ever catch up with A? How long does it take?

Exercise 2.6   A BTP is an Italian Treasury bond.

1. What is the main characteristic of BTPs compared to all other Treasury bonds of the Euro area? compared to US T-bonds?
2. Let us consider the following BTP: coupon 4%, maturity 5.25 years, yield 4.25%. Compute its gross price and its clean price.

Exercise 2.7   1. What is the price of a 5-year bond with a nominal value of $100, a yield to maturity of 7% (with annual compounding frequency), a 10% coupon rate and an annual coupon frequency?
2. Same question for a yield to maturity of 8%, 9% and 10%. Conclude.

Exercise 2.8   1. What is the price of a 5-year bond with a nominal value of $100, a yield to maturity of 7% (with semiannual compounding frequency), a 10% coupon rate, and semiannual coupon payments?
2. Same question for a yield to maturity of 8%, 9% and 10%.

Exercise 2.9   1. What is the price of a 5-year bond with a nominal value of $100, a yield to maturity of 7% (with quarterly compounding frequency), a 10% coupon rate, and quarterly coupon payments?
2. Same question for a yield to maturity of 8%, 9% and 10%.

Exercise 2.10 1. What is the yield to maturity of a 5-year bond with a nominal value of $100, a 10% coupon rate, an annual coupon frequency and a price of 97.856?

2. Same question for a price of 100 and 105.451.

Exercise 2.11 1. What is the yield to maturity of a 5-year bond with a nominal value of $100, a 10% coupon rate, semiannual coupon payments and a price of 97.856?

2. Same question for a price of 100 and 105.451.

Exercise 2.12 1. What is the yield to maturity of a 5-year bond with a nominal value of $100, a 10% coupon rate, quarterly coupon payments and a price of 97.856?

2. Same question for a price of 100 and 105.451.

Exercise 2.13 Consider the following bond: annual coupon 5%, maturity 5 years, annual compounding frequency.

1. What is its relative price change if its required yield increases from 10% to 11%?

2. What is its relative price change if its required yield increases from 5% to 6%?

3. What conclusion can you draw from these examples? Explain why.

Exercise 2.14 We consider the following zero-coupon curve:

Maturity (year)	Zero-coupon rate (%)
1	4.00
2	4.50
3	4.75
4	4.90
5	5.00

1. What is the price of a 5-year bond with a $100 face value, which delivers a 5% annual coupon rate?

2. What is the yield to maturity of this bond?

3. We suppose that the zero-coupon curve increases instantaneously and uniformly by 0.5%. What is the new price and the new yield to maturity of the bond? What is the impact of this rate increase for the bondholder?

4. We suppose now that the zero-coupon curve remains stable over time. You hold the bond until maturity. What is the annual return rate of your investment? Why is this rate different from the yield to maturity?

Exercise 2.15 Let us consider the two following French Treasury bonds whose characteristics are the following:

Name	Maturity (years)	Coupon rate (%)	Price
Bond 1	6	5	100
Bond 2	20	0	31.18

Your investment horizon is 6 years. Which of the two bonds will you select?

Exercise 2.16   1. What is the price of the US Treasury Strip bond with a remaining maturity of 10 years, yielding 5%?
2. What is the price of the Euro Treasury Strip bond with a remaining maturity of 10 years, yielding 5%?
3. What is the equivalent annual yield of the US T-Strip bond, the equivalent semiannual yield of the Euro T-Strip bond?

Exercise 2.17   Consider the US T-bond with coupon 4.625% and maturity date 05/15/2006.
1. Compute the accrued interest of that bond on 01/07/2002.
2. Its quoted price was 101.0625 on 01/07/2002. Calculate its yield to maturity. What is the equivalent annual yield to maturity?
3. Knowing that the repo rate for that bond was 1.67% on 01/07/2002, calculate the daily net funding cost or gain for an investor that is long $1 million of that bond.

Exercise 2.18   We consider three bonds with the following features:

Bond	Maturity (years)	Annual coupon	Price
Bond 1	1	10	106.56
Bond 2	2	8	106.20
Bond 3	3	8	106.45

1. Find the 1-year, 2-year and 3-year zero-coupon rates from the table above.
2. We consider another bond with the following features:

Bond	Maturity	Annual coupon	Price
Bond 4	3 years	9	109.01

Use the zero-coupon curve to price this bond.
3. Find an arbitrage strategy.

Exercise 2.19   An investor wants to invest $1,000 cash for a period of 5 days. He has two alternative choices:
- either invest in a T-bill with a remaining maturity of 10 days
- or roll over his cash using the overnight repo rate.

1. Knowing that the T-bill yields 1.70% at the beginning of the investment period and 1.64% at the end (on a discount basis), and that the overnight repo rate has the following values over the investment period:

- day 1: 1.80%
- day 2: 1.74%
- day 3: 1.70%
- day 4: 1.65%
- day 5: 1.67%

which of the two strategies is the more profitable?
2. What is the interest-rate risk inherent in each strategy?

Exercise 2.20 We consider two bonds with the following features:

Bond	Maturity (years)	Coupon rate (%)	Price	YTM (%)
Bond 1	10	10	1,352.2	5.359
Bond 2	10	5	964.3	5.473

YTM stands for yield to maturity. These two bonds have a $1,000 face value and an annual coupon frequency.

1. An investor buys these two bonds and holds them until maturity. Compute the annual return rate over the period supposing that the yield curve becomes instantaneously flat at a 5.4% level and remains stable at this level during 10 years.
2. What is the rate level such that these two bonds provide the same annual return rate? In this case what is the annual return rate of the two bonds?

Exercise 2.21 Assume that today is 01/01/98. Determine as many points as possible in today's yield curve (or term structure of interest rates), knowing that there are three risk-free bonds with the following characteristics:

- A pure discount bond with face value $1,000 that matures on 06/30/98 is selling today at $980.
- A 6% annual coupon bond with face value $1,000 that matures on 06/30/99 is selling today at $1,010.
- An 8% annual coupon bond with face value $1,000 that matures on 06/30/00 is selling today at $1,050.

Exercise 2.22 Assume today is 01/01/98. The yield compounding frequency is considered annual. A risk-free pure discount bond with face value $1,000 maturing on 12/31/98 is selling today at $940. The forward rate for the period 01/01/99 to 06/30/99 is 7%. Compute the price of a pure discount bond maturing on 06/30/99, with $1,000 face value.

Exercise 2.23 Assume the following information about a Treasury zero-coupon bond yield curve on 09/20/00:

Maturity (years)	Zero-coupon rate (%)	Maturity (years)	Zero-coupon rate (%)
1	5.42	6	6.06
2	5.72	7	6.14
3	5.80	8	6.20
4	5.92	9	6.20
5	5.94	10	6.17

All yields are semiannual.

1. Find the 1-year forward rates starting on each of the dates through 09/20/09.
2. Find the 2-year forward rates starting on each of the dates through 09/20/08.

3. Find the 3-year forward rate starting on 09/20/01.
4. Find the 4-year forward rate starting on 09/20/01.

Exercise 2.24 Assume the following bond yields, compounded semiannually.
6-month Treasury Strip: 5.00%;
1-year Treasury Strip: 5.25%;
18-month Treasury Strip: 5.75%.

1. What is the 6-month forward rate in 6 months?
2. What is the 1-year forward rate in 6 months?
3. What is the price of a semiannual 10% coupon Treasury bond that matures in exactly 18 months?

Exercise 2.25 Assume the following bond yields, compounded semiannually:
1-year Treasury Strip: 6.0%
1-year forward rate, in 1 year: 6.5%
1-year forward rate in 2 years: 7.0%

1. What is the yield on the 2-year Treasury Strip?
2. What is the yield on the 3-year Treasury Strip?
3. Do you have enough information to price a 2-year Treasury note with a 5% semiannual coupon? If not, what further information do you need?

Exercise 2.26 Consider a coupon bond with $n = 20$ semesters (i.e., 10 years) to maturity, an annual coupon rate $c = 6.5\%$ (coupons are paid semiannually), and nominal value $N = \$1,000$. Suppose that the semiannually compounded yield to maturity (YTM) of this bond is $y_2 = 5.5\%$.

1. Compute the current price of the bond using the annuity formula.
2. Compute the annually compounded YTM and the current yield of the bond. Compare them with y_2.
3. If the yield to maturity on the bond does not change over the next semester, what is the Holding Period Return (HPR) obtained from buying the bond now and selling it one semester from now, just after coupon payment? At what price will the bond sell one semester from now just after coupon payment?

Exercise 2.27 Consider the following prices of zero-coupon bonds with nominal value $1,000 and maturities (in semesters) $n = 1, 2, 3, 4 : P_{0,1} = \$968.52, P_{0,2} = \$929.02, P_{0,3} = \$915.15, P_{0,4} = \$905.95$.

1. Compute the yield on a discount basis y_d for the four zero-coupon bonds.
2. Compute the spot rates $R_2(0, 0.5), R_2(0, 1), R_2(0, 1.5), R_2(0, 2)$ implied by the prices given above, and plot the yield curve obtained in this case. What is its shape?
3. Use the spot rates obtained above to compute the price of a coupon bond with maturity $n = 4$, annual coupon rate $c = 7\%$ and face value $N = \$1,000$. Is the bond selling at premium, par or discount?

Exercise 2.28   The spot rates with semiannual compounding for maturities (in semesters) ranging from 1 to 5 are $R_2(0, 0.5) = 5\%$, $R_2(0, 1) = 5.25\%$, $R_2(0, 1.5) = 5.75\%$, $R_2(0, 2) = 6.2\%$, $R_2(0, 2.5) = 6\%$.

1. Use the spot rates given above to compute the forward rates $F_2\left(0, \frac{n-1}{2}, \frac{1}{2}\right)$, for $n = 2, 3, 4, 5$, and plot them on a graph.
2. What positions would you take now in zero-coupon bonds in order to earn for certain an annualized return of 7.55% in the fourth semester (i.e., between times 3 and 4)? Quantify the maturities of the bonds used and the positions taken.
3. What positions would you take now in zero-coupon bonds in order to earn for certain an annualized return of 5.2% in the fifth semester (i.e., between times 4 and 5)? Quantify again the maturities and the positions taken.
4. Compute eventually the positions that you need to take in zero-coupon bonds with maturities 3 and 5 to earn an Effective Annual Yield of 6.47% (observe that $1 + 0.0647 \simeq [1 + (0.0755/2)] \times [1 + (0.052/2)])$ in the year starting 3 semesters from now (i.e., between times 3 and 5).

Exercise 2.29   You are a portfolio manager. You buy at time $t = 0$ a French Treasury bond with annual coupon 6%, and maturity 4 years at a price of 100.5. Your investment horizon is 2.5 years. The reinvestment rate is supposed to be 4%, the yield to maturity of the bond 5.5% at the end of your investment horizon. Determine the annualized total return of the bond over the horizon.

Exercise 2.30   Consider the US floating-rate bond whose coupon rate is set equal to the 6-month US$ Libor rate y_{L6} at the beginning of every coupon period (reset date) and whose maturity value is 100.

1. Calculate its price one coupon period before maturity, two coupon periods before maturity, n coupon periods before maturity (n is an integer).
2. What is the price of the floater between two reset dates?

Term Structure of Interest Rates

PART II

3
Empirical Properties and Classical Theories of the Term Structure

After a presentation of the different yields of the market in Chapter 2, we now define the term structure of interest rates, also called the yield curve, as the graph mapping interest rates corresponding to their respective maturity. The idea of this chapter is to understand what kind of shape it can take, how it evolves over time as well as the answers to these questions given by the classical theories of the term structure of interest rates.

3.1 Definition and Properties of the Term Structure

The term structure of interest rates is the series of interest rates ordered by term-to-maturity at a given time. The nature of interest rates determines the nature of the term structure. Depending on which of the above rates we are interested in, we can get several different types of yield curves. We focus on the following types:

$\theta \longmapsto y(\theta)$, which is the yield to maturity curve at date t with maturity θ

$\theta \longmapsto SR(\theta)$, which is the swap rate curve at date t with maturity θ

$\theta \longmapsto R(t, \theta)$, which is the zero-coupon yield curve at date t with maturity θ

$\theta \longmapsto c(\theta)$, which is the par yield curve at date t with maturity θ

$\theta \longmapsto F(t, s, \theta)$, which is, at date t, the curve of forward rates starting at date s with residual maturity θ

$s \longmapsto f(t, s)$, which is the instantaneous forward term structure at date t, starting at date s with infinitesimal maturity.

For the last curve, note that it is the starting date s that changes but not the maturity of the instantaneous forward rate, which is always infinitesimal (one instant later, see equation (2.4)). Note that yields to maturity and swap yields are market data, whereas zero-coupon, forward and par yields are constructed implicitly using market data. So the first distinction to be made is the one between market curves and implied curves. Besides, the zero-coupon yield curve permits to derive forward curves and the par yield curve using, respectively, equations (2.3, 2.4 and 2.5). In Figure 3.1, we have plotted all these curves (except the yield to maturity curve) on March 11, 1998 for the United States. The forward yield curve is the curve that starts in 1 year. Note how the shapes of the curves differ: the 1-year forward yield curve is upward sloping, whereas the other curves are inverted over the short term (until the 1-year maturity). The difference between the swap curve and the par curve is the term structure of the yield spreads between the interbank market and the Treasury bond market. Like the zero-coupon yield curve from the 1-year maturity onwards, the 1-year forward yield curve is strictly upward sloping. That slope steepens at the 8-year maturity because the zero-coupon yield curve starts to slope upwards in the same maturity band. The slope of the instantaneous forward yield curve is even more pronounced, for the same

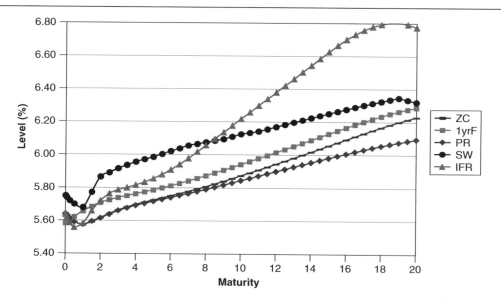

Figure 3.1 Different rate curves—USA—March 11, 1998. ZC = zero-coupon curve, 1yrF = 1-year forward yield curve, IFR = instantaneous forward curve, PR = par yield curve, SW = swap curve.

reasons. The par yield curve follows the same pattern as the zero-coupon curve until the 1-year maturity and, logically, differs thereafter.

We will now focus on the different shapes that the term structure of interest rates may take and the link between the shape of the par yield curve and the relative positions of the corresponding zero-coupon and forward rates.

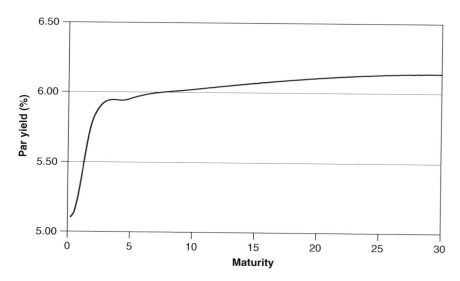

Figure 3.2 US Treasury par yield curve as of 11/03/1999.

3.1.1 What Kind of Shape Can It Take?

The term structure of interest rates can take several varied shapes that can be divided into four standard types:

- *quasi-flat (see Figure 3.2);*

- *increasing (see Figure 3.3);*

- *decreasing (see Figure 3.4);*

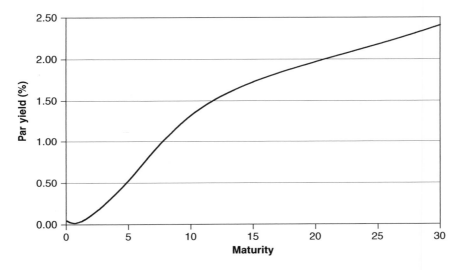

Figure 3.3   Japanese government par yield curve as of 04/27/2001.

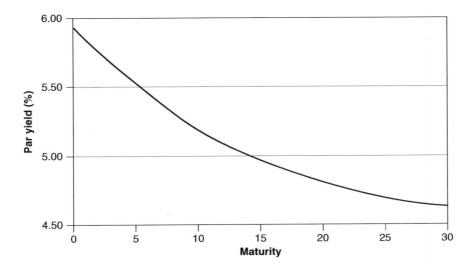

Figure 3.4   UK government par yield curve as of 10/19/2000.

Fixed Income Securities

- *humped [see Figures 3.5 (decreasing on the short end, and then increasing) and 3.6 (increasing on the short end, and then decreasing)].*

In Figures 3.5 and 3.6, note that the Euro government par yield curve as of 04/04/01 is humped, with a global increasing shape, whereas the US Treasury par yield curve as of 02/29/00 is humped with a global decreasing shape.

There exists a direct link between the shape of a par yield curve and the relative positions of the corresponding zero-coupon and forward curves. Two generic cases can be considered, an increasing par yield curve (see Figure 3.7) and a decreasing par yield curve (see Figure 3.8).

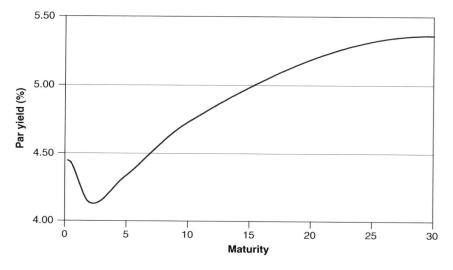

Figure 3.5 Euro government par yield curve as of 04/04/2001 (made of French and German government bonds).

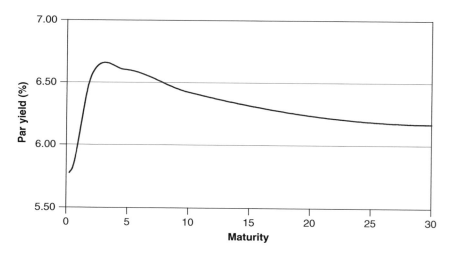

Figure 3.6 US Treasury par yield curve as of 02/29/2000.

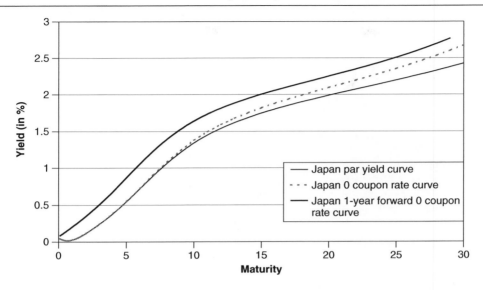

Figure 3.7 Relative positions of par yield, zero-coupon rate and forward zero-coupon rate curves for a rising term structure.

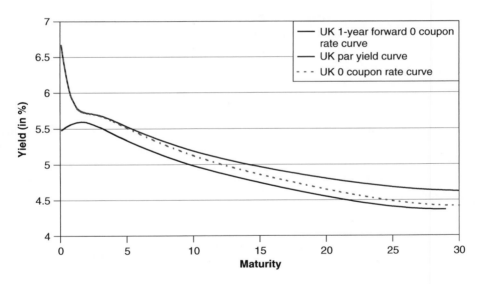

Figure 3.8 Relative positions of par yield, zero-coupon rate and forward zero-coupon rate curves for a falling term structure.

We can see the following from the two graphs:

- *When the current par yield curve is increasing (respectively, decreasing), the current zero-coupon rate curve is above (respectively, below) it, so as to offset the fact that the sum of the coupons discounted at the coupon rate is inferior (respectively, superior) to the sum of the coupons discounted at the zero-coupon rate. We provide a proof of this assertion in the Exercise part.*

Fixed Income Securities

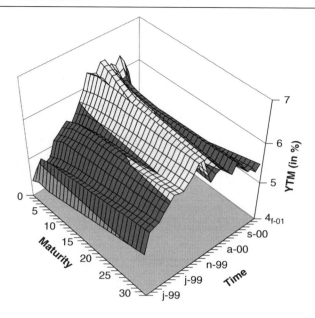

Figure 3.9

Monthly evolution of US government zero-coupon yield curves between January 1999 and March 2001.

- *When the current par yield curve is increasing (respectively, decreasing), the forward zero-coupon rate curve is above (respectively, below) the current zero-coupon rate curve. We provide a proof of this assertion in the Exercise part.*

We clearly see in these examples that curve shapes change over time. The question now is to understand how the term structure of interest rates evolves over time.

3.1.2 How Does It Evolve over Time?

The term structure of interest rates moves over time as is illustrated in Figure 3.9, which shows the monthly evolution of US government yield curves between January 1999 and March 2001.

The historical study of the evolution of the yield curve over time enables to emphasize the five following points:

- *Interest rates are not negative.*

- *Interest rates are affected by mean-reversion effects.*

- *Changes of interest rates are not perfectly correlated.*

- *The volatility of short-term rates is higher than the volatility of long-term rates.*

- *Three main factors explain more than 95% of the changes in the yield curve.*

Interest Rates Are Not Negative

While real interest rates may become negative, generally in a context when the inflation rate is rising exponentially under the effect of external shocks such as a petroleum crisis, and at the same time the economy cannot support too high nominal rates because of the risk of dramatically reducing consumption and consequently growth, nominal interest rates cannot be negative. In fact,

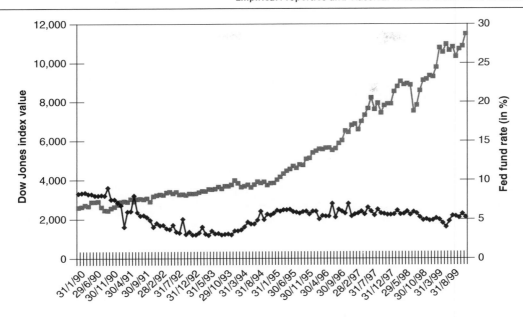

Figure 3.10 Mean reversion of rates compared to the trend followed by equity markets.

it seems crazy to lend money at a negative interest rate.[1] That is why, in particular, interest rates cannot be assumed to be normally distributed.

Mean-Reverting Behavior of Interest Rates

Historical observation shows that when rates reach high levels, they subsequently tend to decline rather than rise still further. Reversion has also been observed when rates fall to unusually low levels. To illustrate that effect, we have plotted in Figure 3.10 the value of the Dow Jones Index alongside the Fed fund rate during the 1990s. We can see clearly that the index price exhibits a rising marked trend, whereas the Fed fund rate hovers around an average value of between 3 and 10%. For this reason, interest rates are often modeled using a mean-reversion process, as described in the following remark.

Remark 3.1   How to Model the Mean-Reversion Effect of Rates?

Vasicek (1977) considers the Ornstein–Uhlenbeck process for the short rate $r(t)$ described by equation (3.1) where $W(t)$ is a Brownian motion capturing the impact of random shocks that affect the term structure of interest rates (see Chapter 12 for a detailed presentation of the Vasicek (1977) model).

$$\mathrm{d}r(t) = a[b - r(t)]\,\mathrm{d}t + \sigma\,\mathrm{d}W(t) \qquad (3.1)$$

---

[1]Note nevertheless that one can encounter negative rates in the repo market when specific stocks are very special.

Fixed Income Securities

Parameter b is the long-term average of the short-term interest rate around which $r(t)$ moves. When $r(t)$ is distanced from b, the expected value of the instantaneous change in $r(t)$, equal to $a(b - r(t))$, is positive if $r(t) < b$. In this case, the short rate tends to rise, approaching the average rate with an intensity that increases with the distance from that average and with the value of parameter a (mean-reversion speed). Conversely, if $r(t) > b$, then the expected value of the instantaneous change in $r(t)$ is negative and $r(t)$ decreases over time to move toward b. That said, $r(t)$ can become negative. To offset this effect, we have to consider the square root process (see Chapter 12), or CIR (Cox, Ingersoll and Ross) [Cox *et al.* (1985)], of equation (3.2)

$$dr(t) = a[b - r(t)]\,dt + \sigma\sqrt{r(t)}\,dW(t) \tag{3.2}$$

Here, the short rate is always positive and benefits from the same mean-reverting effect.

Changes in Interest Rates Are Not Perfectly Correlated

A statistical analysis typically shows that correlations between interest-rate movements are clearly not equal to 1, as shown in Table 3.1, which provides correlations between implied zero-coupon rates with various maturities, derived from the French swap market in 1998.

All correlation coefficients are positive and they are decreasing as the difference in maturity is increasing, which is an intuitive result. In some cases, mostly for the short maturities, correlation coefficients are very close to 1. Hence, when pricing and hedging short-term fixed-income products, (e.g., contingent claims on a bond with maturity less than 1 year), a single-factor model (which would involve a correlation matrix for interest-rate movements in which all the terms are equal to 1) based on the short-rate dynamics may be used with minimal mispricing risk. On the other hand, when dealing with contingent claims on fixed-income securities with longer maturity, one is better-off using multifactor models. This holds, in particular, when one attempts to price an asset involving different segments of the yield curve, such as an option on a short-rate–long-rate spread.

Table 3.1   Correlation Matrix for Zero-Coupon Rates Daily Changes.

	1M	3M	6M	1Y	2Y	3Y	4Y	5Y	6Y	7Y	8Y	9Y	10Y
1M	1												
3M	0.992	1											
6M	0.775	0.775	1										
1Y	0.354	0.3	0.637	1									
2Y	0.214	0.165	0.42	0.901	1								
3Y	0.278	0.246	0.484	0.79	0.946	1							
4Y	0.26	0.225	0.444	0.754	0.913	0.983	1						
5Y	0.224	0.179	0.381	0.737	0.879	0.935	0.981	1					
6Y	0.216	0.168	0.352	0.704	0.837	0.892	0.953	0.991	1				
7Y	0.228	0.182	0.35	0.661	0.792	0.859	0.924	0.969	0.991	1			
8Y	0.241	0.199	0.351	0.614	0.745	0.826	0.892	0.936	0.968	0.992	1		
9Y	0.238	0.198	0.339	0.58	0.712	0.798	0.866	0.913	0.95	0.981	0.996	1	
10Y	0.202	0.158	0.296	0.576	0.705	0.779	0.856	0.915	0.952	0.976	0.985	0.99	1

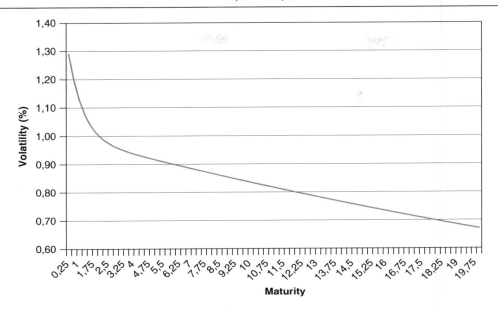

Figure 3.11   Standard form of the term structure of volatility.

Short-Term Rates Are Much More Volatile than Long-Term Rates

We can see that historically

- *the term structure of volatility is a decreasing function (see Figure 3.11 for an example), or an increasing function until the 1-year maturity and a decreasing function for longer maturities, which we call the humped form;*

- *furthermore, there seems to exist some correlation between interest-rate volatility and interest-rate level (see Chapter 12 for more details on that point).*

Three Factors Explain the Quasi-Totality of Rates Changes

Using a principal components analysis (PCA) has become a popular way to study movements of the term structure because it allows one to aggregate the risks in a nonarbitrary way. The concepts behind this powerful statistical technique are fairly simple:

- ***Concept 1***   *Various interest rates for different maturities are highly correlated variables. Even though they are not perfectly correlated (we know this precisely because we witness nonparallel shifts of the yield curve), various interest rates along the yield curve are affected by a limited set of common economic, monetary and financial shocks. As a result, interest rates for various maturities tend to move in the same direction.*

- ***Concept 2***   *Highly correlated variables provide redundant information of one with respect to another. As a consequence, it is tempting to try and identify a set of independent factors that would account for most of the information contained in the time-series of interest-rate variations.*

This is exactly what a PCA does. We will not present the whole theory of this technique, and refer the interested reader to the large statistical literature on the subject [see, for example, Basilevsky

Fixed Income Securities

(1994)]. It is sufficient for us to recall the basic principle. The PCA of a time-series consists in studying the correlation matrix of successive shocks. Its purpose is to explain the behavior of observed variables using a smaller set of unobserved implied variables. From a mathematical standpoint, it consists in transforming a set of m correlated variables into a set of orthogonal variables that reproduce the original information present in the correlation structure. The method allows one to express the interest-rate variations as $\Delta R(t, \theta_k)$, which are highly correlated across different maturities, in terms of new random variables C_t^l, which are statistically uncorrelated

$$\Delta R(t, \theta_k) = \sum_{l=1}^{m} c_{lk} C_t^l$$

An important feature is that, as will be developed later, every empirical investigation shows that the variance of the term structure of interest rates is explained to more than 90% using only the three first components. Hence, we may simply write, where the epsilon term only accounts for less than 10% of the information by doing so,

$$\Delta R(t, \theta_k) = \sum_{l=1}^{3} c_{lk} C_t^l + \varepsilon$$

$$\simeq c_{1k} C_t^1 + c_{2k} C_t^2 + c_{3k} C_t^3$$

where the components have been ordered such that C_t^1 corresponds to the largest fraction of the total variance,[2] C_t^2 corresponds to the second largest fraction of the total variance and C_t^3 corresponds to the third largest fraction of the total variance. The coefficient c_{lk} represents the sensitivity of $\Delta R(t, \theta_k)$ to a variation of C^l. One can show that

$$c_{lk} = \text{corr}(\Delta R(., \theta_k), C^l)$$

Furthermore, these three factors have nice interpretations as being related, respectively, to parallel movement, slope oscillation and curvature of the term structure. The discussion hereafter is illustrated by Figure 3.12, which displays the sensitivity of variations in zero-coupon rates to variations in the factors.

- ***The parallel movement component*** *The data indicate that the component corresponding to the largest eigenvalue (which is selected to be C^1) is such that the function $\theta_k \longmapsto c_{1k}$ is roughly constant, that is, $c_{11} \simeq c_{12} \simeq \cdots \simeq c_{1m}$. This is the reason this component is associated with parallel movements in the interest-rate curve. It can be interpreted as an average rate over shorter and longer maturities. It should be noted that this component always explains more than 60% of the variations in the curve, and provides some justification for simple hedging methods that rely on the assumption of parallel movements. In Figure 3.13, we show upward and downward shift movements, typically implied by a level factor such as the first PCA factor.*

- ***The slope oscillation component*** *The component corresponding to the second largest eigenvalue (which is selected to be C^2) is such that the function $\theta_k \longmapsto c_{2k}$ is roughly increasing or decreasing, that is, $c_{21} \geq c_{22} \geq \cdots \geq c_{2m}$ or $c_{21} \leq c_{22} \leq \cdots \leq c_{2m}$. This function crosses the*

---

[2]It is measured as the ratio of the largest eigenvalue to the sum of all the eigenvalues of the correlation matrix of the interest-rate variations (see the following example extracted from Martellini and Priaulet (2000) for some precisions about that point).

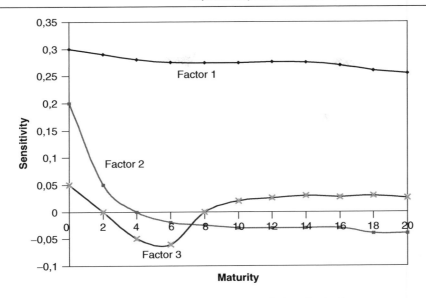

Figure 3.12   Sensitivity of variations in zero-coupon rates to variations in the factors.

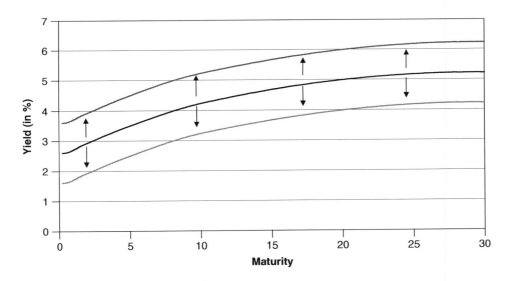

Figure 3.13   Upward and downward shift movements.

x-axis for an interest rate corresponding to a maturity ranging from 2 to 8 years, depending on the period and the country under consideration. This is the reason this component is associated with slope oscillation or a measure of the steepness of the interest-rate curve; that is, it exhibits a differential effect for the short- and the long-term end of the curve. It can be regarded as a short-term/long-term spread, and accounts for 5 to 30% of the changes of the yield curve. In Figure 3.14, we show flattening and steepening twist movements typically implied by a slope factor such as the second PCA factor.

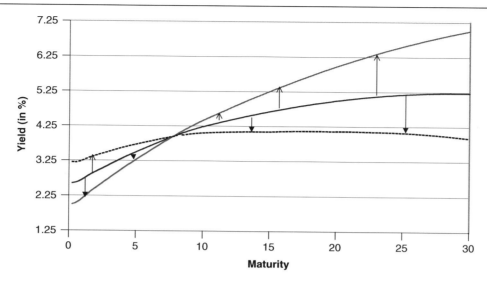

Figure 3.14 Flattening and steepening twist movements.

Note that by combining shift and twist movements, one can define bullish and bearish steepening or flattening movements. A bearish flattening (respectively, steepening) movement is observable when, at the same time, the yield curve shifts upwards and flattens (respectively, steepens). A bullish flattening (respectively, steepening) movement is observable when at the same time the yield curve shifts downwards and flattens (respectively, steepens).

- **The curvature component** *The component corresponding to the third largest eigenvalue (which is selected to be C^3) has a different impact on each of the three segments of the yield curve (short, medium and long term). It brings more or less concavity to the intermediate segment of the curve. Hence, for intermediate values of k (that is, for maturities ranging from 1 to 7 years), c_{3k} is significantly lower or greater than the remaining values of k. This is the reason this component is associated with the curvature of the interest-rate curve. It accounts for 0 to 10% of the yield-curve changes.*

In Figure 3.15, we show concave and convex butterfly movements typically implied by a curvature factor such as the third PCA factor.

In the past few years there have been many studies on the topic of PCA of the interest-rate curves, conducted by both academics and practitioners, including Barber and Copper (BC), Bühler and Zimmermann (BZ), D'Ecclesia and Zenios (DZ), Golub and Tilman (GT), Kanony and Mokrane (KM), Kärki and Reyes (KR), Lardic, Priaulet and Priaulet (LPP), Lekkos (L), Litterman and Scheinkman (LS), Martellini and Priaulet (MP). We summarize their main results in Table 3.2 (where M stands for month and Y for year).

In particular, the last study by Lardic *et al.* (2003) questions the different methodologies that can be adopted when using PCA. Both led on different markets (Treasury and Interbank markets) and different periods of time, it is nevertheless surprising to note that these PCA studies use methodologies sometimes clearly different. Then one can legitimately wonder whether the

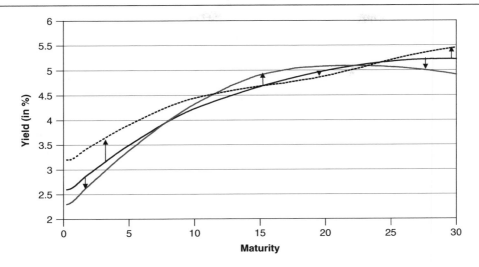

Figure 3.15 Concave and convex butterfly movements.

Table 3.2   Some PCA Results.

Authors	Country (period)—kind of rates	Range	Factors	% of explanation[a]
LS (1991)	USA (1984–1988)—spot	6M–18Y	3	88.04/8.38/1.97
KM (1992)	France (1989–1990)—spot	1Y–25Y	2	93.7/6.1
DZ (1994)	Italy (1988–1992)—spot	6M–7Y	3	93.91/5.49/0.42
KR (1994)	Germany/Switzerland/USA (1990–1994)—spot	3M–10Y	3	Total: 97/98/98
BC (1996)	USA (1985–1991)—spot	1M–20Y	3	80.93/11.85/4.36
BZ (1996)	Germany Switzerland (1988–1996)—spot	1M–10Y	3	71/18/4 75/16/3
GT (1997)	JPMorgan RiskMetrics —09/30/96—spot	3M–30Y	3	92.8/4.8/1.27
L (2000)	USA (1984–1995) Germany (1987–1995) UK (1987–1995) —1 year forward Japan (1987–1995)	1Y–9Y	5	56.5/17.4/9.86/8.12/4.3 50.6/17.3/13.5/8.8/5.8 63.5/6.3/7.5/8.1/5.3 42.8/25.5/17.1/6/4.9
MP (2000)	France (1995–1998)—spot	1M–10Y	3	66.64/20.52/6.96
LPP(2003)	Belgium France Germany (1998–2000)—spot Italy UK	1M–30Y	3	62/27/6 62/21/8 61/23/6 59/24/7 60/24/9

[a]For example, 88.04/8.38/1.97 means that the first factor explains 88.04% of the yield curve deformations, the second 8.38% and the third 1.97%. Sometimes, we also provide the total amount by adding up these terms.

results depend on the methodology choice. Should we use interest-rate levels or interest-rate changes as inputs? For example, Kanony and Mokrane (1992) use interest-rate levels, while other authors prefer to consider interest-rate changes. Should we diagonalize the correlation matrix or the variance–covariance matrix? For example, Barber and Copper (1996) use the variance–covariance matrix as Bühler and Zimmerman (1996) use the correlation matrix. Are the PCA results dependent on the number of inputs and maturities? For example, Golub and Tilman (1997) consider the whole maturity spectrum (they use 10 variables with maturities ranging from 3 months to 30 years), while D'Ecclesia and Zenios (1994) take only the short- and medium-term segments (8 variables with maturities ranging from 6 months to 7 years). Are the PCA results dependent on data frequency? Should we use daily, weekly or monthly data and during which period of time? For example, Barber and Copper (1996) take monthly data from August 1985 to February 1991 as D'Ecclesia and Zenios (1994) consider weekly data from 1988 to 1992.

Using both interest-rate simulated data and historical data (Belgium, France, Germany, Italy and UK), Lardic *et al.* (2003) conclude first that PCA should be implemented with interest-rate changes that are stationary, and second that these variables should be centered and variance-reduced. The number of variables and the maturity spectrum they cover can significantly modify the data set variance percentage explained by the factors. Furthermore, the accuracy of the results is proportional to data frequency. Finally, they show that the differences in sensitivities of rate changes to the first three factors do exist and can potentially affect a fixed-income portfolio hedging strategy based on principal component durations.

In the following example, we concretely examine the PCA results obtained by Martellini and Priaulet (2000).

Example 3.1   The study we examine is extracted from Martellini and Priaulet (2000), and concerns the French market from 1995 to 1998. The yield curves have been derived from daily swap market prices (see Chapter 4 to see in detail how to derive these curves). We have $N = 1011$ observations from early 1995 to the end of 1998. We use zero-coupon rates with 13 different maturities: 1 month, 3 months, 6 months, 1 year ... up to 10 years. We provide tables containing the percentage of explanation by the different factors of the total yield-curve variations. We also provide figures with absolute sensitivities of the spot rates variations with respect to the first four factors. We start with a discussion of the general setup for the PCA.

- **The general setup**
  We have 13 variables (spot rates for 13 different maturities) and 1,011 observations of these variables. We consider the daily interest-rate changes $\Delta R(t, \theta_k) = R(t+1, \theta_k) - R(t, \theta_k)$, and proceed to a PCA of the centered and reduced data, which amounts to using the correlation matrix of the interest-rate changes. The idea is to define

$$\Delta R = (\Delta R_{tk})_{\substack{1 \le t \le 1011 \\ 1 \le k \le 13}} = \left(\frac{\Delta R(t, \theta_k) - \overline{\Delta R(., \theta_k)}}{\sqrt{1011}\, \sigma_{\Delta R(.,\theta_k)}} \right)_{\substack{1 \le t \le 1011 \\ 1 \le k \le 13}}$$

  where $\overline{\Delta R(., \theta_k)}$ and $\sigma_{\Delta R(.,\theta_k)}$ are, respectively, the average value and the standard deviation of changes in the interest rate with maturity θ_k. One may write each element of the matrix ΔR as

$$\frac{\Delta R(t, \theta_k) - \overline{\Delta R(., \theta_k)}}{\sqrt{1011}\, \sigma_{\Delta R(.,\theta_k)}} = \sum_{l=1}^{l=13} \sqrt{\lambda_l}\, V_{tl} U_{lk} \tag{3.3}$$

with

$(U) = (U_{kl})_{1 \le k, l \le 13}$ *being the matrix of the 13 eigenvectors of* $\Delta R^\mathsf{T} \Delta R$, *the correlation matrix of interest-rate changes,*

$(U^\mathsf{T}) = (U_{lk})_{1 \le l, k \le 13}$ *being the transpose of* U,

$(V) = (V_{tl})_{\substack{1 \le t \le 1011 \\ 1 \le l \le 13}}$ *being the matrix of the 13 eigenvectors of* $\Delta R \Delta R^\mathsf{T}$,

λ_l *being the eigenvalue corresponding to the eigenvector* U_l.

Using equation (3.3), we obtain

$$\Delta R(t, \theta_k) = \overline{\Delta R(., \theta_k)} + \sum_{l=1}^{l=13} \sqrt{1011}\, \sigma_{\Delta R(., \theta_k)} \sqrt{\lambda_l}\, V_{tl} U_{lk}$$

or

$$\Delta R(t, \theta_k) = \overline{\Delta R(., \theta_k)} + \sum_{l=1}^{l=13} c_{lk} C_t^l$$

where we denote

$$c_{lk} = \sqrt{1011}\, \sigma_{\Delta R(., \theta_k)} \sqrt{\lambda_l}\, U_{lk}$$

$$V_{tl} = C_t^l$$

with C_t^l *being the lth principal component or the lth factor axis, and* c_{lk} *the coordinate of the interest rate with maturity* θ_k *on the lth factor.*[3] c_{lk} *is also the sensitivity of* $\Delta R(t, \theta_k)$ *with respect to the lth factor, as can be seen through equation (3.4)*

$$\frac{\Delta(\Delta R(t, \theta_k))}{\Delta(C_t^l)} = c_{lk} \qquad (3.4)$$

which amounts to individually applying a, say, 1% variation to each factor, and compute the absolute sensitivity of each zero-coupon yield curve with respect to that unit variation. We may also write

$$\Delta R(t, \theta_k) = \overline{\Delta R(., \theta_k)} + \sum_{l=1}^{M} c_{lk} C_t^l + \sum_{l=M+1}^{13} c_{lk} C_t^l = \overline{\Delta R(., \theta_k)} + \sum_{l=1}^{M} c_{lk} C_t^l + \epsilon_{lk}$$

where M is the number of factors used and ϵ_{lk} *is the residual term assumed to be negligible in interest-rate changes. Finally, we shall use the following relationship for a dynamic hedge of the bond portfolio using a PCA*

$$\Delta R(t, \theta_k) \approx \overline{\Delta R(., \theta_k)} + \sum_{l=1}^{M} c_{lk} C_t^l \qquad (3.5)$$

---

[3]Note that the factors are mutually independent, which translates into orthogonal axes. They are ranked according to a decreasing order in the corresponding eigenvalues.

Fixed Income Securities

Table 3.3 Global Percentage of Explanation by the Factors.

	Factor 1	Factor 2	Factor 3	Factor 4
1995				
Eigenvalue	8.6608	2.6659	0.9065	0.4034
% explained	66.62	20.51	6.97	3.10
% cumulative	66.62	87.13	94.10	97.20
1996				
Eigenvalue	9.6992	2.7101	0.3448	0.1252
% explained	74.61	20.85	2.65	0.96
% cumulative	74.61	95.46	98.11	99.07
1997				
Eigenvalue	9.2186	2.4148	0.8821	0.2489
% explained	70.91	18.58	6.79	1.91
% cumulative	70.91	89.49	96.28	98.19
1998				
Eigenvalue	7.1992	3.1991	1.0992	0.4405
% explained	55.38	24.61	8.45	3.39
% cumulative	55.38	79.99	88.44	91.83
1995–1998				
Eigenvalue	9.0036	2.9830	0.6289	0.1625
% explained	69.26	22.95	4.83	1.25
% cumulative	69.26	92.21	97.04	98.29

- *Percentage of explanation by the factors*

  We first consider the global fraction of the total variance of the zero-coupon yield-curve changes that is accounted for by the factors. For each factor, that percentage is given by $\lambda_l/13$ where λ_l is the lth eigenvalue of the correlation matrix of the raw data (daily interest-rates changes), where 13 is the number of variables. We take below $M = 4$.

  The first 3 factors account for 97.04% of interest-rate changes in the period 1995 to 1998 (see Table 3.3). Note that the results vary for each year. The first factor is more dominant in 1996 and 1997. During these years, the first three factors account for 98.11% and 96.28% of the yield-curve changes. On the other hand, in 1995 and 1998, the first factor is less significant (66.62% and 55.38%), and the second factor relatively more significant (20.51% and 24.61%). The total for these three factors reaches 94.1% in 1995 and 88.44% in 1998, which implies the presence of nonnegligible residuals. Note that the fourth factor accounts for 3.1% of the changes in 1995, and 3.39% in 1998.

  The percentage of explanation R^2_{lk} of the lth factor for the change in the interest rate with maturity k is given by the following ratio

$$R^2_{lk} = \frac{c^2_{lk}}{\displaystyle\sum_{l=1}^{13} c^2_{lk}}$$

Table 3.4 Percentage of Explanation by the Factors for Each Maturity—1995–1998.

Maturity	Factor 1 (%)	Factor 2 (%)	Factor 3 (%)	Factor 4 (%)
1M	8.45	86.25	3.36	0.21
3M	7.92	87.11	3.45	0.11
6M	14.80	78.42	0.25	1.55
1Y	62.38	18.24	14.55	2.60
2Y	79.83	0.10	16.60	2.08
3Y	90.74	0.02	5.13	2.56
4Y	94.67	0.32	0.85	3.96
5Y	95.52	1.76	0.01	1.08
6Y	94.22	3.39	0.50	0.06
7Y	92.33	4.67	2.23	0.05
8Y	88.73	5.48	4.57	0.30
9Y	85.86	6.02	6.12	0.61
10Y	84.90	6.54	5.27	1.08
Mean	**69.26**	**22.95**	**4.83**	**1.25**

For the period 1995 to 1998, the results obtained are summarized in Table 3.4.

We note that the first factor is more significant (>50%) for maturities between 1 and 10 years, and very significant (≥85%) for the maturities ranging from 3 to 10 years. The short rates are significantly affected by the second factor, while that factor is completely negligible for the maturities ranging from 2 to 5 years. The curvature effect, related to the third factor, is not negligible, in particular for the short and long ends of the yield curve, that is, for the portions [1 year, 3 years] and [8 years, 10 years]. Note finally that the mean of R_{lk}^2 with respect to the maturity k gives the percentage of variance explained by the lth factor (see Table 3.4).

- ***Sensitivities of zero-coupon rates—1995 to 1998***

We now display the sensitivities c_{lk} as a function of the interest-rate maturities k for factors 1 and 2 (see Figure 3.16) and factors 3 and 4 (see Figure 3.17).

Over the whole 1995 to 1998 period, the first factor (see Figure 3.16) may actually be regarded as a level factor since it affects all zero-coupon rates in the same way, except for the portion [1 month–6 months], which is less affected. The Figure 3.16 displaying the sensitivity of interest rates with respect to the second factor shows an ascending shape, first negative for maturities less than 3 years, and positive beyond. Hence, it may be regarded as a rotation factor around maturity 3 years. Finally, the third factor (see Figure 3.17) has different effects on intermediate maturities as opposed to extreme maturities (short and long). Hence, it may be interpreted as a curvature factor.

Fixed Income Securities

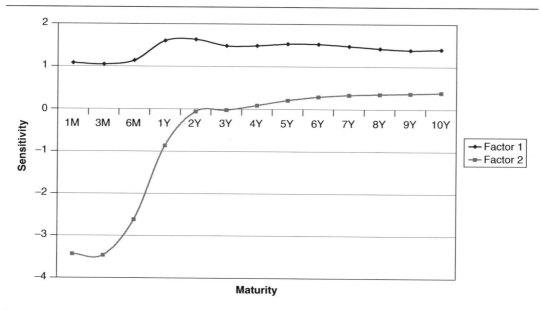

Figure 3.16 Sensitivity of zero-coupon rate changes with respect to factors 1 and 2—1995 to 1998.

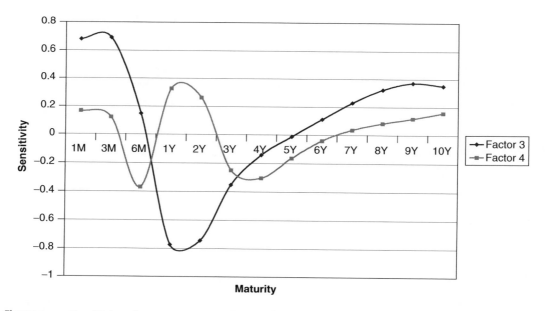

Figure 3.17 Sensitivity of zero-coupon rate changes with respect to factors 3 and 4—1995 to 1998.

We now turn to the classical theories of the term structure whose aim is to explain the future interest-rate expectations implicitly contained in the current term structure of interest rates. We will illustrate in particular the explanation given by these theories about the four classical curve shapes (flat, rising, decreasing and humped), and why they change over time.

3.2   Classical Theories of the Term Structure

Studying the term structure of interest rates boils down to wondering about market participants' preferences (investors, borrowers) for curve maturities. Indeed, if they were indifferent
to these, interest-rate curves would be invariably flat, and the notion of term structure would be
meaningless. Market participants' preferences can be guided by their expectations, the nature of
their liability or asset and the level of the risk premiums they require for offsetting their risk
aversion.

Term structure theories attempt to account for the relationship between interest rates and their
residual maturity. They can be gathered in three categories:

- *The pure expectations theory;*

- *The pure risk premium theories, including the liquidity premium theory and the preferred habitat theory;*

- *The market segmentation theory.*

To these three main types we can add the biased expectations theory, which combines the first
two theories, as well as the stochastic arbitrage approach, which, contrary to the former theories,
postulates that the short-rate evolution is not endogenous to the current term structure.

The first two theories are based on the existence of a close link between interest rates with different
maturities, while the last one postulates that there exists no relationship between short-, medium-
and long-term interest rates.

So as to understand the nature of the endogenous link that the first two theories underscore, one
must notice that long-term rates can be expressed as the average of the current short-term rate and
the forward short-term rates. Formally,

$$1 + R(t, n) = [(1 + R(t, 1))(1 + F(t, t + 1, 1))$$
$$\times (1 + F(t, t + 2, 1)) \cdots (1 + F(t, t + n - 1, 1))]^{1/n}$$

where

$R(t, n)$ is the current rate with maturity n years observed at time t;

$F(t, t + k, 1)$ is the forward rate with maturity 1 year, determined at time t and starting at time
$t + k$.

For simplicity, the short-term rate is taken as the 1-year rate.

The pure expectations theory postulates that forward rates exclusively represent future short-term
rates as expected by the market, whereas the pure risk premium theory postulates that forward
rates exclusively represent the risk premium required by the market to hold longer-term bonds.

The market segmentation theory postulates that each of the two main market investor categories
(the one preferring short bonds, the other long bonds) is invariably located on the same curve
portion (short, long). As a result, short and long curve segments are perfectly impermeable.

Fixed Income Securities

3.2.1 The Pure Expectations Theory

The term structure of interest rates reflects at a given time the market expectations of future short-term rates. An increasing (respectively, flat, respectively, decreasing) structure means that the market expects an increase (respectively, a stagnation, respectively, a decrease) in future short-term rates.

Formally,

$$1 + R(t, n) = [(1 + R(t, 1))(1 + F^a(t, t+1, 1))$$
$$\times (1 + F^a(t, t+2, 1)) \cdots (1 + F^a(t, t+n-1, 1))]^{1/n} \qquad (3.6)$$

where

$R(t, n)$ is the current rate with maturity n years observed at time t;

$F^a(t, t+k, 1)$ is the future short-term rate with maturity 1 year, anticipated by the market at time t and starting at time $t + k$.

The mechanism is as follows. Market participants formulate expectations about the evolution of short-term rates using all the available information, and make their decisions rationally in accordance with it. Their expectations guide their curve position, and hence the long-term rate level. As these expectations prove to be correct on average, *future short-term rates equal forward short-term rates*.

Example 3.2   Change from a flat curve to an increasing curve

Let us assume the interest-rate curve is flat at 5%. Let us assume furthermore that investors expect a 100 bps increase in rates within 1 year. For computation simplicity, we assume that the short (respectively, long) segment of the curve is the 1-year (respectively, 2-year) maturity. Then, under these conditions, the interest-rate curve will not remain flat but will be increasing. Let us explain why.

Consider a long investor with a 2-year investment horizon. His objective consists in maximizing his return in the period. He is indifferent to the strategy that will allow him to reach it. He has to choose one of the following two alternatives:

- *either invest in a long 2-year security;*

- *or invest in a short 1-year security, then reinvest in 1 year the proceeds in another 1-year security.*

Before interest rates adjust at the 6% level, the first alternative provides him with an annual return of 5% over 2 years, whereas the second one returns him 5% the first year and, according to his expectations, 6% the second year, that is to say 5.5% on average per year over 2 years. This is the most profitable. The investor will thus buy short bonds (1 year) rather than long bonds (2 years). Any investor having the same investment horizon will act in the same way. As a result, the price of the 1-year bond will increase (its yield will decrease) and the price of the 2-year bond will decrease (its yield will increase). The curve will steepen.

Analogously, speculators' (short sale of long bonds) and borrowers' (rise in long bonds issuances) behaviors will induce a curve steepening.

In summary, market participants behave collectively to let the relative appeal of one maturity compared to the others disappear. In other words, they neutralize initial preferences for some curve maturities, creating interest-rate differentials along it.

As a result, zero-coupon rate returns equal each other at a given time, whatever their maturity.

However, the pure expectations theory has two limits:

- *It does not take bond price risk into account.*
- *It does not take bond coupon reinvestment risk into account.*

3.2.2 The Pure Risk Premium Theory

In the previous theory, investors behave in accordance with their expectations for the unique purpose of maximizing their investment return. They are risk-neutral. They do not take into account the fact that their expectations may be wrong. The pure risk premium theory includes this contingency. Indeed, if forward rates were perfect predictors of future rates, the future bond prices would be known with certainty. An investment return, whatever its term, would be certain and independent of the invested bond's maturity as well as the date on which the investor wishes to liquidate his position. Unfortunately, it is practically not the case. As future interest rates are unknown and hence also future bond prices, the latter are risky because their return in the future is unknown.

Let us consider the following example.

An investor having a 3-year investment horizon has the three following choices:

- *investing in a 3-year zero-coupon bond and holding it until maturity;*
- *investing in a 5-year zero-coupon bond and selling it in 3 years;*
- *investing in a 10-year zero-coupon bond and selling it in 3 years.*

While he perfectly knows the return on the first investment, he does not know the returns on the others because of the uncertainty affecting the sale price of these instruments in 3 years.

The price of the second (respectively, third) instrument in 3 years will depend on the 2-year (respectively, 7-year) zero-coupon rate in 3 years. As 3-year forward zero-coupon rates with maturities 2 and 7 years, denoted $F(0, 3, 2)$ and $F(0, 3, 7)$, are not perfect predictors of the future zero-coupon rates with the same maturities, the two instruments are affected by price risk. This

Fixed Income Securities

risk is that the price of each of the two zero-coupon bonds is less than the price expected by the market.

At this stage it is worthwhile to notice that a bond price risk (measured by price volatility) tends to increase with maturity in a decreasing proportion. Let us illustrate this through the following example.

Example 3.3 Assume interest rates are at 5% level, and instantaneously increase to 6%. What will be the impact on the price of the 1-year and the 2-year 5% coupon bonds?

The price of these two bonds is 100 before the rates increase. After the rates increase, the price of the 2-year bond will fall to $\frac{5}{1+6\%} + \frac{100+5}{(1+6\%)^2} = 98.17$, whereas the price of the 1-year bond will fall to $\frac{100+5}{1+6\%} = 99.06$. Thus, an instantaneous rise in interest rates from 5 to 6% will induce a fall in the 2-year bond price nearly twice as big as the fall in the 1-year bond price.

According to the pure risk premium theory, the term structure of interest rates reflects at a given time the risk premium that is required by the market for holding long bonds. However, the two versions of this theory differ about the risk premium shape.

The Liquidity Premium

It increases with maturity in a decreasing proportion. In other words, an investor will be interested in holding all the longer bonds as their return contains a substantial risk premium, offsetting their higher volatility. Formally,

$$1 + R(t, n) = [(1 + R(t, 1))(1 + L_2)(1 + L_3) \cdots (1 + L_n)]^{1/n} \tag{3.7}$$

where

$R(t, n)$ is the current yield observed at time t with maturity n years;

$\sum_{j=2}^{k} L_j$ is the liquidity premium required by the market to invest in a bond maturing in k years

$0 < L_2 < L_3 < \cdots < L_n$

$L_2 > L_3 - L_2 > L_4 - L_3 > \cdots > L_n - L_{n-1}$

This theory simultaneously takes into account investors' preference for liquidity and their aversion against the short-term fluctuations of asset prices. Its limits lie in the impossibility of explaining decreasing and humped curves, as well as its ignorance of coupon reinvestment risk.

Let us illustrate this limit by the following example.

An investor having a 3-year investment horizon has the two following choices:

- *investing in a 3-year maturing bond and holding it until maturity;*

- *investing in a 1-year maturing bond, and reinvesting the proceeds in another 1-year bond until covering the whole investment horizon.*

The second alternative is clearly affected by a coupon reinvestment risk.

The Preferred Habitat

It is an improvement of the liquidity premium theory because it postulates that risk premium is not uniformly increasing. Indeed, investors do not all intend to liquidate their investment as soon as possible, as their investment horizon is dictated by the nature of their liabilities. Nevertheless, when bond supply and demand on a specific curve segment do not match, some lenders and borrowers are ready to move to other curve parts where there is the inverse disequilibrium, provided that they receive a risk premium that offsets their price or reinvestment risk aversion. Thus, all curve shapes can be accounted for.

3.2.3 The Market Segmentation Theory

In this framework, there exist different investor categories, each systematically investing on a given curve segment in accordance with its liabilities, without ever moving to other segments. Two of them are usually underlined, because they carry on their own such an overwhelming weight that the other investors' behaviors only have a small impact: commercial banks, which invest on a short-/medium-term basis, and life insurance companies and pension funds, which invest on a long-/very long term basis. Thus, the curve shape is determined by the law of supply and demand on the short-term bond market on the one hand, and on the long-term bond market on the other hand.

Let us detail this point. While life insurance companies and pension funds are structural buyers of long-term bonds, the behavior of commercial banks is more volatile. Indeed, banks prefer to lend money directly to corporations and individuals than to invest in bond securities. Their demand for short-term bonds is influenced by business conditions:

- *during growth periods, banks sell bond securities in order to meet corporations' and individuals' strong demand for loans, hence the relative rise in short-term yields compared to long-term yields;*

- *during slowdown periods, corporations and individuals pay back their loans, thus increasing bank funds and leading them to invest in short-term bond securities, hence the relative fall in short-term yields compared to long-term yields.*

The main limit of this theory lies in its basic assumption, that is, the rigidity of investors' behaviors. Moreover, the assumption of a market segmentation due to regulations is not acceptable in an increasingly internationalized financial environment.

Notice that the market segmentation theory can be viewed as an extreme version of the pure risk premium theory, where risk premia are infinite.

Although they differ from each other, the above-explained theories do not exclude each other. On the contrary, in practice, the effects they emphasize may jointly apply to interest rates.

3.2.4   The Biased Expectations Theory: An Integrated Approach

This theory is a combination of the pure expectations theory and the risk premium theory. It postulates that the term structure of interest rates reflects market expectations of future interest rates as well as permanent liquidity premia that vary over time. Thus, all curve shapes can be accounted for.

Formally,

$$1 + R(t,n) = [(1 + R(t,1)) \cdot (1 + F^a(t, t+1, 1) + L_2) \cdot (1 + F^a(t, t+2, 1) + L_3) \cdots$$
$$+ (1 + F^a(t, t+n-1, 1) + L_n)]^{1/n} \tag{3.8}$$

where

$R(t,n)$ is the current yield observed at time t with maturity n years;

$F^a(t, t+k, 1)$ is the future short-term rate with maturity 1 year, anticipated by the market at time t and starting at time $t+k$;

$\sum_{j=2}^{k} L_j$ is the liquidity premium required by the market to invest in a bond maturing in k years

$0 < L_2 < L_3 < \cdots < L_n$

$L_2 > L_3 - L_2 > L_4 - L_3 > \cdots > L_n - L_{n-1}$

3.2.5   Illustration and Empirical Validation

Let us now illustrate the nature of the explanation given by each of the previous theories for the four classical curve shapes.

Curve type	Pure expectations	Risk premium	Biased expectations	Market segmentation
Quasi-flat curve	The market expects a moderate increase in interest rates.	The risk premium rises with maturity in a decreasing proportion.	The market expects a relative interest-rate stability; the risk premium rises with maturity in a decreasing proportion.	Banks have slightly more funds to invest than insurance companies.
Rising curve	The market expects a great increase in interest rates.	The risk premium rises with maturity.	The market expects a great increase in interest rates; the risk premium rises with maturity in a decreasing proportion.	Banks have much more funds to invest than insurance companies.

Curve type	Pure expectations	Risk premium	Biased expectations	Market segmentation
Falling curve	The market expects a great decrease in interest rates.	The liquidity premium cannot explain it; according to the preferred habitat, the risk premium decreases with maturity.	The market expects a great decrease in interest rates; the risk premium rises with maturity in a decreasing proportion.	Banks have far less funds to invest than insur- ance companies.
Humped curve	The market expects first an increase or decrease in interest rates, and then a decrease or increase in interest rates.	The liquidity premium cannot explain it; according to the preferred habitat, the risk premium increases or decreases with maturity, and then decreases or increases with maturity.	The market expects a decrease followed or not by an increase in interest rates; the risk premium rises with maturity in a decreasing proportion.	Banks and insurance companies have the same amount of funds to invest; their investment segments are disjoint.

Let us now briefly examine the explanatory power of these theories.

All empirical studies, concerning mainly the US market, lead to the following conclusions, which cannot claim to be either universal or definitive:

- *The existence of a positive risk premium seems attested. Its impact seems more pronounced on the short end of the curve, which means that an investor can on average expect to increase the return on his investment by increasing his investment horizon.*

- *This risk premium is not constant over time. Consequently, a change in the curve shape is not necessarily due to a change in market expectations.*

- *Market expectations, which vary over time, seem to have an impact on the term structure of interest rates.*

- *However, their explanatory power is weak.*

3.2.6 Summary and Extensions

We present hereafter a summary of the main financial implications of the two basic theories (pure expectations, pure risk premium) as the others come down to one or a mix of these two types.

	Pure expectations	Risk premium
What information is contained in forward rates?	Forward short rates reflect market's short-rate expectations.	Forward short rates reflect the risk premia required by the market.
What do forward rates forecast?	Forward short rates are unbiased predictors of future short rates.	Forward short rates predict short-term return differentials across bonds.
What is the expected return of a zero coupon over one period?	All zero-coupon bonds, whatever their maturity, have the same expected return over a given period, which is the short rate over this period.	The expected return of a zero coupon maturing in n years at a near-term horizon h is equal to the forward short rate maturing in h years.
What is the best predictor of the future zero-coupon curve?	The forward zero-coupon curve is the best predictor of the future zero coupon.	The current zero-coupon curve is the best predictor of the future zero coupon.

As opposed to these classical theories, the stochastic arbitrage approach takes root in the modelization of uncertainty. In comparison with the previous theories, it assumes that the uncertainty about future interest rates is not implicit in the current term structure of interest rates. In other words, it is difficult to correctly anticipate future interest rates because their evolution is linked to surprise effects. Formally, the evolution of interest rates is modeled as a predictable term plus a stochastic process, whose law is known, but not the value it will generate. This theory represents an alternative to traditional theories.

This approach is generally used for pricing and hedging contingent claims (with uncertain cash flows). Hence, it is based on the absence of arbitrage opportunities (market participants prefer to have "more than less"). We will develop this approach in Chapters 12 and 13.

3.3 End of Chapter Summary

The term structure of interest rates, also called the yield curve, is defined as the graph mapping interest rates corresponding to their respective maturity. The term structure of interest rates can take at any point in time several shapes that can be divided into four standard types: quasi-flat, increasing, decreasing and humped. The key question from a risk management perspective is actually to understand how the term structure of interest rates evolves over time. The historical study of the evolution of the yield curve over time enables us to emphasize the five following important stylized facts: (1) interest rates are not negative; (2) interest rates are mean-reverting; (3) changes of interest rates are not perfectly correlated; (4) the volatility of short-term rates is higher than the volatility of long-term rates. We also argue that three main factors typically explain more than 95% of the changes in the yield curve. These factors are changes in the level, the slope and the curvature of the term structure.

A more ambitious question is to try and understand these changes. Studying the term structure of interest rates boils down to wondering about market participants' preferences (investors, borrowers) for curve maturities. Market participants' preferences can be guided by their expectations, the nature of their liability or asset, and the level of the risk premiums they require for offsetting their risk aversion. We review classical economic theories of the term structure that attempt to account for the relationship between interest rates and their residual maturity. They can be gathered in three categories: (1) the pure expectations theory; (2) the pure risk premium theory (including the liquidity premium theory and the preferred habitat theory) and (3) the market segmentation theory.

The first two theories are based on the existence of a close link between interest rates with different maturities, while the last one postulates that there exists no relationship between short, medium and long-term interest rates.

3.4   References and Further Reading

3.4.1   On the Empirical Behavior of the Yield Curve

Bali, T.G., and S.N. Neftci, 2001, "Estimating the Term Structure of Interest Rate Volatility in Extreme Values", *Journal of Fixed Income*, **10**(4), 7–14.

Chan, K., G.A. Karolyi, F. Longstaff, and A. Sanders, 1992, "An Empirical Comparison of Alternative Models of the Short-Term Interest Rate", *Journal of Finance*, **47**(3), 1209–1227.

Estrella, A., and G.A. Hardouvelis, 1991, "The Term Structure as a Predictor of Real Economic Activity", *Journal of Finance*, **46**(2), 555–576.

Estrella, A., and F.S. Mishkin, 1997, "The Predictive Power of the Term Structure of Interest Rates in Europe and the United States: Implications for the European Central Bank", *European Economic Review*, **41**(7), 1375–1401.

Fama, E.F., 1984, "The Information in the Term Structure", *Journal of Financial Economics*, **13**(4), 509–528.

Fama, E.F., and R.R. Bliss, 1987, "The Information in Long Maturity Forward Rates", *American Economic Review*, **77**(4), 680–692.

Ilmanen, A., and R. Iwanowski, 1997, "Dynamics of the Shape of the Yield Curve", *Journal of Fixed Income*, **7**(2), 47–60.

Koutmos, G., 1998, "The Volatility of Interest Rates Across Maturities and Frequencies", *Journal of Fixed Income*, **8**(3), 27–31.

Lekkos, I., 1999, "Distributional Properties of Spot and Forward Interest Rates: USD, DEM, GBP and JPY", *Journal of Fixed Income*, **8**(4), 35–54.

Mishkin, F.S., 1988, "The Information in the Term Structure: Some Further Results", *Journal of Applied Econometrics*, **3**(4), 307–314.

Papageorgiou, N., and F.S. Skinner, 2002, "Predicting the Direction of Interest Rate Movements", *Journal of Fixed Income*, **11**(4), 87–95.

Phoa, W., 1997, "Can you Derive Market Volatility Forecasts from the Observed Yield Curve Convexity Bias?" *Journal of Fixed Income*, **7**(1), 43–54.

Vasicek, O.A., 1977, "An Equilibrium Characterisation of the Term Structure", *Journal of Financial Economics*, **5**, 177–188.

Wadhwa, P., 1999, "An Empirical Analysis of the Common Factors Governing US Dollar-Libor Implied Volatility Movements", *Journal of Fixed Income*, **9**(3), 61–68.

3.4.2 On the Principal Component Analysis of the Yield Curve

Barber, J.R., and M.L. Copper, 1996, "Immunization Using Principal Component Analysis", *Journal of Portfolio Management*, **23**(1), 99–105.

Basilevsky A., 1994, *Statistical Factor Analysis and Related Methods: Theory and Applications*, Wiley Series in Probability and Mathematical Statistics, Wiley, Chichester.

Bühler, A., and H. Zimmermann, 1996, "A Statistical Analysis of the Term Structure of Interest Rates in Switzerland and Germany", *Journal of Fixed Income*, **6**(3), 55–67.

D'Ecclesia, R.L., and S.A. Zenios, 1994, "Risk Factor Analysis and Portfolio Immunization in the Italian Bond Market", *Journal of Fixed Income*, **4**(2), 51–58.

Golub, B.W., and L.M. Tilman, 1997, "Measuring Yield Curve Risk Using Principal Components Analysis, Value at Risk, and Key Rate Durations", *Journal of Portfolio Management*, **23**(4), 72–84.

James, J., and N. Webber, 2000, *Interest Rate Modeling*, John Wiley & Sons, Chichester.

Kanony, C., and M. Mokrane, 1992, Reconstitution de la courbe des taux, analyse des facteurs d'évolution et couverture factorielle, *Cahiers de la Caisse Autonome de Refinancement*, Vol. 1, Paris.

Kärki, J., and C. Reyes, 1994, "Model Relationship", *Risk*, **7**(12), 32–35.

Knez, R., R. Litterman, and J. Scheinkman, 1994, "Explorations into Factors Explaining Money Market Returns", *Journal of Finance*, **49**(5), 1861–1882.

Lardic, S., P. Priaulet, and S. Priaulet, 2003, "PCA of the Yield Curve Dynamics: Questions of Methodologies", *Journal of Bond Trading and Management*, **1**(4); forthcoming.

Lekkos, I., 2000, "A Critique of Factor Analysis of Interest Rates", *Journal of Derivatives*, **8**(1), 72–83.

Litterman, R., and J. Scheinkman, 1991, "Common Factors Affecting Bond Returns", *Journal of Fixed Income*, **1**(1), 54–61.

Martellini, L., and P. Priaulet, 2000, *Fixed-Income Securities: Dynamic Methods for Interest Rate Risk Pricing and Hedging*, John Wiley & Sons, Chichester.

3.4.3 On the Classical Theories of the Term Structure of Interest Rates

Brennan, M.J., and E.S. Schwartz, 1982, "An Equilibrium Model of Bond Pricing and a Test of Market Efficiency", *Journal of Financial and Quantitative Analysis*, **17**(3), 301–329.

Buser, S.A., G.A. Karolyi, and A.B. Sanders, 1996, "Adjusted Forward Rates as Predictors of Future Spot Rates", *Journal of Fixed Income*, **6**(3), 29–42.

Campbell, J.Y., 1986, "A Defense of Traditional Hypotheses about the Term Structure of Interest Rates", *Journal of Finance*, 183–193.

Chance, D.M., and D. Rich, 2001, "The False Teachings of the Unbiased Expectations Hypothesis", *Journal of Portfolio Management*, **27**(4), 83–95.

Choudhry, M., 2001, *Bond and Money Markets: Strategy, Trading and Analysis*, Butterworth-Heinemann, Woburn, MA.

Constantinides, G., 1992, "A Theory of the Nominal Term Structure of Interest Rates", *Review of Financial Studies*, **5**(4), 531–552.

Cox, J., J. Ingersoll, and S. Ross, 1981, "A Re-examination of Traditional Hypotheses about the Term Structure of Interest Rates", *Journal of Finance*, **36**, 769–799.

Cox, J., J. Ingersoll, and S. Ross, 1985, "A Theory of the Term Structure of Interest Rates", *Econometrica*, **53**, 385–407.

Culbertson, J., 1957, "The Term Structure of Interest Rates", *Quarterly Journal of Economics*, **71**, 489–504.

Fabozzi, F.J., (Editor), 2000, *The Handbook of Fixed Income Securities*, 6th Edition, McGraw-Hill, New York.

Fama, E., 1984, "The Information in the Term Structure", *Journal of Financial Economics*, **13**, 509–528.

Fisher, I., 1896, *Appreciation and Interest*, Publications of the American Economic Association, pp. 23–29, 88–92.

Fisher, M., C. Gilles, 1998, "Around and Around: The Expectations Hypothesis", *Journal of Finance*, **53**, 365–382.

Froot, K., 1989, "New Hope for the Expectations Hypothesis of the Term Structure of Interest Rates", *Journal of Finance*, **44**, 283–305.

Hicks, J.R., 1946, *Value and Capital*, 2nd Edition, Clarendon Press, Oxford.

Huang, R.D., 1984, "Some Alternative Tests of Forward Rates as Predictors of Future Spot Rates", *Journal of International Money and Finance*, **3**, 153–168.

Hull, J., 2000, *Options, Futures and Other Derivatives*, Prentice Hall, New York.

Ilmanen, A., 1996, "Market Rate Expectations and Forward Rates", *Journal of Fixed Income*, **6**(2), 8–22.

Langetieg, T.C., 1980, "A Multivariate Model of the Term Structure", *Journal of Finance*, **35**, 71–97.

Longstaff, F.A., 2000, "Arbitrage and the Expectations Hypotheses", *Journal of Finance*, **60**, 989–994.

Lutz, F.A., 1940, "The Structure of Interest Rates", *Quarterly Journal of Economics*, **55**, 36–63.

McCulloch, J.H., 1993, "A Re-examination of Traditional Hypotheses about the Term Structure of Interest Rates: A Comment", *Journal of Finance*, **63**(2), 779–789.

Modigliani, F., and R. Sutch, 1966, "Innovations in Interest Rate Policy", *American Economic Review*, **56**, 178–197.

Poncet, P., R. Portait, and S. Hayat, 2001, *Mathématiques Financières: Evaluation des Actifs et Analyse du Risque*, 3rd Edition, Paris, Dalloz Gestion.

Stambaugh, R., 1988, "The Information in Forward Rates: Implications for Models of the Term Structure", *Journal of Financial Economics*, **21**, 41–70.

Shiller, R., J. Cambell, and K. Schoenholtz, 1983, Forward Rates and Future Policy: Interpreting the Term Structure of Interest Rates, *Brookings Papers on Economic Activity*, **1**, 173–223.

Van Horne, J.C., 1978, Chapters 4 and 5, *Financial Market Rates and Flows*, Prentice Hall, New York.

3.5 Problems

Exercise 3.1 We consider three zero-coupon bonds (strips) with the following features:

Bond	Maturity	Price
Bond 1	1 year	96.43
Bond 2	2 years	92.47
Bond 3	3 years	87.97

Each strip delivers $100 at maturity.

1. Extract the zero-coupon yield curve from the bond prices.
2. We anticipate a rate increase in 1 year so the prices of strips with residual maturity 1 year, 2 years and 3 years are, respectively, 95.89, 90.97 and 84.23. What is the zero-coupon yield curve anticipated in 1 year?

Exercise 3.2   We consider the following increasing zero-coupon yield curve:

Maturity	$R(0, t)$ (%)	Maturity	$R(0, t)$ (%)
1 year	5.000	6 years	6.550
2 years	5.500	7 years	6.650
3 years	5.900	8 years	6.741
4 years	6.200	9 years	6.830
5 years	6.382	10 years	6.900

where $R(0, t)$ is the zero-coupon rate at date 0 with maturity t.

1. Compute the par yield curve.
2. Compute the forward yield curve in 1 year.
3. Draw the three curves on the same graph. What can you say about their relative position?

Exercise 3.3   We consider the following decreasing zero-coupon yield curve:

Maturity	$R(0, t)$ (%)	Maturity	$R(0, t)$ (%)
1 year	7.000	6 years	6.250
2 years	6.800	7 years	6.200
3 years	6.620	8 years	6.160
4 years	6.460	9 years	6.125
5 years	6.330	10 years	6.100

where $R(0, t)$ is the zero-coupon rate at date 0 with maturity t.

1. Compute the par yield curve.
2. Compute the forward yield curve in 1 year.
3. Draw the three curves on the same graph. What can you say about their relative position?

Exercise 3.4   We consider the following zero-coupon yield curve, which is inverted at the short-term end:

Maturity	$R(0, t)$ (%)	Maturity	$R(0, t)$ (%)
1 year	7.000	6 years	7.650
2 years	6.000	7 years	7.900
3 years	6.500	8 years	8.150
4 years	6.950	9 years	8.250
5 years	7.350	10 years	8.300

where $R(0, t)$ is the zero-coupon rate at date 0 with maturity t.

1. Compute the par yield curve.
2. Compute the forward yield curve in 1 year.
3. Draw the three curves on the same graph. What can you say about their relative position?

Exercise 3.5   We consider the following zero-coupon spot curve:

Maturity	Zero-coupon rate (%)
1 year	3.702
2 years	3.992
3 years	4.365
4 years	4.568
5 years	4.717

1. Compute the forward yield curve in 1 year.
2. Compute the forward yield curve in 2 years.
3. Compute the forward yield curve in 3 years.
4. What does the market expect according to the pure expectations theory?

Exercise 3.6   The goal of this exercise is to give a proof of the relationship between zero-coupon yields and par yields when yields are continuously compounded, and to see the difference obtained when compounding is annual.

1. Annual Compounding
   (a) Recall the relationship between the zero-coupon yield and the discount factor.
   (b) Give a proof of the relationship between the zero-coupon yields and the par yield.

2. Continuous Compounding
   (a) Give a proof of the link between the zero-coupon yield and the discount factor. Find the link between the annual compounded zero-coupon yield and the continuously compounded zero-coupon yield.
   (b) Same question as in question 1.

Exercise 3.7   We consider the following increasing zero-coupon yield curve:

Maturity	$R(0, t)$ (%)	Maturity	$R(0, t)$ (%)
1 year	5.000	6 years	6.550
2 years	5.500	7 years	6.650
3 years	5.900	8 years	6.741
4 years	6.200	9 years	6.830
5 years	6.382	10 years	6.900

where $R(0, t)$ is the annually compounded zero-coupon rate at date 0 with residual maturity t.

1. Find the continuously compounded zero-coupon yield curve.
2. Draw the two curves on the same graph. Conclude.

Exercise 3.8   When the current par yield curve is increasing (respectively, decreasing), the current zero-coupon rate curve is above (respectively, below) it, so as to offset the fact that the sum of the coupons discounted at the coupon rate is inferior (respectively, superior) to the sum of the coupons discounted at the zero-coupon rate. Give a proof of this assertion.

Exercise 3.9   When the current par yield curve is increasing (respectively, decreasing), the forward zero-coupon rate curve is above (respectively, below) the current zero-coupon rate curve. Give a proof of this assertion.

Exercise 3.10   Change from a flat curve to an increasing curve

Let us assume the interest-rate curve is flat at 5%. Let us assume furthermore that investors expect a 100-bp increase in rates within 1 year. For computation simplicity, we assume that the short (respectively, long) segment of the curve is the 1-year (respectively, 2-year) maturity. Then, under these conditions, the interest-rate curve will not remain flat but will be increasing. Show this result from an investor's viewpoint with a 1-year investment horizon.

Exercise 3.11   At date $t = 0$, we observe the following zero-coupon rates in the market:

Maturity	Zero-coupon rate (%)
1 Year	5.00
2 Years	6.00
3 Years	6.50
4 Years	6.80
5 Years	7.00

1. What are the 1-year maturity forward rates implied by the current term structure?
2. Over a long period we observe the mean spreads between 1-year maturity forward rates and 1-year maturity realized rates in the future. We find the following liquidity premiums:

   - $L_2 = 0.1\%$
   - $L_3 = 0.175\%$
   - $L_4 = 0.225\%$
   - $L_5 = 0.250\%$

   Taking into account these liquidity premiums, what are the 1-year maturity future rates expected by the market?

Exercise 3.12   Monetary policy and long-term interest rates

Consider an investor with a 4-year investment horizon. The short-term (long-term, respectively) yield is taken as the 1-year (4-year, respectively) yield. The medium-term yields are taken as the 2-year and 3-year yields. We assume further-more that the assumptions of the pure expectations theory are valid.

For each of the five following scenarios, determine the spot yield curve at date $t = 1$. The yield curve is supposed to be initially flat at the level of 4%, at date $t = 0$.

1. Investors do not expect any Central Bank rate increase over 4 years.
2. The Central Bank increases its prime rate, leading the short-term rate from 4 to 5%. Investors do not expect any other increase over 4 years.
3. The Central Bank increases its prime rate, leading the short-term rate from 4 to 5%. Investors expect another short-term rate increase by 1% at the beginning of the second year, then no other increase over the last two years.
4. The Central Bank increases its prime rate, leading the short-term rate from 4 to 5%. Nevertheless, investors expect a short-term rate decrease by 1% at the beginning of the second year, then no other change over the last two years.
5. The Central Bank increases its prime rate, leading the short-term rate from 4 to 5%. Nevertheless, investors expect a short-term rate decrease by 1% each year, over the three following years.

What conclusions do you draw from this as regards the relationship existing between monetary policy and interest rates?

Exercise 3.13 Explain the basic difference that exists between the preferred habitat theory and the segmentation theory.

Exercise 3.14 Show that the traditional interest-rate theories can be divided into two pure categories.

Exercise 3.15 Let us denote by $R(0, n)$ the zero-coupon yield with maturity n.

1. We assume the validity of the pure expectations theory. Calculate the total return on the zero-coupon with maturity n at horizon h. What is your conclusion?
2. We assume the validity of the pure risk premium theory. Calculate the total return on the zero-coupon with maturity n years at horizon h. What is your conclusion?

Exercise 3.16 Is the market segmentation theory a realistic approach of the term structure of interest rates? Explain why.

Exercise 3.17 Among all traditional theories of the term structure of interest rates, which one best illustrates what practically happens in the market? Explain why.

4

Deriving the Zero-Coupon Yield Curve

Deriving the zero-coupon yield curve is very important in practice because it enables investors at a date t

- *to know the discount factor curve, and consequently to price at this date t any fixed-income security delivering known cash flows in the future (e.g., a fixed coupon bond);*

- *to obtain implicit curves such as the forward rate curve (with forward rates beginning at a future date T > t), the instantaneous forward rate curve and the par yield curve.*

We divide this chapter into three parts:

- *The nondefault Treasury zero-coupon yield curve, which is derived from Treasury bond market prices.*

- *The interbank zero-coupon yield curve, which is derived from money-market rates, futures contracts rates and swap rates.*

- *The risky corporate (or credit) zero-coupon yield curve for a given rating and economic sector, which is derived from corporate bond market prices. Note that by subtracting the Treasury or the interbank zero-coupon yield curve from this curve, we obtain the credit spread zero-coupon yield curve.*

4.1 Deriving the Nondefault Treasury Zero-Coupon Yield Curve

We will see that there exists a simple direct method for extracting zero-coupon prices from the current fixed coupon bearing bond prices. Unfortunately, this method can only be applied under very limited circumstances. Hence, in order to deal with real-life situations, we shall develop the bootstrapping method or some alternative indirect methods to derive those implied zero-coupon bond prices. Direct methods allow the investor to recover exactly the prices of the selected bonds. Indirect methods allow for a very efficient derivation of forward and par yield curves and are very useful for implementing rich–cheap analysis (see Chapter 8 for details about the bond relative value analysis).

4.1.1 How to Select a Basket of Bonds?

Building a General Information Database

To ensure the selection of a coherent basket of bonds, we first need to generate a database gathering a list of information for each bond. Available, for example, from Bloomberg or Reuters, this information concerns the issuer and the characteristics of the issue.

- ***About the issuer:*** *name, country of issuance, S&P and Moody's ratings.*

- ***About the issue:*** *amount issued, amount outstanding, issue date, issue price, maturity, currency, type of coupon, coupon frequency, coupon rate, day-count basis, first coupon date, redemption* *value, presence of option features such as callability, putability, convertibility, pricing source, ask yield to maturity (YTM), bid YTM, ask clean price, bid clean price, mid clean price, daily volume.*

Some Features to Detect

Using this information, the idea is to select bonds that are not concerned with the following:

- *Option features* (*callability, putability, convertibility...*), *because the presence of options can make the price of the bond higher or lower,*[1] *and not homogeneous with bonds that do not contain options.*

- *Pricing errors:* *pricing errors are typically due to an error in the input database. The idea for eliminating bonds with pricing errors is to draw the yield to maturity (YTM) curve. The points that are irrelevant are bonds with pricing errors. They are called "outliers" in the financial jargon.*

- *Illiquidity or overliquidity:* *illiquid bonds must be excluded from the reference baskets, because such bonds typically imply misprices. Besides some bonds may be overliquid at certain periods of time because they are the cheapest-to-deliver bonds of futures contracts or simply benchmark bonds. Assessing the degree of liquidity of a given bond is a challenging task. The idea is to take into account the size of the issue, the nature of the issue (on-the-run or off-the-run), the daily traded volume and so on. For example, JP Morgan publish liquidity states in their Global Bond Index on a monthly basis. They distinguish between three liquidity levels: benchmark, active and traded. A benchmark issue is an "issue recognized as a market indicator, a recent sizable new issue or reopened issue, and a current coupon issue." An active issue is an "issue with significantly daily turnover, a previous benchmark issue." A traded issue is an "issue with prices that change regularly, and for which two-way markets exist." On the basis of these categories, we can define a rule that depends on the size of the local market that is annualized: active bonds are used if there are enough such bonds to cover the whole maturity spectrum. But a mix of active and traded bonds is used if there are not enough active bonds.*

4.1.2 Direct Methods

A Theoretical Method

We have said that one generally does not have a direct access to an exhaustive collection of zero-coupon prices. On the other hand, one would like to have a method of determining a zero-coupon yield curve based on the information supplied by the market. We present here a standard methodology used to extract zero-coupon implied prices from the coupon bond market prices. These coupon bonds form the vast majority of the bonds traded on the financial markets around the world.

If one needs n distinct zero-coupon rates, one needs to first collect the prices of n coupon (or zero-coupon) bonds. Default-free coupon bonds (like US Treasury bonds) are usually preferred, because they provide information about the risk-free[2] structure of interest rates.

Let us denote by

$$P_t = (P_t^1, \ldots, P_t^j, \ldots, P_t^n)^\mathsf{T}$$

---

[1] See Chapter 14 for more details.
[2] Risk-free here means free of default risk.

Fixed Income Securities

an n-dimensional vector of coupon bond prices at time t (here T denotes transposition). We further denote by

$$F \equiv \left(F_{t_i}^{(j)} \right)_{\substack{i=1,\ldots,n \\ j=1,\ldots,n}}$$

the $n \times n$ matrix of the cash flows (coupons and principal) corresponding to these n assets. Here, we have made an overly simplifying assumption that different bonds have the same cash flow dates t_j. Then,

$$B_t = (B(t, t_1), \ldots, B(t, t_n))^{\mathsf{T}}$$

is the n-dimensional vector of the zero-coupon bond prices at time t, which is what we would like to determine here.

In the absence of arbitrage opportunities, the following must hold

$$P_t^j = \sum_{i=1}^{n} F_{t_i}^{(j)} B(t, t_i) \tag{4.1}$$

Writing equation (4.1) for n assets gives the following matrix equation

$$P_t = F \cdot B_t$$

Thus, in order to determine the value of B_t, we need to solve this linear system. We can do it provided F is invertible, or, in other words, no linear dependence in the payoff of the bonds exists. In that case,

$$B_t = F^{-1} \cdot P_t \tag{4.2}$$

Note that the prices we derive this way are not some real market values but, rather, implied zero-coupon bond values consistent with the set of market prices. From these prices, we can easily extract at date t the annual compounded zero-coupon rate $R(t, t_i - t)$ with maturity $t_i - t$ using

$$R(t, t_i - t) = e^{-\frac{1}{t_i - t} \ln[B(t, t_i)]} - 1$$

and its continuously compounded equivalent $R^c(t, t_i - t)$ by using

$$R^c(t, t_i - t) = -\frac{1}{t_i - t} \ln[B(t, t_i)]$$

Example 4.1 At date $t = 0$, we want to derive the zero-coupon curve until the 4-year maturity. For this purpose, we get from the market four bonds with the following features:

	Annual coupon	Maturity (years)	Price
Bond 1	5	1	$P_0^1 = 101$
Bond 2	5.5	2	$P_0^2 = 101.5$
Bond 3	5	3	$P_0^3 = 99$
Bond 4	6	4	$P_0^4 = 100$

Using the no-arbitrage relationship, we obtain the following equations for the four bond prices:

$$\begin{cases} 101 = 105B(0,1) \\ 101.5 = 5.5B(0,1) + 105.5B(0,2) \\ 99 = 5B(0,1) + 5B(0,2) + 105B(0,3) \\ 100 = 6B(0,1) + 6B(0,2) + 6B(0,3) + 106B(0,4) \end{cases}$$

which can be expressed in a matrix form

$$\begin{pmatrix} 101 \\ 101.5 \\ 99 \\ 100 \end{pmatrix} = \begin{pmatrix} 105 & & & \\ 5.5 & 105.5 & & \\ 5 & 5 & 105 & \\ 6 & 6 & 6 & 106 \end{pmatrix} \times \begin{pmatrix} B(0,1) \\ B(0,2) \\ B(0,3) \\ B(0,4) \end{pmatrix}$$

Finally, we get the following discount factors using equation (4.2):

$$\begin{pmatrix} B(0,1) \\ B(0,2) \\ B(0,3) \\ B(0,4) \end{pmatrix} = \begin{pmatrix} 0.9619 \\ 0.91194 \\ 0.85363 \\ 0.78901 \end{pmatrix}$$

from which we find the zero-coupon rates

$$\begin{pmatrix} R(0,1) = 3.96\% \\ R(0,2) = 4.717\% \\ R(0,3) = 5.417\% \\ R(0,4) = 6.103\% \end{pmatrix}$$

This direct method is fairly simple in theory and not computationally intensive. Unfortunately, finding many distinct linearly independent bonds with the same coupon dates is quasi-impossible in practice. This is why practitioners use a common approach known as the *bootstrapping method*.

The Bootstrapping Method

Bootstrapping is the term for generating a zero-coupon yield curve from existing market data such as bond prices. Bootstrapping can be viewed as a repetitive double-step procedure:

- *Firstly, we extract directly zero-coupon rates with maturity inferior or equal to 1 year from corresponding zero-coupon bond prices.*

- *Secondly, we use a linear or cubic interpolation (see next section on "Different Kinds of Interpolation") to draw a continuous zero-coupon yield curve for maturities inferior or equal to 1 year.*

- *Thirdly, we consider the bond with nearest maturity between 1 and 2 years. The bond has two cash flows and its price is logically the discounted value of these two cash flows. We know the first discount factor needed to obtain the discounted value of the first cash flow. The unknown variable is the second discount factor. Solving a nonlinear equation we get this discount factor*

Fixed Income Securities

and the corresponding zero-coupon rate. We begin again with the same process considering the next bond with nearest maturity between 1 and 2 years.

- *Fourthly, we use a linear or cubic interpolation to draw a continuous zero-coupon yield curve for maturities between 1 and 2 years, using the zero-coupon rates obtained from market prices.*

- *Fifthly, we consider the bond with nearest maturity between 2 and 3 years and repeat the same process. The unknown discount factors are always reduced to one and solving one equation enables to determine it as well as the corresponding zero-coupon rate....*

- *And so on.*

Example 4.2 Suppose we know from market prices the following zero-coupon rates with maturities inferior or equal to 1 year:

Maturity	Zero-coupon rate (%)
1 Day	4.40
1 Month	4.50
2 Months	4.60
3 Months	4.70
6 Months	4.90
9 Months	5
1 Year	5.10

Using a linear interpolation (see Figure 4.1), we draw the continuous zero-coupon yield curve for maturities inferior or equal to 1 year. Now, we consider bonds priced by the market until the 3-year maturity:

Maturity	Coupon (%)	Gross price
1 Year and 2 Months	5	103.7
1 Year and 9 Months	6	102
2 Years	5.5	99.5
3 Years	5	97.6

We first extract the one-year-and-two-month zero-coupon rate. In the absence of arbitrage, the price of this bond is the sum of its future discounted cash flows:

$$103.7 = \frac{5}{(1+4.6\%)^{1/6}} + \frac{105}{(1+x)^{1+1/6}}$$

where x is the one-year-and-two-month zero-coupon rate to determine. Solving this equation (for example, with the Excel solver) we obtain 5.41% for x. Applying the same procedure with the one-year-and-nine-month and the 2-year bonds we obtain, respectively, 5.69% and 5.79% for x. Using again a linear interpolation (see Figure 4.1), we draw the continuous zero-coupon yield curve for maturities between 1 and 2 years. Next, we have to extract the

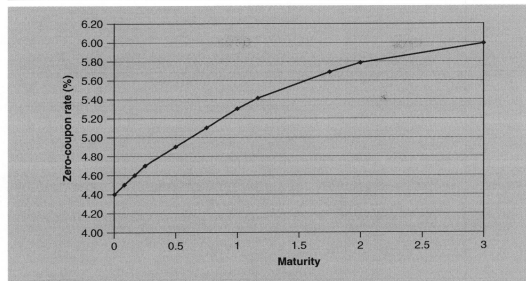

Figure 4.1 Zero-coupon curve using the bootstrapping method.

3-year zero-coupon rate solving the following equation

$$97.6 = \frac{5}{(1 + 5.10\%)} + \frac{5}{(1 + 5.79\%)^2} + \frac{105}{(1 + x\%)^3}$$

x is equal to 5.91%, and we obtain the following zero-coupon curve for maturities inferior or equal to 3 years (see Figure 4.1).

Different Kinds of Interpolation

Using direct methods leads to a discontinuous term structure of interest rates. If we know the 3-year and 4-year maturity zero-coupon rates and if we want to get the three-and-a-half-year maturity zero-coupon rate, we have to interpolate it. There exist many kinds of interpolation. In practice, we use linear or cubic interpolations.

Linear Interpolation Consider that we know $R(0, x)$ and $R(0, z)$, respectively, the x-year and the z-year zero-coupon rates and that we need $R(0, y)$ the y-year zero-coupon rate with $y \in [x; z]$. Using the linear interpolation, $R(0, y)$ is given by the following formula

$$R(0, y) = \frac{(z - y)R(0, x) + (y - x)R(0, z)}{z - x}$$

Example 4.3 The 3-year and 4-year zero-coupon rates are, respectively, given by 5.5% and 6%. Using the linear interpolation, the $3^{3/4}$-year zero-coupon rate $R(0, 3.75)$ is obtained

Fixed Income Securities

as follows:

$$R(0, 3.75) = \frac{0.25 \times 5.5\% + 0.75 \times 6\%}{1} = 5.875\%$$

Cubic Interpolation   We need four zero-coupon rates, respectively, $R(0, v)$, $R(0, x)$, $R(0, y)$ and $R(0, z)$ to implement the cubic interpolation with the condition $v < x < y < z$. The interpolated rate $R(0, w)$ with $w \in [v; z]$ verifies the three-order polynomial equation

$$R(0, w) = aw^3 + bw^2 + cw + d$$

where a, b, c and d satisfy the system

$$\begin{cases} R(0, v) = av^3 + bv^2 + cv + d \\ R(0, x) = ax^3 + bx^2 + cx + d \\ R(0, y) = ay^3 + by^2 + cy + d \\ R(0, z) = az^3 + bz^2 + cz + d \end{cases}$$

This system means simply that the cubic polynomial function contains the four points $(v, R(0, v))$, $(x, R(0, x))$, $(y, R(0, y))$ and $(z, R(0, z))$. a, b, c and d are obtained through the following matrix calculation:

$$\begin{pmatrix} a \\ b \\ c \\ d \end{pmatrix} = \begin{pmatrix} v^3 & v^2 & v & 1 \\ x^3 & x^2 & x & 1 \\ y^3 & y^2 & y & 1 \\ z^3 & z^2 & z & 1 \end{pmatrix}^{-1} \begin{pmatrix} R(0, v) \\ R(0, x) \\ R(0, y) \\ R(0, z) \end{pmatrix}$$

Cubic interpolations are computed using first four points to construct the first part of the curve, then four other points to construct the second part of the curve and so on, which may imply that the slope of the curve is not smooth. Besides, the curve may be concave on one maturity segment and convex on the other.

Example 4.4   The 1-, 2-, 3- and 4-year zero-coupon rates are, respectively, 3%, 5%, 5.5% and 6%. Using the cubic interpolation, the 2.5-year zero-coupon rate is obtained as follows:

$$R(0, 2.5) = a \times 2.5^3 + b \times 2.5^2 + c \times 2.5 + d = 5.34375\%$$

where

$$\begin{pmatrix} a \\ b \\ c \\ d \end{pmatrix} = \begin{pmatrix} 1 & 1 & 1 & 1 \\ 8 & 4 & 2 & 1 \\ 27 & 9 & 3 & 1 \\ 64 & 16 & 4 & 1 \end{pmatrix}^{-1} \begin{pmatrix} 3\% \\ 5\% \\ 5.5\% \\ 6\% \end{pmatrix} = \begin{pmatrix} 0.0025 \\ -0.0225 \\ 0.07 \\ -0.02 \end{pmatrix}$$

Comparison of Linear and Cubic Interpolations

Example 4.5   Using the same data as in the previous example, we compare linear and cubic interpolations in Figure 4.2.

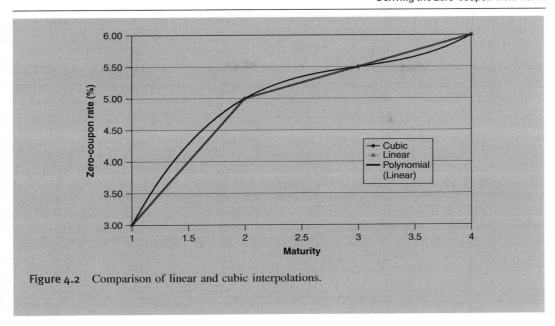

Figure 4.2 Comparison of linear and cubic interpolations.

In the linear case, the slope of the curve is not smooth, whereas the curve is convex for maturities between 3 and 4 years in the cubic interpolation.

4.1.3 Indirect Methods

These difficulties lead us to search for other more practical methods. To that end, indirect methods are developed. The common trait of all indirect models is that they involve fitting the data to a prespecified form of the zero-coupon yield curve. It should be noted that, while indirect models help one avoid the practical difficulties mentioned above, they suffer from the risk of possible misspecification. By that we mean that if one chooses a very bad model for the zero-coupon yield curve, then fitting the data with this model will not give a very reliable framework.

The general approach is as follows. First, one selects a reference set of n default-free bonds with market prices P_t^j and cash flows $F_s^{(j)}$ for some $s \geq t$. They will be used later to estimate the zero-coupon yield curve. Next, one postulates a specific form of the discount function $B(t, s) \equiv f(s - t; \beta_1)$ or the zero-coupon rates $R(t, s - t) \equiv g(s - t; \beta_2)$, where β_1 and β_2 are the vectors of parameters.

The function f is usually defined piecewise in order to allow different sets of parameters for different types of maturities (short, medium and long), under the form of a polynomial or exponential spline functional (see below). The function g is often defined in such a way that the parameters are usually easily interpretable (e.g., close to the solution of a dynamic model such as Vasicek (1977)).

Finally, the set of parameters $\widehat{\beta}^*$ is estimated as the one that best approximates the given market prices, or, in other words, the one that is a solution to the following optimization program

$$\widehat{\beta}^* = \arg\min_{\beta} \sum_{j=1}^{n} (P_t^j - \widehat{P_t^j})^2 \tag{4.3}$$

Fixed Income Securities

where $\widehat{P_t^j}$ are the theoretical prices from the model

$$\widehat{P_t^j} = \sum_s F_s^{(j)} f(s - t; \beta)$$

or

$$\widehat{P_t^j} = \sum_s F_s^{(j)} \exp[-(s - t)g(s - t; \beta)]$$

We now discuss in more detail these two indirect methods for fitting the yield curve, with an emphasis on possible choices of the functions f and g.

Parametrization of the Discount Function as a Spline Function

Let us be more specific now and discuss the particulars of some of the more popular methods, namely, polynomial and exponential splines. We now adopt the following notation:

- *n is the number of bonds used for the estimation of the zero-coupon yield curve.*[3]

- *P_t^j is the market price at date t of the jth bond.*

- *$\widehat{P_t^j}$ is the theoretical price at date t of the jth bond.*

- *The price vectors are $P_t = (P_t^j)_{j=1,\dots,n}$ and $\widehat{P}_t = (\widehat{P_t^j})_{j=1,\dots,n}$, respectively.*

- *T_j is the maturity of the jth bond (in years).*

- *$F_s^{(j)}$ is the coupon and/or principal payment of the jth bond at time $s \geq t$.*

- *α_j is the number of cash flows for the jth bond.*

- *$B(t, s)$ is the discount factor (price at date t of a zero-coupon bond paying \$1 at date s).*
Note that we have the following constraint for the minimization program:

$$B(t, t) = 1$$

In the absence of arbitrage opportunities, the following must hold:

$$\widehat{P_t^j} = \sum_{\substack{s=T_j-\alpha_j+1 \\ s>0}}^{T_j} F_s^{(j)} B(t, s)$$

The model is expressed as

$$P_t = \widehat{P}_t + \varepsilon$$

where the residuals ε satisfy $\forall(j, j') \in \{1, \dots, n\}^2$

$$\mathbb{E}(\varepsilon_j) = 0$$

$$\mathbb{V}ar(\varepsilon_j) = \sigma^2 \omega_j^2$$

$$\mathbb{C}ov(\varepsilon_j, \varepsilon_{j'}) = 0 \text{ for } j \neq j'$$

---

[3]These bonds belong to the reference set used for the optimization procedure, as opposed to the reference set used for verification (which is used for assessing the fitting quality).

Hence, the variance–covariance matrix of the residuals is $\sigma^2 \Omega$ with $\sigma \in \mathbb{R}^+$ and

$$\Omega = \begin{pmatrix} \omega_1^2 & 0 & \cdots & 0 \\ 0 & \omega_2^2 & & \vdots \\ \vdots & & \ddots & 0 \\ 0 & \cdots & 0 & \omega_n^2 \end{pmatrix}$$

The specification of ω_j^2 is actually a crucial point in the procedure. In practice, it consists in overweighting or underweighting some bonds in the minimization program (4.3). Many authors simply consider the homoscedastic case[4] with

$$\omega_j^2 \equiv 1 \quad \forall j \in \{1, \ldots, n\}$$

All bonds have the same weight in the minimization program. In that case, however, the short-term end of the curve [1 day–6 months] is fitted with only approximate precision (see the following remark).

In an attempt to provide a more accurate specification, Vasicek and Fong (1982) have overweighted short bonds in the minimization program. They suggested the following specification for ω_j^2:

$$\omega_j^2 = \left(\frac{dP_t^j}{dy_j(t)} \right)^2 = \frac{D_j^2(t) P_t^j}{(1 + y_j(t))^2}$$

where $y_j(t)$ and $D_j(t)$ are the internal rate of return (or yield to maturity) and the duration of the jth bond at date t, respectively (see Chapter 5 for a definition of duration).

The rationale for this choice follows the intuition that the longer the maturity of a given bond, the more difficult is its price estimation. This difficulty comes from the fact that a bond with maturity shorter than 1 year is priced using a single pure discount rate. On the other hand, pricing a bond with maturity 15 years requires the use of 15 pure discount rates (30 rates if payments are semiannual as for US Treasury bonds). If one wishes to improve the quality of the method for short-term bonds, various specifications for ω_j^2 may be used, such as

$$\omega_j^2 = T_j^2$$

or

$$\omega_j^2 = \frac{D_j(t) P_t^j}{1 + y_j(t)}$$

Remark 4.1   Bad Fit of the Short-Term End of the Curve with Homoscedastic Residuals

As we have seen above, the homoscedastic case implies the same variance for each residual. Nevertheless, the shorter the maturity of a bond, the more precise its price has to be. On

---

[4]In this case, the resolution of the minimization program can be done by the ordinary least squares (OLS) procedure.

Fixed Income Securities

the contrary, the variance of the residuals can be a growing function of a bond's maturity in the heteroscedastic case, so that we can constrain the variance of the residuals to be very small for short maturity bonds. This point is of importance as we can see in the two following examples:

- *We consider a bond with a 1-day maturity, which delivers a cash flow of $100. Its price is, respectively, $99.9866 and $99.9840 if discounted at a rate of 5% and 6%, which shows a very small price difference amounting to $0.0026.*

- *Now, we consider a bond with a 1-week maturity, which delivers a cash flow of $100. Its price is, respectively, $99.888 and $99.879 if discounted at a rate of 6% and 6.5%, which shows a price difference reaching $0.009.*

We see clearly that a 1% change in the 1-day zero-coupon rate or a 0.5% change in the 1-week zero-coupon rate has a negligible impact on the prices of the bonds under consideration. That is why it is important to constrain the variance of the residuals to be small for short maturity bonds so as to prevent the short-term end of the curve from being irrelevant. Besides, bad errors made on short-term rates may lead to mistakes on longer maturity rates because the price of a bond is the sum of its future discounted cash flows.

In Figure 4.3, we consider a concrete example on the French government bond market on 11/28/95. Using a standard basket of bonds, we reconstruct the zero-coupon yield curve implementing a cubic polynomial spline function as the discount function, four splines [0,1], [1,7], [7,10] and [10,20] and two options for the variance of the residuals. The first option denoted CS4O is the homoscedastic case whereas the second denoted CS4G is the Vasicek and Fong heteroscedastic case. Points denoted ZC are the zero-coupon rates extracted directly from the corresponding zero-coupon bond market prices.

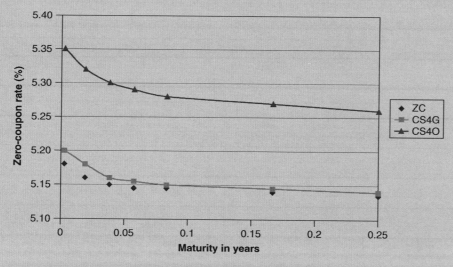

Figure 4.3   Curve differences depending on the choice of residuals.

We can see that CS4G accurately fits the short-term segment of the curve, whereas the CS4O method fits poorly.

We define

- β as the vector of parameters for the discount function we need to estimate;
- $\widehat{\beta}$ as the estimator of β in the absence of the constraint;
- $\widehat{\beta}^*$ as the estimator of β in the presence of the constraint;
- Z as the matrix of the coefficients of the parameters for each bond.

We finally have the following program:

$$\min_{\beta} \sum_{j=1}^{n} (P_t^j - \widehat{P_t^j})^2 \tag{4.4}$$

such that $B(t, t) = 1$. In matrix notation, this is $1 = C^{\mathsf{T}}\beta$.

A direct application of the constrained generalized least squares (GLS)[5] method gives

$$\widehat{\beta}^* = (Z^{\mathsf{T}}\Omega^{-1}Z)^{-1}Z^{\mathsf{T}}\Omega^{-1}P_t + (Z^{\mathsf{T}}\Omega^{-1}Z)^{-1}C^{\mathsf{T}}(C(Z^{\mathsf{T}}\Omega^{-1}Z)^{-1}C^{\mathsf{T}})^{-1}(1\text{-}C\widehat{\beta})$$

or equivalently

$$\widehat{\beta}^* = \widehat{\beta} + (Z^{\mathsf{T}}\Omega^{-1}Z)^{-1}C^{\mathsf{T}}(C(Z^{\mathsf{T}}\Omega^{-1}Z)^{-1}C^{\mathsf{T}})^{-1}(1\text{-}C\widehat{\beta}) \tag{4.5}$$

since

$$\widehat{\beta} = (Z^{\mathsf{T}}\Omega^{-1}Z)^{-1}Z^{\mathsf{T}}\Omega^{-1}P_t$$

Example 4.6   A Two-Order Polynomial Spline

In order to give more flesh to the construction, let us specify the discount factors at date $t = 0$ in terms of polynomial splines, namely,

$$B(0, s) = \begin{cases} B_0(s) = d_0 + c_0 s + b_0 s^2 \text{ for } s \in [0, 5] \\ B_5(s) = d_1 + c_1 s + b_1 s^2 \text{ for } s \in [5, 10] \\ B_{10}(s) = d_2 + c_2 s + b_2 s^2 \text{ for } s \in [10, 20] \end{cases}$$

Then, $\beta = (d_0, c_0, b_0, d_1, c_1, b_1, d_2, c_2, b_2)^{\mathsf{T}} \in \mathbb{R}^9$, $Z = (z_{j,\gamma})$ where $\gamma = 1, \ldots, 9$ and $j = 1, \ldots, n$. For example, if the first of the n bonds is a zero-coupon bond maturing 6 years from now

$$B(0, 6) = B_5(6) = d_1 + 6c_1 + 36b_1$$

---

[5]Note that a GLS program is equivalent to a weighted OLS program.

Fixed Income Securities

then (for $j = 1$)

$$z_{1,1} = 0$$
$$z_{1,2} = 0$$
$$z_{1,3} = 0$$
$$z_{1,4} = 1$$
$$z_{1,5} = 6$$
$$z_{1,6} = 36$$
$$z_{1,7} = 0$$
$$z_{1,8} = 0$$
$$z_{1,9} = 0$$

In particular, if we have $B(0, 0) = d_0$, then $C = (1, 0, 0, 0, 0, 0, 0, 0, 0, 0)^\mathsf{T}$.

We now specify the function $B(t, s)$ as a function of s. Different standard choices will be given, including polynomial and exponential spline functions. In both of these cases, the choice of the spline function stems from the requirement of smoothness in the discount function. More precisely, we attempt to obtain $B(t, s)$ as a $p - 1$ times differentiable function with continuous derivatives if the polynomial used for fitting it is of order p. Hence, for $p = 3$, the function will be continuous and will be twice differentiable. The latter condition ensures a smoothness property in the slope of the instantaneous forward rates. We consider date $t = 0$ and denote $B(0, s) \equiv B(s)$.

Polynomial Splines Polynomial splines have been introduced by McCulloch (1971, 1975). It is of great importance to carefully select the order of the polynomial. A parsimonious choice here is a polynomial spline of order 3, since a spline of order 2 generally implies a discontinuity[6] of the second derivative $B^{(2)}(s)$. Furthermore, choosing a greater order (four or five) leads to an increase in complexity with no real justification about the continuity of the third or fourth derivative. There are two ways of modeling polynomial splines, the standard modelization and the expression in the B-spline basis.

Standard Modelization   It is common to consider, as in the example mentioned above where we model three splines

$$B(s) = \begin{cases} B_0(s) = d_0 + c_0 s + b_0 s^2 + a_0 s^3 & \text{for } s \in [0, 5] \\ B_5(s) = d_1 + c_1 s + b_1 s^2 + a_1 s^3 & \text{for } s \in [5, 10] \\ B_{10}(s) = d_2 + c_2 s + b_2 s^2 + a_2 s^3 & \text{for } s \in [10, 20] \end{cases}$$

In that case, the discount factor function has 12 parameters.

---

[6]This case is illustrated with the following example. We consider the discount factor function $B(s)$:

$$B(s) = \begin{cases} B_0(s) = d_0 + c_0 s + b_0 s^2 & \text{for } s \in [0, 5] \\ B_5(s) = d_1 + c_1 s + b_1 s^2 & \text{for } s \in [5, 10] \\ B_{10}(s) = d_2 + c_2 s + b_2 s^2 & \text{for } s \in [10, 20] \end{cases}$$

The second derivative of the discount factor function is continuous if and only if $b_0 = b_1 = b_2$.

Note that the constraints of smoothness of the function and its derivatives further require

$$B_0^{(i)}(5) = B_5^{(i)}(5)$$

$$B_5^{(i)}(10) = B_{10}^{(i)}(10)$$

$$B_0(0) = 1$$

where $B^{(i)}(.)$ is the ith derivative of the function $B.(.)$ for $i = 0, 1, 2$.

Using these constraints reduces the number of independent parameters to five:

$$B(s) = \begin{cases} B_0(s) = 1 + c_0 s + b_0 s^2 + a_0 s^3 \text{ for } s \in [0, 5] \\ B_5(s) = 1 + c_0 s + b_0 s^2 + a_0 [s^3 - (s-5)^3] \\ \qquad + a_1 (s-5)^3 \text{ for } s \in [5, 10] \\ B_{10}(s) = 1 + c_0 s + b_0 s^2 + a_0 [s^3 - (s-5)^3] \\ \qquad + a_1 [(s-5)^3 - (s-10)^3] + a_2 (s-10)^3 \text{ for } s \in [10, 20] \end{cases} \qquad (4.6)$$

Equation (4.6) may be transformed into

$$B(s) = 1 + c_0 s + b_0 s^2 + a_0 s^3 + (a_1 - a_0) \cdot (s-5)_+^3 + (a_2 - a_1) \cdot (s-10)_+^3 \text{ for } s \in [0, 20]$$

where $(s-5)_+^3$ and $(s-10)_+^3$ are bounded polynomial functions defined as

$$(s - \theta_m)_+^k = [\max(s - \theta_m), 0]^k$$

We see that the basis of the space under consideration is simply $(1, s, s^2, s^3, (s-5)_+^3, (s-10)_+^3)$ and its dimension is equal to six.

In fact, we can create another basis for this space, which is intensively used to model the discount factor function.[7] This is the B-spline basis.

Expression in the B-Spline Basis B-spline functions are linear combinations of bounded polynomial functions. We can write the discount function in this basis in the following manner

$$B(s) = \sum_{l=-3}^{2} c_l B_l^3(s) = \sum_{l=-3}^{2} c_l \left(\sum_{j=l}^{l+4} \left[\prod_{\substack{i=l \\ i \neq j}}^{l+4} \frac{1}{\lambda_i - \lambda_j} \right] (s - \lambda_j)_+^3 \right)$$

where the lambda coefficients are defined according to

$$\lambda_{-3} < \lambda_{-2} < \lambda_{-1} < \lambda_0 = 0 < \lambda_1 = 5 < \lambda_2 = 10 < \lambda_3 = 20 < \lambda_4 < \lambda_5 < \lambda_6$$

Parameters $\lambda_0, \lambda_1, \lambda_2$ and λ_3 are the knot points as parameters $\lambda_{-3}, \lambda_{-2}, \lambda_{-1}, \lambda_4, \lambda_5, \lambda_6$ must only satisfy $\lambda_{-3} < \lambda_{-2} < \lambda_{-1} < 0 < \cdots < 20 < \lambda_4 < \lambda_5 < \lambda_6$ and are defined as mathematical conditions to write B-spline functions $B_l^3(\theta)$.

---

[7]Shea (1984) and Steeley (1991) argue that the B-spline basis is optimal to avoid multicollinearity in the regression matrix.

Fixed Income Securities

The new basis of the space under consideration is $(B^3_{-3}(s), B^3_{-2}(s), B^3_{-1}(s), B^3_0(s), B^3_1(s), B^3_2(s))$. Its dimension equal to 6 is simply the sum of splines plus the degree of the B-spline polynomial, which is $3 + 3$ in our example.

The vector of parameters $\widehat{\beta}^* = (c_{-3}, c_{-2}, c_{-1}, c_0, c_1, c_2)$ is the vector of the problem of minimization (4.4). Note that the classical constraint $B(0) = 1$ becomes

$$B(0) = \sum_{l=-3}^{2} c_l B^3_l(0) = \sum_{l=-3}^{-1} c_l B^3_l(0) = 1$$

because B-spline functions $B^3_0(0)$, $B^3_1(0)$ and $B^3_2(0)$ are all equal to zero.

Note that using the standard modelization or the expression in the B-spline basis provides the same results in terms of the minimization program, that is, we obtain the same results in terms of the spreads between the market price and the theoretical price.

Exponential Splines   Exponential splines have been introduced by Vasicek and Fong (1982) as a potentially efficient model for the zero-coupon yield curve. For the same reasons as above, we consider a third-order exponential spline expressed as

$$B(s) = \begin{cases} B_0(s) = d_0 + c_0 e^{-us} + b_0 e^{-2us} + a_0 e^{-3us} & \text{for } s \in [0, 5] \\ B_5(s) = d_1 + c_1 e^{-us} + b_1 e^{-2us} + a_1 e^{-3us} & \text{for } s \in [5, 10] \\ B_{10}(s) = d_2 + c_2 e^{-us} + b_2 e^{-2us} + a_2 e^{-3us} & \text{for } s \in [10, 20] \end{cases} \tag{4.7}$$

The same constraints as in the case of polynomial splines apply. The next remark provides a further discussion of how to simplify this formulation (4.7) of exponential splines.

Remark 4.2   Simplification of the Exponential Spline Formulation

Vasicek and Fong (1982) define the discount function $B(s)$ as a piecewise third-degree exponential polynomial (see equation (4.7)). The function B is assumed to be of class C^2 on the set $[0, 20]$, and satisfies

$$B^{(i)}_0(5) = B^{(i)}_5(5)$$

$$B^{(i)}_5(10) = B^{(i)}_{10}(10)$$

where $B^{(i)}(.)$ is the ith derivative of the function $B(.)$ for $i = 0, 1, 2$. $B(s)$ is also subject to the constraint $B_0(0) = 1$. Hence, $B(s)$ depends upon 13 parameters and is subject to 7 constraints. We use the constraints to express the function B as a function of 7 parameters under the further constraint $B_0(0) = 1$. Note that $B_0(s)$ is left unchanged.

- *Looking more closely at $B_5(s)$, we have*

$$B_0(5) = B_5(5) \Longleftrightarrow d_1 - d_0 = (c_0 - c_1)e^{-5u} + (b_0 - b_1)e^{-10u} + (a_0 - a_1)e^{-15u}$$

$$B^{(1)}_0(5) = B^{(1)}_5(5) \Longleftrightarrow c_1 - c_0 = 2(b_0 - b_1)e^{-5u} + 3(a_0 - a_1)e^{-10u}$$

$$B^{(2)}_0(5) = B^{(2)}_5(5) \Longleftrightarrow c_1 - c_0 = 4(b_0 - b_1)e^{-5u} + 9(a_0 - a_1)e^{-10u}$$

from which we obtain

$$b_1 - b_0 = 3(a_0 - a_1)e^{-5u}$$

$$c_1 - c_0 = -3(a_0 - a_1)e^{-10u}$$

$$d_1 - d_0 = (a_0 - a_1)e^{-15u}$$

$$B_5(s) = d_0 + c_0 e^{-us} + b_0 e^{-2us} + a_0[e^{-3us} - (e^{-us} - e^{-5u})^3] + a_1[e^{-us} - e^{-5u}]^3$$

- *Looking more closely at $B_{10}(s)$, we have*

$$B_5^{(1)}(10) = B_{10}^{(1)}(10) \Longleftrightarrow c_2 - c_0 = 2(b_0 - b_2)e^{-10u}$$
$$+ 3(a_0 - a_2)e^{-20u} + 3(a_1 - a_0)[e^{-10u} - e^{-5u}]^2$$

$$B_5^{(2)}(10) = B_{10}^{(2)}(10) \Longleftrightarrow c_2 - c_0 = 4(b_0 - b_2)e^{-10u} + 9(a_0 - a_1)e^{-20u}$$
$$+ 3(a_1 - a_0)[e^{-10u} - e^{-5u}][3e^{-10u} - e^{-5u}]$$

from which we obtain

$$b_2 - b_0 = 3(a_0 - a_2)e^{-10u} + 3(a_1 - a_0)[e^{-10u} - e^{-5u}]$$

$$c_2 - c_0 = -3(a_0 - a_2)e^{-20u} + 3(a_0 - a_1)[e^{-20u} - e^{-10u}]$$

$$d_2 - d_0 = (a_0 - a_2)e^{-30u} + (a_0 - a_1)[e^{-15u} - e^{-30u}]$$

$$B_{10}(s) = d_0 + c_0 e^{-us} + b_0 e^{-2us} + a_0[e^{-3us} - (e^{-us} - e^{-5u})^3]$$
$$+ a_1[(e^{-us} - e^{-5u})^3 - (e^{-us} - e^{-10u})^3] + a_2[e^{-us} - e^{-10u}]^3$$

The seven parameters of the function B become $d_0, c_0, b_0, a_0, a_1, a_2$ and u.

Using exponential splines requires one additional step in the estimation procedure. Note that the equation $B(0, s) = B(s)$ is not only a function of s and the set of parameters β but also of u. Even though u can be regarded as just one of the parameters, it also has an interesting economic interpretation. Vasicek and Fong (1982) have shown that

$$u = \lim_{s \to \infty} f(0, s)$$

Hence, u can be considered as the instantaneous forward rate for an infinite horizon.[8]

The optimization procedure (see equation (4.5)) needs to be altered in the following way:
- *Fix initially $f(0, \infty)$ to be a "reasonable" value.*
- *Compute $\widehat{\beta}^*$ using this $f(0, \infty)$.*
- *Optimize over $f(0, \infty)$ using Newton's three-point method (each value of $f(0, \infty)$ corresponds to a different value of $\widehat{\beta}^*$).*

We now address the question of the optimal number of splines.

---

[8] See also Shea (1985).

The Optimal Number of Splines   The question of how many splines should be used is very rarely addressed in academic literature. Vasicek and Fong (1982) do not mention it. Shea (1984) and McCulloch (1971, 1975) argue that one should use a number of splines that is equal to the square root of n, the number of bonds in the reference set.

Kanony and Mokrane (1992) and Deacon and Derry (1994) provide the following two comments:

- *The greater the number of splines, the better the fit in terms of the variance of the residuals, but the curve is less smooth. As the number of splines increases, the curve tends to be much more sensitive to abnormal data. The difference in prices between the actual and the theoretical prices becomes increasingly small. It is then impossible to detect bonds with abnormal prices that one should take out of the reference set.*

- *The lower the number of splines, the smoother the curve. On the other hand, when a small perturbation is introduced, errors become significant, which tends to imply that the quality of fit is not great.*

Priaulet (1997) suggests using an intuitive rule based on the average spreads $\overline{E_{\min}}$ and $\overline{E_{\text{verif}}}$, respectively, obtained on the reference sets used for optimization and verification. $\overline{E_{\min}}$ is defined as

$$\overline{E_{\min}} = \sqrt{\dfrac{\displaystyle\sum_{j=1}^{n}(P_t^j - \widehat{P_t^j})^2}{n}}$$

To assess the robustness of the fit, it is not enough to use bonds from the reference set used in the optimization process. It is desirable to consider another reference set used for checking. A similar quantity $\overline{E_{\text{verif}}}$ is computed on that set and compared with $\overline{E_{\min}}$. The rule is as follows.

We require these two spreads to be lower than 0.10% of the price, which corresponds to a rough approximation of the "bid–ask" spread.[9]

- *If the spreads are not lower than 0.10%, then increase the number of splines until they become so.*

- *If both spreads are lower than 0.10%, compute the difference* $\overline{E_{\min}} - \overline{E_{\text{verif}}}$.[10]

  - *If the difference is "large," then, one concludes that the number of splines is probably too high.*
  - *On the other hand, if the difference is "small" (around 0.02 or 0.03% of the price), then the number of splines can be considered as adequate.*

Note that the implementation of that rule requires a dynamic check of the prices obtained on the reference sets. Also, one should try to exclude illiquid bonds from the reference sets, because such bonds typically imply very large spreads, which do not persist in time.

Finally, one should also carefully select pasting points.

---

[9]More precisely, one could compute the average bid–ask spread on a given market, and use that number instead of the approximate 0.10%.

[10]Note that in principle, one expects to have $\overline{E_{\min}} \leq \overline{E_{\text{verif}}}$.

The Optimal Choice of Pasting (or Knot) Points   Deacon and Derry (1994) show that changing the choice of pasting points implies significant changes in the forward rate curve level (up to 13 basis points). Very few authors, however, address this issue. Shea (1984) simply argues that one should try to have the same numbers of bonds for each spline, which implicitly defines where the pasting points should be. Priaulet (1997) argues, on the other hand, that the choice should reflect a natural segmentation of the bond market. For the French Treasury bond market, he considers four splines:

- A *"short-term" spline [1 day–1 year]*

- A *"medium-term" spline [1 year–7 years]*

- A *"long-term" spline [7 years–10 years]*

- A *"very long-term spline" [10 years–30 years]*.

Priaulet (1997) also argues that one may usefully add a spline where the function is more problematic to fit, which usually corresponds to the segment [1 day–3 years].[11]

The choice of the number of splines and the pasting points is discussed in the following example, where we compare polynomial and exponential splines using data from the French bond market.

Example 4.7   Comparison of Exponential and Polynomial Splines: A Concrete Example

We derive the zero-coupon rate curve using market prices from French Treasury bonds on April 26, 1996. For that, we use a variety of Treasury bonds across a whole range of maturities (from 1 day to 17 years). We use two sets of bonds. One set, which we refer to as the "minimization set," is based upon 25 bonds, and is used to perform the optimization. Another set, which we refer to as the "checking set," is based upon only 10 bonds; it ensures that the zero-coupon rate curve is correctly obtained, a test that can only be performed using assets that do not belong to the optimization set. We consider the following splines: [0,1], [1,7], [7,10] and [10,20] (see above). The exponential spline method is based upon a minimization of a function of eight parameters (three for the order of the exponential polynomial, four for the number of splines, and the parameter u). For the polynomial spline method, we further include the segment [1,3]. It also consists of a minimization program of a function of eight parameters (three for the order of the polynomial, and five for the number of splines). We refer to these methods as VF34 and BS35, respectively. Tables 4.1 and 4.2 summarize the results. They display the spreads between theoretical prices and market prices for each bond, the average spread and also the sum of the squared spreads for each set of bonds. For the two methods, the quality of fit measured on the checking set is very close to the quality of fit as measured on the optimization set, and both are very

---

[11] The standard deviations of yields for pure discount bonds with maturity less than 3 years are usually greater than those obtained for longer maturity bonds.

Table 4.1 Bond Price Spreads—VF34.

Exponential Splines—VF34

Date	04/26/96	
Parameter u	0.1349	
Sum of squared spreads—procedure of minimization		**0.0683**
Sum of squared spreads—checking procedure		**0.0889**
Average spread—procedure of minimization		**0.0523**
Average spread—checking procedure		**0.0943**

Bond	Maturity	Coupon (%)	Market price	Theoretical price VF34	Spread	Spread^2
Procedure of Minimization						
BTF	05/02/96	0	99.9389	99.9391	−0.0002	0.0000
BTF	05/09/96	0	99.8684	99.8681	0.0003	0.0000
BTF	05/23/96	0	99.7277	99.7267	0.001	0.0000
BTF	06/27/96	0	99.3753	99.3753	0	0.0000
BTF	07/25/96	0	99.0958	99.0953	0.0005	0.0000
BTF	09/19/96	0	98.5374	98.5349	0.0025	0.0000
BTF	12/12/96	0	97.7029	97.6828	0.0201	0.0004
BTAN	03/12/97	8.50	104.9479	104.9605	−0.0126	0.0002
BTAN	08/12/97	7.25	109.0547	109.0755	−0.0208	0.0004
BTAN	11/12/97	8.50	110.2058	110.2210	−0.0152	0.0002
BTAN	05/12/98	8	114.5512	114.6069	−0.0557	0.0031
BTAN	11/12/98	5.75	105.3351	105.2850	0.0501	0.0025
BTAN	04/12/99	4.75	100.1822	100.0968	**0.0854**	0.0073
OAT 11,348	05/25/99	8.125	116.8017	116.7481	0.0536	0.0029
OAT 11,641	03/28/00	8.50	112.2653	112.3729	**−0.1076**	0.0116
OAT 11,878	01/25/01	9.50	119.1245	119.1905	−0.066	0.0044
OAT 10,247	11/25/02	8.50	117.7230	117.6070	**0.116**	0.0135
OAT 19,465	10/25/03	6.75	107.3127	107.4022	**−0.0895**	0.0080
OAT 19,537	04/25/04	5.50	95.8651	95.8665	−0.0014	0.0000
OAT 19,603	10/25/04	6.75	106.8927	106.8002	**0.0925**	0.0086
OAT 19,643	04/25/05	7.50	108.3205	108.3632	−0.0427	0.0018
OAT 19,699	10/25/05	7.75	113.9068	113.9560	−0.0492	0.0024
OAT 19,734	04/25/06	7.25	106.5299	106.4963	0.0336	0.0011
OAT 19,377	10/25/08	8.50	121.1949	121.1959	−0.001	0.0000
OAT 10,248	12/26/12	8.50	119.8711	119.8707	0.0004	0.0000
Checking Procedure						
BTF	05/15/96	0	99.8083	99.8075	0.0008	0.0000
BTF	06/20/96	0	99.4455	99.4454	1E-04	0.0000
BTF	10/17/96	0	98.2524	98.2531	−0.0007	0.0000
BTAN	11/12/96	8.50	106.2958	106.3188	−0.023	0.0005
BTAN	04/12/00	7.75	109.4373	109.4080	0.0293	0.0009
BTAN	10/12/00	7	110.3381	110.2413	**0.0968**	0.0094
OAT 11,048	06/25/98	9.50	118.0344	118.1931	**−0.1587**	0.0252
OAT 4,266	05/27/00	10	126.3381	126.5155	**−0.1774**	0.0315
OAT 19,385	04/25/03	8.50	114.2333	114.3444	**−0.1111**	0.0123
OAT 11,351	02/27/04	8.25	114.3536	114.4494	**−0.0958**	0.0092

Table 4.2   Bond Price Spreads—BS35.

Cubic B-Splines—BS35

Date   04/26/96

Sum of squared spreads—procedure of minimization	**0.0813**
Sum of squared spreads—checking procedure	**0.0839**
Average spread—procedure of minimization	**0.0570**
Average spread—checking procedure	**0.0916**

Bond	Maturity	Coupon (%)	Market price	Theoretical price BS35	Spread	Spread^2
Procedure of Minimization						
BTF	05/02/96	0	99.9389	99.9393	−0.0004	0.0000
BTF	05/09/96	0	99.8684	99.8685	−0.0001	0.0000
BTF	05/23/96	0	99.7277	99.7272	0.0005	0.0000
BTF	06/27/96	0	99.3753	99.3753	0	0.0000
BTF	07/25/96	0	99.0958	99.0945	0.0013	0.0000
BTF	09/19/96	0	98.5374	98.5324	0.005	0.0000
BTF	12/12/96	0	97.7029	97.6793	0.0236	0.0006
BTAN	03/12/97	8.50	104.9479	104.9592	−0.0113	0.0001
BTAN	08/12/97	7.25	109.0547	109.0807	−0.026	0.0007
BTAN	11/12/97	8.50	110.2058	110.2278	−0.022	0.0005
BTAN	05/12/98	8	114.5512	114.6121	−0.0609	0.0037
BTAN	11/12/98	5.75	105.3351	105.2834	0.0517	0.0027
BTAN	04/12/99	4.75	100.1822	100.092	**0.0902**	0.0081
OAT 11,348	05/25/99	8.125	116.8017	116.7439	0.0578	0.0033
OAT 11,641	03/28/00	8.50	112.2653	112.3827	**−0.1174**	0.0138
OAT 11,878	01/25/01	9.50	119.1245	119.2075	**−0.083**	0.0069
OAT 10,247	11/25/02	8.50	117.7230	117.5798	**0.1432**	0.0205
OAT 19,465	10/25/03	6.75	107.3127	107.382	−0.0693	0.0048
OAT 19,537	04/25/04	5.50	95.8651	95.8637	0.0014	0.0000
OAT 19,603	10/25/04	6.75	106.8927	106.8117	**0.081**	0.0066
OAT 19,643	04/25/05	7.50	108.3205	108.3806	−0.0601	0.0036
OAT 19,699	10/25/05	7.75	113.9068	113.9673	−0.0605	0.0037
OAT 19,734	04/25/06	7.25	106.5299	106.488	0.0419	0.0018
OAT 19,377	10/25/08	8.50	121.1949	121.1944	0.0005	0.0000
OAT 10,248	12/26/12	8.50	119.8711	119.8711	0	0.0000
Checking Procedure						
BTF	05/15/96	0	99.8083	99.8079	0.0004	0.0000
BTF	06/20/96	0	99.4455	99.4456	−0.0001	0.0000
BTF	10/17/96	0	98.2524	98.2499	0.0025	0.0000
BTAN	11/12/96	8.50	106.2958	106.3149	−0.0191	0.0004
BTAN	04/12/00	7.75	109.4373	109.4184	0.0189	0.0004
BTAN	10/12/00	7	110.3381	110.2577	**0.0804**	0.0065
OAT 11,048	06/25/98	9.50	118.0344	118.1972	**−0.1628**	0.0265
OAT 4,266	05/27/00	10	126.3381	126.5284	**−0.1903**	0.0362
OAT 19,385	04/25/03	8.50	114.2333	114.3137	**−0.0804**	0.0065
OAT 11,351	02/27/04	8.25	114.3536	114.4404	**−0.0868**	0.0075

Fixed Income Securities

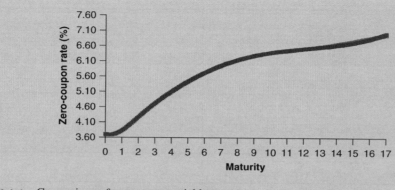

Figure 4.4 Comparison of zero-coupon yield curves.

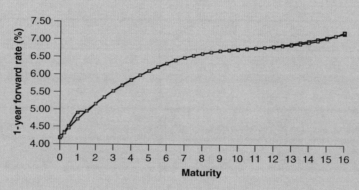

Figure 4.5 Comparison of the 1-year forward yield curves.

good. Hence, we conclude that both methods give excellent results, and these results are somewhat similar:

- *Goodness-of-fit indicators (average spread, sum of the squared spreads) are very close.*

- *Nine of the 10 most significant spreads, which appear in bold face in Tables 4.1 and 4.2, are the same for each method; furthermore, these spreads have the same sign and almost the same absolute value for the two methods.*

- *Finally, the zero-coupon rate curves (see Figure 4.4) and the 1-year forward rate curve (see Figure 4.5) are almost indistinguishable.*

Parametrization of the Zero-Coupon Curve as a Function of Different Parameters

The main drawback of the former, otherwise very useful, approach lies in the fact that most of the estimated parameters (except for u) have no clear economic interpretation. To overcome this, another approach based upon parametrization of the *zero-coupon rate* function has been developed. The procedure is explained below.

While considering the date $t = 0$, we keep the same notation as in the previous section on "Parametrization of the Discount Function as a Spline Function," and introduce ω_j as the weight factor for the jth bond. It is a standard procedure to give more weight to the bonds with shorter maturities in the minimization program (4.8), which explains why the usual choice is again (see previous section)

$$\omega_j = \frac{dP_0^j}{dy_j(0)}$$

The idea is to approximate the different zero-coupon rates $R^c(0, s)$ by a function $G(0, s; u)$, where u is the column vector of parameters that needs to be estimated.

In order to find the best estimate for u, one needs to solve the following (nonlinear) constrained minimization program:

$$\min_u \sum_{j=1}^n \left(\frac{P_0^j - \widehat{P_0^j}}{\omega_j} \right)^2 = \min_u J(u) \tag{4.8}$$

where

$$\widehat{P_0^j} = \sum_{\substack{s=T_j-\alpha_j+1 \\ s>0}}^{T_j} F_s^{(j)} \exp[-sR^c(0, s)]$$

$$= \sum_{\substack{s=T_j-\alpha_j+1 \\ s>0}}^{T_j} F_s^{(j)} \exp[-sG(0, s; u)] \tag{4.9}$$

Such nonlinear optimization problems are solved using modified Newton's optimization techniques (see, for example, Fletcher (1987)). This is the common procedure; the only distinction lies in the choice of the function G. We review some standard choices for G below. In the Appendix of this chapter, we illustrate the useful modified Newton's algorithm using an extended Vasicek model (to be presented below).

There always exists a trade-off between the complexity cost of the increasing number of parameters and the richness of the eligible forms for the zero-coupon yield curve that multiparameter models provide. Over the years, a number of different functional dependencies have been offered, many of them inspired by the solutions of various dynamic models of interest rates (see Martellini and Priaulet (2000) for more details). We give here the most commonly used choices known as *Nelson–Siegel* and *Extended Vasicek* models. Note that we shall not discuss some other well-known models such as the Cox, Ingersoll and Ross (1985) model, which is not flexible enough (some shapes of the term structure cannot be obtained), and Longstaff and Schwartz (1992) or Chen (1996), which require the estimation of too many parameters, 10 and 13, respectively.

Nelson–Siegel and Nelson–Siegel Extended Originally, Nelson and Siegel (1987) derived a similar formula for the solution of an ordinary differential equation describing the dynamics of interest rates. Their solution reads

$$f(0, \theta) = \beta_0 + \beta_1 \exp\left(-\frac{\theta}{\tau_1}\right) + \beta_2 \left(\frac{\theta}{\tau_1}\right) \exp\left(-\frac{\theta}{\tau_1}\right)$$

where $f(0, \theta)$ is the instantaneous forward rate today for the date θ and the parameters β_0, β_1, β_2 and τ_1 are free parameters that need to be estimated.

Using

$$R^c(0, \theta) = \frac{1}{\theta} \int_0^\theta f(0, s)\, ds$$

we get

$$R^c(0, \theta) = \beta_0 + \beta_1 \left[\frac{1 - \exp\left(-\frac{\theta}{\tau_1}\right)}{\frac{\theta}{\tau_1}} \right] + \beta_2 \left[\frac{1 - \exp\left(-\frac{\theta}{\tau_1}\right)}{\frac{\theta}{\tau_1}} - \exp\left(-\frac{\theta}{\tau_1}\right) \right] \qquad (4.10)$$

where

- $R^c(0, \theta)$ *is the continuously compounded zero-coupon rate at time zero with maturity θ.*

- β_0 *is the limit of $R^c(0, \theta)$ as θ goes to infinity. In practice, β_0 should be regarded as a long-term interest rate.*

- β_1 *is the limit of $R^c(0, \theta) - \beta_0$ as θ goes to 0. In practice, β_1 should be regarded as the long-to-short-term spread.*

- β_2 *is a curvature parameter.*

- τ_1 *is a scale parameter that measures the rate at which the short-term and medium-term components decay to zero.*

Example 4.8   Impact of Each Nelson–Siegel's Parameter on the Curve Shape

We start with a base-case increasing curve with parameter values equal to $\beta_0 = 7\%$, $\beta_1 = -2\%$, $\beta_2 = 1\%$ and $\tau_1 = 3.33$ (see Figure 4.6) and we give successively different values to

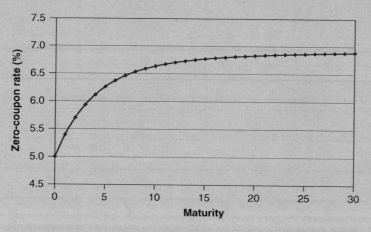

Figure 4.6   Standard zero-coupon curve in the Nelson and Siegel model.

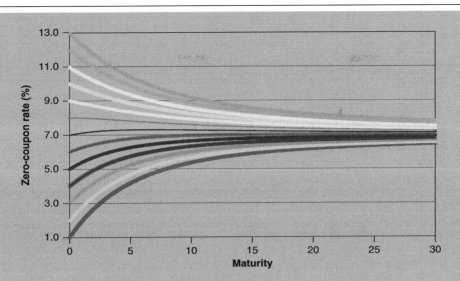

Figure 4.7   Impact of the slope factor in the Nelson and Siegel model.

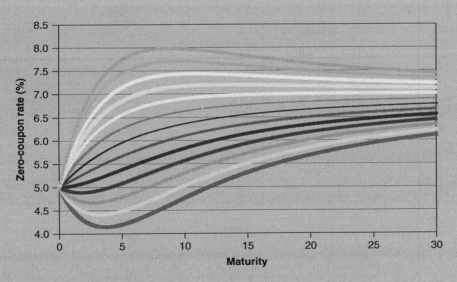

Figure 4.8   Impact of the curvature factor in the Nelson and Siegel model.

β_1 ranging from $\beta_1 = -6$ to $\beta_1 = 6\%$. We obtain the following curves that show graphically (see Figure 4.7) that the parameter β_1 plays the role of a slope factor.

We now give successively different values to β_2 ranging from $\beta_2 = -6\%$ to $\beta_2 = 6\%$. We obtain the following curves that show graphically (see Figure 4.8) that the parameter β_2 plays the role of a curvature factor.

Fixed Income Securities

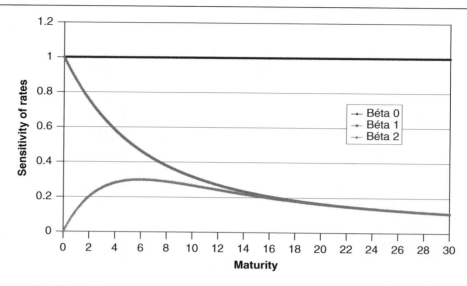

Figure 4.9 Sensitivity of zero-coupon rates to the parameters of the Nelson–Siegel functional form—these sensitivities are obtained by fixing parameter values equal to $\beta_0 = 7\%, \beta_1 = -2\%, \beta_2 = 1\%$ and $\tau_1 = 3.33$.

The advantage of this model is that the three parameters β_0, β_1 and β_2 can directly be linked to parallel shifts, slope shifts and curvature changes in the yield curve as illustrated by Figure 4.9, which shows the sensitivity $S_i = \frac{\partial R^c(0,\theta)}{\partial \beta_i}$ of zero-coupon rates to each parameter β_i for $i = 0, 1, 2$. The level factor S_0 is constant across maturity. The slope factor S_1 is largest for short maturities and declines exponentially toward zero as maturity increases. Beginning at zero for short maturities, the curvature factor S_2 reaches a maximum at the middle of the maturity spectrum and then decreases to zero for longer maturities.

On one hand, this method allows us to obtain four standard shapes for the zero-coupon yield curve (see Figure 4.10): increasing, decreasing, flat and inverted.

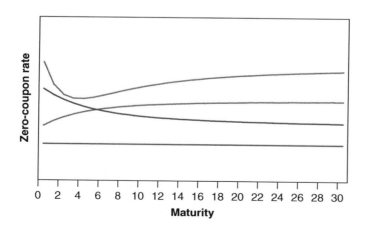

Figure 4.10

Standard curve shapes in the Nelson and Siegel model.

Example 4.9 We implement the Nelson and Siegel method on the French Treasury bond market in 1999 and 2000. ω_j, the weight factor for the jth bond, is taken equal to 1, whatever the value of j. We fix a priori τ_1 equal to 3 and obtain the value of the parameters β_0, β_1 and β_2 through the minimization program. Figure 4.11 represents the evolution of the parameter values.

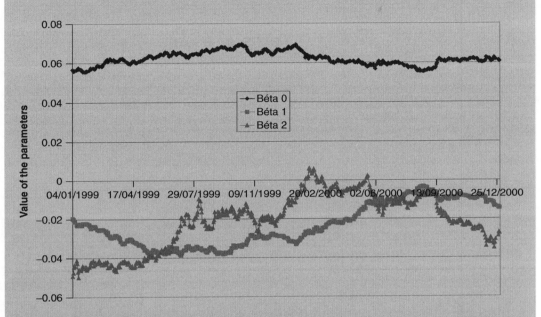

Figure 4.11 Evolution of the Nelson and Siegel parameters on the French market—1999 to 2000.

β_0 oscillates between 5 and 7% and can be regarded as the very long-term rate in the French market. β_1 is the long-term to short-term spread. It varies between −2 and −4% in 1999 and then decreases in absolute value to 0% at the end of 2000. β_2, the curvature parameter, is the more volatile parameter that varies from −5 to 0.7%.

On the other hand, it fails to allow for more involved shapes, such as those described in Figure 4.12 (U-shaped and/or hump-shaped).

To correct this, the method has been extended by Svensson (1994), using the following form

$$R^c(0, \theta) = \beta_0 + \beta_1 \left[\frac{1 - \exp\left(-\frac{\theta}{\tau_1}\right)}{\frac{\theta}{\tau_1}} \right] + \beta_2 \left[\frac{1 - \exp\left(-\frac{\theta}{\tau_1}\right)}{\frac{\theta}{\tau_1}} - \exp\left(-\frac{\theta}{\tau_1}\right) \right]$$

$$+ \beta_3 \left[\frac{1 - \exp\left(-\frac{\theta}{\tau_2}\right)}{\frac{\theta}{\tau_2}} - \exp\left(-\frac{\theta}{\tau_2}\right) \right] \tag{4.11}$$

Fixed Income Securities

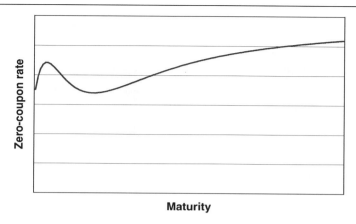

Figure 4.12

Hump-shaped curve in the Nelson and Siegel Extended model.

It is known as the *Nelson–Siegel Extended* form. This extension gives more flexibility to the short-term sector. Parameters τ_1 and τ_2 are set *a priori* and the minimization program is performed over the parameters β_0, β_1, β_2 and β_3.

Example 4.10   Nelson–Siegel Extended—Impact of β_3 on the curve shape

We start with a base-case increasing curve with parameter values equal to $\beta_0 = 7\%$, $\beta_1 = -2\%$, $\beta_2 = 1\%$, $\beta_3 = -1\%$, $\tau_1 = 3.33$ and $\tau_2 = 0.3$ (see Figure 4.13) and we give successively different values to β_3 ranging from $\beta_3 = -6\%$ to $\beta_3 = 6\%$. We obtain the following curves that show graphically (see Figure 4.14) that the parameter β_3 plays the role of a curvature factor in the short-term end of the curve.

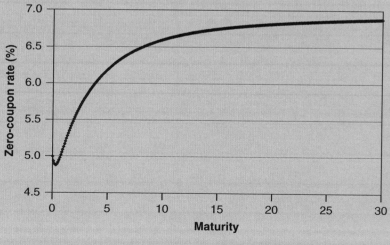

Figure 4.13   Standard zero-coupon curve in the Nelson and Siegel model.

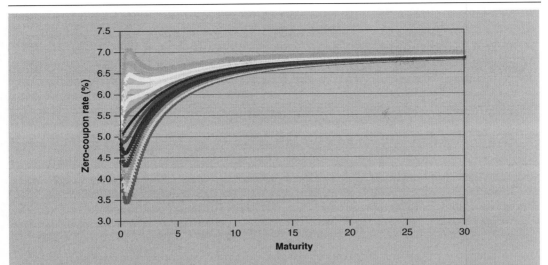

Figure 4.14   Impact of the second curvature factor in the Nelson and Siegel Extended model.

Example 4.11   We implement the Nelson and Siegel Extended method on the French Treasury bond market in 1999 and 2000. ω_j, the weight factor for the jth bond, is taken equal to one, whatever the value of j. We fix a priori τ_1 and τ_2 equal to 3 and 0.3, and obtain the value of the parameters $\beta_0, \beta_1, \beta_2$ and β_3 through the minimization program. Figure 4.15 represents the evolution of the parameter values.

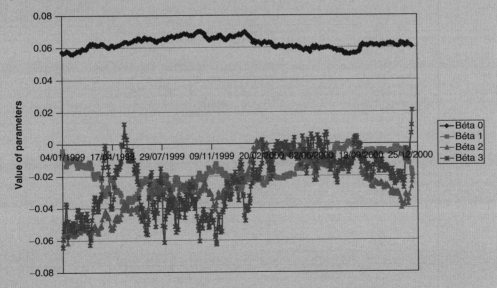

Figure 4.15   Evolution of the Nelson and Siegel Extended parameters on the French market— 1999–2000.

Fixed Income Securities

Evolutions of β_0, β_1 and β_2 parameters are very similar to those obtained in the Nelson and Siegel method. β_3 is a very volatile parameter that varies between -6.5% and 2% and permits to better fit bond market prices.

Note that this method is used, for example, by the French central bank (Banque de France), which makes a pure discount yield curve publicly available on a monthly basis (see Ricart and Sicsic (1995)).

Extended Vasicek   This form is inspired by the solution of the original Vasicek (1977) model, where the short-term rate r_t is assumed to follow an Ornstein–Uhlenbeck diffusion process (see Chapter 12 for more details on this)

$$\mathrm{d}r_t = a(b - r_t)\,\mathrm{d}t + \sigma\,\mathrm{d}W_t$$

In this model (see Martellini and Priaulet (2000)), the zero-coupon function is given by

$$R^c(0, \theta) = R_\infty - (R_\infty - r_0)\left[\frac{1 - \exp(-a\theta)}{a\theta}\right] + \frac{\sigma^2}{a^2}\left[\frac{(1 - \exp(-a\theta))^2}{4a\theta}\right] \tag{4.12}$$

where

$$R_\infty = b + \frac{\lambda\sigma}{a} - \frac{\sigma^2}{2a^2}$$

and λ is a risk premium, assumed to be constant.

It has been extended to the following form of the zero-coupon function (see El Karoui *et al.* (1994))

$$R^c(0, \theta) = G(0, \theta; u)$$

where

$$u = (L_0, S_0, \gamma_0, a)^{\mathsf{T}}$$

and G, which we call Extended Vasicek 1, is such that

$$G(0, \theta; u) = L_0 - S_0\left[\frac{1 - \exp(-a\theta)}{a\theta}\right] + \gamma_0\left[\frac{(1 - \exp(-a\theta))^2}{4a\theta}\right] \tag{4.13}$$

The connection with Vasicek's model (1977)[12] allows for a natural interpretation of the parameters entering function G.

- L_0 is the limit of $R^c(0, \theta)$ as θ goes to infinity. In practice, L_0 should be regarded as a long-term interest rate.

- S_0 is the limit of $L_0 - R^c(0, \theta)$ as θ goes to 0. In practice, S_0 should be regarded as the short-term to long-term spread.

---

[12]Note that in estimating γ_0, we ignore the constraint coming from the Vasicek's model (1977), that is, $\gamma_0 = \frac{\sigma^2}{a^2}$, since such a constraint is not consistent with some possible shapes of the zero-coupon yield curve (for example, those that are inverted in the short-term).

- γ_0 is a curvature parameter related to the volatility σ of the short-term interest rate.[13]

- a is a scale parameter, which may be interpreted as the strength of the reversion of the short-term interest rate toward the long-term mean.[14]

It should be noted that there is a natural connection between this postulated function and what is obtained from empirical principal components analysis (see Chapter 3).

Consider an extension of G of the following type, which we call "Extended Vasicek 2":

$$G(0, \theta; U) = L_0 - S_0 \left[\frac{1 - \exp(-a\theta)}{a\theta} \right] + \gamma_0 \left[\frac{(1 - \exp(-a\theta))^2}{4a\theta} \right] - T_0 \left[\frac{1 - \exp(-b\theta)}{b\theta} \right]$$

$$+ K_0 \left[\frac{(1 - \exp(-b\theta))^2}{4b\theta} \right]$$

Like "Nelson–Siegel Extended," this extension gives more flexibility in the short-term sector. This functional form is also very similar to the solution of the generalized version of Vasicek's model including two stochastic factors (see Martellini and Priaulet (2000) for a detailed description of this model).

Example 4.12 Comparison of Vasicek and Nelson–Siegel Extended Forms: An Example

We derive the zero-coupon rate curve using market prices from French Treasury bonds on April 26, 1996. For that, we use a variety of Treasury bonds across a whole range of maturities (from 1 day to 17 years). We use two sets of bonds. One set, which we refer to as the "minimization set," is based upon 25 bonds, and is used to perform optimization. Another set, which we refer to as the "checking set," is based upon only 10 bonds; it ensures that the zero-coupon rate curve is correctly obtained, a test that can only be performed using assets that do not belong to the optimization set. We consider three different models to derive the zero-coupon curve: Extended Vasicek 1, Extended Vasicek 2 and Nelson and Siegel Extended. In the minimization program we use as weight factors those recommended by Vasicek and Fong (1982). Tables 4.3, 4.4 and 4.5 summarize the results. They display the spreads between theoretical prices and market prices for each bond, the average spread and the weighted average spread, and also the sum of the squared spreads and of the squared weighted spreads for each set of bonds. For the three methods, the quality of fit measured on the checking set is very close to the quality of fit as measured on the optimization set, and all methods are very good except for bonds with a maturity superior to 10 years. Hence, we conclude that the three methods give good results in general, and these results are somewhat similar:

- *Goodness-of-fit indicators (average spread and weighted average spread, sum of the squared spreads and of the squared weighted spreads) are very close.*

---

[13]For additional information concerning the link between curvature and rates volatility, we refer the reader to Ilmanen and Iwanowski (1997).

[14]The parameter a is usually set equal to some arbitrary value between 0.2 and 0.6, and the optimization is performed over the other parameters.

Table 4.3   Bond Price Spreads—Extended Vasicek 1.

Extended Vasicek 1   EV1
Date   04/26/96

Sum of squared spreads—procedure of minimization	**0.5254**
Sum of squared spreads—checking procedure	**0.1462**
Average spread—procedure of minimization	**0.1450**
Average spread—checking procedure	**0.1209**
Sum of weighted squared spreads—procedure of minimization	**1.425E-06**
Sum of weighted squared spreads—checking procedure	**1.198E-06**
Average weighted spread—procedure of minimization	**0.0002387**
Average weighted spread—checking procedure	**0.0003461**

Bond	Maturity	Coupon (%)	Market price	Theoretical price EV1	Spread	Spread^2	Weighted spread^2
Procedure of Minimization							
BTF	05/02/96	0	99.9389	99.9393	−0.0004	0.0000	8.96E-08
BTF	05/09/96	0	99.8684	99.8687	−0.0003	0.0000	9.09E-09
BTF	05/23/96	0	99.7277	99.7277	0	0.0000	2.02E-11
BTF	06/27/96	0	99.3753	99.3764	−0.0011	0.0000	4.61E-09
BTF	07/25/96	0	99.0958	99.0957	0.0001	0.0000	6.49E-12
BTF	09/19/96	0	98.5374	98.5319	0.0055	0.0000	2.06E-08
BTF	12/12/96	0	97.7029	97.6719	0.031	0.0010	**2.74E-07**
BTAN	03/12/97	8.50	104.9479	104.9310	0.0169	0.0003	3.68E-08
BTAN	08/12/97	7.25	109.0547	109.0559	−0.0012	0.0000	8.73E-11
BTAN	11/12/97	8.50	110.2058	110.2173	−0.0115	0.0001	5.54E-09
BTAN	05/12/98	8	114.5512	114.6202	−0.069	0.0048	**1.17E-07**
BTAN	11/12/98	5.75	105.3351	105.3181	0.017	0.0003	4.96E-09
BTAN	04/12/99	4.75	100.1822	100.1198	0.0624	0.0039	5.33E-08
OAT 11,348	05/25/99	8.125	116.8017	116.7712	0.0305	0.0009	**1.05E-08**
OAT 11,641	03/28/00	8.50	112.2653	112.3909	−0.1256	0.0158	**1.13E-07**
OAT 11,878	01/25/01	9.50	119.1245	119.2106	−0.0861	0.0074	3.59E-08
OAT 10,247	11/25/02	8.50	117.7230	117.6628	0.0602	0.0036	**1.07E-08**
OAT 19,465	10/25/03	6.75	107.3127	107.4904	**−0.1777**	0.0316	8.66E-08
OAT 19,537	04/25/04	5.50	95.8651	95.9640	**−0.0989**	0.0098	2.72E-08
OAT 19,603	10/25/04	6.75	106.8927	106.8985	−0.0058	0.0000	7.66E-11
OAT 19,643	04/25/05	7.50	108.3205	108.4180	−0.0975	0.0095	1.89E-08
OAT 19,699	10/25/05	7.75	113.9068	113.9558	−0.049	0.0024	4.32E-09
OAT 19,734	04/25/06	7.25	106.5299	106.3880	0.1419	0.0201	3.54E-08
OAT 19,377	10/25/08	8.50	121.1949	120.5684	**0.6265**	0.3925	**4.49E-07**
OAT 10,248	12/26/12	8.50	119.8711	120.0173	**−0.1462**	0.0214	**1.76E-08**
Checking Procedure							
BTF	05/15/96	0	99.8083	99.8082	0.0001	0.0000	3.97E-11
BTF	06/20/96	0	99.4455	99.4466	−0.0011	0.0000	6.32E-09
BTF	10/17/96	0	98.2524	98.2477	0.0047	0.0000	**1.11E-08**
BTAN	11/12/96	8.50	106.2958	106.3101	−0.0143	0.0002	6.62E-08
BTAN	04/12/00	7.75	109.4373	109.4249	0.0124	0.0002	1.11E-09
BTAN	10/12/00	7	110.3381	110.2576	0.0805	0.0065	3.94E-08
OAT 11,048	06/25/98	9.50	118.0344	118.2127	**−0.1783**	0.0318	**6.68E-07**
OAT 4,266	05/27/00	10	126.3381	126.5319	**−0.1938**	0.0376	**2.34E-07**
OAT 19,385	04/25/03	8.50	114.2333	114.4055	**−0.1722**	0.0297	7.96E-08
OAT 11,351	02/27/04	8.25	114.3536	114.5544	**−0.2008**	0.0403	9.23E-08

Table 4.4   Bond Price Spreads—Vasicek Extended 2.

Extended Vasicek 2 EV2

Date	04/26/96						
Sum of squared spreads—procedure of minimization							**0.4839**
Sum of squared spreads—checking procedure							**0.1257**
Average spread—procedure of minimization							**0.1391**
Average spread—checking procedure							**0.1121**
Sum of weighted squared spreads—procedure of minimization							**1.121E-06**
Sum of weighted squared spreads—checking procedure							**1.242E-06**
Average weighted spread—procedure of minimization							**0.0002117**
Average weighted spread—checking procedure							**0.0003524**

Bond	Maturity	Coupon (%)	Market price	Theoretical price EV2	Spread	Spread^2	Weighted spread^2
Procedure of Minimization							
BTF	05/02/96	0	99.9389	99.9391	−0.0002	0.0000	**1.65E-08**
BTF	05/09/96	0	99.8684	99.8682	0.0002	0.0000	2.47E-09
BTF	05/23/96	0	99.7277	99.7270	0.0007	0.0000	**1.03E-08**
BTF	06/27/96	0	99.3753	99.3764	−0.0011	0.0000	4.83E-09
BTF	07/25/96	0	99.0958	99.0972	−0.0014	0.0000	3.57E-09
BTF	09/19/96	0	98.5374	98.5374	0	0.0000	1.59E-12
BTF	12/12/96	0	97.7029	97.6836	0.0193	0.0004	**1.06E-07**
BTAN	03/12/97	8.50	104.9479	104.9484	−0.0005	0.0000	3.09E-11
BTAN	08/12/97	7.25	109.0547	109.0728	−0.0181	0.0003	1.99E-08
BTAN	11/12/97	8.50	110.2058	110.2304	−0.0246	0.0006	2.50E-08
BTAN	05/12/98	8	114.5512	114.6186	−0.0674	0.0045	**1.12E-07**
BTAN	11/12/98	5.75	105.3351	105.2993	0.0358	0.0013	2.21E-08
BTAN	04/12/99	4.75	100.1822	100.0883	0.0939	0.0088	**1.12E-07**
OAT 11,348	05/25/99	8.125	116.8017	116.7357	0.066	0.0044	4.90E-08
OAT 11,641	03/28/00	8.50	112.2653	112.3382	−0.0729	0.0053	3.80E-08
OAT 11,878	01/25/01	9.50	119.1245	119.1516	−0.0271	0.0007	3.56E-09
OAT 10,247	11/25/02	8.50	117.7230	117.6222	0.1008	0.0102	2.99E-08
OAT 19,465	10/25/03	6.75	107.3127	107.4696	**−0.1569**	0.0246	6.75E-08
OAT 19,537	04/25/04	5.50	95.8651	95.9555	−0.0904	0.0082	2.27E-08
OAT 19,603	10/25/04	6.75	106.8927	106.8985	−0.0058	0.0000	7.47E-11
OAT 19,643	04/25/05	7.50	108.3205	108.4274	**−0.1069**	0.0114	2.28E-08
OAT 19,699	10/25/05	7.75	113.9068	113.9756	−0.0688	0.0047	8.53E-09
OAT 19,734	04/25/06	7.25	106.5299	106.4190	**0.1109**	0.0123	2.16E-08
OAT 19,377	10/25/08	8.50	121.1949	120.6495	**0.5454**	0.2975	**3.40E-07**
OAT 10,248	12/26/12	8.50	119.8711	120.1689	**−0.2978**	0.0887	7.32E-08
Checking Procedure							
BTF	05/15/96	0	99.8083	99.8076	0.0007	0.0000	1.69E-08
BTF	06/20/96	0	99.4455	99.4464	−0.0009	0.0000	4.04E-09
BTF	10/17/96	0	98.2524	98.2554	−0.003	0.0000	4.25E-09
BTAN	11/12/96	8.50	106.2958	106.3206	−0.0248	0.0006	**1.97E-07**
BTAN	04/12/00	7.75	109.4373	109.3721	0.0652	0.0043	3.08E-08
BTAN	10/12/00	7	110.3381	110.2014	**0.1367**	0.0187	**1.14E-07**
OAT 11,048	06/25/98	9.50	118.0344	118.2070	**−0.1726**	0.0298	**6.27E-07**
OAT 4,266	05/27/00	10	126.3381	126.4760	**−0.1379**	0.0190	**1.18E-07**
OAT 19,385	04/25/03	8.50	114.2333	114.3721	**−0.1388**	0.0193	5.18E-08
OAT 11,351	02/27/04	8.25	114.3536	114.5381	**−0.1845**	0.0340	7.79E-08

Fixed Income Securities

Table 4.5 Bond Price Spreads—Nelson–Siegel Extended.

Nelson–Siegel Extended NSE

Date	04/26/96						
Sum of squared spreads—procedure of minimization							**0.5458**
Sum of squared spreads—checking procedure							**0.1436**
Average spread—procedure of minimization							**0.1478**
Average spread—checking procedure							**0.1198**
Sum of weighted squared spreads—procedure of minimization							**1.274E-06**
Sum of weighted squared spreads—checking procedure							**1.294E-06**
Average weighted spread—procedure of minimization							**0.0002257**
Average weighted spread—checking procedure							**0.0003597**

Bond	Maturity	Coupon (%)	Market price	Theoretical price NSE	Spread	Spread^2	Weighted Spread^2
Procedure of Minimization							
BTF	05/02/96	0	99.9389	99.9389	0	0.0000	8.95E-10
BTF	05/09/96	0	99.8684	99.8680	0.0004	0.0000	9.26E-09
BTF	05/23/96	0	99.7277	99.7273	0.0004	0.0000	4.36E-09
BTF	06/27/96	0	99.3753	99.3788	−0.0035	0.0000	4.56E-08
BTF	07/25/96	0	99.0958	99.1010	−0.0052	0.0000	4.98E-08
BTF	09/19/96	0	98.5374	98.5417	−0.0043	0.0000	**1.28E-08**
BTF	12/12/96	0	97.7029	97.6819	0.021	0.0004	**1.26E-07**
BTAN	03/12/97	8.50	104.9479	104.9355	0.0124	0.0002	1.96E-08
BTAN	08/12/97	7.25	109.0547	109.0475	0.0072	0.0001	3.10E-09
BTAN	11/12/97	8.50	110.2058	110.2036	0.0022	0.0000	1.90E-10
BTAN	05/12/98	8	114.5512	114.6024	−0.0512	0.0026	6.43E-08
BTAN	11/12/98	5.75	105.3351	105.3054	0.0297	0.0009	**1.52E-08**
BTAN	04/12/99	4.75	100.1822	100.1133	0.0689	0.0047	6.49E-08
OAT 11,348	05/25/99	8.125	116.8017	116.7658	0.0359	0.0013	**1.45E-08**
OAT 11,641	03/28/00	8.50	112.2653	112.3981	−0.1328	0.0176	**1.26E-07**
OAT 11,878	01/25/01	9.50	119.1245	119.2243	−0.0998	0.0100	4.82E-08
OAT 10,247	11/25/02	8.50	117.7230	117.6714	0.0516	0.0027	7.84E-09
OAT 19,465	10/25/03	6.75	107.3127	107.4920	−0.1793	0.0321	8.81E-08
OAT 19,537	04/25/04	5.50	95.8651	95.9616	−0.0965	0.0093	2.59E-08
OAT 19,603	10/25/04	6.75	106.8927	106.8935	−0.0008	0.0000	1.26E-12
OAT 19,643	04/25/05	7.50	108.3205	108.4098	−0.0893	0.0080	1.59E-08
OAT 19,699	10/25/05	7.75	113.9068	113.9458	−0.039	0.0015	2.73E-09
OAT 19,734	04/25/06	7.25	106.5299	106.3756	**0.1543**	0.0238	4.18E-08
OAT 19,377	10/25/08	8.50	121.1949	120.5526	**0.6423**	0.4125	**4.72E-07**
OAT 10,248	12/26/12	8.50	119.8711	120.0051	−0.134	0.0180	**1.48E-08**
Checking Procedure							
BTF	05/15/96	0	99.8083	99.8076	0.0007	0.0000	1.91E-08
BTF	06/20/96	0	99.4455	99.4483	−0.0028	0.0000	3.79E-08
BTF	10/17/96	0	98.2524	98.2583	−0.0059	0.0000	1.73E-08
BTAN	11/12/96	8.50	106.2958	106.3218	−0.026	0.0007	**2.17E-07**
BTAN	04/12/00	7.75	109.4373	109.4326	0.0047	0.0000	1.60E-10
BTAN	10/12/00	7	110.3381	110.2700	0.0681	0.0046	2.82E-08
OAT 11,048	06/25/98	9.50	118.0344	118.1951	−0.1607	0.0258	**5.43E-07**
OAT 4,266	05/27/00	10	126.3381	126.5404	−0.2023	0.0409	**2.55E-07**
OAT 19,385	04/25/03	8.50	114.2333	114.4106	−0.1773	0.0314	8.44E-08
OAT 11,351	02/27/04	8.25	114.3536	114.5536	−0.2	0.0400	9.16E-08

- *The ten most significant spreads, which appear in bold face in Tables 4.3, 4.4 and 4.5, are quite the same for each method; they concern, in particular, OATs 19465, 19734, 19377, 10248, 11048, 4266, 19385 and 11351. Furthermore, these spreads have the same sign and almost the same absolute value for the three methods.*

- *The ten most significant weighted spreads, which also appear in bold face in Tables 4.3, 4.4 and 4.5, are not the same for each method.*

- *The gain in terms of the sum of the squared weighted spreads from Vasicek Extended 2 to Vasicek Extended 1 is 21.38%.*

- *Finally, the three methods generate very similar zero-coupon yield and 1-year forward yield curves. We remark that the curves exhibit a systematic concavity on the long-term end (starting from 7 years of maturity), which consequently induces a fit of poorer quality for long-term maturity bonds compared to the fit obtained with a spline method (see the example "Comparison of Exponential and Polynomial Splines: A Concrete Example" in the section on "Parametrization of the Discount Function as a Spline Function").*

Discussion and Comparison of the Methods

From a theoretical standpoint, one shortcoming of fitting the model to the current term structure is that one loses a model of the dynamic of prices. The model changes everyday because the parameters are chosen to fit the zero-coupon yield curve, but there is no model predicting how the parameters tomorrow are related to the parameters today (see Chapter 12 and Martellini and Priaulet (2000) for dynamic models of the zero-coupon yield curve). This comment applies of course to both methods, fitting the discount function and fitting the zero-coupon yield curve. Note also that the vast majority of such models are not consistent with dynamics models of the zero-coupon yield curve. By consistency, we mean here that the dynamic model should produce future curves belonging to the family of reconstructed yield curves. As shown by Björk and Christensen (1999), the Nelson and Siegel Extended yield curve model is consistent with the Hull and White (1990) dynamic model (see Chapter 12).

Moreover, always from a theoretical standpoint, fitting the zero-coupon yield curve is clearly better than fitting the discount function. In particular, it allows for a clearer interpretation of the parameters. Also, it requires fewer parameters. This makes any attempt to hedge a bond portfolio by setting the sensitivity to zero with respect to these parameters more convenient (see Chapter 6). However, it is difficult to implement from a computation standpoint, because it requires solving nonlinear optimization algorithms, which are often slow to converge. Finally, it exhibits a systematic concavity on the long-term end of the curve (starting from 7 years to maturity). This is arguably the main drawback, and Priaulet (1997) shows that long-term bonds are priced with lower accuracy by this method. In particular, when making rich and cheap analysis, spline methods are the most flexible methods; they enable to recover bond prices with a quasi-perfect accuracy.

4.2 Deriving the Interbank Zero-Coupon Rate Curve

4.2.1 How to Select the Basket of Instruments?

The basket of inputs contains three kinds of instruments: money-market rates, futures contracts and swaps.

Money-Market Rates

We consider money-market rates with maturities ranging from 1 day to 1 year, for example, Euribor or Libor rates. These rates, expressed on an Actual/360 (or 365) basis, are first converted into equivalent zero-coupon rates with Actual/365 (or 30/360) basis. For example, on 01/01/99, we assume that the 1-month Libor rate was equal to 2.5%. Using the Actual/365 basis, the equivalent zero-coupon rate (denoted by $R(0, 1/12)$) is given by

$$R(0, 1/12) = \left(1 + \frac{31}{360} \cdot 2.5\%\right)^{\frac{365}{31}} - 1$$

Futures Contracts[15]

At this stage, we only need to consider futures contracts depending on money-market rates, for example, 3-month Libor or 3-month Euribor contracts, and find zero-coupon rates from raw data. The price of a 3-month Libor contract is given by 100 minus the underlying 3-month forward rate.[16] For example, on 03/15/99, the 3-month Libor rate was 3%, and the 3-month Libor contract with maturity date June 1999 had a price equal to 96.5. Hence on 03/15/99, the 3-month forward rate, starting on 06/15/99, is 3.5%. The 6-month spot rate (denoted by $R(0, 6/12)$) is obtained as follows:

$$R(0, 6/12) = \left[\left(1 + \frac{92}{360} \cdot 3\%\right)\left(1 + \frac{92}{360} \cdot 3.5\%\right)\right]^{\frac{365}{184}} - 1$$

Similarly, from the prices of futures contracts with maturity date September 1999, December 1999 and March 2000, respectively, we can obtain the zero-coupon rates $R(0, 9/12)$, $R(0, 1)$ and $R(0, 15/12)$.

Swaps[17]

We consider 3-or-6-month Libor (or Euribor) swap yields with maturities ranging from 1 year to 30 years and find recursively equivalent zero-coupon rates. Swap yields are par yields; so the zero-coupon rate with maturity 2 years $R(0, 2)$ is obtained as the solution to the following equation[18]

$$\frac{SR(2)}{1 + R(0, 1)} + \frac{1 + SR(2)}{(1 + R(0, 2))^2} = 1$$

---

[15] For a detailed description of futures contracts, we refer the reader to Chapter 11, which is entirely devoted to that matter.
[16] See Chapter 11 devoted to forward and futures contracts.
[17] For a detailed description of swaps, we refer the reader to Chapter 10, which is entirely devoted to that matter.
[18] See Chapter 10 devoted to swaps.

where $SR(2)$ is the 2-year swap yield and $R(0, 1)$ is equal to $SR(1)$. Spot rates $R(0, 3), \ldots, R(0, 10)$ are obtained recursively in a similar fashion.

Example 4.13 We give below an example of a real basket on 05/31/2001 in the euro interbank market:

- *Euribor rates:*

Maturity	Euribor rate
1 day	4.56%
1 week	4.57%
1 month	4.574%

- *Three-month Euribor futures contracts:*

Maturity	Bid–ask prices	Maturity	Bid–ask prices
June 2001	95.52–95.5275	June 2002	95.58–95.5825
September 2001	95.73–95.7350	September 2002	95.45–95.4525
December 2001	95.68–95.6825	December 2002	95.29–95.2925
March 2002	95.71–95.7175	March 2003	95.26–95.2675

- *Six-month Euribor swap yields:*

Maturity	Swap rate (%)	Maturity (years)	Swap rate (%)
27 Months	4.634	10	5.583
30 Months	4.669	11	5.65
33 Months	4.714	12	5.711
3 Years	4.762	13	5.765
4 Years	4.914	14	5.813
5 Years	5.059	15	5.856
6 Years	5.193	20	5.983
7 Years	5.319	25	6.052
8 Years	5.426	30	6.056
9 Years	5.511	—	—

We need to pay attention to the connections between money-market rates and futures contracts on one hand, and between futures contracts and swaps on the other. For example, the 9-month zero-coupon rate as derived from the money market may be different from the 9-month zero-coupon rate as derived from futures contracts. We are confronted by three different segments with different actors and, because of all sorts of friction costs (transaction costs, bid–ask spread...), tax considerations and calculation conventions, some differences may appear and cannot be arbitraged. As a simple rule, the maturity of the last zero-coupon rate deduced from the money market and the maturity of the first zero-coupon deduced from futures contracts have to be different by a minimum of 1 month. The same rule is applied for the connection between futures contracts and swaps.

4.2.2 Interpolation Methods

Linear and Cubic Interpolations

In the above example, our basket contains 30 instruments with maturities ranging from 1 day to 30 years, which enables us to derive 30 zero-coupon rates with maturities ranging from 1 day to 30 years. If we need a continuous zero-coupon term structure, we can use either linear or cubic interpolations, as explained in the previous section on "Different Kinds of Interpolation", or we can use another interpolation that is a log-linear interpolation of the discount factors.

Log-Linear Interpolation

Consider that we know at date $t = 0$ the two discount factors $B(0, x)$ and $B(0, z)$ and need to know $B(0, y)$ with $y \in [x; z]$. Using the log-linear interpolation with discount factors, $B(0, y)$ is given by the following formula:

$$\ln[B(0, y)] = \left(\frac{z - y}{z - x}\right) \times \ln[B(0, x)] + \left(\frac{y - x}{z - x}\right) \times \ln[B(0, z)] \qquad (4.14)$$

Using the following expression where $R^c(0, y)$ is the continuously compounded zero-coupon rate at date $t = 0$ with maturity y

$$B(0, y) = e^{-y R^c(0, y)}$$

equation (4.14) becomes

$$R^c(0, y) \times y = \left(\frac{z - y}{z - x}\right) \times R^c(0, x) \times x + \left(\frac{y - x}{z - x}\right) \times R^c(0, z) \times z$$

We observe that the quantity $R^c(0, y) \cdot y$ is obtained by the linear interpolation between $R^c(0, x) \times x$ and $R^c(0, z) \times z$.

4.2.3 Least Squares Methods Based on Rates

Least squares methods used to derive the current interbank curve are very similar to those used to derive the current nondefault Treasury curve. After converting market data into equivalent zero-coupon rates, the zero-coupon yield curve is derived using a two-stage process:

1. writing zero-coupon rates as a B-spline function;

2. fitting them through an ordinary least squares (OLS) method.

Writing Zero-Coupon Rates in Terms of B-Spline Functions

We have N equivalent zero-coupon rates denoted by $R(0, n)$ for $n = 1, \dots, N$. Using standard notation, we denote by $\widehat{R}(0, \theta)$ the theoretical zero-coupon rate with maturity date θ. $\widehat{R}(0, \theta)$ may be written as a sum of cubic B-spline functions, which ensures the achievement of perfectly smooth spot and forward curves:

$$\widehat{R}(0, \theta) = \sum_l a_l B_l^3(\theta) = \sum_l a_l \left(\sum_{j=l}^{l+4} \left[\prod_{\substack{i=l \\ i \neq j}}^{l+4} \frac{1}{\lambda_i - \lambda_j} \right] (\theta - \lambda_j)_+^3 \right) \qquad (4.15)$$

When the idea is to reconstruct the interbank curve for maturities between 1 day and 10 years, a standard choice for splines may be [0, 1/2], [1/2, 1], [1, 2], [2, 3], [3, 4], [4, 5], [5, 6], [6, 8] and [8, 10]. In that case, we write specifically

$$\widehat{R}(0,\theta) = \sum_{l=-3}^{8} a_l B_l^3(\theta) = \sum_{l=-3}^{8} a_l \left(\sum_{j=l}^{l+4} \left[\prod_{\substack{i=l \\ i\neq j}}^{l+4} \frac{1}{\lambda_i - \lambda_j} \right] (\theta - \lambda_j)_+^3 \right)$$

where $\lambda_{-3} = -3, \lambda_{-2} = -2, \lambda_{-1} = -1, \lambda_0 = 0, \lambda_1 = 1/2, \lambda_2 = 1, \lambda_3 = 2, \lambda_4 = 3, \lambda_5 = 4, \lambda_6 = 5, \lambda_7 = 6, \lambda_8 = 8, \lambda_9 = 10, \lambda_{10} = 11, \lambda_{11} = 12$ and $\lambda_{12} = 13$. Recall that parameters $\lambda_{-3}, \lambda_{-2}, \lambda_{-1}, \lambda_{10}, \lambda_{11}, \lambda_{12}$ must only satisfy $\lambda_{-3} < \lambda_{-2} < \lambda_{-1} < 0 < \ldots < 10 < \lambda_{10} < \lambda_{11} < \lambda_{12}$ and are defined as mathematical conditions for writing B-spline functions $B_l^3(\theta)$.

This method allows the fitting function to be a quasi-perfect match for all the $R(0, n)$ points. Note that it is possible to be fully consistent with all market points by choosing as many splines as market points.

Fitting that Function through an Ordinary Least Squares Method

The last step consists in minimizing the sum of the squares spreads between market rates and theoretical rates according to the following program

$$\underset{a_l}{Min} \sum_{n=1}^{N} (R(0, n) - \widehat{R}(0, n))^2$$

4.2.4 Least Squares Methods Based on Prices

This method is an original method that consists in transforming rates into prices. After converting market data into equivalent zero-coupon rates, the derivation of a zero-coupon yield curve is a three-stage process:

1. *transforming market data into bond prices;*

2. *writing the discount function as a B-spline function;*

3. *fitting prices through a generalized least squares (GLS) method.*

Transforming Market Data into Bond Prices

All quoted yields (money-market rates, futures contracts rates and swap yields) are first homogenized on a bond basis:

- *Money-market rates are first converted into equivalent zero-coupon rates, and then into a zero-coupon bond delivering $100 at maturity. For example, on 02/01/00, we assume that the 3-month Libor rate was equal to 3%. The equivalent in terms of zero-coupon rate (denoted by $R(0, 3/12)$) is given by*

$$R(0, 3/12) = \left(1 + \frac{90}{360} \times 3\% \right)^{\frac{365}{90}} - 1$$

and we convert this zero-coupon rate into a zero-coupon bond delivering $100 on 05/01/00 whose price P on 02/01/00 is given by

$$P = 100 \times B(0, 3/12) = \frac{100}{[1 + R(0, 3/12)]^{90/365}}$$

- *Zero-coupon rates (with maturity inferior or equal to 1 year) as derived from futures contracts are transformed in the same way as zero-coupon bonds.*

- *Finally, as swap rates are par yields, swap prices equal $100 (assuming a $100 notional principal).*

Writing the Discount Function in Terms of a B-Spline Function

The idea is then to write the discount function $B(0, \theta)$ (or the price of the zero-coupon bond paying $1 at maturity θ) as a sum of cubic B-splines:

$$B(0, \theta) = \sum_k a_k B_k^3(\theta) = \sum_k a_k \left(\sum_{j=k}^{k+4} \left[\prod_{\substack{i=k \\ i \neq j}}^{k+4} \frac{1}{\lambda_i - \lambda_j} \right] (\theta - \lambda_j)_+^3 \right) \tag{4.16}$$

Fitting Prices through a Generalized Least Squares Method

The last step consists in minimizing the sum of the squares spreads between market prices P_n and theoretical prices $\widehat{P_n}$ according to the following program

$$\underset{a_k}{Min} \sum_{n=1}^{N} (P_n - \widehat{P_n})^2 \tag{4.17}$$

where, for $n = 1, \ldots, N$, P_n are market prices and $\widehat{P_n}$ are theoretical prices obtained as the sum of discounted cash flows using the discount function $B(0, \theta)$.

Example 4.14 10/19/2000—Euro Interbank Market—Reconstructing the Zero-Coupon Yield Curve Using Cubic B-Splines

We derive the Euribor swap zero-coupon rate curve as of October 19, 2000 (see Figure 4.16), using both the least squares method based on rates (see Table 4.6) and based on prices (see Table 4.7). We consider the following splines in both cases: [0,1/2], [1/2,1], [1,2], [2,3], [3,4], [4,5], [5,6], [6,8] and [8,10].

Note that the first method is rather dedicated to the pricing of instruments and the computation of asset swap spreads, while the second one is convenient for the estimation of credit spread term structures when using a joint estimation model. In terms of fitting power (see Tables 4.6 and 4.7), both methods prove to be efficient, especially the first one (see the sum of squared errors). The second one is less accurate in restituting the short end of the curve [0,3]. This difference is due to the fact that the second method is based on price fitting, while short-term instruments are best fitted in terms of yields. Indeed, a very good fit of prices can

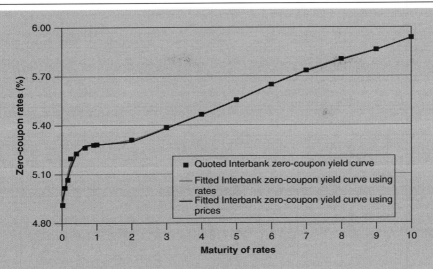

Figure 4.16 Comparison of the zero-coupon curves obtained with the two methods.

Table 4.6 Results of the Least Squares Method Based on Rates.

Interbank Curve—Cubic B-Splines
Least Squares Method Based on Rates

Date	10/19/00			
Sum of squared spreads	2.3971E-07			
Average spread	0.012%			
Rate or instrument	Maturity	Market ZC rate (%)	Theoretical ZC rate (%)	Spread (%)
Procedure of Minimization				
1-week Euribor	10/26/00	4.911	4.910	0.001
1-month Euribor	11/20/00	5.017	5.007	0.009
2-month Euribor	12/19/00	5.066	5.102	−0.036
3-month Euribor	01/19/01	5.198	5.167	0.031
Euribor futures contract Dec 00	03/19/01	5.228	5.232	−0.004
Euribor futures contract Mar 01	06/18/01	5.263	5.266	−0.003
Euribor futures contract June 01	09/17/01	5.280	5.279	0.001
Euribor futures contract Sept 01	12/17/01	5.287	5.283	0.004
2-year swap	10/21/02	5.311	5.311	0.000
3-year swap	10/20/03	5.384	5.384	0.000
4-year swap	10/19/04	5.465	5.465	0.000
5-year swap	10/19/05	5.552	5.552	0.000
6-year swap	10/19/06	5.648	5.648	0.000
7-year swap	10/19/07	5.733	5.733	0.000
8-year swap	10/20/08	5.803	5.803	0.000
9-year swap	10/19/09	5.861	5.861	0.000
10-year swap	10/19/10	5.935	5.935	0.000

Fixed Income Securities

Table 4.7 Results of the Least Squares Method Based on Prices.

Interbank Curve—Cubic B-Splines

Least Squares Method Based on Prices

Date	10/19/00				
Sum of squared spreads	**0.0003**				
Average spread	**0.0045**				
Rate or instrument	Maturity	Coupon (%)	Market price	Theoretical price	Spread
Procedure of Minimization					
1-week Euribor	10/26/00	0	99.908	99.907	0.001
1-month Euribor	11/20/00	0	99.573	99.572	0.001
2-month Euribor	12/19/00	0	99.180	99.175	0.004
3-month Euribor	01/19/01	0	98.734	98.744	−0.010
Euribor futures contract Dec 00	03/19/01	0	97.914	97.915	−0.001
Euribor futures contract Mar 01	06/18/01	0	96.657	96.649	0.008
Euribor futures contract June 01	09/17/01	0	95.415	95.413	0.002
Euribor futures contract Sept 01	12/17/01	0	94.191	94.198	−0.007
2-year swap	10/21/02	5.31	100.000	99.997	0.003
3-year swap	10/20/03	5.38	100.000	100.001	−0.001
4-year swap	10/19/04	5.45	100.000	99.999	0.001
5-year swap	10/19/05	5.53	100.000	100.002	−0.002
6-year swap	10/19/06	5.62	100.000	99.995	0.005
7-year swap	10/19/07	5.69	100.000	100.007	−0.007
8-year swap	10/20/08	5.76	100.000	99.995	0.005
9-year swap	10/19/09	5.81	100.000	100.002	−0.002
10-year swap	10/19/10	5.86	100.000	100.000	0.000

hide an inadequate fit of yields, because of the very small duration of short-term instruments. For example, a 10-bps change in the yield of a 3-month instrument approximately results in a 2.5 cents price change, or put differently, a 1 cent price error is equivalent to a 4-bps yield error.

4.3 Deriving Credit Spread Term Structures

The term structure of credit spreads for a given rating class and a given economic sector can be derived from market data through two different methods: the disjoint method and the joint method. The first one consists in separately deriving the term structure of nondefault zero-coupon yields and the term structure of risky zero-coupon yields so as to obtain by differentiation the term structure of zero-coupon credit spreads. In contrast, the second one consists in generating both term structures of zero-coupon yields through a one-step procedure.

4.3.1 Disjoint Methods

For a given risky rating class and a given economic sector, deriving the current term structure of credit spreads by using the disjoint method is a three-step procedure:

- *First, derive the benchmark zero-coupon yield curve. It can be taken as either the Treasury zero-coupon yield curve or the Interbank zero-coupon yield curve, using one of the methods explained in Sections 4.1 and 4.2.*

- *Then, constitute a homogeneous basket of bonds for the risky class studied, using the method described in the section on "How to Select a Basket of Bonds?", and derive the corresponding zero-coupon yield curve using the same methods as those presented in Section 4.1.*

- *Finally, obtain the zero-coupon credit spread curve by subtracting the benchmark zero-coupon yield curve from the risky zero-coupon yield curve.*

The drawback of this method is that estimated credit spreads (1) are sensitive to model assumptions like the choice of the discount function, the number of splines and the localization of pasting points and (2) may be unsmooth functions of time to maturity, which is not realistic and contradictory to the smooth functions (monotonically increasing, hump-shaped or downward sloping) obtained in the theoretical models of credit bond prices like the models by Merton (1974), Black and Cox (1976), Longstaff and Schwartz (1995) and others (see Chapter 13).

4.3.2 Joint Methods

Suppose we want to jointly derive the current credit spread term structures of n different risky classes with respect to a benchmark zero-coupon yield curve. We denote

- J_i *is the number of bonds of the ith risky class for $i = 1, 2, \ldots, n$. J_0 is the number of bonds of the benchmark class.*

- $P_t^{j_i}$ *is the market price at date t of the jth bond of the ith risky class.*

- $\widehat{P_t^{j_i}}$ *is the theoretical price at date t of the jth bond of the ith risky class.*

- *The price vectors are $P_t^i = (P_t^{j_i})_{j_i = 1, \ldots, J_i}$ and $\widehat{P_t^i} = (\widehat{P_t^{j_i}})_{j_i = 1, \ldots, J_i}$, respectively.*

- T_{j_i} *is the maturity of the jth bond (in years) of the ith risky class.*

- $F_s^{(j_i)}$ *is the coupon and/or principal payment of the jth bond of the ith risky class at time $s \geq t$.*

- α_{j_i} *is the number of cash flows for the jth bond of the ith risky class.*

- $B_i(t, s)$ *is the discount factor associated to the ith risky class (price at date t of a zero-coupon bond of the ith class paying \$1 at date s). $B_0(t, s)$ is the discount function associated with the benchmark class. Note that we have the following constraint for the minimization program $\forall i = 0, 1, 2, \ldots, n$*

$$B_i(t, t) = 1$$

There are two ways of modeling the relationship between discount factors:

- *The discount function associated with the ith risky class is the sum of the discount function of the benchmark class plus a spread function*

$$B_i(t, s) = B_0(t, s) + S_i(t, s)$$

where $S_i(t, s)$ is the discount spread function associated with the ith risky class and $S_0(t, s) = 0$.

- *The discount function associated with the ith risky class is the multiplication of the discount function of the benchmark class by a spread function*

$$B_i(t,s) = B_0(t,s) \times T_i(t,s)$$

where $T_i(t,s)$ is the discount spread function associated with the ith risky class and $T_0(t,s) = 1$.

The advantage of the first model is that we keep the linear character of the problem for the minimization program if we write the discount function as a linear function of the parameters to be estimated. In contrast, the second model leads to a nonlinear minimization program but is more intuitive in the sense that we can write the risky zero-coupon rate as the sum of the benchmark zero-coupon rate plus a spread[19]

$$R_i^c(t, s-t) = R^c(t, s-t) + t_i^c(t, s-t)$$

where $R_i^c(t, s-t)$ is the continuously compounded zero-coupon rate of the ith risky class at date t with maturity $s-t$, and $t_i^c(t, s-t)$ is the spread at date t for maturity $s-t$ between the risky zero-coupon rate and the benchmark zero-coupon rate.

In the absence of arbitrage opportunities, the following relationship must hold

$$\widehat{P_t^{j_i}} = \sum_{\substack{s=T_{j_i}-\alpha_{j_i}+1 \\ s>0}}^{T_{j_i}} F_s^{(j_i)} B_i(t,s)$$

Using an Additive Spread

When we model the discount function associated with the ith risky class as the sum of the discount function of the benchmark class plus a spread function, we are confronted by the same minimization problem as previously exposed in the section on "Parametrization of the Discount Function as a Spline Function." In fact, we obtain

$$\widehat{P_t^{j_i}} = \sum_{\substack{s=T_{j_i}-\alpha_{j_i}+1 \\ s>0}}^{T_{j_i}} F_s^{(j_i)} (B_0(t,s) + S_i(t,s))$$

Houweling *et al.* (1999) propose to model the discount functions with B-splines. For example, we may use the following parametrization at date $t = 0$

$$\begin{cases} B_0(0,s) = B_0(s) = \sum_{k=-3}^{4} a_{0,k} \left(\sum_{m=k}^{k+4} \left[\prod_{\substack{l=k \\ l \neq m}}^{k+4} \frac{1}{\lambda_l - \lambda_m} \right] (s - \lambda_m)_+^3 \right) \\ \\ S_i(0,s) = S_i(s) = \sum_{k=-3}^{4} a_{i,k} \left(\sum_{m=k}^{k+4} \left[\prod_{\substack{l=k \\ l \neq m}}^{k+4} \frac{1}{\lambda_l - \lambda_m} \right] (s - \lambda_m)_+^3 \right) \end{cases} \tag{4.18}$$

---

[19]This equation is obtained using

$$e^{-(s-t) \cdot R_i^c(t,s-t)} = e^{-(s-t) \cdot R^c(t,s-t)} \times e^{-(s-t) \cdot t_i^c(t,s-t)}.$$

Here, the discount function as well as the discount spread function are modeled in the same manner using cubic B-splines and the same number of pasting points. We may change the localization of pasting points, the number of pasting points and choose two-order B-splines instead of cubic B-splines to model the discount spread function.

Discount functions may also be modeled using exponential splines. In the equation (4.18), you simply have to replace s by $e^{-\alpha s}$ to obtain exponential spline discount functions. The idea is to jointly estimate in a one-step procedure the parameters $a_{0,k}$ and $a_{i,k} \forall i, \forall k$, which best fit the market prices of the bonds of the n risky classes and instruments of the benchmark curve. This is done by using a GLS program as previously exposed in the section on "Parametrization of the Discount Function as a Spline Function."

Using a Multiplicative Spread

When we model the discount function associated with the ith risky class as the product of the discount function of the benchmark class by a spread function, we can write the risky zero-coupon rate as the sum of the benchmark zero-coupon rate plus a spread

$$R_i(t, s - t) = R(t, s - t) + t_i(t, s - t)$$

where $R_i(t, s - t)$ is the zero-coupon rate of the ith risky class at date t with maturity $s - t$, and $t_i(t, s - t)$ is the spread at date t for maturity $s - t$ between the risky zero-coupon rate and the benchmark zero-coupon rate.

$R(t, s - t)$ might be directly modeled in the same manner as we have written zero-coupon rates in terms of cubic B-splines (see equation (4.15)), when our goal was to derive the inter-bank zero-coupon yield curve. That modelization is all the more coherent since the benchmark curve is the interbank zero-coupon yield curve. Almeida *et al.* (1998, 2000) show that the spread $t_i(t, s - t)$ can be modeled with success using Legendre polynomials; so we obtain at date $t = 0$

$$\begin{cases} R(0, s) = \sum_{k=-3}^{4} a_{0,k} \left(\sum_{m=k}^{k+4} \left[\prod_{\substack{l=k \\ l \neq m}}^{k+4} \frac{1}{\lambda_l - \lambda_m} \right] (s - \lambda_m)_+^3 \right) \\ t_i(0, s) = \sum_{p \geq 0} c_{i,p} P_p \left(\frac{2s}{M} - 1 \right) \end{cases}$$

where the Legendre polynomial $P_p(x)$ is defined as follows:

$$P_p(x) = \frac{1}{2^p p!} \frac{\partial^p}{\partial x^n} [(x^2 - 1)^p] \quad \forall p = 0, 1, 2, \ldots,$$

For example, the first four Legendre polynomials are

$$\begin{cases} P_0(x) = 1 \\ P_1(x) = x \\ P_2(x) = \frac{1}{2}(3x^2 - 1) \\ P_3(x) = \frac{1}{2}(5x^3 - 3x) \end{cases}$$

Note that other orthogonal polynomials may be used too. In the absence of arbitrage opportunities, the following relationship must hold:

$$\widehat{P_t^{j_i}} = \sum_{\substack{s=T_{j_i}-\alpha_{j_i}+1 \\ s>0}}^{T_{j_i}} F_s^{(j_i)} e^{-(s-t)\times(R_i^c(t,s-t))} = \sum_{\substack{s=T_{j_i}-\alpha_{j_i}+1 \\ s>0}}^{T_{j_i}} F_s^{(j_i)} e^{-(s-t)\times(R^c(t,s-t)+t_i^c(t,s-t))}$$

A least squares program[20] is used to estimate the parameters $a_{0,k}$ and $c_{i,p} \forall i, \forall k, \forall p$, which best fit the bond market prices of the n risky classes and of the benchmark curve. The program is nonlinear and so more time-consuming than a simple linear program. Note that Jankowitsch and Pichler (2002) propose to model the benchmark zero-coupon rate $R^c(t, s - t)$ with the Svensson (1994) functional form, and the credit spread $t_i^c(t, s - t)$ with the Nelson and Siegel (1987) form.

We provide hereafter a comparison of joint and disjoint methods.

Example 4.15   Comparison of the Disjoint and Joint Methods

We derive the zero-coupon spread curve for the bank sector in the Eurozone as of May 31, 2000, using the interbank zero-coupon curve as benchmark curve. For that purpose, we use two different methods:

- **The disjoint method.**   *We consider the standard cubic B-splines to model the two discount functions associated, respectively, with the risky zero-coupon yield curve and the benchmark curve. We consider the following splines [0;1], [1;5], [5;10] for the benchmark curve and [0;3], [3;10] for the risky class. As there are no short risky bonds quoted on the market, we add 20 bps to the short-term segment of the risky zero-coupon curve compared to the benchmark curve. Results in terms of prices are summarized in Table 4.8*

Table 4.8   Bond Price Spreads—Disjoint Method.

Disjoint Method—Cubic B-Splines

Date		05/31/00		
Sum of squared spreads		**0.595**		
Average spread		**0.146**		
Rate or instrument	Maturity	Market price	Theoretical price	Spread
Procedure of Minimization				
1-week Euribor	06/07/00	99.918	99.917	0.002
1-month Euribor	06/30/00	99.646	99.639	0.007
2-month Euribor	07/31/00	99.267	99.256	0.011
3-month Euribor	08/31/00	98.874	98.865	0.009
6-month derived from Euribor futures contract	11/30/00	97.648	97.674	−0.026

---

[20]The least squares program is typically a weighted least squares program because the longer the maturity of the bond, the more difficult its price to estimate.

Table 4.8 *(continued)*

Disjoint Method—Cubic B-Splines

Date	05/31/00
Sum of squared spreads	**0.595**
Average spread	**0.146**

Rate or instrument	Maturity	Market price	Theoretical price	Spread
9-month derived from Euribor futures contract	02/28/01	96.418	96.455	−0.036
1-year derived from Euribor futures contract	05/31/01	95.189	95.189	0.000
2-year swap	05/31/02	100.000	99.994	0.006
3-year swap	05/30/03	100.000	100.015	−0.015
4-year swap	05/31/04	100.000	99.999	0.006
5-year swap	05/31/05	100.000	100.011	−0.011
6-year swap	05/31/06	100.000	99.993	0.007
7-year swap	05/31/07	100.000	99.990	0.010
8-year swap	05/30/08	100.000	100.001	−0.001
9-year swap	05/29/09	100.000	100.012	−0.012
10-year swap	05/31/10	100.000	99.994	0.006
BNP PARIBAS 6 07/06/01	06/07/01	106.666	106.763	−0.097
CREDIT NATIONAL 9.25 10/02/01	10/02/01	111.033	111.115	−0.082
CREDIT NATIONAL 7.25 05/14/03	05/14/03	104.643	104.384	0.259
SNS BANK 4.75 09/21/04	09/21/04	99.411	99.338	0.074
CREDIT NATIONAL 6 11/22/04	11/22/04	103.733	103.851	−0.118
BNP PARIBAS 6.5 12/03/04	12/03/04	106.184	105.857	0.327
BNP PARIBAS 5.75 08/06/07	08/06/07	103.457	103.368	0.089
ING BANK NV 6 10/01/07	10/01/07	103.467	103.929	−0.462
ING BANK NV 5.375 03/10/08	03/10/08	96.582	96.813	−0.230
COMMERZBANK AG 4.75 04/21/09	04/21/09	89.518	89.347	0.171
BSCH ISSUANCES 5.125 07/06/09	07/06/09	95.564	95.315	0.249
BANK OF SCOTLAND 5.5 07/27/09	07/27/09	97.591	97.720	−0.129

- *The joint method.* *We consider the joint method using an additive spread and use again the standard cubic B-splines to model the discount function associated with the benchmark curve and the spread function associated with the risky spread curve. As there are no short risky bonds quoted on the market, we add 20 bps to the short-term segment of the risky zero-coupon curve compared to the benchmark curve. We consider the same splines as in the disjoint method. Results in terms of prices are summarized in Table 4.9.*

In our example, the quality of fit is better in the disjoint method compared to the joint method, but the form of the zero-coupon spread structure seems erratic (see Figure 4.17). In contrast, the spread curve obtained by the joint method is a very smooth function (see Figure 4.17). We conclude that the joint method is the best compromise between the quality of fit and the robustness.

Fixed Income Securities

Table 4.9 Bond Price Spreads—Joint Method.

Joint Method—Cubic B-Splines

Date	05/31/00			
Sum of squared spreads	**1.818**			
Average spread	**0.255**			
Rate or instrument	Maturity	Market price	Theoretical price	Spread
Procedure of Minimization				
1-week Euribor	06/07/00	99.918	99.918	0.000
1-month Euribor	06/30/00	99.646	99.645	0.001
2-month Euribor	07/31/00	99.267	99.266	0.001
3-month Euribor	08/31/00	98.874	98.876	−0.003
6-month derived from Euribor futures contract	11/30/00	97.648	97.680	−0.032
9-month derived from Euribor futures contract	02/28/01	96.418	96.445	−0.027
1-year derived from Euribor futures contract	05/31/01	95.189	95.163	0.026
2-year swap	05/31/02	100.000	99.934	0.066
3-year swap	05/30/03	100.000	99.961	0.039
4-year swap	05/31/04	100.000	100.021	−0.021
5-year swap	05/31/05	100.000	100.090	−0.090
6-year swap	05/31/06	100.000	100.111	−0.111
7-year swap	05/31/07	100.000	100.115	−0.115
8-year swap	05/30/08	100.000	100.083	−0.083
9-year swap	05/29/09	100.000	99.976	0.024
10-year swap	05/31/10	100.000	99.784	0.216
BNP PARIBAS 6 07/06/01	06/07/01	106.666	106.643	0.024
CREDIT NATIONAL 9.25 10/02/01	10/02/01	111.033	111.004	0.029
CREDIT NATIONAL 7.25 05/14/03	05/14/03	104.643	104.770	−0.127
SNS BANK 4.75 09/21/04	09/21/04	99.411	99.626	−0.214
CREDIT NATIONAL 6 11/22/04	11/22/04	103.733	104.088	−0.355
BNP PARIBAS 6.5 12/03/04	12/03/04	106.184	106.085	0.099
BNP PARIBAS 5.75 08/06/07	08/06/07	103.457	102.605	0.852
ING BANK NV 6 10/01/07	10/01/07	103.467	103.168	0.298
ING BANK NV 5.375 03/10/08	03/10/08	96.582	96.141	0.441
COMMERZBANK AG 4.75 04/21/09	04/21/09	89.518	89.532	−0.015
BSCH ISSUANCES 5.125 07/06/09	07/06/09	95.564	95.784	−0.220
BANK OF SCOTLAND 5.5 07/27/09	07/27/09	97.591	98.272	−0.682

4.4 End of Chapter Summary

Bond pricing is typically performed by taking the discounted value of the bond cash flows. Information about discount rates is usually extracted from market sources. This is known as *relative pricing*: the price of a bond is obtained in such a way that it is consistent with prices of other bonds in a reference set. Because there is no abundance of zero-coupon bonds traded in the market, one cannot extract directly the zero-coupon yield curve. A robust methodology for extracting implied zero-coupon prices or rates from bond market prices is therefore needed.

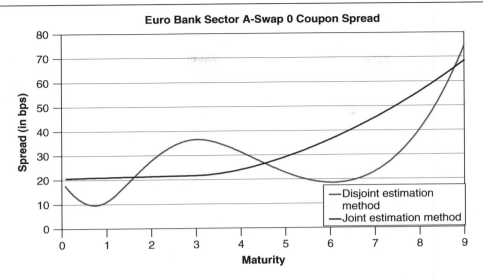

Figure 4.17 Comparison of zero-coupon credit spread term structure by using a disjoint method and a joint method.

There is a direct method to fit a default-free yield curve, known as the bootstrapping method, but it somewhat lacks in robustness. Indirect methods are therefore usually preferred. The common character of all indirect models is that they involve fitting data to a prespecified form of the zero-coupon yield curve. The general approach is to first select a reference set of bonds with market prices and cash flows taken as given. Then, one postulates a specific form of the discount function or the zero-coupon rates, where the function is usually defined in a piecewise manner in order to allow different sets of parameters for different types of maturities (short, medium and long), under the form of a polynomial or exponential spline functional. Finally, the set of parameters is estimated as the one that best approximates given market prices.

In the context of interest-rate risk management, fitting the zero-coupon yield curve is generally better than fitting the discount function because it allows for a clearer interpretation of the parameters. Also, it usually requires a smaller number of parameters. However, models for the zero-coupon yield curve are difficult to implement from a computational standpoint, and they usually do not have enough flexibility to account for all possible shapes of the term structure encountered in practice. Therefore, when the emphasis is on pricing (as opposed to hedging) fixed-income portfolios, spline models of the discount factors are usually preferred; they enable investors to recover bond prices with a quasi-perfect accuracy.

The term structure of credit spreads for a given rating class and a given economic sector can also be derived from market data. Two different methods exist, the disjoint method and the joint method. The first one consists in separately deriving the term structure of nondefault zero-coupon yields and the term structure of risky zero-coupon yields so as to obtain by differentiation the term structure of zero-coupon credit spreads. In contrast, the second one consists in generating both term structures of zero-coupon yields through a one-step procedure, using an additive or a multiplicative spread model.

4.5 References and Further Reading

Almeida, C.I.R., A.M. Duarte, and C.A.C. Fernandes, 1998, "Decomposing and Simulating the Movements of the Term Structure of Interest Rates in Emerging Eurobond Markets", *Journal of Fixed Income*, **1**, 21–31.

Almeida, C.I.R., A.M. Duarte, and C.A.C. Fernandes, 2000, "Credit Spread Arbitrage in Emerging Eurobond Markets", *Journal of Fixed Income*, **10**(3), 100–111.

Anderson, N, F. Breedon, M. Deacon, and A. Derry, 1996, *Estimating and Interpreting the Yield Curve, Series in Financial Economics and Quantitative Analysis*, John Wiley & Sons, New York.

Balduzzi, P., S.R. Das, S. Foresi, and R. Sundaram, 1996, "A Simple Approach to Three-Factor Affine Term Structure Models", *Journal of Fixed Income*, **6**(3), 43–53.

Barrett, B., T. Gosnell, and A. Heuson, 1995, "Yield Curve Shifts and the Selection of Immunization Strategies", *Journal of Fixed Income*, **5**(2), 53–64.

Björk, T., and B.J. Christensen, 1999, "Interest Rate Dynamics and Consistent Forward Rate Curves", *Mathematical Finance*, **9**(4), 323–348.

Black, F., and J.C. Cox, 1976, "Valuing Corporate Securities: Some Effects of Bond Indenture Provisions", *Journal of Finance*, **31**, 351–367.

Bliss, R., 1997, "Testing Term Structure Estimation Methods", *Advances in Futures and Options Research*, **9**, 197–232.

Brooks, R., and D.Y. Yan, 1999 "London Inter-Bank Offer Rate (LIBOR) versus Treasury Rate: Evidence from the Parsimonious Term Structure Model", *Journal of Fixed Income*, **9**(1), 71–83.

Brown, S.J., and P.H. Dybvig, 1986, "The Empirical Implications of the Cox, Ingersoll, Ross Theory of the Term Structure of Interest Rates", *Journal of Finance*, **41**(3), 617–632.

Brown, R.H., S.M. Schaefer, 1994, "The Term Structure of Real Interest Rates and the Cox, Ingersoll, Ross Model", *Journal of Financial Economics*, **35**(1), 3–42.

Chen, L., 1996, "Stochastic Mean and Stochastic Volatility—A Three Factor Model of the Term Structure of Interest Rates and its Applications in Derivatives Pricing and Risk Management", *Financial Markets, Institutions and Instruments*, **5**(1), 1–87.

Cox, J.C., J.E. Ingersoll, and S.A. Ross, 1985, "A Theory of the Term Structure of Interest Rates", *Econometrica*, **53**(2), 385–407.

Dahlquist, M., and L.E.O. Svensson, 1996, "Estimating the Term Structure of Interest Rates for Monetary Analysis", *Scandinavian Journal of Economics*, **98**(2), 163–183.

Deacon M., and A. Derry, 1994, Estimating the Term Structure of Interest Rates, Working Paper Series 24, Bank of England.

Diaz, A., and F.S. Skinner, 2001, "Estimating Corporate Yield Curves", *Journal of Fixed Income*, **11**(2), 95–103.

Dierckx, P., 1997, *Curve and Surface Fitting with Splines*, Oxford University Press, Oxford.

Düllman, K., and M. Windfuhr, 2000, Credit Spreads Between German and Italian Sovereign Bonds—Do Affine Models Work?, Working Paper, University of Mannheim.

El Karoui, N., T. Chérif, J.A. Dicoum, and K. Savidan, 1994, Modélisation de la Structure par Terme des Taux d'Intérêt: Tests et Applications, *Cahiers de la Caisse Autonome de Refinancement*, Vol. 6, Paris.

Ferguson, R., and S. Raymar, 1998, "A Comparative Analysis of Several Popular Term Structure Estimation Models", *Journal of Fixed Income*, **7**(4), 17–33.

Fletcher, R., 1987, *Practical Methods of Optimization*, John Wiley & Sons, Chichester.

Geyer, A., S, Kossmeier and S. Pichler, 2001, Empirical Analysis of European Government Yield Spreads, Working Paper, Vienna University of Technology.

Houweling, P., J. Hoek, and F. Kleibergen, 1999, The Joint Estimation of Term Structures and Credit Spreads, Working Paper, Erasmus University Rotterdam.

Hull, J., and A. White, 1990, "Pricing Interest Rate Derivative Securities", *Review of Financial Studies*, **3**(4), 573–592.

Ilmanen, A., and R. Iwanowski, 1997, "Dynamics of the Shape of the Yield Curve", *Journal of Fixed Income*, **7**(2), 47–60.

Jankowitsch, R., and S. Pichler, 2002, Parsimonious Estimation of Credit Spreads, Working Paper, Vienna University of Technology.

Jankowitsch, R., H. Mösenbacher, and S. Pichler, 2002, Measuring the Liquidity Impact on EMU Government Bond Prices, Working Paper, Vienna University of Technology.

Litzenberger, R.H., and J. Rolfo, 1984, "An International Study of Tax Effects on Government Bonds", *Journal of Finance*, **39**(1), 1–22.

Longstaff, F.A., and E.S. Schwartz, 1992, "Interest Rate Volatility and the Term Structure: A Two-Factor General Equilibrium Model", *Journal of Finance*, **47**(4), 1259–1282.

Longstaff, F.A., and E.S. Schwartz, 1995, "A Simple Approach to Valuing Risky Fixed and Floating Rate Debt", *Journal of Finance*, **50**(3), 789–819.

Mc Culloch, J.H., 1971, "Measuring the Term Structure of Interest Rates", *Journal of Business*, **44**, 19–31.

Mc Culloch, J.H., 1975, "The Tax-Adjusted Yield Curve", *Journal of Finance*, **30**(3), 811–830.

Martellini, L., and P. Priaulet, 2000, *Fixed-Income Securities: Dynamic Methods for Interest Rate Risk Pricing and Hedging*, John Wiley & Sons, Chichester.

Merton, R.C., 1974, "On the Pricing of Corporate Debt: The Risk Structure of Interest Rates", *Journal of Finance*, **29**, 449–470.

Nelson, C.R., and A.F. Siegel, 1987, "Parsimonious Modeling of Yield Curves", *Journal of Business*, **60**(4), 473–489.

Priaulet, P., 1997, Structure par Terme des Taux d'Intérêt: Reconstitution, Modélisation et Couverture, Thèse de Doctorat en Sciences Economiques, Université Paris IX-Dauphine.

Ricart, R., and P. Sicsic, 1995, "Estimation d'une Structure par Termes des Taux d'Intérêt sur Données Françaises", *Bulletin de la Banque de France*, **22**, 117–128.

Shea, G.S., 1984, "Pitfalls in Smoothing Interest Rate Term Structure Data: Equilibrium Models and Spline Approximations", *Journal of Financial and Quantitative Analysis*, **19**(3), 253–269.

Shea, G.S., 1985, "Interest Rate Term Structure Estimation with Exponential Splines: A Note", *Journal of Finance*, **40**(1), 319–325.

Steeley, J.M., 1991, "Estimating the Gilt-Edged Term Structure: Basis Splines and Confidence Intervals", *Journal of Business Finance and Accounting*, **18**(4), 512–529.

Subramanian K.V., 2001, "Term Structure Estimation in Illiquid Markets", *Journal of Fixed Income*, **11**(1), 77–86.

Svensson, L., 1994, Estimating and Interpreting Forward Interest Rates: Sweden 1992–94, CEPR Discussion Paper 1051.

Vasicek, O.A., 1977, "An Equilibrium Characterisation of the Term Structure", *Journal of Financial Economics*, **5**, 177–188.

Vasicek, O.A., and H.G. Fong, 1982, "Term Structure Modeling using Exponential Splines", *Journal of Finance*, **37**(2), 339–348.

Waggoner, F.D., 1997, Spline Methods for Extracting Interest Rate Curves from Coupon Bond Prices, Working Paper, Federal Reserve Bank of Atlanta.

Willner, R., 1996, "A New Tool for Portfolio Managers: Level, Slope and Curvature Durations", *Journal of Fixed Income*, **6**(1), 48–59.

4.6 Problems

Exercise 4.1   At date $t = 0$, we consider five bonds with the following features:

	Annual coupon (%)	Maturity (years)	Price
Bond 1	6	1	$P_0^1 = 103$
Bond 2	5	2	$P_0^2 = 102$
Bond 3	4	3	$P_0^3 = 100$
Bond 4	6	4	$P_0^4 = 104$
Bond 5	5	5	$P_0^5 = 99$

Derive the zero-coupon curve until the 5-year maturity.

Exercise 4.2   At date $t = 0$, we consider three bonds with the following features:

	Annual coupon (%)	Maturity (years)	Price
Bond 1	10	2	$P_0^1 = 108.00$
Bond 2	7.5	3	$P_0^2 = 100.85$
Bond 3	8.5	3	$P_0^3 = 103.50$

Derive the zero-coupon curve until the 3-year maturity.

Exercise 4.3   Suppose we know from market prices the following zero-coupon rates with maturities inferior or equal to 1 year:

Maturity	Zero-coupon rate (%)
1 Day	3.20
1 Month	3.30
2 Months	3.40
3 Months	3.50
6 Months	3.60
9 Months	3.80
1 Year	4.00

Now, we consider the following bonds priced by the market until the 4-year maturity:

Maturity	Annual coupon (%)	Gross price
1 Year and 3 Months	4	102.8
1 Year and 6 Months	4.5	102.5
2 Years	3.5	98.3
3 Years	4	98.7
4 Years	5	101.6

The compounding frequency is assumed to be annual.

1. Using the bootstrapping method, compute the zero-coupon rates for the following maturities: 1 year and 3 months, 1 year and 6 months, 2 years, 3 years and 4 years.
2. Draw the zero-coupon yield curve using a linear interpolation.

Exercise 4.4

1. The 10-year and 12-year zero-coupon rates are, respectively, equal to 4% and 4.5%. Compute the $11^{1/4}$- and $11^{3/4}$-year zero-coupon rates using the linear interpolation.
2. Same question when you know the 10-year and 15-year zero-coupon rates, which are, respectively, equal to 8.6% and 9%.

Exercise 4.5   The 1-, 2-, 3- and 4-year zero-coupon rates are, respectively, 7%, 8%, 8.5% and 9%. Compute the $3^{1/4}$-year zero-coupon rate using the cubic interpolation.

Exercise 4.6   We consider the discount function modeled as a three-order polynomial spline with the two following splines:

$$B(s) = \begin{cases} B_0(s) = d_0 + c_0 s + b_0 s^2 + a_0 s^3 \text{ for } s \in [0, 10] \\ B_{10}(s) = d_1 + c_1 s + b_1 s^2 + a_1 s^3 \text{ for } s \in [10, 30] \end{cases}$$

In that case, the discount function has 8 parameters. Using the standard constraints for that modelization, show that the discount function can be written as

$$B(s) = \begin{cases} B_0(s) = 1 + c_0 s + b_0 s^2 + a_0 s^3 \text{ for } s \in [0, 10] \\ B_{10}(s) = 1 + c_0 s + b_0 s^2 + a_0 [s^3 - (s - 10)^3] + a_1 (s - 10)^3 \\ \qquad \text{for } s \in [10, 30] \end{cases}$$

Exercise 4.7   From the prices of zero-coupon bonds quoted in the market, we obtain the following zero-coupon curve:

Maturity (years)	Zero-coupon rate $R(0, t)$	Discount factor $B(0, t)$
1	5.000%	0.95238
2	5.500%	0.89845
3	5.900%	0.84200
4	6.200%	0.78614
5	?	?
6	6.550%	0.68341
7	6.650%	0.63720
8	?	?
9	6.830%	0.55177
10	6.900%	0.51312

where $R(0, t)$ is the zero-coupon rate at date 0 for maturity t and $B(0, t)$ is the discount factor at date 0 for maturity t.

We need to know the value for the 5-year and the 8-year zero-coupon rates. We have to estimate them, and test four different methods.

1. We use a linear interpolation with the zero-coupon rates. Find $R(0, 5)$, $R(0, 8)$ and the corresponding values for $B(0, 5)$ and $B(0, 8)$.
2. We use a linear interpolation with the discount factors. Find $B(0, 5)$, $B(0, 8)$ and the corresponding values for $R(0, 5)$ and $R(0, 8)$.
3. We postulate the following form for the zero-coupon rate function $\bar{R}(0, t)$:

$$\bar{R}(0, t) = a + bt + ct^2 + dt^3$$

Estimate the coefficients a, b, c and d, which best approximate the given zero-coupon rates, using the following optimization program:

$$\underset{a,b,c,d}{Min} \sum_i (R(0, i) - \bar{R}(0, i))^2$$

where $R(0, i)$ are the zero-coupon rates given by the market.

Find the value for $R(0, 5) = \bar{R}(0, 5)$, $R(0, 8) = \bar{R}(0, 8)$, and the corresponding values for $B(0, 5)$ and $B(0, 8)$.

4. We postulate the following form for the discount function $\bar{B}(0, t)$:

$$\bar{B}(0, t) = a + bt + ct^2 + dt^3$$

Estimate the coefficients a, b, c and d, which best approximate the given discount factors, using the following optimization program:

$$\underset{a,b,c,d}{Min} \sum_i (B(0, i) - \bar{B}(0, i))^2$$

where $B(0, i)$ are the discount factors given by the market.

Obtain the value for $B(0, 5) = \bar{B}(0, 5)$, $B(0, 8) = \bar{B}(0, 8)$, and the corresponding values for $R(0, 5)$ and $R(0, 8)$.

5. Conclude.

Exercise 4.8   From the prices of zero-coupon bonds quoted in the market, we obtain the following zero-coupon curve:

Maturity (years)	$R(0, t)$ (%)
0.5	7.500
1	7.130
1.25	7.200
2	7.652
3	8.023
4	8.289
5	8.516
6	8.724
7	8.846
8	8.915
10	8.967

where $R(0, t)$ is the zero-coupon rate at date 0 with maturity t and $B(0, t)$ is the discount factor at date 0 with maturity t.

We need to know the value for $R(0, 0.8)$, $R(0, 1.5)$, $R(0, 3.4)$, $R(0, 5.25)$, $R(0, 8.3)$ and $R(0, 9)$ where $R(0, i)$ is the zero-coupon rate at date 0 with maturity i. We have to estimate them and test two different methods.

1. We postulate the following form for the zero-coupon rate function $\bar{R}(0, t)$:

$$\bar{R}(0, t) = a + bt + ct^2 + dt^3$$

   a) Estimate the coefficients a, b, c and d, which best approximate the given zero-coupon rates, using the following optimization program:

$$\underset{a,b,c,d}{Min} \sum_i (R(0, i) - \bar{R}(0, i))^2$$

   where $R(0, i)$ are the zero-coupon rates given by the market. Compare these rates $R(0, i)$ to the rates $\bar{R}(0, i)$ given by the model.

   b) Find the value for the six zero-coupon rates that we are looking for.

   c) Draw the two following curves on the same graph:

- the market curve by plotting the market points and
- the theoretical curve as derived from the prespecified functional form.

2. Same question as the previous one. But we now postulate the following form for the discount function $\bar{B}(0, t)$:

$$\bar{B}(0, t) = a + bt + ct^2 + dt^3$$

Estimate the coefficients a, b, c and d, which best approximate the given discount factors, using the following optimization program:

$$\underset{a,b,c,d}{Min} \sum_i (B(0, i) - \bar{B}(0, i))^2$$

where $B(0, i)$ are the discount factors given by the market.

3. Conclude.

Exercise 4.9   Data are the same as in the previous exercise. We now use different forms for the zero-coupon rate function $\bar{R}(0, t)$.

1. We first postulate a four-order polynomial form for the zero-coupon rate function $\bar{R}(0, t)$

$$\bar{R}(0, t) = a + bt + ct^2 + dt^3 + et^4$$

   a) Estimate the coefficients a, b, c, d and e, which best approximate the given zero-coupon rates, using the following optimization program:

$$\underset{a,b,c,d,e}{Min} \sum_i (R(0, i) - \bar{R}(0, i))^2$$

where $R(0, i)$ are the zero-coupon rates given by the market. Compare these rates $R(0, i)$ to the rates $\bar{R}(0, i)$ given by the model.

b) Find the value for the six zero-coupon rates that we are looking for.

c) Draw the two following curves on the same graph:

- the market curve by plotting the market points and
- the theoretical curve as derived from the prespecified functional form.

2. We now consider the Nelson–Siegel functional form for the annually compounded zero-coupon rate $\bar{R}(0, t)$ (note that Nelson and Siegel (1987) consider the following functional form for the continuously compounded zero-coupon rate in their model) as written below:

$$\bar{R}(0, t) = \beta_0 + \beta_1 \left[\frac{1 - \exp\left(-\dfrac{\theta}{\tau}\right)}{\dfrac{\theta}{\tau}} \right] + \beta_2 \left[\frac{1 - \exp\left(-\dfrac{\theta}{\tau}\right)}{\dfrac{\theta}{\tau}} - \exp\left(-\dfrac{\theta}{\tau}\right) \right]$$

a) Estimate the coefficients β_0, β_1 and β_2, which best approximate the given zero-coupon rates, using the following optimization program:

$$\underset{\beta_0, \beta_1, \beta_2}{Min} \sum_i (R(0, i) - \bar{R}(0, i))^2$$

where $R(0, i)$ are the zero-coupon rates given by the market. First, fix a value for τ, and then optimize over this parameter using the "Solver" function from Excel.

b) Compute $\sum_i (R(0, i) - \bar{R}(0, i))^2$.

c) Compare the market rates $R(0, i)$ to the rates $\bar{R}(0, i)$ given by the model.

d) Find the value for the six zero-coupon rates that we are looking for.

e) Draw the two following curves on the same graph:

- the market curve by plotting the market points;
- and the theoretical curve as derived from the prespecified functional form.

3. We now consider the Nelson–Siegel Extended functional form for the annually compounded zero-coupon rate $\bar{R}(0, t)$ (note that Svensson (1994) considers the following functional form for the continuously compounded zero-coupon rate in his model) as written below:

$$\bar{R}(0, t) = \beta_0 + \beta_1 \left[\frac{1 - \exp\left(-\dfrac{\theta}{\tau_1}\right)}{\dfrac{\theta}{\tau_1}} \right] + \beta_2 \left[\frac{1 - \exp\left(-\dfrac{\theta}{\tau_1}\right)}{\dfrac{\theta}{\tau_1}} - \exp\left(-\dfrac{\theta}{\tau_1}\right) \right]$$

$$+ \beta_3 \left[\frac{1 - \exp\left(-\dfrac{\theta}{\tau_2}\right)}{\dfrac{\theta}{\tau_2}} - \exp\left(-\dfrac{\theta}{\tau_2}\right) \right]$$

a) Estimate the coefficients β_0, β_1, β_2 and β_3, which best approximate the given zero-coupon rates, using the following optimization program:

$$\underset{\beta_0,\beta_1,\beta_2,\beta_3}{Min} \sum_i (R(0,i) - \bar{R}(0,i))^2$$

where $R(0,i)$ are the zero-coupon rates given by the market. First, fix a couple of values for (τ_1, τ_2), and then optimize over these parameters using the "Solver" function from Excel.

b) Compute $\sum_i (R(0,i) - \bar{R}(0,i))^2$ and compare it to the value obtained with the Nelson and Siegel form.

c) Compare the market rates $R(0,i)$ to the rates $\bar{R}(0,i)$ given by the model.

d) Find the value for the six zero-coupon rates that we are looking for.

e) Draw the two following curves on the same graph:

- the market curve by plotting the market points and
- the theoretical curve as derived from the prespecified functional form.

4. Conclude.

Exercise 4.10 Consider the Nelson and Siegel model

$$R^c(0,\theta) = \beta_0 + \beta_1 \left[\frac{1 - \exp\left(-\dfrac{\theta}{\tau}\right)}{\dfrac{\theta}{\tau}} \right] + \beta_2 \left[\frac{1 - \exp\left(-\dfrac{\theta}{\tau}\right)}{\dfrac{\theta}{\tau}} - \exp\left(-\dfrac{\theta}{\tau}\right) \right]$$

Our goal is to analyze the impact of the parameter $1/\tau$ on the zero-coupon curve for three different configurations, an increasing curve, a decreasing curve and an inverted curve at the short-term end.

1. We consider the increasing curve corresponding to the following base-case parameter values: $\beta_0 = 8\%$, $\beta_1 = -3\%$, $\beta_2 = 1\%$ and $1/\tau = 0.3$. We give successively five different values to the parameter $1/\tau$: $1/\tau = 0.1$, $1/\tau = 0.2$, $1/\tau = 0.3$, $1/\tau = 0.4$ and $1/\tau = 0.5$. The other parameters are fixed. Draw the five different yield curves to estimate the effect of the parameter $1/\tau$.

2. We consider the decreasing curve corresponding to the following base-case parameter values: $\beta_0 = 8\%$, $\beta_1 = 3\%$, $\beta_2 = 1\%$ and $1/\tau = 0.3$. We give successively five different values to the parameter $1/\tau$: $1/\tau = 0.1$, $1/\tau = 0.2$, $1/\tau = 0.3$, $1/\tau = 0.4$ and $1/\tau = 0.5$. The other parameters are fixed. Draw the five different yield curves to estimate the effect of the parameter $1/\tau$.

3. We consider the inverted curve corresponding to the following base-case parameter values: $\beta_0 = 8\%$, $\beta_1 = -1\%$, $\beta_2 = -2\%$ and $1/\tau = 0.3$. We give successively five different values to the parameter $1/\tau$: $1/\tau = 0.1$, $1/\tau = 0.2$, $1/\tau = 0.3$, $1/\tau = 0.4$ and $1/\tau = 0.5$. The other parameters are fixed. Draw the five different yield curves to estimate the effect of the parameter $1/\tau$.

Exercise 4.11 We want to derive the current zero-coupon yield curve for maturities inferior to 10 years. For that purpose, we use a basket of bonds quoted by the market and a discount function modeled as a three-order polynomial spline. The features of the bonds used to derive this curve are summarized in the following table:

Bond	Coupon rate (%)	Maturity (years)	Market price
Bond 1	0	7/365	99.92
Bond 2	0	1/12	99.65
Bond 3	0	0.25	98.92
Bond 4	0	0.5	97.77
Bond 5	5	1	100.02
Bond 6	6	2	101.56
Bond 7	5	2.5	101.72
Bond 8	7	3.25	109.72
Bond 9	8	4	108.65
Bond 10	5	4.5	100.26
Bond 11	7	5.5	109.89
Bond 12	7	7	107.55
Bond 13	6	8.75	102.75
Bond 14	7	10	108.21

The coupon frequency of these bonds is annual and the face value is Eur 100.

We model the discount function $B(0, s)$ as a standard polynomial spline with two splines:

$$B(0, s) = \begin{cases} B_0(s) = 1 + c_0 s + b_0 s^2 + a_0 s^3 \text{ for } s \in [0, 3] \\ B_{10}(s) = 1 + c_0 s + b_0 s^2 + a_0[s^3 - (s - 3)^3] + a_1(s - 3)^3 \\ \text{for } s \in [3, 10] \end{cases}$$

1. Write the theoretical price of bond 1.
2. Calculate the coefficients behind each parameter and the constant number for bond 1.
3. Do the same job for bond 2 to bond 14.
4. Estimate the coefficients c_0, b_0, a_0 and a_1, which best approximate the market prices of the given bonds, using the following optimization program:

$$\underset{c_0, b_0, a_0, a_1}{Min} \sum_{i=1}^{14} (P_i - \bar{P}_i)^2$$

where P_i are the market prices and $\bar{P}_i$ the theoretical prices. We suppose that residuals are homoscedastic so that each bond has the same weight in the minimization program.

5. Calculate $\sum_{i=1}^{14} (P_i - \bar{P}_i)^2$.
6. For each bond, calculate the spread between the market price and the theoretical price.
7. Draw the graph of the zero-coupon yield curve.
8. Draw the graph of the forward yield curve in 1, 2 and 3 months.

Exercise 4.12   We take the same data as in the previous exercise. Our goal is to derive the zero-coupon curve using the bootstrap method and the linear interpolation between the points.

1. Derive the zero-coupon yield curve using the bootstrap method.
2. Compare it with the curve derived in the previous exercise by modeling the discount function as a three-order polynomial spline. Conclude.

Exercise 4.13   We take the same data as in the two previous exercises. Our goal is to derive the zero-coupon curve in the same manner as in the first exercise where we model the discount function as a three-order polynomial function. But here instead of considering the homoscedasticity of residuals, we overweight the bonds with short maturity in the minimization program.

We model the discount function $B(0, s)$ as a standard polynomial spline with two splines

$$B(0, s) = \begin{cases} B_0(s) = 1 + c_0 s + b_0 s^2 + a_0 s^3 \text{ for } s \in [0, 3] \\ B_{10}(s) = 1 + c_0 s + b_0 s^2 + a_0[s^3 - (s\text{-}3)^3] + a_1(s\text{-}3)^3 \text{ for } s \in [3, 10] \end{cases}$$

and we estimate the coefficients c_0, b_0, a_0 and a_1, which best approximate the market prices of the given bonds, using the following optimization program:

$$\underset{c_0, b_0, a_0, a_1}{Min} \sum_{i=1}^{14} \left(\frac{P_i - \bar{P}_i}{T_i} \right)^2 = \underset{c_0, b_0, a_0, a_1}{Min} \sum_{i=1}^{14} \left(\frac{\varepsilon_i}{T_i} \right)^2$$

where P_i is the market price of bond i, $\bar{P}_i$ its theoretical price, ε_i the difference between the two prices or the residual and T_i its time to maturity.

Note that this minimization program is equivalent to the following program

$$\underset{c_0, b_0, a_0, a_1}{Min} \sum_{i=1}^{14} (P_i - \bar{P}_i)^2$$ where we suppose that residuals are heteroscedastic with

$$\mathbb{V}ar(\varepsilon_i) = \sigma^2 . T_i^2$$

and where we use the GLS (Generalized Least Squares) method to obtain the vector of parameters β.

1. Calculate the coefficients behind each parameter and the constant number for bond 1.
2. Do the same job for bond 2 to bond 14.
3. Estimate the coefficients c_0, b_0, a_0 and a_1.
4. Calculate $\sum_{i=1}^{14} \left(\frac{P_i - \bar{P}_i}{T_i} \right)^2$ and $\sum_{i=1}^{14} (P_i - \bar{P}_i)^2$.
5. For each bond, calculate the weighted spread and the spread between the market price and the theoretical price.

154

6. Draw the graph of the zero-coupon yield curve and compare it to those obtained in the two previous exercises using the same minimization program but the homoscedasticity of residuals, and the bootstrap method to derive it.
7. Draw the graph of the forward yield curve in 3 months and compare it to that obtained in the previous exercise where we used the same minimization program, but the homoscedasticity of residuals.

Exercise 4.14 Consider the Nelson and Siegel model

$$R^c(0, \theta) = \beta_0 + \beta_1 \left[\frac{1 - \exp\left(-\frac{\theta}{\tau}\right)}{\frac{\theta}{\tau}} \right] + \beta_2 \left[\frac{1 - \exp\left(-\frac{\theta}{\tau}\right)}{\frac{\theta}{\tau}} - \exp\left(-\frac{\theta}{\tau}\right) \right]$$

with the following base-case parameter values: $\beta_0 = 8\%$, $\beta_1 = -3\%$, $\beta_2 = 1\%$ and $1/\tau = 0.3$.

1. We give successively five different values to the parameter β_0 : $\beta_0 = 6\%$, $\beta_0 = 7\%$, $\beta_0 = 8\%$, $\beta_0 = 9\%$ and $\beta_0 = 10\%$. The other parameters are fixed. Draw the five different yield curves to estimate the effect of the level factor β_0.
2. We give successively five different values to the parameter β_1 : $\beta_1 = -1\%$, $\beta_1 = -2\%$, $\beta_1 = -3\%$, $\beta_1 = -4\%$ and $\beta_1 = -5\%$. The other parameters are fixed. Draw the five different yield curves to estimate the effect of the slope factor β_1.
3. We give successively five different values to the parameter β_2: $\beta_2 = 0\%$, $\beta_2 = 0.5\%$, $\beta_2 = 1\%$, $\beta_2 = 1.5\%$ and $\beta_2 = 2\%$. The other parameters are fixed. Draw the five different yield curves to estimate the effect of the curvature factor β_2.

Exercise 4.15 Consider the Nelson and Siegel Extended model

$$R^c(0, \theta) = \beta_0 + \beta_1 \left[\frac{1 - \exp\left(-\frac{\theta}{\tau_1}\right)}{\frac{\theta}{\tau_1}} \right] + \beta_2 \left[\frac{1 - \exp\left(-\frac{\theta}{\tau_1}\right)}{\frac{\theta}{\tau_1}} - \exp\left(-\frac{\theta}{\tau_1}\right) \right]$$

$$+ \beta_3 \left[\frac{1 - \exp\left(-\frac{\theta}{\tau_2}\right)}{\frac{\theta}{\tau_2}} - \exp\left(-\frac{\theta}{\tau_2}\right) \right]$$

with the following base-case parameter values: $\beta_0 = 8\%$, $\beta_1 = -3\%$, $\beta_2 = 1\%$, $\beta_3 = -1\%$, $1/\tau_1 = 0.3$ and $1/\tau_2 = 3$.

We give successively five different values to the parameter β_3 : $\beta_3 = -3\%$, $\beta_3 = -2\%$, $\beta_3 = -1\%$, $\beta_3 = 0\%$ and $\beta_3 = 1\%$. The other parameters are fixed. Draw the five different yield curves to estimate the effect of the curvature factor β_3.

Exercise 4.16 Deriving the Interbank Zero-Coupon Yield Curve
On 03/15/02, we get from the market the following Euribor rates, futures contract prices and swap rates (see Chapters 10 and 11 for more details about swaps and futures)

Maturity	Euribor (%) rate	Contract maturity	Futures price	Maturity	Swap (%) rate
03/22/02	4.07	06/15/02	95.2	03/15/04	5.20
03/29/02	4.11	09/15/02	95.13	03/15/05	5.36
04/15/02	4.15	12/15/02	94.93	03/15/06	5.49
05/15/02	4.26	03/15/03	94.79	03/15/07	5.61
06/15/02	4.34	06/15/03	94.69	03/15/08	5.71
07/15/02	4.44	09/15/03	94.54	03/15/09	5.75
08/15/02	4.53	—	—	03/15/10	5.79
—	—	—	—	03/15/11	5.82
—	—	—	—	03/15/12	5.84

Note that the underlying asset of the futures contract is a 3-month Euribor rate. For example, the first contract matures on 06/15/02, and the underlying asset matures 3 months later on 09/15/02.

1. Extract the implied zero-coupon rates from market data.
2. Draw the zero-coupon yield curve by building a linear interpolation between the implied zero-coupon rates.

Exercise 4.17   We define the following cubic B-spline

$$B_0^3(x) = \sum_{j=0}^{j=4} \left[\prod_{\substack{i=0 \\ i \neq j}}^{i=4} \frac{1}{(\lambda_i - \lambda_j)} \right] (x - \lambda_j)_+^3$$

where $\lambda_0 = 0$, $\lambda_1 = 1$, $\lambda_2 = 3$, $\lambda_3 = 7$ and $\lambda_4 = 10$ are the knots of the modelization, and $(x - \lambda_j)_+^3 = Max[0; (x - \lambda_j)_+^3]$.

1. Calculate the quantity $\prod_{\substack{i=0 \\ i \neq j}}^{i=4} \frac{1}{(\lambda_i - \lambda_j)}$ for $j = 0, 1, 2, 3, 4$.
2. Draw the graph of $B_0^3(x)$ on the segment $[-5; 15]$
3. Same two questions when $\lambda_4 = 15$.

4.7   Appendix: A Useful Modified Newton's Algorithm

Let us consider the function G, which provides the spot zero-coupon yield rates as obtained through the "extended Vasicek" model (see equation (4.13))

$$G(0, \theta; u) = L_0 - S_0 \left[\frac{1 - e^{-a\theta}}{a\theta} \right] + \gamma_0 \left[\frac{(1 - e^{-a\theta})^2}{4a\theta} \right]$$

We recall that the optimization problem is defined by equations (4.8) to (4.9), which can be solved via the use of a so-called "modified Newton algorithm." This algorithm is also commonly used for the calibration of the interest-rate models discussed in Chapter 12.

Fixed Income Securities

Newton Algorithm

We consider a given starting point $(u^{(0)})^{\mathsf{T}} = (L_0^{(0)}, S_0^{(0)}, \gamma_0^{(0)})$, for a given value of the parameter a (known as a *scale* parameter). The algorithm is based upon the Newton method. We first obtain a second-order Taylor expansion of the function J around the value $u^{(0)}$. We actually consider a quadratic approximation $J^{(0)}$ for J around $u^{(0)}$:

$$J^{(0)}(u) = J(u^{(0)}) + \nabla J(u^{(0)})^{\mathsf{T}} \cdot (u - u^{(0)}) + \tfrac{1}{2}(u - u^{(0)})^{\mathsf{T}} \cdot \nabla^2 J(u^{(0)}) \cdot (u - u^{(0)})$$

where $\nabla J(u^{(0)})$ denotes the gradient of J in $u^{(0)}$, that is, the vector of first-order derivatives of J:

$$\nabla J(u^{(0)}) = \begin{pmatrix} \dfrac{\partial J}{\partial L}(u^{(0)}) \\ \dfrac{\partial J}{\partial S}(u^{(0)}) \\ \dfrac{\partial J}{\partial \gamma}(u^{(0)}) \end{pmatrix}$$

$\nabla^2 J(u^{(0)})$ is the Hessian matrix of J in $u^{(0)}$, that is, the symmetric matrix containing the second-order derivatives of J:

$$\nabla^2 J(u^{(0)}) = \begin{pmatrix} \dfrac{\partial^2 J}{\partial L^2}(u^{(0)}) & \dfrac{\partial^2 J}{\partial L \partial S}(u^{(0)}) & \dfrac{\partial^2 J}{\partial L \partial \gamma}(u^{(0)}) \\ \dfrac{\partial^2 J}{\partial S \partial L}(u^{(0)}) & \dfrac{\partial^2 J}{\partial S^2}(u^{(0)}) & \dfrac{\partial^2 J}{\partial S \partial \gamma}(u^{(0)}) \\ \dfrac{\partial^2 J}{\partial \gamma \partial L}(u^{(0)}) & \dfrac{\partial^2 J}{\partial \gamma \partial S}(u^{(0)}) & \dfrac{\partial^2 J}{\partial \gamma^2}(u^{(0)}) \end{pmatrix}$$

We try to minimize $J^{(0)}(u)$, which we denote by $F(u)$. This amounts to finding the column vector satisfying

$$F'(u^{(1)}) = 0$$

or equivalently

$$(1, 1, 1) \cdot \nabla J(u^{(0)}) + (1, 1, 1) \cdot \nabla^2 J(u^{(0)}) \cdot (u^{(1)} - u^{(0)}) = 0$$

$u^{(1)}$ is thus a solution to the following linear system:

$$u^{(1)} = u^{(0)} - (\nabla^2 J(u^{(0)}))^{-1} \nabla J(u^{(0)})$$

At step k, we consider $J^{(k)}$, the quadratic approximation of J around $u^{(k)}$, which we minimize to obtain $u^{(k+1)}$ defined by

$$u^{(k+1)} = u^{(k)} - (\nabla^2 J(u^{(k)}))^{-1} \nabla J(u^{(k)})$$

Note, however, that the method may provide local maxima as well as saddle points for the function J. In other words, the direction, or "Newton direction" $-(\nabla^2 J(u^{(k)}))^{-1} \nabla J(u^{(k)})$, denoted by $-\delta^{(k)}$, is not necessarily a descent direction. Therefore, the algorithm needs to be adjusted so that J decreases after each step. The local minimization of J is based upon a descent along the Newton direction.

Linear Optimization along the Newton Direction

Starting from $(u^{(0)})^{\mathsf{T}} = (L_0^{(0)}, S_0^{(0)}, \gamma_0^{(0)})$, we build the series of points $u^{(k)}$ such that

$$u^{(k+1)} = u^{(k)} + \alpha^{(k)} \delta^{(k)}$$

$\alpha^{(k)}$ is chosen so that

- $J(u^{(k+1)}) \leq J(u^{(k)})$ *(hence, the value actually decreases at each step)*;

- $J(u^{(k+1)})$ *takes on the smallest possible value.*

Since one cannot directly obtain the value $\alpha^{(k)}$ that realizes the minimum for $J(u^{(k+1)})$, one needs to minimize the quadratic approximation of $J(u^{(k+1)})$ again, which we denote by $J^{(k)}(u^{(k+1)})$, based upon a second-order Taylor expansion around $u^{(k)}$:

$$J^{(k)}(u^{(k+1)}) = J(u^{(k)}) + \nabla J(u^{(k)})^{\mathsf{T}} \cdot (u^{(k+1)} - u^{(k)})$$
$$+ \tfrac{1}{2}(u^{(k+1)} - u^{(k)})^{\mathsf{T}} \cdot \nabla^2 J(u^{(k)}) \cdot (u^{(k+1)} - u^{(k)})$$

Hence, minimizing $J^{(k)}(u^{(k+1)})$ amounts to minimizing

$$\nabla J(u^{(k)})^{\mathsf{T}} \cdot (u^{(k+1)} - u^{(k)}) + \tfrac{1}{2}(u^{(k+1)} - u^{(k)})^{\mathsf{T}} \cdot \nabla^2 J(u^{(k)}) \cdot (u^{(k+1)} - u^{(k)})$$

or equivalently

$$\alpha^{(k)} \cdot \nabla J(u^{(k)})^{\mathsf{T}} \cdot (\nabla^2 J(u^{(k)}))^{-1} \cdot \nabla J(u^{(k)})$$
$$+ \frac{(\alpha^{(k)})^2}{2} \nabla J(u^{(k)})^{\mathsf{T}} \cdot (\nabla^2 J(u^{(k)}))^{-1} \cdot \nabla J(u^{(k)})$$

which can be written

$$H(\alpha^{(k)}) = \left(\alpha^{(k)} + \frac{(\alpha^{(k)})^2}{2} \right) \eta^{(k)}$$

with

$$\eta^{(k)} = \nabla J(u^{(k)})^{\mathsf{T}} \cdot (\nabla^2 J(u^{(k)}))^{-1} \cdot \nabla J(u^{(k)})$$

One needs to distinguish between two cases in this minimization of $H(\alpha^{(k)})$:

1. if $\eta^{(k)} > 0$, the function $H(\alpha^{(k)})$ reaches its minimum at -1; we denote $u_0^{(k+1)} = u^{(k)} - \delta^{(k)}$;
   - *if $J(u_0^{(k+1)}) < J(u^{(k)})$, we denote $u^{(k+1)} = u^{(k)} - \delta^{(k)}$;*

   - *if $J(u_0^{(k+1)}) \geq J(u^{(k)})$, we denote $u_1^{(k+1)} = u^{(k)} - \dfrac{\delta^{(k)}}{2}$ and again one compares $J(u_1^{(k+1)})$ to $J(u^{(k)})$;*

   - *if $J(u_1^{(k+1)}) < J(u^{(k)})$, we denote $u^{(k+1)} = u^{(k)} - \dfrac{\delta^{(k)}}{2}$;*

   - *if $J(u_1^{(k+1)}) \geq J(u^{(k)})$, we denote $u_2^{(k+1)} = u^{(k)} - \dfrac{\delta^{(k)}}{2^2}$ and again one compares $J(u_2^{(k+1)})$ to $J(u^{(k)})$ ...*

The procedure is iterated until one obtains $u^{(k+1)} = u_i^{(k+1)} = u^{(k)} - \dfrac{\delta^{(k)}}{2^i}$, as the first $u_i^{(k+1)}$, such that $J(u_i^{(k+1)}) < J(u^{(k)})$.

2. *if $\eta^{(k)} < 0$, the function $H(\alpha^{(k)})$ reaches its maximum at $-\infty$ and $+\infty$.*

   In this case, set $\alpha^{(k)} = \dfrac{0.01}{\|(\nabla^2 J(u^{(k)}))^{-1} \cdot \nabla J(u^{(k)})\|}$ and $u_0^{(k+1)} = u^{(k)} + \alpha^{(k)}\delta^{(k)}$.

As defined above, $\alpha^{(k)}$ takes on very large values. The procedure discussed in 1) is used until one obtains $u^{(k+1)} = u_i^{(k+1)} = u^{(k)} - \dfrac{\delta^{(k)}}{2^i}$, the first $u_i^{(k+1)}$ such that $J(u_i^{(k+1)}) < J(u^{(k)})$.

Here, we divide the descent direction by two at each step. One may have used any other number. The larger that number, the slower one gets away from the value $u^{(k)}$. In any case, the algorithm requires a specification for a stopping rule. For example, the minimization could be stopped whenever the $\mathbb{L}^2$ distance between two successive points $\|u^{(k+1)} - u^{(k)}\|$ becomes smaller than 10^{-7}.

Hedging Interest-Rate Risk

PART III

Before turning to passive and active fixed-income strategies, one needs to first provide a comprehensive coverage of the risks involved in fixed-income investing and how to manage them.

A stock risk is usually proxied by its beta, which is a measure of the stock sensitivity to market movements. In the same vein, bond price risk is, most often, measured in terms of the bond interest-rate sensitivity, or duration. This is a one-dimensional measure of the bond's sensitivity to interest-rate movements. There is one complication, however: as seen in the previous chapters, the value of a bond, or a bond portfolio, is affected by changes in interest rates of all possible maturities. In other words, there is more than one risk factor, and simple methods based upon a one-dimensional measure of risk will not allow investors to properly manage interest-rate risks.

In the world of equity investment, it has long been recognized that there may be more than one rewarded risk factor [see, for example, the seminal work by Fama and French (1992)]. A variety of more general multifactor models, economically justified either by equilibrium (Merton, 1973) or arbitrage (Ross, 1976) arguments, have been applied to risk management and portfolio performance evaluation. In this part we survey the multifactor models used for interest-rate risk management. All these models have been designed to better account for the complex nature of interest-rate risk. Because it is never easy to hedge the risk associated with too many sources of uncertainty, it is always desirable to try and reduce the number of risk factors, and identify a limited number of common factors. There are several ways in which this can be done and all of them are to some extent arbitrary. In that context, it is important to know the exact assumptions one has to make in the process, and try to evaluate the robustness of these assumptions with respect to the specific scenario an investor has in mind.

We first review in Chapter 5 the traditional duration hedging method that is intensively used by practitioners. That approach is based on a series of very restrictive and simplistic assumptions, the assumptions of a small and parallel shift in the yield-to-maturity curve. As seen in Chapter 3, we know, however, that large variations can affect the yield-to-maturity curve and that three main factors (level, slope and curvature) have been found to drive the dynamics of the yield curve [see Litterman and Scheinkman (1991)]. This strongly suggests that duration hedging is inefficient in many circumstances. That is why we will see in Chapter 6 hedging methods that go "beyond duration" by relaxing the two fundamental assumptions of duration hedging, and show that satisfactory hedging results can be achieved by using a three-factor model for the yield curve.

5

Hedging Interest-Rate Risk with Duration

Before implementing any kind of hedging method against the interest-rate risk, we need to understand how bond prices change, given a change in interest rates. This is critical to successful bond management.

5.1 Basics of Interest-Rate Risk: Qualitative Insights

The basics of bond price movements as a result of interest-rate changes are perhaps best summarized by the five theorems on the relationship between bond prices and yields. As an illustration (see Table 5.1), let us consider the percentage price change for 4 bonds with different annual coupon rates (8% and 5%) and different maturities (5 years and 25 years), starting with a common 8% yield-to-maturity (YTM), and assuming successively a new yield of 5%, 7%, 7.99%, 8.01%, 9% and 11%.

From this example, we can make the following observations. Using the bond valuation model, one can show the changes that occur in the price of a bond (i.e., its volatility), given a change in yields, as a result of bond variables such as time to maturity and coupon, and show that these observations actually hold in all generalities. For now, we simply state these "theorems." More detailed comments about these elements will follow. We leave the proof of these theorems as an exercise to the mathematically oriented reader.

Table 5.1 Percentage Price Change for 4 Bonds, Starting with a Common 8% YTM.

New yield (%)	Change (bps)	8%/25 (%)	8%/5 (%)	5%/25 (%)	5%/5 (%)
5.00	−300	42.28	12.99	47.11	13.61
7.00	−100	11.65	4.10	12.82	4.29
7.99	−1	0.11	0.04	0.12	0.04
8.01	+1	−0.11	−0.04	−0.12	−0.04
9.00	+100	−9.82	−3.89	−10.69	−4.07
11.00	+300	−25.27	−11.09	−27.22	−11.58

5.1.1 The Five Theorems of Bond Pricing

- *Bond prices move inversely to interest rates. Investors must always keep in mind a fundamental fact about the relationship between bond prices and bond yields: bond prices move inversely to market yields. When the level of required yields demanded by investors on new issues changes, the required yields on all bonds already outstanding will also change. For these yields to change, the prices of these bonds must change. This inverse relationship is the basis for understanding, valuing and managing bonds.*

- *Holding maturity constant, a decrease in rates will raise bond prices on a percentage basis more than a corresponding increase in rates will lower bond prices. Obviously, bond price volatility can work for, as well as against, investors. Money can be made, and lost, in risk-free Treasury securities as well as in riskier corporate bonds.*

- *All things being equal, bond price volatility is an increasing function of maturity. Long-term bond prices fluctuate more than short-term bond prices. Although the inverse relationship between bond prices and interest rates is the basis of all bond analysis, a complete understanding of bond price changes as a result of interest-rate changes requires additional information. An increase in interest rates will cause bond prices to decline, but the exact amount of decline will depend on important variables unique to each bond such as time to maturity and coupon. An important principle is that for a given change in market yields, changes in bond prices are directly related to time to maturity. Therefore, as interest rates change, the prices of longer-term bonds will change more than the prices of shorter-term bonds, everything else being equal.*

- *A related principle regarding maturity is as follows: the percentage price change that occurs as a result of the direct relationship between a bond's maturity and its price volatility increases at a decreasing rate as time to maturity increases. In other words, the percentage of price change resulting from an increase in time to maturity increases, but at a decreasing rate. Put simply, a doubling of the time to maturity will not result in a doubling of the percentage price change resulting from a change in market yields.*

- *In addition to the maturity effect, the change in the price of a bond as a result of a change in interest rates depends on the coupon rate of the bond. We can state this principle as (other things equal): bond price fluctuations (volatility) and bond coupon rates are inversely related. Note that we are talking about percentage price fluctuations; this relationship does not necessarily hold if we measure volatility in terms of dollar price changes rather than percentage price changes.*

These principles lead to the practical conclusion that the two bond variables of major importance in assessing the change in the price of a bond, given a change in interest rates, are its coupon and its maturity. This conclusion can be summarized as follows: A decline (rise) in interest rates will cause a rise (decline) in bond prices, with the maximum volatility in bond prices occurring in longer maturity bonds and in bonds with low coupons. Therefore, a bond buyer, in order to receive the maximum price impact of an expected change in interest rates, should purchase low-coupon, long-maturity bonds. If an increase in interest rates is expected (or feared), investors contemplating their purchase should consider those bonds with large coupons or short maturities, or both.

These relationships provide useful information for bond investors by demonstrating how the price of a bond changes as interest rates change. Although investors have no control over the change and direction in market rates, they can exercise control over the coupon and maturity, both of which have significant effects on bond price changes.

An important distinction needs to be made between two kinds of risk, reinvestment risk and capital gain risk.

5.1.2 Reinvestment Risk

It is important to understand that the YTM is a promised yield, because investors earn the indicated yield only if the bond is held to maturity and the coupons are reinvested at the calculated YTM (yield to maturity). Obviously, no trading can be done for a particular bond if the YTM is to be earned. The investor simply buys and holds. What is not so obvious to many investors, however, is the reinvestment implications of the YTM measure. Because of the importance of the reinvestment rate, we consider it in more detail by analyzing the reinvestment risk.

The YTM calculation assumes that the investor reinvests all coupons received from a bond at a rate equal to the computed YTM on that bond, thereby earning interest on interest over the life of the bond at the computed YTM rate.

If the investor spends the coupons, or reinvests them at a rate different from the YTM, the realized yield that will actually be earned at the termination of the investment in the bond will differ from the promised YTM. In fact, coupons almost always will be reinvested at rates higher or lower than the computed YTM, resulting in a realized yield that differs from the promised yield. This gives rise to reinvestment rate risk.

This interest-on-interest concept significantly affects the potential total dollar return. The exact impact is a function of coupon and time to maturity, with reinvestment becoming more important as either coupon or time to maturity, or both, rise. Specifically,

- *holding everything else constant, the longer the maturity of a bond, the greater the reinvestment risk;*

- *holding everything else constant, the higher the coupon rate, the greater the dependence of the total dollar return from the bond on the reinvestment of the coupon payments.*

Lets look at realized yields under different assumed reinvestment rates for a 20-year bullet bond purchased at a $100 face value, which delivers an annual 10% coupon rate. If the reinvestment rate exactly equals 10% YTM, the investor would realize a 10% compound return when the bond is held to maturity, with $372.75 of the total dollar return from the bond attributable to the reinvestment of the coupon payments. At a 12% reinvestment rate, the investor would realize an 11.10% compound return, with 63.4% of the total return coming from interest on interest ($520.52/$820.52). With no reinvestment of coupons (spending them as received), the investor would achieve only a 5.65% return. In all cases, the bond is held to maturity.

Clearly, the reinvestment portion of the YTM concept is critical. In fact, for long-term bonds the interest-on-interest component of the total realized yield may account for more than three-fourths of the bond's total dollar return.

5.1.3 Capital Gain Risk

As bond yield drops, bond price rises, and vice versa.

Example 5.1 Consider a 2-year, 10% coupon bond with a $1,000 face value, and a yield of 8.8%, which pays a semiannual coupon. The price of the bond equals $1,021.58:

$$\frac{50}{(1+4.4\%)} + \frac{50}{(1+4.4\%)^2} + \frac{50}{(1+4.4\%)^3} + \frac{1,050}{(1+4.4\%)^4} = \$1,021.58$$

Suppose the market interest rate drops instantaneously to 7.8%. The market price is now $1,040.02:

$$\frac{50}{(1+3.9\%)} + \frac{50}{(1+3.9\%)^2} + \frac{50}{(1+3.9\%)^3} + \frac{1,050}{(1+3.9\%)^4} = \$1,040.02$$

There is an interplay between capital gain risk and reinvestment risk.

Example 5.2 An investor with a horizon of 1 year buys the 2-year, 10% coupon bond of the previous example. The bond yield is 8%.

- *Scenario 1:* *The interest rate drops to 7.8%, soon after the bond is purchased, and stays there. The bond price rises immediately to 1,040.02. After 6 months, the bond price rises to 1,040.02 × 1.039 = 1,080.58. At this time, a coupon of $50 is paid, whereupon the price of the bond drops by an equal amount to 1,030.58. The bond increases in value at the end of the year to 1,030.58 × 1.039 = 1,070.78, while the $50 coupon has been reinvested at an annual yield of 7.8% and has grown to 50 × 1.039 = 51.95, for a total of 1,122.73.*

- *Scenario 2:* *The interest rate rises to 8.2%, and stays there. The price immediately drops to 1,032.59. However, the bond and coupons thereafter rise at the rate of 4.1% every 6 months, culminating in a value of 1,119.00 at the end of the investment horizon.*

What we can see is that if interest rates drop and stay there, there is an immediate appreciation in the value of the portfolio, but the portfolio then grows at a slower rate; on the other hand, if interest rates rise and stay there, there is a capital loss, but the portfolio then appreciates more rapidly. Hence, there is some investment horizon D, such that investors with that horizon will not care if interest rates drop or rise (as long as the changes are small). We will see below that the value of this horizon depends on the characteristics of the bond portfolio; specifically, we will see that D is simply the duration of the bond portfolio.

Despite the usefulness of the qualitative insights obtained above, quantitative tools must be introduced to provide investors with more definite answers to the most important question they face: what is the dollar impact of a given change in market conditions on the value of my bond portfolio? That is why we have to first qualify the interest-rate risk.

5.1.4 Qualifying Interest-Rate Risk

A portfolio manager aims at hedging the value of a fixed-income portfolio that delivers certain (or deterministic) cash flows in the future, typically cash flows from straight bonds with a fixed-coupon rate. Even if these cash flows are known in advance, the portfolio price changes in time, which leaves an investor exposed to a potentially significant capital loss.

To fix the notation, we consider at date t a portfolio of fixed-income securities that delivers m certain cash flows F_i at future dates t_i for $i = 1, \ldots, m$. The price P of the portfolio (in $ value) can be written as the sum of the future cash flows discounted with the appropriate zero-coupon rate with maturity corresponding to the maturity of each cash flow:

$$P_t = \sum_{i=1}^{m} F_i B(t, t_i) = \sum_{i=1}^{m} \frac{F_i}{[1 + R(t, t_i - t)]^{t_i - t}} \qquad (5.1)$$

where $B(t, t_i)$ is the price at date t of a zero-coupon bond paying \$1 at date t_i (also called the *discount factor*) and $R(t, t_i - t)$ is the associated zero-coupon rate, starting at date t for a residual maturity of $t_i - t$ years.

We can see in equation (5.1) that the price P_t is a function of m interest-rate variables $R(t, t_i - t)$ and of the time variable t. This suggests that the value of the portfolio is subject to a potentially large number m of risk factors. For example, a bond with annual cash flows up to a 10-year maturity is affected by potential changes in 10 zero-coupon rates. To hedge a position in this bond, we need to be hedged against a change in all of these 10 factor risks.

In practice, it is not easy to hedge the risk of so many variables. We must create a global portfolio containing the portfolio to be hedged in such a way that the portfolio is insensitive to all sources of risk (the m interest-rate variables and the time variable t).[1] One suitable way to simplify the hedging problematic is to reduce the number of risk variables. Duration hedging of a portfolio is based on a single risk variable, the yield to maturity of this portfolio.

5.2 Hedging with Duration

The whole idea behind duration hedging is to bypass the complication of a multidimensional interest-rate risk by identifying a single risk factor, the yield to maturity of the portfolio, which will serve as a "proxy" for the whole term structure. We study the sensitivity of the price of the bond to changes in this yield using a one-order Taylor expansion.

5.2.1 Using a One-Order Taylor Expansion

The first step consists in writing the price of the portfolio P_t in \$ value as a function of a single source of interest-rate risk, its yield to maturity y_t (see equation (5.2)):

$$P_t = P(y_t) = \sum_{i=1}^{m} \frac{F_i}{[1 + y_t]^{t_i - t}} \qquad (5.2)$$

Remark 5.1 For semiannual coupon-bearing bonds, the formula above should be expressed as

$$P_t = \sum_{i=1}^{m} \frac{F_i}{\left(1 + \dfrac{y_t}{2}\right)^{2(t_i - t)}} \qquad (5.3)$$

where y_t is a semiannual compounded yield and $t_i - t$ a fraction of the year before cash flow i is paid. As an example, we consider a \$1,000 face value 2-year bond with 8% coupon and

---

[1] Hereafter, we do not consider the change in value due to time because it is a deterministic term [for details about the time-value of a bond, see Chance and Jordan (1996)]. We only consider changes in value due to interest-rate variations.

Fixed Income Securities

a yield to maturity $y = 6\%$. The bond price is obtained as

$$P = \frac{40}{1 + \frac{y}{2}} + \frac{40}{\left(1 + \frac{y}{2}\right)^2} + \frac{40}{\left(1 + \frac{y}{2}\right)^3} + \frac{1{,}040}{\left(1 + \frac{y}{2}\right)^4} = \$1{,}037.17$$

Therefore, equation (5.3) should rather be written as

$$P_t = \sum_{i=1}^{m} \frac{F_i}{(1 + y_t')^{\theta_i}}$$

with the convention $y_t' = \frac{y_t}{2}$, and $\theta_i = 2(t_i - t)$ being a number of half-years. For notational simplicity, we choose to maintain equation (5.2) instead with y and $t_i - t$. We hope not to confuse the reader by doing so.

In this case, we can see clearly that the interest-rate risk is (imperfectly) summarized by changes in the yield to maturity y_t. Of course, this can only be achieved by losing much generality and imposing important, rather arbitrary and simplifying assumptions. The yield to maturity is a complex average of the whole term structure, and it can be regarded as the term structure if and only if the term structure is flat.

A second step involves the derivation of a Taylor expansion of the value of the portfolio P as an attempt to quantify the magnitude of value changes dP that are triggered by small changes dy in yield. We get an approximation of the *absolute* change in the value of the portfolio as

$$dP(y) = P(y + dy) - P(y) = P'(y)\,dy + o(y) \simeq \$Dur(P(y))\,dy \tag{5.4}$$

where

$$P'(y) = -\sum_{i=1}^{m} \frac{(t_i - t)F_i}{[1 + y_t]^{t_i - t + 1}}$$

The derivative of the bond value function with respect to the yield to maturity is known as the *$duration* (or *sensitivity*) of portfolio P, and $o(y)$ a negligible term. From equation (5.4), we confirm an important result discussed in the qualitative approach to the problem: $\$Dur < 0$. What this means is that the relationship between price and yield is negative; higher yields imply lower prices.

Dividing equation (5.4) by $P(y)$, we obtain an approximation of the *relative* change in value of the portfolio as

$$\frac{dP(y)}{P(y)} = \frac{P'(y)}{P(y)}\,dy + o_1(y) \simeq -MD(P(y))\,dy \tag{5.5}$$

where

$$MD(P(y)) = -\frac{P'(y)}{P(y)}$$

is known as the *modified duration (MD)*[2] of portfolio P.

---

[2]Note that the opposite quantity of the modified duration is known as the *relative sensitivity*.

The $duration and the modified duration enable us to compute the absolute P&L and the relative P&L of portfolio P for a small change Δy of the yield to maturity (for example, 10 bps or 0.1% as expressed in percentage):

$$\text{Absolute } P\&L \simeq \$Dur \times \Delta y$$

$$\text{Relative } P\&L \simeq -MD \times \Delta y$$

The $duration and the modified duration are also measures of the volatility of a bond portfolio.

Another standard measure is the basis point value (BPV), which is the change in the bond price given a basis point change in the bond's yield. BPV is given by the following equation:

$$BPV = \frac{MD \times P}{10,000} = \frac{-\$Dur}{10,000}$$

BPV is typically used for hedging bond positions.

Example 5.3 $Duration, Modified Duration and Basis Point Value

Consider below a bond with the following features:

- *maturity:* 10 years
- *coupon rate:* 6%
- *YTM:* 5% *(or price: $107.72)*

Coupon frequency and compounding frequency are assumed to be annual.

The $duration of this bond is equal to -809.67, the BPV is 0.0809 and the modified duration is equal to 7.52. If the YTM increases by 0.1%, the holder of the bond will incur in first approximation an absolute loss equal to

$$\text{Absolute Loss} = -809.67 \times 0.1\% = -\$0.80967$$

Its relative loss expressed in percentage is

$$\text{Relative Loss} = -7.52 \times 0.1\% = -0.752\%$$

Remark 5.2 $Duration and Modified Duration of a Bond with Semiannual Payments

Considering the price of a bond with semiannual payments given by equation (5.3), we obtain the following expression for $P'(y)$, which is the derivative of the bond price with respect to the yield to maturity y

$$P'(y) = -\sum_{i=1}^{m} \frac{(t_i - t)F_i}{\left[1 + \frac{y_t}{2}\right]^{2(t_i - t)+1}}$$

We now consider the same bond as in the previous example (maturity = 10 years; coupon rate = 6%; YTM = 5%) except that coupon frequency and compounding frequency are now assumed to be semiannual.

The price, $duration and modified duration of this bond are equal to $107.79, −816.27 and 7.57, respectively.

5.2.2 Duration, $Duration and Modified Duration

Different Notions of Duration

There are three different notions of duration. We already have seen two of them, the $duration and the modified duration, which are used to compute the absolute P&L and the relative P&L of the bond portfolio for a small change in the yield to maturity. The third one is the Macaulay duration, simply called *duration*. The duration of bond P is defined as

$$D \equiv D(P(y)) \equiv -(1+y)\frac{P'(y)}{P(y)} = \frac{\displaystyle\sum_{i=1}^{m} \frac{(t_i - t)F_i}{[1+y]^{t_i-t}}}{P(y)} \tag{5.6}$$

The duration may be interpreted as a weighted average maturity for the portfolio. The weighted coefficient for each maturity $t_i - t$ is equal to

$$w = \frac{F_i}{P(y)(1+y)^{t_i-t}}$$

It is easy to check that the duration is always less than or equal to the maturity, and is equal to it if and only if the portfolio has only one cash flow (e.g., zero-coupon bond). Duration is very easy to compute in practice, as can be seen through the following example.

Example 5.4   Calculation of Bond Duration

We consider a bond paying 10 annual cash flows, with a coupon rate $c = 5.34\%$ and a yield to maturity $y = 5.34\%$ (with annual compounding frequency). We compute the duration as $D = 8$ (see Table 5.2). This tells us that the cash flow–weighted average maturity is 8 years. In other words, this 10-year coupon bond essentially behaves, in terms of sensitivity to interest-rate changes, as an 8-year pure discount bond.

The duration of a bond or bond portfolio is the investment horizon such that investors with that horizon will not care if interest rates drop or rise as long as changes are small. In other words, capital gain risk is offset by reinvestment risk as is shown now in the following example.

Example 5.5   Duration = Neutral Investment Horizon

Consider a 3-year standard bond with a 5% YTM and a $100 face value, which delivers a 5% coupon rate. Coupon frequency and compounding frequency are assumed to be annual. Its

Table 5.2 Calculation of Bond Duration.

Time of cash flow (t)	Cash flow F_t	$w_t = \frac{1}{P} \times \frac{F_t}{(1+y)^t}$	$t \times w_t$
1	53.4	0.0506930	0.0506930
2	53.4	0.0481232	0.0962464
3	53.4	0.0456837	0.1370511
4	53.4	0.0433679	0.1734714
5	53.4	0.0411694	0.2058471
6	53.4	0.0390824	0.2344945
7	53.4	0.0371012	0.2597085
8	53.4	0.0352204	0.2817635
9	53.4	0.0334350	0.3009151
10	1053.4	0.6261237	6.2612374
		Total	8.0014280

$$\Rightarrow D = \sum_{t=1} t \times w_t \cong 8$$

price is \$100 and its duration is equal to 2.86. We assume that YTM changes instantaneously and stays at this level during the life of the bond. Whatever the change in this YTM, we show in the following table that the sum of the bond price and the reinvested coupons after 2.86 years is always the same, equal to 114.972 or 114.971.

YTM (%)	Bond price	Reinvested coupons	Total
4	104.422	10.550	114.972
4.5	104.352	10.619	114.971
5	104.282	10.689	114.971
5.5	104.212	10.759	114.971
6	104.143	10.829	114.972

Relationships between the Different Duration Measures

Note that there is a set of simple relationships between the three different durations:

$$MD = \frac{D}{1+y}$$

$$\$Dur = -\frac{D}{1+y} \times P = -MD \times P$$

Remark 5.3 When the coupon frequency and the compounding frequency of a bond are assumed to be semiannual, these two relationships are affected in the following manner:

$$MD = \frac{D}{1+\frac{y}{2}}$$

$$\$Dur = -\frac{D}{1+\frac{y}{2}} \times P = -MD \times P$$

Properties of the Different Duration Measures

The main properties of duration, modified duration and $duration measures are as follows:

1. *The duration of a zero-coupon bond equals its time to maturity.*
2. *Holding the maturity and the YTM of a bond constant, the bond's duration (modified duration or $duration) is higher when the coupon rate is lower.*
3. *Holding the coupon rate and the YTM of a bond constant, its duration (or modified duration) increases with its time to maturity as $duration decreases.*
4. *Holding other factors constant, the duration (or modified duration) of a coupon bond is higher as $duration is lower when the bond's YTM is lower.*

Example 5.6   To illustrate points (2), (3) and (4), we consider a base-case bond with maturity 10 years, a 6% annual coupon rate, a 6% YTM (with annual compounding frequency) and a $100 face value.

Holding the maturity and the YTM of this bond constant, we give different values to the coupon rate and can see clearly that the lower the coupon rate, the higher the duration (modified duration and $duration).

Coupon rate (%)	Duration	$Duration	Modified duration
3	8.59	−631.40	8.10
4	8.28	−666.27	7.81
5	8.02	−701.14	7.57
6	7.80	−736.01	7.36
7	7.61	−770.88	7.18
8	7.45	−805.75	7.02
9	7.30	−840.62	6.89

Example 5.7   Holding the coupon rate and the YTM of this bond constant, we give different values to the maturity and can see that clearly the higher the maturity, the higher the duration (and modified duration), and the lower the $duration.

Maturity (years)	Duration	$Duration	Modified duration
7	5.92	−558.24	5.58
8	6.58	−620.98	6.21
9	7.21	−680.17	6.80
10	7.80	−736.01	7.36
11	8.36	−788.69	7.89
12	8.89	−838.38	8.38
13	9.38	−885.27	8.85

Holding the maturity and the coupon rate of this bond constant, we give different values to the YTM and can see clearly that the lower the YTM, the higher the duration (and modified duration), and the lower the $duration.

YTM (%)	Duration	$Duration	Modified duration
3	8.07	−983.62	7.83
4	7.98	−891.84	7.67
5	7.89	−809.67	7.52
6	7.80	−736.01	7.36
7	7.71	−669.89	7.20
8	7.62	−610.48	7.05
9	7.52	−557.02	6.90

5. The duration of a perpetual bond that delivers an annual coupon c over an unlimited horizon and with a YTM equal to y is $(1 + y)/y$.

6. Another convenient property of duration is that it is a linear operator. In other words, the duration of a portfolio P invested in n bonds denominated in the same currency with weights w_i is the weighted average of each bond's duration:

$$D_p = \sum_{i=1}^{n} w_i D_i \qquad (5.7)$$

A proof of these two last propositions can be found in the Exercise part.

Remark 5.4 Note that this property of linearity, also true for modified duration, is only true in the context of a flat curve. When the YTM curve is no longer flat, this property becomes false and may only be used as an approximation of the true duration (or modified duration).

5.2.3 How to Hedge in Practice?

We attempt to hedge a bond portfolio with yield to maturity y and price (in $ value) denoted by $P(y)$. The idea is to consider one hedging asset with yield to maturity y_1 (a priori different from y), whose price is denoted by $H(y_1)$, and to build a global portfolio with value P^* invested in the initial portfolio and some quantity ϕ of the hedging instrument.

$$P^* = P(y) + \phi H(y_1)$$

The goal is to make the global portfolio insensitive to small interest-rate variations. Using equation (5.4) and assuming that the YTM curve is only affected by parallel shifts so that $dy = dy_1$, we obtain

$$dP^* \simeq [P'(y) + \phi H'(y_1)] dy = 0$$

Fixed Income Securities

which translates into

$$\phi \$Dur(H(y_1)) = -\$Dur(P(y))$$

or

$$\phi H(y_1) MD(H(y_1)) = -P(y) MD(P(y))$$

and we finally get

$$\phi = -\frac{\$Dur(P(y))}{\$Dur(H(y_1))} = -\frac{P(y)MD(P(y))}{H(y_1)MD(H(y_1))} \qquad (5.8)$$

The optimal amount invested in the hedging asset is simply equal to the opposite of the ratio of the \$duration of the bond portfolio to be hedged by the \$duration of the hedging instrument. Recall that the hedge requires taking an opposite position in the hedging instrument. The idea is that any loss (gain) with the bond has to be offset by a gain (loss) with the hedging instrument.

> **Remark 5.5** When the yield curve is flat, which means that $y = y_1$, we can also use the Macaulay Duration to construct the hedge of the instrument. In this particular case, the hedge ratio (HR) ϕ given by equation (5.8) is also equal to
>
> $$\phi = -\frac{P(y)D(P(y))}{H(y)D(H(y))}$$
>
> where the Macaulay duration $D(P(y))$ is defined in equation (5.6).

In practice, it is preferable to use futures contracts or swaps instead of bonds to hedge a bond portfolio because of significantly lower costs and higher liquidity. Using standard swaps as hedging instruments[3], the HR ϕ_s is

$$\phi_s = -\frac{\$Dur_P}{\$Dur_S} \qquad (5.9)$$

where $\$Dur_S$ is the \$duration of the fixed-coupon bond contained in the swap.

Using futures as hedging instruments[4], the HR ϕ_f is equal to

$$\phi_f = -\frac{\$Dur_P}{\$Dur_{CTD}} \times CF \qquad (5.10)$$

where $\$Dur_{CTD}$ is the \$duration of the cheapest-to-deliver bond, and CF the conversion factor.

We will see practical examples of hedges using swaps and futures in Chapters 10 and 11.

---

[3] See Chapter 10 for a complete description of interest-rate risk hedging methods with swaps.
[4] See Chapter 11 for a complete description of interest-rate risk hedging methods with futures.

Example 5.8 Hedging a Bond Position

An investor holds a bond portfolio, whose features are summarized in the following table, and wishes to be hedged against a rise in interest rates.

YTM	MD	Price
5.143%	6.760	$328,635

The characteristics of the hedging instrument, which is a bond here, are the following:

YTM	MD	Price
4.779%	5.486	$118.786

We then obtain the quantity ϕ of the hedging instrument using equation (5.8):

$$\phi = -\frac{328,635 \times 6.760}{118.786 \times 5.486} = -3,409$$

The investor has to sell 3,409 units of the hedging instrument.

Another measure commonly used by market participants to hedge their bond positions is the basis point value (BPV) measure.

Example 5.9 Hedging a Bond Position Using BPV

We calculate the hedge ratio denoted as HR, which gives the size of the hedge position

$$HR = \frac{BPV_b}{BPV_h} \times \frac{Change\ in\ bond\ yield}{Change\ in\ yield\ for\ the\ hedging\ instrument}$$

where BPV_b and BPV_h are, respectively, the basis point value of the bond to be hedged and of the hedging instrument. The second ratio in the equation is sometimes called the *yield ratio*.

For example, if $BPV_b = 0.0809$ and $BPV_h = 0.05$ and if we assume that the YTM curve is affected by a parallel shift of the same magnitude, which implies that the yield ratio is equal to 1, then the HR is 1.618. For a $10,000 long position in the bond we have to take a $16,180 short position in the hedging instrument.

5.3 End of Chapter Summary

A decline (rise) in interest rates will cause a rise (decline) in bond prices, with the most volatility in bond prices occurring in longer maturity bonds and bonds with low coupons. As a stock risk is usually proxied by its beta, which is a measure of the stock sensitivity to market movements, bond price risk is most often measured in terms of the bond interest-rate sensitivity, or duration.

This is a one-dimensional measure of the bond's sensitivity to interest-rate movements. There are actually three related notions of duration: Macaulay duration, $duration and modified duration. Macaulay duration, often simply called *duration*, is defined as a weighted average maturity for the portfolio. The duration of a bond or bond portfolio is the investment horizon such that investors with that horizon will not care if interest rates drop or rise as long as changes are small, as capital gain risk is offset by reinvestment risk on the period. $duration and modified duration are used to compute, respectively, the absolute P&L and the relative P&L of a bond portfolio for a small change in the yield to maturity. $duration also provides us with a convenient hedging strategy: to offset the risks related to a small change in the level of the yield curve, one should optimally invest in a hedging asset a proportion equal to the opposite of the ratio of the $duration of the bond portfolio to be hedged by the $duration of the hedging instrument.

5.4 References and Further Reading

5.4.1 Books

Bierwag, G.O., 1987, *Duration Analysis: Managing Interest Rate Risk*, Ballinger Publishing Company, Cambridge, MA.

Chambers, D.R., and S.K. Nawalkha (Editors), 1999, *Interest Rate Risk Measurement and Management*, Institutional Investor, New York.

Fabozzi, F.J., 1996, *Fixed-Income Mathematics*, 3rd Edition, McGraw-Hill, New York.

Fabozzi, F.J., 1999, *Duration, Convexity and Other Bond Risk Measures*, John Wiley & Sons, Chichester.

Martellini, L., and P. Priaulet, 2000, *Fixed-Income Securities: Dynamic Methods for Interest Rate Risk Pricing and Hedging*, John Wiley & Sons, Chichester.

Macaulay, F.R., 1938, *The Movements of Interest Rates, Bond Yields, and Stock Prices in the United States Since 1859*, Columbia University Press, NBER, New York.

5.4.2 Papers

Bierwag, G.O., 1977, "Immunization, Duration and the Term Structure of Interest Rates", *Journal of Financial and Quantitative Analysis*, **12**, 725–742.

Bierwag, G.O., G.G. Kaufman, and A. Toevs, 1983, "Duration: Its Development and Use in Bond Portfolio Management", *Financial Analysts Journal*, **39**, 15–35.

Chance D.M., and J.V. Jordan, 1996, "Duration, Convexity, and Time as Components of Bond Returns", *Journal of Fixed Income*, **6**(2), 88–96.

Christensen P.O., and B.G. Sorensen, 1994, "Duration, Convexity and Time Value", *Journal of Portfolio Management*, **20**(2), 51–60.

Fama, E.F., and K.R. French, 1992, "The Cross-Section of Expected Stock Returns", *Journal of Finance*, **47**(2), 427–465.

Grove, M.A., 1974, "On Duration and the Optimal Maturity Structure of the Balance Sheet", *Bell Journal of Economics and Management Science*, **5**, 696–709.

Ilmanen, A., 1996, "Does Duration Extension Enhance Long-Term Expected Returns?" *Journal of Fixed Income*, **6**(2), 23–36.

Ingersoll, J.E., J. Skelton, and R.L. Weil, 1978, "Duration Forty Years After", *Journal of Financial and Quantitative Analysis*, **34**, 627–648.

Litterman, R., and J. Scheinkman, 1991, "Common Factors Affecting Bond Returns", *Journal of Fixed Income*, **1**(1), 54–61.

Merton, R.C., 1973, "An Intertemporal Capital Asset Pricing Model", *Econometrica*, **41**, 867–888.

Rendleman, R.J., 1999, "Duration-Based Hedging with Treasury Bond Futures", *Journal of Fixed Income*, **9**(1), 84–91.

Ross, S., 1976, "The Arbitrage Theory of Capital Asset Pricing", *Journal of Economic Theory*, **13**, 341–360.

5.5 Problems

Exercise 5.1   Calculate the percentage price change for 4 bonds with different annual coupon rates (5% and 10%) and different maturities (3 years and 10 years), starting with a common 7.5% YTM (with annual compounding frequency), and assuming successively a new yield of 5%, 7%, 7.49%, 7.51%, 8% and 10%.

Exercise 5.2   Suppose that the Treasury department issues a new 2-year bond that settles today and matures in exactly 2 years. It has a yield of 6% and a coupon rate of 6%. Coupon frequency and compounding frequency are assumed to be semiannual. There are 182 days in the first coupon period. Answer the following questions.

1. What is the price of the bond?
2. What is the accrued interest?
3. What is the duration and modified duration?

Exercise 5.3   We consider a base-case bond with maturity 8 years, a 5% annual coupon rate, a 5% YTM (with annual compounding frequency) and a $100 face value.

1. Holding the maturity and the YTM of this bond constant, compute its duration, $duration and modified duration by giving different values to the coupon rate between 2 and 8%.
2. Holding the coupon rate and the YTM of this bond constant, compute its duration, $duration and modified duration by giving different values to the maturity between 5 and 11 years.
3. Holding the maturity and the coupon rate of this bond constant, compute its duration, $duration and modified duration by giving different values to the YTM between 2 and 8%.

Exercise 5.4   Show that the duration of a perpetual bond delivering annually a coupon c with a YTM equal to y is $\frac{1+y}{y}$.

Exercise 5.5   Show that the duration of a portfolio P invested in n bonds with weights w_i, denominated in the same currency, is the weighted average of each bond's duration:

$$D_p = \sum_{i=1}^{n} w_i D_i$$

Exercise 5.6   Is the duration of a multicurrency portfolio the linear combination of the durations of its currency components? Explain why.

Exercise 5.7   Compute the dirty price, the duration, the modified duration, the $duration and the BPV (basis point value) of the following bonds with $100 face value assuming that coupon frequency and compounding frequency are (1) annual; (2) semiannual and (3) quarterly.

Bond	Maturity (years)	Coupon rate (%)	YTM (%)
Bond 1	1	5	5
Bond 2	1	10	6
Bond 3	5	5	5
Bond 4	5	10	6
Bond 5	5	5	7
Bond 6	5	10	8
Bond 7	20	5	5
Bond 8	20	10	6
Bond 9	20	5	7
Bond 10	20	10	8

Exercise 5.8   Assume the following information about a Treasury bond:
Coupon Rate: 7%; maturity: November 15, 2002; settlement date: September 13, 2000; last coupon paid: May 15, 2000; yield: 6.75%; nominal value: $100. Coupon frequency and compounding frequency are assumed to be semiannual.

1. Compute the accrued interest, the (dirty) price, the clean price and the modified duration of this bond.
2. Using the modified duration, what is the approximate percentage change in price for a 25 basis point change in yield?
3. Find the price if the yield is 7%. Why is the total cost not equal to par? Find the price if the yield is 6.5%. Did the price change by more or less than was predicted? Why?

Exercise 5.9   Repeat the previous exercise for a bond that has the same characteristics except that it has a coupon rate of 10%.

Exercise 5.10   Repeat the previous exercise for a bond that has the same characteristics (coupon rate = 7%) except that its maturity date is November 15, 2003.

Exercise 5.11   Zero-Coupon Bonds

1. What is the price of a zero-coupon bond with $100 face value that matures in 7 years and has a yield of 7%? We assume that the compounding frequency is semiannual.
2. What is the bond's modified duration?
3. Use the modified duration to find the approximate change in price if the bond yield rises by 15 basis points.

Exercise 5.12   You own a 10% Treasury bond with $100 face value that has a modified duration of 9.5. The clean price is 115.25. You have just received a coupon payment 28 days ago. Coupons are received semiannually.

    1. If there are 183 days in this coupon period, what is the accrued interest?

    2. Is the yield greater than the coupon rate or less than the coupon rate? How do you know?

    3. Use the modified duration to find the approximate change in price if the yield were to suddenly fall by 7 basis points.

    4. Will the actual value change by more or less than this amount? Why?

Exercise 5.13   You own a 7% Treasury bond with $100 face value that has a modified duration of 6.3. The clean price is 95.25. You have just received a coupon payment 12 days ago. Coupons are received semiannually.

    1. If there are 182 days in this coupon period, what is the accrued interest?

    2. Is the yield greater than the coupon rate or less than the coupon rate? How do you know?

    3. Use the modified duration to find the approximate change in value if the yield were to suddenly rise by 8 basis points.

    4. Will the actual value change by more or less than this amount? Why?

Exercise 5.14   What is the modified duration of a zero-coupon bond with a remaining maturity of 10.5 years and a bond yield of 10%? What is the price?

Exercise 5.15   Today is 01/01/98. On 06/30/99 we make a payment of $100. We can only invest in a risk-free pure discount bond (nominal $100) that matures on 12/31/98 and in a risk-free coupon bond (nominal $100) that pays an annual interest (on 12/31) of 8% and matures on 12/31/00. Assume a flat term structure of 7%. How many units of each of the bonds should we buy in order to be perfectly immunized?

Exercise 5.16   Consider a 3-year standard bond with a 6% YTM and a $100 face value, which delivers a 10% coupon rate. Coupon frequency and compounding frequency are assumed to be annual. Its price is $110.69 and its duration is equal to 2.75. We assume that YTM changes instantaneously to become 5%, 5.5%, 6.5% or 7% and stays at this level during the life of the bond. Whatever the change in this YTM, show that the sum of the bond price and the reinvested coupons after 2.75 years is always the same.

Exercise 5.17   Provide a rigorous proof of the three following theorems about bond prices and yield changes:

    1. Bond prices move inversely to interest rates.

    2. Holding maturity constant, a decrease in rates will raise bond prices on a percentage basis more than a corresponding increase in rates will lower bond prices.

    3. Other things being equal, bond price volatility measured by its modified duration (denoted by MD) is an increasing function of maturity.

Exercise 5.18   We consider a portfolio composed of 60% of bond A and 40% of bond B, whose features are given below.

Bond A:

Maturity: 2 years

Coupon: 4% (annual frequency)

Yield to maturity: 5% (annual compounding frequency)

Bond B:

Maturity: 5 years

Coupon: 5% (annual frequency)

Yield to maturity: 6% (annual compounding frequency)

1. Compute the YTM of the portfolio.
2. Compare it with the average yield and the $duration weighted yield of the portfolio. What is your conclusion?

Exercise 5.19 An investor holds 100,000 units of a bond whose features are summarized in the following table. He wishes to be hedged against a rise in interest rates.

Maturity	Coupon rate	YTM	Duration	Price
18 Years	9.5%	8%	9.5055	$114.181

Characteristics of the hedging instrument, which is a bond here, are as follows:

Maturity	Coupon rate	YTM	Duration	Price
20 Years	10%	8%	9.8703	$119.792

Coupon frequency and compounding frequency are assumed to be semiannual. YTM stands for yield to maturity. The YTM curve is flat at an 8% level.

1. What is the quantity ϕ of the hedging instrument that the investor has to sell?
2. We suppose that the YTM curve increases instantaneously by 0.1%.

   (a) What happens if the bond portfolio has not been hedged?
   (b) And if it has been hedged?

3. Same question as the previous one when the YTM curve increases instantaneously by 2%.
4. Conclude.

Exercise 5.20 Same exercise as the previous one except that we now consider a nonflat YTM curve. The YTM of the bond with maturity 18 years is 7.5%, and the YTM of the bond with maturity 20 years is still 8%.

Exercise 5.21 The BPV_b and BPV_h of the bond to be hedged and of the hedging instrument are equal, respectively, to 0.12064 and 0.1049. We assume that the YTM curve is affected by a uniform parallel shift. For a long position of $10,000,000 in the bond, what is the position to take in the hedging instrument?

Exercise 5.22 A trader implements a duration-neutral strategy that consists in buying a cheap bond and selling a rich bond. This is the rich and cheap bond strategy. Today, the rich and cheap bonds have the following characteristics:

Bond	Coupon (%)	Maturity (years)	YTM (%)
Rich	5	10	7.50
Cheap	5.5	12	7.75

Coupon frequency and compounding frequency are assumed to be annual. Face value is $100 for the two bonds.

Compute the BPV of the two bonds and find the hedge position.

6

Beyond Duration

Duration hedging is very simple. However, one should be aware that the method is based upon the following, very restrictive, assumptions:

- *It is explicitly assumed that the value of the portfolio could be approximated by its first-order Taylor expansion. This assumption is all the more critical, as the changes in interest rates are larger. In other words, the method relies on the assumption of small yield-to-maturity changes. This is why the hedge portfolio should be readjusted reasonably often.*

- *It is also assumed that the yield curve is only affected by parallel shifts. In other words, the interest-rate risk is simply considered as a risk on the general level of interest rates.*

In this chapter,[1] we attempt to relax both assumptions to account for more realistic changes in the term structure of interest rates.

6.1 Relaxing the Assumption of a Small Shift

We have argued in Chapter 5 that $duration provides a convenient way to estimate the impact of a *small* change dy in yield on the value of a bond or a bond portfolio. We take the same notations as in Chapter 5.

6.1.1 Using a Second-Order Taylor Expansion

Duration hedging only works for small yield changes, because the price of a bond as a function of yield is nonlinear. In other words, the $duration of a bond changes as its yield changes. When a portfolio manager expects a potentially large shift in the term structure, a convexity term should be introduced. The price approximation can be improved if one can account for such nonlinearity by explicitly introducing a convexity term. Let us take the following example to illustrate this point.

> **Example 6.1** We consider a 10-year maturity and 6% annual coupon bond traded at par. Coupon frequency and compounding frequency are assumed to be annual. Its modified duration is equal to 7.36. We assume that the yield to maturity goes suddenly from 6 to 8% and we reprice the bond after this large change:
>
> - *The new price of the bond, obtained by discounting its future cash flows, is equal to $86.58, and the exact change in value amounts to −$13.42 (= $86.58 − $100).*
>
> - *Using a first-order Taylor expansion, the change in value is approximated by −$14.72 (= −$100 × 7.36 × 0.02); so we overestimate the decrease in price by $1.30.*

---

[1]Some parts of this chapter first appeared in the Journal of Bond Trading and Management. See Martellini *et al.* (2002b).

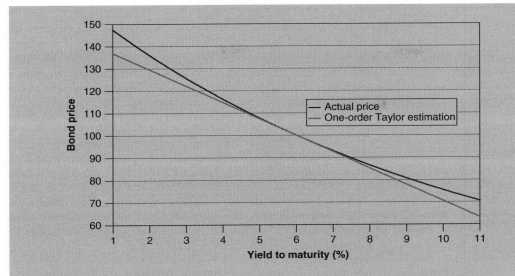

Figure 6.1 The convexity of the bond price.

We conclude that the first-order Taylor expansion gives a good approximation of the bond price change only when the variation of its yield to maturity is small. Figure 6.1 illustrates graphically this point by showing that the relationship between the bond price and its yield to maturity is nonlinear but convex.

If one is concerned about the impact of a larger move dy on a bond portfolio value, one needs to write (at least) a second-order version of the Taylor expansion:

$$dP(y) = P'(y)dy + \frac{1}{2}P''(y)(dy)^2 + o((dy)^2)$$

$$\simeq \$Dur(P(y))dy + \frac{1}{2}\$Conv(P(y))(dy)^2 \qquad (6.1)$$

where

$$P''(y) = \sum_{i=1}^{m} \frac{(t_i - t)(t_i - t + 1)F_i}{[1 + y_t]^{t_i - t + 2}}$$

the second derivative of the bond value function with respect to yield to maturity, also denoted by $\$Conv(P(y))$ is known as the $convexity of the bond P.

Dividing equation (6.1) by $P(y)$, we obtain an approximation of the *relative* change in the value of the portfolio as

$$\frac{dP(y)}{P(y)} \simeq -MD(P(y))dy + \frac{1}{2}RC(P(y))(dy)^2$$

where

$$RC(P(y)) = \frac{P''(y)}{P(y)}$$

is called the *(relative) convexity* of portfolio P.

We now reconsider the previous example and approximate the bond price change by using equation (6.1). The bond convexity is equal to 69.74 and the bond price change is now approximated by $-\$13.33$ ($= -\$14.72 + (\$100 \times 69.74 \times 0.02^2/2)$). We conclude that the second-order approximation is well suited for large interest-rate deviations.

Example 6.2   \$Convexity and Convexity

The \$convexity and the (relative) convexity of a bond with price P are very useful for practitioners because they provide the absolute and the relative change in price due to convexity for a change in the yield to maturity y (for example, 50 bps or 0.5% as expressed in percentage).

Consider a bond with the following features:

- *maturity: 10 years*

- *coupon rate: 6%*

- *YTM: 5% (or price: $107.72)*

Coupon frequency and compounding frequency are assumed to be annual.

The \$convexity of this bond is equal to 7,774.68 as the (relative) convexity is equal to 72.17. If the YTM increases or decreases by 0.5%, the bondholder will obtain an absolute gain due to convexity, expressed in $ equal to

$$absolute\ gain\ due\ to\ convexity = \$7{,}774.68 \times (0.5\%)^2/2 = \$0.097$$

The relative gain due to convexity expressed in percentage is

$$relative\ gain\ due\ to\ convexity = 72.17 \times (0.5\%)^2/2 = 0.09\%$$

Remark 6.1   \$Convexity and Convexity of a Bond with Semiannual Payments

Considering the price of a bond with semiannual payments given by equation (5.3), we obtain the following expression for $P''(y)$, which is the second derivative of the bond price with respect to the yield to maturity y:

$$P''(y) = \sum_{i=1}^{m} \frac{(t_i - t) \times [(t_i - t) + 1/2] \times F_i}{\left[1 + \frac{y_t}{2}\right]^{2(t_i - t) + 2}}$$

We now consider the same bond as in the previous example (maturity $= 10$ years; coupon rate $= 6\%$; YTM $= 5\%$) except that coupon frequency and compounding frequency are now assumed to be semiannual.

The price, \$convexity and convexity of this bond are equal to $107.79, 7615.63 and 70.65, respectively.

6.1.2 Properties of Convexity

The main properties of the convexity and $convexity measures are as follows:

1. *For a given bond, the change in value due to the convexity term is always positive.*

2. *Holding the maturity and the YTM of a bond constant, the lower the coupon rate, the higher its convexity and the lower its $convexity.*

3. *Holding the coupon rate and the YTM of a bond constant, its convexity and $convexity increase with its time to maturity.*

4. *Holding other factors constant, the convexity and $convexity of a coupon bond are higher when the bond's yield to maturity is lower.*

Example 6.3 To illustrate points 2, 3 and 4, we consider a base-case bond with maturity 10 years, a 6% coupon rate, a 6% YTM and a $100 face value. Coupon frequency and compounding frequency are assumed to be annual.

Holding the maturity and the YTM of this bond constant, we give different values to the coupon rate. We can see clearly that the lower the coupon rate, the higher the convexity and the lower the $convexity.

Coupon rate (%)	Convexity	$Convexity
3	79.83	6,220.35
4	75.89	6,471.58
5	72.57	6,722.81
6	69.74	6,974.04
7	67.30	7,225.27
8	65.17	7,476.50
9	63.3	7,727.73

Holding the coupon rate and the YTM of this bond constant, we give different values to maturity. We can see clearly that the higher the maturity, the higher the convexity and the $convexity.

Maturity (years)	Convexity	$Convexity
7	39.68	3,968.31
8	49.15	4,915.35
9	59.20	5,920.46
10	69.74	6,974.04
11	80.67	8,067.37
12	91.93	9,192.59
13	103.43	10,342.57

Holding the maturity and the coupon rate of this bond constant, we give different values to YTM. We can see clearly that the lower the YTM, the higher the convexity and the $convexity.

YTM (%)	Convexity	$Convexity
3	77.22	9,698.02
4	74.67	8,677.86
5	72.17	7,774.68
6	69.74	6,974.04
7	67.37	6,263.42
8	65.05	5,631.91
9	62.79	5,070.04

5. *Another convenient property of convexity is that it is a linear operator. In other words, the convexity of a portfolio P invested in n bonds denominated in the same currency with weights w_i is the weighted average of each bond's convexity:*

$$RC_p = \sum_{i=1}^{n} w_i RC_i \qquad (6.2)$$

Remark 6.2   Duration, Modified Duration and Convexity of a Portfolio of Bonds When the Curve is Nonflat

As for duration and modified duration, this property of linearity is only true in the context of a flat curve. When the YTM curve is no longer flat, this property becomes false and may only be used as an approximation of the true convexity. This point is illustrated in the following example.

Consider three bonds with the following features:

	Price ($)	Coupon rate (%)	Maturity (years)	YTM (%)	Duration	MD	Convexity
Bond 1	100	5	2	5	1.952	1.859	5.269
Bond 2	91.773	5	7	6.5	6.029	5.661	40.354
Bond 3	77.932	5	15	7.5	10.286	9.568	123.808

Coupon frequency and compounding frequency are assumed to be annual.

Now we create a bond portfolio with a unit quantity of each of these three bonds and we want to know the modified duration and the convexity of this portfolio. We first use the weighted average of the bond's duration, modified duration and convexity as in equations (5.7 and 6.2), which is an approximation of the real values. Real values are calculated by searching for the

YTM of the portfolio and then using the standard formula of duration, modified duration and convexity. The YTM of the bond portfolio is equal to 6.844%.

Results are given in the following table:

	Duration	MD	Convexity
Approximation	5.747	5.38	51.46
True method	5.925	5.545	54.594
Absolute difference	−0.178	−0.165	−3.134
Difference in %	−3%	−2.98%	−5.74%

Using approximation in this example, we can see that we underestimate the duration by 3%, the modified duration by 2.98% and the convexity by 5.74%.

6.1.3 Hedging Method

One needs to introduce two hedging assets with prices in \$ denoted by H_1 and H_2, and YTM by y_1 and y_2, respectively, in order to hedge at the first and second order, the interest-rate risk of a portfolio with price in \$ denoted by P, and YTM by y. The goal is to obtain a portfolio that is both \$duration-neutral and \$convexity-neutral. The optimal quantity (ϕ_1, ϕ_2) of these two assets to hold is then given by the solution to the following system of equations, at each date, assuming that $dy = dy_1 = dy_2$:

$$\begin{cases} \phi_1 H_1'(y_1) + \phi_2 H_2'(y_2) = -P'(y) \\ \phi_1 H_1''(y_1) + \phi_2 H_2''(y_2) = -P''(y) \end{cases}$$

which translates into

$$\begin{cases} \phi_1 \$Dur(H_1(y_1)) + \phi_2 \$Dur(H_2(y_2)) = -\$Dur(P(y)) \\ \phi_1 \$Conv(H_1(y_1)) + \phi_2 \$Conv(H_2(y_2)) = -\$Conv(P(y)) \end{cases} \quad (6.3)$$

or

$$\begin{cases} \phi_1 H_1(y_1)MD(H_1(y_1)) + \phi_2 H_2(y_2)MD(H_2(y_2)) = -P(y)MD(P(y)) \\ \phi_1 H_1(y_1)RC(H_1(y_1)) + \phi_2 H_2(y_2)RC(H_2(y_2)) = -P(y)RC(P(y)) \end{cases}$$

Example 6.4 Modified Duration/Convexity Bond Portfolio Hedge

At date t, the portfolio to be hedged is a Treasury-bond portfolio with bonds with various possible maturities. Its characteristics are given by

Price	YTM	MD	Convexity
\$32,863,500	5.143%	6.76	85.329

Fixed Income Securities

We consider Treasury bonds as hedging assets, and at date t we force the hedging portfolio to have the opposite value of the portfolio to be hedged. Because of this additional restriction, we need the number of hedging assets to be equal to three. They have the following features:

Asset	Price ($)	Coupon rate (%)	Maturity date (years)	YTM (%)	MD	Convexity
Asset 1	108.038	7	3	4.098	2.705	10.168
Asset 2	118.786	8	7	4.779	5.486	38.962
Asset 3	97.962	5	12	5.233	8.813	99.081

We then are looking for the quantities ϕ_1, ϕ_2 and ϕ_3 of each of the hedging assets 1, 2, 3 as solutions to the following linear system (see equation (6.3)[2]):

$$\begin{pmatrix} \phi_1 \\ \phi_2 \\ \phi_3 \end{pmatrix} = \begin{pmatrix} 108.038 & 118.786 & 97.962 \\ -292.231 & -651.669 & -863.372 \\ 1098.574 & 4628.157 & 9706.147 \end{pmatrix}^{-1} \begin{pmatrix} -32,863,500 \\ 222,157,260 \\ -2,804,209,592 \end{pmatrix} = \begin{pmatrix} -330,991 \\ 381,941 \\ -433,568 \end{pmatrix}$$

6.2 Relaxing the Assumption of a Parallel Shift

6.2.1 A Common Principle

A major shortcoming of single-factor models is that they imply that all possible zero-coupon rates are perfectly correlated, making bonds redundant assets. We know, however, that rates with different maturities do not always change in the same way. In particular, long-term rates tend to be less volatile than short-term rates. An empirical analysis of the dynamics of the interest-rate term structure shows that two or three factors account for most of the yield-curve changes. They can be interpreted, respectively, as level, slope and curvature factors (see Chapter 3). This strongly suggests that a multifactor approach should be used for pricing and hedging fixed-income securities.

There are different ways to generalize the above method to account for nonparallel deformations of the term structure. The common principle behind all techniques is the following. Let us express the price in $ of the portfolio using the whole curve of zero-coupon rates, where we now make explicit the time-dependency of the variables:

$$P_t = \sum_{i=1}^{m} \frac{F_i}{(1 + R(t, t_i - t))^{t_i - t}}$$

Hence, we consider P_t to be a function of the zero-coupon rates $R(t, t_i - t)$, which will be denoted by R_t^i in this section for simplicity of exposition. The risk factor is the yield curve as a whole,

---

[2]The first equation of the system guarantees that the value of the hedging portfolio is the opposite of the portfolio to be hedged.

represented *a priori* by m components, as opposed to a single variable, the yield to maturity y. The whole point is to narrow down this number of factors in the least arbitrary way. The starting point is, as usual, a (second-order) Taylor expansion of the portfolio value. We treat this as a function of different variables $P_t = P(R_t^1, \dots, R_t^m)$:

$$dP_t \simeq \sum_{i=1}^m \frac{\partial P_t}{\partial R_t^i} dR_t^i + \frac{1}{2} \sum_{i,i'=1}^m \frac{\partial^2 P_t}{\partial R_t^i \partial R_t^{i'}} dR_t^i dR_t^{i'}$$

If we merely consider the first-order terms, then we get

$$dP_t \simeq \sum_{i=1}^m \frac{\partial P_t}{\partial R_t^i} dR_t^i$$

Let us further assume that the investor is willing to use as many hedging assets, with price in \$ denoted by H^j, as there are different risk factors, which is m in this case. This assumption is quite restrictive because, as we have already said, it is not very convenient, and may prove to be very expensive, to use more than a few hedging assets, and will be relaxed below. The price of each of these hedging assets will obviously also be a function of the different rates R_t^i. This is precisely why we may use them as hedging assets! So we have for $j = 1, \dots, m$

$$dH_t^j \simeq \sum_{i=1}^m \frac{\partial H_t^j}{\partial R_t^i} dR_t^i$$

Then we construct our global hedge portfolio

$$P_t^* = P_t + \sum_{j=1}^m \phi_t^j H_t^j$$

such that, up to the first order,

$$dP_t^* = 0$$

We have

$$dP_t^* \simeq \sum_{i=1}^m \frac{\partial P_t}{\partial R_t^i} dR_t^i + \sum_{j=1}^m \phi_t^j \sum_{i=1}^m \frac{\partial H_t^j}{\partial R_t^i} dR_t^i$$

or equivalently

$$dP_t^* \simeq \sum_{i=1}^m \left(\frac{\partial P_t}{\partial R_t^i} + \sum_{j=1}^m \phi_t^j \frac{\partial H_t^j}{\partial R_t^i} \right) dR_t^i$$

A sufficient and necessary condition to have $dP_t^* = 0$ up to a first-order approximation for any set of (small) variations dR_t^i is, to take for any i,

$$\frac{\partial P_t}{\partial R_t^i} + \sum_{j=1}^m \phi_t^j \frac{\partial H_t^j}{\partial R_t^i} = 0$$

Solving this linear system for ϕ_t^j, $j = 1, \dots, m$ at each trading date gives the optimal hedging strategy.

If we now denote

$$H'_t = \left(\frac{\partial H_t^j}{\partial R_t^i}\right)_{\substack{i=1,\dots,m \\ j=1,\dots,m}} = \begin{pmatrix} \dfrac{\partial H_t^1}{\partial R_t^1} & \cdots & \dfrac{\partial H_t^m}{\partial R_t^1} \\ \vdots & & \vdots \\ \dfrac{\partial H_t^1}{\partial R_t^m} & \cdots & \dfrac{\partial H_t^m}{\partial R_t^m} \end{pmatrix} ; \Phi_t = \begin{pmatrix} \phi_t^1 \\ \vdots \\ \phi_t^m \end{pmatrix} \text{ and } P'_t = \begin{pmatrix} -\dfrac{\partial P_t}{\partial R_t^1} \\ \vdots \\ -\dfrac{\partial P_t}{\partial R_t^m} \end{pmatrix}$$

then we finally have the following system:

$$H'_t \cdot \Phi_t = P'_t$$

The solution is given by

$$\Phi_t = (H'_t)^{-1} \cdot P'_t$$

if we further assume that the matrix H'_t is invertible, which means that no hedging asset price may be a linear combination of the other $m - 1$.

Remark 6.3   Cross-Hedge Risk

It sometimes happens that the value of the hedging assets may depend on risk factors slightly different from those affecting the hedged portfolio. This is called *correlation risk* or *cross-hedge risk*. Let us assume for the sake of simplicity that there is only one risk factor, which we denote by R_t. We write

$$P_t = P(R_t) \text{ and } H_t = H(R'_t)$$

where R'_t is *a priori* (slightly) different from R_t. A priori one should always try to minimize that difference. The question is: once the hedging asset has been selected, what can be done *a posteriori* to improve the hedge efficiency? We have

$$dP_t^* \simeq \frac{\partial P_t}{\partial R_t} dR_t + \phi_t \frac{\partial H_t}{\partial R'_t} dR'_t$$

In that case, the usual prescription

$$\phi_t = -\frac{\dfrac{\partial P_t}{\partial R_t}}{\dfrac{\partial H_t}{\partial R'_t}}$$

will fail to apply successfully because dR'_t may be different from dR_t, which is precisely what *correlation risk* is all about. One may handle the situation in the following way. Let us first consider the convenient situation in which one could express R'_t as some function of R_t:

$$R'_t = f(R_t)$$

In that case, we have

$$dP_t^* \simeq \frac{\partial P_t}{\partial R_t} dR_t + \phi_t \frac{\partial H_t}{\partial R'_t} f'(R_t) dR_t$$

Then

$$dP_t^* \simeq 0 \Longleftrightarrow \phi_t = -\dfrac{\dfrac{\partial P_t}{\partial R_t}}{\dfrac{\partial H_t}{\partial R_t'} f'(R_t)}$$

Hence, we may keep the usual prescription provided we amend it in order to account for the sensitivity of one factor with respect to the other. Unfortunately, it is not generally possible to express R_t' as a function of R_t. However, a satisfying solution may be found using a statistical estimation of the function $f(R_t)$. We may, for example, assume a simple linear relationship:[3]

$$R_t' = f(R_t) = aR_t + b + \varepsilon_t$$

where ε_t is the usual error term, and the parameters are estimated using standard statistical tools. Then, taking the error term equal to zero, we get

$$dR_t' = df(R_t) = adR_t$$

Hence, we should amend the hedge ratio in the following way:

$$\phi_t = -\dfrac{\dfrac{\partial P_t}{\partial R_t}}{\dfrac{\partial H_t}{\partial R_t'} a}$$

Of course, the method is as accurate as the quality of the approximation (measured through the squared correlation factor). This will change the hedging strategy and improve the efficiency of the method in the case when a is significantly different from 1.

Example 6.5 A portfolio manager invests a nominal amount of $50,000,000 in a bond A whose gross price (in % of the nominal amount) and modified duration are, respectively, 93.274 and 8.319. He fears a rate increase and wants to protect his investment. Suppose that the hedging instrument is a bond B whose gross price (in % of the nominal amount) and modified duration are, respectively, 105.264 and 7.04. Its nominal amount is $1,000.

We suppose that changes in yields are not equal and that the relationship between the yield to maturity of bond A denoted by y_A and the yield to maturity of bond B denoted by y_B is equal to

$$\Delta y_A \simeq 1.18 \times \Delta y_B$$

---

[3] Because of cointegration and nonstationarity of the series, it is better to consider a linear relationship in variations rather than in level. We should write

$$dR_t' = a \, dR_t + b + \varepsilon_t$$

For example, a 10-bp move of the yield y_B will be accompanied by a 1.18×10 bps $= 11.8$ bps change in the yield y_A.

We find the number n of units of bond B that the investor has to sell as given by the following ratio

$$n = \frac{8.319 \times 93.274 \times 50,000,000}{7.04 \times 105.264 \times 1,000} \times 1.18 = 61,777.6$$

The investor has to sell 61,778 units of bond B.

In practice, one should consider a more realistic case, namely, a situation in which the hedger does not want to use as many hedging assets as there are different risk factors. The principle is invariably to aggregate the risks in the most sensible way. There is actually a systematic method to do so using results from a principal components analysis (PCA) of the interest-rate variations, as will be explained now. This is the state-of-the-art technique for dynamic interest-rate hedging.

6.2.2 Regrouping Risk Factors through a Principal Component Analysis

The purpose of PCA is to explain the behavior of observed variables using a smaller set of unobserved implied variables. From a mathematical standpoint, it consists of transforming a set of m correlated variables into a reduced set of orthogonal variables that reproduces the original information present in the correlation structure. This tool can yield interesting results, especially for the pricing and risk management of correlated positions. Using PCA with historical zero-coupon rate curves (both from the Treasury and Interbank markets), one can observe that the first three principal components of spot curve changes explain the main part of the return variations on fixed-income securities over time (see Chapter 3 on this point where we detail the method and summarize the results of some studies on the topic of PCA of interest curves led both by academics and practitioners).

These three factors, namely, level, slope and curvature, are believed to drive interest-rate dynamics and can be formulated in terms of interest-rate shocks, which can be used to compute principal component durations.

We express the change $\Delta R(t, \theta_i) = R(t + dt, \theta_i) - R(t, \theta_i)$ of the zero-coupon rate $R(t, \theta_i)$ with maturity θ_i at date t such that

$$\Delta R(t, \theta_i) = \sum_{l=1}^{p<m} c_{li} C_t^l + \varepsilon_{ti} \tag{6.4}$$

where c_{li} is the sensitivity of the ith variable to the lth factor defined as

$$\frac{\Delta(\Delta R(t, \theta_i))}{\Delta(C_t^l)} = c_{li}$$

which amounts to individually applying a, say, 1% variation to each factor, and computing the absolute sensitivity of each zero-coupon yield curve with respect to that unit variation. These sensitivities are commonly called the *principal component $durations*.

C_t^l is the value of the *l*th factor at date t, and ε_{ti} is the residual part of $\Delta R(t, \theta_i)$ that is not explained by the factor model.

One can easily see why this method has become popular. Its main achievement is that it allows for the reduction of the number of risk factors without losing much information, that is, to proceed in the least possible arbitrary way. Since these three factors (parallel movement, slope oscillation and curvature), regarded as risk factors, explain most of the variance in interest-rate variations, we can now use just three hedging assets. We now write the change in the value of a fixed-income portfolio as

$$\Delta P_t^* \simeq \sum_{i=1}^m \left(\frac{\partial P_t}{\partial R(t, \theta_i)} + \sum_{j=1}^3 \phi_t^j \frac{\partial H_t^j}{\partial R(t, \theta_i)} \right) \Delta R(t, \theta_i)$$

We then use $\Delta R(t, \theta_i) \simeq \sum_{l=1}^3 c_{li} C_t^l$ to obtain

$$\Delta P_t^* \simeq \sum_{i=1}^m \left(\left(\frac{\partial P_t}{\partial R(t, \theta_i)} + \sum_{j=1}^3 \phi_t^j \frac{\partial H_t^j}{\partial R(t, \theta_i)} \right) \sum_{l=1}^3 c_{li} C_t^l \right)$$

or

$$dP_t^* \simeq \sum_{i=1}^m \left(c_{1i} \frac{\partial P_t}{\partial R(t, \theta_i)} + \sum_{j=1}^3 \phi_t^j c_{1i} \frac{\partial H_t^j}{\partial R(t, \theta_i)} \right) C_t^1$$

$$+ \sum_{i=1}^m \left(c_{2i} \frac{\partial P_t}{\partial R(t, \theta_i)} + \sum_{j=1}^3 \phi_t^j c_{2i} \frac{\partial H_t^j}{\partial R(t, \theta_i)} \right) C_t^2$$

$$+ \sum_{i=1}^m \left(c_{3i} \frac{\partial P_t}{\partial R(t, \theta_i)} + \sum_{j=1}^3 \phi_t^j c_{3i} \frac{\partial H_t^j}{\partial R(t, \theta_i)} \right) C_t^3$$

The quantity $\sum_{i=1}^m \left(c_{1i} \frac{\partial P_t}{\partial R(t, \theta_i)} + \sum_{j=1}^3 \phi_t^j c_{1i} \frac{\partial H_t^j}{\partial R(t, \theta_i)} \right)$ is commonly called the *principal component \$duration* of portfolio P^* with respect to factor 1.

If we want to set the (first-order) variations in the hedged portfolio P_t^* to zero for any possible evolution of the interest rates $\Delta R(t, \theta_i)$, or equivalently for any possible evolution of the C_t^l, a sufficient condition for this is to take

$$\sum_{i=1}^m \left(c_{li} \frac{\partial P_t}{\partial R(t, \theta_i)} + \sum_{j=1}^3 \phi_t^j c_{li} \frac{\partial H_t^j}{\partial R(t, \theta_i)} \right) = 0 \quad \text{for } l = 1, 2, 3 \qquad (6.5)$$

that is, neutral principal component \$durations.

Finally, on each possible date, we are left with three unknowns ϕ_t^j and three linear equations. The system may be represented in the following way. Let us introduce

$$H_t' = \begin{pmatrix} \sum_{i=1}^{m} c_{1i} \frac{\partial H_t^1}{\partial R(t,\theta_i)} & \sum_{i=1}^{m} c_{1i} \frac{\partial H_t^2}{\partial R(t,\theta_i)} & \sum_{i=1}^{m} c_{1i} \frac{\partial H_t^3}{\partial R(t,\theta_i)} \\ \sum_{i=1}^{m} c_{2i} \frac{\partial H_t^1}{\partial R(t,\theta_i)} & \sum_{i=1}^{m} c_{2i} \frac{\partial H_t^2}{\partial R(t,\theta_i)} & \sum_{i=1}^{m} c_{2i} \frac{\partial H_t^3}{\partial R(t,\theta_i)} \\ \sum_{i=1}^{m} c_{3i} \frac{\partial H_t^1}{\partial R(t,\theta_i)} & \sum_{i=1}^{m} c_{3i} \frac{\partial H_t^2}{\partial R(t,\theta_i)} & \sum_{i=1}^{m} c_{3i} \frac{\partial H_t^3}{\partial R(t,\theta_i)} \end{pmatrix} ; \Phi_t = \begin{pmatrix} \phi_t^1 \\ \phi_t^2 \\ \phi_t^3 \end{pmatrix} ; P_t' = \begin{pmatrix} -\sum_{i=1}^{m} c_{1i} \frac{\partial P_t}{\partial R(t,\theta_i)} \\ -\sum_{i=1}^{m} c_{2i} \frac{\partial P_t}{\partial R(t,\theta_i)} \\ -\sum_{i=1}^{m} c_{3i} \frac{\partial P_t}{\partial R(t,\theta_i)} \end{pmatrix}$$

We then have the following system:

$$H_t' \cdot \Phi_t = P_t'$$

The solution is given by

$$\Phi_t = (H_t')^{-1} \cdot P_t'$$

In the following example, we show how PCA can be applied to hedging a bond portfolio.

Example 6.6 We now discuss how one may use a PCA of the yield curve changes for hedging purposes. At date t, the portfolio to be hedged P_t contains a set of Treasury bonds with various maturities. The price P_t of that portfolio at date t is given by

$$P_t = \sum_{i=1}^{m} F_{t+\theta_i} B(t, t+\theta_i) = \sum_{i=1}^{m} \frac{F_{t+\theta_i}}{(1 + R(t, \theta_i))^{\theta_i}}$$

where $(F_{t+\theta_i})_{i=1,\dots,m}$ are the cash flows of portfolio P to be received at dates $t+\theta_i$, $B(t, t+\theta_i)$ are the discount factors at date t for maturities $t+\theta_i$, and $R(t, \theta_i)$ are the corresponding zero-coupon rates. We obtain the portfolio value change ΔP_t between dates t and $t+1$:

$$\Delta P_t = P_{t+1} - P_t = \sum_{i=1}^{m} \frac{\partial P_t}{\partial R(t, \theta_i)} \Delta R(t, \theta_i) = \sum_{i=1}^{m} \left(\frac{-\theta_i F_{t+\theta_i}}{(1 + R(t, \theta_i))^{\theta_i+1}} \right) \Delta R(t, \theta_i)$$

Using the factor representation given by equation (6.4), we obtain

$$\Delta P_t = \sum_{i=1}^{m} \left(\frac{-\theta_i F_{t+\theta_i}}{(1 + R(t, \theta_i))^{\theta_i+1}} \right) \Delta R(t, \theta_i) \approx \sum_{i=1}^{m} \left(\frac{-\theta_i F_{t+\theta_i}}{(1 + R(t, \theta_i))^{\theta_i+1}} \right) \left(\sum_{l=1}^{p} c_{li} C_t^l \right)$$

We only hedge the first three factors so that we obtain

$$\Delta P_t = -\sum_{l=1}^{3} \left(\sum_{i=1}^{m} c_{li} \left(\frac{\theta_i F_{t+\theta_i}}{(1 + R(t, \theta_i))^{\theta_i+1}} \right) \right) C_t^l = -\sum_{l=1}^{3} \left(\sum_{i=1}^{m} \beta_{li} \right) C_t^l = -\sum_{l=1}^{3} \beta_l^P C_t^l$$

Let us consider at date t, the hedging portfolio H_t containing assets with price H_t^j and quantities ϕ_t^j. Given the self-financing constraint, the hedging portfolio contains four assets. Using a similar reasoning as above, the variation in the hedging portfolio value ΔH_t is given by

$$\Delta H_t = -\sum_{j=1}^{4} \sum_{l=1}^{3} \phi_t^j \beta_l^{H_t^j} C_t^l$$

The idea is to set the sensitivity of the global portfolio to zero (when the global portfolio is the portfolio to be hedged plus the hedging portfolio) with respect to the factors C_t^l. A sufficient condition for this is (where the global portfolio value is zero at date t)

$$\begin{cases} \Delta P_t + \Delta H_t = 0 \\ P_t + H_t = 0 \end{cases}$$

or

$$\begin{cases} -\sum_{l=1}^{3} \left(\beta_l^P + \sum_{j=1}^{4} \phi_t^j \beta_l^{H^j} \right) C_t^l = 0 \\ P_t + H_t = 0 \end{cases}$$

that is

$$\begin{cases} \beta_l^P + \sum_{j=1}^{4} \phi_t^j \beta_l^{H^j} = 0 \quad \forall l = 1, 2, 3 \\ P_t + H_t = 0 \end{cases}$$

This system is similar to the one given in equation (6.5), subject to the fact that we have included the self-financing constraint $P_t + H_t = 0$. The quantities ϕ_t^j to hold in the hedging assets are the solutions to that linear system.

In practice, we need to estimate the principal component \$durations used at date t. They are derived from a PCA performed on a period prior to t, for example, $[t - 3 \text{ months}, t]$. Hence, the result of the method is strongly sample-dependent. In fact, and for estimation purposes, it is more convenient to use some functional specification for the zero-coupon yield curve that is consistent with results from a PCA.

6.2.3 Hedging Using a Three-Factor Model of the Yield Curve

The idea here consists of using a model for the zero-coupon rate function. We detail below the Nelson and Siegel (1987) as well as the extended Nelson–Siegel [or Svensson (1994)] models. One can also alternatively use the Vasicek (1977) model, the Extended Vasicek model, or the CIR (1985) model, among others.[4]

Nelson–Siegel and Svensson Models

Nelson and Siegel (1987) have suggested to model the continuously compounded zero-coupon rate $R^c(0, \theta)$ as

$$R^c(0, \theta) = \beta_0 + \beta_1 \left[\frac{1 - \exp\left(-\dfrac{\theta}{\tau_1}\right)}{\dfrac{\theta}{\tau_1}} \right] + \beta_2 \left[\frac{1 - \exp\left(-\dfrac{\theta}{\tau_1}\right)}{\dfrac{\theta}{\tau_1}} - \exp\left(-\dfrac{\theta}{\tau_1}\right) \right]$$

[4] See Chapters 4 and 12 for details about these zero-coupon functions.

Fixed Income Securities

a form that was later extended by Svensson (1994) as

$$R^c(0, \theta) = \beta_0 + \beta_1 \left[\frac{1 - \exp\left(-\dfrac{\theta}{\tau_1}\right)}{\dfrac{\theta}{\tau_1}} \right] + \beta_2 \left[\frac{1 - \exp\left(-\dfrac{\theta}{\tau_1}\right)}{\dfrac{\theta}{\tau_1}} - \exp\left(-\dfrac{\theta}{\tau_1}\right) \right]$$

$$+ \beta_3 \left[\frac{1 - \exp\left(-\dfrac{\theta}{\tau_2}\right)}{\dfrac{\theta}{\tau_2}} - \exp\left(-\dfrac{\theta}{\tau_2}\right) \right]$$

where

$R^c(0, \theta)$ is the continuously compounded zero-coupon rate at time zero with maturity θ;

β_0 is the limit of $R^c(0, \theta)$ as θ goes to infinity. In practice, β_0 should be regarded as a long-term interest rate;

β_1 is the limit of $R^c(0, \theta) - \beta_0$ as θ goes to 0. In practice, β_1 should be regarded as the long- to short-term spread;

β_2 and β_3 are curvature parameters;

τ_1 and τ_2 are scale parameters that measure the rate at which the short-term and medium-term components decay to zero.

As shown by Svensson (1994), the extended form allows for more flexibility in yield-curve estimation, in particular at the short-term end of the curve, because it allows for more complex shapes such as U-shaped and hump-shaped curves. The parameters β_0, β_1, β_2 and β_3 are estimated daily by using an OLS (Ordinary Least Squares) optimization program, which consists, for a basket of bonds, in minimizing the sum of the squared spreads between the market price and the theoretical price of the bonds as obtained with the model (see Chapter 4 for more details).

We can see that the evolution of the zero-coupon rate $R^c(t, \theta)$ is entirely driven by the evolution of the beta parameters, the scale parameters being fixed. In an attempt to hedge a bond, for example, one should build a global portfolio with the bond and a hedging instrument, so that the global portfolio achieves a neutral sensitivity to each of the beta parameters. Before the method can be implemented, one therefore needs to compute the sensitivities of any arbitrary portfolio of bonds to each of the beta parameters.

Consider a bond that delivers principal or coupon and principal denoted by F_i at dates θ_i. Its price in \$ at date $t = 0$, denoted by P_0, is given by the following formula:

$$P_0 = \sum_i F_i\, e^{-\theta_i R^c(0, \theta_i)}$$

In the Nelson and Siegel (1987) and Svensson (1994) models, we can calculate at date $t = 0$, the \$durations $D_i = \frac{\partial P_0}{\partial \beta_i}$ for $i = 0, 1, 2, 3$ of the bond P to the parameters β_0, β_1, β_2 and β_3. They are given by the following formulas:[5]

---

[5]Of course, \$duration D_3 is only obtained in the Svensson (1994) model.

$$
\begin{cases}
D_0 = -\sum_i \theta_i F_i e^{-\theta_i R^c(0,\theta_i)} \\[2ex]
D_1 = -\sum_i \theta_i \left[\dfrac{1 - \exp\left(-\dfrac{\theta_i}{\tau_1}\right)}{\dfrac{\theta_i}{\tau_1}} \right] F_i e^{-\theta_i R^c(0,\theta_i)} \\[3ex]
D_2 = -\sum_i \theta_i \left[\dfrac{1 - \exp\left(-\dfrac{\theta_i}{\tau_1}\right)}{\dfrac{\theta_i}{\tau_1}} - \exp\left(-\dfrac{\theta_i}{\tau_1}\right) \right] F_i e^{-\theta_i R^c(0,\theta_i)} \\[3ex]
D_3 = -\sum_i \theta_i \left[\dfrac{1 - \exp\left(-\dfrac{\theta_i}{\tau_2}\right)}{\dfrac{\theta_i}{\tau_2}} - \exp\left(-\dfrac{\theta_i}{\tau_2}\right) \right] F_i e^{-\theta_i R^c(0,\theta_i)}
\end{cases}
\tag{6.6}
$$

We provide below an example where we compute the level, slope and curvature \$durations of a bond portfolio with the Nelson and Siegel (1987) model.

Example 6.7   Computing the Level, Slope and Curvature \$Durations of a Portfolio of Bonds with the Nelson and Siegel Model

At date $t = 0$, the values of the parameters are as follows:

β_0	β_1	β_2	τ_1
8%	−3%	−1%	3

We consider three bonds with the following features (coupon frequency is annual), and calculate the \$durations using equations (6.6). We also calculate the same \$durations for a portfolio composed of one unit of bond 1, bond 2 and bond 3:

	Maturity (years)	Coupon (%)	Price ($)	D_0	D_1	D_2
Bond 1	2	5	98.627	−192.51	−141.08	−41.28
Bond 2	7	5	90.786	−545.42	−224.78	−156.73
Bond 3	15	5	79.606	−812.61	−207.2	−173.03
Portfolio	—	—	269.019	−1,550.54	−573.06	−371.04

We can very simply interpret the beta sensitivities. For example, D_0, which is called the \$level duration (or \$$\beta_0$ duration), means that for a 1% increase of the β_0 parameter, the price of bond 1 (in our example) will decrease by $1.9251 (−192.51 × 1%). Besides, we note that the beta sensitivities of a bond portfolio are equal to the sum of the beta sensitivities of each bond weighted by the number of each bond present in the portfolio.

Hedging Method

The idea of the hedge in the Svensson (1994) model is to create a global portfolio with the bond portfolio to be hedged, whose price in $ is denoted by P, and four hedging instruments, whose prices in $ are denoted by G_i for $i = 1, 2, 3$ and 4, and to make it neutral to changes in parameters $\beta_0, \beta_1, \beta_2$ and β_3.

We therefore look for the quantities q_1, q_2, q_3 and q_4 to invest, respectively, in the four hedging instruments G_1, G_2, G_3 and G_4, which satisfy the following linear system:

$$\begin{cases} q_1 \dfrac{\partial G_1}{\partial \beta_0} + q_2 \dfrac{\partial G_2}{\partial \beta_0} + q_3 \dfrac{\partial G_3}{\partial \beta_0} + q_4 \dfrac{\partial G_4}{\partial \beta_0} = -D_0 \\[2mm] q_1 \dfrac{\partial G_1}{\partial \beta_1} + q_2 \dfrac{\partial G_2}{\partial \beta_1} + q_3 \dfrac{\partial G_3}{\partial \beta_1} + q_4 \dfrac{\partial G_4}{\partial \beta_1} = -D_1 \\[2mm] q_1 \dfrac{\partial G_1}{\partial \beta_2} + q_2 \dfrac{\partial G_2}{\partial \beta_2} + q_3 \dfrac{\partial G_3}{\partial \beta_2} + q_4 \dfrac{\partial G_4}{\partial \beta_2} = -D_2 \\[2mm] q_1 \dfrac{\partial G_1}{\partial \beta_3} + q_2 \dfrac{\partial G_2}{\partial \beta_3} + q_3 \dfrac{\partial G_3}{\partial \beta_3} + q_4 \dfrac{\partial G_4}{\partial \beta_3} = -D_3 \end{cases} \qquad (6.7)$$

In the Nelson and Siegel (1987) model, we only have three hedging instruments because there are only three parameters. Then $q_4 = 0$, and the last equation of system (6.7) disappears.

Example 6.8 We consider the Extended Vasicek zero-coupon rate function (see Chapter 4 for more details on that):

$$R^c(t, \theta) = L_t - S_t \left[\frac{1 - e^{-a\theta}}{a\theta} \right] + \gamma_t \left[\frac{(1 - e^{-a\theta})^2}{4a\theta} \right]$$

At date t, the model is calibrated, the parameters L_t, S_t and γ_t being obtained using market prices, as discussed in Chapter 4. Their values are

L_t	S_t	γ_t
0.06	0.025	−0.05

The scale parameter a is equal to 0.4. At the same date, the portfolio P to be hedged has the following features:

Price	D_L	D_S	D_γ
$32, 863,500	−224,016,404	63,538,154	−13,264,994

where $D_L = \frac{\partial P}{\partial L}(L_t, S_t, \gamma_t)$, $D_S = \frac{\partial P}{\partial S}(L_t, S_t, \gamma_t)$ and $D_\gamma = \frac{\partial P}{\partial \gamma}(L_t, S_t, \gamma_t)$ are the level, slope and curvature $durations of P in the Extended Vasicek model.

We consider Treasury bonds as hedging assets, and at date t, we force the hedging portfolio to have the opposite value of the portfolio to be hedged. Because of this additional restriction, we need the number of hedging assets to be equal to four. They have the following features (coupon frequency is annual):

	Coupon rate (%)	Maturity (years)	Price ($)	D_L^1	D_S^2	D_γ^3
Asset 1	7	3	108.039	−304.125	180.112	−30.621
Asset 2	8	7	118.786	−680.671	251.662	−55.549
Asset 3	5	12	97.962	−901.951	221.454	−51.88
Asset 4	6	18	106.439	−1,224.863	239.101	−55.878

We are looking for the quantities ϕ_1, ϕ_2, ϕ_3 and ϕ_4 of each of the hedging asset as solutions to the following linear system:

$$\begin{pmatrix} \phi_1 \\ \phi_2 \\ \phi_3 \\ \phi_4 \end{pmatrix} = \begin{pmatrix} -304.125 & -680.671 & -901.951 & -1,224.863 \\ 180.112 & 251.662 & 221.454 & 239.101 \\ -30.621 & -55.549 & -51.88 & -55.878 \\ 108.039 & 118.786 & 97.962 & 106.439 \end{pmatrix}^{-1} \begin{pmatrix} 224,016,404 \\ -63,538,154 \\ 13,264,994 \\ -32,863,500 \end{pmatrix} = \begin{pmatrix} -518,667 \\ 1,247,532 \\ -2,321,721 \\ 962,266 \end{pmatrix}$$

This part has addressed the problem of hedging a bond portfolio. Because there is ample empirical evidence that changes in the yield curve can be large and multidimensional, duration hedging techniques achieve limited efficiency in most market conditions (see Martellini *et al.* (2002b) for a comparative analysis of various hedging techniques). Besides, by implementing semihedged strategies based on three-factor models, a portfolio manager can take specific bets on particular changes in the yield curve while being hedged against the others (see Martellini *et al.* (2002a) for such an implementation in the case of a butterfly strategy).

6.3   End of Chapter Summary

Duration hedging is very simple, but it is based upon the following, very restrictive, assumptions: (1) it is explicitly assumed that changes in the yield curve will be small and (2) it is also assumed that the yield curve is only affected by parallel shifts. As seen in Chapter 3, we know however, that large variations can affect the yield-to-maturity curve and that three main factors (level, slope and curvature) have been found to drive the dynamics of the yield curve. This strongly suggests that duration hedging is inefficient in many circumstances. In this chapter, we go "beyond duration" by relaxing the two aforementioned assumptions.

Relaxing the assumption of a small change in the yield curve can be performed though the introduction of a convexity adjustment in the hedging procedure. Convexity is a measure of the sensitivity of $duration with respect to yield changes.

Accounting for general, nonparallel deformations of the term structure is not easy because it increases the dimensionality of the problem. Because it is never easy to hedge the risk associated with too many sources of uncertainty, it is always desirable to try and reduce the number of risk factors and identify a limited number of common factors. This can be done in a systematic way by using an appropriate statistical analysis of the yield-curve dynamics. Alternatively, one may choose to use a model for the discount rate function.

6.4 References and Further Reading

Barber, J.R., and M.L. Copper, 1996, "Immunization Using Principal Component Analysis" *Journal of Portfolio Management*, **23**(1), 99–105.

Barber, J.R., and M.L. Copper, 1997, "Is Bond Convexity a Free Lunch?" *Journal of Portfolio Management*, **24**(1), 113–119.

Barrett W., T. Gosnell Jr., and A. Heuson, 1995, "Yield Curve Shifts and the Selection of Immunization Strategies", *Journal of Fixed Income*, **5**(2), 53–64.

Chambers, D.R., W.T. Carleton, and R.W. Mc Enally, 1988, "Immunizing Default-Free Bond Portfolios with a Duration Vector", *Journal of Financial and Quantitative Analysis*, **23**, 89–104.

Chambers, D.R., and S.K. Nawalkha, (Editors), 1999, *Interest Rate Risk Measurement and Management*, Institutional Investor, New York.

Chance, D.M., and J.V. Jordan, 1996, "Duration, Convexity, and Time as Components of Bond Returns", *Journal of Fixed Income*, **6**(2), 88–96.

Christensen, P.O., and B.G. Sorensen, 1994, "Duration, Convexity and Time Value", *Journal of Portfolio Management*, **20**(2), 51–60.

Cox, J.C., J.E. Ingersoll, and S.A. Ross, 1985, "A Theory of the Term Structure of Interest Rates", *Econometrica*, **53**(2), 385–407.

Dynkin, L., J. Hyman, and P. Lindner, 2002, "Hedging and Replication of Fixed-Income Portfolios", *Journal of Fixed Income*, **11**(4), 43–63.

Golub, B.W., and L.M. Tilman, 1997, "Measuring Yield Curve Risk Using Principal Components Analysis, Value at Risk, and Key Rate Durations", *Journal of Portfolio Management*, **23**(4), 72–84.

Grantier, B.J., 1988, "Convexity and Bond Performance: The Benter the Better", *Financial Analysts Journal*, **44**(6), 79–81.

Fabozzi, F.J., 1996, *Fixed-Income Mathematics*, 3rd Edition, McGraw-Hill, New York.

Fabozzi, F.J., 1999, *Duration, Convexity and Other Bond Risk Measures*, John Wiley & Sons, Chichester.

Falkenstein, E., and J. Hanweck, 1997, "Minimizing Basis Risk from Non-Parallel Shifts in the Yield Curve—Part II: Principal Components", *Journal of Fixed Income*, **7**(1), 85–90.

Hill, C.F., and S. Vaysman, 1998, "An Approach to Scenario Hedging", *Journal of Portfolio Management*, **24**(2), 83–92.

Ho, T.S.Y., 1992, "Key Rate Durations: Measures of Interest Rate Risks", *Journal of Fixed Income*, **2**(2), 29–44.

Kahn, R.N., and D. Gulrajani, 1993, "Risk and Return in the Canadian Bond Market", *Journal of Portfolio Management*, **19**(3), 86–93.

Kang, J.C., and A.H. Chen, 2002, "Evidence on Theta and Convexity in Treasury Returns", *Journal of Fixed Income*, **12**(1), 41–50.

Klaffky, T.E., Y.Y. Ma, and A. Nozari, 1992, "Managing Yield Curve Exposure: Introducing Reshaping Duration's", *Journal of Fixed Income*, **2**(3), 39–46.

Litterman, R., and J. Scheinkman, 1991, "Common Factors Affecting Bond Returns", *Journal of Fixed Income*, **1**(1), 54–61.

Martellini, L., and P. Priaulet, 2000, *Fixed-Income Securities: Dynamic Methods for Interest Rate Risk Pricing and Hedging*, John Wiley & Sons, Chichester.

Martellini, L., P. Priaulet, and S. Priaulet, 2002a, "Understanding the Butterfly Strategy", *Journal of Bond Trading and Management*, **1**(1), 9–19.

Martellini, L., P. Priaulet, and S. Priaulet, 2002b, "Beyond Duration", *Journal of Bond Trading and Management*, **1**(2), 103–119.

Nelson, C.R., and A.F. Siegel, 1987, "Parsimonious Modeling of Yield Curves", *Journal of Business*, **60**(4), 473–489.

Reitano, R.R., 1992, "Non-Parallel Yield Curve Shifts and Immunization", *Journal of Portfolio Management*, **18**(3), 37–43.

Svensson, L., 1994, Estimating and Interpreting Forward Interest Rates: Sweden 1992–94, CEPR Discussion Paper 1051.

Vasicek, O.A., 1977, "An Equilibrium Characterisation of the Term Structure", *Journal of Financial Economics*, **5**(2), 177–188.

Willner, R., 1996, "A New Tool for Portfolio Managers: Level, Slope and Curvature Durations", *Journal of Fixed Income*, **6**(1), 48–59.

6.5 Problems

Exercise 6.1 We consider a 20-year zero-coupon bond with a 6% YTM and $100 face value. Compounding frequency is assumed to be annual.

1. Compute its price, modified duration, $duration, convexity and $convexity?
2. On the same graph, draw the price change of the bond when YTM goes from 1 to 11%

   (a) by using the exact pricing formula;
   (b) by using the one-order Taylor estimation;
   (c) by using the second-order Taylor estimation.

Exercise 6.2 On 01/08/99, we consider a base-case bond with maturity 8 years, a 5% coupon rate, a 5% YTM and a $100 face value. Coupon frequency and compounding frequency are assumed to be annual.

1. Holding the maturity and the YTM of this bond constant, compute its convexity and $convexity by giving different values to its coupon rate between 2 and 8%.
2. Holding the coupon rate and the YTM of this bond constant, compute its convexity and $convexity by giving different values to its maturity between 5 and 11 years.
3. Holding the maturity and the coupon rate of this bond constant, compute its convexity and $convexity by giving different values to its YTM between 2 and 8%.

Exercise 6.3 1. Compute the modified duration and convexity of a 6%, 25-year bond selling at a yield of 9%. Coupon frequency and compounding frequency are assumed to be semiannual.
2. What is its estimated percentage price change for a yield change from 9 to 11% using the one-order Taylor expansion? Using the two-order Taylor expansion? Compare both of them with the actual change.
3. Same question when the yield decreases by 200 basis points. Conclude.

Exercise 6.4   We consider three bonds with the following features:

Bond	Maturity (years)	Coupon rate (%)	YTM (%)
Bond 1	2	5	5
Bond 2	10	6	5.5
Bond 3	30	7	6

Coupon frequency and compounding frequency are assumed to be annual.

1. Compute the dirty price and the modified duration of each bond.
2. (a) The YTM of each bond decreases instantaneously by 0.2%. Compute the exact new price of each bond, the price approximation using the first-order Taylor expansion and the difference between these two prices.
   (b) Same question if the YTM of each bond decreases instantaneously by 1%. Conclude.
   (c) For bond 3, draw the difference between the two prices depending on YTM change.
3. Compute the convexity of each bond.
4. We suppose that the YTM of each bond decreases instantaneously by 1%. Compute the price approximation using the second-order Taylor expansion. Compare it with the exact price.

Exercise 6.5   Consider a situation in which the spot yield curve is flat at level 5.5%, and consider a par coupon bond (i.e., $c = 5.5\%$) with a 2-year maturity and a $1,000 face value. Coupon frequency and compounding frequency are assumed to be semi-annual.

1. Compute the duration D, modified duration MD and convexity RC of the bond.
2. Suppose that the spot rate increases to 7%. Compute the percentage change in the bond price, using first only duration and then adjusting for convexity. Comment on how significant the difference between the two methods is in this case.

Exercise 6.6   Assume a 2-year Euro-note, with a $100,000 face value, a coupon rate of 10% and a convexity of 4.53, if today's YTM is 11.5% and term structure is flat. Coupon frequency and compounding frequency are assumed to be annual.

1. What is the Macaulay duration of this bond?
2. What does convexity measure? Why does convexity differ among bonds? What happens to convexity when interest rates rise? Why?
3. What is the exact price change in dollars if interest rates increase by 10 basis points (a uniform shift)?
4. Use the duration model to calculate the approximate price change in dollars if interest rates increase by 10 basis points.
5. Incorporate convexity to calculate the approximate price change in dollars if interest rates increase by 10 basis points.

Exercise 6.7   Duration, Modified Duration and Convexity of a Bond Portfolio
Consider five bonds with the following features on 01/08/99:

	Price	Coupon rate (%)	Maturity (%)	YTM	Duration	MD	Convexity
Bond 1	95.762	4	01/08/03	5.201	3.770	3.583	16.689
Bond 2	89.563	4.50	01/08/07	6.194	6.819	6.421	51.462
Bond 3	85.456	5	01/08/09	7.078	7.928	7.404	70.012
Bond 4	78.254	5	01/08/15	7.357	10.707	9.974	135.884
Bond 5	77.755	5.50	01/08/25	7.462	12.903	12.007	225.083

Coupon frequency and compounding frequency are assumed to be annual.
You create a bond portfolio with a unit quantity of each of these five bonds.

1. Compute the duration, modified duration and convexity of this portfolio using the weighted averages of the bond's duration, modified duration and convexity as in equations (5.7 and 6.2), which are proxies for actual values.
2. Compute the YTM of the portfolio.
3. Calculate the actual values of the portfolio duration, modified duration and convexity using the standard formula of duration, modified duration and convexity. Conclude.

Exercise 6.8   Modified Duration/Convexity Bond Portfolio Hedge
At date t, the portfolio P to be hedged is a portfolio of Treasury bonds with various possible maturities. Its characteristics are as follows:

Price	YTM	MD	Convexity
$28,296,919	7.511%	5.906	67.578

We consider Treasury bonds as hedging assets, with the following features:

Bond	Price ($)	Coupon rate (%)	Maturity date (years)
Bond 1	108.039	7	3
Bond 2	118.786	8	7
Bond 3	97.962	5	12

Coupon frequency and compounding frequency are assumed to be annual. At date t we force the hedging portfolio to have the opposite value of the portfolio to be hedged.

1. What is the number of hedging instruments necessary to implement a modified duration/convexity hedge?
2. Compute the YTM, modified duration and convexity of the three hedging assets.
3. Which quantities ϕ_1, ϕ_2 and ϕ_3 of each of the hedging asset 1, 2, 3 do we have to consider to hedge the portfolio P?

Exercise 6.9   Computing the Level, Slope and Curvature $Durations of a Bond Portfolio in the Nelson and Siegel Model

1. At date $t = 0$, the values of the Nelson and Siegel parameters are as follows:

β_0	β_1	β_2	τ_1
9%	−2%	−0.5%	4

Recall from Chapter 4 that the continuously compounded zero-coupon rate $R^c(0, \theta)$ is given by the following formula:

$$R^c(0, \theta) = \beta_0 + \beta_1 \left[\frac{1 - \exp\left(-\frac{\theta}{\tau_1}\right)}{\frac{\theta}{\tau_1}} \right] + \beta_2 \left[\frac{1 - \exp\left(-\frac{\theta}{\tau_1}\right)}{\frac{\theta}{\tau_1}} - \exp\left(-\frac{\theta}{\tau_1}\right) \right]$$

We consider three bonds with the following features. Coupon frequency is semi-annual.

	Maturity (years)	Coupon (%)
Bond 1	1	8
Bond 2	5	8
Bond 3	10	8

Compute the price and the level, slope and curvature $durations of each bond. Compute also the same $durations for a portfolio with two units of bond 1, three units of bond 2 and one unit of bond 3.

2. Same question when the coupon frequency is annual.

Exercise 6.10   Computing the Level, Slope and Curvature $Durations of a Bond Portfolio using the Nelson and Siegel Extended Model

On 09/02/02, the values of the Nelson and Siegel Extended parameters are as follows

β_0	β_1	β_2	τ_1	β_3	τ_2
5.9%	−1.6%	−0.5%	5	1%	0.5

Recall from Chapter 4 that the continuously compounded zero-coupon rate $R^c(0, \theta)$ is given by the following formula:

$$R^c(0, \theta) = \beta_0 + \beta_1 \left[\frac{1 - \exp\left(-\frac{\theta}{\tau_1}\right)}{\frac{\theta}{\tau_1}} \right] + \beta_2 \left[\frac{1 - \exp\left(-\frac{\theta}{\tau_1}\right)}{\frac{\theta}{\tau_1}} - \exp\left(-\frac{\theta}{\tau_1}\right) \right]$$

$$+ \beta_3 \left[\frac{1 - \exp\left(-\frac{\theta}{\tau_2}\right)}{\frac{\theta}{\tau_2}} - \exp\left(-\frac{\theta}{\tau_2}\right) \right]$$

1. Draw the zero-coupon yield curve associated with this set of parameters.

2. We consider three bonds with the following features. Coupon frequency is annual.

	Maturity (years)	Coupon (%)
Bond 1	3	4
Bond 2	7	5
Bond 3	15	6

Compute the price and the level, slope and curvature $durations of each bond. Compute also the same $durations for a portfolio with 100 units of bond 1, 200 units of bond 2 and 100 units of bond 3.

3. The parameters of the Nelson and Siegel Extended model change instantaneously to become

β_0	β_1	β_2	τ_1	β_3	τ_2
5.5%	−1%	0.1%	5	2%	0.5

(a) Draw the new zero-coupon yield curve.
(b) Compute the new price of the bond portfolio and compare it with the value given by the following equation:

$$New\ estimated\ price\ =\ former\ price\ +\Delta\beta_0 \cdot D_{0,P} + \Delta\beta_1 \cdot D_{1,P}$$

$$+\ \Delta\beta_2 \cdot D_{2,P} + \Delta\beta_3 \cdot D_{3,P}$$

where $\Delta\beta_i$ is the change in value of parameter β_i, and $D_{i,P}$ is the $duration of the bond portfolio associated with parameter β_i.

4. Same questions when the coupon frequency is semiannual.

Exercise 6.11   Bond Portfolio Hedge using the Extended Vasicek Model
We consider the Extended Vasicek zero-coupon rate function (see Chapter 4 for more details on this)

$$R^c(t, \theta) = L_t - S_t \left[\frac{1 - e^{-a\theta}}{a\theta} \right] + \gamma_t \left[\frac{(1 - e^{-a\theta})^2}{4a\theta} \right]$$

where $R^c(t, \theta)$ is the continuously compounded zero-coupon rate at date t with maturity θ.
At date t, the model is calibrated, parameters L_t, S_t and γ_t being as follows:

L_t	S_t	γ_t
0.08	0.015	−0.05

The scale parameter a is equal to 0.4. At the same date, the portfolio P to be hedged has the following features:

Price	D_L	D_S	D_γ
$28,296,919	−172,982,410	53,228,324	−10,864,919

where $D_L = \frac{\partial P}{\partial L}(L_t, S_t, \gamma_t)$, $D_S = \frac{\partial P}{\partial S}(L_t, S_t, \gamma_t)$ and $D\gamma = \frac{\partial P}{\partial \gamma}(L_t, S_t, \gamma_t)$ are the level, slope and curvature \$durations of P in the Extended Vasicek model.

We consider Treasury bonds as hedging instruments, with the following features:

Bond	Coupon rate (%)	Maturity (years)	Price ($)
Bond 1	7	3	100.445
Bond 2	8	7	103.808
Bond 3	5	12	79.929
Bond 4	6	18	83.376

Coupons are assumed to be paid annually. At date t, we force the hedging portfolio to have the opposite value of the portfolio to be hedged.

1. What is the number of hedging instruments necessary to implement the Extended Vasicek hedge?
2. Compute the level, slope and curvature \$durations of the four hedging assets.
3. Which quantities ϕ_1, ϕ_2, ϕ_3 and ϕ_4 of each hedging asset 1, 2, 3, 4 do we have to consider to hedge the portfolio P?

Exercise 6.12 Bond Portfolio Hedge using the Nelson–Siegel Extended Model
We consider the Nelson–Siegel Extended zero-coupon rate function

$$R^c(t, \theta) = \beta_0 + \beta_1 \left[\frac{1 - \exp\left(-\frac{\theta}{\tau_1}\right)}{\frac{\theta}{\tau_1}} \right] + \beta_2 \left[\frac{1 - \exp\left(-\frac{\theta}{\tau_1}\right)}{\frac{\theta}{\tau_1}} - \exp\left(-\frac{\theta}{\tau_1}\right) \right]$$
$$+ \beta_3 \left[\frac{1 - \exp\left(-\frac{\theta}{\tau_2}\right)}{\frac{\theta}{\tau_2}} - \exp\left(-\frac{\theta}{\tau_2}\right) \right]$$

where $R^c(t, \theta)$ is the continuously compounded zero-coupon rate at date t with maturity θ.

On 09/02/02, the model is calibrated, parameters being as follows:

β_0	β_1	β_2	τ_1	β_3	τ_2
5.9%	−1.6%	−0.5%	5	1%	0.5

At the same date, a manager wants to hedge its bond portfolio P against interest-rate risk. The portfolio contains the following Treasury bonds (delivering annual coupons, with a $100 face value):

Bond	Maturity	Coupon	Quantity
Bond 1	01/12/05	4	10,000
Bond 2	04/12/06	7.75	10,000
Bond 3	07/12/07	4	10,000

Bond	Maturity	Coupon	Quantity
Bond 4	10/12/08	7	10,000
Bond 5	03/12/09	5.75	10,000
Bond 6	10/12/10	5.5	10,000
Bond 7	01/12/12	4	10,000
Bond 8	03/12/15	4.75	10,000
Bond 9	07/12/20	4.5	10,000
Bond 10	01/12/25	5	10,000
Bond 11	07/12/30	4.5	10,000
Bond 12	01/12/31	4	10,000
Bond 13	07/12/32	5	10,000

We consider Treasury bonds as hedging instruments with the following features:

Hedging asset	Coupon	Maturity
Hedging asset 1	4.5	04/15/06
Hedging asset 2	5	12/28/12
Hedging asset 3	6	10/05/15
Hedging asset 4	6	10/10/20
Hedging asset 5	6.5	10/10/31

Coupons are assumed to be paid annually, and the face value of each bond is $100. At date t, we force the hedging portfolio to have the opposite value of the portfolio to be hedged.

1. Compute the price and level, slope and curvature $durations of portfolio P.
2. Compute the price and level, slope and curvature $durations of the five hedging assets.
3. Which quantities $\phi_1, \phi_2, \phi_3, \phi_4$ and ϕ_5 of each hedging asset 1, 2, 3, 4 and 5 do we have to consider to hedge the portfolio P?
4. The parameters of the Nelson and Siegel Extended model change instantaneously to become:

β_0	β_1	β_2	τ_1	β_3	τ_2
6.5%	−1%	0.1%	5	2%	0.5

(a) What is the price of the bond portfolio after this change? If the manager has not hedged its portfolio, how much money has he lost?
(b) What is the variation in price of the global portfolio (where the global portfolio is the bond portfolio plus the hedging instruments)?
(c) Conclusion.

Investment Strategies

PART IV

One of the most profound ideas affecting the investment decision process, and indeed all of finance, is that the security markets, equity and fixed-income are efficient. In an efficient market, the prices of securities do not depart for any length of time from the justified economic values that investors calculate for them. Economic values for securities are determined by investor expectations about earnings, risks and so on, as investors grapple with the uncertain future. If the market price of a security does depart from its estimated economic value, investors act to bring the two values together. Thus, as new information arrives in an efficient marketplace, causing a revision in the estimated economic value of a security, its price adjusts to this information quickly and, on balance, correctly. In other words, securities are efficiently priced on a continuous basis.

An efficient market does not have to be perfectly efficient to have a profound impact on investors. All that is required is that the market be *economically* efficient. That is, after acting on information to trade securities and subtracting all costs (transaction costs and taxes, to name two), the investor would have been as well off with a simple buy-and-hold strategy. If the market were economically efficient, securities could depart somewhat from their economic (justified) values, but it would not pay investors to take advantage of these small discrepancies.

A natural outcome of a belief in efficient markets is to use some type of passive strategy in owning and managing portfolios. Passive strategies do not seek to outperform the market but simply to do as well as the market. The emphasis is on minimizing transaction costs and time spent in managing the portfolio because any expected benefits from active trading or analysis are likely to be less than costs. Passive investors act as if the market were efficient and take the consensus estimates of return and risk, accepting current market price as the best estimate of a security's value. If the market were totally efficient, no active strategy should be able to beat the market on a risk-adjusted basis.

On the other hand, investors who do not accept the EMH (Efficient Market Hypothesis), or have serious doubts about it, pursue active investment strategies, believing that they can identify undervalued securities and that lags exist in the market adjustment of these securities' prices to new (better) information. These investors generate more search costs (both in time and money) and more transaction costs, but they believe that the marginal benefit outweighs the marginal costs incurred. Following an active strategy assumes that investors possess some advantage relative to other market participants. Such advantages could include superior analytical or judgmental skills, superior information, or the ability or willingness to do what other investors, particularly institutions, are unable to do.

7 Passive Fixed-Income Portfolio Management

Many investors manage portfolios (or parts of portfolios) to match index returns. Even active managers may fall back to passive index tracking in times when they have no definite views. The simplest way to replicate an index is to buy most of the securities in the index in the proper proportions. However, this method is practical only for the largest index funds. For smaller portfolios, maintaining the necessary proportions of a large number of bonds would necessitate buying odd lots and lead to overwhelming transaction costs. Investors with smaller portfolios often build index proxies, that is, portfolios that contain only a small number of securities yet deviate minimally from the returns of much larger target indices. This is known as *bond indexing*.

The first bond index fund was in the early conceptual stages in 1985 when an article in Forbes magazine discussing the inability of high-cost bond fund managers to match the bond market indices asked, "Vanguard, where are you when we need you?" By the next year Vanguard's Total Bond Market Index(VBMFX) was up and running. SEI Funds also started a bond index fund that year. In 1991, Galaxy Funds opened an index fund of government long bonds and Mainstay Funds started its long-term bond index. Also in 1991, Charles Schwab Co. opened its Short-Term Bond Market Index. In 1994, Vanguard created the first series of bond index funds of varying maturities—short, intermediate and long.

Today there are a large number of bond index funds. Although their customer base has not grown as fast as that in stock index funds, bond index fund managers had handled more than $20 billion at the end of 2001. Bond index fund assets have grown slowly in part because report of the virtues of fund indexing has for the most part spread through word of mouth, and because low-cost index funds rarely budget much for sales and marketing. Bond index funds occupy a fairly small niche in the world of mutual funds; only approximately 3% of all bond fund assets are in bond index funds, and these assets are held disproportionately by institutional investors, who keep about 25% of their bond fund assets in bond index funds.

We now present the techniques used for bond indexing.

7.1 Straightforward Replication

As recalled in the introduction to this section, the most straightforward replication technique involves duplicating the target index precisely, holding all its securities in their exact proportions. Once replication is achieved, trading in the indexed portfolio becomes necessary only when the makeup of the index changes or as a way of reinvesting cash flows. While this approach is often preferred for equities, it is not practical with bonds. (The good news is that it is not necessary either, as other methods can efficiently be applied, which we describe below). Bond Market index funds, like those managed by Vanguard and Charles Schwab Co., as well as intermediate bond indices, like the Maxim Bond Index, usually aim to trace the performance of the Lehman Brothers

Aggregate Bond Index. This benchmark is a collection of 5,545 bonds (as of 12/31/99) from the Treasury, corporate, mortgage-backed and international US dollar-denominated debt sectors with an overall intermediate to long-range dollar-weighted average maturity. The range was 8.4 to 9.0 years for the last five years ending December 31, 1999, although it varied with market conditions (see Lehman Brothers's note on "Quantitative Management of Bond Portfolios"—Fixed-Income Research—May 2001). Now, it would not be cost-efficient for managers to include, say, all 5,545 issues from the Lehman Brothers Aggregate index, among other reasons because they would forgo very substantial volume discounts at auction. Other difficulties include the following points:

- *Many of the bonds in the indices are thinly traded.*

- *The composition of the index changes regularly, as the bonds mature.*

Given that the cost of owning and trading such a large number of securities would be prohibitive, an alternative approach, known as *optimization* or *sampling*, seeks to reproduce the overall attributes of the index (yield, credit quality, duration, convexity, etc.) with a limited number of issues. While this may sound simple in theory, it is difficult to achieve in practice. Passive does not mean inactive. In fact, it takes a very active portfolio management process to deliver reliable index performance with low tracking error. It requires extensive portfolio modeling and monitoring, together with very disciplined and cost-conscious trading capabilities. Under this approach, fund managers will consider each broad segment of the benchmark (government bonds, mortgages and corporate issues), and within each segment select a set of US dollar-denominated bonds that is representative of key benchmark traits. The most important of these traits are interest-rate sensitivity, credit quality and sector diversification, although other characteristics will be reflected.

There are three basic approaches to index replication other than straightforward replication: cell-matching or stratified sampling, tracking error minimization and factor-based replication. The cell-matching approach consists in replicating index attributes, while the tracking error approach consists in replicating index returns directly. Factor-based replication consists in matching the exposure of the replicating portfolio with respect to a set of common factors with that of the benchmark.

7.2 Replication by Stratified Sampling

The *stratified sampling bond indexing* techniques are the "common sense approach." To replicate an index, one has to represent every important component that it has with a few securities. The holdings of securities in a particular cell are usually computed to match that cell's contribution to the overall duration. First, a portfolio manager maps a benchmark onto an arbitrary grid and then sets portfolio allocations to each of the cells that match those of the benchmark. In other words, it consists in dividing the index into cells, each cell representing a different characteristic, and then buying bonds to match those characteristics.

Examples of identifying characteristics are

- *duration,*

- *coupon rate,*

- *maturity,*

- *market sectors (Treasury, corporate, mortgage-backed, etc.),*

- *credit rating,*

- *call factors,*

- *sinking fund features.*

The objective is then to select from all of the issues in the index, one or more issues in each cell that can be used to represent the entire cell. The more securities are selected in each cell, the more closely the resulting portfolio tracks the index.

Example 7.1 In a Lehman Brothers note entitled "High yield index replication" (March 2001), it is explained how this approach can be successfully applied to replicate the Lehman Brothers high-yield index. Three sets of strategies have been studied:

- *Issuer strategy: it consists in selecting the largest (by % market value) securities from the list of the largest issuers in the index. The issuer strategy assumes that idiosyncratic risk is a key component of returns in the high-yield market. This assumption is based on the fact that only a small fraction of high-yield total return volatility is explained by the Treasury-bond term-structure volatility.*

- *Structure strategy: it consists in dividing the high-yield index into industry and credit "buckets" and then selecting bonds to populate each bucket. The replicating proxy portfolio is constructed so that in each bucket, the market weights and contributions to spread duration match those of the index. In addition, this strategy also matches both Treasury duration and convexity of the index. Because idiosyncratic risk is an important factor in a high-yield bond's return variability, the strategy imposes a set of eligible criteria to avoid bonds with a potential for high-return volatility. The number of bonds in each bucket (a diversification constraint) is also based on the bucket's historical behavior.*

- *Structured-issuer strategy: it is similar to the structured strategy except that this strategy filters the list of eligible bonds further. The final list contains only the largest value security from every issuer in the index to force issuer diversification. Otherwise, this strategy follows the same methodology as the structure strategy.*

The total dollar amount invested in each cell will typically depend upon the share of that cell in the entire universe of securities represented in the index. The number of cells used will depend on the dollar amount of the portfolio to be indexed. A portfolio with a small dollar value will have fewer cells, so as not to increase tracking error due to transaction costs.

The stratified sampling bond indexing method is sometimes coupled with an optimization procedure. The optimization approach is also a cellular one; however, the choice of securities from each cell is made with a view to achieving some other objective, such as maximizing yield to maturity, maximizing convexity and so on. Mathematical programming is used to achieve this goal.

7.3   Tracking-Error Minimization

Risk models allow us to replicate indices by creating minimum tracking error portfolios. These models rely on historical volatilities and correlations between returns on different asset classes or different risk factors in the market.

The Variance Minimization approach uses historical data to estimate the variance of the tracking error for each issue in the index, and then uses that to minimize the total variance of the tracking error. The tracking error variance of a given security is obtained by estimating the price function for that security as a function of its cash flows, duration and other sector characteristics. Quadratic programming is then used to find the optimal index portfolio in terms of minimized tracking error. Since it is difficult to get enough data on each security, this approach is very difficult.

A fund manager will typically invest substantially all fund assets in bonds specifically represented in the index. In general, they own US government and agency obligations, mortgage- and asset-backed securities, corporate bonds and US dollar-denominated securities of foreign issuers. Other securities may also be purchased, such as collateralized mortgage obligations(CMOs) and certain types of derivatives, provided they have similar characteristics to index securities and potentially offer more attractive prices, yields or liquidity. Derivatives, such as futures and options, will not exceed 10% of the fund's total assets. This flexibility in investing is intended to help the manager keep the fund's composition in line with the index and minimize deviations in performance between the fund and the index.

Typically, investment managers expect the correlation between the fund and the index to be at least 0.95. A correlation of 1.00 means that the returns of the fund and the index move in the same direction (but not necessarily by the same amount). A correlation of 0.00 means movements in the fund are unrelated to movements in the index. The fund may sell securities to better align the portfolio with the characteristics of its benchmark or to satisfy redemption requests. However, the fund is not required to sell specific bond issues that have been removed from the index.

The technique involves two separate steps: the estimation of the bond return covariance matrix, and the use of that covariance matrix for tracking error optimization.

7.3.1   Optimization Procedure

The problem is to replicate as closely as possible a bond index return with a portfolio invested in N individual bonds. We denote by R_B the return on the benchmark (i.e., the index), $w_1, \ldots, w_N$ the weights of N bonds in the replicating portfolio, $S = (\sigma_{ij})_{i,j=1,\ldots,N}$ the variance–covariance matrix of these bonds, and R_P the return on the replicating portfolio. We have

$$R_P = \sum_{i=1}^{N} w_i R_i$$

Mathematically, the problem can be stated as

$$\underset{w_1,\ldots,w_N}{Min} \; \mathbb{V}ar(R_P - R_B) = \sum_{i=i,j}^{N} w_i w_j \sigma_{ij} - 2 \sum_{i=1}^{N} w_i \sigma_{iB} + \sigma_B^2 \qquad (7.1)$$

where σ_{iB} is the covariance between the return on the ith bond in the replicating portfolio and the benchmark return, and σ_B the volatility of the benchmark. Mathematical programming is used to solve this optimization program. It can also be implemented via the Microsoft Excel^{TM} solver function.

In the absence of constraints on the sign of the weights and when the volatility of the replicating portfolio is required to be equal to that of the benchmark, we obtain a classic (constrained) linear regression (zero intercept)

$$R_{tB} = \sum_{i=1}^{N} w_i R_{ti} + \varepsilon_t$$

where R_{tB} (respectively, R_{ti}) denotes the return on the benchmark (respectively, asset i) at date t. In that case, we also obtain confidence intervals on optimal portfolio weights.

The quality of replication is measured by *tracking error* (denoted by TE), that is, standard deviation of the difference between the return on the portfolio and that of the benchmark, that is,

$$TE = \sqrt{\mathbb{V}\mathrm{ar}(R_P - R_B)}$$

Note that this was precisely the quantity that was minimized by the optimization procedure.

The choice of securities in the replicating portfolio is a straightforward task when the number M of candidate securities in the universe is small and the number N of securities to be included in the replicating portfolio is small. When M increases and N approaches $M/2$, it becomes a complex optimization problem. The idea is to form equally weighted portfolios using N among M securities and find best candidates; this is known as an *integer programming problem*, which can be solved using some specific genetic algorithm.

7.3.2 Bond Return Covariance Matrix Estimation

As can be seen from equation (7.1), the key input to the optimization procedure is the variance–covariance matrix $(\sigma_{ij})_{i,j=1,\ldots,N}$ of bond returns. Several methods for asset return covariance matrix estimation have been suggested in the literature. They fall within the following three categories: sample covariance matrix estimators, factor models based estimators and shrinkage estimators.[1]

Sample Covariance Matrix

The most common estimator of return covariance matrix is the sample covariance matrix of historical returns

$$S = \frac{1}{T-1} \sum_{t=1}^{T} (R_t - \overline{R})(R_t - \overline{R})^{\top}$$

---

[1] Another set of methods incorporate prior information, and use forecast models for the variance–covariance matrix. Such solutions are more typically implemented in the context of tactical allocation models.

where T is the sample size, N is the number of assets in the portfolio, R_t is the N-vector of bond returns in period t, and $\overline{R}$ is the N-vector of the average of these returns over time. We denote by S_{ij} the (i, j) entry of S.

Example 7.2 We consider in this example the following eight T-Bonds bonds with coupon rate and maturity date:

6.25; 31-Jan-2002

4.75; 15-Feb-2004

5.875; 15-Nov-2005

6.125; 15-Aug-2007

6.5; 15-Feb-2010

5; 15-Aug-2011

6.25; 15-May-2030

5.375; 15-Feb-2031

We collect data on daily returns on these bonds, as well as on daily returns on the JP Morgan T-Bond index from 08/03/01 to 01/30/02 that we use as a benchmark. On the basis of that information, we estimate the correlation matrix (see Table 7.1) that contains all pair-wise correlations.

As we can see, most bond returns are fairly highly correlated with the return on the index, and medium maturity bonds tend to post higher correlation with the index. This can be explained by the fact that the Macaulay duration of the index turns out to be 6.73 on average over the period. Using $\sigma_{ij} = \sigma_i \sigma_j \rho_{ij}$, where σ_{ij} (respectively, ρ_{ij}) is the covariance (respectively, the correlation) between the return on bond i and bond j, and σ_i is the volatility of bond i, we can easily obtain the variance–covariance matrix (see Table 7.2).

From there, we perform the following optimization:

$$\text{Min}_{w_1,\ldots,w_8} TE = \sqrt{\mathbb{V}\text{ar}(R_P - R_B)} = \sqrt{\sum_{i=i,j}^{8} w_i w_j \sigma_{ij} - 2\sum_{i=1}^{8} w_i \sigma_{iB} + \sigma_B^2} \qquad (7.2)$$

subject to the constraint

$$\sum_{i=1}^{8} w_i = 1$$

An additional short sales constraint $w_i \geq 0$ for all $i = 1, \ldots, 8$ can be further added. This can be solved using Excel solver function, which gives the optimal portfolio, as shown in Table 7.3.

Table 7.1   Estimated Correlation Matrix.

	Benchmark	Bond 1	Bond 2	Bond 3	Bond 4	Bond 5	Bond 6	Bond 7	Bond 8
Benchmark	1	—	—	—	—	—	—	—	—
Bond 1	0.035340992	1	—	—	—	—	—	—	—
Bond 2	0.570480252	0.037162337	1	—	—	—	—	—	—
Bond 3	0.762486545	0.03232004	0.539232667	1	—	—	—	—	—
Bond 4	0.80490507	0.030394112	0.928891982	0.675469702	1	—	—	—	—
Bond 5	0.873289816	0.023278035	0.865561277	0.698241657	0.982726525	1	—	—	—
Bond 6	0.987947611	0.03032363	0.573606745	0.771601295	0.810561264	0.880679105	1	—	—
Bond 7	0.932169847	0.023653633	0.439369201	0.782454722	0.684073945	0.774954075	0.89795721	1	—
Bond 8	0.912529511	0.022592811	0.586354587	0.608825075	0.788072503	0.858459264	0.866043218	0.932159141	1

Table 7.2   Estimated Variance–Covariance Matrix.

	Benchmark	Bond 1	Bond 2	Bond 3	Bond 4	Bond 5	Bond 6	Bond 7	Bond 8
Benchmark	2.1025E-05	4.49009E-07	7.64749E-06	1.47276E-05	1.74099E-05	2.26991E-05	2.57709E-05	4.09206E-05	4.16176E-05
Bond 1	4.49009E-07	7.67745E-06	3.01039E-07	3.77236E-07	3.97268E-07	3.65626E-07	4.77989E-07	6.27459E-07	6.22645E-07
Bond 2	7.64749E-06	3.01039E-07	8.54715E-06	6.64079E-06	1.28104E-05	1.43447E-05	9.54011E-06	1.22976E-05	1.70503E-05
Bond 3	1.47276E-05	3.77236E-07	6.64079E-06	1.77446E-05	1.34222E-05	1.66733E-05	1.84907E-05	3.15552E-05	2.55087E-05
Bond 4	1.74099E-05	3.97268E-07	1.28104E-05	1.34222E-05	2.22521E-05	2.62785E-05	2.1752E-05	3.08935E-05	3.69755E-05
Bond 5	2.26991E-05	3.65626E-07	1.43447E-05	1.66733E-05	2.62785E-05	3.2134E-05	2.84006E-05	4.20569E-05	4.84021E-05
Bond 6	2.57709E-05	4.77989E-07	9.54011E-06	1.84907E-05	2.1752E-05	2.84006E-05	3.23636E-05	4.89061E-05	4.90038E-05
Bond 7	4.09206E-05	6.27459E-07	1.22976E-05	3.15552E-05	3.08935E-05	4.20569E-05	4.89061E-05	9.16555E-05	8.87629E-05
Bond 8	4.16176E-05	6.22645E-07	1.70503E-05	2.55087E-05	3.69755E-05	4.84021E-05	4.90038E-05	8.87629E-05	9.89292E-05

Table 7.3 Optimized Portfolios with and without Short Sale Constraints.

Sample covariance matrix	Bond 1	Bond 2	Bond 3	Bond 4	Bond 5	Bond 6	Bond 7	Bond 8
With short sales constraints (%)	12.93	14.19	0.00	0.00	0.00	62.41	8.33	2.13
Without short sales constraints (%)	1.99	39.92	−1.43	20.93	−62.38	83.59	3.44	13.93

To get a better insight about whether portfolio optimization allows for a significant improvement in tracking error, we compute the tracking error of an arbitrary equally weighted portfolio of the eight bonds, and it comes out to be a daily 0.14%. The interpretation is that the replicating portfolio will deviate on average by a daily 0.14% from the target. When portfolio optimization is used, on the other hand, we obtain a 0.07% and a 0.04% tracking error for the optimal portfolio in the presence and in the absence of short sale constraints, respectively. These results strongly suggest that portfolio optimization allows for a significant improvement in a passive portfolio strategy since the tracking error is reduced by a factor of 0.14%/0.07% = 2 and 0.14%/0.04% = 3.5. The improvement in terms of quality of replication can be seen from the following three pictures that display the evolution of $100 invested in the benchmark, and three different kinds of replicating portfolios, an equally weighted portfolio (see Figure 7.1), an optimized portfolio with short sale constraints (see Figure 7.2) and an optimized portfolio without short sale constraints (see Figure 7.3).

One problem with that estimator is typically that a covariance matrix may have too many parameters compared to the available data, and this leads to having too few degrees of freedom relative to the number of parameters that have to be estimated, and results in excessive sampling errors. If the number of assets in the portfolio is N, there are indeed $\frac{N(N-1)}{2}$ different covariance terms

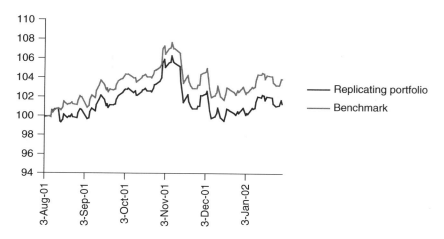

Figure 7.1 Benchmark and equally weighted replicating portfolio.

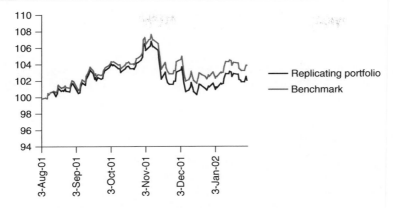

Figure 7.2 Benchmark and optimized portfolio with short sale constraints.

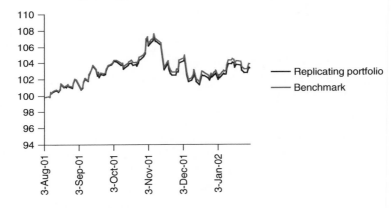

Figure 7.3 Benchmark and optimized portfolio without short sale constraints.

to be estimated. For example, the covariance matrix of the returns of 50 bonds will have 1,225 distinct parameters. It obviously takes a very long history of bond returns to estimate as many as 1,225 parameters with any accuracy. This is a problem because going far back in time to gather more data implies using outdated information.

One possible generalization/improvement to this sample covariance matrix estimation is to allow for declining weights assigned to observations as they go further back in time [see Litterman and Winkelmann (1998)].

$$S = \sum_{t=1}^{T} p_t (R_t - \overline{R})(R_t - \overline{R})^{\top}$$

When $p_t = \frac{1}{T-1}$ for all t, we get back to the usual sample covariance matrix estimator. Typically, the weights are taken to decline exponentially

$$p_t = \frac{\lambda^{T-t+1}}{\displaystyle\sum_{t=1}^{T} \lambda^t}$$

Fixed Income Securities

where the decay rate λ is a calibrated parameter. A commonly used value is $\lambda = 0.94$ [see JP Morgan (1996) or Walter and Lopez (2000)].

Example 7.3 Using the same data as in the previous example, we implement the exponentially weighted estimator of the variance–covariance matrix with $\lambda = 0.94$, and obtain the following optimal portfolios, with and without short sale constraints (see Table 7.4), after resolving the minimization program (7.2).

Table 7.4 Optimized Portfolios with and without Short sale Constraints.

Exponentially weighted estimator	Bond 1	Bond 2	Bond 3	Bond 4	Bond 5	Bond 6	Bond 7	Bond 8
With short sales constraints (%)	0.37	34.44	0.27	4.02	0.00	44.79	0.00	16.10
Without short sales constraints (%)	0.20	29.00	5.21	18.80	−23.80	54.74	−4.97	20.82

When portfolio optimization is used, we obtain a 0.02% and a 0.01% tracking error for the optimal portfolio in the presence and in the absence of short sale constraints, respectively. Because the variance–covariance matrix is different from the sample estimate previously used, such numbers cannot be compared to what was obtained before. The tracking error for the equally weighted portfolio turns out to be 0.12%, while it was equal to 0.14% when the sample estimate of the variance–covariance matrix was used. A first comparison can still be drawn in terms of relative improvement, and we obtain here that tracking error has been reduced by a factor of $0.12\%/0.02\% = 6$ and $0.12\%/0.01\% = 12$, respectively, as opposed to 2 and 3.5 in the case of the sample estimate (see the previous example). A better understanding of the performance of various estimators of the variance–covariance matrixes in this context can actually be achieved by running a horse race on an out-of-sample basis. More specifically, one would have to divide the data set in two subperiods, one used for calibration, the other for back-testing. The different estimators would be calibrated using, say, two-thirds of the available data, perform the optimization, and then record the performance of the replicating portfolio on the remaining one-third of the data. Finally, an ex-post tracking error can be derived as the standard deviation of the excess return of the replicating portfolio compared to the benchmark portfolio. This exercise is left as a problem (see the section called "Problems" in this chapter).

Factor-Based Covariance Matrix

The traditional estimator, the sample covariance matrix, is seldom used because it imposes too little structure. One possible cure to the curse of dimensionality in covariance matrix estimation is to impose some structure on the covariance matrix to reduce the number of parameters to be estimated. In the case of asset returns, a low-dimensional linear factor structure seems natural and consistent with standard asset pricing theory, as linear multifactor models can be economically justified through equilibrium arguments [cf. Merton's Intertemporal Capital Asset Pricing Model (CAPM) (1973)] or arbitrage arguments [cf. Ross's Arbitrage Pricing Theory (1976)]. Therefore, in what follows, we shall focus on a J-factor model with uncorrelated residuals.[2] Of course, this leaves two very important questions: *how much structure should we impose?* (the fewer the factors, the stronger the structure) and *what factors should we use?*

There are two types of factor models, one being a single-index model estimator where the single factor is taken to be a market index, the other being a multiple-index implicit factor model.

One-Factor Market Model   Sharpe's (1963) single-index model assumes that asset returns are generated by

$$h_t = \alpha + \beta m_t + \varepsilon_t$$

where β is the factor loading vector, ε_t a vector of residuals ε_{it} that are assumed to be uncorrelated to market return, denoted by m_t, and to one another. The covariance matrix implied by this model is

$$F = \sigma_m^2 \beta\beta^\top + \Delta$$

where σ_m^2 is the variance of the market portfolio, and Δ is the diagonal matrix containing residual variances. We denote by δ_{ij} the (i, j) entry of Δ and by f_{ij} the (i, j) entry of F.

It is, of course, important to note that the exact composition of the market portfolio is unknown. In particular, no existing market index captures both equity and fixed-income investment opportunities worldwide. The exact composition of the market portfolio, however, is not as critical here as it is for testing the CAPM [see Roll (1977)]. All we need is to explain a significant amount of the variance of most assets (bond returns). As a practical matter, for simplicity, one may take the market index as the equal-weighted portfolio of the N bonds in the sample.

$$m_t = \frac{1}{N} \sum_{i=1}^{N} R_{it}$$

This is similar to Ledoit (1999). Alternatively, a broad-based index can be used as a proxy for the market portfolio.

Example 7.4   Using the same data as in the previous example, we implement a version of the market model by regressing the return on each of the eight bonds in the replicating portfolio on the index return. Table 7.5 records the betas of these bonds, as well as the optimal replicating portfolios with and without short sale constraints, after resolving the minimization program (7.2).

In this case, the presence of short sale constraints does not affect the results of the optimization because short sale constraints are not binding in the first place. We note that the optimal portfolio is now significantly different from the one obtained with the sample estimate and

[2]Another way to impose structure on the covariance matrix is the constant correlation model (Elton and Gruber, 1973). This model can actually be thought of as a James–Stein estimator that shrinks each pair-wise correlation to the global mean correlation.

Fixed Income Securities

Table 7.5   Betas and Optimized Portfolios with and without Short sale Constraints.

Single-index covariance matrix	Bond 1	Bond 2	Bond 3	Bond 4	Bond 5	Bond 6	Bond 7	Bond 8
Beta	0.021	0.361	0.695	0.821	1.071	1.216	1.930	1.963
With short sales constraints (%)	8.20	10.84	8.29	7.81	7.85	48.73	4.74	3.53
Without short sales constraints (%)	8.20	10.84	8.29	7.81	7.85	48.73	4.74	3.53

the exponentially weighted estimate of the variance–covariance matrix. In this context, the number of parameters to be estimated is relatively low. Therefore, the specification risk that is induced by using an index model may be larger than any improvement in estimation risk that can be achieved from that approach.

Multifactor Model   There are two types of multifactor models: explicit factor models and implicit factor models. We have previously discussed the benefits of using a Principle Component Analysis (PCA) to extract a set of implicit factors (see Chapter 3). Let us recall that a PCA consists in transforming a set of K correlated variables into a set of orthogonal variables, or implicit factors, which reproduces the original information present in the correlation structure. Each implicit factor is defined as a linear combination of original variables.

Let us define R as the following matrix:

$$R = (R_{tk})_{\substack{1 \leq t \leq T \\ 1 \leq k \leq K}}$$

We have K variables R_k for $k = 1, \ldots, K$, that is, monthly returns for K different bonds, and T observations of these variables.[3] The idea is that we can describe each variable as a linear function of a reduced number of factors as follows:

$$R_{tk} = \sum_{j=1}^{K} s_{jk} F_{tj}$$

where the K factors F_j are a set of orthogonal variables, and s_{jk} is the sensitivity of the kth variable to the jth factor defined as

$$\frac{\Delta(R_{tk})}{\Delta(F_{tj})} = s_{jk}$$

PCA enables us to decompose R_{tk} as follows:

$$R_{tk} = \sum_{j=1}^{K} \sqrt{\lambda_j} U_{jk} V_{tj}$$

---

[3] The asset returns have first been normalized to have zero mean and unit variance.

where

$(U) = (U_{jk})_{1 \leq j, k \leq K}$ is the matrix of the K eigenvectors of $R^\top R$.

$(U^\top) = (U_{kj})_{1 \leq k, j \leq K}$ is the transpose of U.

$(V) = (V_{tj})_{\substack{1 \leq t \leq T \\ 1 \leq j \leq K}}$ is the matrix of the K eigenvectors of $RR^\top$.

Note that these K eigenvectors are orthonormal. λ_j is the eigenvalue (ordered by degree of magnitude) corresponding to the eigenvector U_j and we denote $s_{jk} = \sqrt{\lambda_j} U_{jk}$ and $V_{tj} = F_{tj}$. s_{jk} is called *the principal component's sensitivity of the kth variable to the jth factor*.

The main challenge is to select a number of factors $J < K$ such that the first J factors capture a large fraction of asset return variance, while the remaining part can be regarded as statistical noise.

$$R_{tk} = \sum_{j=1}^{J} s_{jk} F_{tj} + \sum_{j=J+1}^{K} s_{jk} F_{tj} = \sum_{j=1}^{J} s_{jk} F_{tj} + \varepsilon_{tk}$$

where the residuals ε_{tk} are assumed to be uncorrelated to one another.

The total data set variance percentage explained by the first J factors is given by $\frac{\sum_{j=1}^{J} \lambda_j}{\sum_{j=1}^{K} \lambda_j}$.

We have previously seen that two or three factors typically account for a very large fraction of bond return variations (see Chapter 3).

Shrinkage Estimators

Shrinkage estimators combine two estimators, the sample covariance estimator (which contains large estimation risk but no model risk) and a factor-based estimator (which contains model risk but lower estimation risk) to achieve optimal balance between sampling error and specification error. There are two types of shrinkage estimators that have been introduced in the literature.

- *The first approach is due to Jorion (1985, 1986) who argues that the class of shrinkage estimators as proposed by Stein (1955) handles the problem of parameter uncertainty in portfolio selection appropriately. The estimator suggested for the covariance matrix under suitable assumptions is*

$$S_{\text{Jorion}} = \left(\frac{T-1}{T-N-2} S \right) \left(1 + \frac{1}{T+p} \right) + \frac{p}{T(T+1+p)} \frac{\mathbf{1} \mathbf{1}'}{\mathbf{1}' \left(\frac{T-1}{T-N-2} S \right)^{-1} \mathbf{1}}$$

where S is the sample covariance matrix, $\mathbf{1}$ is a $N \times 1$ vector of ones, and p is some precision parameter defined as $p = \frac{wT}{1-w}$, where w is the shrinkage coefficient

$$w = \frac{N+2}{(N+2) + (\bar{R} - \bar{R}_0 \mathbf{1})' T \left(\frac{T-1}{T-N-2} S \right)^{-1} (\bar{R} - \bar{R}_0 \mathbf{1})}$$

where $\bar{R}_0$ is the grand mean, that is, in this context, the mean of the minimum variance portfolio estimated, obtained using the sample covariance matrix.

Fixed Income Securities

- *Ledoit (1999) offers a new approach to a shrinkage estimator of the variance–covariance matrix by proposing an estimator that optimally shrinks the sample covariance matrix toward the one-factor model covariance matrix*

$$S_{\text{Ledoit}} = \frac{a}{T}(\sigma_m^2 \beta \beta^\top + \Delta) + \left(1 - \frac{a}{T}\right) S$$

where $a = (p - r)/c$, with

$$p = \sum_{i,j=1}^{N} p_{ij} \text{ and } p_{ij} = \frac{1}{T} \sum_{t=1}^{T} [(R_{it} - \overline{R_i})(R_{jt} - \overline{R_j}) - s_{ij}]$$

$$c = \sum_{i,j=1}^{N} c_{ij} \text{ and } c_{ij} = (f_{ij} - s_{ij})^2$$

$$r = \sum_{i,j=1}^{N} r_{ij} \text{ and } r_{ij} = \sum_{t=1}^{T} r_{ijt}$$

and

$$r_{ijt} = \left[\frac{1}{\sigma_m^4} s_{jm} \sigma_m^2 (R_{it} - \overline{R_i}) + s_{im} \sigma_m^2 (R_{jt} - \overline{R_j}) - s_{im} s_{jm} (m_t - \overline{m}) \right]$$
$$\times (R_{it} - \overline{R_i})(R_{jt} - \overline{R_j})(m_t - \overline{m}) - f_{ij} s_{ij}$$

Portfolio Constraints

In a recent paper, Jagannathan and Ma (2000) show that imposing portfolio weight constraints is equivalent to shrinking the extreme covariance estimates toward the average estimates. To the extent that these extreme estimates are more likely to be plagued by estimation error, this shrinking can reduce the sampling error. Hence, they provide formal justification to the well-known fact that imposing portfolio weight constraints actually reduces estimation error.

7.4 Factor-Based Replication

Index replication may also be based upon the risk decomposition allowed by a factor model. Let us recall that a principal component analysis of the term-structure of interest rates allows us to select a small number of (implicit) factors J such that the first J factors capture a large fraction of asset return variance, while the remaining part can be regarded as statistical noise. Let us assume for simplicity that $J = 3$. In that case, each bond return R_{ti} can be written as

$$R_{ti} = s_{1i} F_{t1} + s_{2i} F_{t2} + s_{3i} F_{t3} + \varepsilon_{ti}$$

where the residuals ε_{ti} are assumed to be uncorrelated to one another. Adding over different bond returns, the return on a bond portfolio P can be written as

$$R_{tP} = s_{1P} F_{t1} + s_{2P} F_{t2} + s_{3P} F_{t3} + \varepsilon_{tP}$$

with, for $j = 1, 2, 3$,

$$s_{jP} = \sum_{i=1}^{N} w_i s_{ji}$$

where N is the number of bonds in the bond portfolio P.

Similarly, the return on the benchmark (bond index) can be written as

$$R_{tB} = s_{1B} F_{t1} + s_{2B} F_{t2} + s_{3B} F_{t3} + \varepsilon_{tB}$$

The factor-based replication technique consists in choosing the portfolio weights so as to match the portfolio's and the benchmark's exposure to the common factors:

$$\sum_{i=1}^{N} w_i s_{1i} = s_{1B}$$

$$\sum_{i=1}^{N} w_i s_{2i} = s_{2B}$$

$$\sum_{i=1}^{N} w_i s_{3i} = s_{3B}$$

This is a system of 3 equations (more generally, J equations in case of a J-factor model) and N unknown values in the optimal weights w_i^* for $i = 1, \ldots, N$. It admits more than one solution if $J > N$. The goal is then to choose the weights so that the tracking-error is minimized.

Example 7.5 Using the same data as in the previous example, we regress the return on each of the eight bonds and the benchmark on two factors. Here we use explicit factors for convenience. The first factor is the change in 3-month interest rate, regarded as a proxy for changes in the level of the term-structure, while the second factor is the change in the spread between the 30-year rate and the 3-month rate, regarded as a proxy for changes in the slope of the term-structure. We know from our previous discussion on the term-structure that these two factors usually account for a very large fraction of bond return variation. As an example, Table 7.6 displays the result of this regression when the left-hand variable is the return on the benchmark.

The R-squared for that regression is 0.91, suggesting that more than 90% of the time variation in the return on the benchmark is captured by the time variation in the two aforementioned factors. This provides us with a motivation to use factor-based replication; if we manage to find a portfolio with exactly the same exposure to these two risk factors as the benchmark, then the behavior of that portfolio will be close to that of the benchmark. Table 7.7 records the betas of the bonds and the benchmark with respect to the two risk factors.

We now perform the same analysis as before, using the sample estimate of the variance–covariance matrix[4] to perform the following optimization program

$$\mathrm{Min}_{w_1, \ldots, w_8} TE = \sqrt{\mathbb{V}\mathrm{ar}(R_P - R_B)} = \sqrt{\sum_{i=i,j}^{8} w_i w_j \sigma_{ij} - 2 \sum_{i=1}^{8} w_i \sigma_{iB} + \sigma_B^2}$$

---

[4] A similar optimization could be run with any of the competing estimators for the variance–covariance matrix.

Table 7.6 Regression Results.

	Coefficients
Intercept	6.14942E-05
Factor 1	−27.0865211
Factor 2	−22.2656083

Table 7.7 Betas of the Bonds and the Benchmark with Respect to the Two Risk Factors.

	Beta 1	Beta 2
Benchmark	−27.0865211	−22.26560827
Bond 1	−2.81376114	−1.084816042
Bond 2	−11.1461975	−5.759743001
Bond 3	−19.9855764	−13.46348007
Bond 4	−23.1662469	−15.95768661
Bond 5	−28.7309262	−22.18051504
Bond 6	−32.4878358	−26.25424263
Bond 7	−50.8107969	−48.54826524
Bond 8	−52.2945817	−50.57663054

subject to the constraint

$$\sum_{i=1}^{8} w_i = 1$$

and

$$\sum_{i=i}^{8} w_i s_{1i} = -27.0865211$$

$$\sum_{i=i}^{8} w_i s_{2i} = -22.26560827$$

where s_{1i} (respectively, s_{2i}) is the sensitivity of bond i with respect to the first (respectively, second) factor. The corresponding optimal replicating portfolios in the presence and in the absence of short sale constraints are given in Table 7.8.

Table 7.8 Optimized Portfolios with and without Short sale Constraints.

Factor-based replication	Bond 1	Bond 2	Bond 3	Bond 4	Bond 5	Bond 6	Bond 7	Bond 8
With short sales constraints (%)	16.70	13.71	0.00	0.00	0.00	56.31	10.14	3.14
Without short sales constraints (%)	2.66	46.10	−3.22	8.67	−54.77	82.12	5.21	13.22

These portfolio weights are actually fairly close to what was obtained in the case of the sample covariance matrix estimate, and the in-sample tracking-error is roughly the same (0.07% and 0.04% in the presence and in the absence of short sale constraints, respectively). The usefulness of the factor-based replication approach is that it allows for more robustness, that is, for potential improvement of the out-of-sample tracking-error, because we attempt to replicate what explains the return on the benchmark, as opposed to replicating the return on the benchmark regarded as a black box.

7.5 Derivatives-Based Replication

The replicating portfolio does not necessarily consist of securities sampled out of the index being replicated. A very practical alternative is using futures and swaps, which are liquid market instruments with return characteristics similar to many of the index securities. We refer the reader to Chapters 10 and 11 for more details on these instruments. A variation of the cell-matching technique can actually be applied to replicate the term-structure exposure of any fixed-income index with Treasury futures. Futures are widely used as a duration adjustment tool because of advantages such as no portfolio disruption, ease of establishing and unwinding positions, and low transaction costs. For funds with frequent and significant cash inflows and outflows, replication of benchmark returns with exchange-traded futures is often an attractive strategy. By taking a long or short position in a single contract, investors can match the duration of any benchmark. However, meaningfully replicating the performance of a broad-based market index requires matching its exposures to all segments of the yield curve. A methodology, currently implemented by a number of investors, uses four Treasury futures contracts (2-, 5-, 10- and 30-year) to replicate the curve allocation of an index. By analyzing the distribution of security durations in the index, one may determine the required mix of contracts. The first step is to divide the index into four duration cells. We then compute the allocation and dollar duration within each cell of a perfectly indexed investment of the desired size. Each cell's market value and dollar duration are then matched with a combination of a cash investment and a position in the appropriate futures contract. The cash is usually invested in Treasury bills, though portfolio managers are free to choose other alternatives, such as commercial paper or short-term asset-backed securities, as a source of extra return. Term-structure exposure can be hedged effectively with Treasury futures. Spread risk, inherent in the Credit and Mortgage indices, needs to be hedged separately. Eurodollar futures and swaps can be used in a similar methodology to replicate spread indices.

The same technique has been applied to a broad-based index such as the Lehman Brothers Global Aggregate Index. Its diversity of exposures to currency, yield curve and spread risks makes replication with derivatives a natural choice for this index. Replication strategies using combinations of Treasury-bond futures, money-market futures, and swaps in four currencies—US dollar, euro, yen and sterling—have been tested by Lehman Brothers (see "Quantitative Management of Bond Portfolios," Lehman Brothers Fixed-Income Research Publication, 2001). These four markets make up over 95% of the Global Aggregate Index. Attempts to fully replicate all the other currencies have been shown to yield diminishing returns, as tracking-error declines by no more than 1 to 2 bp/month, while transaction costs increase dramatically.

7.6 Pros and Cons of Stratified Sampling versus Tracking-Error Minimization

The cell-matching approach consists in replicating index attributes, while the tracking-error approach consists in replicating index returns, either directly or through replication of factors explaining a large fraction of index returns.

- *One problem with cell matching is that a mismatch to the benchmark in any cell appears to be equally important. In reality, matching some cells is more critical than matching others because the return (or spread) volatility associated with them is higher.*

- *Sampling technique also ignores correlations among cells that sometimes cause risk from an overweight in one cell to be canceled with an overweight in another.*

- *Tracking-error minimization techniques rely on historical volatilities and correlations between returns on different asset classes or different risk factors in the market. Therefore, the model's "knowledge" is limited to the historical experience observed over the calibration period. Such models may ignore a significant structural change that historically has not yet resulted in return volatility. In other words, it tends to be a backward-looking technique.*

Rather than regarding them as competing methods, we tend to view them as complementary. For example, experienced portfolio managers may be alerted to a possible shift in market conditions by stratified sampling techniques, and may wish to take corrective measures based on their expectations that are not necessarily reflective of history. This makes potentially tracking-error models more reliable for out-of-sample replication.

7.7 End of Chapter Summary

Many investors manage portfolios to match index returns. Even active managers may fall back to passive index tracking in times when they have no definite views. In the context of fixed-income securities, this is known as *bond indexing*. The simplest way to replicate an index is to buy most of the securities in the index in the proper proportions. While this approach is often preferred for equities, it is not practical with bonds.

Fortunately, other methods can efficiently be applied to the problem of bond indexing. There are three basic approaches to index replication other than straightforward replication: cell-matching or stratified sampling, tracking-error minimization and factor-based replication. The cell-matching approach consists in replicating index attributes, while the tracking-error approach consists in replicating index returns directly. Factor-based replication consists in matching the exposure of the replicating portfolio with respect to a set of common factors with that of the benchmark. Good estimates of the variance–covariance matrix of bond returns are needed for tracking-error minimization and factor-based replication. We review in this chapter some of the advanced techniques that can be used to improve variance–covariance matrix estimates.

The replicating portfolio does not necessarily consist of securities sampled out of the index being replicated. A very practical alternative is using futures and swaps, which are liquid market instruments with return characteristics similar to many of the index securities.

7.8 References and Further Reading

7.8.1 Books and Papers

Elton, E., and M. Gruber, 1973, "Estimating the Dependence Structure of Share Prices: Implications for Portfolio Selection", *Journal of Finance*, **28**, 1203–1232.

Fabozzi, F.J., 2001, *Bond Portfolio Management*, 2nd Edition, F.J. Fabozzi Associates, New Hope, Pa.

Jagannathan, R., and T. Ma, 2000, *Covariance Matrix Estimation: Myth and Reality*, Working Paper, Northwestern University.

Morgan, J.P., 1996, J.P. Morgan/Reuters Riskmetrics[TM], Technical Document, New York.

Jorion, P., 1985, "International Portfolio Diversification with Estimation Risk", *Journal of Business*, **58**, 259–278.

Jorion, P., 1986, "Bayes-Stein Estimation for Portfolio Analysis", *Journal of Financial and Quantitative Analysis*, **21**(3), 279–292.

Ledoit, O., 1999, *Improved Estimation of the Covariance Matrix of Stock Returns with an Application to Portfolio Selection*, Working Paper, UCLA.

Lehman Brothers, 1997, *Replicating the MBS Index Risk and Return Characteristics Using Proxy Portfolios*, Lehman Brothers Fixed-Income Research Publication.

Lehman Brothers, 2001, *Quantitative Management of Bond Portfolios*, Lehman Brothers Fixed-Income Research Publication.

Litterman, R., and K. Winkelmann, 1998, Estimating Covariance Matrices, *Goldman Sachs Risk Management Series*.

Merton, R.C., 1973, "An Intertemporal Capital Asset Pricing Model", *Econometrica*, **41**, 867–888.

Roll, R., 1977, "A Critique of the Asset Pricing Theory's Tests—Part 1: On Past and Potential Testability of the Theory", *Journal of Financial Economics*, **4**, 129–176.

Roll, R., 1992, "A Mean/Variance Analysis of Tracking Error", *Journal of Portfolio Management*, **18**(4), 13–22.

Ross, S., 1976, "The Arbitrage Theory of Capital Asset Pricing", *Journal of Economic Theory*, **13**, 341–360.

Sharpe, W., 1963, "A Simplified Model for Portfolio Analysis", *Management Science*, **9**, 277–293.

Stein, C., 1955, Inadmissibility of the Usual Estimator for the Mean of a Multivariate Normal Distribution, *Proceedings of the 3rd Berkeley Symposium on Probability and Statistics*, University of California Press, Berkeley, pp. 197–206.

Walter, C., and J.A. Lopez, 2000, "Is Implied Correlation Worth Calculating? Evidence from Foreign Exchange Option Prices", *Journal of Derivatives*, **7**(3), 65–82.

7.8.2 Websites

www.indexfunds.com/articles/20,000,630_bonds_iss_sect_SH.htm.

7.9 Problems

Exercise 7.1   Would you say it is easier to track a bond index or a stock index? Why or why not?

Exercise 7.2   What are the pros and cons of popular indexing methodologies in the fixed-income universe?

Exercise 7.3   What are the major features of passive fixed-income management and active fixed-income management in terms of philosophy and objective? How do these two types of fixed-income management implement their objective?

Exercise 7.4   What is enhanced index management? In what type of interest-rate context is it potentially most rewarding? Explain why.

Exercise 7.5   What does tracking error mean? Why is it not equal to zero in passive index management?

Exercise 7.6   To what extent is the construction of a bond benchmark portfolio more difficult but also easier than the construction of an equity benchmark portfolio?

Exercise 7.7   This exercise focuses on the impact of changes in the number of bonds used in the replicating portfolio. The data is the same as the one used in the examples for this chapter (see excel file passive_bond_portfolio_strategies.xls).

1. Assume you can only use three bonds, instead of eight, to replicate the performance of the benchmark. Explain which bonds you would select and why.
2. Using the selection of bonds from Question 1, compute the best replicating portfolio using the sample estimate of the variance–covariance matrix, and compare the performance of that portfolio with what was obtained by the portfolio invested in eight bonds.

Exercise 7.8   This exercise focuses on out-of-sample testing of the quality of replicating portfolios obtained using different methods.

1. Use the first two-thirds of the data from excel file Lecture06_passive_bond_portfolio_ strategies.xls (i.e., from 08/03/01 to 12/03/01 included) for calibration of the following estimates of the covariance matrix: sample estimate, exponentially weighted estimate, single-index estimate. On the basis of those estimates, compute the best replicating portfolio in the presence and in the absence of short sale constraints. Also derive the best replicating portfolio when imposing the constraints that the beta of the replicating portfolio with respect to level and slope factors match those of the index.
2. Record the performance of these optimal portfolios on the back-testing period, that is, the last one-third of the original data set (from 12/04/01 to 01/30/02 included). Compute the standard deviation of the excess return of these portfolios over the return on the benchmark. This quantity is known as *out-of-sample tracking error*. Conclude.

8

Active Fixed-Income Portfolio Management

Active fixed-income portfolio managers work under the assumption that investment as well as arbitrage opportunities exist, which yield on average a higher return than the cost incurred to implement them. So as to identify these opportunities, portfolio managers put forward relative advantages to their competitors like information advantage, technical or judgemental skills. Their objective is to have their portfolios outperform their benchmark index. Typically, there are two kinds of active strategies:

- *Trading on interest-rate predictions, which is called market timing.*

- *Trading on market inefficiencies, which is called bond picking.*

In the text that follows we will go through each of these strategies.

8.1 Market Timing: Trading on Interest-Rate Predictions

Active portfolio managers clearly make some bets on changes in the yield curve or one particular segment of the yield curve. We distinguish three kinds of bets:

- *Timing bets based on no change in the yield curve.*

- *Timing bets based on interest-rate level.*

- *Timing bets based on both slope and curvature movements of the yield curve.*

These bets apply to a specific rating class, for example, the term structure of default-free rates. We also discuss systematic bets on bond indices representative of various classes (Treasury, Corporate Investment Grade, High Yield) that are based on econometric analysis. These are known as *tactical style allocation* (TSA) decisions, which constitute a modern form of bond timing strategy.

These bets emphasize the need for building decision-making helping tools, which consist in providing portfolio managers with landmarks they can compare their expectations with. Typically such tools are referred to as *scenario analysis tools*. For a given strategy, a set of scenarios allows for the following two analyses: first, the evaluation of the break-even point from which the strategy will start making or losing money; second, the assessment of the risk that the expectations are not realized. In short, portfolio managers can estimate the return and the risk of the strategy that is implied by their expectations, and thus act coherently in accordance with them.

8.1.1 Timing Bets on No Change in the Yield Curve or "Riding the Yield Curve"

Analyzing the Strategy

When an investor invests in a fixed-income security with a maturity different from his desired holding period, he is exposed to either reinvestment risk or capital risk. Consider, for example, a portfolio manager who has a given amount to invest over 9 months. If he buys a 6-month T-bill, he incurs a reinvestment risk because the 3-month rate at which he will invest his funds in 6 months is not known today. And if he buys a 1-year T-bill, he incurs a risk of capital loss because the price at which he can sell it in 9 months is not known today.

Riding the yield curve is a technique that fixed-income portfolio managers traditionally use in order to enhance returns. When the yield curve is upward sloping and is supposed to remain unchanged, it enables an investor to earn a higher rate of return by purchasing fixed-income securities with maturities longer than the desired holding period, and selling them to profit from falling bond yields as maturities decrease over time. We give below an example of riding the yield curve.

Example 8.1 Riding the Yield Curve Using Bonds

We consider at time $t = 0$ the following zero-coupon curve and five bonds with the same $1,000,000 nominal value and a 6% annual coupon rate. The prices of these bonds are given at time $t = 0$ and 1 year later at time $t = 1$, assuming that the zero-coupon yield curve has remained stable (see table below).

Maturity (Years)	Zero-coupon rate (%)	Bond price at $t = 0$	Bond price at $t = 1$
1	3.90	102.021	102.021
2	4.50	102.842	102.842
3	4.90	103.098	103.098
4	5.25	102.848	102.848
5	5.60	102.077	—

A portfolio manager who has $1,020,770 cash at disposal for 1 year buys 1 unit of the 5-year bond at a market price of 102.077%, and sells it 1 year later at a price of 102.848%. The total return, denoted by TR, of the buy-and-sell strategy is given by the following formula:

$$TR = \left(\frac{102.848 + 6}{102.077} \right) - 1 = 6.633\%$$

Over the same period, a 1-year investment would have just returned 3.90%. The portfolio manager has made 2.733% surplus profit out of his ride. Of course, the calculation is based on the assumption that future interest rates are unchanged. If rates had risen, then the investment would have returned less than 6.633% and might even have returned less than the 1-year rate. Reciprocally, the steeper the curve's slope at the outset, the lower the interest rates when the position is liquidated, and the higher the return on the strategy.

We calculate the total return for different "riding the yield curve" strategies:

- **Strategy one:** *buy the 4-year maturity bond and sell it 1 year later.*

- **Strategy two:** *buy the 3-year maturity bond and sell it 1 year later.*

- **Strategy three:** *buy the 2-year maturity bond and sell it 1 year later.*

Results in terms of total return are summarized in the table below. They show in this example that the longer the maturity of the bond bought at the outset the higher the return on the strategy.

Strategy	Total return (%)
1	6.077
2	5.571
3	5.036

Is the Strategy Performing Well?

It should be noted that if the expectations theory of the term structure holds in practice, then an upward sloping yield curve indicates that future short rates are expected to rise. Therefore, an investor will not earn higher returns by holding long bonds rather than short bonds. In other words, investors should expect to earn about the same amount on short-term or long-term bonds over any horizon. In practice, however, the expectations theory of the term structure may not hold perfectly, and a steep increasing yield curve might mean that expected returns on long-term bonds are higher than on short-term bonds over a given horizon.

Many authors have actually attempted to answer the fundamental question: Is riding down the yield curve a profitable strategy on average? The outcomes of their studies are contrasted:

- *Using a sample of weekly US T-bill prices over the 1970 to 1975 period, Dyl and Joehnk (1981) show that riding the yield curve provides a rate of return higher than the prevailing short-term interest rate without a corresponding increase in risk. They also show that longer-term bills are better than shorter-term bills at providing these returns.*

- *Using prices for implied zero-coupon bonds in the US market over the 1949 to 1988 period, Grieves and Marcus (1992) find, over several subperiods, that riding the yield curve using 6-month zero-coupon bonds stochastically dominates the distribution from buying and holding 3-month zero-coupon bonds.*

- *Chandy and Hsueh (1995) show in the US market over the 1981 to 1985 period that it is not possible to enhance returns by riding the yield curve.*

- *Ang et al. (1998) examine the profitability of riding the yield curve in Australia, Canada, the United Kingdom and the United States over the 1985 to 1997 period with 3-month holding periods and 6-month instruments, and 1-year holding periods and 2-year instruments. With 6-month bills, the buy-and-hold strategy stochastically dominates the riding strategy in the United*

States, as there is no stochastic dominance in Australia, Canada and the United Kingdom. With 2-year bonds, there is no stochastic dominance of one particular strategy in any of the countries. Besides, they show that riding the yield curve using 2-year bonds is less risky than using 6-month bills.

- Using US T-bills over the 1987 to 1997 period, Grieves et al. (1999) examine two holding periods, 3 and 6 months. They find that riding the bill curve on average enhances return over a given holding period compared to a buy-and-hold strategy. This additional return comes at the expense of higher risk but they show that only the most risk-averse investors would reject the riding strategy. Conditioning the ride on the steepness of the yield curve does not really improve the performance for most rides.

8.1.2 Timing Bets on Interest-Rate Level

Strategies based on changes in the level of interest rates are very naive. They are based on the yield-to-maturity curve assuming that one single factor is at the origin of all deviations of the yield curve, only affected by parallel shifts. There are only two possible movements, a decreasing movement and an increasing movement.

When Rates Are Expected to Decrease

If you think that interest rates will decrease in level, you will lengthen the $duration or modified duration of your portfolio by buying bonds or futures contracts (or holding them if you already have these securities in your portfolio) so as to optimize your absolute capital gains or your relative capital gains.

Recall from Chapter 5 that $duration and modified duration enable a portfolio manager to estimate, respectively, the absolute and relative P&L of his bond portfolio after a small yield-to-maturity change. In particular,

- the longer the maturity and the higher the coupon rate, the higher the $duration of a bond;
- the longer the maturity and the lower the coupon rate, the higher the modified duration of a bond.

On date t, the idea is then to build a portfolio with bonds having a long maturity and a high coupon rate if you want to optimize your absolute gain, and a portfolio with bonds having a long maturity and a low coupon rate if you want to optimize your relative gain. We now move on to a specific example.

Example 8.2 Choosing a Portfolio with the Maximum $Duration or Modified Duration Possible

Consider on date t a flat 5% curve and five bonds delivering annual coupon rates with the following features (see table below):

Maturity (Years)	CR (%)	YTM (%)	Price	MD	$Dur	Absolute gain ($)	Relative gain (%)
2	5	5	100	1.859	−185.9	0.936	0.936
10	5	5	100	7.722	−772.2	3.956	3.956
30	5	5	100	15.372	−1,537.2	8.144	8.144
30	7.5	5	138.43	14.269	−1,975.3	10.436	7.538
30	10	5	176.86	13.646	−2,413.4	12.727	7.196

CR stands for coupon rate, YTM for yield to maturity, MD for modified duration and $Dur for $duration.

A portfolio manager thinks that the YTM curve level will very rapidly decrease by 0.5% to reach 4.5%. He calculates the absolute gain and the relative gain he will earn with each of these five bonds. If he wants to maximize his absolute gain, he will choose the 30-year bond with 10% coupon rate. On the contrary, if he prefers to maximize his relative gain, he will invest in the 30-year bond with 5% coupon rate. Note that the difference in terms of relative gain reaches 7.208% between the 30-year bond and the 2-year bond with 5% coupon rate.

When Rates Are Expected to Increase

On the contrary, if you think that interest rates will increase in level, you will shorten the $duration or modified duration of your portfolio by selling bonds or futures contracts, or alternatively you will hold short-term instruments until maturity and roll over at higher rates. This strategy is known as *rollover*. We now present an example of such a strategy.

Example 8.3   Rollover Strategy

Consider at time $t = 0$ a flat 5% yield-to-maturity curve. A portfolio manager has money to invest over a 5-year horizon. He anticipates an interest rate increase by 1% in 1 year. Instead of buying directly a 5-year bond (Scenario 1), he buys a 1-year bond, holds it until maturity and buys in 1 year a 4-year bond (Scenario 2). Suppose now that his anticipation is correct:

- *Scenario 1: if he buys a 5-year bond with a 5% annual coupon rate at a $100 price, the total return rate of his investment after 1 year is*

$$\text{Total Return Rate} = \frac{96.535 + 5 - 100}{100} = 1.53\%$$

where $96.535 is the price of the 5-year bond after 1 year, discounted at a 6% rate.

After 1 year, he gains a 1.53% annual total return rate and he holds a 4-year maturity bond with a 5% coupon rate.

- **Scenario 2:** *if he adopts the rollover strategy, the total return of his investment after 1 year is*

$$\text{Total Return Rate} = \frac{105 - 100}{100} = 5\%$$

After 1 year, he gains a 5% annual total return rate and he holds a 4-year maturity bond with a 6% coupon rate and $5 in cash.

Suppose now that the yield-to-maturity curve remains stable at 6% over the next four years. We are able to calculate the annual total return of his investment over the 5-year period in the two cases, assuming that he has reinvested the intermediary cash flows he has received at an annual rate of 6%.

- **Scenario 1:** *the portfolio manager receives the following cash flows:*

Time	0	1Y later	2Y later	3Y later	4Y later	5Y later
Cash flows ($)	−100	5	5	5	5	105

and the annual total return over the period is

$$\text{Total Return Rate} = \left(\frac{128.185}{100}\right)^{1/5} - 1 = 5.092\%$$

where $128.185 is, 5 years later, the sum obtained by the portfolio manager after reinvesting the intermediary cash flows at a 6% annual rate.

- **Scenario 2:** *the portfolio manager receives the following cash flows:*

Time	0	1Y later	2Y later	3Y later	4Y later	5Y later
Cash flows ($)	−100	5	6	6	6	106

Note that 1 year later he receives $105 and reinvests $100 to buy a 4-year maturity bond with a 6% coupon rate; so the net cash flow is $5. The annual total return over the period is

$$\text{Total Return Rate} = \left(\frac{132.56}{100}\right)^{1/5} - 1 = 5.8\%$$

where $132.56 is, 5 years later, the sum obtained by the portfolio manager after reinvesting the intermediary cash flows at a 6% annual rate.

8.1.3   Timing Bets on Specific Changes in the Yield Curve

We know, however, that the yield curve is potentially affected by many other movements than parallel shifts. These include, in particular, pure slope and curvature movements, as well as combinations of level, slope and curvature movements [see, for example, Litterman and Scheinkman (1991)]. It is in general fairly complex to know under what exact market conditions a given strategy might generate a positive or a negative payoff when all these possible movements are accounted for. Our objective here is to understand this point. We first define very standard strategies like bullet and barbell strategies. We then move on to discuss more complex strategies like butterfly strategies and other semihedged strategies.

Bullet, Barbell and Ladder Strategies

- *A bullet portfolio is constructed by concentrating investments on a particular maturity of the yield curve.*

Example 8.4 A portfolio invested 100% in the 5-year maturity T-bond is an example of a bullet.

- *A barbell portfolio is constructed by concentrating investments at the short-term and the long-term ends of the yield curve.*

Example 8.5 A portfolio invested half in the 6-month maturity T-bill and half in the 30-year maturity T-bond is an example of a barbell.

A barbell is known to be more convex than a bullet with the same duration, as illustrated in the following remark.

Remark 8.1 A Barbell is More Convex than a Bullet with the Same Duration

Let us consider Figure 8.1 representing the relationship between the convexity and the Macaulay duration of a zero-coupon bond, the yield curve is assumed to be flat at 5% (but the relationship still holds for other curve shapes).

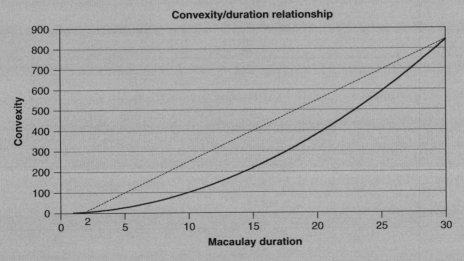

Figure 8.1 Convexity/duration relationship.

As this relationship is convex, any straight line linking one point of the curve to another one is above the curve. In our example, the line connecting the 2-year duration point to the 30-year duration point corresponds to the various combinations of the two zero-coupon bonds with, respectively, 2-year and 30-year maturity in a barbell structure for different Macaulay duration values. It follows that the convexity of a barbell portfolio is higher than the convexity of a Macaulay duration matched bullet portfolio.

- *A ladder portfolio is constructed by investing equal amounts in bonds with different maturity dates.*

Example 8.6 A portfolio invested for 20% in the 1-year T-bond, 20% in the 2-year T-bond, 20% in the 3-year T-bond, 20% in the 4-year T-bond and finally, 20% in the 5-year T-bond is an example of a ladder.

We can construct very different ladders depending on the maturity of the bonds we invest in; for example, a ladder whose investments are concentrated at the short-term end of the yield curve (maturities between 1 month and 1 year) is very different from a ladder whose investments are equally distributed between short-term, medium-term and long-term maturities.

Butterfly Strategy[1]

A *butterfly* is one of the most common fixed-income active strategies used by practitioners.[2] It is the combination of a barbell (called *the wings of the butterfly*) and a bullet (called *the body of the butterfly*). The purpose of the trade is to adjust the weights of these components so that the transaction is cash-neutral and has a $duration equal to zero. The latter property guarantees a quasi-perfect interest-rate neutrality when only small parallel shifts affect the yield curve. Besides, the butterfly, which is usually structured so as to display a positive convexity, generates a positive gain if large parallel shifts occur. On the other hand, as we let the yield curve be affected by more complex movements than parallel shifts, including slope and curvature movements, the performance of the strategy can be drastically impacted. It is in general fairly complex to know under which exact market conditions a given butterfly generates positive or negative payoffs when all these possible movements are accounted for. In what follows, we show that there actually exist many different kinds of butterflies (some of which are not cash-neutral), which are structured so as to generate a positive payoff in case a particular move of the yield curve occurs. Finally, we address the question of measuring the performance and the risk of a butterfly.

A Convex Trade When only parallel shifts affect the yield curve, the strategy is structured so as to have a positive convexity. An investor is then certain to enjoy a positive payoff if the yield curve is affected by a positive or a negative parallel shift. This point is illustrated in the following example.

---

[1] A version of this section first appeared in Journal of Bond Trading and Management in 2002. See Martellini *et al.* (2002).
[2] See Choudhry (2001) for a description of this strategy including, in particular, an example of a butterfly analysis on Bloomberg.

Example 8.7 We consider three bonds with short, medium and long maturities whose features are summarized in the following table.

Maturity (Years)	Coupon rate (%)	YTM (%)	Bond price	$Duration	Quantity
2	5	5	100	−185.9	q_s
5	5	5	100	−432.9	−1,000
10	5	5	100	−772.2	q_l

These bonds are hypothetical bonds assumed to be default-risk free.

The bonds' face value is normalized to be $100, YTM stands for yield to maturity, bond prices are dirty prices and we assume a flat yield-to-maturity curve in this example. We structure a butterfly in the following way:

- *we sell 1,000 5-year maturity bonds;*
- *we buy q_s 2-year maturity bonds and q_l 10-year maturity bonds.*

The quantities q_s and q_l are determined so that the butterfly is cash- and $duration-neutral, that is, we impose that they satisfy the following system:

$$\begin{cases} (q_s \times 185.9) + (q_l \times 772.2) = 1,000 \times 432.9 \\ (q_s \times 100) + (q_l \times 100) = 1,000 \times 100 \end{cases}$$

whose solution is

$$\begin{pmatrix} q_s \\ q_l \end{pmatrix} = \begin{pmatrix} 185.9 & 772.2 \\ 100 & 100 \end{pmatrix}^{-1} \times \begin{pmatrix} 432,900 \\ 100,000 \end{pmatrix} = \begin{pmatrix} 578.65 \\ 421.35 \end{pmatrix}$$

Of course, in a real market situation, we would buy 579 2-year maturity bonds and 421 10-year maturity bonds.[3] We now draw the profile of the strategy gain depending on the value of the yield to maturity (see Figure 8.2).

The butterfly has a positive convexity. Whatever the value of the yield to maturity, the strategy always generates a gain. This gain is all the more substantial as the yield to maturity reaches a level further away from 5%. The gain has a convex profile with a perfect symmetry around the 5% x-axis. For example, the total return reaches $57 when the yield to maturity is 4%.

We know, however, that the yield curve is potentially affected by many movements other than parallel shifts. It is in general fairly complex to know under what exact market conditions a given butterfly might generate a positive or a negative payoff when all these possible movements are accounted for [see Mann and Ramanlal (1997)]. Some butterflies are structured so as to payoff if a particular move of the yield curve occurs.

---

[3]On the market you actually buy bonds in terms of amount and not in terms of number of securities. You will or not round the amount you want to buy, depending on the minimum amount of the security that can be purchased. Here, for simplicity, the quantity of bonds is measured in terms of number.

Fixed Income Securities

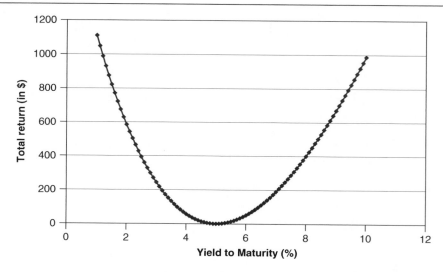

Figure 8.2 Profile of the P&L's butterfly strategy depending on the value of the yield to maturity.

Different Kinds of Butterflies   While a feature common to all butterflies is that they always have a $duration equal to zero, they actually come in many very different shapes and forms that we now examine in detail. In the case of a standard butterfly, the barbell is a combination of a short-term bond and a long-term bond and the bullet is typically a medium-term bond. α, the quantity of the medium-term bond in the portfolio, is defined at date 0 by the investor.

Maturity	Bond price	Quantity	$Duration
Short	P_s	q_s	D_s
Medium	P_m	$q_m = \alpha$	D_m
Long	P_l	q_l	D_l

Cash- and $duration-Neutral Weighting   The idea is to adjust the weights so that the transaction has a zero $duration, and the initial net cost of the portfolio is also zero, which can be written as

$$\begin{cases} q_s D_s + q_l D_l + \alpha D_m = 0 \\ q_s P_s + q_l P_l + \alpha P_m = 0 \end{cases} \tag{8.1}$$

Solving this linear system yields the quantities q_s and q_l to hold in the short-term and the long-term bonds, respectively.

Example 8.8   We consider three bonds with the following features

Maturity (Years)	YTM (%)	Bond price ($)	Quantity	$Duration
2	4.5	100.936	q_s	−188.6
5	5.5	97.865	−10,000	−421.17
10	6	92.64	q_l	−701.14

These bonds are again hypothetical bonds, assumed to be default-risk free.

We structure a butterfly in the following way:

- *we sell 10,000 5-year maturity bonds;*
- *we buy q_s 2-year maturity bonds and q_l 10-year maturity bonds.*

Quantities q_s and q_l are determined so that the butterfly satisfies the system (8.1):

$$\begin{cases} (q_s \times 188.6) + (q_l \times 701.14) = (10,000 \times 421.17) \\ (q_s \times 100.936) + (q_l \times 92.64) = (10,000 \times 97.865) \end{cases}$$

Solving the system, we obtain q_s and q_l

$$\begin{pmatrix} q_s \\ q_l \end{pmatrix} = \begin{pmatrix} 188.6 & 701.14 \\ 100.936 & 92.64 \end{pmatrix}^{-1} \times \begin{pmatrix} 4,211,734 \\ 978,649 \end{pmatrix} = \begin{pmatrix} 5,553.5 \\ 4,513.1 \end{pmatrix}$$

Some strategies do not require a zero initial cash flow. In this case, there is an initial cost of financing. Three classic strategies are the fifty–fifty weighting butterfly, the regression-weighting butterfly as first described by Grieves (1999) and the maturity-weighting butterfly.

Fifty–Fifty Weighting The idea is to adjust the weights so that the transaction has a zero \$duration and the same \$duration on each wing so as to satisfy the two following equations:

$$\begin{cases} q_s D_s + q_l D_l + \alpha D_m = 0 \\ q_s D_s = q_l D_l = \dfrac{-\alpha D_m}{2} \end{cases} \tag{8.2}$$

The aim of this butterfly is to make the trade neutral to some small steepening and flattening movements. In terms of yield to maturity (YTM), if the spread change between the body and the short wing is equal to the spread change between the long wing and the body, a fifty–fifty weighting butterfly is neutral to such curve movements. Then, for a steepening scenario "−30/0/30," which means that the short wing YTM decreases by 30 bps and the long wing YTM increases by 30 bps while the body YTM does not move, the trade is quasi-curve-neutral. The same would apply for a flattening scenario "30/0/−30."

Example 8.9 We consider the same components of the butterfly as in the previous example.

The quantities q_s and q_l are determined so that the butterfly satisfies the system (8.2):

$$\begin{cases} (q_s \times 188.6) + (q_l \times 701.14) = (10,000 \times 421.17) \\ (q_s \times 188.6) - (q_l \times 701.14) = 0 \end{cases}$$

Solving the system, we obtain q_s and q_l

$$\begin{pmatrix} q_s \\ q_l \end{pmatrix} = \begin{pmatrix} 188.6 & 701.14 \\ 188.6 & -701.14 \end{pmatrix}^{-1} \times \begin{pmatrix} 4,211,734 \\ 0 \end{pmatrix} = \begin{pmatrix} 11,165.7 \\ 3,003.5 \end{pmatrix}$$

The fifty–fifty weighting butterfly is not cash-neutral. In the example above, the portfolio manager has to pay $426,623, and if he carries the position during 1 day, he will have to support a financing cost equal to $46, assuming a 1-day short rate equal to 4%.

Regression-Weighting The idea is to adjust the weights so that the transaction has a zero $duration, and so as to satisfy the two following equations:

$$\begin{cases} q_s D_s + q_1 D_1 + \alpha D_m = 0 \\ q_s D_s \times (1/\beta) = q_1 D_1 \end{cases} \tag{8.3}$$

As short-term rates are much more volatile than long-term rates, we normally expect the short wing to move more from the body than the long wing. This stylized fact motivates the introduction of a coefficient β obtained by regressing changes in the spread between the long wing and the body on changes in the spread between the body and the short wing. This coefficient is of course dependent on the data frequency used (daily, weekly or monthly changes). Assuming that we obtain a value of, say, 0.5 for the regression coefficient, it means that for a 20-bps spread change between the body and the short wing, we obtain on average a 10-bps spread change between the long wing and the body. Then, for a steepening scenario "−30/0/15," which means that the short wing YTM decreases by 30 bps, the body YTM does not move and the long wing YTM increases by 15 bps, or for a flattening scenario "30/0/−15," the trade is quasi-curve-neutral. Note finally that the fifty–fifty weighting butterfly is equivalent to a regression-weighting butterfly with a regression coefficient equal to 1.

Example 8.10 We consider the same components of the butterfly as in the two previous examples.

Quantities q_s and q_1 are determined so that the butterfly satisfies the system (8.3):

$$\begin{cases} (q_s \times 188.6) + (q_1 \times 701.14) = (10,000 \times 421.17) \\ (q_s \times 188.6) - (0.5 \times q_1 \times 701.14) = 0 \end{cases}$$

with a solution

$$\begin{pmatrix} q_s \\ q_1 \end{pmatrix} = \begin{pmatrix} 188.6 & 701.14 \\ 188.6 & -350.57 \end{pmatrix}^{-1} \times \begin{pmatrix} 4,211,734 \\ 0 \end{pmatrix} = \begin{pmatrix} 7,443.8 \\ 4,004.7 \end{pmatrix}$$

In the example above, the portfolio manager has to pay $143,695, and if he carries the position during 1 day, he will have to incur a financing cost equal to $15, assuming a 1-day short rate equal to 4%.

Maturity-Weighting The idea is to adjust the weights so that the transaction has a zero $duration and so as to satisfy the following three equations:

$$\begin{cases} q_s D_s + q_1 D_1 + \alpha D_m = 0 \\ q_s D_s = -\alpha \left(\dfrac{M_m - M_s}{M_1 - M_s} \right) D_m \\ q_1 D_1 = -\alpha \left(\dfrac{M_1 - M_m}{M_1 - M_s} \right) D_m \end{cases} \tag{8.4}$$

where M_s, M_m and M_l are the maturities of the short-term, the medium-term and the long-term bonds, respectively.

Maturity-weighting butterflies are structured similarly to regression-weighting butterflies, but instead of searching for a regression coefficient β that is dependent on historical data, the idea is to weight each wing of the butterfly with a coefficient depending on the maturities of the three bonds. In fact using equation (8.4) we show that

$$q_s D_s = \left(\frac{M_m - M_s}{M_l - M_m} \right) q_l D_l$$

Finally, a maturity-weighting butterfly is equivalent to a regression-weighting butterfly with a regression coefficient equal to $\beta = \frac{M_m - M_s}{M_l - M_m}$.

Example 8.11 We consider the same components of the butterfly as in the three previous examples.

The quantities q_s and q_l are determined so that the butterfly satisfies the system (8.4):

$$\begin{cases} (q_s \times 188.6) + (q_l \times 701.14) = (10{,}000 \times 421.17) \\ (q_s \times 188.6) = (10{,}000 \times (3/8) \times 421.17) \end{cases}$$

Solving the system, we obtain q_s and q_l

$$\begin{pmatrix} q_s \\ q_l \end{pmatrix} = \begin{pmatrix} 188.6 & 701.14 \\ 188.6 & 0 \end{pmatrix}^{-1} \times \begin{pmatrix} 4{,}211{,}734 \\ 1{,}579{,}400 \end{pmatrix} = \begin{pmatrix} 8{,}374.3 \\ 3{,}754.4 \end{pmatrix}$$

In the above example, the portfolio manager has to pay $214,427, and if he carries the position during 1 day, he will have to support a financing cost equal to $23, assuming a 1-day short rate equal to 4%.

How to Measure the Performance and the Risk of a Butterfly? There are two possible ways of detecting interesting opportunities for a butterfly strategy. The first indicator, the total return indicator, may also be applied to other types of strategies. The second indicator is based upon an analysis of historical spreads.

Total Return Measure In an attempt to measure the abnormal performance of a given strategy with respect to another given strategy for a specific scenario of yield curve evolution, one needs to perform a total return analysis. This implies taking into account the profit in terms of price changes, interest paid, and reinvestment on interest and principal paid. The total return in $ from date t to date $t + dt$ is given by

Total Return in $ = (sell price at date $t + dt$ − buy price at date t + received coupons from date t to date $t + dt$ + interest gain from reinvested payments from date t to date $t + dt$).

When the butterfly generates a nonzero initial cash flow, we calculate the net total return in $ by subtracting the financing cost from the total return in $:

Net Total Return in $ = Total Return in $ − Financing Cost in $

Example 8.12   Taking into account the four kinds of butterfly strategies, we consider again the same components of the butterfly as in the four previous examples.

We always structure the butterfly so as to sell the body and buy the wings, and assume seven different movements of the term structure:

- *no movement ("Unch" for unchanged);*

- *parallel movements with a uniform change of +20 bps or −20 bps for the three YTMs;*

- *steepening and flattening movements in which the curve rotates around the body; for example, −30/0/30 meaning that the short wing YTM decreases by 30 bps, the body YTM does not move and the long wing YTM increases by 30 bps.*

Table 8.1 displays net total returns in $ for the four different butterflies carried for only 1 day. Besides we assume that the cost of carry is 4%.

For an unchanged curve, the net total return in $ for each of the butterflies is very low as we may expect since the position is carried out during just 1 day.

In the second and third columns of the table, we increase and decrease, respectively, all three YTMs by 20 bps. Because the four strategies are $duration-neutral, the net returns are very close to zero. The wings, which exhibit larger convexity, outperform the body for parallel shifts, except for the fifty–fifty weighting because of the cost of carry.

The fourth to seventh columns of the table show the results for different steepening and flattening scenarios. The net total return is very different from one butterfly to another. We note the following:

- *The cash- and $duration-neutral weighting butterfly has a negative return for a steepening and a positive return for a flattening. This is because the major part of the $duration of the trade is in the long wing. When the move of the long wing YTM goes from 30 to 15 bps, the net return increases from −$6,214 to −$1,569 and inversely decreases from $6,495 to $1,646 when the long wing YTM goes from −30 to −15 bps.*

- *For the fifty–fifty weighting butterfly, when the changes between the body and the short wing on the one hand, and between the long wing and the body on the other hand, are equal, the net total return is very close to zero. This is because the butterfly is structured so as to have the same $duration in each wing. Besides we note that returns are positive because of the difference in convexity between the body and the wings. The fifty–fifty weighting butterfly has a positive return for a steepening and a negative return for a flattening.*

Table 8.1   Overnight Butterfly Trades (sell the body, buy the wings)—Daily Net Total Return in $.

Kinds of butterfly	Unch	+20	−20	−30/0/30	30/0/−30	−30/0/15	30/0/−15
Cash-neutral	−9	11	11	−6,214	6,495	−1,569	1,646
Fifty–fifty weighting	−9	−1	−5	140	116	3,192	−3,110
Regression-weighting	−9	7	6	−4,087	4,347	35	44
Maturity-weighting	−9	5	3	−3,040	3,289	824	−744

- As expected, the regression-weighting butterfly with a regression coefficient equal to 0.5 is quasi-curve-neutral to the two scenarios for which it was structured ("−30/0/15" and "30/0/−15"). Returns are positive because of a difference of convexity between the body and the wings. It has a negative return for the steepening scenario "−30/0/30" as it has a positive return for the flattening scenario "30/0/−30" because most of the $duration is in the long wing.

- The maturity-weighting scenario has about the same profile as the regression-weighting butterfly. In fact, it corresponds to a regression-weighting butterfly with a regression coefficient equal to 0.6 [(5 − 2)/(10 − 5)]. For a flattening scenario (30/0/−18) and a steepening scenario (−30/0/18), it would be curve-neutral.

Spread Measures   Spread measures provide very good estimates of total returns in dollars. This indicator applies to all kinds of butterfly except for the cash- and $duration-neutral combination.

- For a fifty–fifty-weighting butterfly, the approximate total return in $ is given by

$$\text{Total Return in } \$ \simeq \alpha D_m \triangle R_m + q_s D_s \triangle R_s + q_l D_l \triangle R_l$$

which translates into, using equation (8.2)

$$\text{Total Return in } \$ \simeq \alpha D_m \left[\triangle R_m - \frac{(\triangle R_s + \triangle R_l)}{2} \right]$$

This is used to determine the following spread:

$$R_m - \left(\frac{R_s + R_l}{2} \right)$$

- For a regression-weighting butterfly, the approximate total return in $ is given by

$$\text{Total Return in } \$ \simeq \alpha D_m \triangle R_m + q_s D_s \triangle R_s + q_l D_l \triangle R_l$$

From equation (8.3), we obtain

$$\text{Total Return in } \$ \simeq \alpha D_m \left[\triangle R_m - \left(\frac{\beta}{\beta + 1} \right) \triangle R_s - \left(\frac{1}{\beta + 1} \right) \triangle R_l \right]$$

which is used to determine the following spread:

$$R_m - \left(\frac{\beta}{\beta + 1} \right) R_s - \left(\frac{1}{\beta + 1} \right) R_l$$

- For a strategy with a maturity-weighting butterfly, the approximate total return in $ is also given by

$$\text{Total Return in } \$ \simeq \alpha D_m \triangle R_m + q_s D_s \triangle R_s + q_l D_l \triangle R_l$$

From equation (8.4), we obtain

$$\text{Total Return in } \$ \simeq \alpha D_m \left[\triangle R_m - \left(\frac{M_m - M_s}{M_l - M_s} \right) \triangle R_s - \left(\frac{M_l - M_m}{M_l - M_s} \right) \triangle R_l \right]$$

which yields the following spread:

$$R_m - \left(\frac{M_m - M_s}{M_l - M_s} \right) R_s - \left(\frac{M_l - M_m}{M_l - M_s} \right) R_l$$

Table 8.2   Overnight Butterfly Trades (sell the body, buy the wings)—Approximative Total Return in \$ Using Spread Indicators.

Kinds of butterfly	Unch	+20	−20	−30/0/30	30/0/−30	−30/0/15	30/0/−15
Fifty–fifty weighting	0	0	0	0	0	3,159	−3,159
Regression-weighting	0	0	0	−4,212	4,212	0	0
Maturity-weighting	0	0	0	−3,159	3,159	790	−790

Using these three spread indicators, we calculate the approximate total returns in \$ for the butterflies examined in the previous example. Results are summarized in Table 8.2. From a comparison with the total returns in \$ obtained in Table 8.1, we can see that spread indicators provide a very accurate estimate of the total returns in \$.

A historical analysis of these spreads gives an indication of the highest or the lowest values, which may be used as indicators of opportunities to enter a butterfly strategy. Note that this spread analysis does not take into account the effect of received coupons and financing costs of the trades.

Level, Slope and Curvature \$Duration Risk Measures   One way to measure the sensitivity of a butterfly to interest-rate risk is to compute the level, slope and curvature \$durations in the Nelson and Siegel (1987) model (see Chapter 4 for a detailed presentation of this model, and Chapter 6 to see how to hedge a bond portfolio using level, slope and curvature \$durations).

The price P_t at date t of a butterfly (sell the body and buy the wings) is the sum of its n future discounted cash flows C_i multiplied by the amount invested q_i (for example, q_i is −1,000 for the cash flows of the body if we sell 1,000 of the medium-term bond). Some of these cash flows are of course negative because we sell the body. The price is expressed as follows:

$$P_t = \sum_{i=1}^{n} q_i \cdot C_i \cdot e^{-\theta_i R^c(t,\theta_i)}$$

Using equation (6.6), the butterfly level, slope and curvature \$durations, denoted respectively by D_0, D_1 and D_2, are given by

$$\begin{cases} D_{0,t} = \dfrac{\partial P_t}{\partial \beta_0} = -\sum q_i \cdot \theta_i C_i e^{-\theta_i R^c(t,\theta_i)} \\[2em] D_{1,t} = \dfrac{\partial P_t}{\partial \beta_1} = -\sum q_i \cdot \theta_i \left[\dfrac{1 - \exp\left(-\dfrac{\theta_i}{\tau}\right)}{\dfrac{\theta_i}{\tau}} \right] C_i e^{-\theta_i R^c(t,\theta_i)} \\[2em] D_{2,t} = \dfrac{\partial P_t}{\partial \beta_2} = -\sum q_i \cdot \theta_i \left[\dfrac{1 - \exp\left(-\dfrac{\theta_i}{\tau}\right)}{\dfrac{\theta_i}{\tau}} - \exp\left(-\dfrac{\theta_i}{\tau}\right) \right] C_i e^{-\theta_i R^c(t,\theta_i)} \end{cases} \quad (8.5)$$

At any date t, from a derivation of the zero-coupon yield curve based on this model, one can compute the level, slope and curvature \$durations of the butterfly. Of course, the \$duration D_0 is expected to be very small because the butterfly is structured so as to be neutral to small parallel shifts. The $duration D_1 provides the exposure of the trade to the slope factor. Finally, the $duration D_2 quantifies the curvature risk of the butterfly that can be neutralized by proper hedging.

> **Example 8.13** We compute below the level, slope and curvature $durations of a butterfly in the Nelson and Siegel (1987) model.
>
> At date $t = 0$, the values of the parameters are the following:
>
> | β_0 | β_1 | β_2 | τ |
> |------|------|------|---|
> | 8% | −3% | −1% | 3 |
>
> We consider three hypothetical default risk-free bonds with the following features. The face value of bonds is $100. We structure a cash- and $duration-neutral butterfly by selling the body and buying the wings. We compute the level, slope and curvature $durations of the butterfly from equations (8.5).
>
> | | Maturity (years) | Coupon (%) | Quantity | Price | Level D_0 | Slope D_1 | Curvature D_2 |
> |---|---|---|---|---|---|---|---|
> | Bond 1 | 2 | 5 | 472 | 98.627 | −192.51 | −141.08 | −41.28 |
> | Bond 2 | 7 | 5 | −1,000 | 90.786 | −545.42 | −224.78 | −156.73 |
> | Bond 3 | 15 | 5 | 556 | 79.606 | −812.61 | −207.2 | −173.03 |
> | Butterfly | — | — | — | $0 | 2,744 | 42,987 | 41,041 |
>
> The interpretation of these results is straightforward. For example, based on the butterfly slope $duration D_1, one expects a 0.1% increase of the β_1 parameter to increase the value of the butterfly by 42.987$ ($42,987 \times 0.1\%$). As expected, we can see, in particular, that the level $duration is small compared to the slope and curvature $durations.

While being neutral to small parallel shifts of the yield curve, the purpose of a butterfly strategy is to take specific bets on particular changes in the yield curve. There exist four different types of butterflies, the cash- and $duration-neutral weighting butterfly, the fifty–fifty weighting regression, the regression-weighting butterfly and the maturity-weighting butterfly. We have shown that they have a positive payoff in case the particular flattening or steepening move of the yield curve they were structured for occurs. We have also argued that spread indicators offer a convenient way of detecting the opportunity to enter a specific butterfly. One convenient method to hedge the risk of a butterfly is to use the Nelson and Siegel (1987) model. The idea is to compute the level, slope and curvature durations of the butterfly in this model, and then to construct semihedged strategies. A portfolio manager structuring, for example, a fifty–fifty weighting butterfly (by selling the body and buying the wings) is then able to take a particular bet on a steepening move of the yield curve while being hedged against the curvature risk. We now move on to other kinds of semihedged strategies.

Semihedged Strategies

The idea is still to make a particular bet on a movement of the yield curve while being hedged against all other movements or some of them by using the level, slope and curvature $durations of the Nelson and Siegel (1987) model. We develop below the example of a ladder hedged against a slope movement. Of course, many different products can be structured in a similar way.

Example 8.14   A Ladder Hedged Against a Slope Movement

A portfolio manager who anticipates a parallel decrease in the zero-coupon yield curve creates a ladder that has equal amounts of securities with a maturity between 1 and 10 years. But he fears a slope movement of the curve and then seeks to be hedged against a change in the β_1 parameter, which is responsible for the slope variations. Recall that the Nelson–Siegel functional form gives the zero-coupon rate $R^c(0,\theta)$ at time $t = 0$ with maturity θ as follows:

$$R^c(0,\theta) = \beta_0 + \beta_1 \left[\frac{1 - \exp\left(-\dfrac{\theta}{\tau_1}\right)}{\dfrac{\theta}{\tau_1}} \right] + \beta_2 \left[\frac{1 - \exp\left(-\dfrac{\theta}{\tau_1}\right)}{\dfrac{\theta}{\tau_1}} - \exp\left(-\dfrac{\theta}{\tau_1}\right) \right]$$

Suppose at time $t = 0$ that the Nelson and Siegel parameters are given by $\beta_0 = 8\%$, $\beta_1 = -3.5\%$, $\beta_1 = 0.1\%$ and $\tau_1 = 3$ so that we obtain the following zero-coupon yield curve (expressed on an annual compounding frequency basis) and discounted factors for maturities between 1 and 10 years:

Maturity	Zero-coupon rate (%)	Discounted factors
1	5.166	0.95088
2	5.619	0.89642
3	5.986	0.83994
4	6.285	0.78362
5	6.531	0.72883
6	6.734	0.67639
7	6.902	0.62675
8	7.044	0.58011
9	7.163	0.53653
10	7.265	0.49595

A portfolio manager creates a ladder with the following bonds whose maturity, coupon rate and price are given in the following table:

Maturity	Coupon rate (%)	Price ($)	Maturity	Coupon rate (%)	Price ($)
1	5	9,984.217	6	10	11,639.930
2	4	9,703.161	7	6	9,569.164
3	6	10,011.787	8	4	8,234.310
4	8	10,612.880	9	8	10,660.888
5	9	11,067.976	10	5	8,517.199

The price of this ladder, as the sum of each of its constituents, is \$100,001.514. The portfolio manager anticipates a rapid decrease of the curve and wants to be hedged against a slope movement. More precisely he anticipates a change in the value of the β_0 parameter from 8 to 7.5% and wants to be hedged against any deviation of the β_1 parameter. Under the parallel shift scenario when β_0 goes from 8 to 7.5%, the price of the ladder becomes \$102,293.385, and the portfolio manager gains \$2,291.871, which represents a total return equal to 2.29%. But if the yield curve is affected by a flattening movement and if, for example, β_1 goes from -3.5 to -3%, the price of the ladder becomes \$98,978.403, which means that the portfolio manager loses \$1,023.111.

The portfolio manager wants to be hedged against any slope movement. The idea is to construct a global portfolio with the ladder and a bond serving as hedging instrument[4] to be hedged against any deviation of the β_1 parameter. The hedging instrument is a 5-year maturity bond with coupon rate 6% and a price of \$9,808.069. The \$duration of the ladder to the β_1 parameter at time $t = 0$ is $-203,629.365$. We calculate also the \$duration of the hedging instrument to the β_1 parameter, which is $-22,063.868$. We make the global portfolio (ladder $+$ a q quantity of the hedging instrument to be determined) globally insensitive to any variation of the β_1 parameter, which means we have to solve the following equation:

$$-203,629.365 + q \times -22,063.868 = 0$$

so that we obtain q, the quantity of the hedging instrument to sell

$$q = -9.22909$$

At time $t = 0$, the price of the global portfolio is \$9,481.986. If β_1 goes from -3.5 to -3% (slope move), then the price of the global portfolio becomes \$9,471.114, which means that the loss of the portfolio manager is only \$10.872, a quasi-perfect hedge. But if β_0 goes from 8 to 7.5% the price of the global portfolio becomes \$9,734.661, which means that the portfolio manager gains \$252.675, a total return equal to 2.66%.

To conclude, our product is perfectly hedged against a slope move, while it still benefits from a decrease in the level of the zero-coupon yield curve.

8.1.4 Scenario Analysis

What Is Scenario Analysis?

When you make active investment decisions, you need to know exactly which strategy will be the most beneficial in the scenario you anticipate. But of course your priors on yield curve changes are subject to errors as you are never a perfect predictor. Therefore, you also need to imagine the outcome of your bets under the assumption of alternative scenarios. This is what we call *scenario analysis*. Assuming you have made a realistic scenario analysis, you are able to know the worst possible loss you might incur as well as the mean total return rate of your position and its volatility.

---

[4]Of course, we can also use futures contracts and swaps as hedging instruments (see Chapters 10 and 11).

Scenario analysis is in general performed as a two-step process:

- *First, the portfolio manager specifies a few yield curve scenarios for a given horizon and computes the total return rate of his strategy under each scenario.*

- *Second, the portfolio manager assigns subjective probabilities to the different scenarios and computes the probability-weighted expected total return rate for his strategy and its volatility.*

Example 8.15 We consider at time $t = 0$ the following zero-coupon yield curve:

Maturity	1Y	2Y	3Y	4Y	5Y
Zero-coupon rate (%)	4	4.5	4.75	5	5.2

and a bond portfolio with the following features:

Bond	Maturity (years)	Coupon rate (%)	Price ($)	Quantity
Bond 1	1	4	100	100,000
Bond 2	3	6	103.49	100,000
Bond 3	5	5	99.34	100,000

A portfolio manager has an investing horizon of 1 year and imagines six different scenarios at this horizon:

Zero-coupon rate	1Y (%)	2Y (%)	3Y (%)	4Y (%)	5Y (%)
Bear-level	5	5.5	5.75	6	6.2
Bull-level	3	3.5	3.75	4	4.2
Unchanged	4	4.5	4.75	5	5.2
Flattening	4.3	4.6	4.75	4.85	5
Steepening	3.8	4.3	4.75	5.2	5.5
Curvature	4.2	4.5	4.75	5	5.1

He computes the 1-year total return rate of his portfolio in each scenario. Results are given below:

Scenario	Bond 1 (%)	Bond 2 (%)	Bond 3 (%)	Portfolio (%)
Bear-level	4	3.35	2.33	3.23
Bull-level	4	7.04	9.48	6.84
Unchanged	4	5.17	5.82	5
Flattening	4	4.97	6.29	5.08
Steepening	4	5.54	5.19	4.91
Curvature	4	5.16	5.81	4.99

Assigning an equal probability of 1/6 to each scenario, the portfolio manager is able to compute the portfolio's probability-weighted expected return, denoted by $\mathbb{E}(P)$, and its standard-error $\sigma(P)$:

$$\begin{cases} \mathbb{E}(P) = \frac{1}{6}(3.23\% + 6.84\% + 5\% + 5.08\% + 4.91\% + 4.99\%) = 5.01\% \\ \sigma(P) = 1.04\% \end{cases}$$

How to Construct Scenario Analysis?

The construction of a valid scenario analysis is actually not an easy exercise. There are three main steps to deal with:

- *First, gather the maximum amount of information about the macroeconomic context, the monetary policy of Central Banks, and also econometric studies concerning key financial variables, opinions of economic experts around the world and so on.*

- *Then, make a synthesis of all this information and formulate anticipations over a given horizon of time.*

- *Finally, translate these anticipations into a model of the yield curve.*

We develop below the third step that consists in using a model of the zero-coupon yield curve to implement scenario analysis. Using, for example, the Nelson and Siegel yield curve model (see Chapter 4 for a detailed presentation of this functional form), we are able to simulate different scenarios of the zero-coupon yield curve. Considering an initial zero-coupon curve at date $t = 0$, that means an initial set of parameters β_0, β_1, β_2 and τ, the idea behind the simulation is to add every day (every week, every month or every year...) a random term to each parameter because the parameters β_0, β_1, β_2 and τ are responsible for the distortion of the zero-coupon yield curve. Formally we write

$$\beta_i(t_j) = \beta_i(t_{j-1}) + \sigma_i X_i \quad \text{for } i = 0, 1, 2$$

where $\beta_i(t_j)$ is the value of β_i at time t_j and $t_j - t_{j-1} = 1/365$ or $1/52$ or $1/12$ or 1 or any possible period frequency depending on the investor horizon. σ_i is the daily, weekly, monthly or annual standard deviation of β_i depending on the value of $t_j - t_{j-1}$. Consider, for example, an investor with a 1-year horizon who wants to calculate the 1-year total return rate of a portfolio. He takes $t_j - t_{j-1} = 1$ and σ_i is the annual standard deviation of $\beta_i \cdot X_i$ follows a Gaussian process with mean 0 and variance 1. According to Willner (1996), we can postulate that the correlation between the changes in the level and curvature parameters is insignificant and can be treated independently. Changes in level and slope parameters are probably correlated, but only to a very weak degree, and can be ignored without any consequence. On the contrary, changes in the slope and curvature factors are historically correlated with a significant positive coefficient. Then we can consider that all the processes are independent except for X_1 and X_2, which are correlated with a coefficient of 0.3. Of course other choices are possible.

Example 8.16 Using the Nelson and Siegel extended form, we simulate 10,000 scenarios for the zero-coupon yield curve over a 1-year horizon and record the terminal value of each zero-coupon yield 1 year later. The initial curve is obtained with the following parameter

Fixed Income Securities

set: $\beta_0 = 7\%$, $\beta_1 = -2\%$, $\beta_2 = 1\%$, $\tau = 3.33$. This set of parameters corresponds to a standard increasing form with a spread of 2% between the very short- and long-term maturities. So as to obtain realistic standard deviations of rate changes, we fix the following values for $\sigma_0 = 1\%$, $\sigma_1 = 1.5\%$ and $\sigma_2 = 1\%$. These are the annual standard deviations of parameters β_0, β_1 and β_2, respectively. As an example, we provide below the first 10 values of Gaussian variables X_0, X_1, and X_2 we have simulated and consequently the parameter values we have obtained for β_0, β_1 and β_2 1 year later.

X_0	X_1	X_2	$\beta_0(\%)$	$\beta_1(\%)$	$\beta_2(\%)$
0.94609	−0.79892	−0.17100	7.946	−3.198	0.829
−1.75589	−0.30225	−0.18102	5.244	−2.453	0.819
−0.87887	0.43819	0.31922	6.121	−1.343	1.319
2.65269	−0.49391	−1.72018	9.653	−2.741	−0.720
0.14571	−0.36995	0.22236	7.146	−2.555	1.222
0.07497	−0.35838	0.14148	7.075	−2.538	1.141
−0.30337	−0.93128	0.74128	6.697	−3.397	1.741
−0.50094	0.33320	0.53526	6.499	−1.500	1.535
0.37996	0.13183	1.80647	7.380	−1.802	2.806
0.43879	0.53296	1.09350	7.439	−1.201	2.094

This enables us to draw the 10 first zero-coupon yield curves we simulate 1 year later and to compare them with the initial yield curve (cf. Figure 8.3).

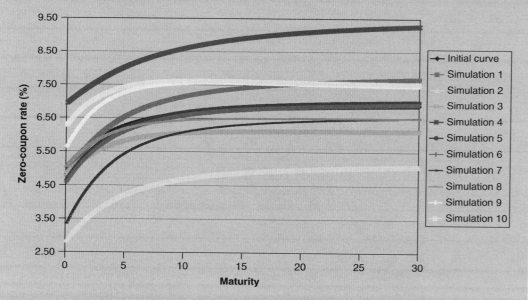

Figure 8.3 10 Zero-coupon yield curve scenarios simulated with the Nelson–Siegel model.

Of course we are now able to compute the 1-year total return rate of any bond portfolio in each scenario.

8.1.5 Active Fixed-Income Style Allocation Decisions

There is now a consensus in empirical finance that expected asset returns, and also variances and covariances, are, to some extent, predictable. Pioneering work on the predictability of asset class returns in the US market was carried out by Keim and Stambaugh (1986), Campbell (1987), Campbell and Shiller (1988), Fama and French (1989), and Ferson and Harvey (1991). More recently, some authors started to investigate this phenomenon on an international basis by studying the predictability of asset class returns in various national markets [see, for example, Bekaert and Hodrick (1992), Ferson and Harvey (1993, 1995), Harvey (1995), and Harasty and Roulet (2000)]. The use of predetermined variables to predict asset returns has produced new insights into asset pricing models, and the literature on optimal portfolio selection has recognized that these insights can be exploited to improve on existing policies based upon unconditional estimates. For example, Kandel and Stambaugh (1996) argue that even a low level of statistical predictability can generate economic significance and abnormal returns may be attained even if the market is successfully timed only 1 out of 100 times (see the reference section for more research on optimal portfolio decisions in the presence of predictable returns). Practitioners also recognized the potential significance of return predictability and started to engage in tactical asset allocation (TAA) strategies as early as the 1970s. The exact amount of investment currently engaged in TAA is not clear, but it is certainly growing very rapidly. For example, Philip et al. (1996) estimated that around $48 billion was allocated to domestic TAA in 1994, while Lee (2000) estimates that more than $100 billion was dedicated to domestic TAA at the end of 1999.

TAA strategies were traditionally concerned with allocating wealth between two asset classes, typically shifting between stocks and bonds. More recently, more complex style timing strategies have been successfully tested and implemented.

On the one hand, several authors have recently shown that various equity style returns were at least as much predictable as a broad market index, and emphasized the benefits of active strategies that focus on tactical style timing only. In particular, Kao and Shumaker (1999) and Amenc et al. (2002) have underlined the performance of strategies that involve dynamic trading in various equity styles [see also Fan (1995), Sorensen and Lazzara (1995) and Avramov (2002)]. On the fixed-income side, various authors have also studied the predictability of the return on bond portfolios [e.g., Campbell (1987), Fama and French (1989), Bekaert et al. (1997), Lekkos and Milas (2001)], but they mostly have done so in a context of timing stocks versus bonds, with no emphasis on the timing of the different classes of credit ratings. More recently, Amenc et al. (2002) have investigated the predictability of fixed-income portfolio returns. They emphasize the benefits of a market-neutral strategy that generates abnormal return from timing between traditional Treasury, Corporate and High-Yield bond indices, while maintaining a zero exposure with respect to a global bond index. In this section, which borrows largely from Amenc et al. (2002), we report some of that evidence. The focus on a market neutral strategy allows us to better isolate the benefits of style timing as a way to generate abnormal profits in a fixed-income environment.

Table 8.3   Descriptive Statistics for the Fixed-Income Indices.

	T-Bond	Investment grade	High yield
T-Bond	1.00		
Investment grade	0.77	1.00	
High yield	0.12	0.24	1.00
Mean	0.37%	0.40%	0.22%
Standard deviation	4.92%	5.60%	6.64%

Factor Analysis of Bond Index Returns

Investors have an intuitive understanding that different bond indices have contrasted performance at different points of the business cycle. To confirm and test the validity of such an intuition, we have used monthly data on the period 1991 to 2001 for three broad-based bond indices by Lehman Brothers, the Lehman T-Bond index, the Lehman investment grade corporate bond index (which we also refer to as the "credit bond index" in this section) and the Lehman high-yield bond index.

The following table reports correlations, means and standard deviations for the fixed-income indices based on monthly data over the period 1991 to 2001.

The relatively low correlations between T-Bond and Investment Grade indices and the high-yield index reported in Table 8.3 suggest that different fixed-income strategies perform better at different points in time. While unconditional correlations suggest potential economic value in timing bond indices, conditional correlations are perhaps more indicative.

From an intuitive standpoint, the notion of *flight-to-quality* suggests, for example, that during times of increased stock uncertainty, the price of US Treasury bonds tends to increase relative to stocks and also corporate bonds. This strongly suggests that using a predictive variable such as a proxy for stock market volatility can help in the appreciation of the future relative performance of various bond indices. Before providing formal evidence of predictability in bond indices, we first document how bond indices perform under various economic conditions.

Economic conditions are described in terms of the values of a shortlist of financial and macroeconomic factors. Some of these factors have been shown to be useful in predicting the performance of traditional asset classes and/or explaining a significant fraction of the cross-sectional differences in various stock and bond index returns.

The financial factors are as follows:

- *3-month T-Bill yield. Fama (1981) and Fama and Schwert (1977) show that this variable is negatively correlated with future stock market returns. It serves as a proxy for expectations of future economic activity.*

- *Dividend yield (proxied by the dividend yield on S&P stocks). It has been shown to be associated with slow mean reversion in stock returns across several economic cycles (Keim and Stambaugh, 1986, Campbell and Shiller, 1998, Fama and French, 1989). It serves as a proxy for time variation in the unobservable risk premium since a high dividend yield indicates that dividends have been discounted at a higher rate.*

- *Default spread (proxied by changes in the monthly observations of the difference between the yield on long-term Baa bonds and the yield on long-term AAA bonds). This captures the effect of default premium. Default premiums track long-term business cycle conditions: higher during recessions, lower during expansions (Fama and French, 1998).*

- *Term spread (proxied by monthly observations of the difference between the yield on 3-month Treasuries and 10-year Treasuries).*

- *Implied volatility (proxied by changes in the average of intramonth values of the chicago board options exchange OEX volatility index (VIX)).*[5]

- *Market volume (proxied by changes in the monthly market volume on the then New York Stock Exchange (NYSE)).*

- *US equity factor (proxied by the return on the S&P 500 index).*

The economic factors are as follows:

- *Inflation (proxied by Consumer Price Index).*

- *Money supply (proxied by M1 monetary aggregate).*

- *Economic growth (proxied by real quarterly Gross Domestic Product).*

Two general sets of results are discussed below. First, we discuss the performance of these strategies under different contemporaneous levels as well as changes in each of the factors. Next, we discuss the performance of the same strategies using a 3-month lag between observing the economic factors and performance of various strategies. The goal is to see if lagged values of economic factors affect the subsequent performance of various strategies. We study the performance of bond indices under various levels of these factors as well as changes in them.

We first report the results on a contemporaneous analysis for the example of changes in implied volatility based on monthly data over the period 1991–2001 (see Table 8.4).

These results allow for interesting interpretations. For example, the 1/3 largest decreases in implied volatility on equity corresponds to drops ranging from −33.15 to −4.39%. Under these conditions, the Lehman high-yield index performs rather well, since on an annual basis it outperforms the Lehman Investment grade index by 6.53% more than the unconditional annualized mean, a small negative −0.18%. On the other hand, when implied volatility on equity is increasing significantly (from +4.46 to +59.22%), on average the Lehman high-yield index underperforms the Lehman Investment grade index by 7.64% more than the unconditional mean. This is consistent with the intuition that high-yield bonds are a good investment in periods of low uncertainty, but are dominated by higher quality bonds in periods of higher uncertainty.

Table 8.5 provides a summary of such an analysis for a selection of these variables.

From such an analysis, we conclude, for example, that high-yield bonds tend to outperform investment grade bonds in our sample when

---

[5]VIX, introduced by CBOE in 1993, measures the volatility of the US equity market. It provides investors with up-to-the-minute market estimates of expected volatility by using real-time OEX index option bid–ask quotes. This index is calculated by taking a weighted average of the implied volatilities of eight OEX calls and puts. The chosen options have an average time to maturity of 30 days.

Table 8.4 Performance of Bond Indices under Different Contemporaneous Economic Conditions—The Example of Changes in Implied Volatility.

Change in implicit volatility Difference between conditional values and unconditional values	Low Minimum −33.15% Maximum −4.39%		Medium Minimum −3.80% Maximum 4.45%		High Minimum 4.46% Maximum 59.22%		Unconditional values		
	Mean (%)	Stdev (%)	Mean (%)	Stdev (%)	Mean (%)	Stdev (%)	Mean (%)	Stdev (%)	Correlation
CREDIT BOND INDEX—LEHMAN AGGREGATE	0.87	0.26	0.45	−0.31	−1.32	−0.02	0.25	1.73	−0.33
HIGH-YIELD BOND INDEX—LEHMAN AGGREGATE	7.40	−0.42	1.56	−0.31	−8.96	0.10	0.07	7.40	−0.44
TREASURY BOND INDEX—LEHMAN AGGREGATE	0.14	0.01	2.89	−0.20	−3.03	−0.01	0.21	2.89	0.00
HIGH-YIELD BOND INDEX—CREDIT BOND INDEX	6.53	−0.17	1.11	−0.21	−7.64	−0.02	−0.18	7.59	−0.36

Table 8.5 Performance of Bond Indices under Different Contemporaneous Economic Conditions—Synthesis.

	US Treasury bill 3 month			Change in T-Bill			Dividend yield			Change in dividend yield			Default spread		
	Low	Med	High	Low	Med	High	Low	Med	High	Low	Med	High	Low	Med	High
CREDIT BOND INDEX—LEHMAN AGGREGATE	M	M	M	M	M	M	M	M	M	M	M	M	M	M	M
HIGH YIELD BOND INDEX—LEHMAN AGGREGATE	H	M	L	M	H	L	M	L	M	H	H	L	L	M	M
TREASURY BOND INDEX—LEHMAN AGGREGATE	M	M	M	M	M	M	M	M	M	M	M	M	M	M	M
HIGH YIELD BOND INDEX—CREDIT BOND INDEX	H	M	L	L	H	L	M	L	M	H	H	L	L	M	M

(continued overleaf)

Table 8.5 (continued)

	Implicit volatility			Change in implicit volatility			S&P 500 index return			Market volume			Change in market volume		
	Low	Med	High	Low	Med	High	Low	Med	High	Low	Med	High	Low	Med	High
CREDIT BOND INDEX—LEHMAN AGGREGATE	M	M	M	M	M	M	M	M	M	M	M	M	M	M	M
HIGH YIELD BOND INDEX—LEHMAN AGGREGATE	M	M	L	H	M	L	L	M	H	M	M	M	M	M	M
TREASURY BOND INDEX—LEHMAN AGGREGATE	M	M	M	M	M	L	M	M	M	M	M	M	M	M	M
HIGH YIELD BOND INDEX—CREDIT BOND INDEX	M	M	L	H	M	L	L	H	H	M	M	M	M	M	M

Note: H corresponds to values greater than 3%; L corresponds to values lower than −3% and M to values between −3% and 3%.

- *short-term rates are low and do not change much;*

- *the dividend yield is decreasing or remaining stable;*

- *the yield curve is very upward sloping;*

- *implied volatility is decreasing significantly and the S&P is increasing;*

- *inflation is low and economic growth is high.*

We next report the results of a 1-month lagged analysis, in the example of the term spread (Table 8.6).

For example, the 1/3 lowest values for the term spread range from −0.61 to 0.99%. Under these conditions, the Lehman high-yield index performs rather poorly, since on an annual basis it underperforms the Lehman Aggregate bond index, −3.17% below the unconditional annualized mean, a small positive 0.05%. On the other hand, when the yield curve is very upward sloping (term spread ranging from 2.48 to 3.01%), on average the Lehman high-yield index outperforms the Lehman Aggregate bond index by 3.90% more than the unconditional mean. This is consistent with the intuition that an upward sloping yield curve signals expectations of increasing short-term rates, typically associated with scenarios of economic recovery, conditions under which high-yield bonds tend to outperform safer bonds.

Table 8.7 provides a summary of such an analysis for all variables.

From such an analysis, we conclude, for example, that high-yield bonds tend to outperform investment grade bonds with a 1-month lag when

- *short-term rates are low and decreasing;*

- *the dividend yield is decreasing;*

- *the default spread is high and decreasing;*

- *the yield curve is very upward sloping and steepening;*

- *market volume is significantly increasing;*

- *the S&P return is high.*

Contemporaneous and lagged factor analysis are a very useful tool for helping an asset allocator in his/her discretionary decision-making process. On the other hand, the objective of a systematic tactical allocator is to set up an econometric model able to predict when a given fixed-income strategy is going to outperform other strategies. We now turn to formal econometric evidence of predictability in bond index returns.

Evidence of Predictability in Bond Index Returns

In this section, we describe an econometric model that can be used in an attempt to search for evidence of predictability in bond index returns. This is a simplified approach to the problem of searching for evidence of predictability in fixed-income portfolio returns.[6]

---

[6]See Amenc *et al.* (2002) for more details.

Table 8.6 Performance of Bond Indices under Different Contemporaneous Economic Conditions—The Example of the Term Spread.

Term spread Difference between conditional values and unconditional values	Low		Medium		High		Unconditional values		
	Minimum −0.61% Mean (%)	Maximum −0.99% Stdev (%)	Minimum −1.03% Mean (%)	Maximum −2.35% Stdev (%)	Minimum −2.48% Mean (%)	Maximum −3.91% Stdev (%)	Mean (%)	Stdev (%)	Correlation
CREDIT BOND INDEX—LEHMAN AGGREGATE	−0.81	0.54	0.52	−0.49	0.29	−20	0.24	1.75	0.09
HIGH-YIELD BOND INDEX—LEHMAN AGGREGATE	−3.17	1.52	−0.73	−0.18	3.90	−1.64	0.05	7.44	0.12
TREASURY BOND INDEX—LEHMAN AGGREGATE	0.33	−1.42	−0.04	0.41	−0.29	0.63	0.26	2.92	−0.03
HIGH-YIELD BOND INDEX—CREDIT BOND INDEX	−2.37	1.28	−1.25	−0.26	3.61	−1.14	−0.19	7.62	0.10

Table 8.7 Performance of Bond Indices under Different 1-Month Lagged Economic Conditions —Synthesis.

	US Treasury bill 3 month		Change in T-Bill			Dividend yield			Change in dividend yield			Default spread			Change in default spread			Term spread			Change in term spread		
	Low	High	Low	Med	High	Low	Med	High	Low	Med	High	Low	Med	High	Low	Med	High	Low	Med	High	Low	Med	High
CREDIT BOND INDEX-LEHMAN AGGREGATE	M	M	M	M	M	M	M	M	M	M	M	M	M	M	M	M	M	M	M	M	M	M	M
HIGH-YIELD BOND INDEX-LEHMAN AGGREGATE	H	M	H	L	M	L	M	M	H	H	L	L	M	H	H	L	M	L	M	H	M	M	H
TREASURY BOND INDEX-LEHMAN AGGREGATE	M	M	M	M	M	M	M	M	M	M	M	M	M	M	M	M	M	M	M	M	M	M	M
HIGH-YIELD BOND INDEX-CREDIT BOND INDEX	H	M	H	L	M	L	M	M	H	H	L	L	M	H	H	L	M	M	M	H	M	M	H

(continued overleaf)

Table 8.7 *(continued)*

	Implicit volatility			Change in implicit volatility			Market volume			Change in market volume			S&P 500 index return			Rate of inflation (CPI)			Real quarterly GDP		
	Low	Med	High	Low	Med	High	Low	Med	High	Low	Med	High	Low	Med	High	Low	Med	High	Low	Med	High
CREDIT BOND INDEX-LEHMAN AGGREGATE	M	M	M	M	M	M	M	M	M	M	M	M	M	M	M	M	M	M	M	M	M
HIGH-YIELD BOND INDEX-LEHMAN AGGREGATE	M	M	M	M	H	L	M	M	M	L	M	H	L	M	H	M	M	M	M	M	M
TREASURY BOND INDEX-LEHMAN AGGREGATE	M	M	M	M	M	M	M	M	M	M	M	M	H	L	M	M	M	M	M	M	M
HIGH-YIELD BOND INDEX-CREDIT BOND INDEX	M	M	M	M	M	M	M	M	M	L	M	H	L	M	H	M	M	M	M	M	M

Note: H corresponds to values greater than 3%; L corresponds to values lower than −3% and M to values between −3% and 3%.

Selecting the Variables   Rather than trying to screen hundreds of variables through stepwise regression techniques, which usually leads to high in-sample R-squared but low out-of-sample R-squared (robustness problem), it is instead usually better to select a shortlist of economically meaningful variables. These variables are those used in the factor analysis from the section on "Factor Analysis of Bond Index Returns", to which we add the lagged return on each index as a potential regressor.

To select a shortlist of useful variables for each index, one typically distinguishes between two subperiods:

- *Calibration period:*   *for each index and each predictive variable, use a rolling window of data (say of 4 years) to calibrate the model, that is, estimate the coefficients in a linear regression of the bond indices on the selected variables.*

- *Back-testing period:*   *for each index and each predictive variable, use a rolling window of data to generate forecasts and compute hit ratios. Hit ratios are the percentage of times the predicted sign equals the actual sign of the style return.*

For each index, one may select a shortlist of very few variables according to usual criteria such as the quality of fit and/or hit ratio.

Selecting the Models   The process for model selection is similar to the one used for variable selection. From the selected short list of variables for a given index, form multivariate linear models based on at most five variables.[7]

For each index, we then select a model on the basis of various criteria representing the model's quality-of-fit and/or predictive performance. Once the model has been built, various improvements/tests can be performed. Apart from standard heteroscedasticity tests, which are designed to test whether the variance of the error term changes through time or across a cross section of data (leading to inefficiency of the least squares estimator), one may want to test for the presence of autocorrelation and/or cointegration, and adjust the models accordingly when needed. It is far beyond the scope of this book to cover such techniques, and we refer the reader to Hamilton (1994) for more details.

Using the Models   The next step is to use the model, or perform out-of-sample testing of the models. The methodology is as follows: calibrate the models displayed above using a rolling window of the previous 48 months, that is, dynamically reestimate the coefficients each month using the past 48 months of observation, and generate forecasts for the consecutive months. The model forecasting ability can be measured by out-of-sample hit ratios, which designate the percentage of time the predicted direction is valid, that is, the index goes up (respectively, down) when the model predicts it will go up (respectively, down).

---

[7]One should systematically seek to avoid multicolinearity, that is, include correlated variables in a given regression. It is indeed well known that in the presence of multicolinearity, it becomes very difficult to determine the relative influences of the independent variables and the coefficient estimates could be sensitive to the block of data used (robustness problem). For more details on that point see Gujarati (2002).

Using a sophisticated version of the procedure described above (including more advanced econometric techniques), Amenc *et al.* (2002) report strong evidence of predictability in bond index returns on the period ranging from January 1999 to December 2001.[8] They find out-of-sample hit ratios are statistically greater than $\frac{1}{2}$ (case of no predictive power of the models). This suggests that there is clear in-sample and out-of-sample statistical evidence of predictability in bond index returns. The next step for the portfolio manager is then to test whether there is also economic significance in the predictability of bond index return. This test can be performed in terms of implementation of a TAA model.

Implications for Tactical Style Allocation

Tactical asset allocation (TAA) is a form of conditional asset allocation, which consists in rebalancing portfolios around long run asset weights depending on conditional information. We first provide some evidence of the economic significance of the performance of hedge fund style timing models by comparing the performance of a market timer with perfect forecast ability in the alternative investment universe versus the traditional universe. We then present the performance of a realistic style timing model.

Performance of a Style Timer with Perfect Forecast Ability Different fixed-income investment strategies perform somewhat differently in different times. In an attempt to assess the performance of a style timer with perfect forecast ability in the fixed-income universe, we compute the annual return on fixed-income indices such as Lehman Brothers T-Bond, corporate, high-yield and global bond indices. We also display the performance of a style timer with perfect forecast ability who invests 100% of a portfolio at the beginning of the year in the best performing style for the year. The results appear in Table 8.8.

From Table 8.8, the benefits of timing are very obvious. A perfect style timer has an average return of 2.16% with 7.19% volatility. This compares very favorably with the performance of each of the traditional and alternative fixed-income indices. Furthermore, a perfect style timer would generate a return very significantly higher than the one on the Global Bond Index with a slightly higher volatility.

Despite their illustrative power, these experiments obviously do not provide a fair understanding of what the performance of a realistic style timing model could be. On the one hand, they are based upon the assumption of perfect forecast ability, which, of course, is not achievable in practice. On the other hand, they are based upon annual data, while further benefits of timing can be achieved by working with monthly returns. In an attempt to test the economic significance of predictability in bond index returns through their use for TSA decisions, one may implement a realistic style timing model in the alternative investment area that is based on monthly returns and forecast ability generated by the econometric models presented above.

Performance of a Realistic Style Timing Model We report here the results of a test conducted by Amenc *et al.* (2002). They use their econometric models to generate predictions

---

[8]See Amenc *et al.* (2002) for some evidence of predictability in alternative fixed-income strategies such as fixed-income arbitrage and convertible arbitrage.

Table 8.8 Performance of a Style Timer with Perfect Forecast Ability in the Fixed-Income Universe.

Year	T-Bond (%)	Corporate (%)	High yield (%)	LGBI (%)	Perfect timer (%)
1994	−10.22	−12.42	−11.39	−10.86	−10.22
1995	10.90	13.08	9.45	10.24	13.08
1996	−4.61	−5.14	0.20	−4.03	0.20
1997	3.72	4.51	2.63	3.49	4.51
1998	2.31	−1.41	−9.00	0.37	2.31
1999	−8.07	−8.68	−6.80	−7.70	−6.80
2000	8.32	5.19	−7.46	5.95	8.32
2001	−1.34	2.07	5.89	0.09	5.89
Average	**0.12**	**−0.35**	**−2.06**	**−0.31**	**2.16**
Std. dev.	**7.07**	**7.74**	**7.15**	**6.57**	**7.19**

Note: This table features the annual return on various traditional and alternative fixed-income indices from 1995–2001, and also the annual average return and volatility over the period, as well as similar performance measures for a style timer with perfect forecast ability who invests the totality of a portfolio at the beginning of the year in the best performing style for the year. The return on the best performing style for each year appears in italic.

on expected returns for the three traditional bond indices by Lehman Brothers, a Lehman T-Bond index, a Lehman investment grade corporate bond index and a Lehman high-yield bond index.

They turn econometric bets into market-neutral portfolio decisions, following an approach introduced by Treynor and Black (1973) and extended by Cvitanic *et al.* (2002) to allow, among other things, for the presence of dollar or market-neutrality constraints.[9] Focusing on market-neutral strategies allows one to better assess the economic significance of the presence of predictability in bond index returns.

More specifically, they have implemented a market-neutral strategy that generates abnormal return from timing between these three indexes, while maintaining a zero exposure with respect to the Lehman global bond index and a target level of leverage. The goal is to deliver absolute return over the full business cycle ensured through systematic style timing and market-neutrality. The performance of the portfolio is detailed in Table 8.9. We note that, as a result of dollar-neutrality, 100% of the wealth is always invested in the risk-free asset, here proxied by an investment at Libor rate.

The performance of the tactical allocation models is spectacular, in terms of return as well as risk; downside deviation is also limited, as can be seen from Table 8.10 (see Amenc *et al.* (2002) for more details).

This emphasizes the benefits of a market-neutral strategy that generates abnormal return from timing between traditional Treasury, Corporate and High-Yield bond indices, while maintaining

---

[9]Market-neutral can imply dollar-neutral, beta-neutral or both.

Table 8.9   Performance of TSA Portfolio.

Year	Jan (%)	Feb (%)	Mar (%)	Apr (%)	May (%)	Jun (%)	Jul (%)	Aug (%)	Sep (%)	Oct (%)	Nov (%)	Dec (%)
1999	0.27	1.20	0.26	−0.40	0.53	0.30	0.89	0.40	−0.53	0.03	1.19	1.14
2000	0.50	0.97	1.11	0.77	0.64	0.73	0.47	0.59	−0.06	2.18	3.26	0.59
2001	4.55	0.57	1.50	0.26	1.51	0.84	0.71	0.11	4.18	0.66	−2.08	1.51

Note: This table features the monthly return from January 1999 to December 2001 for a TSA portfolio based on the econometric models presented in the section on "Using the Models", and dollar neutrality with a level of leverage equal to 2.

Table 8.10   Risk/Return Analysis of TSA Portfolio.

Risk return analysis	TSA fund	Lehman Brothers Global
Cumulative return	36.31%	−2.65%
Annualized return	10.45%	−0.84%
Annualized std. deviation	4.16%	3.46%
Downside deviation (3.0%)	2.56%	3.46%
Sortino (3.0%)	2.91	−1.11
Sharpe (Risk-free rate = 3.0%)	1.79	−1.11
1st Centile	−1.54%	−2.30%
% Negative returns	11.11%	52.78%
Up months in up market	88.24%	
Down months in down market	10.53%	
Up market outperformance	52.94%	
Down market outperformance	89.47%	
Worst monthly drawdown	−2.08%	−2.48%
Maximum drawdown	−2.08%	−6.75%
Months in max drawdown	1	7
Months to recover	in progress	26

Note: This table features the monthly return from January 1999 to December 2001 for a TSA dollar neutrality portfolio with a level of leverage equal to 2.

a zero exposure with respect to a global bond index. Similar timing strategies can also involve different maturities (short-, medium- and long-term bond indices) within a given rating class. These portfolio decisions can be implemented by using investible supports for bond indices, like futures contracts[10] and/or Exchange-Traded Funds (ETFs), when available.

8.2   Trading on Market Inefficiencies

Another approach to active bond portfolio management consists in trying to detect mispriced securities (bond picking). We now describe several techniques designed to generate abnormal profits from the trading on such market inefficiencies. We distinguish here two kinds of trading:

- *The first one which takes place within a given market is called the bond relative value analysis.*

- *The second one is across markets. It concerns both spread and convergence trades.*

---

[10]See Chapter 11 devoted to futures contracts.

8.2.1   Trading within a Given Market: The Bond Relative Value Analysis

Bond relative value is a technique that consists in detecting bonds that are underpriced by the market in order to buy them and bonds that are overpriced by the market in order to sell them. Two methods exist that are very different in nature.

- *The first method consists in comparing the prices of two instruments that are equivalent in terms of future cash flows. These two products are a bond and the sum of the strips that reconstitute exactly the bond. If the prices of these two products are not equal, there is a risk-free arbitrage opportunity because they provide the same cash flows in the future.*

- *The goal of the second method is to detect rich and cheap securities that historically present abnormal yields to maturity, taking as reference a theoretical zero-coupon yield curve fitted with bond prices.*

Comparing a Bond with a Portfolio of Strips

Strips (Separate Trading of Registered Interest and Principal) are zero-coupon securities mainly issued by Treasury departments of the G7 countries (see Chapter 1). The Treasury strip market is very important in the United States where more than 150 Treasury strips were traded on September 2001 and enabled to reconstruct more than 50 Treasury bonds. In the other G7 countries, Treasury strips markets are less developed. For example, in France, Treasury strips were about 80 on September 2001 and enabled to reconstruct only 25 Treasury bonds.

Recall that the price of a bond can be expressed in the absence of arbitrage opportunity as the sum of its discounted future cash flows:

$$P_t = \sum_{\substack{s=T-\alpha+1 \\ s>0}}^{T} F_s B(t, s) \tag{8.6}$$

where:

- P_t is the market price of the bond at time t;

- T is the maturity of the bond expressed in years;

- F_s is the coupon and/or principal payment of the bond at time $s \geq t$;

- α is the number of cash flows of the bond;

- $B(t, s)$ is the discount factor or price at date t of a zero-coupon bond paying $1 at time s.

In the previous formula, we can see in the absence of arbitrage opportunities that the bond is necessarily equal to the weighted sum of zero-coupon bonds or strips. If not, there is an arbitrage opportunity.

Example 8.17   On 09/14/01, we suppose that the price of strips with maturity 02/15/02, 02/15/03 and 02/15/04 are, respectively, 99.07, 96.06 and 92.54. The principal amount of strips is $1,000. At the same time the price of the bond with maturity 02/15/04, coupon rate 10% and principal amount $10,000 is 121.5. The price of the reconstructed bond using

strips is 121.307:
$$10 \times 0.9907 + 10 \times 0.9606 + 110 \times 0.9254 = 121.307$$

A trader then decides to sell the bond and buy the strips. He sells a quantity of 1,000 bonds, buys a quantity of 1,000 strips with maturity 02/15/02, 1,000 strips with maturity 02/15/03 and 11,000 strips with maturity 02/15/04. The gain of the trader is

$$\$10,000 \times 1,000 \times (121.5 - 121.307)\% = \$19,300$$

Actually, the arbitrage is not so easy to detect because the trader has to take into account bid–ask spreads as well as the repo rate in his calculation. Jordan *et al.* (2000) have studied the potential for arbitrage in the US Treasury Strips market. On the basis of an examination of over 90,000 price quotes on strippable US Treasury notes and bonds and their component strip portfolios covering the period January 1990 through September 1996, they find that significant arbitrage opportunities arising from price differences across the two markets appear to be rare. When price differences occur, they are usually small and too short-lived to be exploited.

Using a Theoretical Yield Curve

Bond rich and cheap analysis is a common market practice. The idea is to obtain a relative value for bonds, which is based upon a comparison with a homogeneous reference.

To What Kind of Assets It Can Be Applied?   We can develop a rich–cheap analysis for the following:

- *Treasury bonds of a specified country using the Treasury zero-coupon yield curve of this country as a reference.*

Example 8.18   French Treasury bonds using OAT, BTAN and BTF to construct the French Treasury yield curve. US Treasury bonds using T-bills and T-bonds to construct the US Treasury yield curve.

- *Treasury bonds of a financial unified zone (with a unique currency) using the bonds issued in this zone to obtain the adequate zero-coupon yield curve.*

Example 8.19   Euro Treasury bonds using French, German and Dutch bonds to construct the Euro Treasury yield curve.

- *Corporate bonds of a specified country or financial unified zone with the same rating and economic sector.*

Example 8.20   BBB-rated Telecom bonds of the Euro zone using the same kind of bonds to construct the Euro BBB Telecom yield curve.

- *Corporate bonds of a single firm.*

Example 8.21 France Telecom bonds using all the France Telecom bond issues to construct the France Telecom yield curve.

How It Works? Whatever the possible application, rich–cheap analysis proceeds in five steps.

- *First, construct an adequate current zero-coupon yield curve using data for assets with the same characteristics in terms of liquidity and risk (see Chapter 4, which deals in detail with how to derive current zero-coupon yield curves and credit spread term structures).*

- *Then, compute a theoretical price for each asset as the sum of its discounted cash flows using zero-coupon rates with comparable maturity; then calculate the market yield to maturity and compare it to the theoretical yield to maturity; this spread (market yield–theoretical yield) allows for the identification of an expensive asset (negative spread) or a cheap asset (positive spread).*

- *The analysis is then improved by means of a statistical analysis of historical spreads for each asset so as to distinguish actual inefficiencies from abnormal yields related to specific features of a given asset (liquidity effect, benchmark effect, coupon effect, etc. . .). This statistical analysis known as Z-Score analysis provides signals of short or long positions to take in the market.*

- *Short and long positions are unwound according to a criterion that is defined a priori.*

Focus on the Z-Score Analysis One can use a 30-, 60- or 90-working day period, which allows the generation of the 30, 60 or 90 last spreads. Two criteria can then be applied. The first criterion is based upon the assumption of normally distributed spreads. The second criterion is based upon some historical distribution of spreads.

Criterion 1

- *First compute the expected value m and the standard deviation σ of the last 60 spreads, for example.*

- *Assume that the theoretical spread S is approximately normally distributed with mean m and standard deviation σ, then define the new spread $U = \frac{S-m}{2\sigma}$. In particular, we have*

$$P(-1 \leq U \leq 1) = 0.9544$$

- *Denote by $\hat{S}$ the spread obtained and $\hat{U} = \frac{\hat{S}-m}{2\sigma}$.*

- *If $\hat{U} > 1$, the bond can be regarded as relatively cheap and can be bought; on the other hand, if $\hat{U} < -1$, the bond can be regarded as expensive and can be sold; for $-1 \leq \hat{U} \leq 1$, one can conclude that the bond is fairly priced.*

Taking $U = \frac{S-m}{\alpha\sigma}$, with $\alpha > 2$, the confidence level for buy or sell signals is even stronger, since, taking for example, $\alpha = 3$, we obtain

$$\mathbb{P}(-1 \leq U \leq 1) = 0.9973$$

Example 8.22 Suppose a bond whose expected value m and standard deviation σ of the 60 last spreads are: $m = 0.03\%$ and $\sigma = 0.04\%$. One day later, the new spread is -0.11%.

Considering a confidence level with $\alpha = 3$, we obtain $\hat{U} = \frac{\hat{S}-m}{3\sigma} = -1.166$ and conclude that this bond is expensive and can be sold.

Criterion 2

- We define the value *Min* such that $\alpha\%$ of the spreads are below that value, and the value *Max* such that $\alpha\%$ of the spreads are above that value. α may be equal to 10, 5, 1, or any other value, depending upon the confidence level the investor requires for that decision rule.

- When $\frac{\hat{S}-Min}{Max-Min}$ converges to 1 or exceeds 1, the bond is considered cheap, and can be bought; on the other hand, when $\frac{\hat{S}-Min}{Max-Min}$ converges to 0 or becomes negative, the bond is considered expensive and can be sold; for other values of this ratio, one can conclude that the bond is fairly priced.

Example 8.23 Suppose we obtain the following historical distribution for the spread of a given bond over the last 60 working days (Figure 8.4):

The value *Min*, such that 5% of the spreads are below that value, is $Min = -0.0888\%$, and the value *Max*, such that 5% of the spreads are above that value, is $Max = 0.0677\%$. One day later, the new spread is 0.0775% and we obtain $\frac{\hat{S}-Min}{Max-Min} = 1.063$. We conclude that this bond is cheap and can be bought.

When to Unwind the Position? The issue lies in the decision timing to reverse the position in the market. Many choices are possible. We expose here two of them:

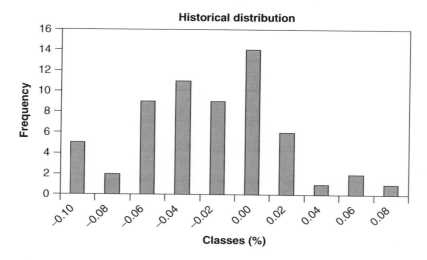

Figure 8.4

- It can be the first time when the position generates a profit net of transaction costs (in fact the bid–ask spread).

- Another idea is to define new values Min (Max) such that $\beta\%$ of the spreads are below (above) this value. For example, if the signal is detected for $\alpha = 1$, the position can be reversed in the market for $\beta = 15$, which means that the spread has now a more normal level.

Note finally that these methods seek to benefit from inefficiencies or relative mispricings detected in the market, considering that the theoretical yield curves are the good ones and that spreads will mean-revert around zero level or some other normal level. This normal level is obtained as the historical mean of spreads computed over the past 1, 2, 3 months or more. The difficulty of these methods for the bank or investment company lies in the ability to correctly model the different yield curves. Besides, the choice of the period to set up the Z-score analysis may severely modify the results. By combining short and long positions, it is possible to create portfolios that are quasi-insensitive to an increase or a decrease in the level of the yield curve. In this respect it can be regarded as a technique belonging to alternative investment methods. We give below some results of the bond relative value analysis on the French market.

Example 8.24 Some Results of the Bond Relative Value Analysis on the French Market

We back-test the method on the French Treasury bond market in 1995 and 1996. Hypotheses of the back-test are the following:

- The basket of instruments used to recover the zero-coupon yield curve is composed of BTF[11], BTAN[12] and OAT.[13]

- We use a cubic B-spline method with seven splines to recover the French Treasury zero-coupon yield curve.

- Bid–ask spreads in price are two cents for a BTAN and five cents for an OAT. We do not take any position on BTFs.

- The Z-score analysis is performed over a 100-day period. The value x, which provides signals for short and long positions is equal to 1%. The fixed level y, which is chosen to reverse the position is equal to 15%.

- Short and long positions are financed by means of the repo market.[14] For each transaction, we buy or sell for Eur10 million.

- When a signal is detected on a bond, we take the opposite position on the next maturity bond so as to obtain a global position which is $duration-neutral.

[11]BTF means "Bon à Taux Fixe." It is a French T-bill.
[12]BTAN means "Bon à Taux Annuel Normalisé." It is a French T-bond, always issued with a maturity between 2 and 5 years.
[13]OAT means "Obligation Assimilable du Trésor." It is a French medium- to long-term Treasury bond.
[14]For convenience, we use a fixed 4% rate on the period.

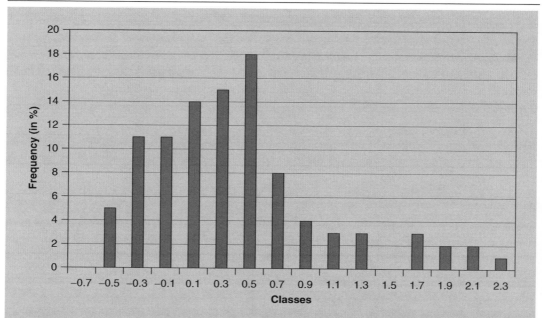

Figure 8.5

1- Description of a standard arbitrage as detected by the model

On 10/07/96, we detect an opportunity to buy the OAT 02/27/04. On 10/04/96, the value Min, such that 1% of the spreads are below that value, and the value Max, such that 1% of the spreads are above, are, respectively, −0.65 and 2.16. We show the graph of the historical distribution on 10/04/96 in Figure 8.5.

The spread value on 10/07/96 is 3.17. The ratio $\frac{\hat{S}-Min}{Max-Min}$ is equal to 1.359. It provides a signal to become long of the bond.

So we buy the OAT 02/27/04 for Eur9,999,977 and sell the OAT 10/25/04 for Eur9,276,006 so that the position is $duration-neutral. This position is summarized in the following table

Bond	Price	MD	YTM	Position	Investment
OAT 02/27/04	120.4	5.39	5.64	Long	−9,999,977
OAT 10/25/04	112.81	5.82	5.74	Short	9,276,006

YTM stands for yield to maturity, and MD for modified duration.

On 10/04/96, the value Max, such that 15% of the spreads are above that value, is 1. The first time when the spread goes below that value we close the position by selling the OAT

02/27/04 and buying the OAT 10/25/04. This happens on 10/17/04 when the spread value is equal to 0.67. The profit and loss generated by the transaction is given in the following table:

Date	Bond	Price	Position	Investment	TC	FC	Profit and loss
10/07/96	OAT 02/27/04	120.4	Long	−9,999,977	2,500	—	—
10/07/96	OAT 10/25/04	112.81	Short	9,276,006	2,319	—	—
10/17/96	OAT 02/27/04	120.92	Short	10,042,836	2,511	—	—
10/17/96	OAT 10/25/04	112.97	Long	−9,289,568	2,322	—	—
Total	—	—	—	29,297	9,652	−804	18,840

TC stands for transaction costs, and FC for financing cost.

2- Comparison of the net asset value (NAV) of a pure monetary fund and a combined monetary and bond rich and cheap fund

In Figure 8.6, we provide the following:

- *The net asset value (NAV) of a fund with an initial cash of Eur40 million, which is only invested at Eonia (for convenience we suppose a fixed 4% Eonia over the period).*

- *The NAV of a combined fund with the same initial cash of Eur40 million invested both at Eonia and in the bond rich and cheap strategy.*

The evolution of the two funds is the same at the beginning because we take a 100-day period to implement the Z-score analysis. We can see that the fund "Eonia + Bond Rich-Cheap"

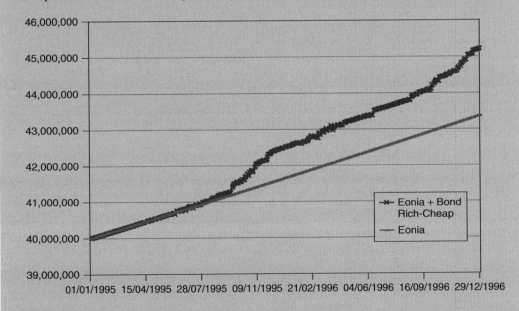

Figure 8.6

outperforms the fund "Eonia." The two final NAV of the two funds are, respectively, Eur45,214,440 and Eur43,364,807. The total return of the two funds are, respectively, 6.318% and 4.121%.

3- Risks of Such a Method

We see three kinds of risks linked to the implementation of such a strategy:

- *the interest-rate risk which can be badly measured using only the $duration concept;*

- *the liquidity risk which can affect the accuracy of the zero-coupon curve and the Z-score analysis, and is also the squeeze risk for an investor with a short position;*

- *and finally the operational risk.*

Interest-rate risk. One of the principles of the method is to combine long and short positions in order to obtain a global position that is $duration-neutral, and then guarantee a perfect immunization against small parallel changes. But we also have to measure the slope and the curvature risk. One way to achieve this goal is to use the slope and curvature $durations of the Nelson and Siegel (1987) model (see Chapter 6 and the section on "Level, Slope and Curvature $Duration Risk Measures" about the butterfly strategy in this chapter).

Liquidity risk. It is linked either to the illiquidity or the overliquidity of the bonds used to derive the zero-coupon yield curve and also the Z-score analysis. For example, a bond seems to be cheap on a given date, but if it is not liquid it will not probably mean-revert around what is considered as its normal level. The illiquidity risk is generally linked to small bond issues and/or small volumes in the market. It is then necessary to take a precise look at these parameters and at the bid-ask spread that can be sometimes an indicator of illiquidity. The overliquidity risk can appear on the cheapest-to-deliver bonds that futures sellers want to deliver. The liquidity risk (or liquidity squeeze) can also affect an investor in a short position who cannot repurchase the bond at a fair price.

Operational risk. It is linked to price errors that can be contained in the database. Also bonds with embedded options can be mistaken for straight bonds. Then it is necessary to rigorously select the securities used to implement the strategy.

8.2.2 Trading across Markets: Spread and Convergence Trades

Trading across markets is essentially made of spread and convergence trades. Note that we recommend you read Chapter 10, entirely devoted to swaps, before reading this section.

Spread Trades

Spread trades designate swap-Treasury spread trades and corporate-swap spread trades.

Swap-Treasury Spread Trades   This kind of trade consists in detecting the time when swap spreads[15] are high (which means that credit is cheap in general) and when they are low (which means that credit is rich in general). The statistical technique used for judging the cheapness or richness of swap spreads is basically the same as the one used to perform bond relative value analysis (see Section 8.2.1). A swap spread is computed as the difference between the swap yield and the Treasury bond par fitted yield with the same maturity. For example, the 10-year swap spread is equal to the difference between the 10-year swap yield and the 10-year T-bond par fitted yield. The latter can be obtained by using one of the models developed in Chapter 4 for reconstructing a zero-coupon yield curve. The par yield curve is directly deduced from the zero-coupon yield curve with the bootstrapping method. This way of computing a swap spread is recommended because the T-bond yield must be homogeneous to the swap yield, that is, it must be a par yield as well as a constant maturity yield. The use of market yields to maturity is not appropriate in this respect. Indeed, they do not have a constant maturity. Furthermore, for a given maturity, choosing a benchmark or an off-the-run security does not yield the same result.

> **Example 8.25**   Suppose the current Euro 10-year swap spread amounts to 40 bps. Assume furthermore that its mean and standard deviation over the last 60 working days amount to, respectively, 25 bps and 5 bps. Hence the corresponding Z-score[16] is equal to $(40-25)/5 = 3$. So the swap spread can be considered cheap. As a result, a portfolio manager can go long a AA 10-year corporate bond and short a 10-year Treasury bond in order to lock in a high spread. Suppose that 3 months later the swap spread amounts to 20 bps. Its 60-day mean and standard deviation are equal to, respectively, 25 bps and 2 bps. The corresponding Z-score is equal to $(20 - 25)/2 = -2.5$. So the swap spread can be considered rich. The portfolio manager will unwind his position and take his profit, which is approximately equal to
>
> $$\frac{swap\ spread\ change \times \$duration\ of\ a\ 10\text{-}year\ bond}{4}$$
>
> that is, $0.2 \times 7.5/4 = 0.375$ cent per 1\$ invested.[17]

Corporate-Swap Spread Trades   These trades are based upon the use of relative value tools like those developed for Treasury bonds. Corporate bonds are analyzed relatively to a swap curve rather than to a Treasury curve. There are at least two reasons for this. First, a swap curve is an unambiguously defined reference, while there does not exist one single Treasury curve (several choices have to be made: basically, the basket of bonds for reconstructing the curve and the model). The use of a Treasury curve would hence involve a model error. Second, the spread between a corporate bond yield and a swap yield can be considered the specific credit risk premium of the bond, which is exactly what we want to analyze. In contrast, the spread between a corporate bond yield and a Treasury bond yield represents the total credit risk premium of the bond (systematic + specific).

---

[15] See Chapter 10 for a definition.

[16] See Section 8.2.1, where we detail the Z-score analysis.

[17] Here we consider, as an example, the dollar duration of a 10-year bond with an annual coupon equal to 5% and quoting approximately par.

But the systematic risk premium, that is the swap spread, is another issue that must be separately addressed.

Building a reliable relative value tool for corporate bonds is not an easy task. We recommend the use of a joint estimation method (see Chapter 4) so as to obtain realistic spread curve shapes. As regards the selection of corporate bonds to reconstruct the curve, an efficient way consists in applying a screening method. First, select the corporate bonds according to issuance currency, issuer rating and industry sector (if you want to reconstruct sector spread curves). Second, gather a substantial amount of historical yields for these bonds and check that, for each historical date, yields are homogeneously distributed around a curve. Identify the outliers and leave them aside. Lastly, add to your short-term references a spread that accounts for the rating of the corporate bonds.

Example 8.26   Suppose that the Euro 10-year BBB-AA spread[18] amounts to 120 bps. The corresponding 60-day mean and standard deviation are equal to 90 bps and 10 bps. The Z-score is equal to 3, which means that 10-year BBB-bonds are cheap relatively to the 10-year swap. A portfolio manager can go long a 10-year BBB bond and swap the fixed rate against floating rates (He enters a swap where he pays the 10-year BBB and receives Libor +120 bps.), locking in an asset swap spread of 120 bps. He will wait for a reverse Z-score signal (meaning an improvement of the credit of BBB rated bonds) to unwind his position and make his profit.

Convergence Trades

When a portfolio manager expects a country to join a unified economic area (unique currency) or a set of countries to merge into a unified economic area, as was the case for the Euro area, he can choose to initiate a so-called convergence trade. This enables him to take advantage of the financial implications of the unification, that is the merge of swap yield curves into a single swap yield curve as well as the convergence of Treasury yield curves on the benchmark Treasury yield curve of the area. A recent example has been Greece joining the Euro area in January 2001. The UK case, which is still topical, is another example that we are going to develop. There are different types of convergence trades, two of which are very popular among portfolio managers: forward rate trades and yield curve trades. For our explanation, we consider a portfolio manager who expects in the near-term the spread between the sterling swap yield curve and the euro swap yield curve to narrow. He can decide to express his convergence views through one trade or the other.

Forward Rate Trades   Forward rate trades are implemented through the use of forward rates. In our example, the portfolio manager decides to expose his portfolio to convergence through entering forward swap transactions. The idea is to detect the largest divergence in the forward path of swap spreads between the United Kingdom and the Euro area. Once the term to maturity is chosen and the forward period is identified, the portfolio manager enters the forward swap transaction allowing him to profit from the expected convergence movement.

We give hereafter a detailed example of such a trade.

---

[18]This spread corresponds to the spread between 10-year BBB rated instruments and 10-year swap instruments.

A forward swap[19] is a swap with a fixed leg being a forward swap yield, and a floating leg being made of forward interbank yields (typically 6-month). The convergence strategy consists in buying the swap[20] in the currency for which interest rates are lower and selling the swap in the currency for which interest rates are higher. Indeed, both swaps equal zero at inception. When unwinding your swap positions, you expect to have won money on the long position as well as on the short position or at least to have won more on one than lost on the other. The long position will be profitable if the yields on the floating leg will have increased, and conversely for the short position. Remember that the value of a long swap position equals the difference between the discounted fixed leg and the discounted floating leg, and conversely for a short position.[21] Now, let us take the following example.

Example 8.27 On October 1, 2001, you note a large distortion between the sterling and the euro 5-year forward 5-year swap yields, which you expect to dwindle in the very next future (say 1 month). The euro 5-year forward 5-year swap yield is equal to 6.06%; the sterling 5-year forward 5-year swap yield is equal to 5.74%. So as to implement this view, you will go short a 5-year forward swap on the euro 5-year yield and go long a 5-year forward swap on the sterling 5-year yield for, let us say, a notional principal amount of Eur1 million. If your expectation is correct, you are going to win money when unwinding your position 1 month later on October 31, 2001.

Strategy: Short the 5-year forward 5-year Euro swap for Eur1 million

Long the 5-year forward 5-year sterling swap for Eur1 million

Trade date	01-oct-01
Settlement date	03-oct-01
5-year forward 5-year Euro swap yield at inception	6.06%
5-year forward 5-year Sterling swap yield at inception	5.74%
4-year and 11-month 5-year Euro swap yield at the end	5.54%
4-year and 11-month 5-year Sterling swap yield at the end	5.31%
€/£ exchange rate on October 1	0.6201
€/£ exchange rate on October 31	0.6191

In order to compute your gain or loss, you can use two different methods:

First Method: Forward Rate Projection

- *Determine the forward fixed yield as well as the forward floating yields on each swap transaction (This can be done using the forward curve (FWCV) page on Bloomberg: make sure you select the coupon swap curve).*

---

[19] See Chapter 10 for more details.

[20] Buying a swap means receiving the floating leg and paying the fixed leg; and selling a swap means paying the floating leg and receiving the fixed leg (see Chapter 10).

[21] Usually, the profit/loss on each of the two forward swaps is left currency unhedged. Indeed, the currency will only impact the Net Present Value (NPV) of each swap, the magnitude of the currency risk being very often much lower than that of the profit/loss on the swaps.

- *From the zero-coupon swap curve determine the discount factors having the same maturity as the floating and fixed yields of the swap transactions. This will enable you to value each swap transaction. Note that, at inception the value of each of your swaps equals 0, and that at the time the transaction is unwound, the value is no longer equal to 0. The difference between these values represents your gain or loss. You must of course take into account the exchange rates at the beginning and at the end of the transaction so as to convert all values into one single currency. The table hereafter sums up your positions at inception and at the end, 1 month later.*

First Method : Forward Rate Projection
On October 31st

	Discount factors	Floating leg	NPV floating	Fixed leg	NPV fixed
Euro leg					
03-avr-07	0.801639511	25,980	20,826		
03-oct-07	0.781317077	26,231	20,495	60,572	47,326
03-avr-08	0.760840349	26,825	20,410		
03-oct-08	0.740249763	27,009	19,993	60,572	44,838
03-avr-09	0.720989631	27,385	19,744		
05-oct-09	0.701721827	27,002	18,948	60,572	42,505
06-avr-10	0.68276314	27,119	18,516		
04-oct-10	0.664129702	28,450	18,894	60,572	40,228
04-avr-11	0.645530294	28,894	18,652		
03-oct-11	0.627086081	27,924	17,510	60,572	37,984
	NPV		193,988		212,881
	Profit/loss (NPV fixed-NPV floating)		18,892		
Sterling leg					
03-avr-07	0.764471364	26,927	20,585	28,687	21,930
03-oct-07	0.744841828	26,682	19,873	28,687	21,367
03-avr-08	0.72557331	26,654	19,339	28,687	20,814
03-oct-08	0.706664008	26,562	18,770	28,687	20,272
03-avr-09	0.688797034	26,534	18,277	28,687	19,759
05-oct-09	0.671155321	26,297	17,649	28,687	19,253
06-avr-10	0.654108896	26,200	17,138	28,687	18,764
04-oct-10	0.637636533	26,354	16,804	28,687	18,292
04-avr-11	0.621454115	26,328	16,361	28,687	17,827
03-oct-11	0.605645946	25,620	15,517	28,687	17,374
	NPV		180,314		195,652
	Profit/loss (NPV floating-NPV fixed)		−15,338		

Profit on the Euro position (in €)	18,892
Profit on the Sterling position (in €)	−15,338
Net profit (in €)	3,554

Second Method: Substitution

- *It consists in offsetting the initial swaps by symmetrical swaps (in our example, the initial short one by a long one and the initial long one by a short one) so as to neutralize the floating leg of each of them. As a result, we have fixed payments that are discounted with the corresponding swap discount factors.*

The table hereafter sums up your positions at inception and at the end, 1 month later.

Second Method: Substitution
On October 31

Fixed leg	Discounted fixed leg
5,200	4,063
5,200	3,849
5,200	3,649
5,200	3,453
5,200	3,261
NPV	18,275

Fixed leg	Discounted fixed leg
−2,150	−1,644
−2,150	−1,601
−2,150	−1,560
−2,150	−1,519
−2,150	−1,481
−2,150	−1,443
−2,150	−1,406
−2,150	−1,371
−2,150	−1,336
−2,150	−1,302
NPV	−14,664
Profit on the Euro position (in €)	18,275
Profit on the Sterling position (in €)	−14,687
Net profit (in €)	**3,588**

Your net profit amounts to about Eur3,500. Note that while you have won on the short position, you have lost on the long one. Indeed, both curve movements have been downwards. Note furthermore that the two methods give approximately the same results.

Yield Curve Trades   Yield curve trades are implemented through yield curve trading. The convergence of the sterling yield curve on the Euro yield curve implies a "steepening" of the sterling yield curve (at the time of writing). Hence a portfolio manager will overweight his portfolio at the short end of the UK yield curve and underweight it at the long end. He can also enter a cash- and $duration-neutral butterfly trade, being long the bullet (for example, 5Y) and short the barbell (for example, 2Y and 10Y). Indeed, remind that a bullet tends to outperform a barbell under "steepening" curve environments.[22] For an example of such a trade, we refer to Section 8.1.3.

8.3   End of Chapter Summary

Active fixed-income portfolio managers' objective is clearly to have their portfolios beat their benchmark index. As in equity investing, there are two broad kinds of active fixed-income portfolio strategies: (1) trading on interest-rate predictions ("market timing") and (2) trading on market inefficiencies ("bond picking").

Most active portfolio managers are taking timing bets on changes of the yield curve or one particular segment of the yield curve. We distinguish three kinds of bets: (1) timing bets based on no change in the yield curve (sometimes referred to as *riding the yield curve*); (2) timing bets based on interest-rate level and (3) timing bets based both on slope and curvature movements of the yield curve. Riding the yield curve is a technique that fixed-income portfolio managers traditionally use to enhance returns. When the yield curve is upward sloping and is supposed to remain unchanged, it enables an investor to earn a higher rate of return by purchasing fixed-income securities with maturities longer than the desired holding period, and selling them to profit from falling bond yields as maturities decrease with time. Strategies based on changes in the level of interest rates are very naive; they only account for two possible changes in the yield curve, a decrease in the level of interest rates (which typically leads an active manager to increase the portfolio duration) and an increase in the level of interest rates (which typically leads an active manager to *roll over*, that is, to shorten the portfolio duration). More complex strategies such as *bullet*, *barbell* and *butterfly* strategies can also be designed to take advantage of timing bets based both on slope and curvature movements of the yield curve.

These bets apply to a specific rating class, for example, the term structure of default-free rates. Systematic bets can also be made on bond indices representative of various classes (Treasury, Corporate Investment Grade, High Yield) based on econometric analysis. This is a modern form of bond timing strategy known as *tactical style allocation*.

Another approach to active bond portfolio management consists in trying to detect mispriced securities. Bond portfolio managers typically distinguish trades that take place within a given market (this is called *bond relative value analysis*) from trades across markets (this includes in particular, *spread* trades and *convergence* trades.). Bond relative value is a technique that consists in detecting bonds that are underpriced by the market in order to buy them, and bonds that are overpriced by the market in order to sell them. Two methods exist that are very different in nature. The first method consists in comparing the price of two instruments that are equivalent in terms

---

[22]See the section on "Butterfly Strategy" in this chapter.

of future cash flows. These two instruments are a bond and the sum of the strips that reconstitute exactly the bond. If the prices of these two instruments are not equal, there is a risk-free arbitrage opportunity because they provide the same cash flows in the future. The goal of the second method is to detect *rich* and *cheap* securities that historically present abnormal yield to maturity taking as reference a theoretical zero-coupon yield curve fitted with bond prices.

Some active bond portfolio managers can go short and long, and/or use derivatives to hedge away the overall exposure of the portfolio with respect to interest-rate risk. A number of hedge funds that perform fixed-income arbitrage follow such alternative forms of investment strategies.

8.4 References and Further Reading

8.4.1 On Active Fixed-Income Strategies

Almeida, C.I.R., A.M. Duarte, and C.A.C. Fernandes, 2000, "Credit Spread Arbitrage in Emerging Eurobond Markets", *Journal of Fixed Income*, **10**(3), 100–111.

Ang, S., L. Alles, and D. Allen, 1998 "Riding the Yield Curve: An Analysis of International Evidence", *Journal of Fixed Income*, **8**(3), 57–74.

Barrett, B., T. Gosnell, and A. Heuson, 1995, "Yield Curve Shifts and the Selection of Immunization Strategies", *Journal of Fixed Income*, **5**(2), 53–64.

Choudhry, M., 2001, *Bond Market Securities*, Prentice Hall, New York.

Dolan, C.P., 1999, "Forecasting the Yield Curve Shape, Evidence in Global Markets", *Journal of Fixed Income*, **9**(1), 92–99.

Dyl, E.A., and M.D. Joehnk, 1981, "Riding the Yield Curve: Does it Work ?" *Journal of Portfolio Management*, **7**(3), 13–17.

Fabozzi, F.J., 2001, *Bond Portfolio Management*, 2nd Edition, Frank J. Fabozzi and Associates.

Grieves, R., 1999, "Butterfly Trades", *Journal of Portfolio Management*, **26**(1), 87–95.

Grieves, R., S.V. Mann, A.J. Marcus, and P. Ramanlal, 1999, "Riding the Bill Curve", *Journal of Portfolio Management*, **25**(3), 74–82.

Grieves, R., and A.J. Marcus, 1992, "Riding the Yield Curve: Reprise", *Journal of Portfolio Management*, **18**(4), 67–76.

Hill, C.F., and S. Vaysman, 1998, "An Approach to Scenario Hedging", *Journal of Portfolio Management*, **24**(2), 83–92.

Ilmanen, A., 1997, "Forecasting US Bond Returns", *Journal of Fixed Income*, **7**(1), 22–37.

Jones, F., 1991, "Yield Curve Strategies", *Journal of Fixed Income*, **1**(2), 43–51.

Jordan, B.D., R.D. Jorgensen, and D.R. Kuipers, 2000, "The Relative Pricing of US Treasury STRIPS: Empirical Evidence", *Journal of Financial Economics*, **56**(1), 89–123.

Litterman, R., and J. Scheinkman, 1991, "Common Factors Affecting Bond Returns", *Journal of Fixed Income*, **1**(1), 54–61.

Mann, S.V., and P. Ramanlal, 1997, "The Relative Performance of Yield Curve Strategies", *Journal of Portfolio Management*, **23**(4), 64–70.

Martellini, L., and P. Priaulet, 2000, *Fixed-Income Securities: Dynamic Methods for Interest Rate Risk Pricing and Hedging*, John Wiley & Sons, Chichester.

Martellini, L., P. Priaulet, and S. Priaulet, 2002, "Understanding the Butterfly Strategy", *Journal of Bond Trading and Management*, **1**(1), 9–19.

Nelson, C.R., and A.F. Siegel, 1987, "Parsimonious Modeling of Yield Curves", *Journal of Business*, **60**(4), 473–489.

Papageorgiou, N., and F.S. Skinner, 2002, "Predicting the Direction of Interest Rate Movements", *Journal of Fixed Income*, **11**(4), 87–95.

Prendergast, J.R., 2000, "Predicting the Ten-Year Libor Swap Spread: The Role and Limitations of Rich/Cheap Analysis", *Journal of Fixed Income*, **10**(3), 86–99.

Sorensen, E.H., K.L. Miller, and V. Samak, 1998, "Allocating between Active and Passive Management", *Financial Analysts Journal*, **September/October**, 18–31.

Willner, R., 1996, "A New Tool for Portfolio Managers: Level, Slope and Curvature Durations", *Journal of Fixed Income*, **6**(1), 48–59.

8.4.2   On Active Asset Allocation Decisions

Ahmed, P., L. Lockwood, and S. Nanda, 2002, "Multistyle Rotation Strategies", *Journal of Portfolio Management*, **28**(3), 17–29.

Amenc, N., S. El Bied, and L. Martellini, 2003, "Evidence of Predictability in Hedge Fund Returns and Multi-Style Multi-Class Style Allocation Decisions", *Financial Analysts Journal*, forthcoming.

Amenc, N., L. Martellini, P. Malaise, and D. Sfeir, 2002, *Tactical Style Allocation, a New Form of Market Neutral Strategy*, Working Paper, USC.

Amenc, N., L. Martellini, and D. Sfeir, 2002, *Evidence of Predictability in Bond Indices and Implications for Fixed-Income Tactical Style Allocation Decisions*, Working Paper, USC.

Avramov, D., 2002, "Stock Return Predictability and Model Uncertainty", *Journal of Financial Economics*, **64**(3), 423–458.

Barberis, N., 2000, "Investing for the Long Run when Returns are Predictable", *Journal of Finance*, **55**, 225–264.

Bekaert, G., and R. Hodrick, 1992, "Characterizing Predictable Components in Excess Returns on Equity and Foreign Exchange Markets", *Journal of Finance*, **47**, 467–509.

Bekaert, G., R. Hodrick, and D. Marshall, 1997, "On Biases in Tests of the Expectations Hypothesis of the Term Structure of Interest Rates", *Journal of Financial Economics*, **44**, 309–348.

Brandt, M., 1999, "Estimating Portfolio and Consumption Choice: a Conditional Euler Equations Approach", *Journal of Finance*, **54**, 1609–1645.

Brennan, M., E. Schwartz, and R. Lagnado, 1997, "Strategic Asset Allocation", *Journal of Economic Dynamics and Control*, **21**, 1377–1403.

Campbell, J., 1987, "Stock Returns and the Term Structure", *Journal of Financial Economics*, **18**, 373–399.

Campbell, J., Y. Chan, and L. Viceira, 2000, *A Multivariate Model of Strategic Asset Allocation*, Working Paper, Harvard University.

Campbell, J., and R. Shiller, 1988, "Stock Prices, Earnings, and Expected Dividends", *Journal of Finance*, **43**, 661–676.

Campbell, J., and L. Viceira, 1998, *Who Should Buy Long-Term Bonds ?* NBER Working Paper 6801.

Chow, G, 1960, "Tests of Equality Between Sets of Coefficients in Two Linear Regressions", *Econometrica*, **28**, 591–605.

Fama, E., 1981, "Stock Returns, Real Activity, Inflation, and Money", *American Economic Review*, **71**(4), 545–565.

Fama, E., and K. French, 1989, "Business Conditions and Expected Returns on Stocks and Bonds", *Journal of Financial Economics*, **25**, 23–49.

Fama, E., and W. Schwert, 1977, "Asset Returns and Inflation", *Journal of Financial Economics*, **5**, 115–146.

Fan, S., 1995, *Equity Style Timing and Allocation, Chapter 14 from Equity Style Management*, Irwin Publishing.

Ferson, W., and C. Harvey, 1991, "Sources of Predictability in Portfolio Returns", *Financial Analysts Journal*, **3**, 49–56.

Ferson, W., and C. Harvey, 1993, "The Risk and Predictability of International Equity Returns", *Review of Financial Studies*, **6**, 527–566.

Ferson, W., and C. Harvey, 1995, "Predictability and Time-Varying Risk in World Equity Markets", *Research in Finance*, **13**, 25–88.

Gujarati, D.N., 2002, *Basic Econometrics*, 4th Edition, McGraw-Hill/Irwin Publishing, New York.

Hamilton, J., 1994, *Time Series Analysis*, Princeton University Press, NJ.

Harasty, H., and J. Roulet, 2000, "Modelling Stock Market Returns: An Error Correction Model", *Journal of Portfolio Management*, **26**(2), 33–46.

Harvey, C., 1989, "Time-Varying Conditional Covariances in Tests of Asset Pricing Models", *Journal of Financial Economics*, **24**, 289–317.

Harvey, C., 1995, "Predictable Risk and Returns in Emerging Markets", *Review of Financial Studies*, **8**(3), 773–816.

Johansen, S., 1991, "Estimation and Hypothesis Testing of Cointegration Vectors in Gaussian Vector Autoregressive Models", *Econometrica*, **59**, 1551–1580.

Johansen, S., 1995, *Likelihood-Based Inference in Cointegrated Vector Autoregressive Models*, Oxford University Press, New York.

Kandel, S., and R. Stambaugh, 1996, "On the Predictability of Stock Returns: An Asset Allocation Perspective", *Journal of Finance*, **51**, 385–424.

Keim, D., and R. Stambaugh, 1986, "Predicting Returns in the Stock and Bond Markets", *Journal of Financial Economics*, **17**, 357–390.

Lee, W., 2000, *Advanced Theory and Methodology of Tactical Asset Allocation*, Frank J. Fabozzi and Associates.

Lekkos, I., and C. Milas, 2001, *The Predictability of Excess Return on UK Bonds: A Non Linear Approach*, Working Paper, Brunel University.

Lynch, A., 2000, *Portfolio Choice and Equity Characteristics: Characterizing the Hedging Demands Induced by Return Predictability*, Working Paper, NYU.

Lynch, A., and P. Balduzzi, 2000, "Predictability and Transaction Costs: The Impact on Rebalancing Rules and Behavior", *Journal of Finance*, **55**, 2285–2310.

Merton, R.C., 1969, "Lifetime Portfolio Selection Under Uncertainty: The Continuous-Time Case", *Review of Economics and Statistics*, **51**, 247–257.

Merton, R.C., 1971, "Optimal Consumption and Portfolio Rules in a Continuous-Time Model", *Journal of Economic Theory*, **3**, 373–413.

Merton, R.C., 1973, "An Intertemporal Capital Asset Pricing Model", *Econometrica*, **41**, 867–888.

Philip, T., G. Rogers, and R. Capaldi, 1996, "Tactical Asset Allocation: 1977-1994", *Journal of Portfolio Management*, **23**(1), 57–64.

Samuelson, P., 1969, "Lifetime Portfolio Selection by Dynamic Stochastic Programming", *Review of Economics and Statistics*, **51**, 239–246.

Sorensen, E., and C. Lazzara, 1995, *Equity Style Management: the Case of Growth and Value, Chapter 4 from Equity Style Management*, Irwin Publishing.

8.4.3   Others

See HSBV, the Bloomberg site of the global fixed-income strategy of HSBC.

8.5   Problems

Exercise 8.1   Describe the types of bets made by active fixed-income managers to beat the market and explain how they are implemented in portfolios.

Exercise 8.2   Choosing a portfolio with the maximum $ Duration or Modified Duration, consider at time t five bonds delivering annual coupon rates with the following features:

Maturity (Years)	CR (%)	YTM (%)	Price
5	7	4	113.355
7	6	4.5	108.839
15	8	5	131.139
20	5	5.25	96.949
22	7	5.35	121.042

Note: CR stands for coupon rate and YTM for yield to maturity.

A portfolio manager believes that the YTM curve will very rapidly decrease by 0.3% in level. Which of these bonds provides the maximum absolute gain? Which of these bonds provides the maximum relative gain?

Exercise 8.3   Riding the Yield Curve

At time $t = 0$, we consider the following zero-coupon curve for the short-term segment which is upward sloping.

Maturity (days)	Zero-coupon rate (%)	Zero-coupon bond price ($)
91	4.00	99.027
183	4.50	97.817
274	4.80	96.542

An investor has funds to invest for 6 months. He has two different opportunities:
- buying a 183-day T-bill and holding it until the maturity or
- riding down the yield curve by buying a 274-day T-bill and selling it 6 months later (183 days later).

1. Calculate the total return rate of these two strategies assuming that the zero-coupon curve remains stable.
2. If the zero-coupon yield curve rises by 2% after time $t = 0$ and remains stable at this level, what would be the total return rate of riding down the yield curve?

Exercise 8.4   Rollover Strategy

An investor has funds to invest over 1 year. He anticipates a 1% increase in the curve in 6 months. Six-month and 1-year zero-coupon rates are, respectively, 3% and 3.2%. He has two different opportunities:
- he can buy the 1-year zero-coupon T-bond and hold it until maturity or

- he can choose a rollover strategy by buying the 6-month T-bill, holding it until maturity, and buying a new 6-month T-bill in 6 months, and holding it until maturity.

1. Calculate the annualized total return rate of these two strategies assuming that the investor's anticipation is correct.
2. Same question when interest rates decrease by 1% after 6 months.

Exercise 8.5   Scenario Analysis

We consider at time $t = 0$ the following zero-coupon curve:

Maturity rate (Years)	Zero-coupon rate (%)
1	4.30
2	4.70
3	5.00
4	5.25
5	5.50
6	5.70
7	5.85
8	5.90
9	5.95
10	6.00

and five bonds with the same $100 face value, which deliver annual coupon rate and whose features are summarized in the following table:

Bond	Bond maturity (Years)	Coupon rate (%)
1	2	5
2	5	5
3	7	6
4	10	4
5	10	6

A portfolio manager who has funds at disposal for 1 year anticipates that the zero-coupon yield curve will remain stable until time $t = 1$. He chooses to adopt the riding strategy, that is, he buys bonds with longer maturity than 1 year and sells them 1 year later.

1. Calculate the total return rate of this strategy for each bond.
2. The portfolio manager is not sure that the yield curve will remain stable 1 year later. He constructs three other scenarios for the zero-coupon yield curve at time $t = 1$ (see the following table). Curve 1 is obtained after a flattening movement. Curve 2 is obtained after a steepening movement as curve 3 is an inverted curve.

Maturity rate (Years)	Curve 1 ZC rate (%)	Curve 2 ZC rate (%)	Curve 3 ZC rate (%)
1	5.25	3.20	5.90
2	5.35	3.70	5.80
3	5.40	4.40	5.70
4	5.45	5.00	5.60
5	5.50	5.50	5.50
6	5.55	5.90	5.40
7	5.60	6.20	5.20
8	5.62	6.50	5.00
9	5.65	6.75	4.80
10	5.66	7.00	4.60

1. Draw the four possible curves at time $t = 1$.
2. Calculate the total return rate of the riding strategy for each bond in the three new curve scenarios. Conclude.

Exercise 8.6   Bond versus Strips Arbitrage

On 05/15/02, we suppose that the price of Strips with maturity 05/15/03, 05/15/04, 05/15/05 and 05/15/06 are, respectively, 96.05, 91.23, 86.5 and 81.1. The principal amount of Strips is $100. At the same time the price of the bond with maturity 05/15/06, annual coupon rate 5% and principal amount $1,000 is 98.75.

1. Compute the price of the reconstructed bond.
2. A trader wants to buy 10,000 bonds. Is there an arbitrage opportunity he can benefit from ?

Exercise 8.7   Butterfly

We consider three bonds with short, medium and long maturities whose features are summarized in the following table:

Maturity (Years)	Coupon rate (%)	YTM (%)	Bond price ($)	$Duration	Quantity
2	6	6	100	−183.34	q_s
10	6	6	100	−736.01	−10,000
30	6	6	100	−1,376.48	q_l

YTM stands for yield to maturity, bond prices are dirty prices, and we assume a flat yield-to-maturity curve in the exercise. We structure a butterfly in the following way:

- we sell 10,000 10-year bonds;
- we buy q_s 2-year bonds and q_l 30-year bonds.

1. Determine the quantities q_s and q_l so that the butterfly is cash- and $duration-neutral.

2. What is the P&L of the butterfly if the yield-to-maturity curve goes up to a 7% level? And down to a 5% level?

3. Draw the P&L of the butterfly depending on the value of the yield to maturity.

Exercise 8.8   Z-Score Analysis

The spread S of a bond is defined as the difference between the market yield to maturity and the theoretical yield to maturity given by a yield curve model. We suppose that historical spreads are normally distributed with mean m and standard deviation σ.

We define $U = \frac{S-m}{2\sigma}$. In particular, we have $P(-1 \leq U \leq 1) = 0.9544$. If $U > 1$, the bond can be regarded as relatively cheap and can be bought; on the other hand, if $U < -1$, the bond can be regarded as expensive and can be sold; for $-1 \leq U \leq 1$, one can conclude that the bond is fairly priced.

Consider a bond whose expected value m and standard deviation σ of the last 100 spreads are $m = 0.01\%$ and $\sigma = 0.02\%$. One day later, the new spread is 0.07%. Is the bond expensive or cheap? Same question if the new spread becomes -0.02%.

Exercise 8.9   Cash- and $Duration-Neutral Butterfly

We consider three bonds with short, medium and long maturities, whose features are summarized in the following table:

Maturity (Years)	Coupon rate (%)	YTM (%)
5	5.50	5
10	6	6
30	6	6.5

The face value of bonds is $100, YTM stands for yield to maturity, coupons are received annually. We structure a butterfly in the following way:

- we sell 10,000 10-year maturity bonds;
- we buy q_s 5-year maturity bonds and q_l 30-year maturity bonds.

1. Determine the dirty price, the modified duration (denoted MD) and the $duration of each bond.

2. Determine the quantities q_s and q_l so that the butterfly is cash- and $duration-neutral.

3. One month later, the YTM curve has changed. A flattening movement has happened so that the curve rotates around the body. We consider the following movement "+20/0/−20" meaning that the short wing YTM increases by 20 bps, the body does not move and the long wing YTM decreases by 20 bps. Compute the total return of the butterfly.

4. Same question with a steepening movement "−20/0/+20."

5. Same question if the YTM does not change, if a uniform parallel movement of +20 bps and of −20 bps affects the original YTM curve.

Exercise 8.10 Fifty–Fifty Weighting Butterfly

Answer the same questions as in the previous exercise for a fifty–fifty butterfly. We assume a 1-month 5% rate to finance the position. Compute also the net total return for the two following scenarios "−20/0/10" and "20/0/−10." In each case, give an approximation of the net total return by using the spread measure.

Exercise 8.11 Regression-Weighting Butterfly

Answer the same questions as in the previous exercise for a regression-weighting butterfly. We consider that the regression coefficient is equal to 0.5.

Exercise 8.12 Forward Yield

The forward yield curve provides a benchmark with which an active portfolio manager can compare his expectations on future short rates.

On 05/15/01 the US Treasury zero-coupon curve was as follows:

Maturity	Zero-coupon rate	Maturity	Zero-coupon rate
1	4.01	16	6.18
2	4.44	17	6.22
3	4.74	18	6.24
4	4.96	19	6.25
5	5.14	20	6.26
6	5.29	21	6.25
7	5.42	22	6.24
8	5.54	23	6.22
9	5.64	24	6.19
10	5.75	25	6.16
11	5.84	26	6.13
12	5.93	27	6.09
13	6.01	28	6.06
14	6.08	29	6.02
15	6.13	30	5.99

Assume you are an investor with a 1-year investment horizon.

1. Compute the 1-year forward zero-coupon rates as well as the 1-year rolling zero-coupon rates.
2. You expect a rise in the 1-year rate by 50 bps in 1 year. Which strategy will you implement in your portfolio? If the curve remains unchanged, which will be the most profitable maturity?

Exercise 8.13 We denote today's zero-coupon yield curve by $(R(0, t))_{t \in [0,T]}$. We assume that it has a decreasing shape. So, for $m < n$, $R(0, m) > R(0, n)$. We assume that the price of the m-year zero-coupon bond, $P_{0,m}$, is equal to the price of the n-year zero-coupon bond, $P_{0,n}$. We furthermore denote by $SP_{m,n}(k)$ the spread between the n-year zero-coupon yield and the m-year zero-coupon yield observed at time *k*. As an active manager, you make a bet on the shape of the yield curve over the horizon *h*, expecting a steepening movement of the [*m* years, *n* years] part of it.

1. What simple strategy can you implement in your portfolio in order to reflect your expectations?
2. Determine the break-even steepening yield spread of this strategy.
3. Show that it can be divided into two components: a pure time effect component and a pure yield effect component. What is the name of the first component?

Exercise 8.14   We denote today's zero-coupon yield curve by $(R(0, t))_{t \in [0, T]}$. Let us consider a cash- and \$duration-neutral butterfly strategy with zero-coupon bonds.

        Under what condition can the break-even flattening yield spread of the strategy over a given horizon *h* be simply expressed using forward yields starting at time *h*? Give a numerical example. Is it realistic?

Exercise 8.15   We consider country A and country B, with respectively currency *c*(*A*) and currency *c*(*B*). The yield and coupon calculation convention in both countries is supposed to be annual. At time 0, the par swap curve in each country is as follows:

Country A
time t = 0

Maturity (in years)	Swap par yield (%)
1	6
2	5.00
3	4.50
4	4.25

Country B
time t = 0

Maturity (in years)	Swap par yield (%)
1	4
2	5.00
3	5.50
4	5.75

One year later, at time 1, the two curves are as follows:

Country A
time t = 1

Maturity (in years)	Swap par yield (%)
1	5.50
2	5
3	4.75
4	4.63

Country B time t = 1	
Maturity (in years)	Swap par yield (%)
1	4.50
2	4.75
3	4.88
4	4.94

For the sake of simplicity, the underlying floating rate of the swaps is supposed to be annual. Furthermore, we suppose that at time $t = 0$, the exchange rate is as follows:

$$1c(A) = 1c(B)$$

At time $t = 1$, it becomes:

$$1c(A) = 0.9c(B)$$

Assume you have entered a forward rate trade at time $t = 0$ over a 1-year horizon for a nominal amount N denominated in $c(A)$, expecting the large, positive spread between the 2-year forward 2-year swap yield in currency $c(A)$ and the 2-year forward 2-year swap yield in currency c(B) to sharply decrease.

1. Describe the forward rate trade you have implemented.
2. Calculate the gain or loss of the trade in currency $c(A)$ at time $t = 1$ according to the forward rate projection method as well as the substitution method.

9 Performance Measurement on Fixed-Income Portfolios

There are two steps involved in assessing the performance of a bond portfolio—one is measuring the performance of the portfolio and the other is applying some risk adjustment to that raw performance measure.

9.1 Return Measures

It is not completely trivial to measure the return on an investment, in particular when that investment involves more than one time period. For one-period horizon (between date t and $t + 1$), the return is composed of cash distributions and capital gain/loss, and one just needs to apply the usual formula

$$r_{t,t+1} = \frac{V_{t+1} - V_t + D_{t,t+1}}{V_t}$$

where V_t is the value of the portfolio at date t, and $D_{t,t+1}$ is the cash-flow distribution between t and $t + 1$. For multiperiod horizon, cash may be added to, or withdrawn from, the fund and the issue is whether to recognize timing of cash flows or not. Several options are possible.

9.1.1 Arithmetic Rate of Return

The arithmetic rate of return is the simplest option. It consists in taking a simple equally weighted average of return over different time periods. This may lead, however, to misleading interpretations, as can be seen from the example below.

Example 9.1 The rates of return for the first 4 months of the year are January -50%, February $+50\%$, March -50%, April $+50\%$. If one looks just at the rates of return for these 4 months and calculates the total arithmetic rate of return, one obtains: $(-50\% +50\% -50\% +50\%)/4 = 0\%$. In other words, the average rate of return is 0%. A quick look at that number might suggest that, over these 4 months, one would break even. This is, however, a misleading conclusion. If one would have invested \$1,000,000 at the end of December, one would have \$562,500 at the end of April. This can be seen from the following computation:

$$\$1,000,000 \times 0.50 \times 1.50 \times 0.50 \times 1.50 = \$562,500$$

The reason the investor does not break even, even when the average rate of return is 0%, is that the gains and losses of 1 month must be reinvested at the beginning of the next one. As an even more extreme example, imagine that the rate of return is -100% in January. One may earn a subsequent $+100\%$ in February but still would not have any money on the first of March!

9.1.2 Geometric Rate of Return

The example above shows that it is certainly desirable to use geometric, and not arithmetic, averages to compute the return on a bond portfolio in a multiperiod setting. This is similar to using compounded, versus simple, interest rates. Geometric rates of return actually come under two forms—one is value-weighted and the other is time-weighted geometric average.

The value-weighted rate of return (or dollar-weighted rate of return) is equivalent to finding the internal rate of return on a series of cash flows. Formally, solve for r the following equation:

$$V_0 = \sum_{t=1}^{T} \frac{CF_t}{(1+r)^t} + \frac{V_T}{(1+r)^T}$$

where

CF_t are the net cash flows (cash inflows minus cash outflows) from the bond portfolio for dates $t = 1, \ldots, T$.

V_0 is the initial market value of the portfolio.

V_T is the terminal value of the portfolio.

The time-weighted rate of return is a measure of the compounded rate of growth of a portfolio. It is normally used to compare the returns of investment managers because the method eliminates the distorting effects of new money inflows. When calculating, the effect of varying cash inflows is eliminated by assuming a single investment at the beginning of a period and measuring the growth or loss of market value to the end of the period. It is assumed that all cash distributions are reinvested in the portfolio, and exactly the same periods are used for comparisons. The time-weighted rate of return reflects reinvestment from one period to the next. To calculate a time-weighted rate of return, compute the returns between withdrawals, assume that inflows and outflows take place at the end of a given period (say a week or a month), then compound the returns (geometric average). If the horizon considered is less than a year, one needs also to annualize the performance.

Example 9.2 Compute the value-weighted and time-weighted rates of return for the two following investments.

1. *Initial investment is 50 (initial market value of the portfolio = 50); after 1 year, the value of the portfolio is 100.*

   We first compute the annual value-weighted rate of return denoted by r^{vw}:

   $$50 = \frac{100}{(1+r^{vw})}$$

   The solution is $r^{vw} = 100\%$.

   We now compute the annual time-weighted rate of return denoted by r^{tw}:

   $$r^{tw} = \frac{100 - 50}{50} = 100\%$$

2. *Initial investment is 50 (initial market value of the portfolio = 50); after 6 months, the net cash flow is −25 (cash outflow). After 1 year, the value of the portfolio is 100.*

We first compute the annual value-weighted rate of return denoted by r^{vw}:

$$50 = -\frac{25}{(1+r^{vw})^{0.5}} + \frac{100}{(1+r^{vw})}$$

The solution is $r^{vw} = 40.69\%$.

We now compute the annual time-weighted rate of return denoted by r^{tw}:

$$r_1 = \frac{25-50}{50} = -50\%$$

$$r_2 = \frac{100-25}{25} = 300\%$$

where r_1 and r_2 are, respectively, the time-weighted rates of return for the first 6 months and the last 6 months of the period. We then obtain the annual time-weighted rate r^{tw}

$$r^{tw} = [(1+r_1)(1+r_2)] - 1 = 100\%$$

The value-weighted rate of return and the time-weighted rate of return are equivalent if there are no withdrawals or contributions over the evaluation period and all investment is reinvested. It appears that the dollar-weighted rate of return is a better measure of performance when the manager has control over inflows/outflows of money: the manager should be rewarded (penalized) when he makes good (bad) decisions and add (withdraw) money into (from) the portfolio when he/she believes the value of the portfolio is going to increase (decrease). In other situations, when the manager has no control over inflows/outflows of money (typically the case of a pension fund manager), the time-weighted geometric average should instead be used.

9.2 Risk-Adjusted Performance Evaluation

Sound investment decisions rest on identifying and selecting portfolio managers who are expected to deliver superior performance. Portfolio excess return can be decomposed into a passive and active component. The passive return component is based on public information: noninformed investors can earn this return by investing in the benchmark portfolio and in the risk-free assets according to their risk preferences. Passive return is an indicator for the diversification capabilities of the portfolio manager, that is, his ability to construct a mean-variance-efficient portfolio based upon public information (see Chapter 7 on passive strategies). The active part of excess return includes the performance components based on selection and on timing information (see Chapter 8 on active strategies). The goal of performance analysis is the identification of active and passive return components. Active return is further broken down into a timing and a selectivity return component. Statistical techniques are then used to distinguish these systematic performance effects from pure chance and to account for the risks taken to earn them.

Measuring the performance of portfolio managers is a challenging task because performance must be evaluated in a risk-adjusted sense and a relevant benchmark must be used for this. The best manager is not necessarily the one with the highest return! Before the 1960s, risk adjustment took the form of asset-type classifications, imprecise and not very analytical. The development of modern portfolio theory in the past 40 to 50 years has provided us with a much better understanding of the notion of risk and risk adjustments.

9.2.1 Absolute Risk-Adjusted Performance Evaluation

We first review measures of risk-adjusted performance that depends solely on the attributes (return, risk) of the manager's portfolio. In the next section, we shall review methods for risk-adjusted performance evaluation that are relative, in the sense that the manager's performance is compared to that of other managers or risk factors.

Volatility as a Measure of Risk and Sharpe Ratio as a Measure of Risk-Adjusted Return

In his seminal paper, Markowitz (1952) has introduced volatility as a natural measure of risk. Volatility, denoted by σ, is the standard deviation of returns, that is, the square root of the average squared deviation with respect to mean return, or $\sigma = \frac{1}{T} \sum_{t=1}^{T} (R_t - \overline{R})^2$.

One commonly used method for risk-adjusting the performance of a portfolio is to normalize the excess return over the risk-free rate of the portfolio by the volatility of the portfolio. This is known as the Sharpe ratio

$$SR = \frac{E(R_p) - r_f}{\sigma_p}$$

where $E(R_p)$ is the mean return on the portfolio, σ_p is the portfolio volatility and r_f the risk-free rate. Hence, the Sharpe index penalizes managers for taking risks.

Although the ratio has the advantage of being simple, robust, and above all, not depending on any reference index, it does not allow the many dimensions of risk to be captured satisfactorily. The Sharpe ratio, for example, completely hides the existence of third- and fourth-order moments (i.e., skewness and kurtosis), which are nonetheless frequently unfavorable to the investor in the alternative world. By only considering the first- and second-order moments of the distribution function of bond portfolio performances, a large part of the risk being run is ignored. This is particularly true for alternative fixed-income strategies, in which the low level of volatility achieved by some hedge-fund managers is only obtained in exchange for fatter distribution tails. The price to be paid for risk-adjusted performances that seem to be significantly better than those of traditional assets is therefore an increased probability of having to put up with extreme losses (notably due to liquidity and credit risk). To this is added the ease with which it is possible to manipulate the Sharpe ratio by transferring part of the risk from the first- and second-order moments to the third- and fourth-order moments [see, for example, Lo (2001)].[1]

---

[1] By selling out-of-the-money put options (strike price on average 7% below the market price) on the S&P 500, with a maturity of 3 months or less, Lo (2001) manages to obtain a Sharpe ratio of 1.94 for the period from January 1992 to December 1999 (compared to 0.98 for the S&P 500!). Of course, the downside of this strategy is the very significant increase in the risks of extreme loss, which only appear in moments greater than 2 (skewness and kurtosis) and which are therefore not taken into account in the Sharpe ratio. In Lo's example, the maximal loss recorded by the "Capital Decimation Partners" fund is 18.3%, compared to 8.9% for the S&P 500.

Accounting for Higher Moments

As a result of taking their nonlinear and non-Gaussian character into account, the investor generally displays a nontrivial preference for the third- and fourth-order moments of return distribution (skewness and kurtosis), as is evidenced, furthermore, by the development of measures of extreme risk such as the VaR (Value-at-Risk) (see below).

It is possible to obtain two probability distributions with the same mean and the same variance, but with entirely different skewness and kurtosis. For example, an equally weighted mixture of a Gaussian with a mean of 0.5 and a standard deviation of 0.5 and a Gaussian with a mean of −0.5 and a standard deviation 1.32 exhibits the same mean and variance as a standardized Gaussian (0 and 1, respectively), but a skewness of −0.75 and a kurtosis of 6.06, compared to 0 and 3, respectively, for the standardized Gaussian (see Figure 9.1 below). Only by taking into account the third- and fourth-order moments can we truly distinguish the funds with returns that follow those probability distributions.

Because actual return distributions deviate from the Gaussian model along two dimensions, skewness and kurtosis, modern financial theory and practice have tried to account for these two aspects to improve on existing measures of risk-adjusted portfolio performance.

Accounting for Skewness   The skewness problem is perhaps the most straightforward. Investors dislike negative returns: they need a measure of the downside risk, for example, semivariance. Semivariance is defined as $\frac{1}{T^-} \sum\limits_{t \text{ s.t. } R_t \leq \overline{R}} (R_t - \overline{R})^2$, where T^- is the number of returns below the mean in the sample.

This can be generalized in terms of any Minimum Acceptable Return (MAR), where the MAR term replaces the average return in the above expression. There exists an analog to the Sharpe

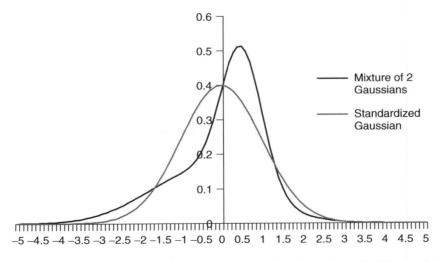

Figure 9.1   Two probability distributions with the same mean and variance, but with different skewness and kurtosis.

ratio, known as the *Sortino ratio*, that penalizes managers for taking on negative risks

$$Sortino = \frac{\mathbb{E}(R_p) - MAR}{\sqrt{\frac{1}{T^{MAR}} \sum_{t \text{ s.t. } R_t \leq MAR} (R_t - MAR)^2}}$$

where T^{MAR} is the number of returns below the MAR in the sample.

Accounting for Kurtosis   Risk management literature has recently focused on extreme risks, as opposed to average risk measured by volatility. Extreme risk is commonly measured in terms of Value-at-Risk (VaR), a statistical measure of risk that quantifies the possible loss on a position with a certain degree of probability. More precisely, VaR estimates the potential loss (expressed in currency units) that may result from holding a portfolio of financial products for a given period of time (1 day, 1 week, etc.), with a confidence level set *a priori* (95%, 99%, etc.) and with market fluctuations similar to those observed in the past. Financial regulators require a confidence interval of 99% so that, statistically, actual losses should exceed VaR in only one out of a hundred cases. Moreover, the regulatory 10-day holding period corresponds to the estimated time period needed to reverse the position in the market.

Consequently, 10-day VaR with a 99% confidence interval is simply the quantile of order 1% of the probability distribution of changes in a portfolio's market value over 10 days (see Figure 9.2).

Calculating VaR therefore comes down to estimating a quantile for this distribution. Three methods are currently used to estimate VaR: the historical method, based on observed data; the parametric method, which uses a given model in order to deduce closed formulae; and the Monte Carlo simulation method.

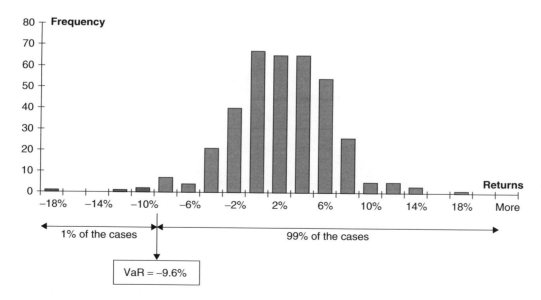

Figure 9.2   10-day VaR with a 99% confidence interval.

- *With the historical method, which is the most intuitive of the three, the distribution of future shifts in risk factors is treated in the same way as prior-period distributions. This means that past shifts are used to revalue the portfolio and simulate its profits and losses (P&Ls). VaR is then obtained by reading the relevant quantile off the histogram of simulated returns. On a historical observation period of 500 daily P&Ls, the 1-day 99% VaR of the portfolio is simply equal to the fifth largest loss observed during that period.*

- *The parametric method is based on the assumption that the joint distribution of risk factors can be approximated by an a priori theoretical distribution, the mathematical expression of which depends on a smaller number of parameters. The properties of this theoretical distribution are used to estimate the quantile of the distribution and hence the VaR of a position or a portfolio. Normal, or Gaussian, distribution is often used because of its simplicity. Unfortunately, using a Gaussian approximation results in a sometimes dramatic underestimation of real VaR. It is possible to use other parametric assumptions, and to consider in particular probability distributions such as Student or Pareto-Levy, for example, which exhibit the kind of fat tails that we find in actual financial data.*

- *Estimating VaR via Monte Carlo simulations is similar in some respects to applying the historical and the parametric methods. First, the joint distribution of risk factors is specified and used to generate a large number of risk-factor variation scenarios. These scenarios are then used to compute the hypothetical results of the portfolio. Last, VaR is determined in the same way as historical VaR but on the basis of the simulated sample.*

It is actually beyond the scope of the present book to describe in detail those approaches, and we refer the interested reader to Jorion (2000) for a comprehensive coverage of Value-at-Risk.

Once a reliable estimate on the VaR has been computed using either of the aforementioned methods, it can be used to define an analog to the Sharpe ratio that penalizes managers for taking on extreme risks, as opposed to average risk. This is a ratio of Ratio Return/VaR, or R/VaR

$$Ratio \ R/VaR = \frac{\mathbb{E}(R_p) - r_f}{|VaR_p|}$$

Whatever the measure of risk used, previous ratios (Sharpe ratio, Sortino Ratio, Ratio Return/VaR) were assessing the performance in absolute terms. One problem with such an approach is the following: if T-bonds perform better than corporate bonds, Sharpe (or Sortino) ratio of a poor T-Bond manager is likely to be higher than Sharpe ratio of a good corporate bond manager. In other words, absolute evaluation measures as much the performance of an asset class as that of the manager!

9.2.2 Relative Risk-Adjusted Performance Evaluation

In the light of the above remark, it seems desirable to perform relative performance evaluation, that is, measure the manager performance with respect to the performance of comparable managers or with respect to broad-based indices or benchmarks.

Factor Models for Performance Evaluation

More generally, relative risk-adjusted performance evaluation consists in using a factor model to compare the overall performance of a manager to the performance he/she should get from being

Fixed Income Securities

exposed to rewarded sources of risk. These models allow us to decompose mutual fund (excess) returns into two components.

$$\text{Total (excess) return} = \text{Normal return} + \text{Abnormal return (skill)}$$

Normal return is generated as a fair reward for the risk(s) taken by mutual fund managers. Abnormal return (aka alpha) is generated through the managers' unique ability to "beat the market" in a risk-adjusted sense (market timing and/or security selection skills). Abnormal return therefore appears as a natural way to assess managers' risk-adjusted performance. While total return is readily observable, the challenge is to measure normal return (not observable). We need a model to measure normal return. The Capital Asset Pricing Model (CAPM) of Sharpe (1964) is the reference model for measuring normal return, and was later extended in the form of multifactor models.

As recalled above, factor models can be used to measure abnormal returns, that is, returns above and beyond the fair return from being exposed to the kind of risks the manager was exposed to. This is formalized by the following equation, the theoretical foundations of which are based on the Arbitrage Pricing Theory (Ross, 1976)

$$\alpha_i = \overline{r_i} - r_f - \sum_{k=1}^{K} \beta_{ik}\lambda_k \tag{9.1}$$

where α_i is the risk-adjusted return for fund i, $\overline{r_i}$ is the average return on the fund, r_f is the risk-free rate, β_{ik} is the sensitivity (measure of exposure) of fund i with respect to factor k and λ_k is the risk premium associated with factor k.

The CAPM security market line equation is a specific case of equation (9.1), which reads

$$\alpha_i = \overline{r_i} - r_f - \beta_i(\overline{r_M} - r_f)$$

where $\overline{r_M}$ is the average return on the market portfolio (often proxied by a broad-based index), β_i is the sensitivity of fund i with respect to the market portfolio and $\lambda = \overline{r_M} - r_f$ is the risk premium associated with the market portfolio.

In the classical CAPM framework, the expected return on an asset is related to the beta of the asset with respect to market portfolio. For instance, an asset with the beta of 2 is expected to have a risk premium that is twice as high as the market portfolio's risk premium. We have empirical evidence that a single factor (i.e., the market portfolio) may not be capable of properly measuring the riskiness of various asset classes. For this reason, it is, in general, better to use a multifactor model for measuring the normal return on a bond portfolio.

While equation (9.1) provides us with a theoretically satisfying answer to the problem of risk-adjusted performance measurement, an important question remains in practice: the choice of the factors. There are four types of factor models.

1. *Implicit factor model   In this approach, some factor analysis (e.g., a principal component analysis) is performed to statistically extract the factors from the return's time series [see, for example, Connor and Korajczyk (1993)]. It is perhaps the best approach because it is free of problems such as inclusion of spurious factors and omission of true factors. However, factors may not be easily interpretable.*

2. *Macro factor model*   *In this approach, macroeconomic variables are used as factors. For example, Chen et al. (1986) use inflation rate, growth in industrial production, spread long–short treasuries, spread high–low grade corporate interest rate.*

3. *Micro factor model*   *In this approach, microeconomic attributes are used as factors. A commonly used industrial application of such a model is provided by BARRA, a California-based financial software company.*

4. *Index factor model*   *In this approach, stock market indices are used as factors. This is consistent with the idea of using portfolio returns as factors. The most popular example of this approach is the CAPM (Sharpe, 1964), where the return on the market portfolio, proxied by a broad-based index is used as a factor. The idea of using "mimicking portfolios" as a proxy for the true unknown factor is also present in Fama and French (1992).*

In the example that follows (see the next section), we shall use the return on broad indices as factors. This is a pragmatic approach to the problem since index returns are readily observable, as we now explain.

Fixed-Income Indices

There are many bond index providers. In what follows, we provide a detailed description of the criteria that a good index should meet, and we also list the most commonly used bond indices.

Characteristics of a Good Index   The following is a list of important items an investor should take into account when choosing a fixed-income index:

- *Relevance*   *An index should be relevant to investors. At a minimum, it should track those markets and market segments of most interest to investors.*

- *Comprehensiveness*   *An index should include all opportunities that are realistically available to market participants under normal market conditions while measuring the performance of new investments and existing holdings.*

- *Replicability*   *The total returns reported for an index should be replicable by market participants. It must be fair to investment managers who are measured against it and to sponsors who pay fees or award management assignments based on performance relative to it. Furthermore, over time, an index must represent a realistic baseline strategy that a passive investor could have followed. Accordingly, information about index composition and historical returns should be readily available.*

- *Stability*   *An index should not change composition very often, and all changes should be easily understood and highly predictable. It should not be subject to opinions about which bonds or equities to include on any particular day. However, index composition must change occasionally to ensure that it accurately reflects the structure of the market. A key virtue of an index is to provide a passive benchmark; investors should not be forced to execute a significant number of transactions just to keep pace.*

- **Barriers to entry** *The markets or market segments included in an index should not contain significant barriers to entry. This guideline is especially applicable to an international index in which an included country may discourage foreign ownership of its bonds or participation in its equity market.*

- **Expenses** *In the normal course of investing, expenses related to withholding tax, safekeeping and transactions are incurred. For a market or market segment to be included, these ancillary expenses should be well understood by market participants and should not be excessive. For example, if expenses are unpredictable or inconsistently applied, an index cannot hope to fairly measure market performance.*

- **Simple and objective selection criteria** *There should be a clear set of rules governing inclusion of bonds, equities or markets in an index, and investors should be able to forecast and agree on changes in composition.*

This list of desirable characteristics may not be exhaustive, and different investors may place different emphasis on each.

In any case, it is critical that an index follows objective rules that are well defined so that all interested parties can understand how to apply the information to their particular situation.

Providers of Bonds Indices There are many bond index providers. In what follows, we list the most commonly used bond indices, and provide some brief information on how the indices are built.

- **Merrill Lynch** *The month-to-date Index return is equal to the sum of the individual bond returns times their beginning of month capitalization weights.*

$$TR_n = \sum_i TR_{n,i} \times w_{i,n-1}$$

where:

TR_n = *index month-to-date total return on day n;*

$TR_{n,i}$ = *month-to-date total return on day n of bond i;*

$w_{i,n-1}$ = *prior month-end capitalization weight of bond i.*

- **Salomon Smith Barney** *Total returns are computed on the assumption that each security is purchased at the beginning of the period and sold at the end of the period. An issue's total rate of return is the percentage change in its total value over the measurement period. The total returns are market-capitalization-weighted using the security's beginning-of-period market value.*

Beginning-of-Period Value = (beginning price + beginning accrued) × beginning par amount outstanding

End-of-period value = ((ending price + ending accrued) × (beginning par amount outstanding − principal payments)) + coupon payments + principal payments + reinvestment income.

Total rate of return (%) = ((end-of-period value/beginning-of-period value) −1) × 100

- **Lehman Brothers**   *Perhaps the most heavily used provider of bond indices. Indices are rebalanced monthly by market capitalization.*

- **JP Morgan**   *JP Morgan includes only government debt issued by sovereign or sovereign-guaranteed issuers in one index. This index focuses on large, liquid agency bullet issues so as to provide investors a somewhat different kind of index from the other US agency indices that are currently being published by other index providers.*

Another important provider is Salomon Brothers, and we use their indices in the example in the next section. In Europe, we find some providers in the above list, plus specific European providers such as Comité de Normalisation Obligataire. They publish an index, CNO-ETRIX, which measures the total return of fixed-rate liquid bonds issued by Governments within the euro zone. The total return of the global index is then calculated as the average of the maturity bands' total return indices weighted by the representativity coefficients of the various maturity bands. As a simplified example, if there were only two maturity bands A and B, A weighting 90% and B 10%, the total return of the global index would be 90% of the total return of maturity band A and 10% of the total return of maturity band B.

$$Total\ Return\ of\ the\ Global\ Index = Total\ Return(Indice_i) \times CR_i$$

where CR is calculated as a ratio of the market capitalization of the qualifying bonds in a maturity band to the market capitalization of the qualifying bonds in all maturity bands.

Benchmarks for Alternative Fixed-Income Strategies   Indices also exist for alternative fixed-income strategies, known as *fixed-income arbitrage* and *convertible arbitrage*.[2] They provide a quick overview of the return on a portfolio of hedge-fund managers following a given investment style. One serious problem there is that fixed-income hedge-fund indices come in very different shapes and forms. The existence of a profound heterogeneity in the set of assets under consideration, as well as some heterogeneity in the index construction methods may result in some dramatic heterogeneity in the returns.[3] As a result, hedge-fund style indices tend to convey a somewhat confusing view of the alternative investments universe [see Amenc and Martellini (2001)]. This is because the collection of such indices is neither collectively exhaustive, nor mutually exclusive (see Figure 9.3 for an illustration).[4]

There are at least a dozen competing hedge-fund index providers (see Table 9.1) that differ in the construction methods they use, in terms of selection criteria (examples of selection criteria

---

[2]For more information on fixed-income arbitrage, see Chapter 8. For more information on convertible arbitrage strategies, see Chapter 14.

[3]This applies, but to a lesser extent, in the context of bond indices. Reilly, Kao and Wright (1992) find that the correlation of annual returns between the three main providers of broad-based bond indices (Lehman Brothers, Merrill Lynch and Salomon Brothers) to be around a comforting 98%. The authors found, however, sizable return differences at the monthly level, as well as for the specialized sectors covered by the three dealer firms.

[4]As a simple evidence of the lack of collective exhaustivity, it perhaps suffices to say that one of the most frequently used hedge-fund indices, the EACM 100, does not account for more than a few percent of all existing hedge funds.

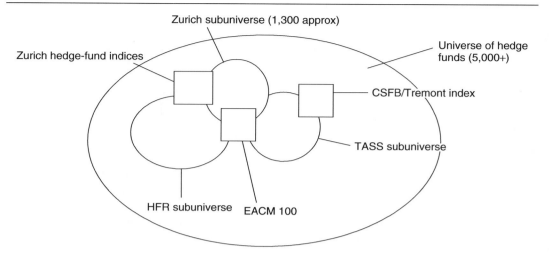

Figure 9.3 Hedge-Fund universe. The hedge-fund universe is made up of more than 5,000 funds. Several competing indices exist, none of which fully represent the entire universe.

Table 9.1   Competing Indices in Hedge-Fund Universe.

Providers	nb of indices	Website
EACM	13	eacmalternative.com
HFR	7	hfr.com
CSFB/Tremont	9	hedgeindex.com
Zürich Capital	5	zcmgroup.com
MSCI	4	msci.com
Van Hedge	12	vanhedge.com
Henessee Group	22	hedgefnd.com
Hedgefund.net	33	hedgefund.net
LJH Global Investment	16	ljh.com
MAR	15	marhedge.com
Altvest	13	altvest.com
Magnum	8	magnum.com

Note: This table provides a listing of competing hedge-fund index providers, with information on the number of indices and websites.

include length of track record, assets under management and restrictions on new investment), style classification (manager's self-proclaimed styles versus objective statistical-based classification), weighting scheme (equally weighted versus value-weighted) and rebalancing scheme (e.g., monthly versus annually).

Concerning the fixed-income universe, we have listed in Table 9.2 various competing indices for the two dominant styles.

As a result of such differences in the construction methods, competing index providers offer a very contrasted picture of hedge-fund returns, and differences in monthly returns can be higher

Table 9.2   Competing Indices in Hedge-Fund Fixed-Income Universe.

Subuniverse	List of competing indices	Range
Convertible arbitrage	CSFB, HFR, EACM, Zürich, Henessee, HF Net	01/98–12/00
Fixed-income arbitrage	CSFB, HFR, Van Hedge, Henessee, HF Net	01/96–12/00

Note: This table provides a listing of competing indices in the fixed-income universe with details on the competing indices and the data range.

Table 9.3   Measures of Heterogeneity in Hedge-Fund Indices (1).

Subuniverse	Max difference (with dates and indices)
Convertible arbitrage	4.75% (Oct 98; CSFB (−4.67)/Henessee (0.08))
Fixed-income arbitrage	10.98% (Oct 98; HF Net (−10.78)/Van Hedge (0.2))

Note: This table provides the maximum monthly return difference between competing indices for the same style.

Table 9.4   Measures of Heterogeneity in Hedge-Fund Indices (2).

Subuniverse	Average correlation	Median correlation	Heterogeneity index
Convertible arbitrage	0.8183	0.8319	0.1817
Fixed-income arbitrage	0.5407	0.4968	0.4592

Note: This table provides three measures of heterogeneity in the hedge-fund index universe [average correlation, median correlation and a percentage heterogeneity index (1-average correlation)].

than 10%! For example, HF Net fixed-income arbitrage index posts a −10.78% performance in October 1998, while Van Hedge index achieves a small positive 0.2% (see Table 9.3).

We also compute the average and median correlation between various indices in each given universe. We also compute a customized heterogeneity index aimed at representing the percentage heterogeneity in the subuniverse. For that we simply compute

$$HI = 1 - \frac{\sum_{i,j=1}^{K} \rho_{i,j}}{K}$$

Assume that a universe is made of K perfectly homogeneous indices. In that case, the correlation matrix is entirely made of 1, and the heterogeneity index is equal to $1 - 1 = 0\%$ heterogeneity. In general, this yields a number between 0 and 1 that can be regarded as a percentage heterogeneity in the subuniverse under consideration. Table 9.4 summarizes that information for fixed-oriented alternative strategies.

There is evidence of strong heterogeneity in the information conveyed by competing indices. For example, the mean correlation between competing indices within a particular style can be as low as less than 0.6. In particular, fixed-income arbitrage strategies exhibit a low 0.5407 average correlation. Fixed-income arbitrage managers tend to follow a pure alpha strategy with little, if any, systematic exposure to pervasive risk factors, which leads to a high heterogeneity in the returns. On the other hand, convertible arbitrage managers maintain an exposure to standard risk factors (in particular, equity volatility risk and bond default risk) in a way that makes them more similar.

Customized Benchmarks (Normal Portfolios)

When an investment policy requires specific allocations to selected sectors or imposes other restrictions, a standard market-weighted index may not be an appropriate benchmark. To measure the manager's performance fairly under such an investment policy, the benchmark should be subjected to similar restrictions. The challenge is to make the benchmark as broad-based and well diversified as possible, and at the same time meeting all requirements of the investment policy.

Decomposition-Based Customized Benchmark Construction In a simple case, a customized index merely changes relative weights of a standard index's components. Such a benchmark consists solely of securities in the standard index, but weights them according to the preferred allocation scheme rather than by market capitalization. For instance, a money manager might receive a mandate specifying equal investments in government and corporate bonds. As corporate bonds compose only about one-third of a typical Government/Credit Index such as the Lehman Brothers Government/Credit Index, a more appropriate benchmark for this portfolio would be a customized index containing two equal parts representing the Government Index and the Credit Index.

Benchmark construction can be more complex as one needs to account for the presence of many potential constraints in the mandate of the portfolio manager. Examples of such constraints are as follows:[5]

- *Portfolio duration must be within +/−6 months of benchmark duration.*

- *Between 20 and 30% of the portfolio should be invested in corporate bonds.*

- *The corporate spread duration must be within +/−1 year of the benchmark spread duration.*

- *Up to 10% of the portfolio may be invested in high-yield bonds with a minimum rating of B.*

- *No single issue may account for more than 3% of the portfolio.*

- *No single corporate issuer may constitute more than 5% of the portfolio.*

- *No futures, options or other derivative securities may be purchased.*

- *No callable bonds are allowed.*

It is a real challenge to translate such investment policy constraints into a specific market-observable benchmark that meets all these criteria. The method consists in applying the rules that define a specific benchmark to a historical index data, and retroactively created time series of benchmark returns (as well as sensitivities to a set of risk factors). The decomposition-based approach to the construction of customized benchmarks requires a significant amount of information.

- *First, it is a daunting task to reconstruct a customized benchmark in that way, even for the provider of the original index. Now, any other investor or manager may not be able to get access to the source of data that was used by the index provider, so that it is generally not feasible to adjust the index according to specific constraints unless one is the index provider.*

---

[5]These examples are borrowed from "Quantitative Management of Bond Portfolios," Lehman Brothers Fixed-Income Research Publication, 2001.

- *Also, some institutions do not follow any formal benchmark, but historically have maintained a certain asset mix.*

- *Finally, one needs to be able to know what is the strategy that the manager is following. This, however, is not always feasible. In particular, some managers do not exactly follow their self-proclaimed investment style and/or shift their investment styles. This can occur, for example, as market conditions may prevent a manager from implementing his favorite portfolio strategy. The situation is even worse in the case of alternative investment strategies, where it is usually not feasible to know what a manager is doing, because he is using proprietary models and investment strategies that are the essence of his competitive advantage in the market place.*

Fortunately, other methods exist for customized index construction, which are easier to implement.

Return-Based Customized Benchmark Construction It is widely agreed that asset allocation accounts for a large part of the variability in the return on a typical bond portfolio. Asset allocation is generally defined as the allocation of an investor's portfolio among a number of major asset classes or styles (e.g., Treasuries, corporate bonds, investment grades, etc.). Sharpe (1988, 1992) has introduced the following model to provide an objective assessment of a manager's effective style mix, as opposed to the manager's declared style mix. This is known as return-based style analysis, and does not require details on the exact portfolio holdings. The style analysis model reads

$$r_{it} = \sum_{k=1}^{K} w_{ik} I_{kt} + \varepsilon_{it}$$

where r_{it} is the (net of fees) excess return on a given portfolio or fund, I_{kt} is the return on index k for the period t, w_{ik} is the style weight (add up to 1), and ε_{it} is an error term. For a manager, a customized benchmark or normal portfolio can then be defined as $\sum_{k=1}^{K} w_{ik} I_{kt}$, that is, the passive investment strategy in the desired styles that best replicate the performance of the manager's portfolio. The difference ε_{it} between the normal portfolio and the actual portfolio is a manifestation of a manager's active bets.

In the context of assessing the performance of traditional fixed-income portfolio managers, one may use a set of indices representative of various segments of the market, and in particular long-term Treasury bond index, medium-term Treasury bond index, long-term corporate bond index, medium-term corporate bond index, high-yield bond index, mortgage-backed securities index. This set of indices is consistent with what was used in academic studies of bond portfolio performance [see, for example, Elton *et al.* (1993)].

Style analysis is a specific case of a (multiple) linear regression analysis (statistical terminology) and of a factor model (financial terminology). Such factor models are typically evaluated on the basis of their ability to explain the returns of the assets in question (i.e., the r_{it}). A useful metric is the proportion of variance "explained" by the selected asset classes. Using the traditional definition, for manager i

$$R_i^2 = 1 - \frac{\mathbb{V}ar(\varepsilon_i)}{\mathbb{V}ar(r_i)}$$

The right-hand side of this equation equals 1 minus the proportion of variance "unexplained." The resulting R-squared value thus indicates the proportion of the variance of r_i "explained" by the K asset classes/styles. On a technical note, the optimal style weights are actually obtained as the solution to a program of minimization of the variance of the residual term; this is the traditional approach of "least square estimation" (statistical terminology) or "tracking error minimization" (financial terminology). What makes style analysis specific with respect to standard linear regression is that specific constraints are imposed on the coefficients so that they can be naturally interpreted as weights:[6]

- **Portfolio constraint:** the coefficients w_{ik} are constrained to add up to 1;

- **Positivity constraint:** the coefficients w_{ik} are constrained to be positive.

There are also some caveats with return-based style analysis. First and foremost, style analysis is a backward-looking technique because data from the past are used to infer a manager's current asset allocation. Because the out-of-sample performance of in-sample estimates is not clear, it is often suggested to use the recent past data and give more weight to recent observations. It is also typical to perform style analysis with a rolling window of observation to try and determine what style drifts, if any, have occurred during a given time period.

In the context of defining a customized portfolio for alternative fixed-income strategies such as fixed-income arbitrage or convertible arbitrage, return-based style analysis yields somewhat unsatisfactory results. For example, Fung and Hsieh (1997ab, 2000) report that almost half of the hedge funds in their sample (409 funds from the AIG Global Investors, TASS Management and Paradigm LDC databases with 3 years of monthly returns with at least $5 million of assets under management) have R-squared below 30%. On the other hand, when they apply style analysis in the traditional investment universe (funds in Morningstar's database), they find that 73% of mutual funds have R-squared above 80% and 56% have above 90%. In other words, for traditional managers, where they invest, as opposed to how they invest, is the key component. On the other hand, the payoff of hedge funds arises from three types of factors:

- *Location factors (buy-and-hold policy): Sharpe's traditional factors*

- *Trading strategy factor (optionlike payoff): market timing*

- *Leverage factor (scaling of payoff due to gearing).*

This is a justification of the "alternative" in "alternative investment" strategies. How hedge-fund managers invest is at least as important as where they invest. Hedge funds typically exhibit nonlinear optionlike exposures to standard asset classes (Fung and Hsieh, 1997ab, 2000; Agarwal and Naik, 2000) because they can use derivatives and they follow dynamic trading strategies, and also because of the explicit sharing of the upside profits (postfee returns have optionlike element

---

[6]It should be noted that the presence of these constraints distorts standard regression results. In particular, confidence intervals for coefficients are no longer readily available in closed form. These may, however, be numerically estimated [see Lobosco and DiBartolomeo (1997)]. Portfolio and positivity constraints may actually sometimes be relaxed, in particular when performing style analysis for hedge funds, because of the ability of hedge-fund managers to use leveraged position and take long but also short positions in traditional asset classes [see Agarwal and Naik (2000)]. Style analysis without positivity constraints is sometimes referred to as semistrong style analysis, while style analysis with no constraints is referred to as weak style analysis.

even if prefee returns do not). Given that dynamic trading strategies and the presence of derivatives introduce nonlinear dependence of hedge fund with respect to standard bond indices, a standard return-based style analysis type of regression on standard indices such as long-term Treasury bond index, medium-term Treasury bond index, long-term corporate bond index, medium-term corporate bond index, high-yield bond index, mortgage-backed securities index... may not yield satisfying results. One solution[7] to try and capture such a nonlinear dependence is to include new regressors with nonlinear exposure to standard bond indices to proxy dynamic trading strategies in a linear regression. Candidates for new regressors are buy-and-hold positions in derivatives (Agarwal and Naik, 2000) or hedge-fund indices (Amenc and Martellini, 2001, Lhabitant, 2001).

In summary, both decomposition-based and return-based style analysis have shortcomings. Return-based style analysis is usually regarded as a better, more objective, way to assess what a manager's normal portfolio is when compared to broad benchmarks or manager's self-proclaimed styles, the idea being to assess the style of a manager by checking the footprints of the manager returns. This is perhaps best illustrated by William Sharpe's famous quote: "If it acts like a duck, assume it's a duck." On the other hand, decomposition-based style analysis is more backward looking than return-based style analysis. Both methods actually perform best when combined. For example, before running a return-based style analysis regression, it is useful to start with a qualitative assessment approach: interview or questionnaire that allows the manager to describe his investment philosophy, and also, if possible, analyze the manager's current holding to guarantee the respect of prespecified constraints and style consistency of the manager on a timely basis.

In what follows, we present an example of application of style analysis to performance evaluation of bond portfolio managers.

9.3 Application of Style Analysis to Performance Evaluation of Bond Portfolio Managers: An Example

We have seen that many different methods can be applied to perform risk adjustment. Here we present a method developed in Amenc *et al.* (2001), which is a multistep adaptation of style analysis to performance valuation. It can also be regarded as a specific case of a multi-index factor model.

We have recalled above the details of Sharpe's ((1988), (1992)) style analysis model

$$r_{it} = \sum_{k=1}^{K} w_{ik} I_{kt} + \varepsilon_{it}$$

where r_{it} is the (net of fees) excess return on a given portfolio or fund, I_{kt} is the return on index k for the period t, w_{ik} is the style weight (add up to 1), and ε_{it} is an error term. It is tempting to interpret the "skill" or total excess return term ε_{it} in a style analysis as a measure of abnormal return.

---

[7] Another solution would be to allow for a nonlinear analysis of standard asset classes. This, however, implies a stronger departure with respect to standard techniques used in portfolio theory.

It should be noted that the presence of these constraints distorts standard regression results. In particular, confidence intervals for coefficients are no longer readily available in closed form. These may, however, be numerically estimated using a method introduced by Lobosco and DiBartolomeo (1997).

It is possible to represent each fund by a vector of the fund's style weights, and then perform cluster-based peer grouping by minimizing intragroup and maximizing extragroup distance between funds, where distance is defined in terms of an appropriate metric in the space of the fund's style weights. Cluster analysis routines are readily available in statistical software, and we have used SAS for this computation. All cluster analysis methods are based on the usual agglomerative hierarchical clustering procedure. Each observation begins in a cluster by itself. The two closest clusters are merged to form a new cluster that replaces the two old clusters. Merging of the two closest clusters is repeated until only one cluster is left. The various clustering methods differ in how the distance between two clusters is computed. We use the Ward's minimum-variance method by which squared Euclidean distances are used in the combinatorial distance formulas. We have exogenously imposed a limited number of clusters, so as to ensure that a reasonable number of different classes be obtained.

We illustrate the method on a set of 252 French fixed-income managers who report themselves as investing in the international bond markets. We have obtained weekly returns on these funds from early June 1999 to end of May 2002. We have used the following set of indices as regressors: short-term, medium-term and long-term maturity Treasury indices, plus one general corporate and one high yield to capture the fraction of performance that can be attributable to exposure to credit risk. These indices are as follows:

- *Salomon Brothers Global Short-Term Treasury Bond Index*
- *Salomon Brothers Global Medium-Term Treasury Bond Index*
- *Salomon Brothers Global Long-Term Treasury bond Index*
- *Salomon Brothers Global Investment-Grade Corporate Bond Index*
- *Salomon Brothers Global High-Yield Bond Index.*

The results of the analysis are displayed in the following Table 9.5, where we display the average value of the style weight for each cluster in each geographical zone.

From Table 9.5, it appears that the first cluster contains 153 managers who invest almost exclusively in Treasury bonds of various maturities. In cluster 2, we find 26 managers with strong exposure to high-yield bonds, while a third cluster contains 73 managers who invest mostly in investment-grade corporate bonds.

9.3.1 Alpha Analysis

It is tempting to interpret the "skill" or total excess return term ε_{it} in a style analysis as a measure of abnormal return. There are two important caveats, however. First, the introduction of portfolio and positivity constraints in style analysis distorts the standard regression results. As a result, standard desirable properties of linear regression models do not hold. In particular, the correlation

Table 9.5 Average Value of the Style Weight for each Cluster in each Geographical Zone.

	Global Short-Term Treasury Bond Index	Global Medium-Term Treasury Bond Index	Global Long-Term Treasury Bond Index	Global Investment-Grade Corporate Bond	Global High-Yield Bond Index	Number of funds	Style interpretation
Cluster 1	**0.313**	**0.427**	**0.172**	0.055	0.033	153	Treasury
Cluster 2	**0.103**	0.000	**0.010**	**0.140**	**0.746**	26	High Yield
Cluster 3	**0.107**	0.003	0.017	**0.825**	0.048	73	Corporate

between error term and benchmark asset may not be zero (Deroon *et al.*, 2000). Secondly, such an analysis does not provide us with an understanding of abnormal return, in a risk-adjusted sense. One needs to use instead a full-fledged multifactor model, which provides a measurement of a fund abnormal return as the excess mean return over the "normal return" given by the following relationship (straightforward generalization of the CAPM security market line):

$$\alpha_i = \overline{r_i} - r_f - \sum_{k=1}^{K} \beta_{ik}\lambda_k$$

In this approach, stock market indices are used as factors. This is consistent with the idea of using portfolio returns as factors. The most popular example of this approach is the CAPM (Sharpe, 1964), where the return on the market portfolio, proxied by a broad-based index is used as a factor. The idea of using "mimicking portfolios" as a proxy for the true unknown factor is also present in Fama and French (1992). In this context, one possible option is to address both problems of shortcomings of style analysis (distortion of linear factor model results because of the presence of constraints, and lack of proper risk adjustment) by using an Index Multifactor Model, which can be written as

$$r_{it} - r_{ft} = \alpha_i + \sum_{k=1}^{K} \beta_{ik}(F_{kt} - r_{ft}) + \zeta_{it}$$

This factor model is similar in spirit to the one used by Elton *et al.* (1993) to assess the managers' fund performance. This equation can be regarded as a weak form of style analysis, consisting in relaxing the positivity and portfolio constraints, and including a constant term in the regression. We also work in terms of excess returns. On a practical standpoint, this approach therefore allows us to address the question of benchmarking and performance measurement in a unified setup: once suitable indices have been selected, they can be used both for return-based style analysis (strong form of style analysis with positivity and portfolio constraints) and abnormal return measurement (weak form applied to excess returns).

One solution is therefore to measure risk-adjusted performance as the intercept (with T-statistic for assessment of statistical significance) of an unconstrained regression of the fund's excess return on the different indices' excess return. We first perform some peer grouping, that is, we first represent each fund by a vector of the fund's style weights, and then perform cluster-based peer grouping by minimizing intragroup and maximizing extragroup distance between funds, where distance is defined in terms of an appropriate metric in the space of fund's style weights. In order to avoid over-fitting and multicolinearity problems, an extra step might involve the selection, for each fund, of the subset of subindices that have been identified as more than marginally contributing to explaining the fund return (e.g., style weights larger than 10%). In particular, we suggest using potentially different models (i.e., different sets of indices) for different groups, but the same model (i.e., same set of indices) within a given group. In the example of the set of 252 French fixed-income managers, we use the following indices for the alpha analysis.

- ***Cluster 1, where the dominant style is T-Bonds***   Salomon Brothers Global Short-Term Treasury Bond Index, Salomon Brothers Global Medium-Term Treasury Bond Index, Salomon Brothers Global Long-Term Treasury Bond Index.

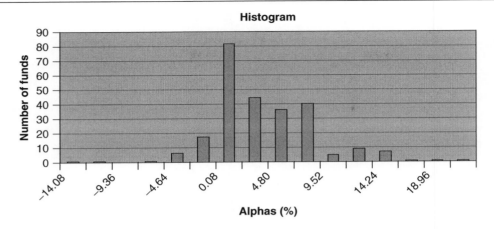

Figure 9.4 Distribution of annual alphas.

- ***Cluster 2, where the dominant style is High Yield*** *Salomon Brothers Global Short-Term Treasury Bond Index, Salomon Brothers Global Long-Term Treasury Bond Index, Salomon Brothers Global Investment Grade Corporate Bond Index, Salomon Brothers Global High Yield Bond Index.*

- ***Cluster 3, where the dominant style is Corporate Bonds*** *Salomon Brothers Global Short-Term Treasury Bond Index, Salomon Brothers Global Investment Grade Corporate Bond Index.*

In Figure 9.4, we display the distribution of annual alphas across the set of 252 French fixed-income managers. We found that 150 out of 252 funds did exhibit a positive alpha in this period. Only 73 out of these 150 were statistically significant at the 5% level (T-stat greater than 2). The average value for the annual alpha is 1.95%, while the standard deviation is 4.69%.

9.3.2 Passive Versus Active Managers

It is tempting to try and provide a quantitative estimate of the position of bond portfolio managers in terms of whether they follow passive versus active strategies. Sharpe's style analysis model can be used to that end. The model essentially divides the fund return into two components. The first component is "style": $\sum_{k=1}^{K} w_{ik} I_{kt}$ (part attributable to market movements), while the second component is "skill": ε_{it} (part unique to the manager). The skill term itself may be attributable to either the manager's exposure to other asset classes not included in the analysis or the manager's active bets (active picking within classes and/or class timing). One may use $\frac{\mathbb{V}ar(\varepsilon_{it})}{\mathbb{V}ar(r_{it})}$ as a proxy for the percentage of the performance that emanates from the manager's active bets. This is equivalent to an R-squared in a standard, unconstrained regression. If that ratio is equal to zero, it means that we are dealing with a manager passively investing in the set of style indices. In Figure 9.5, we display the distribution of this ratio across the set of 252 French fixed-income managers. We see that a significant fraction of the managers' returns is explained by the model. The average value for the R-squared is 59.04%, while the standard deviation is 30%. Therefore, on average, French managers in the sample can be regarded as 60% passive and 40% active.

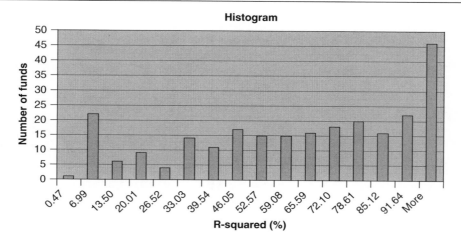

Figure 9.5 Distribution of the performance that emanates from the manager active bets across a set of 252 French fixed-income managers.

9.4 End of Chapter Summary

There are two steps involved in assessing the performance of a bond portfolio—one is measuring the performance of the portfolio and the other is applying some risk adjustment to raw performance measure.

Measuring returns is not a trivial task for multiperiod horizons, when cash may be added to or withdrawn from the fund. The arithmetic rate of return is the simplest option to compute a return in a multiperiod context. It consists in taking a simple equally weighted average of return over different time periods. This may lead, however, to misleading interpretations. It is desirable to use geometric, and not arithmetic, averages to compute the return on a bond portfolio in a multiperiod setting. Geometric rates of return actually come under two forms—one is the value-weighted and the other is the time-weighted geometric average. Dollar-weighted rate of return is a better measure of performance when the manager has control over inflows/outflows of money. In other situations, when the manager has no control over inflows/outflows of money, the time-weighted geometric average should instead be used.

Measuring the performance of portfolio managers is a challenging task because performance must be evaluated in a risk-adjusted sense and a relevant benchmark must be used for this. The development of modern portfolio theory in the past 40 to 50 years has provided us with a much better understanding of the notion of risk and risk adjustments. Investors often use the ratio of excess return on a bond portfolio over the risk-free rate divided by some measure of risk (volatility, downside risk, VaR, etc.) to measure the risk-adjusted performance of the fund.

Investors typically want to appreciate not only the absolute performance of a fund but also its relative performance with respect to a benchmark. Sometimes, a standard market-weighted index may not be an appropriate benchmark for a given fund. Style analysis can be used to compute a specific benchmark for a given bond portfolio manager. Style analysis can also be used to perform a risk-adjusted performance evaluation.

9.5 References and Further Reading

9.5.1 Books and Papers

Agarwal, V., and N.Y. Naik, 2000, "On Taking the Alternative Route: Risks, Rewards, and Performance Persistence of Hedge Funds", *Journal of Alternative Investments*, **2**(4), 6–23.

Amenc, N., and V., Lesourd, 2003, *Portfolio Theory and Performance Evaluation*, John Wiley, Europe.

Amenc, N., S. Curtis, and L. Martellini, 2001, The Alpha and Omega of Hedge Fund Performance Measurement, Working Paper, EDHEC-MISYS Risk and Asset Management Research Center.

Amenc, N., and L. Martellini, 2001, The Brave New World of Hedge Fund Indices, Working Paper, EDHEC-MISYS Risk and Asset Management Research Center.

Amenc, N., L. Martellini, and D. Sfeir, 2002, Do French Managers Invest with Style? Yes–But Only When They Invest Abroad!, Working Paper, EDHEC-MISYS Risk and Asset Management Research Center.

Brinson, G.P., L.R. Hood, and G.L. Beebower, 1986, "Determinants of Portfolio Performance", *Financial Analysts Journal*, **July/August**, 39–44.

Brinson, G.P., B.D. Singer, and G.L. Beebower, 1991, "Determinants of Portfolio Performance II: An Update", *Financial Analysts Journal*, **May/June**, 40–48.

Brown, D.T., and W.J. Marshall, 2001, "Assessing Fixed-Income Fund Manager Style and Performance from Historical Returns", *Journal of Fixed Income*, **10**(4), 15–25.

Chen, N., R. Roll, and S. Ross, 1986, "Economic Forces and the Stock Market", *Journal of Business*, **59**, 383–403.

Connor, G., and R. Korajczyk, 1993, A Test for the Number of Factors in an Approximate Factor Model, *Journal of Finance*, **48**, 1263–1291.

Deroon, F., T. Nijman, and J. Terhorst, 2000, Evaluating Style Analysis, Working Paper, Quantitative Investment Research Europe.

Elton, E., M. Gruber, S. Das, and M. Hlavka, 1993, "Efficiency with Costly Information: a Reinterpretation of Evidence from Managed Portfolios", *Review of Financial Studies*, **6**(1), 1–22.

Fabozzi, F.J., 1996, *Fixed-Income Mathematics*, 3rd Edition, McGraw-Hill, New York.

Fama, E., and K. French, 1992, "The Cross-Section of Expected Stock Returns", *Journal of Finance*, **47**, 442–465.

Fjelstad, M., 1999, "Modeling the Performance of Active Managers in the Euroland Bond Market", *Journal of Fixed Income*, **9**(1), 32–46.

Fung, W., and D.A. Hsieh, 1997a, "Empirical Characteristics of Dynamic Trading Strategies", *Review of Financial Studies*, **10**, 275–302.

Fung, W., and D.A. Hsieh, 1997b, "Survivorship Bias and Investment Style in the Returns of CTAs", *Journal of Portfolio Management*, **24**(1), 30–41.

Fung, W., and D.A. Hsieh, 2000, "Performance Characteristics of Hedge Funds and CTA Funds: Natural Versus Spurious Biases", *Journal of Financial and Quantitative Analysis*, **35**(3), 291–307.

Jorion, P., 2000, *Value-at-Risk: The New Benchmark for Managing Financial Risk*, McGraw-Hill, New York.

Keller, U., and A. Schlatter, 1999, "Telescopic Sums: A New Method for Performance Analysis of Bond Portfolios", *Journal of Fixed Income*, **9**(2), 88–91.

Lhabitant, F., 2001, Hedge Funds Investing: A Quantitative Look Inside the Black Box, Working Paper, Union Bancaire Privée.

Lo, A., 2001, "Risk Management for Hedge Funds, Introduction and Overview", *Financial Analysts Journal*, **March/April**, 16–23.

Lobosco, A., and D. DiBartolomeo, 1997, "Approximating the Confidence Intervals for Sharpe Style Weights", *Financial Analysts Journal*, **July/August**, 80–85.

Markowitz, H., 1952, "Portfolio Selection", *Journal of Finance*, **7**, 77–91.

Ross, S., 1976, "The Arbitrage Theory of Capital Asset Pricing", *Journal of Economic Theory*, **13**, 341–360.

Sharpe, W., 1964, "Capital Asset Prices: A Theory of Market Equilibrium Under Conditions of Risk", *Journal of Finance*, **19**, 425–442.

Sharpe, W., 1988, "Determining a Fund's Effective Asset Mix", *Investment Management Review*, **2**(6), 56–69.

Sharpe, W., 1992, "Asset allocation: Management Style and Performance Model", *Journal of Portfolio Management*, **Winter**, 7–20.

9.5.2 Websites

www.eacmalternative.com.

www.hfr.com.

www.hedgeindex.com.

www.zcmgroup.com.

www.msci.com.

www.vanhedge.com.

www.hedgefnd.com.

www.hedgefund.net.

www.ljh.com.

www.marhedge.com.

www.altvest.com.

www.magnum.com.

9.6 Problems

Exercise 9.1 How can the return of an international fixed-income portfolio that is not hedged with respect to currency risk be broadly decomposed?

Exercise 9.2 We have registered each month the end-of-month value of a bond index, which are as follows:

Month	Index value	Month	Index value	Month	Index value
January	98	May	111	September	111
February	101	June	110	October	112
March	104	July	112	November	110
April	107	August	110	December	113

At the beginning of January, the index value is equal to 100.

1. Compute the arithmetic average rate of return denoted by AARR, and calculate the final index value by using the following formula:

$$\text{Final Index Value} = 100 \times (1 + AARR)^{12}$$

2. Compute the time-weighted rate of return denoted by TWRR, and calculate the final index value by using the following formula:

$$\text{Final Index Value} = 100 \times (1 + TWRR)^{12}$$

3. Same question with the following index values:

Month	Index value	Month	Index value
January	85	July	115
February	110	August	130
March	120	September	145
April	135	October	160
May	115	November	145
June	100	December	160

4. Conclude.

Exercise 9.3 An investor buys 3 bonds from a given issuer at the beginning of 1995, buys another 2 bonds at the beginning of 1996, sells one bond at the beginning of 1997, and sells all 4 remaining bonds at the beginning of 1998. The history of prices and coupon payments on the bond portfolio is as follows:

Year	Beginning-of-year price ($)	End-of-year coupon payment ($)
1995	100	4
1996	120	4
1997	90	4
1998	100	4

1. What is the time-weighted average rate of return?
2. What is the dollar-weighted rate of return?

Exercise 9.4 A firm buys 10 bonds at the beginning of year 1, sells 5 bonds at the beginning of year 2, buys 15 bonds at the beginning of year 5, buys 25 bonds at the beginning of year 7, sells 25 bonds at the beginning of year 9 and sells 20 bonds at the beginning of year 10.

The bond is a 10% fixed-coupon bond whose beginning-of-year prices are given below:

Year	Beginning-of-year price ($)	Year	Beginning-of-year price ($)
1	105.02	6	108.85
2	110.07	7	107.99
3	112.52	8	107.02
4	113.54	9	109.05
5	109.98	10	115.82

Compute the dollar-weighted rate of return of this investment.

Exercise 9.5   The excel file performance_evaluation_problem.xls contains the following data:

- weekly return on four money managers investing in international fixed-income markets;
- weekly return on Salomon Brothers Global Short-term Treasury bond index (1–3 Y), Salomon Brothers Global Medium-term Treasury bond index (3–7 Y), Salomon Brothers Global Long-term Treasury bond index (7–10 Y), Salomon Brothers Global Investment grade corporate bond index, Salomon Brothers Global High-yield bond index;
- weekly values of the Euribor rate that can be used as a proxy for the risk-free rate for a European investor.

For each fund in the excel file, perform a Sharpe-based performance analysis to try and guess what type of investment strategies these managers follow. Comment the results.

Exercise 9.6   Using the same data, estimate the abnormal return (alpha) on these four portfolio managers. Make sure you use the relevant set of indices for each manager. Please also compute T-stats to check for the significance of the alphas.

Exercise 9.7   Using the same data, compute the annual Sharpe ratio for each fund, and compare the ranking in terms of Sharpe ratio to the ranking in terms of abnormal return.

Exercise 9.8   Using the same data, provide a quantitative estimate of the positioning of the managers on the active versus passive spectrum.

Exercise 9.9   You want to assess the effect of changes in interest rates on the value of your fixed-income portfolio, which consists in a straight 3-year Treasury bond with face value $5,000 and (annual) coupon rate 5%. The interest rates are now at 4%. We assume for simplicity a flat yield curve.

1. What are the cash flows?
2. What is the present value of these cash flows, that is, the value of your bond portfolio?
3. In a more general framework, what would be the other possible sources of risk? Quantifying market risk: find on the Internet a series of 100 weekly data concerning interest rates level in the past (ordered from the most recent to

the most ancient data). On the basis of that information, you have to assess what is the *daily* risk, that is, how much you might lose in one day on that position because of changes in interest rates.

4. Average risk: you first have to get an idea about the *average* amount of risk that you are facing. A possible way of proceeding is to use the standard deviation of interest-rate changes as a measure of average risk. *Can you imagine other possible measures of average risk?*

5. Find the standard deviation of interest rates changes using the time series (weekly data).

6. Turn it into a daily equivalent (using the square root of time law).

7. How much money do you expect to lose if interest rates rise tomorrow by an amount precisely equal to that average amount of monthly risk as measured in question 6?

8. Marginal risk. You are now interested in assessing what is your *marginal* exposure to interest-rate risk, that is, how much money you expect to lose or gain in case of some infinitesimal change in interest rates. Compute the $ duration V' for your bond portfolio (also called sensitivity of the portfolio).

9. How much money do you expect to lose if interest rates rise by one basis point, that is, if interest rates increase from 4 to 4.01%?

10. What is the percentage change in the value of your portfolio?

11. Can you express this percentage change in the bond portfolio value in terms of its duration?

12. Compute the duration of your bond. How does it compare to the bond maturity? In which very specific case is the duration equal to the bond maturity?

13. How much money do you expect to lose if interest rates rise by one hundred basis points, that is if interest rates increase from 4 to 5%?

14. Numerical Procedure: We now consider a situation in which the investor is really math-averse and does not want to hear about taking derivatives. One can suggest the following numerical procedure in order to approximate the sensitivity of the bond

$$V' \approx \frac{V(r + \varepsilon) - V(r - \varepsilon)}{2\varepsilon}$$

Compute the numerical approximation to V' using $\varepsilon = 1$ basis point. How does it compare to the value obtained in question 8?

15. In the same fashion, suggest a numerical procedure to get an approximate value of V''.

16. Extreme risk. On the basis of the simple idea that what really hurts is never a small deviation in the risk factor, we now have to investigate what risk we are facing in case of a major move in interest rates. We first assume that interest-rate changes are normally distributed. What can you object to in such an assumption?

17. Using your estimate of the standard deviation of interest-rate changes and assuming normality, find the positive number which is such that with 5% chances positive interest-rate changes will be larger than this number.

18. How much money do you expect to lose if interest rates rise by the amount computed in question 17? That amount is called the weekly VaR of your bond portfolio for a 5% confidence interval.
19. What would be a daily VaR?
20. If you do not want to assume a normal distribution for interest-rate changes (for reasons developed in question 16), you may use the data to get an estimation of the same numbers. Merely using the data and without assuming normality, find the positive number which is such that with 5% chances positive interest-rate changes will be larger than this number. How does it compare with the answer to question 17?

Exercise 9.10   Mr. Genius is regarded as the best bond portfolio manager available in the street. Over the last 5 years, a portfolio managed by Mr. Genius has produced an average annual return of 16.8% while the average annual risk-free return was 7.4% and the average annual return on a broad bond index have been, respectively, 15.2%. Moreover, the estimated beta of the portfolio with respect to the index is 1.1. What is the Jensen alpha of that portfolio?

Swaps and Futures

PART V

Under the word "derivatives," we commonly gather swaps, futures, options and credit derivatives. These products are built using more standard products. Unlike the other "derivatives," swaps and futures have the particularity that they do not contain any optionality clause. We now focus on these two products and particularly, on their definition, terminology, prices, market quotes and uses in practice.

10

Swaps

10.1 Description of Swaps

10.1.1 Definition

A swap contract is a cash-flow transaction with no capital exchange that enables two counterparts to swap financial cash flows originated by loans or investments. Calculated on a notional principal, these cash-flow swaps take place on predetermined dates.

We distinguish many different types of swaps (accrediting, amortizing and roller-coaster swaps, basis swaps, CMS swaps...) and we will describe all of these swaps in Section 10.4. Now let us move on to standard or plain vanilla swaps. In fact, a standard or plain vanilla swap is an interest-rate swap,

- *exchanging a fixed leg whose payments depend on a fixed rate for a floating leg whose payments depend on a floating rate;*

- *in which the notional principal remains constant over the life of the contract;*

- *and where the maturity of the floating-rate index is identical to the payment frequency of the floating-leg flows.*

We give below an example of a plain vanilla swap.

Example 10.1 The 6-month Libor swap, starting on date T_0, maturing on date T_{2n} with notional principal N, which has the following maturity profile on date T_0, is a plain vanilla swap:

Fixed leg			$-N \cdot F$		$-N \cdot F$			$-N \cdot F$
Date	T_0	T_1	T_2	T_3	T_4	...	...	T_{2n}
Floating leg		$N \cdot V_0/2$	$N \cdot V_1/2$	$N \cdot V_2/2$	$N \cdot V_3/2$			$N \cdot V_{2n-1}/2$

Every 6 months on date T_i ($T_i - T_{i-1} = 6$ months) for $i = 1$ to $2n$, and prorated for the period, the borrower receives the 6-month Libor V_{i-1} observed 6 months earlier multiplied by the principal and pays a fixed rate F every year on date T_{2i} for $i = 1$ to n multiplied by the principal. Note in this example that the swap is structured so that we receive the floating leg and pay the fixed leg. But, of course, we can structure the opposite swap in which we receive the fixed leg and pay the floating leg.

10.1.2 Terminology and Conventions

All swaps are traded under the legal terms and conditions fixed by the International Swap Dealer Association (ISDA). The terms of the trade include especially the maturity and notional amount of the swap, the fixed and floating interest rate and the payment bases of both legs of the swap.

Recall that a swap consists of two legs: a fixed leg whose payments depend on a fixed rate and a floating leg whose payments depend on a floating rate.

- *The notional principal allows to calculate the actual amount of the different payments on the two legs of the swap.*

> **Example 10.2** Consider a 3-year swap exchanging the 1-year Libor for fixed 5%. The notional principal is $10 million. Payments on the two legs are annual. Every year, the amount paid on the fixed leg is equal to 5%·$10 million = $500,000 as the amount received on the floating leg is the 1-year Libor multiplied by $10 million.

- *Payments on each leg take place on predetermined dates. The trade date is the date on which the swap is traded. The effective date, in general, two working days after the trading date, is used to calculate the interest payments of the swap. When the payments do not take place on anniversary dates, they have to be prorated for the period.*

- *The day-count basis for the prorated period depends on the country or area. For example, dollar and euro-denominated swaps use an Actual/360 day-count basis while sterling swaps use an Actual/365 day-count basis.*

The floating rate for each period is fixed at the beginning of the period, so that the first interest payment of the swap is known in advance by both parties.

Note that even if both parties pay and receive interest payments, on a payment date, only the net difference between the two interest payments is exchanged.

10.2 Pricing and Market Quotes

10.2.1 Pricing of Swaps

The Basic Principle

A plain vanilla swap contract consists in the exchange of a fixed-rate for a floating-rate security. Initially, both should have the same value, otherwise it would not be a fair deal, and therefore swap contracts have a zero initial value. Later on, prices can differ depending on the evolution of the term structure. Fixed-rate notes have longer duration and therefore a rise (decline) in interest rates tends to lower (increase) the value of the fixed leg more than that of the variable leg. This raises (lowers) the value of the swap to the buyer and lowers (raises) the value of the swap to the seller. The value of the swap at date t (for the party that pays fixed) is the difference in value at date t between the value of the fixed leg and the value of the floating leg. The value of the fixed leg is easy to obtain as the present value of future payments discounted at the corresponding spot rates. For the floating leg, on the other hand, we only know the next payment; later payments are unknown as of today as they depend upon the future value of the benchmark rate. The trick consists in noting that those payments will be at the prevailing market rate. If we assume for simplicity of exposure that the notional is also exchanged, then the floating leg will pay notional plus market rate. Now, the present value of notional plus market rate discounted at the market rate should be the notional value. Therefore, the price of a floating-rate note on each and every coupon date is equal to par.

Example 10.3 Today is January 1st. The swap residual maturity is 9 months. The notional principal is $1,000. You receive 5% fixed semiannual payments and pay semiannual cash flows based on the 6-month Libor rate on March 31st and September 30th. Next payment is based on Libor at 6%. The current term structure is $R(0,0.25) = 5\%$ and $R(0,0.75) = 7\%$. The value of the fixed leg is

$$F = \frac{50}{(1+0.05)^{\frac{1}{4}}} + \frac{1,050}{(1+0.07)^{\frac{3}{4}}} = 1,047.44$$

while the value of the floating leg is

$$F = \frac{30}{(1+0.05)^{\frac{1}{4}}} + \frac{1,000}{(1+0.05)^{\frac{1}{4}}} = 1,017.51$$

Finally, the value of the swap is $1047.44 - 1017.51 = 29.93$.

This method is sometimes called the *zero-coupon method* because a swap price can be regarded as the difference between the price of a coupon-bearing bond maturing at the maturity date of the swap and the price of a zero-coupon maturing at the next floating cash-flow payment (both with principal amount equal to the swap nominal amount).

Practitioners often use an alternative method, known as the *forward projection method*, which is based upon the assumption that the future floating rates of the floating leg are equal to the forward rates. One can actually show that both methods agree when we consider plain vanilla swaps for which the difference between the measurement date and the payment date is equal to the maturity of the reference index (see the section on "Equivalence between the Forward Projection Approach and the Zero-Coupon Method" below).

The Forward Projection Market Approach

This is the standard pricing approach used by the market, which is based upon the assumption that the future floating rates of the floating leg are equal to the forward rates.[1] We now turn to the pricing of swaps using the forward projection.

Consider a swap whose price at date t is denoted by $SWAP_t$. At date t, the price $SWAP_t$ of this swap is given by the difference between the present value of the fixed leg and the present value

---

[1] We argue below that this assumption is correct for plain vanilla swap contracts. For these contracts, the difference between the measurement date and the payment date is equal to the maturity of the reference index. In this specific case, the forward rate is equal to the expected value of the future rate, and the market approach is perfectly consistent. However, for nonstandard swap contracts, it is necessary to apply a convexity adjustment to the forward rate.

of the floating leg.

$$SWAP_t = N \times \left(\sum_{i=1}^{n} F \left(\frac{T_{ki} - T_{k(i-1)}}{360} \right) B(t, T_{ki}) - \sum_{j=1}^{m} V_{j-1} \left(\frac{T_j - T_{j-1}}{360} \right) B(t, T_j) \right)$$

where

N is the notional principal,

V_{j-1} is the value of the floating rate at date T_{j-1} and paid at date T_j,

m is the number of cash flows of the floating leg delivered at date T_j with $j = 1, \ldots, m$,

F is the fixed rate of the fixed leg,

n is the number of cash flows of the fixed leg delivered at date T_{ki} with $i = 1, \ldots, n$. k is a coefficient equal to the payment frequency on the variable leg divided by the payment frequency on the fixed leg. We have, in particular, the following relation $kn = m$.

$T_j - T_{j-1}$ is simply the number of days between the jth and the $(j-1)$th payments. Note that we assume here an Actual/360 day-count basis.

The idea of the pricing is simply to replace V_{j-1} by its forward value $F(t, V_{j-1})$ at date t to obtain

$$SWAP_t = N \times \left(\sum_{i=1}^{n} F \left(\frac{T_{ki} - T_{k(i-1)}}{360} \right) B(t, T_{ki}) - \sum_{j=1}^{m} F(t, V_{j-1}) \left(\frac{T_j - T_{j-1}}{360} \right) B(t, T_j) \right)$$

(10.1)

Example 10.4 On 06/21/01, we consider a 6-month Libor swap with maturity 2 years and notional principal N, with the following cash-flow schedule:

Fixed leg		$N \times F$		$N \times F$
Date	$T_1 = 12/21/01$	$T_2 = 06/21/02$	$T_3 = 12/21/02$	$T_4 = 06/21/03$
Floating leg	$-\frac{N}{2} \times L_{06/21/01}$	$-\frac{N}{2} \times L_{12/21/01}$	$-\frac{N}{2} \times L_{06/21/02}$	$-\frac{N}{2} \times L_{12/21/02}$

Note that $T_0 = 06/21/01$. We assume an Actual/Actual day-count basis on the fixed leg.

On 06/21/01 the swap price is

$$SWAP_{06/21/01} = N \times \left(\sum_{i=1}^{2} F \times B(06/21/01, T_{2i}) - \frac{1}{2} \sum_{j=1}^{4} L_{j-1} \times B(06/21/01, T_j) \right)$$

where

L_{j-1} is the 6-month Libor at date T_{j-1},

$\frac{T_j - T_{j-1}}{360}$ is assumed to be equal to $1/2$, $\forall j = 1, \ldots, 4$,

k is equal to 2.

Using the forward projection, L_{j-1} is replaced by $F(06/21/01, T_{j-1}, T_j)$, which is the 6-month Libor forward rate determined on 06/21/01, starting at date T_{j-1} and finishing at date T_j.

So the swap price is

$$SWAP_{06/21/01} = N \times \left(\begin{array}{c} \displaystyle\sum_{i=1}^{2} F \times B(06/21/01, T_{2i}) \\ \displaystyle -\frac{1}{2} \sum_{j=1}^{4} F(06/21/01, T_{j-1}, T_j) \times B(06/21/01, T_j) \end{array} \right)$$

Equivalence between the Forward Projection Approach and the Zero-Coupon Method

When we consider plain vanilla swaps for which the difference between the measurement date and the payment date is equal to the maturity of the reference index, and still using the forward projection, we obtain a simplification and a new formula for the swap price that only depends on zero-coupon price. This is what we call the *zero-coupon method*. In this case, $F(t, V_{j-1})$, the forward value of V_{j-1} at date t, may be expressed as

$$F(t, V_{j-1}) = \left(\frac{B(t, T_{j-1})}{B(t, T_j)} - 1 \right) \cdot \frac{360}{T_j - T_{j-1}}$$

and using equation (10.1), the swap price is

$$SWAP_t = N \times \left(\sum_{i=1}^{n} F \left(\frac{T_{ki} - T_{k(i-1)}}{360} \right) B(t, T_{ki}) - \sum_{j=1}^{m} (B(t, T_{j-1}) - B(t, T_j)) \right)$$

and we finally obtain

$$SWAP_t = N \times \left(\sum_{i=1}^{n} F \left(\frac{T_{ki} - T_{k(i-1)}}{360} \right) B(t, T_{ki}) - B(t, T_0) + B(t, T_m) \right)$$

or

$$SWAP_t = N \times \left(\sum_{i=1}^{n} F \left(\frac{T_{ki} - T_{k(i-1)}}{360} \right) B(t, T_{ki}) + B(t, T_m) \right) - N.B(t, T_0)$$

Note that the swap is then the difference between two bonds:

- *an F coupon-bearing bond maturing at date T_m with N as principal amount;*

- *minus a zero-coupon maturing at date T_0 with N as principal amount.*

In particular, when $t = T_0$, we obtain

$$SWAP_t = N \times \left(\sum_{i=1}^{n} F \left(\frac{T_{ki} - T_{k(i-1)}}{360} \right) B(t, T_{ki}) + B(t, T_m) \right) - N \qquad (10.2)$$

so that the swap is the F coupon-bearing bond maturing at date T_m with N as principal amount minus the principal amount N.

In terms of hedging, the advantage of a plain vanilla swap compared to a coupon-bearing bond is that its price is very much lower than that of the coupon-bearing bond while it has the same sensitivity to rate changes.

Example 10.5 On 06/21/01, we consider a 3-month Libor swap with maturity 2 years and notional principal N with the following cash-flow schedule:

Fixed leg				$N \times F$
Date	$T_1 = 09/21/01$	$T_2 = 12/21/01$	$T_3 = 03/21/02$	$T_4 = 06/21/02$
Variable leg	$-\frac{N}{4} \times L_{06/21/01}$	$-\frac{N}{4} \times L_{09/21/01}$	$-\frac{N}{4} \times L_{12/21/01}$	$-\frac{N}{4} \times L_{03/21/02}$
Fixed leg				$N \times F$
Date	$T_5 = 09/21/02$	$T_6 = 12/21/02$	$T_7 = 03/21/03$	$T_8 = 06/21/03$
Variable leg	$-\frac{N}{4} \times L_{06/21/02}$	$-\frac{N}{4} \times L_{09/21/02}$	$-\frac{N}{4} \times L_{12/21/02}$	$-\frac{N}{4} \times L_{03/21/03}$

Note that $T_0 = 06/21/01$. We assume an Actual/Actual day-count basis on the fixed leg, and for convenience $\frac{T_j - T_{j-1}}{360} = \frac{1}{4}, \forall j = 1, \ldots, 8$ (see the previous table).

On 06/21/01 the price of this swap is

$$SWAP_{06/21/01} = N \times \left(\sum_{i=1}^{2} F \times B(06/21/01, T_{4i}) - \sum_{j=1}^{8} L_{j-1} \right.$$

$$\left. \times \left(\frac{T_j - T_{j-1}}{360} \right) \times B(06/21/01, T_j) \right)$$

where L_{j-1} is the 3-month Libor at date T_{j-1}.

Using the forward projection, L_{j-1} is replaced by $F(06/21/01, T_{j-1}, T_j)$, which is the 3-month Libor forward rate determined on 06/21/01, starting at date T_{j-1} and finishing at date T_j. $F(06/21/01, T_{j-1}, T_j)$ is obtained from the spot zero-coupon yield curve through the following equation:

$$F(06/21/01, T_{j-1}, T_j) = \left(\frac{B(06/21/01, T_{j-1})}{B(06/21/01, T_j)} - 1 \right) \times \frac{360}{T_j - T_{j-1}}$$

So, the price of the swap is

$$SWAP_{06/21/01} = N \times \left(\sum_{i=1}^{2} F \times B(06/21/01, T_{4i}) - 1 + B(06/21/01, 06/21/03) \right)$$

We can see clearly in the previous equation that the swap price depends only on zero-coupon prices. Note that this formula is perfectly correct for a plain vanilla swap.

A Pricing Example

We develop below a concrete example of plain vanilla swap pricing.

Example 10.6   Pricing a 3-Month Libor Swap

As an illustration of the pricing of swaps, we consider, below one standard asset from the market. This is a 3-month Libor swap contract where the floating leg is received and the fixed leg is paid.

We consider at date t, a 3-month Libor swap contract with maturity 4 years[2] with the following cash-flow schedule:

		$-F_1$					$-F_2$					$-F_3$				$-F_4$
t	T_0	T_1	T_2	T_3	T_4	T_5	T_6	T_7	T_8	T_9	T_{10}	T_{11}	T_{12}	T_{13}	T_{14}	T_{15}	T_{16}
	V_0	V_1	V_2	V_3	V_4	V_5	V_6	V_7	V_8	V_9	V_{10}	V_{11}	V_{12}	V_{13}	V_{14}	V_{15}

We assume an Actual/Actual day-count basis on the fixed leg and $\frac{T_{j+1}-T_j}{360} = \frac{1}{4}, \forall j \in \{0, 1, 2, \ldots, 15\}$.

We try to derive the price at date t of that swap which starts at date T_0. The price is given by

$$SWAP_t = Nominal \times \left(\frac{1}{4} \sum_{j=1}^{16} V_{j-1} \times B(t, T_j) - \sum_{i=1}^{4} F \times B(t, T_{4i}) \right)$$

Using the two methods previously exposed, we price this swap with the forward projection method and the zero-coupon method.

This implies that the following are known:

- *The spot zero-coupon yield curve at date t*

- *The 3-month Libor forward rates.*

We now further assume that

- *the swap face value is $100 million and*

- *the swap fixed rate F is 5.5%.*

The spot zero-coupon yield curve at date t is obtained using the cubic B-spline method discussed in Chapter 4. The discount factor for maturity θ is

$$B(t, \theta) = B(\theta) = \sum_{l=-3}^{4} a_l B_l^3(\theta) = \sum_{l=-3}^{4} a_l \left(\sum_{j=l}^{l+4} \left[\prod_{\substack{i=l \\ i \neq j}}^{l+4} \frac{1}{\lambda_i - \lambda_j} \right] (\theta - \lambda_j)_+^3 \right)$$

---

[2]This example may easily be extended to the case of a swap with any given maturity.

where the parameters are such that

a_{-3}	a_{-2}	a_{-1}	a_0	a_1	a_2	a_3	a_4
4.1553	5.0031	7.5571	8.2673	12.5071	7.3256	4.922	1.6997

The 3-month Libor forward rates are obtained from the spot zero-coupon yield curve through the following equation:

$$F(t, T_{j-1}, T_j) = \left(\frac{B(t, T_{j-1})}{B(t, T_j)} - 1 \right) \times \frac{360}{T_j - T_{j-1}}$$

where $F(t, T_{j-1}, T_j)$ is the 3-month Libor forward rates computed at date t, starting at date T_{j-1}, with maturity date T_j. These two yield curves are given in Table 10.1 below.

Table 10.1   Swap Pricing.

Maturity	$B(t, T_i)$	$F(t, T_{j-1}, T_j)$	$\frac{1}{4}F(t, T_{j-1}, T_j)B(t, T_j)$	$-F \times B(t, T_{4i})$
T_0	0.99664			
T_1	0.98641	0.0415	0.0102	
T_2	0.9759	0.0431	0.0105	
T_3	0.96509	0.0448	0.0108	
T_4	0.95393	0.0468	0.0112	−0.0525
T_5	0.94244	0.0488	0.0115	
T_6	0.93063	0.0508	0.0118	
T_7	0.91853	0.0527	0.0121	
T_8	0.90618	0.0545	0.0124	−0.0498
T_9	0.8936	0.0563	0.0126	
T_{10}	0.88082	0.058	0.0128	
T_{11}	0.86788	0.0597	0.0129	
T_{12}	0.8548	0.0612	0.0131	−0.047
T_{13}	0.84161	0.0627	0.0132	
T_{14}	0.82833	0.0641	0.0133	
T_{15}	0.81498	0.0655	0.0134	
T_{16}	0.80158	0.0669	0.0134	−0.0441

- *Using the forward rate projection method, the swap price is given by*

$$SWAP_t = 10^8 \times \left(\frac{1}{4} \sum_{j=1}^{16} F(t, T_{j-1}, T_j) \times B(t, T_j) - \sum_{i=1}^{4} F \times B(t, T_{4i}) \right) = \$166,159$$

- *Using the zero-coupon rate method, the swap price is given by*

$$SWAP_t = 10^8 \times \left(B(t, T_0) - B(t, T_{16}) - \sum_{i=1}^{4} F \times B(t, T_{4i}) \right) = \$166,000$$

The two methods give, of course, the same price results.[3]

---

[3]The small price difference is due to rounded-off numbers.

We have, so far, only considered standard "plain vanilla" swap contracts. For these contracts, the difference between the measurement date and the payment date (3 months in our example) is equal to the maturity of the reference index (in our example the 3-month Libor contract). In this specific case, the forward rate is equal to the expected value of the future rate, and the market approach discussed below is perfectly consistent. However, for nonstandard swap contracts,[4] it is necessary to apply a convexity adjustment to the forward rate. We refer the reader to El Karoui and Geman (1994), Rainelli-Le Montagner (1996), Hull (2002) and Brigo and Mercurio (2001) for more details about the pricing of this term.

10.2.2 Market Quotes

For a given maturity, the market quote convention consists for the swap market maker in setting the floating leg at Libor and then quoting the fixed rate, called the *swap rate*, that makes the value of the swap equal to zero. The *swap rate* is then the value of the fixed rate that makes the swap's fixed leg equal to its floating leg because the swap value is very simply the difference between the sum of the discounted cash flows of one leg and the sum of the discounted cash flows of the other leg. To illustrate this convention, consider the following 7-year 3-month Libor swap quoted by a market maker:

- *Floating-rate payer:* pay 3-month Libor and receive fixed rate of 6%.

- *Fixed-rate payer:* pay a fixed rate of 6.05% and receive 3-month Libor.

The bid price quoted by the market maker is 6% to pay the fixed rate as the ask price to receive the fixed rate is 6.05%.

A swap is also quoted as a swap spread. The *swap spread* of a swap with a certain maturity is equal to the difference between the fixed rate of the swap and the Treasury benchmark bond yield of the same maturity. It is expressed as a number of basis points. We consider, for example, a 7-year 3-month Libor swap. A market maker quotes 45–50, which means that he is willing to enter a swap paying fixed 45 points above the 7-year benchmark bond yield and receiving the 3-month Libor, or receiving fixed 50 basis points above the 7-year bond yield and paying the Libor.

We give below an example of swap rate and swap spread quotes as can be seen on a Bloomberg terminal (IRSB function).

Example 10.7   Swap Rate and Swap Spread Quotes

The Bloomberg screen (Figure 10.1) below provides swap rate and swap spread quotes on 12/04/01. Swaps quoted are US Libor 3-month plain vanilla swaps. On the fixed leg, the frequency of payment is semiannual as the day-count basis is 30/360. On the floating leg, payments are quarterly and the day-count basis is Act/360. Bloomberg provides on this

---

[4]In particular, one may consider swap contracts with no difference between the measurement date and payment date, or swap contracts with a difference not equal to the maturity of the reference index. See Section 10.4.

```
Press 98<GO> to make a copy, 99<GO> to clear news alerts.     Comdty IRSB
19:41                    US  SWAP  RATES                      Page 1 / 2
94<GO> View News.
  SECURITY  Bid      Ask      CHANGE     SECURITY  Bid      Ask      CHANGE

  US Semi 30/360                         US Spreads 30/360
   3)2  YR  3.2600   3.2800   -.0230    23)2YR    49.00    51.00    n.a.
   4)3  YR  3.9200   3.9600   -.0300    24)3YR    76.50    78.50    n.a.
   5)4  YR  4.3500   4.3700   -.0370    25)4YR    78.50    80.50    n.a.
   6)5  YR  4.6400   4.6530   -.0375    26)5YR    68.00    70.00    n.a.
   7)6  YR  4.8220   4.8620   -.0590    27)6YR    74.50    76.50    n.a.
   8)7  YR  4.9900   5.0300   -.0600    28)7YR    78.00    80.00    n.a.
   9)8  YR  5.1210   5.1610   -.0660    29)8YR    76.50    78.50    n.a.
  10)9  YR  5.2120   5.2520   -.0750    30)9YR    72.50    74.50    n.a.
  11)10 YR  5.3020   5.3420   -.0740    31)10YR   67.50    69.50    n.a.
  12)15 YR  5.6500   5.6700   -.0780    32)15YR   87.00    89.00    n.a.
  13)20 YR  5.8000   5.8410   -.0630    33)20YR   88.00    90.00    n.a.
  14)30 YR  5.8350   5.8750   -.0740    34)30YR   64.00    66.00    n.a.
  Change on Day                         Change on Day
  IYC4 I52<GO>                          IYC4 I48<GO>
  Change on Month                       Change on Month
  IYC6 I52<GO>                          IYC6 I48<GO>

  Page for ANN Rates
Australia 61 2 9777 8600      Brazil 5511 3048 4500      Europe 44 20 7330 7500      Germany 49 69 92041210
Hong Kong 852 2977 6000 Japan 81 3 3201 8900 Singapore 65 212 1000 U.S. 1 212 318 2000  Copyright 2001 Bloomberg L.P.
                                                                                       I356-711-0 04-Dec-01 19:41:39
```

Figure 10.1 © 2003 Bloomberg L.P. All rights reserved. Reprinted with permission.

screen the bid–ask swap rate and the bid–ask swap spread as well as the percentage change compared to the last price of the previous day.

On the next screen (Figure 10.2), Bloomberg provides the same information on 12/04/01. Swaps quoted are still US Libor 3-month plain vanilla swaps. But the payment frequency on the fixed leg is annual as the day-count basis is Act/360. On the floating leg, payments are still quarterly and the day-count basis is Act/360.

Note finally that a *margin swap* is a swap where there is a margin above or below the floating leg and that the *prime swap*, expressed as a percentage of the notional principal and in general equal to zero, is the price difference between the fixed leg and the floating leg that makes up the swap agreement.

10.3 Uses of Swaps

Swaps can be used to optimize the financial conditions of a debt, to convert the financial conditions of a debt, to create new synthetic assets or to hedge a portfolio of fixed-income securities against any change in the yield curve.

```
19:42                    US  SWAP  RATES                        Page 2 / 2
94<GO> View News.
```

SECURITY	Bid	Ask	CHANGE	SECURITY	Bid	Ask	CHANGE
Ann Act/360 Rates				Ann Act/360 Spread			
3)2YR	3.2500	3.2700	-.0050	23)2YR	48.0000	51.0000	-2.0000
4)3YR	3.9300	3.9500	-.0355	24)3YR	76.0000	79.0000	-.2500
5)4YR	4.3400	4.3600	-.0510	25)4YR	79.0000	82.0000	-2.7500
6)5YR	4.7000	4.7200	+.0340	26)5YR	67.0000	69.0000	-3.2500
7)6YR	4.8090	4.8500	-.0940	27)6YR	73.0000	76.0000	-3.5000
8)7YR	5.0100	5.0180	-.0995	28)7YR	76.0000	79.0000	-7.2500
9)8YR	5.1100	5.1510	-.0945	29)8YR	75.0000	78.0000	-4.0000
10)9YR	5.2030	5.2430	-.1045	30)9YR	71.0000	74.0000	-2.5000
11)10YR	5.3140	5.3340	-.0880	31)10YR	66.5000	68.5000	-3.2500
12)15YR	5.6390	5.6790	-.0835	32)15YR	98.0000	101.0000	-.5000
13)20YR	5.7980	5.8380	-.0760	33)20YR	112.0000	115.0000	+1.5000
14)30YR	5.8330	5.8730	-.0885	34)30YR	61.0000	65.0000	-6.5000

```
Change on Day                        Change on Day
IYC4 I205<GO>                        IYC4 I207<GO>
Change on Month                      Change on Month
IYC6 I205<GO>                        IYC6 I207<GO>
```

```
Australia 61 2 9777 8600        Brazil 5511 3048 4500      Europe 44 20 7330 7500     Germany 49 69 92041210
Hong Kong 852 2977 6000 Japan 81 3 3201 8900 Singapore 65 212 1000 U.S. 1 212 318 2000 Copyright 2001 Bloomberg L.P.
                                                                                      I356-711-0 04-Dec-01 19:42:05
```

Figure 10.2 © 2003 Bloomberg L.P. All rights reserved. Reprinted with permission.

10.3.1 Optimizing the Financial Conditions of a Debt

Firms have different financial conditions in the market. Consider two firms A and B. When the spread between the conditions obtained by firm A and firm B on a fixed rate is different from the spread between the conditions obtained by firm A and firm B on a floating rate, firm A and firm B can optimize their financial conditions by structuring a swap together.

Example 10.8 We consider two firms A and B, which have the same financial needs in terms of maturity and principal. The two firms can borrow money in the market under the following conditions:

- *Firm A:* *10% at a fixed rate or Libor + 1.5% for a $10 million loan and a 5-year maturity.*

- *Firm B:* *8.5% at a fixed rate or Libor + 0.5% for a $10 million loan and a 5-year maturity.*

Firm B has 1.5% better conditions at a fixed rate and 1% better conditions at a floating rate than firm A. The spread between the conditions obtained by firm A and firm B at a fixed rate and the spread between the conditions obtained by firm A and firm B at a floating rate is different from 0.5%.

Suppose now that firm B prefers a floating-rate debt as firm A prefers a fixed-rate debt. There are two solutions:

- **Solution 1**

  Firm B borrows money at a Libor + 0.5% floating rate and firm A contracts a loan at a 10% fixed rate.

- **Solution 2**

  Firm B borrows money at an 8.5% fixed rate, firm A contracts a loan at a Libor + 1.5% floating rate and they structure the following swap. Firm B pays Libor + 0.75% and receives the fixed 9% as firm A receives Libor+0.75% and pays the fixed 9%. The financing operation is summarized in the following table:

	Firm A	Firm B
Initial financing (1)	Libor + 1.5%	8.5%
Swap A to B (2)	−9%	9%
Swap B to A (3)	Libor + 0.75%	−(Libor + 0.75%)
Financing cost (4) = (1) − (2) − (3)	9.75%	Libor + 0.25%
Financing cost without swap (5)	10%	Libor + 0.5%
Gain (6) = (5) − (4)	0.25%	0.25%

By structuring a swap, firm A and firm B have optimized their financial conditions and gained 0.25%. They have equally shared the 0.5% difference between the two spreads, the spread between the conditions obtained by firm A and firm B at a fixed rate and the spread between the conditions obtained by firm A and firm B at a floating rate.

10.3.2 Converting the Financial Conditions of a Debt

To finance their needs, most firms issue long-term fixed-coupon bonds because of the large liquidity of these bonds. A treasurer expects a decrease in interest rates and so wishes to transform its fixed-rate debt into a floating-rate debt. The idea is to contract a swap in which he will receive the fixed rate and pay the floating rate.

Example 10.9 On 05/25/00, firm A issues a 5-year maturity bond at a 7% fixed rate with a notional principal of $10 million. The issuer who expects a decrease in interest rates in 1 year wishes to transform its debt into a floating-rate debt. Market conditions for a 4-year 6-month Libor swap beginning in 1 year are the following: Libor against 5.5% or Libor + 1.5% against 7%.

The issuer enters a 4-year maturity swap with a notional amount of $10 million to pay Libor + 1.5% and receive 7%. That means firm A will pay every 6 months and prorated for the period the 6-month-Libor observed 6 months earlier and will receive the fixed rate every year. The profile of this swap for firm A is as follows:

Fixed leg		$700,000
Date	11/25/01	05/25/02
Floating leg	$-\frac{1}{2}(L_{05/25/01} + 1.5\%) \cdot \$10m$	$-\frac{1}{2}(L_{11/25/01} + 1.5\%) \cdot \$10m$
Fixed leg		$700,000
Date	11/25/02	05/25/03
Floating leg	$-\frac{1}{2}(L_{05/25/02} + 1.5\%) \cdot \$10m$	$-\frac{1}{2}(L_{11/25/02} + 1.5\%) \cdot \$10m$
Fixed leg		$700,000
Date	11/25/03	05/25/04
Floating leg	$-\frac{1}{2}(L_{05/25/03} + 1.5\%) \cdot \$10m$	$-\frac{1}{2}(L_{11/25/03} + 1.5\%) \cdot \$10m$
Fixed leg		$700,000
Date	11/25/04	05/25/05
Floating leg	$-\frac{1}{2}(L_{05/25/04} + 1.5\%) \cdot \$10m$	$-\frac{1}{2}(L_{11/25/04} + 1.5\%) \cdot \$10m$

where L_t is the 6-month Libor rate on date t and m stands for million.

Converting the financial conditions of a debt may also be used by a firm to optimize the matching of assets and liabilities.

Example 10.10 Consider a bank that has a portfolio consisting of 4-year bonds with a 7% fixed-coupon rate and a $10 million principal value. Coupons are paid semiannually. To fund this portfolio, the bank has issued CDs at the 6-month Libor rate + 0.2%.

If the 6-month Libor goes up to 6.8% or more, the cost of funds will exceed the interest rate earned on the portfolio. That is why the bank wants to lock in the margin over its costs of funds and enters a 4-year 6-month Libor swap, where it receives the floating rate and pays the fixed rate. Suppose that the swap rate for such a swap is 6%, then the bank will lock in 0.8% over the costs of its funds.

10.3.3 Creating New Assets Using Swaps

Swaps can be used to create new assets that do not exist in the market. The transaction is called *an asset swap*. We detail below the mechanism of a par asset swap.

Remark 10.1 Mechanism of a Par Asset Swap

A par asset swap is a combination of two trades:

- *the asset swap buyer purchases a bond from the asset swap seller for a gross price GP in return for par 1.*

- *The asset swap buyer then swaps the cash flows of his bond to receive Libor, plus a spread S above or below Libor.*

We give below an example of a par asset swap.

> **Example 10.11** Consider a firm with a BBB rating that has issued bonds with a 10% fixed coupon and a 4-year maturity. An investor who thinks that this firm is an interesting one, but at the same time expects a rise in short-term interest rates can create a synthetic bond of this firm that delivers a 1-year Libor coupon plus a spread. The idea is to buy the 10% fixed-coupon bond with maturity 4 years in return for par, and to enter a swap where the investor receives the 1-year Libor + S and pays the fixed rate. Suppose now that $S = 4\%$ and that the investor has financed his transaction at Libor + 3.75%, his gain is then 0.25%.

We now explain how to calculate the spread of a par asset swap.

> **Remark 10.2 Calculation of the Asset Swap Spread**
>
> Following Remark 10.1, we must have at date t:
>
> $$GP_t = 1 + V_t$$
>
> where V_t is the asset swap value.
>
> More explicitly, and considering that there are n annual payments F on the fixed leg, we have (see Section 10.2.1 for the notation):
>
> $$GP_t = 1 + \left(\sum_{i=1}^{n} FB(t, T_{ki}) - \sum_{j=1}^{m} (V_{j-1} + S) \cdot \left(\frac{T_j - T_{j-1}}{360} \right) B(t, T_j) \right)$$
>
> where
>
> S is the asset swap spread,
>
> $B(t, T)$ is the discount factor derived from the interbank zero-coupon yield curve (see Chapter 4).
>
> This formula simplifies into:
>
> $$GP_t = 1 + \left(\sum_{i=1}^{n} FB(t, T_{ki}) - \sum_{j=1}^{m} V_{j-1} \cdot \left(\frac{T_j - T_{j-1}}{360} \right) B(t, T_j) \right.$$
> $$\left. - \sum_{j=1}^{m} S \cdot \left(\frac{T_j - T_{j-1}}{360} \right) B(t, T_j) \right)$$
>
> We finally obtain
>
> $$\sum_{i=1}^{n} FB(t, T_{ki}) + B(t, T_m) - GP_t = \sum_{j=1}^{m} S \cdot \left(\frac{T_j - T_{j-1}}{360} \right) B(t, T_j)$$

and

$$S = \frac{\sum_{i=1}^{n} FB(t, T_{ki}) + B(t, T_m) - GP_t}{\sum_{j=1}^{m} \left(\frac{T_j - T_{j-1}}{360}\right) B(t, T_j)}$$

The asset swap spread is then a function of the difference between the gross price of the bond and the cash flows of this same bond discounted with the interbank zero-coupon yield curve.

10.3.4 Hedging Interest-Rate Risk Using Swaps

Recall that the price formula for a plain vanilla swap on the fixed leg is given by

$$SWAP_t = N \cdot \left(\sum_{i=1}^{n} F \cdot \left(\frac{T_{ki} - T_{k(i-1)}}{360}\right) \cdot B(t, T_{ki}) + B(t, T_m)\right) - N \qquad (10.3)$$

so that the swap is the F coupon-bearing bond maturing at date T_m with N as principal amount, minus the principal amount N. In terms of hedging, the advantage of a plain vanilla swap compared to a coupon rate bond is that its price is very much lower than that of the coupon-bearing bond while it has the same sensitivity to rate changes. We now consider a portfolio P of bonds and hedge it with swaps using the three main hedging approaches we have seen in Chapters 5 and 6: the duration hedge, the duration/convexity hedge and the hedge using a three-factor model.

Duration Hedge

We use a one-order Taylor expansion to approximate the price change of portfolio P and of the swap (see Chapter 5 for a complete description of the method). The hedge ratio denoted ϕ_s is

$$\phi_s = -\frac{\$Dur_P}{\$Dur_S} \qquad (10.4)$$

where $\$Dur_P$ and $\$Dur_S$ are, respectively, the $duration of portfolio P and of the fixed-coupon bond contained in the swap.

Example 10.12 Consider now an investor who holds a bond portfolio whose price and modified duration are, respectively, $10,200,000 and 8.35. He wishes to be hedged against a rise in interest rates. The yield curve is flat at a 5% level and he uses as hedging instrument a 10-year plain vanilla swap whose features are as follows:

- *Principal value: $1,000,000.*
- *The fixed leg pays coupon annually at a 5% rate.*
- *The price of the swap as expressed in percentage of the principal value is equal to 100 − 100 = 0.*

The price of the bond contained in the swap is equal to $1,000,000, and its modified duration is equal to 7.7217.

We consider that the bond portfolio and the swap instrument present the same default risk so that we are not concerned with that additional source of uncertainty, and we can use the same yield curve to price them.

So, we find the hedge ratio ϕ_s

$$\phi_s = -\frac{\$Dur_P}{\$Dur_S} = -\frac{10,200,000}{1,000,000} \times \frac{8.35}{7.7217} = -11$$

In the example, the investor has to sell 11 swaps.

Duration/Convexity Hedge

We now use a two-order Taylor expansion to approximate the price change of portfolio P and of the swap (see Chapter 6 for a complete description of the method). The idea of the hedge is to obtain a global portfolio that is both $duration-neutral and $convexity-neutral. Then we have to determine quantities ϕ_1 and ϕ_2 to buy or sell in swaps S_1 and S_2 so that

$$\begin{cases} \phi_1 \$Dur_{S_1} + \phi_2 \$Dur_{S_2} = -\$Dur_P \\ \phi_1 \$Conv_{S_1} + \phi_2 \$Conv_{S_2} = -\$Conv_P \end{cases} \tag{10.5}$$

where $\$Dur_P (\$Conv_P)$, $\$Dur_{S_1} (\$Conv_{S_1})$ and $\$Dur_{S_2} (\$Conv_{S_2})$ are, respectively, the $duration ($convexity) of portfolio P and of the fixed-coupon bond contained in swaps S_1 and S_2.

Example 10.13 We consider a bond portfolio whose features are summarized in the following table. The price is expressed in percentage of the face value which is equal to $100,000,000. We compute the yield to maturity (YTM), the $duration and the $convexity (expressed in percentage of the face value):

Price	YTM	$Duration	$Convexity
1,092.43	5.417%	−7,570.54	117,511.14

To hedge the bond portfolio, we use two plain vanilla 6-month Libor swaps whose features are summarized in the following table. $duration and $convexity (expressed in percentage of the principal amount) are those of the fixed-coupon bond contained in the swap. The principal amount of the swaps is $1,000,000.

Maturity (years)	Price	Swap rate (%)	$Duration	$Convexity
7	0	5.001	−634.55	4,377.76
15	0	5.407	−1,195.95	14,498.05

We consider that the bond portfolio and the swap instruments present the same default risk so that we are not concerned with that additional source of uncertainty, and we can use the same yield curve to price them.

Using equation (10.5), we obtain

$$\begin{pmatrix} \phi_1 \\ \phi_2 \end{pmatrix} = \begin{pmatrix} 634,553,017 & 1,195,950,909 \\ 4,377,760,207 & 1.4498E+10 \end{pmatrix}^{-1} \cdot \begin{pmatrix} -7.5705E+11 \\ -1.1751E+13 \end{pmatrix} = \begin{pmatrix} 776 \\ -1,045 \end{pmatrix}$$

The Duration/Convexity hedge is performed by buying 776 7-year swaps and selling 1,045 15-year swaps.

Hedge in a Three-Factor Model

The idea of the hedge is to create a global portfolio with portfolio P and three swaps, and to make it neutral to changes of the three level, slope and curvature factors denoted by β_0, β_1 and β_2 (see Chapter 6 for a complete description of the method). Then, we have to determine quantities ϕ_1, ϕ_2 and ϕ_3 to buy or sell in swaps S_1, S_2 and S_3 so that

$$\begin{cases} \phi_1 \dfrac{\partial S_1}{\partial \beta_0} + \phi_2 \dfrac{\partial S_2}{\partial \beta_0} + \phi_3 \dfrac{\partial S_3}{\partial \beta_0} = -\dfrac{\partial P}{\partial \beta_0} \\ \phi_1 \dfrac{\partial S_1}{\partial \beta_1} + \phi_2 \dfrac{\partial S_2}{\partial \beta_1} + \phi_3 \dfrac{\partial S_3}{\partial \beta_1} = -\dfrac{\partial P}{\partial \beta_1} \\ \phi_1 \dfrac{\partial S_1}{\partial \beta_2} + \phi_2 \dfrac{\partial S_2}{\partial \beta_2} + \phi_3 \dfrac{\partial S_3}{\partial \beta_2} = -\dfrac{\partial P}{\partial \beta_2} \end{cases} \qquad (10.6)$$

where $\frac{\partial P}{\partial \beta_j}$, $\frac{\partial S_1}{\partial \beta_j}$, $\frac{\partial S_2}{\partial \beta_j}$ and $\frac{\partial S_3}{\partial \beta_j}$ are, respectively, the sensitivity of portfolio P and of swaps S_1, S_2 and S_3 with respect to factors β_j for $j = 0, 1, 2$.

Example 10.14 At date $t = 0$, the continuously compounded zero-coupon yield curve is described by the following set of parameters of the Nelson and Siegel model:

β_0	β_1	β_2	τ
6%	−2%	−1%	3

This corresponds to a standard increasing curve. We consider a bond portfolio whose features are summarized in the following table. The price is expressed in percentage of the face value, which is equal to $100,000,000. We compute the yield to maturity (YTM), and the level, slope and curvature $durations (expressed in percentage of the face value) of the bond portfolio as given by equation (6.6) in Chapter 6.

Price	YTM	Level D_0	Slope D_1	Curvature D_2
1,092.43	5.417%	−7,980.61	−2,155.55	−1,543.82

To hedge the bond portfolio, we use three plain vanilla 6-month Libor swaps whose features are summarized in the following table. Level, slope and curvature $durations (expressed in percentage of the face value) are those of the fixed-coupon bond contained in the swap. The principal amount of the swaps is $1,000,000.

Maturity (years)	Price	Swap rate (%)	Level D_0	Slope D_1	Curvature D_2
2	0	4.414	−199.48	−146.26	−42.72
7	0	5.001	−643.17	−268.02	−184.58
15	0	5.407	−1,182.91	−307.59	−255.09

We consider that the bond portfolio and the swap instruments present the same default risk so that we are not concerned with that additional source of uncertainty, and we can use the same yield curve to price them.

Using equation (10.6), we obtain

$$\begin{pmatrix} \phi_1 \\ \phi_2 \\ \phi_3 \end{pmatrix} = \begin{pmatrix} -199,480,538 & -643,170,361 & -1,182,905,220 \\ -146,259,937 & -268,016,373 & -307,592,595 \\ -42,723,912 & -184,576,754 & -255,094,498 \end{pmatrix}^{-1}$$
$$\cdot \begin{pmatrix} 7.98061E+11 \\ 2.15555E+11 \\ 1.54382E+11 \end{pmatrix} = \begin{pmatrix} -494 \\ 383 \\ -800 \end{pmatrix}$$

The Nelson and Siegel hedge is performed by selling 494 2-year swaps, buying 383 7-year swaps and selling 800 15-year swaps.

Note finally that hedging interest-rate risk of a bond portfolio with swaps is an efficient way when they have exactly the same default risk. If not, a default risk still exists that is not hedged.

10.4 Nonplain Vanilla Swaps

10.4.1 Accrediting, Amortizing and Roller Coaster Swaps

In a plain vanilla swap, the notional principal remains unchanged over the life of the swap. Thus, it is referred to as a *bullet swap*. On the contrary, an accrediting swap is one in which the notional amount increases over time, whereas an amortizing swap is one in which the notional amount decreases in a predetermined way over the life of the swap. A roller-coaster swap is one in which the notional amount may rise or fall from one period to another.

Example 10.15 One year ago, a firm issued a 1-year Libor amortizing bond with maturity 5 years and $10 million notional amount. The notional amount of the bond is equally amortized so that each year $2 million is paid off. But now this firm expects an increase in the

1-year Libor and wants to enter an amortizing swap with the same amortization schedule as the bond's and where it receives the 1-year Libor and pays the fixed rate.

10.4.2 Basis Swap

A basis swap is a floating-for-floating interest-rate swap that exchanges the floating rates of two different markets or that exchanges the same floating rate but with different maturities or that exchanges the floating rates of two different markets and with different maturities.

Example 10.16   The 6-month Libor exchanged for the 3-month CD rate is an example of a basis swap. The 6-month Libor exchanged for the 1-month Libor is another example of a basis swap. Note in this last case that if one counterparty pays on a monthly basis, it receives semiannual cash flows, which means that it would have made six interest payments before receiving one in return.

When one of the legs is calculated in a different currency, the basis swap is called a *differential swap*.

10.4.3 Constant Maturity Swap and Constant Maturity Treasury Swap

A Constant Maturity Swap (CMS) is a floating-for-floating interest-rate swap exchanging a Libor rate for a particular swap rate as a Constant Maturity Treasury Swap (CMT) is a floating-for-floating interest-rate swap exchanging a Libor rate for a particular Treasury-bond rate.

Example 10.17   The 3-month Libor exchanged for the 10-year swap rate is an example of a Constant Maturity Swap. The 6-month Libor exchanged for the 5-year Treasury-bond rate is an example of a Constant Maturity Treasury swap.

It is also possible to exchange a constant swap rate against a constant Treasury-bond rate.

Example 10.18   Consider the following 5-year swap beginning on 02/02/01, where a firm pays quarterly to a bank the 10-year CMT rate+20 bps and receives quarterly from this bank the 10-year CMS rate. This swap is equivalent to receive CMS–CMT and to pay 0.20%. Assuming there is a positive correlation between the evolution of the spread CMS–CMT and the spread between the yield of risky bonds and default-free Treasury bonds, it is a valid hedging instrument for issuers who are exposed for their financing cost to an increase in the spread between the yield of risky bonds and default-free Treasury bonds.

Fixed Income Securities

10.4.4 Forward-Starting Swap

A forward-starting swap does not start on the current date but allows the counterparties to initiate it on a specified deferred date. Firms typically use this kind of swap when they want to fix a hedge or cost of borrowing for a specified period starting in the future.

> **Example 10.19**   We are now on 06/05/01. One-and-a-half years ago a firm issued a 3-month Libor floating-rate debt with maturity 5 years and expects now a rise in the 3-month Libor but only in 6 months. Then, it enters today a 3-year forward-starting swap beginning on 12/05/01 where it will pay the fixed rate and receive the 3-month Libor.

10.4.5 Inflation-Linked Swap

Inflation-linked swaps are often used by issuers of inflation-linked bonds (see Chapter 1) who want to be swapped into Libor (or Euribor...).

> **Example 10.20**   Consider a swap where an issuer of inflation-linked bonds receives each year the inflation leg and pays semiannually the 6-month Euribor rate. The issuer receives each year at date t before maturity $N \times RC \times \left(\frac{DIR_t}{DIR_{\text{initial}}} \right)$, and $N \times (1 + RC) \times \left(\frac{DIR_T}{DIR_{\text{initial}}} \right)$ at the maturity date T
>
> where
>
> N is the nominal amount;
>
> RC is the real coupon;
>
> DIR_t and DIR_{initial} are the daily inflation reference at date t and on the initial date (see Chapter 1 for the terminology of inflation-linked bonds).
>
> With the swap, the issuer of inflation-linked bonds has transformed his debt into a classical floating-rate debt.

10.4.6 Libor in Arrears Swap

As opposed to standard swaps where the floating rate is set in advance and paid in arrears, Libor in arrears swap is a swap where the floating rate is set in arrears and paid in arrears. These products are priced by adjusting the forward rate with a convexity term. This convexity term can be calculated in the Black model (see Chapter 15) or in a term-structure model (see Chapter 12).[5]

---

[5] See Hull (2002), Brigo and Mercurio (2001), and Martellini and Priaulet (2000) where a convexity adjustment is calculated for a CMT bond.

Example 10.21 We consider a 6-month Libor in arrears swap with a 3-year maturity, which starts on 11/27/02. The first cash flow CF of the floating leg, received on 05/27/03, is equal to

$$CF = N \times \frac{181}{360} \times L_{05/27/03}$$

where N is the notional amount, L_t is the 6-month Libor at date t, and we choose an Actual/360 day-count basis.

In a plain vanilla swap, this cash flow would be

$$CF = N \times \frac{181}{360} \times L_{11/27/02}$$

10.4.7 Yield-Curve Swap

A yield-curve swap is a floating-for-floating interest-rate swap where the counterparts exchange the difference between interest rates at two points on a given yield curve. This swap enables a firm to make bets on a spread between two rates of a given yield curve.

Example 10.22 The 6-month T-bill rate exchanged for the 5-year CMT rate is an example of a yield-curve swap. Suppose on 05/08/01 that the yield curve is flat at 5%. Firm A, which expects for a certain time a decrease in the short-term interest rates and an increase in the medium-term interest rates, enters a 3-year swap where it pays the 6-month T-bill rate and receives the 5-year CMT on a yearly basis. One year later, the 6-month T-Bill rate is 4% while the 5-year CMT is 6%. Firm A has gained 2%.

10.4.8 Zero-Coupon Swap

A zero-coupon swap is a swap that makes it possible to exchange a fixed or floating index that delivers regular coupons for an index that delivers only one coupon at the beginning or at the end of the swap. A zero-coupon swap is used to guarantee a rate for a given period because it avoids the problem of reinvesting coupons on future dates.

Example 10.23 On 05/06/01, we consider the 3-year zero-coupon swap that exchanges 7% fixed with an annual frequency for a unique F payment on 05/06/04. This swap has the following payment profile:

Fixed leg (%)	7	7	7
Date	05/06/02	05/06/03	05/06/04
Zero-coupon leg			$-F$

> **Remark 10.3** In the absence of arbitrage opportunities, the discounted value of F is equal to the sum of the three discounted cash flows of the fixed leg. So we get for F
>
> $$F = \frac{7\%[B(05/06/01, 05/06/02) + B(05/06/01, 05/06/03) + B(05/06/01, 05/06/04)]}{B(05/06/01, 05/06/04)}$$
>
> where $B(t, T)$ is the value on date t of \$1 received on date T.

10.5 End of Chapter Summary

A swap contract is a cash-flow transaction with no capital exchange that enables two counterparts to swap financial cash flows originated by loans or investments. Calculated on a notional principal, these cash-flow swaps take place on predetermined dates. Plain vanilla swaps are interest-rate swaps based on the exchange of a fixed leg whose payments depend on a fixed rate for a floating leg whose payments depend on a floating rate, in which the notional principal remains constant over the life of the contract, and where the maturity of the floating-rate index is identical to the payment frequency of the floating-leg flows. There also exist many different types of swaps, including, among others, accrediting, amortizing and roller-coaster swaps, basis swaps, constant maturity swaps, forward-starting swaps, inflation-linked swaps and so on.

Pricing a swap essentially amounts to calculating the difference between the price of a coupon-bearing bond maturing at the maturity date of the swap and the price of a zero-coupon maturing at the next floating cash-flow payment (both with principal amount equal to the swap nominal amount). This is known as the *zero-coupon method*. Practitioners often use an alternative method, known as the *forward projection method*, which is based upon the assumption that the future floating rates of the floating leg are equal to the forward rates. Both methods agree for plain vanilla swaps. On the other hand, for nonstandard swap contracts, it is necessary to apply a convexity adjustment to the forward rate.

The convention for quotes in the market is for the swap market maker to set the floating leg at Libor and then quote the fixed rate called the *swap rate* that makes the value of the swap equal to zero. Swaps are also quoted in terms of a swap spread, which is the difference between the fixed rate of the swap and the benchmark Treasury-bond yield of the same maturity as the swap.

Swaps may be used to (1) optimize the financial conditions of a debt; (2) convert the financial conditions of a debt; (3) create new synthetic assets; and (4) hedge a fixed-income portfolio against unexpected changes in the yield curve.

10.6 References and Further Reading

10.6.1 Books and Papers

Bicksler, J., and A.H. Chen, 1986, "An Economic Analysis of Interest Rate Swaps", *Journal of Finance*, **41**(3), 645–655.

Brigo, D., and F. Mercurio, 2001, *Interest Rate Models: Theory and Practice*, Springer Verlag, Heidelberg.

Brown, R., F. In, and V. Fang, 2002, "Modeling the Determinants of Swap Spreads", *Journal of Fixed Income*, **12**(1), 29–40.

Buetow, G.W., and F.J. Fabozzi, 2000, *Valuation of Interest Rate Swaps and Swaptions*, John Wiley & Sons, Chichester.

Chazot, C. and P. Claude, 1995, *Les Swaps*, Economica, Paris.

Choudhry, M., 2001, *Bond and Money Markets: Strategy, Trading and Analysis*, Butterworth-Heinemann, MA.

Das, S., 2000, *Structured Products and Hybrid Securities*, 2nd Edition, *John Wiley & Sons*, Chichester.

Dynkin, L., J. Hyman, and P. Lindner, 2002, "Hedging and Replication of Fixed-Income Portfolios", *Journal of Fixed Income*, **11**(4), 43–63.

El Karoui, N., and H. Geman, 1994, "A Probabilistic Approach to the Valuation of General Floating-Rate Notes with an Application to Interest Rate Swaps", *Advances in Futures and Options Research*, **7**, 47–64.

Fabozzi, F.J., (Editor), 2000, *The Handbook of Fixed Income Securities*, 6th Edition, McGraw-Hill, New York.

Hull, J., 2002, *Options, Futures and Other Derivatives*, 5th Edition, Prentice Hall, New York.

Marshall, J.F., and K.R. Kapner, 1993, *Understanding Swaps*, John Wiley & Sons, Chichester.

Martellini, L., P. Priaulet, and S. Priaulet, 2002, "Beyond Duration", *Journal of Bond Trading and Management*, **1**(2), 103–119.

Rainelli-Le Montagner, H., 1996, "Evaluation des Swaps de Taux: Théorie et Tratique", *Banque et Marchés*, **22**, 12–21.

Turnbull, S.M., 1987, "Swaps: A Zero Sum Game", *Financial Management*, **16**, 15–21.

10.6.2 Websites

www.isda.org.

www.bloomberg.com.

www.reuters.com.

10.7 Problems

Exercise 10.1   What are the four main uses of interest-rate swaps?

Exercise 10.2   Explain what is an asset swap.

Exercise 10.3   On 06/15/01, a firm issues a 3-year maturity bond at a 5% fixed rate with a notional principal of $10 million. The issuer who expects a decrease in interest rates in 1 year wishes to transform its debt into a floating-rate debt. Market conditions for a 2-year 6-month Libor swap beginning in 1 year are the following: Libor against 4.5% or Libor+0.5% against 5%. What is the swap he enters? Give the detail of the swap cash flows.

Exercise 10.4   We consider two firms A and B that have the same financial needs in terms of maturity and principal. The two firms can borrow money in the market at the following conditions:

- **Firm A:** 11% at a fixed rate or Libor + 2% for a $10 million loan and a 5-year maturity.
- **Firm B:** 9% at a fixed rate or Libor + 0.25% for a $10 million loan and a 5-year maturity.

1. We suppose that firm B prefers a floating-rate debt as firm A prefers a fixed-rate debt. What is the swap they will structure to optimize their financial conditions?
2. If firm B prefers a fixed-rate debt as firm A prefers a floating-rate debt, is there a swap to structure so that the two firms optimize their financial conditions?
3. Conclude.

Exercise 10.5 We consider at date T_0, a 3-month Libor swap contract with maturity 2 years with the following cash-flow schedule:

				F				F
T_0	T_1	T_2	T_3	T_4	T_5	T_6	T_7	T_8
	$-V_0$	$-V_1$	$-V_2$	$-V_3$	$-V_4$	$-V_5$	$-V_6$	$-V_7$

Note that $T_{j+1} - T_j = 3$ months $= 90$ days, $\forall j \in \{0, 1, 2, \ldots, 7\}$. We suppose that the swap nominal amount is $10 million and that the rate F of the fixed leg is 6.12%. Recall that V_{j-1} is the value of the floating rate at date T_{j-1} and paid at date T_j.

At date T_0, zero-coupon rates for maturities $T_1, T_2, \ldots T_8$ are given in the following table:

Maturity	ZC rates (%)	Maturity	ZC rates (%)
T_1	5.553	T_5	6.123
T_2	5.756	T_6	6.235
T_3	5.893	T_7	6.321
T_4	6.012	T_8	6.399

1. What is the price formula of this swap using the forward projection method and the zero-coupon method?
2. For $j = \{1, \ldots, 8\}$, compute the discount factors $B(T_0, T_j)$ and the forward rates $F(T_0, V_{j-1})$ used in the forward rate projection method.
3. Give the price of this swap using the forward projection method.
4. Give the price of this swap using the zero-coupon method.
5. Conclude.

Exercise 10.6 We consider at date T_0, a 6-month Libor standard swap contract with maturity 6 years with the following cash-flow schedule:

		F		F		F		F		F		F
T_0	T_1	T_2	T_3	T_4	T_5	T_6	T_7	T_8	T_9	T_{10}	T_{11}	T_{12}
	$-V_0$	$-V_1$	$-V_2$	$-V_3$	$-V_4$	$-V_5$	$-V_6$	$-V_7$	$-V_8$	$-V_9$	$-V_{10}$	$-V_{11}$

Note that $T_{i+1} - T_i = 6$ months, $\forall i \in \{0, 1, 2, \ldots, 11\}$. We suppose that the swap nominal amount is \$1 million and that the rate F of the fixed leg is 6%.

At date T_0, zero-coupon rates with maturities $T_1, T_2, \ldots T_{12}$ are given in the following table:

Maturity	ZC rates (%)	Maturity	ZC rates (%)
T_1	4.005	T_7	5.785
T_2	4.575	T_8	5.896
T_3	4.925	T_9	6.001
T_4	5.134	T_{10}	6.069
T_5	5.412	T_{11}	6.121
T_6	5.599	T_{12}	6.148

1. What is the pricing formula for this plain vanilla swap using the zero-coupon method?
2. Compute the discount factors for maturities $T_1, T_2, \ldots T_{12}$.
3. Give the price of this swap.
4. What is the swap rate such that the price of this swap is zero?
5. An investor has bought 100,000 5-year bond with a 7.2% annual coupon rate and a nominal amount of \$1,000. What is the price, the yield to maturity and the modified duration of this bond?
6. The investor fears a rates increase. How many swaps must he sell to protect his bond portfolio?
7. The yield to maturity curve increases uniformly by 0.3%. What is his new position with and without the hedge?

Exercise 10.7 We consider at date T_0, a 1-year Libor swap contract with maturity 10 years and with the following cash-flow schedule:

	F	F	F	F	F	F	F	F	F	F
T_0	T_1	T_2	T_3	T_4	T_5	T_6	T_7	T_8	T_9	T_{10}
	$-V_0$	$-V_1$	$-V_2$	$-V_3$	$-V_4$	$-V_5$	$-V_6$	$-V_7$	$-V_8$	$-V_9$

Note that $T_{i+1} - T_i = 1$ year, $\forall i \in \{0, 1, 2, \ldots, 9\}$. We suppose that the swap nominal amount is \$10 million and that the rate F of the fixed leg is 9.55%.

At date T_0, zero-coupon rates with maturities $T_1, T_2, \ldots T_{10}$ are given in the following table:

Maturity	ZC rates (%)	Maturity	ZC rates (%)
T_1	8.005	T_6	9.235
T_2	7.856	T_7	9.478
T_3	8.235	T_8	9.656
T_4	8.669	T_9	9.789
T_5	8.963	T_{10}	9.883

1. Give the price of this swap.
2. What is the swap rate such that the price of this swap is zero?
3. An investor holds a bond portfolio whose price, yield to maturity and modified duration are, respectively, $9,991,565,452, 9.2% and 5.92. He wants to be protected against an increase in rates. How many swaps must he sell to protect his bond portfolio?

Exercise 10.8   Deriving the current interbank zero-coupon yield curve with the Nelson and Siegel model (see Chapter 4 for a description of this model) we obtain the following parameter values:

β_0	β_1	β_2	τ
6.9%	−3.5%	−1%	3

The goal of this exercise is to obtain the Nelson and Siegel level, slope and curvature $durations of some plain vanilla swaps and to hedge a bond portfolio against a change in these parameters.

1. Compute the price and the Nelson and Siegel level, slope and curvature $durations of the three following swaps:

   (a) the 6-month Libor plain vanilla swap with a nominal amount of $1,000,000, a maturity of 2 years, semiannual payments on the fixed leg and a fixed rate equal to 4%.
   (b) the 6-month Libor plain vanilla swap with a nominal amount of $1,000,000, a maturity of 5 years, semiannual payments on the fixed leg and a fixed rate equal to 5%.
   (c) the 6-month Libor plain vanilla swap with a nominal amount of $1,000,000, a maturity of 10 years, semiannual payments on the fixed leg and a fixed rate equal to 5.50%.

2. An investor wants to hedge a bond portfolio whose level, slope and curvature $ durations are, respectively, −789,456,145, −142,256,548 and −97,897,254. He decides to use the three swaps to hedge his position. How many of these three swaps must he buy or sell?
3. Compute the financing cost of the hedge by assuming that the investor hedges his position during 14 days with no rebalancing. The 2-week Libor is equal to 3.5%.
4. Explain why hedging with swaps is better than hedging with bonds.

Exercise 10.9   At date $t = 0$, we consider the 5-year zero-coupon swap with $1,000,000 face value that exchanges 7% fixed with an annual frequency for a unique F payment in 5 years.

1. What is the payment profile of this swap?
2. Determine the value F assuming the following discount factor curve:

Maturity	Discount factor
$t = 1$	0.909
$t = 2$	0.825
$t = 3$	0.755
$t = 4$	0.672
$t = 5$	0.637

Exercise 10.10 The objective of this exercise is to analyze the hedging performance of three methods, the duration hedge, the duration/convexity hedge and the Nelson–Siegel $durations hedge in the context of a specific bond portfolio. At date $t = 0$, the continuously compounded zero-coupon yield curve is described by the following set of parameters of the Nelson and Siegel model (see Chapter 4 for a description of this model):

β_0	β_1	β_2	τ
8%	−3%	−1%	3

This corresponds to a standard increasing curve. We consider a bond portfolio whose features are summarized in the following table. The price is expressed in percentage of the face value, which is equal to $100,000,000. We compute the yield to maturity (YTM), the $duration, the $convexity, and the level, slope and curvature $durations of the bond portfolio as given by equation (6.6). Note that the $duration, the $convexity and the level, slope and curvature $durations are expressed in percentage of the bond portfolio face value.

Price	YTM	$Duration	$Convexity	Level D_0	Slope D_1	Curvature D_2
972.376	7.169%	−5,709.59	79,662.17	−6,118.91	−1,820.02	−1,243.28

To hedge the bond portfolio, we use three plain vanilla 6-month Libor swaps whose features are summarized in the following table. $duration, $convexity, level, slope and curvature $durations are those of the fixed-coupon bond contained in the swap. The principal amount of the swaps is $1,000,000.

Maturity (years)	Price	Swap rate (%)	$Duration	$Convexity	Level D_0	Slope D_1	Curvature D_2
2	0	5.7451	−184.00	517.09	−194.55	−142.66	−41.66
7	0	6.6717	−545.15	3,809.39	−579.80	−242.66	−166.22
15	0	7.2309	−897.66	11,002.57	−948.31	−254.58	−206.69

We consider that the bond portfolio and the swap instruments present the same default risk so that we are not concerned with that additional source of uncertainty, and we can use the same yield curve to price them. This curve is the one described above with the Nelson and Siegel parameters.

1. Duration hedging is performed with the 7-year swap. What is the quantity of this swap to be sold so as to hedge the bond portfolio?

2. Duration/Convexity hedging is performed with the 7- and 15-year swaps. What are the quantities of each of them to be bought or sold so as to hedge the bond portfolio?

3. Nelson and Siegel $durations hedge is performed with the three swaps. What are the quantities of each of them to be bought or sold so as to hedge the bond portfolio?

4. To measure the performance of the three hedge methods, we assume 10 different movements of the yield curve. These 10 scenarios are obtained by assuming the following changes in the beta parameters in the Nelson and Siegel model:

   (a) Small parallel shifts with $\beta_0 = +0.1\%$ and -0.1%.
   (b) Large parallel shifts with $\beta_0 = +1\%$ and -1%.
   (c) Decrease and increase in the long- to short-term spread with $\beta_1 = +1\%$ and -1%.
   (d) Curvature moves with $\beta_2 = +0.6\%$ and -0.6%.
   (e) Flattening and steepening move of the yield curve with ($\beta_0 = -0.4\%$, $\beta_1 = +1.2\%$) and ($\beta_0 = +0.4\%$, $\beta_1 = -1.2\%$).

      Draw the last six yield-curve scenarios that represent nonparallel shifts.

5. In each scenario, calculate the variation in the value of the bond portfolio.

6. In each scenario, calculate the hedging error of the three different methods.

7. Conclude.

11 Forwards and Futures

11.1 Definition

A *forward contract* or a *futures contract* is an agreement made on a date t to buy (long position) or to sell (short position) a security on a future date T called the *delivery date* and at a given price F_t^T called the *forward* or *futures price*. The forward or futures price F_t^T is computed so that the value of the contract on date t is equal to zero. Then on date T, the seller of the contract delivers the security to the buyer at the futures price F_t^T. Note that if the long side of a contract gains, the short side loses so that it is a zero-sum game.

> **Example 11.1** We consider on 03/12/01 a forward contract whose underlying asset is a 3-month T-bill. The maturity of the contract is one month and its price 98.6. The seller of the contract delivers the 3-month T-bill to the buyer of the contract on 04/12/01 at a 98.6 price.

Futures contracts are similar to forward contracts but are standardized and exchanged on recognized futures markets. On the contrary, forward contracts are designed to meet specific individual requirements and traded over the counter. We distinguish three types of interest-rate futures contracts depending on the underlying reference of the contract, which can be directly an interest rate like the 3-month Libor, a Treasury bill such as the 13-week T-bill or a bond such as the 10-year T-bond.

Futures contracts are traded all over the world. The main markets of interest-rate futures contracts in the world are the International Money Market of the Chicago Mercantile Exchange (CME) (see www.cme.com), the Chicago Board of Trade (CBOT) (see www.cbot.com), the Sydney Futures Exchange (see www.sfe.com), the Montreal Stock Exchange Futures (see www.me.org), the London International Financial Futures Exchange (LIFFE) (see www.liffe.com), the Tokyo International Financial Futures Exchange (see www.tiffe.org.jp), the Marché à Terme International de France MATIF (see www.matif.fr), Eurex (see www.eurexchange.com), the Hong-Kong Futures Exchange (see www.hkfe.com) and so on.

We give in Tables 11.1 and 11.2 the list of contracts traded on 09/03/01 in the CME (Chicago Mercantile Exchange), CBOT (Chicago Board of Trade), LIFFE (London International Financial Futures and Options), EUREX (the European Derivatives Market) and MATIF (Marché à Terme International de France). Most of them are contracts written on Treasury bonds (T-bill, T-bond, Gilt, OAT, Bund, Bobl or Schatz etc.) or assimilated (agency notes, municipal bond index), interest rates (Libor, Euribor etc.), swapnotes or more exotic products such as Brady bonds.

The whole description of these contracts can be obtained on Bloomberg (see CEM (Contract Exchange Menu) function), on Reuters or on websites of futures markets.

Fixed Income Securities

Table 11.1   CME, CBOT and LIFFE Interest-Rate Futures.

CME	CBOT	LIFFE
Eurodollar Futures	30-Year US Treasury Bonds	Long Gilt Contract
13-Week Treasury Bill Futures	10-Year US Treasury Notes	German Government Bond Contract
Libor Futures	5-Year US Treasury Notes	Japanese Government Bond Contract
Fed Funds Turn Futures	2-Year US Treasury Notes	3-Month Euribor Futures
10-Year Agency Futures	10-Year Agency Notes	3-Month Euro Libor Futures
5-Year Agency Futures	5-Year Agency Notes	3-Month Sterling Futures
Argentine 2X FRB Brady Bond Futures	Long-term Municipal Bond Index	3-Month Euro Swiss Franc Futures
Argentine Par Bond Futures	30-Day Federal Funds Mortgage	3-Month Euroyen (Tibor) Futures
Brazilian 2X C Brady Bond Futures		3-Month Euroyen (Libor) Futures
Brazilian 2X EI Brady Bond Futures		2-Year Euro Swapnote
Mexican 2X Brady Bond Futures		5-Year Euro Swapnote
Euro Yen Futures		10-Year Euro Swapnote
Japanese Government Bond Futures		
Euro Yen Libor Futures		
Mexican TIIE Futures		
Mexican CETES Futures		

Table 11.2   EUREX and MATIF Interest-Rate Futures.

EUREX	MATIF
1-Month Euribor Futures	30-Year E-Bond Futures
3-Month Euribor Futures	Euro Notional Futures
Euro-Schatz Futures	5-Year Euro Futures
Euro Bobl Futures	2-Year E-Note Futures
Euro Bund Futures	3-Month Euribor Futures
Euro Buxl Futures	
Conf Futures	

11.2   Terminology, Conventions and Market Quotes

A futures contract is an agreement between two parties that specifies the characteristics of this contract like any agreement.

11.2.1   Terminology and Conventions

The Underlying Asset

It is the asset that the seller delivers to the buyer at the end of the contract. It may exist, as is the case for an interest rate or a bill, or not, as is the case for a bond. In the last case, there is a difference between the fictitious underlying asset of the contract and the asset that will be actually delivered. Therefore, a contract stipulates the *grades* of the underlying assets that are acceptable for delivering.

Example 11.2   The underlying asset of the CBOT 30-year US Treasury-bond futures is a fictitious 30-year maturity US Treasury bond with 6% coupon rate. Deliverable grades are US Treasury bonds that, if callable, are not callable for at least 15 years from the first day of the delivery month or, if not callable, have a maturity of at least 15 years from the first day of the delivery month.

The Contract Size

The contract size corresponds to the notional amount of the asset that has to be delivered.

Example 11.3   The notional amount of the CME 13-week T-bill futures contract is $1,000,000. The notional amount of the CBOT 30-year US T-bond futures contract is $100,000. The notional amount of the Matif 3-month Euribor futures contract to be delivered is Eur1,000,000.

Delivery Month

The *delivery month* is the month when the contract expires.

Example 11.4   The Matif Euro Notional futures contract has three successive quarterly contract cycles out of March, June, September and December.

For each delivery month of a contract, there is a calendar specifying the *last trading day*, and if necessary, the *repartition* or *allotment day* when sellers determine which assets they will deliver to buyers, the *delivery day* (or sometimes the *delivery period*) when assets are delivered, days we refer to calculate the conversion factor and accrued interest.

Example 11.5   Matif Euro Notional Futures—Calendar for the September 2001 Futures Contract

Last trading day	September 17, 2001
Repartition day	September 18, 2001
Delivery day	September 21, 2001
Conversion factor calculated referring to	September 18, 2001
Accrued interest referring to	September 21, 2001

Example 11.6   CME 13-Week T-Bill Futures—Calendar for the June 2003 Futures Contract

Fixed Income Securities

First trade date	June 18, 2002
Last trade date	June 16, 2003
Delivery date	June 16, 2003

11.2.2 Quotes

The *futures price* is quoted differently depending on the nature of the underlying asset, an interest rate, a bill or a bond. When the underlying asset is an interest rate, the futures price is quoted with three decimals as 100 minus this interest rate. When the underlying asset is a bill, the futures price is quoted with two decimals as 100 minus the yield on a discount basis (see Chapter 1 for a definition of this yield). When the underlying asset is a bond, it is quoted in the same way as a bond, that is, in percentage of the nominal value of the underlying asset with two decimals. Par is quoted on the basis of 100 points. The *tick* is the minimum price fluctuation that can occur in trading.

> **Example 11.7** The Matif 3-month Euribor futures contract maturing in two months is quoted as 100%—the 3-month Euribor futures rate in two months. The tick of this contract is 1/5 bp, which is equal to 5 euros. The CME 13-week T-bill futures contract is quoted as 100—the yield on a discount basis. The tick of this contract is 1/2 bp, which represents $12.5. The CBOT 30-year US T-bond futures contract is quoted in percentage of the nominal value of the underlying asset. The tick for this contract is about 1/32 of a point which represents $31.25. For example, 80-16 equals 80 16/32.

Sometimes *daily price movement limits* as well as *position limits* are specified by the exchange. Note that on the expiration date of the contract the futures price as well as the forward price is equal to the price of the underlying asset.

> **Example 11.8** The Matif 3-month Euribor futures contract has a daily price movement limit equal to +/−16 bps. The position limit for the CBOT Mortgage futures is 5,000 contracts.

The *regular initial margin* is the minimum dollar amount deposit per contract as specified by the exchange. To take a position on a futures contract with a given size, you only need to deposit a percentage of this size, which may be cash or a security such as a T-bill. This enables the investor in the futures market to benefit from a *leverage effect*. The leverage effect of a contract is calculated by dividing its contract size by its regular initial margin.

> **Example 11.9** The Matif Euro Notional futures contract has a regular deposit margin of Eur1,500 and its contract size is Eur100,000. The leverage effect of this contract is 100,000/1,500 = 66.66. The Matif 3-month Euribor futures contract has a regular deposit margin of Eur500 and its contract size is Eur1,000,000. The leverage effect of this contract is 1,000,000/500 = 2,000.

Example 11.10 CBOT US 10-Year Note Futures Contract

We now focus on the CBOT US 10-year futures contract. The futures contract description is given on the Bloomberg screen in Figure 11.1. In particular, we obtain the following information:

- *The delivery month: March 2002*

- *The Bloomberg ticker: TYH2*

- *The underlying asset: US 10-year Treasury note with a 6% fixed coupon rate*

- *The contract size: $100,000*

- *The value of 1 point: $1,000*

- *The tick value: $15.625*

- *The futures price: 107-23 or 107.71875*

- *The grades of the underlying asset: US Treasury notes maturing in at least 6 1/2 years, but not more than 10 years, from the first day of the delivery month*

- *The last trading day: 03/19/2002, the first delivery day: 03/01/2002, the last delivery day: 03/28/2002, the first trading day: 12/20/2000.*

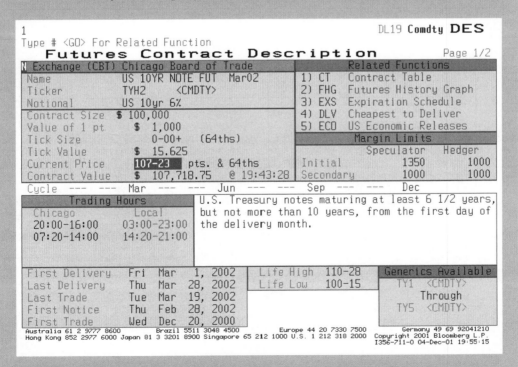

Figure 11.1 © 2003 Bloomberg L.P. All rights reserved. Reprinted with permission.

Fixed Income Securities

11.3   Margin Requirements and the Role of the Clearing House

When two traders agree to exchange an asset for a certain price in the future, a risk is that one of them may not have the financial resources to honor the agreement. The role of the clearing house is to minimize this risk of default. The initial margin required by the clearing house and deposited in a *margin account* is an insurance against this risk. But as the price of futures contracts moves, the initial margin required may be inferior to the loss incurred. The *maintenance margin*, inferior to the initial margin is set up so that if the balance in the margin account falls below the maintenance margin intraday, the trader is requested to bring back the balance of his margin account to the maintenance margin level in a very short time. Besides, at the end of each trading day, the trader's gain or loss is added to the margin account. If the balance of the margin account is below the initial margin, the trader is requested to readjust the margin account to the initial margin level. In this case, the additional margin deposited is called the *variation margin*. Unlike the initial margin, the variation margin must be only in cash and not in interest-bearing instruments.

Example 11.11   Consider a trader who sells 100 units of a Matif Euro Notional futures contract at a price of 104.64% on 06/04/01. The trader deposits an initial margin of Eur150,000 (100 × 1,500) on his margin account. Remember that the contract size is Eur100,000 and that a 0.01% nominal variation of the futures contract represents a value of Eur10. The following table represents the daily P&L and the variation margins[1] generated by this position

Date	Future price (%)	Daily P&L (Eur)	Variation margin (Eur)
06/05/01	104.86	−22,000	22,000
06/06/01	104.52	34,000	−22,000
06/07/01	104.23	29,000	—
06/08/01	103.89	34,000	—
06/11/01	104.12	−23,000	—
06/12/01	103.68	44,000	—
06/13/01	104.23	−55,000	—
06/14/01	104.89	−66,000	25,000
06/15/01	105.45	−56,000	56,000
06/18/01	104.35	110,000	−81,000
06/19/01	104.34	1,000	—
Total	—	**Eur30,000**	—

On 06/19/01, the trader closes his position by buying 100 units of the futures contract at a price of 104.34%. The total gain of his trade is Eur30,000.

[1]In this example, we assume that excess margin over the initial margin is paid back to the trader.

11.4 Conversion Factor and the Cheapest-to-Deliver Bond

When the underlying asset of a futures contract is fictitious, the seller of the contract has to deliver a real asset that may differ from the fictitious asset in terms of coupon rate and maturity. That is why we compute a *conversion factor* whose goal is to equate the value of the two assets, the fictitious bond and the bond to be delivered. The conversion factor is computed in general on the allotment date. Given a futures contract and a real asset to be delivered, it is a constant factor that is known in advance. Conversion factors for the next contracts to mature are available on websites of futures markets. Let us now move on to the method used to compute the conversion factor.

Consider a futures contract whose fictitious underlying asset is an m-year bond with a coupon rate equal to r. We suppose that the real asset delivered by the seller of the futures contract is an x-year bond with a coupon rate equal to c. Expressed as a percentage of the nominal value, the conversion factor denoted by CF is calculated referring to the allotment date and is formally equal to

$$CF = PV - AC$$

where PV is on the allotment date the present value of the real asset discounted at rate r and AC is the amount of the accrued interest of the same asset.

Example 11.12 We consider a futures contract whose underlying asset is a fictitious 10-year bond with a 6% annual coupon rate. Suppose that the real asset to be delivered on the allotment date is an 8.5-year bond with a 7% annual coupon rate whose accrued interest is 3.5% of the nominal amount. The conversion factor is equal to

$$CF = \sum_{i=0.5}^{8.5} \frac{7\%}{(1+6\%)^i} + \frac{100\%}{(1+6\%)^{8.5}} - 3.5\% = 109.959\% - 3.5\% = 106.459\%$$

Given a futures contract and a real asset to be delivered, this is a constant factor because the coupon rate of the bond, the rate used to discount cash flows and the allotment date are fixed.

Example 11.13   Conversion Factors of the CBOT US 10-Year Note Futures Contract

The Bloomberg screen in Figure 11.2 provides conversion factors for the next CBOT US 10-year note futures contracts maturing on March 2002 (TYH2), June 2002 (TYM2) and September 2002 (TYU2). For example, the conversion factor associated with TYH2 for the 6 1/2 fixed-coupon Treasury note maturing on 02/15/2010 is 103.05%.

The conversion factor is used to calculate the *invoice price* that the buyer of the futures contract must pay to the seller when a bond is delivered. The invoice price denoted by IP is defined as

$$IP = \text{contract size} \times [\text{futures price} \times CF + AC]$$

```
<HELP> for explanation, <MENU> for similar functions.      DL19 Comdty FAC
Enter all values and hit <GO>.
                        Conversion Factors               Page 1 of 1
      Coupon or Maturity order M        Ascending or Descending D
      Bonds     Futures:  TYH2      TYM2      TYU2      TYZ2
   1)T 5 08/15/11        .9297     .9312     .9326     n.a.
   2)T 5 02/15/11        .9326     .9342     .9356     n.a.
   3)T 5 ¾ 08/15/10      .9838     .9843     .9846     n.a.
   4)T 6 ½ 02/15/10     1.0305    1.0298    1.0289     n.a.
   5)T 6 08/15/09        .9999    1.0000     .9999     n.a.
   6)T 5 ½ 05/15/09      .9718     .9725     .9734     n.a.
   7)T 4 ¾ 11/15/08      .9335     n.a.      n.a.      n.a.


   Australia 61 2 9777 8600      Brazil 5511 3048 4500      Europe 44 20 7330 7500      Germany 49 69 92041210
   Hong Kong 852 2977 6000 Japan 81 3 3201 8900 Singapore 65 212 1000 U.S. 1 212 318 2000  Copyright 2001 Bloomberg L.P.
                                                                      I356-711-0 04-Dec-01 19:55:53
```

Figure 11.2 © 2003 Bloomberg L.P. All rights reserved. Reprinted with permission.

Example 11.14 Suppose a futures contract whose size is $100,000 and price is 98. The conversion factor is equal to 106.459% and the accrued interest is 3.5%. The invoice price IP is equal to

$$IP = \$100,000 \times [98\% \times 106.459\% + 3.5\%] = \$107,829.82$$

11.4.1 The Cheapest to Deliver on the Repartition Date

On the repartition date, there are, in general, many bonds that may be delivered by the seller of the futures contract. These bonds vary in terms of maturity and coupon rate. Because the conversion factor is an imperfect measure, the seller may choose which of the available bonds is the cheapest to deliver. The seller of the futures contract receives from the buyer the invoice price, and the cost of purchasing the bond denoted by CP is

$$CP = \text{contract size} \times [\text{quoted price} + AC]$$

The cheapest to deliver for the seller is then the bond that maximizes the difference between the invoice price IP and the cost of purchasing the bond CP, that is

$$\text{Max}\,(IP - CP) = \text{Max}\,(\text{futures price} \times CF - \text{quoted price})$$

Example 11.15 Suppose a futures contract with $100,000 size whose price is 97%, and three bonds denoted A, B and C with the following features. We look for the bond that maximizes the quantity $IP - CP$.

	Quoted price	Conversion factor (%)	$IP - CP$ ($)
Bond A	103.90	107.145	30.65
Bond B	118.90	122.512	−63.36
Bond C	131.25	135,355	44.35

The seller of the futures contract will choose to deliver Bond C.

11.4.2 The Cheapest to Deliver before the Repartition Date

The *implied repo rate* is defined as the return earned on purchasing a cash bond and selling the futures contract, with the intention of delivering that particular bond in the future. Therefore, the bond with the highest implied repo rate is the cheapest to deliver. The higher the implied repo rate, the cheaper the bond to deliver. The implied repo rate denoted by r satisfies the following equation

$$GP \cdot \left(1 + \frac{r.D_1}{360}\right) = IC \cdot \left(1 + \frac{r.D_2}{360}\right) + FP.CF + AC \qquad (11.1)$$

where

FP is the futures price;

CF is the conversion factor;

AC is the accrued interest of the bond at the futures delivery date;

GP is the gross price of the bond;

IC is the interim coupon received (0 if no coupon received);

D_1 is the number of days from the settlement date to the futures delivery date;

D_2 is the number of days from the last coupon date (after the settlement date) to the futures delivery date.

More precisely, the implied repo rate is the rate that permits to equate the cash out, which is the cost of purchasing and financing the bond, to the cash in, which is the sum of the invoice price and reinvested earnings plus the amount received from contract delivery and the accrued interest of the bond.

Using equation (11.1) we obtain for r

$$r = \frac{(FP.CF + AC - GP + IC)}{GP \cdot \dfrac{D_1}{360} - IC \cdot \dfrac{D_2}{360}} \qquad (11.2)$$

We give below an example of the cheapest to deliver obtained from Bloomberg.

Fixed Income Securities

```
<HELP> for explanation.                                    DL19 Comdty DLV
Hit {NUMBER} <GO> to view Historical Basis/Repo
Cheapest  to  Deliver              Trade 12/ 7/01 Dlv 3/28/02
   US 10YR NOTE FUT  Mar02   TYH2 104.1406     Set 12/10/01 Cheapest IRP= .60
                                              DECIMAL  108 Days Act/360  DECIMAL
  PRICES AS DECIMALS? Y  (Mid)           Conv.  Gross Implied  Actual  Net
     Order DR re-sort? Y Price Source Yield C.Factor Basis Repo%  Repo%  Basis
            MASTER:                                                1.73
  1) T 6 ¹₂ 02/15/10  109.0391 BGN  5.132 1.0305  1.722   .60    1.73   .373
  2) T 6    08/15/09  105.7891 BGN  5.079  .9999  1.659   .35    1.73   .440
  3) T 5 ¹₂ 05/15/09  102.8672 BGN  5.032  .9718  1.663  -.07    1.73   .558
  4) T 5 ³₄ 08/15/10  104.1797 BGN  5.146  .9838  1.726  -.09    1.73   .573
  5) T 4 ³₄ 11/15/08   98.8203 BGN  4.953  .9335  1.605  -.63    1.73   .702
  6) T 5    02/15/11   98.8828 BGN  5.153  .9326  1.761  -.95    1.73   .801
  7) T 5    08/15/11   98.9688 BGN  5.136  .9297  2.149 -2.25    1.73  1.190

Australia 61 2 9777 8600      Brazil 5511 3048 4500       Europe 44 20 7330 7500      Germany 49 69 92041210
Hong Kong 852 2977 6000 Japan 81 3 3201 8900 Singapore 65 212 1000 U.S. 1 212 318 2000 Copyright 2001 Bloomberg L.P.
                                                                       I356-711-0 07-Dec-01 20:38:47
```

Figure 11.3   © 2003 Bloomberg L.P. All rights reserved. Reprinted with permission.

Example 11.16   The Cheapest to Deliver

The Bloomberg screen below (Figure 11.3) provides the cheapest bond to deliver on 12/07/01 for the US 10-year note futures contract maturing on March 2002 (TYH2). The gross basis is obtained as the difference between the bond price and the futures price multiplied by the conversion factor. The implied repo rate is calculated using equation (11.2). We can see that the Treasury note delivering a 6 1/2 coupon rate and maturing on 02/15/10 is the cheapest to deliver for that futures contract on 12/07/01.

We will see next in Section 11.6 how to take profit of arbitrage opportunities when the implied repo rate in equation (11.2) is different from the repo rate on the market. This is what we call cash-and-carry arbitrage and reverse cash-and-carry arbitrage.

11.5   Pricing of Forwards and Futures

11.5.1   Forward-Spot Parity or How to Price a Forward Contract?

Suppose at date t an investor who wants to hold at a future date T one unit of a bond B whose coupon rate and price (expressed in percentage of the face value) at date t are, respectively, c and P_t. He faces the following alternative:

- *either he buys at date t a forward contract from a seller who will deliver at date T one unit of this bond B at a determined price of F_t;*

- *or he borrows money in the market to buy this bond at date t.*

The cash flows implied by these two operations are the following:

Date	t	T
Buy a forward contract written on 1 unit of bond B	0	F_t
Borrow money to buy 1 unit of bond B	P_t	$-P_t \times \left[1 + r\left(\dfrac{T-t}{360}\right)\right]$
Buy 1 unit of bond B	$-P_t$	$AC = 100 \times c \times \left(\dfrac{T-t}{365}\right)$

where r is the interest rate to borrow money, expressed as a linear rate in the Actual/360 day-count basis, and AC the accrued interest of bond B.

We note that these two operations have a cost equal to zero at date t. In the absence of arbitrage opportunities, the cash flows generated by the two operations at date T must be equal. So we obtain

$$F_t = P_t \times \left[1 + r\left(\frac{T-t}{360}\right)\right] - 100 \times c \times \left(\frac{T-t}{365}\right)$$

If we define R as the interest rate which satisfies

$$R\left(\frac{T-t}{365}\right) = r\left(\frac{T-t}{360}\right)$$

and C as

$$C = \frac{100 \times c}{P_t}$$

we finally obtain

$$F_t = P_t \times \left[1 + (R - C)\left(\frac{T-t}{365}\right)\right] \qquad (11.3)$$

Example 11.17 Pricing of a Forward Contract Written on a Bond

On 05/01/01, we consider a forward contract maturing in 6 months, written on a bond whose coupon rate and price are, respectively, 10% and 115. Assuming that the interest rate r to borrow money is equal to 7%, the forward price $F_{05/01/01}$ is equal to

$$F_{05/01/01} = 115.\left(1 + 7\%.\frac{184}{360}\right) - 100 \times 10\% \times \left(\frac{184}{365}\right) = 114.07$$

Example 11.18 Pricing of a Forward Contract Written on an Interest Rate

In this case, we simply have to determine the forward rate that can be guaranteed now on a transaction occurring in the future. Take a simple example. Suppose an investor who wants now to guarantee the 1-year zero-coupon rate for a $10,000 loan starting in one year. He has two alternatives:

- *either he buys a forward contract with $10,000 principal value maturing in one year written on the 1-year zero-coupon rate $R(0,1)$ at a determined rate $F(0,1,1)$, which is the forward rate calculated at date $t = 0$, beginning in one year and maturing one year after;*

- *or he simultaneously borrows and lends $10,000 repayable at the end of year 2 and year 1, respectively.*

The cash flows generated by this transaction are as follows:

	Today	In 1 year	In 2 years
Borrow	10,000	—	$-10,000 \cdot (1 + R(0, 2))^2$
Lend	$-10,000$	$10,000 \cdot [1 + R(0, 1)]$	—
Total	0	$10,000 \cdot [1 + R(0, 1)]$	$-10,000 \cdot (1 + R(0, 2))^2$

This is equivalent to borrowing $10,000 \cdot [1 + R(0, 1)]$ in one year, repayable in two years as $10,000 \cdot [1 + R(0, 2)]^2$. The implied rate on the loan given by the following equation is the forward rate $F(0, 1, 1)$:

$$10,000 \cdot [1 + R(0, 1)] \cdot [1 + F(0, 1, 1)] = 10,000 \cdot [1 + R(0, 2)]^2$$

or, equivalently,

$$F(0, 1, 1) = \frac{[1 + R(0, 2)]^2}{1 + R(0, 1)} - 1$$

11.5.2 The Forward Contract Payoff

Taking the point of view of the seller, the forward contract payoff is equal to:

$$\text{Payoff} = F_t - P_T$$

Example 11.19
Consider a forward contract maturing at date T written on a bond whose coupon rate and price at date t are 6% and 105, respectively. The interest rate R to borrow money is equal to 5% and $T - t = 91$. Using equation (11.3), we draw below (Figure 11.4) the payoff for this forward contract taking the point of view of the seller.

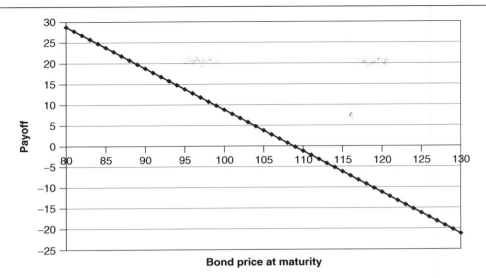

Figure 11.4   Forward contract payoff.

11.5.3   Relation between Forward and Futures Prices

There are no intermediary cash flows in a forward contract. On the other hand, because of the existence of margins in a futures contract designed to insure the default risk, there are the initial margin and intermediary cash flows that are the variation margins. As a consequence, forward and futures prices are not the same except in the case when interest rates are certain. We give the proof of this assertion in the appendix of this chapter.

11.6   Uses of Forwards and Futures

Forwards and futures can be used to fix today the financial conditions of a loan or investment in the future, to detect riskless arbitrage opportunities and to hedge a portfolio of fixed-income securities against any change in the yield curve. Futures also can be used to create pure speculation with leverage effect.

11.6.1   Pure Speculation with Leverage Effect

Like classic bonds, futures contracts move in the opposite direction to interest rates. This is why a speculator expecting a fall (rise) in interest rates will buy (sell) futures contracts. Besides futures contracts have three main advantages compared to classic bonds:

- *Because of small margin requirements, investors can benefit from substantial leverage effects.*

- *Short sales are much easier in the futures market than in the bond market.*

- *Transaction costs are very low.*

Example 11.20   Today, the gross price of a 5-year bond with $1,000 principal amount is 103.199. At the same moment, the price of the 5-year futures contract that expires in three months is 101.521. Its nominal amount is $1,000,000, and the deposit margin is $5,000. Two months later the price of the bond is 105.227 as the futures price is 103.537.

An investor with $1,000,000 at disposal anticipates that rates will decrease in a short-term period. He can either invest in the bond or in the futures contract:

- *With a position in the bond, he will gain $19,651 over the period:*

$$Absolute\ Gain = \frac{\$1,000,000}{\$1,000 \times 103.199\%} \times \$1,000 \times [105.227 - 103.199]\% = \$19,651$$

The quantity $\frac{\$1,000,000}{\$1,000 \times 103.199\%}$ gives him the number of bonds he invests in, which is 969 in our example.

- *With a position in the futures contract, he will gain $3,971,520 over the period:*

$$Absolute\ Gain = \frac{\$1,000,000}{\$5,000 \times 101.521\%} \times \$1,000,000 \times [103.537 - 101.521]\%$$

$$= \$3,971,520$$

The quantity $\frac{\$1,000,000}{\$5,000 \times 101.521\%}$ gives him the number of futures contract he invests in, which is 197 in our example.

The return rate of his investment is 1.965% with the bond and 397.16% with the futures contract. The difference of performance is due to the leverage effect of the futures contract, which is equal to $\frac{1,000,000}{5,000} = 200$ in the example.

11.6.2 Fixing Today the Financial Conditions of a Loan or Investment in the Future

Futures contracts as well as forward contracts can also be used to:

Fix Today the Financial Cost for a Loan in the Future

This is perhaps best understood through an example.

Example 11.21 On 04/05/01 a firm knows that it has to borrow $10 million on 06/15/01 for a 6-month period. This firm sells 10 futures contracts maturing on 06/15/01 whose underlying reference is the 6-month Libor and price 94. The contract size is equal to $1 million.

On 06/15/01, the 6-month Libor is 7%.

- *The firm borrows $10 million at a 7% rate and pays*

$$\$10,000,000 \times 7\% \times \frac{183}{360} = \$355,833$$

- *Its gain with the futures contract amounts to*

$$10 \times (7\% - 6\%) \times \frac{183}{360} \times \$1,000,000 = \$50,833$$

so that the net payment is equal to $305,000 which means a 6% guaranteed interest rate for the loan of the firm.

Fix Today the Total Return of an Investment in the Future

We illustrate that point through an example.

Example 11.22 On 04/05/01 a firm knows that it has to invest $1 million on 09/15/01 for a 3-month period. This firm buys a futures contract with size $1 million, maturing on 09/15/01 whose underlying asset is the 3-month Libor and price 95. So, it has guaranteed a 5% interest rate for its investment on 09/15/01.

11.6.3 Detecting Riskless Arbitrage Opportunities Using Futures

Arbitrage is a riskless transaction whose aim is to make profit by tracking abnormal price differences between products whose prices are linked by a strong relationship. By using a forward or a futures contract and the underlying asset of this contract, we can detect such opportunities and build such transactions. We distinguish two kinds of arbitrage:

- *Cash-and-carry arbitrage, which consists in buying the underlying asset and selling the forward or futures contract; this global transaction amounts to lending cash at a certain interest rate X. There is an arbitrage opportunity when the financing cost on the market is inferior to the lending rate X.*

- *Reverse cash-and-carry arbitrage, which consists in selling (short) the underlying asset and buying the forward or futures contract; this global transaction amounts to borrowing cash at a certain interest rate Y. There is an arbitrage opportunity when the investment rate on the market is superior to the borrowing rate Y.*

We now turn to an example of cash-and-carry arbitrage with T-bills, futures and repo.

Example 11.23   Cash-and-Carry Arbitrage with T-Bill, Futures and Repo

A pure arbitrageur observes the following prices on November 15, 2001:

- *The quoted price on a T-bill futures that expires on November 30 is 94.5. This contract delivers a 91-day T-bill at maturity.*

- *The 106-day T-bill yield that expires on March 1, 2002 is equal to 5.53%.*

- *The repo rate for 15 days is an annualized 5.3%.*

The T-bill yield r_f implied by the futures price is then given by the following formula:

$$r_f = 100 - 94.5 = 5.5\%$$

The arbitrageur first creates a synthetic loan by buying the T-bill and taking a short position on the T-bill futures:

- *he buys the 106-day T-bill at a price P of*

$$P = \$10,000,000 \times \left(1 - 5.53\%.\frac{106}{360}\right) = \$9,837,172$$

- *he shorts the T-bill futures at a price P_F of*

$$P_F = \$10,000,000 \times \left(1 - 5.5\%.\frac{91}{360}\right) = \$9,860,972$$

On November 30, he delivers the T-bill into the futures contract. Finally, this strategy creates a synthetic loan where the arbitrageur pays \$9,837,172 on November 15 and receives \$9,860,972 on November 30. The implied repo rate of this transaction over 15 days is given by the following formula:

$$\textit{Implied Repo Rate} = \frac{\$9,860,972 - \$9,837,172}{\$9,837,172} = 0.242\%$$

equivalent to an annualized rate of 5.807%

$$\textit{Annualized Rate} = 0.242\% \times \left(\frac{360}{15}\right) = 5.807\%$$

The next step of the arbitrage is to finance the long position in the T-bill between November 15 and November 30 on the repo market. The cost for the arbitrageur is the repo rate over the 15-day period, that is,

$$5.3\% \times \left(\frac{15}{360}\right) = 0.22\%$$

The arbitrageur has to pay a total of \$9,858,896:

$$\$9,837,172 \times (1 + 0.22\%) = \$9,858,896$$

The pure arbitrage is then equal to \$2,076:

$$\$9,860,972 - \$9,858,896 = \$2,076$$

Cash-and-carry arbitrage and reverse cash-and-carry arbitrage can also be detected by using bonds, futures and repo. In particular, when the implied repo rate given by equation (11.2) is superior to the repo rate on the market, there is an opportunity of cash-and-carry arbitrage. On the contrary, when the implied repo rate is inferior to the repo rate on the market, there is an opportunity of reverse cash-and-carry arbitrage.

11.6.4 Hedging Interest-Rate Risk Using Futures

Because of high liquidity and low cost due to low margin requirements, futures contracts are actually very often used in practice for hedging purposes.

We now consider a portfolio P of bonds and hedge it with futures using the three main hedging approaches we have seen in Chapters 5 and 6: the duration hedge, the duration/convexity hedge and the hedge using a three-factor model.

Duration Hedge

We use a one-order Taylor expansion to approximate the price change of portfolio P and of the futures contract (see Chapter 5 for a complete description of the method). As the underlying asset of the futures contract is fictive in general, we replace it with the grades of the underlying asset that are acceptable for delivering. In this case, the hedge ratio denoted by ϕ_f is

$$\phi_f = -\frac{\$Dur_P}{\$Dur_B} \times CF \qquad (11.4)$$

where $\$Dur_P$ and $\$Dur_B$ are the \$duration of portfolio P and the \$duration of the bond B (contained in the grades of the underlying assets and which can be the cheapest-to-deliver bond) as CF is the conversion factor of this bond.

Example 11.24 Consider now an investor who holds a bond portfolio whose principal value, price (in percentage of the face value) and modified duration are, respectively, $10,000,000, 102 and 8. He wishes to be hedged against a rise in interest rates. He uses as hedging instrument a futures contract whose features are the following:

- *size: $100,000*

- *$duration of bond B (contained in the grades of the underlying asset): −760.24 (in % of the size)*

- *conversion factor: 112.74%*

We find the hedge ratio ϕ_f

$$\phi_f = -\frac{10,000,000}{100,000} \times \frac{816}{760.24} \times 112.74\% \simeq 121$$

In the example, the investor has to sell 121 futures contracts.

Duration/Convexity Hedge

We now use a two-order Taylor expansion to approximate the price change of portfolio P and of the futures contract (see Chapter 6 for a complete description of the method). The idea of the hedge is to obtain a global portfolio that is both \$duration-neutral and \$convexity-neutral. Then we have to determine the quantities ϕ_1 and ϕ_2 to buy or sell in futures contracts F_1 and F_2 so that

$$\begin{cases} \phi_1 \dfrac{\$Dur_{B_1}}{CF_1} + \phi_2 \dfrac{\$Dur_{B_2}}{CF_2} = -\$Dur_P \\[2mm] \phi_1 \dfrac{\$Conv_{B_1}}{CF_1} + \phi_2 \dfrac{\$Conv_{B_2}}{CF_2} = -\$Conv_P \end{cases}$$

where $\$Dur_P (\$Conv_P)$, $\$Dur_{B_1}(\$Conv_{B_1})$ and $\$Dur_{B_2}(\$Conv_{B_2})$ are, respectively, the \$duration ($\$convexity) of portfolio P and of the two bonds B_1 and B_2, which are contained in the grades of the underlying asset of futures contracts F_1 and F_2. CF_1 and CF_2 are the two conversion factors associated with the two bonds B_1 and B_2.

Examples of similar hedges have been previously developed in Chapters 6 and 10 when using bonds and swaps as hedging instruments.

Hedge in a Three-Factor Model

The idea of the hedge is to create a global portfolio with portfolio P and three futures contracts, and to make it neutral to changes in the three level, slope and curvature factors denoted by β_0, β_1 and β_2 (see Chapter 6 for a complete description of the method). Then we have to determine the quantities ϕ_1, ϕ_2 and ϕ_3 to buy or sell in futures contracts F_1, F_2 and F_3 so that

$$
\begin{cases}
\dfrac{\phi_1}{CF_1}\dfrac{\partial B_1}{\partial \beta_0} + \dfrac{\phi_2}{CF_2}\dfrac{\partial B_2}{\partial \beta_0} + \dfrac{\phi_3}{CF_3}\dfrac{\partial B_3}{\partial \beta_0} = -\dfrac{\partial P}{\partial \beta_0} \\[2ex]
\dfrac{\phi_1}{CF_1}\dfrac{\partial B_1}{\partial \beta_1} + \dfrac{\phi_2}{CF_2}\dfrac{\partial B_2}{\partial \beta_1} + \dfrac{\phi_3}{CF_3}\dfrac{\partial B_3}{\partial \beta_1} = -\dfrac{\partial P}{\partial \beta_1} \\[2ex]
\dfrac{\phi_1}{CF_1}\dfrac{\partial B_1}{\partial \beta_2} + \dfrac{\phi_2}{CF_2}\dfrac{\partial B_2}{\partial \beta_2} + \dfrac{\phi_3}{CF_3}\dfrac{\partial B_3}{\partial \beta_2} = -\dfrac{\partial P}{\partial \beta_2}
\end{cases}
$$

where $\frac{\partial P}{\partial \beta_j}$, $\frac{\partial B_1}{\partial \beta_j}$, $\frac{\partial B_2}{\partial \beta_j}$ and $\frac{\partial B_3}{\partial \beta_j}$ are, respectively, the sensitivity of portfolio P and of bonds B_1, B_2 and B_3 with respect to factors β_j for $j = 0, 1, 2$. Bonds B_1, B_2 and B_3 are contained in the grades of the underlying asset of futures contracts F_1, F_2 and F_3. CF_1, CF_2 and CF_3 are the three conversion factors associated with the three bonds B_1, B_2 and B_3.

Examples of similar hedges have been previously developed in Chapters 6 and 10 when using bonds and swaps as hedging instruments.

11.7 End of Chapter Summary

A *forward contract* or a *futures contract* is an agreement made on some initial date to buy (long position) or to sell (short position) a security on a future date called the *delivery date* and at a given price called the *forward* or *futures price*. The forward or futures price is computed so that the value of the contract on the initial date is equal to zero. Futures contracts are similar to forward contracts but are standardized and exchanged on recognized futures markets with a clearing house ensuring that default risk is minimized. On the contrary, forward contracts are designed to meet specific individual requirements and traded over the counter. Because there are no intermediary cash flows in a forward contract, while futures contracts are subject to margin calls, forward and futures prices are not the same, except in the case when interest rates are certain.

The underlying reference of the contract can be an interest rate like the 3-month Libor rate, a Treasury bill such as the 13-week T-bill or a bond such as the 10-year T-bond. When the underlying asset is an interest rate, the futures price is quoted as 100 minus this interest rate. When the underlying asset is a bill, the futures price is quoted as 100 minus the yield on a discount basis. When the underlying asset is a bond, it is quoted in the same way as a bond, that is, in percentage of the nominal value of the underlying asset.

When the underlying asset of a futures contract is fictitious, the seller of the contract has to deliver a real asset that may differ from the fictitious asset in terms of coupon rate and maturity. That is why we compute a *conversion factor*. The conversion factor tells you how many units of the actual assets are worth as much as one unit of the fictive underlying asset. Because the conversion factor is an imperfect measure, the seller may choose which of the available bonds is the *cheapest to deliver*.

Forwards and futures can be used to fix today the financial conditions of a loan or investment in the future, to perform arbitrage trades (cash-and-carry arbitrage or reverse cash-and-carry arbitrage), and to hedge a portfolio of fixed-income securities against any change in the yield curve. Futures can also be used to create pure speculation with leverage effect.

11.8 References and Further Reading

11.8.1 Books and Papers

Black, F., 1976, "The Pricing of Commodity Contracts", *Journal of Financial Economics*, **3**(1/2), 167–179.

Clare, A., M. Ioannides, and F.S. Skinner, 2000, "Hedging Corporate Bonds with Stock Index Futures: A Word of Caution", *Journal of Fixed Income*, **10**(2), 25–34.

Cox, J.C., J.E. Ingersoll, and S.A. Ross, 1981, "The Relation between Forward Prices and Futures Prices", *Journal of Financial Economics*, **9**(4), 321–346.

Dynkin, L., J. Hyman, and P. Lindner, 2002, "Hedging and Replication of Fixed-Income Portfolios", *Journal of Fixed Income*, **11**(4), 43–63.

Fabozzi, F.J., (Editor), 2000, *The Handbook of Fixed Income Securities*, 6th Edition, McGraw-Hill, New York.

Hull, J., 2000, *Options, Futures and Other Derivatives*, Prentice Hall, New York.

Kishimoto, N., 1998, "Duration and Convexity of Coupon Bond Futures", *Journal of Fixed Income*, **8**(1), 79–83.

Kolb, R.W., and R. Chiang, 1981, "Improving Hedging Performance Using Interest Rate Futures", *Financial Management*, **10**, 72–79.

Kolb, R.W., and R. Chiang, 1982, "Duration, Immunization and Hedging with Interest Rate Futures", *Journal of Financial Research*, **5**(2), 161–170.

Mussavian, M., 2002, "When Should Investors Trade in the European Futures Markets?" *Journal of Alternative Investments*, **5**(1), 43–54.

Poncet, P., R. Portait, and S. Hayat, 2001, *Mathématiques Financières: Evaluation des Actifs et Analyse du Risque*, 3rd Edition, Dalloz, Paris.

Rendleman, R.J., 1999, "Duration-Based Hedging with Treasury Bond Futures", *Journal of Fixed Income*, **9**(1), 84–91.

Senchak, A.J., and J.C. Easterwood, 1983, "Cross Hedging CDs with Treasury Bill Futures", *Journal of Futures Markets*, **3**, 429–438.

Siegel, D.R., and D.F. Siegel, 1990, *Futures Markets*, Dryden Press, Chicago.

11.8.2 Websites of Futures Markets and of the Futures Industry Association

www.cme.com.

www.cbot.com.

www.sfe.com.

Fixed Income Securities

www.tiffe.org.jp.

www.hkfe.com.

www.me.org.

www.eurexchange.com.

www.liffe.com.

www.matif.fr.

www.futuresindustry.org.

11.9 Problems

Exercise 11.1   The Cheapest to Deliver on the Repartition Date

We are on the repartition date. Consider a futures contract with size Eur100,000 whose price is 95% and three bonds denoted by A, B and C with the following features. What is the bond that the seller of the futures contract will choose to deliver?

	Clean price (%)	Conversion factor (%)
Bond A	112.67	119.96
Bond B	111.54	118.66
Bond C	111.47	119.78

Exercise 11.2   Forward Price of a Contract Written on a Bond

On 05/30/01, we consider a forward contract maturing in 3 months written on a bond whose nominal value, coupon rate and price are, respectively, $1,000, 10% and 125. Assuming that the 3-month Euribor is equal to 5%, what is the forward price of this contract?

Exercise 11.3   We consider a forward contract maturing at date T written on a bond whose nominal value, coupon rate and price at date t are $1,000, 4% and 99, respectively. $T - t = 26$ days, and the 26-day Euribor is 3.5%. Draw below the payoff for this forward contract taking the point of view of the buyer.

Exercise 11.4   An investor holds a bond portfolio with principal value $10,000,000 whose price and modified duration are, respectively, 112 and 9.21. He wishes to be hedged against a rise in interest rates by selling futures contracts written on a bond. Suppose the futures price of the contract is 105.2. The contract size is $100,000. The conversion factor for the cheapest to deliver is equal to 98.1%. The cheapest to deliver has a modified duration equal to 8.

1. Give a proof of the hedge ratio ϕ_f as obtained in equation (11.4).
2. Determine the number of contracts ϕ_f he has to sell.

Exercise 11.5   The treasurer of a firm knows today that he will have to invest a nominal amount of Eur50,000,000 in a particular bond A in one month. Today, this bond quotes 116.414 (the accrued interest is included in the price). He fears a decrease in rates and then uses the futures market to hedge his interest-rate risk. The price of the 10-year futures contract that expires in one month is 98.55. Its nominal amount is Eur100,000. The conversion factor for bond A is 1.18125.

1. Does the treasurer have to buy or sell futures contracts to hedge his interest-rate risk?
2. What is the position he has to take on the futures market?
3. One month later, the price of bond A is 121.137 as the price of the futures contract is 102.55. What is the result of the hedge transaction for the treasurer?

Exercise 11.6   Hedging a Bond Position Using Eurodollar Futures
Suppose that you are a bond trader. You have just sold $10,000,000 par value of a 10% coupon bond that matures in exactly 3/4 of a year. The yield is 6.5%. Compounding frequency is semiannual. You do not have the bond in inventory, but think you can purchase it in the market tomorrow. You want to hedge your interest-rate risk overnight with Eurodollar futures. Do you buy or sell? How many contracts do you need?

Exercise 11.7   For the following problems, assume that you are a T-bill trader at an investment bank. The dollar value of your inventory is $7,500,000. The modified duration of your inventory position is 0.7 years.

1. You consider hedging your interest-rate risk with Eurodollar futures. Do you buy or sell? How many contracts do you buy or sell? We assume that the Eurodollar futures buyer loses $25 for every basis point the interest rate goes up.
2. You consider hedging your interest-rate risk with T-bill futures. Do you buy or sell? How many contracts do you buy or sell? We assume that the T-bill futures buyer loses $25 for every basis point the interest rate goes up.
3. Is one of these methods any better than the other? Why?

Exercise 11.8   An investor has a nominal amount of $50,000,000 in a bullet bond A whose gross price (in % of the face value) and modified duration are, respectively, 92.971 and 7.56. We consider a futures contract on a coupon bond whose characteristics are the following:

- contract size: $100,000;
- gross price (in % of the face value) and modified duration of the cheapest to deliver: 107.625 and 7.61, respectively;
- conversion factor: 1.5312.

1. We estimate the relationship between the yield to maturity of bond A, denoted by y_A, and the yield to maturity of the cheapest to deliver, denoted by y_{CTD}. The result is:

$$\Delta y_A \simeq 1.21 \times \Delta y_{CTD}$$

What does it mean?
2. What is the number of futures contracts that the investor has to sell?

Exercise 11.9   A firm intends to issue in two months a bullet bond debt with Eur200,000,000 principal amount. Features of the bond are the following:

- annual coupon rate: 8%
- maturity: 9 years.

Today, rates (with no default risk) are at a 7% level.

1. Which change in rates is unfavorable for the issuer?
2. We suppose that a futures contract exists on the market with a 2-month maturity. Explain why a correct position taken on this contract enables the firm to hedge its interest-rate risk.
3. The futures contract delivers a bond with a 10-year maturity and a 10% annual coupon rate. Its nominal amount is Eur1,000,000. The price of the futures contract is 121.105 and the modified duration of the underlying bond is 6.6057. What is the position that the firm has to take in order to hedge interest-rate risk?

Exercise 11.10   Speculation with Futures

Today, the gross price of a 10-year bond with $1,000 principal amount is 116.277. At the same moment, the price of the 10-year futures contract that expires in 2 months is 98.03. Its nominal amount is $100,000, and the deposit margin is $1,000. One month later, the price of the bond is 120.815 as the futures price is 102.24.

1. What is the leverage effect on this futures contract?
2. An investor anticipates that rates will decrease in a short-term period. His cash at disposal is $100,000.

   (a) What is the position he can take on the market using the bond? What is his absolute gain after one month? What is the return rate of his investment?
   (b) Same question as the previous one using the futures contract?
   (c) Conclude.

Exercise 11.11   Cash-and-Carry Arbitrage with T-Bill, Futures and Repo

A pure arbitrageur observes the following prices on December 13, 2000:

- The quoted price on a T-bill futures that expires on December 30 is 97.7. This contract delivers a 92-day T-bill at maturity.
- The 109-day T-bill yield that expires on April 1, 2001, is equal to 2.4%.
- The repo rate for 17 days is an annualized 2.2%.

1. What is the T-bill yield implied by the futures price?
2. Describe the cash-and-carry arbitrage using T-bill, futures and repo for a $100 million face value.

Exercise 11.12   Consider on 11/14/01 a futures contract whose nominal amount, price and maturity are, respectively, $1,000,000, 106.59 and 12/14/01. Three bonds are acceptable for delivery whose features are the following:

Bond	Maturity	Coupon rate (%)	Clean price	Conversion factor
Bond 1	10/25/10	5.50	106.51	99.69
Bond 2	04/25/11	5.25	104.89	98.28
Bond 3	10/25/11	8.50	130.45	122.13

These three bonds deliver annual coupon.

1. What is the cheapest to deliver?
2. The 2-month repo rate is 3.66%. Is there any cash-and-carry arbitrage? For any of them, give the gain for a $100 million face value.

Exercise 11.13   Deriving the Interbank Zero-Coupon Yield Curve
On 07/15/02, we get from the market the following Euribor rates, futures contract prices and swap rates:

Maturity	Euribor rate (%)	Contract maturity	Futures price	Maturity	Swap rate (%)
07/22/02	6.51	08/15/02	94.21	07/15/04	6.31
07/29/02	6.37	11/15/02	94.29	07/15/05	6.45
08/15/02	6.21	02/15/03	94.31	07/15/06	6.55
09/15/02	6.13	05/15/03	94.09	07/15/07	6.64
10/15/02	6.02	08/15/03	93.88	07/15/08	6.73
—	—	11/15/03	93.74	07/15/09	6.80
—	—	02/15/04	93.20	07/15/10	6.85
—	—	—	—	07/15/11	6.87
—	—	—	—	07/15/12	6.88

Note that the underlying asset of the futures contract is a 3-month Euribor rate. For example, the first contract matures on 08/15/02, and the underlying asset matures three months later on 11/15/02.

1. Find the implied zero-coupon rates from the market data.
2. Draw the zero-coupon yield curve by building a linear interpolation between the implied zero-coupon rates.

11.10 Appendix: Forward and Futures Prices Are Identical When Interest Rates Are Constant

Consider a forward contract and a futures contract beginning at date $t = 0$ and maturing at date T. These two contracts are written on the same asset. The forward and futures price at date $t = 0$ are, respectively, G_0 and F_0. Besides, we suppose that there is no initial investment, that the risk-free arbitrage opportunities are absent, that any number of contracts may be traded (including noninteger numbers) and that interest rates at a level of r, whatever the maturity, stay constant between $t = 0$ and T. This is not really true in the case of the futures contract because of the existence of the initial margin. Besides, arbitrage opportunities may exist in the market, we can only trade integer numbers of contracts and interest rates are uncertain.

Fixed Income Securities

- *The first strategy consists in buying* $\left(1 + \frac{rT}{365}\right)$ *forward contracts that delivers at maturity* $(P_T - G_0) \times \left(1 + \frac{rT}{365}\right)$.

- *The second strategy consists in buying several futures contracts at different dates in the future, closing them one day later and investing or borrowing the net position in the market:*

  - *We buy* $\left(1 + \frac{r}{365}\right)$ *futures contract at date* $t = 0$, *which allows to receive* $F_1 - F_0$ *at date* $t = 1$. *The position is closed out at date* $t = 1$ *and the net cash flow is invested or borrowed in the market up to the expiry date* T *to finally generate the payoff* $(F_1 - F_0) \times \left(1 + \frac{rT}{365}\right)$.

  - *We buy* $\left(1 + \frac{2r}{365}\right)$ *futures contract at date* $t = 1$, *which allows to receive* $F_2 - F_1$ *at date* $t = 2$. *The position is closed out at date* $t = 2$ *and the net cash flow is invested or borrowed in the market up to the expiry date* T *to finally generate the payoff* $(F_2 - F_1) \times \left(1 + \frac{rT}{365}\right)$.

  - ...

  - *We buy* $\left(1 + \frac{(j+1)r}{365}\right)$ *futures contract at date* $t = j$, *which allows to receive* $F_{j+1} - F_j$ *at date* $t = j + 1$. *The position is closed out at date* $t = j + 1$ *and the net cash flow is invested or borrowed in the market up to the expiry date* T *to finally generate the payoff* $(F_{j+1} - F_j) \times \left(1 + \frac{rT}{365}\right)$.

  - ...

  - *We buy* $\left(1 + \frac{rT}{365}\right)$ *futures contract at date* $t = T - 1$, *which allows to receive* $P_T - F_{T-1}$ *at date* $t = T$. *The position closed out at date* $t = T$ *to finally generate the payoff* $(P_T - F_{T-1}) \times \left(1 + \frac{rT}{365}\right)$.

The sum at date T of all these cash flows is equal to:

$$(F_1 - F_0) \times \left(1 + \frac{rT}{365}\right) + (F_2 - F_1) \times \left(1 + \frac{rT}{365}\right) + \cdots + (P_T - F_{T-1}) \times \left(1 + \frac{rT}{365}\right)$$

$$= (P_T - F_0) \times \left(1 + \frac{rT}{365}\right)$$

The two strategies have a zero cash outlay and are self-financing. In the absence of arbitrage opportunities, the cash flows generated at date T must be the same. So we obtain

$$(P_T - G_0) \times \left(1 + \frac{rT}{365}\right) = (P_T - F_0) \times \left(1 + \frac{rT}{365}\right)$$

and finally

$$G_0 = F_0$$

which concludes the proof.

Modeling the Term Structure of Interest Rates and Credit Spreads

PART VI

Pricing interest-rate derivatives is a challenging task that not only requires the use of the current term structure of interest rates, as would be the case for pricing straight bonds, but also a model that describes how the term structure is going to evolve over time. This is because the payoff of these instruments is contingent upon the future values of interest rates. In Chapter 12, we introduce a series of popular interest-rate models. In Chapter 13, we present an application of dynamic models to the analysis of credit spreads.

Generally speaking, the material devoted to modeling the term structure and pricing interest-rate derivatives is more technical. To alleviate the burden for the nontechnically oriented reader, we have consistently favored intuition and economic analysis over mathematical developments. We have also chosen to focus most of our attention to discrete-time models, the understanding of which only requires a relatively limited level of mathematical sophistication (it essentially includes basic notions of calculus and statistics), while only the main results have been introduced for their continuous-time counterparts, and some of the most technical aspects have been relegated to a dedicated appendix (see Appendix 2 of Chapter 12). Even though a good understanding of the concepts behind the models of the term structure is a key to understanding the pricing and hedging of fixed-income derivatives (which we cover in Chapters 14, 15 and 16), the appendices and parts of Section 12.3 of Chapter 12 can nonetheless be skipped by the nonquantitatively oriented reader without impeding his/her ability to understand most of the remaining material.

12 Modeling the Yield Curve Dynamics

We have argued in previous chapters that the pricing (and hedging) of assets paying cash flows that are known with certainty at the present date (e.g., plain vanilla bonds) boils down to a computation of the sum of these cash flows, discounted at a suitable rate. The challenge for the bond portfolio manager is therefore limited to being able to have access to a robust methodology for extracting implied zero-coupon prices from market prices. This is covered in detail in Chapter 4.

On the other hand, pricing and hedging fixed-income securities that pay uncertain cash flows (e.g., options on bonds) is more involved. It requires not only the knowledge on discount factors at the present date but also some kind of understanding of how these discount factors (i.e., the term structure of pure discount rates) are going to evolve over time. In particular, one needs to account for potential correlations between the discount factor and the promised payoff. Some dynamic model of the term structure of interest rates is therefore needed to describe the explicit nature of the variables of interest in the valuation formula.[1]

Merton's (1973) model and Vasicek's (1977) model are the first examples of attempts to model the yield-curve dynamics. Since then, many models have been introduced in the literature, and it has become a somewhat daunting task for the practitioner to decide which to use. We borrow from Rogers (1995) the following list of criteria that a good model should satisfy. In order to price and hedge fixed-income derivatives efficiently, a model should be

- *flexible enough to capture a variety of situations that might be encountered in practice (in particular, a variety of possible shapes of the term structure of interest rates);*

- *well specified, in the sense that the model inputs should be observable or at least easy to estimate;*

- *consistent with reference market prices;*

- *simple enough to allow for fast numerical computation;*

- *realistic (e.g., it excludes the possibility of negative values for the interest rate); and*

- *coherent, from a theoretical standpoint (e.g., it excludes the possibility of arbitrage opportunity).*

---

[1]Practitioners still widely use Black's (1976) model, although it is not an interest-rate model. This model has become a benchmark for the pricing of futures options, caps, floors and swaptions (see Chapter 15) in early days, when there were no real interest-rate models that were plausible alternatives. It has remained so popular among practitioners that it is actually now used in the calibration of other interest-rate models (see Chapter 15, Appendix 5 for a description of Brace, Gatarek and Musiela (1997) and Jamshidian (1997) "market models.").

In what follows, we attempt to provide the reader with a synthetic overview of existing models, while emphasizing the pros and cons of competing approaches. We first consider a discrete-time binomial setting, and then discuss some popular continuous-time models, starting with single-factor models, and then moving to multifactor specifications. Finally, we cover the more recently introduced *arbitrage models*, which enjoy an appealing built-in property of generating bond prices consistent with market prices.

12.1 The Binomial Interest-Rate Tree Methodology

This way of modeling interest-rate dynamics is most frequently used in the market place. The interest-rate tree concept it is based on is a simple description of the evolution of the short-term interest rate over time.[2]

12.1.1 Building an Interest-Rate Tree

In a binomial interest-rate tree model, it is assumed that, given today's level of the short-term interest rate r, the next-period short interest rate, in period 1, can take on only two possible values: an upper value r_u (where the subscript u stands for upper) and a lower value r_l (where the subscript l stands for lower) with equal probability .5. In period 2, the short-term interest rate can take on four possible values: r_{uu}, r_{lu}, r_{ul} and r_{ll}. More generally, in period n, the short-term interest rate can take on 2^n values.

The implementation of such a tree, which is called a *nonrecombining tree*, is very time-consuming and computationally inefficient. For instance, pricing a 30-year callable bond (see Chapter 14) with annual coupon payments would require the computation of over 1 billion interest-rate values in period 30. For a 30-year bond with semiannual coupon payments, the number of values to be calculated in period 60 would be even greater than 10^{18}!

In practice, market participants prefer to use a recombining binomial interest-rate tree, which means that an upward–downward sequence leads to the same result as a downward–upward sequence. For example, $r_{lu} = r_{ul}$. All in all, the short-term interest rate takes only 3, as opposed to 4, values on period 2. There is a .25 probability of reaching the node r_{uu} or the node r_{ll}, while there is a .5 probability to reach the intermediate state, since $r_{lu} = r_{ul}$. This is a binomial distribution. In period n, it can take on $n + 1$ values with the probability of reaching node $r_{ku,(n-k)l}$ given by $C_n^k \times \left(\frac{1}{2}\right)^k \times \left(\frac{1}{2}\right)^{n-k}$, where $C_n^k = \frac{n!}{k!(n-k)!}$ is the number of paths with k up moves and $n - k$ down moves in n steps. This simplification greatly reduces the number of values to estimate on period 30 (respectively, period 60) for a 30-year callable bond with annual (respectively, semiannual) coupon payments to 31 (respectively, 61).

---

[2] We focus in this section on binomial trees, but there also exist trinomial interest-rate trees (see Appendix 1 of this chapter, where we detail the Hull and White (1994a, 1994b, 1994c, 1995, 1996) trinomial lattice).

Formally, we have

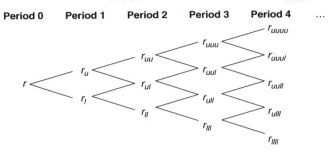

Another way to describe this process is to write down that the changes in the short-term interest rate r are generated from the following equation

$$\Delta r_t = r_{t+\Delta t} - r_t = \sigma \varepsilon_t \sqrt{\Delta t}$$

or more generally

$$\Delta r_t = r_{t+\Delta t} - r_t = \mu \Delta t + \sigma \varepsilon_t \sqrt{\Delta t} \tag{12.1}$$

where

Δr designates the change in the short-term interest rate over one period;

Δt designates the change in time from one period to another;

μ designates the expected absolute change on the short-term interest rate per time unit, which in general can be a function of time t, the short-term interest rate r and potentially some other state variable (in the binomial setting presented above, we have actually considered for simplicity that $\mu = 0$; this can be seen from the fact that the probability of an up and a down move were both equal to $1/2$);

σ designates the magnitude, or standard deviation of the absolute change in the short-term interest rate per time unit, which in general can be a function of time t, the short-term interest rate r and potentially some other state variable;

ε_t designates independent Bernoulli distributed variables that take on the values $+1$ and -1 with equal probabilities.

Because the binomial distribution converges to a Gaussian distribution as we let the number of time steps increase, we guess that the binomial process and the one described in equation (12.1) are very similar. One might wonder what exactly is the limit of the process described in equation (12.1) when Δt goes to zero, that is, when we go from a discrete-time to a continuous-time setting. We shall discuss this in Section 12.2, devoted to continuous-time models.

We sometimes prefer to use the following model:

$$\Delta \ln r_t = \ln r_{t+\Delta t} - \ln r_t = \mu \Delta t + \sigma \varepsilon_t \sqrt{\Delta t} \tag{12.2}$$

This is similar to the model in equation (12.1), except that it is written on relative changes of interest rates (proxied by $\ln r_{t+\Delta t} - \ln r_t = \ln \frac{r_{t+\Delta t}}{r_t} \simeq \frac{r_{t+\Delta t}}{r_t} - 1$), as opposed to focusing on absolute changes on interest rates ($\Delta r_t = r_{t+\Delta t} - r_t$). The reason we generally prefer to model the changes in the natural log of the interest rates is that it prevents interest rates from becoming negative with positive probability. It is actually easy to see that one shortcoming of model (12.1) is that after a sufficiently large number of down moves, the interest rates can become negative with positive probability, whatever the initial value of interest rates. A model written on relative changes of interest rates allows us to avoid this undesirable feature.

12.1.2 Calibrating an Interest-Rate Tree

The next step is to calibrate the model in such a way that it is consistent with the actual dynamics of the short-term interest rate. The determinant characteristic of an arbitrage-free interest-rate tree is that it is calibrated to the current zero-coupon fitted term structure of Treasury bonds or Interbank instruments. In what follows, we explain how to perform this calibration exercise in the context of a model written on relative changes of interest rates, as in equation (12.2).

Let us now examine how the upper and lower values are determined. We denote by σ the assumed volatility of the short-term interest rate, T the maturity (expressed in periods) of the bond to be priced and n the number of periods of the tree. From equation (12.2), we have at date 0

$$\Delta \ln r_0 = \ln r_{\Delta t} - \ln r_0 = \mu \Delta t + \sigma \varepsilon_0 \sqrt{\frac{T}{n}}$$

or

$$\ln r_u = \ln r_0 + \mu \Delta t + \sigma \sqrt{\frac{T}{n}}$$

$$\ln r_l = \ln r_0 + \mu \Delta t - \sigma \sqrt{\frac{T}{n}}$$

Therefore,

$$\ln r_u - \ln r_l = 2\sigma \sqrt{\frac{T}{n}} \Leftrightarrow r_u = r_l \exp\left(2\sigma \sqrt{\frac{T}{n}}\right)$$

More generally, we have on period k

$$r_{(k+1)u} = r_{(k+1)l} \exp\left(2(k+1)\sigma \sqrt{\frac{T}{n}}\right)$$

where $r_{(k+1)u} = r_{\underbrace{uu...u}_{k+1}}$ and $r_{(k+1)l} = r_{\underbrace{ll...l}_{k+1}}$.

We may now proceed to the calibration of the interest-rate tree. We assume for simplicity that the time span between two periods is $\frac{T}{n} = 1$ year. The risk-free interest-rate tree is constructed by using constant maturity Treasury-bond zero-coupon yields derived from highly liquid bonds. The process is an iterative one. First, the values of the 1-year risk-free rate a year from now are determined using a 2-year Treasury par yield bond. Then, the values of the 1-year risk-free rate 2 years from now are determined using a 3-year Treasury par yield bond and so on.

We denote by y_n the par Treasury-bond yield maturing in n years. First of all, we must choose an arbitrary value for the 1-year interest-rate volatility σ. We can, for example, use some estimate of the historical volatility over the last 1 year. We start by determining r_u, the value of the short-term interest rate one step ahead in case of an up move, and r_l, the value of the short-term interest rate one step ahead in case of a down move. The price 1 year from now of the 2-year par Treasury bond can take 2 values: a value P_u associated with r_u and a value P_l associated with r_l. We have

$$P_u = \frac{100 + y_2}{(1 + r_u)}$$

and

$$P_l = \frac{100 + y_2}{(1 + r_l)}$$

The current price of the 2-year par Treasury bond is equal to 100. So, as the probability of the r_u state and the probability of the r_l state are assumed to be equal to .5, we can write[3]

$$\frac{1}{2}\left(\frac{P_u + y_2}{1 + y_1} + \frac{P_l + y_2}{1 + y_1}\right) = 100$$

$$\frac{1}{2}\left(\frac{\frac{100 + y_2}{(1 + r_u)} + y_2}{1 + y_1} + \frac{\frac{100 + y_2}{(1 + r_l)} + y_2}{1 + y_1}\right) = 100$$

As

$$r_u = r_l \exp(2\sigma)$$

we have

$$\frac{1}{2}\left(\frac{\frac{100 + y_2}{(1 + r_l \exp(2\sigma))} + y_2}{1 + y_1} + \frac{\frac{100 + y_2}{(1 + r_l)} + y_2}{1 + y_1}\right) = 100$$

From this equation, we find the values of r_l, with y_1, y_2, and σ being known.

Let us now move on to the computation of r_{uu}, r_{ul} and r_{ll}. The price 2 years from now of the 3-year par Treasury bond can take 3 values: a value P'_{uu} associated with r_{uu}, a value P'_{ul} associated with r_{ul} and a value P'_{ll} associated with r_{ll}. We have

$$P'_{uu} = \frac{100 + y_3}{(1 + r_{uu})}$$

$$P'_{ul} = \frac{100 + y_3}{(1 + r_{ul})}$$

and

$$P'_{ll} = \frac{100 + y_3}{(1 + r_{ll})}$$

The price 1 year from now of the 3-year par Treasury bond can take 2 values: a value P'_u associated with r_u and a value P'_l associated with r_l. We have

$$P'_u = \frac{1}{2}\left(\frac{P'_{uu} + y_3}{1 + r_u} + \frac{P'_{ul} + y_3}{1 + r_u}\right)$$

---

[3]This is based upon the assumption of risk-neutrality. In general, the formula still applies, except that the price is equal to the discounted expected value of the cash flow, where expectation is taken with respect to a set of risk-adjusted probabilities, as opposed to actual probabilities. For more on risk-adjusted probabilities, we refer the reader to Ho and Lee's (1986) discrete-time arbitrage model in Section 12.3.1 for an example of risk-adjustment in a binomial model of bond prices, and to the exposition of the binomial model for stock prices in Section 14.5.2 in Chapter 14.

Fixed Income Securities

and

$$P_l' = \frac{1}{2}\left(\frac{P_{ul}' + y_3}{1 + r_l} + \frac{P_{ll}' + y_3}{1 + r_l}\right)$$

The current price of the 3-year par Treasury bond is equal to 100. So,

$$\frac{1}{2}\left(\frac{P_u' + y_3}{1 + y_1} + \frac{P_l' + y_3}{1 + y_1}\right) = 100$$

$$\frac{1}{2}\left(\frac{\frac{1}{2}\left(\frac{\frac{100 + y_3}{(1 + r_{uu})} + y_3}{1 + r_u} + \frac{\frac{100 + y_3}{(1 + r_{ul})} + y_3}{1 + r_u}\right) + y_3}{1 + y_1}\right.$$

$$\left. + \frac{\frac{1}{2}\left(\frac{\frac{100 + y_3}{(1 + r_{ul})} + y_3}{1 + r_l} + \frac{\frac{100 + y_3}{(1 + r_{ll})} + y_3}{1 + r_l}\right) + y_3}{1 + y_1}\right) = 100$$

As

$$r_{uu} = r_{ll}\exp(4\sigma)$$

and

$$r_{ul} = r_{ll}\exp(2\sigma)$$

we have

$$\frac{1}{2}\left(\frac{\frac{1}{2}\left(\frac{\frac{100 + y_3}{(1 + r_{ll}\exp(4\sigma))} + y_3}{1 + r_u} + \frac{\frac{100 + y_3}{(1 + r_{ll}\exp(2\sigma))} + y_3}{1 + r_u}\right) + y_3}{1 + y_1}\right.$$

$$\left. + \frac{\frac{1}{2}\left(\frac{\frac{100 + y_3}{(1 + r_{ll}\exp(2\sigma))} + y_3}{1 + r_l} + \frac{\frac{100 + y_3}{(1 + r_{ll})} + y_3}{1 + r_l}\right) + y_3}{1 + y_1}\right) = 100$$

From this equation, we find the values of r_{ll}, with y_1, y_2, y_3, r_u, r_l and σ being already known. We keep repeating this process until the longest maturity of the term structure of interest rates. We now turn to an example.

Example 12.1 We consider today's Treasury-bond par yield curve

Maturity (in years)	Par yield (%)
1	4.00
2	4.30
3	4.50

We want to compute a 3-year binomial interest-rate tree, assuming a volatility of 1% for the 1-year interest rate. We have $T = 3$ and $n = 3$. Let us begin with the computation of r_u and r_l. Using the above formulas, we have

$$\frac{1}{2}\left(\frac{\dfrac{100 + 4.3}{(1 + r_l\exp(2/100))} + 4.3}{1 + 4\%} + \frac{\dfrac{100 + 4.3}{(1 + r_l)} + 4.3}{1 + 4\%} \right) = 100$$

which gives

$$r_l = 4.57\%$$

and

$$r_u = r_l\exp(2/100) = 4.66\%$$

Applying the above formulas, we find similarly

$$r_{ll} = 4.83\%$$

$$r_{ul} = r_{ll}\exp(2/100) = 4.93\%$$

and

$$r_{uu} = r_{ll}\exp(4/100) = 5.03\%$$

We now turn to continuous-time interest-rate models.

12.2 Continuous-Time Models

A general (one-factor) continuous-time model for short-term interest-rate changes may be given in the following form:

$$dr_t = \mu(t, r_t)\,dt + \sigma(t, r_t)\,dW_t \tag{12.3}$$

This equation (which is known under the fancy name of *stochastic differential equation (SDE)*) should simply be thought of as the limit of equation (12.1) when Δt goes to zero, that is, as we let the time increment become infinitesimal (hence the term *continuous time*).[4] Here, $\mu(t, r_t)$ and $\sigma(t, r_t)$ are the expected value and the standard deviation of the instantaneous interest-rate variation, respectively. W is known as a *Brownian motion*, a process with independent normally distributed increments. Intuitively, $dW_t = W_{t+dt} - W_t$ can be thought of as $\varepsilon_t \sqrt{dt}$, where ε_t are independent normally distributed random variables with zero mean and a unit variance. We give a formal content to these intuitions, and provide the reader with an introduction to the theory of stochastic processes in continuous time, in a dedicated appendix (see Appendix 2 of this chapter).

In what follows, we take a look at a series of special cases of such continuous-time models, starting with single-factor models, and then moving to multifactor models.

12.2.1 Single-Factor Models

The idea common to all one-factor models of the term structure is to consider the whole yield curve as a function of a single state variable. There is a consensus about the fact that if there is only one factor, then the short-term interest rate should be that factor. Single-factor models only differ in that they are based on different models for short-term rate dynamics. The intuition for such models comes from the fact that, to a first-order approximation, prices of bonds of different maturities tend to move in a correlated way, in response to variations in the short-term interest rate (viewed as the rate of return on a default-free short-term bond, namely, a T-bill with short residual maturity). In other words, changes in the short rate are used as a proxy for changes in the level of the term structure, which, as argued in Chapter 3, accounts for a large fraction of the dynamics of the term structure.

Classification of Various Models

Empirical studies of yield-curve dynamics have allowed us to obtain useful insights into the features any consistent model should display (see Chapter 3). In particular, the important requirements, which a model should satisfy to be consistent with stylized empirical facts, are as follows:

- *(Real) interest rates cannot be negative [this feature is captured in the squared root process used in Cox, Ingersoll and Ross (1985), for example].*

- *High (low) values of interest rates are more likely to be followed by lower (higher) values, rather than higher (lower) values [this feature is captured in the mean-reverting process used in Vasicek (1977), for example].*

- *Interest-rate volatility tends to be higher for short-term rates compared with long-term rates; furthermore, a non-zero correlation seems to exist between interest rate volatility and interest-rate level.*

Empirical studies have provided useful insights to researchers. Since the first model offered in Merton (1973), many improvements have been made. In Table 12.1, we provide a list of some popular models for the short-term process, which can all fit into the following specification of equation (12.3):

$$dr_t = (\mu_1 + \mu_2 r_t)\, dt + (\sigma_1 + \sigma_2 r_t)^\alpha\, dW_t$$

---

[4]Even though this general model is written on absolute changes in the level of interest rates, one may use a suitable specification of the drift and volatility processes to ensure that interest rates cannot take on negative values with positive probability (see, for example, Cox, Ingersoll and Ross's (1985) model below).

Table 12.1   Short-Rate SDE.

Model	μ_1	μ_2	σ_1	σ_2	α
Brennan–Schwartz (1980)	•	•	—	•	1
Cox–Ingersoll–Ross (1985)	•	•	—	•	0.5
Dothan (1978)	—	—	—	•	1
Merton (1973)	•	—	•	—	1
Pearson–Sun (1994)	•	•	•	•	0.5
Vasicek (1977)	•	•	•	—	1

where μ_i, σ_j and α are constant parameters, and $\alpha \in [0.5; 1]$. The presence of the corresponding parameter in the SDE is denoted by • in Table 12.1.

We now provide a critical analysis of these models.[5] When possible, we give the corresponding continuously compounded zero-coupon rate $R(t, \theta)$ and the zero-coupon rate volatility $V(t, \theta)$ functions.

A Classic Example: Vasicek (1977)

Vasicek (1977) postulates a so-called Ornstein–Uhlenbeck process for the short-term interest rate

$$\mathrm{d}r_t = (\mu_1 + \mu_2 r_t)\,\mathrm{d}t + \sigma_1\,\mathrm{d}W_t = a(b - r_t)\,\mathrm{d}t + \sigma\,\mathrm{d}W_t$$

Note that this process contains a mean-reverting feature, which is close to what is empirically observed. The parameter b may be regarded as the equilibrium level of the short-term interest rate, around which it stochastically evolves. When r_t falls far below its long-term value b, the expected instantaneous variation in r_t, given by $a(b - r_t)$ is positive (since $r_t < b$). In this case, the short-term rate will tend to move up. It will move toward its long-term value quickly when it is far from it and when the parameter a (speed of return to the long-term mean value) is high. Conversely, if $r_t > b$, the expected value of the instantaneous interest-rate change $\mathrm{d}r_t$ is negative, then r_t will be more likely to fall quickly to get back to b. Assuming a constant price for interest-rate risk denoted as λ (see Appendix 2 of this chapter for more details), Vasicek (1977) finds that $R^c(t, \theta)$, the continuously compounded pure discount rate at date t for maturity $t + \theta$, is given by [see, for example, Martellini and Priaulet (2000) for a proof of that result][6]

$$R^c(t, \theta) = R_\infty - (R_\infty - r_t)\left(\frac{1 - \mathrm{e}^{-a\theta}}{\theta}\right) + \frac{\sigma^2}{4a^3\theta}(1 - \mathrm{e}^{-a\theta})^2$$

with

$$R_\infty = b - \frac{\sigma\lambda}{a} - \frac{\sigma^2}{2a^2}$$

Under Vasicek (1977) specification, the zero-coupon curve may be flat, increasing or decreasing. On the other hand, it does not allow for the possibility of inverted yield curves, U-shaped curves

---

[5]Duffie and Kan (1996) have shown that the Merton (1973), Vasicek (1977), CIR (1985) and Pearson and Sun (1994) models all belong to a general class known as *the affine class*. The name comes from the fact that, for all models in this class, zero-coupon rates are affine functions of the short rate (see Martellini and Priaulet (2000) for more details).

[6]Note that the functional form that was exogenously specified for the zero-coupon rate curve in equation (4.12) from Chapter 4 may be recognized here.

or hump-shaped curves (see Chapter 4). $R(t, \infty)$ is a constant, which makes the right end of the yield curve fixed for a given choice of the parameters. The zero-coupon rate volatility $V(t, \theta)$ is given by

$$V(t, \theta) = V(\theta) = \sigma \left(\frac{e^{a\theta} - 1}{a\theta} \right)$$

It is decreasing in θ, which implies that long rates are less volatile than short rates, a feature often observed in practice. The parameter a, which specifies the speed of return to the mean, intuitively plays an important role in the volatility of interest rates. The larger this parameter is, the faster interest rates are brought back to their long-term level, and consequently, the smaller is their volatility. Note that in this model, the short rate may take on negative values with positive probability.

Other Classic Examples

Merton (1973)   Merton introduced in 1973 the following model for interest rates

$$dr_t = \mu_1 \, dt + \sigma_1 \, dW_t = \mu \, dt + \sigma \, dW_t$$

Assuming a zero market price for interest-rate risk, Merton (1973) derived the following zero-coupon rate function:

$$R^c(t, \theta) = r_t + \frac{\mu}{2}\theta - \frac{\sigma^2}{6}\theta^2$$

This form only allows for very specific shapes of the zero-coupon yield curve. As θ goes to ∞, $R^c(t, \infty)$ goes to $-\infty$. Zero-coupon rate volatility $V(t, \theta)$ is a constant equal to σ. In this model, the short rate may also take on negative values with positive probability.

Cox–Ingersoll–Ross (1985)   Cox *et al.* (1985) have introduced a square root process for the short rate $r(t)$ that enjoys the property of not allowing for negative interest rates. This process, which they endogenously derive in a general equilibrium setting, is written as

$$dr_t = (\mu_1 + \mu_2 r_t) \, dt + \sqrt{\sigma_2 r_t} \, dW_t$$

Assuming a constant market price for interest-rate risk λ, Cox *et al.* (1985) find

$$R^c(t, \theta) = \frac{-2\mu_1}{\sigma_2^4 \theta} \ln A(\theta) + \frac{r_t}{\theta} D(\theta)$$

with

$$A(\theta) = \frac{2\gamma \exp\left[\frac{(-\mu_2 + \lambda + \gamma)\theta}{2} \right]}{(-\mu_2 + \lambda + \gamma)[\exp(\gamma\theta) - 1] + 2\gamma} \tag{12.4}$$

$$D(\theta) = \frac{2[\exp(\gamma\theta) - 1]}{(-\mu_2 + \lambda + \gamma)[\exp(\gamma\theta) - 1] + 2\gamma} \tag{12.5}$$

$$\gamma = \sqrt{(-\mu_2 + \lambda)^2 + 2\sigma_2^4} \tag{12.6}$$

While this specification allows for inverted shapes at the short end of the curve, it fails in capturing curves with either a U-shape or a hump. The longer end of the curve is also asymptotic to a constant.

Finally, the zero-coupon rate volatility function is decreasing in maturity and is proportional to the square root of the short-term rate, as can be seen from the following result:

$$V(t, \theta) = \frac{\sigma_2 \sqrt{r_t} D(\theta)}{\theta}$$

This model has been empirically tested by Brown and Dybvig (1986) and by Brown and Schaefer (1994). These authors have shown that the volatility of the short-term rate conforms relatively well to empirical observations, but they argue that the model is not flexible enough to capture the variety of shapes encountered in practice.

The other models in Table 12.1 do not allow for closed-form solutions of discount bond prices, and thus require numerical computation. One advantage is that they allow for an explicit specification of the short-term volatility as a function of the short-term rate. However, Chan *et al.* (1992), using data from the T-bills market on the period 1964–1989, argue that the parameter α should be taken as larger than 1.

Shortcomings of the Single-Factor Models

Single-factor models achieve very little flexibility in capturing the variety of possible yield-curve shapes and dynamics observed in practice. As mentioned earlier, the Merton (1973) and Vasicek (1977) models even allow negative rates with a positive probability. Rogers (1996) discussed the pricing implications of this latter shortcoming. He uses a Vasicek (1977) model to price both a standard bond and the same bond with an embedded "knockout" option. This means that the bond pays off the promised amount at maturity only if the short rate has remained positive during the bond's lifetime. In practice, real rates cannot go negative (that would be an obvious arbitrage opportunity), and prices of these two bonds should be identical. The model, however, provides a significantly lower price for the bond with the knockout option, and the difference in price increases with the short-rate volatility and the bond maturity.

Furthermore, the models do not perform well in terms of pricing error measurement. It is not uncommon to obtain model-generated theoretical bond prices that differ from actual prices by more than 1%. These errors are then amplified when it comes to pricing fixed-income derivatives (around 20% and 30%). From a practical perspective, the magnitude of the pricing error is not acceptable.

More generally, a professional trading activity in fixed-income products requires

- *the use of a reliable model in which traders can have faith;*

- *the ability to implement dynamic trading strategies allowing the seller of derivative products to replicate the contingent payoff using other fixed-income securities, an objective that cannot be achieved when the model used implies significant pricing errors; and*

- *the ability to use the model from a risk-management perspective.*

Finally, let us note that a major shortcoming of single-factor models is that they imply that all possible zero-coupon rates are perfectly correlated, making bonds redundant assets. To see this, compute the correlation between zero-coupon rate changes for different maturities $dR^c(t, T_1 - t)$ and $dR^c(t, T_2 - t)$, which is equal to 1, since there is only one source of randomness in the model. This element is obviously counterfactual, as we have already seen from Table 3.1 (see Chapter 3 and comments below Table 3.1).

Fixed Income Securities

12.2.2 Multifactor Models

As mentioned above, an empirical analysis of the dynamics of the interest-rate term structure strongly suggests the use of a multifactor model.[7]

Some Popular Models

Table 12.2 contains a list of some popular multifactor models.[8] The principle behind multifactor models is to exogenously specify a model for the dynamics of variables of interest, such as

Table 12.2 Multifactor Linear Models.

State variables	Author(s)
Short rate $$dr(t) = \alpha(\bar{r} - r(t))\,dt + \sqrt{v(t)}\,dW_1(t)$$ **Short-rate volatility** $$dv(t) = \gamma(\bar{v} - v(t))\,dt + \xi\sqrt{v(t)}\,dW_2(t)$$	Fong and Vasicek (1991)
Short rate $$dr(t) = \left(\alpha\gamma + \beta\eta - \frac{\beta\delta - \alpha\xi}{\beta - \alpha}r(t) - \frac{\xi - \delta}{\beta - \alpha}v(t)\right)dt + \alpha\sqrt{\frac{\beta r(t) - v(t)}{\alpha(\beta - \alpha)}}\,dW_1(t) + \beta\sqrt{\frac{v(t) - \alpha r(t)}{\beta(\beta - \alpha)}}\,dW_2(t)$$ **Short-rate volatility** $$dv(t) = \left(\alpha^2\gamma + \beta^2\eta - \frac{\alpha\beta(\delta - \xi)}{\beta - \alpha}r(t) - \frac{\beta\xi - \alpha\delta}{\beta - \alpha}v(t)\right)dt + \alpha^2\sqrt{\frac{\beta r(t) - v(t)}{\alpha(\beta - \alpha)}}\,dW_1(t) + \beta^2\sqrt{\frac{v(t) - \alpha r(t)}{\beta(\beta - \alpha)}}\,dW_2(t)$$	Longstaff and Schwartz (1992)
Short rate $$dr(t) = k(\theta(t) - r(t))\,dt + \sqrt{v(t)}\sqrt{r(t)}\,dW_1(t)$$ **Short-rate mean** $$d\theta(t) = \alpha(\bar{\theta} - \theta(t))\,dt + \zeta\sqrt{\theta(t)}\,dW_2(t)$$ **Short-rate volatility** $$dv(t) = \mu(\bar{v} - v(t))\,dt + \eta\sqrt{v(t)}\,dW_3(t)$$	Chen (1996)
Short rate $$dr(t) = k(\theta(t) - r(t))\,dt + \sqrt{v(t)}\,dW_1(t)$$ **Short-rate mean** $$d\theta(t) = \alpha(\bar{\theta} - \theta(t))\,dt + \zeta\,dW_2(t)$$ **Short-rate volatility** $$dv(t) = \mu(\bar{v} - v(t))\,dt + \eta\sqrt{v(t)}\,dW_3(t)$$	Balduzzi *et al.* (1996)

---

[7] See in particular, principal components analysis (PCA) on interest-rate changes (see Chapter 3) and correlation coefficients in Table 3.1 (see Chapter 3).

[8] These models also belong to the so-called "affine" class. A key point in favor of these models is that they can be made to match results from a PCA of the yield curve dynamics (see Chapter 3).

the short-term interest rate (as in single-factor models), but also introduce a modelization for its volatility or mean value.[9]

We now provide more detailed comments on some of the most popular models.

The Fong and Vasicek (1991) Model Fong and Vasicek (1991) take the short rate and its volatility as two state variables. The variance of the short-rate changes is actually a key element in the pricing of fixed-income securities. A two-factor model also allows modeling of the imperfect correlations between interest rates and their volatility. This contrasts with single-factor models such as Brennan and Schwartz (1980), Cox, Ingersoll and Ross (1985), Dothan (1978) and Pearson and Sun (1994). As noted by Strickland (1996a, 1996b), the model still allows negative values for the short rate with positive probability. $\bar{r}$ and $\bar{v}$ are the long-term mean values of the short-term and the variance of its variations. The model also implies an added complexity, which prevents the authors from obtaining a closed-form solution for the price of a discount bond.

The Longstaff and Schwartz (1992) Model Longstaff and Schwartz (1992) use the same two state variables, but with a different specification that allows them to get a closed-form solution for the price of a discount bond and a call option on a discount bond.[10] They obtain the following zero-coupon rate function:

$$R^c(t, \theta) = -\kappa - \left[\frac{C(\theta)r(t) + D(\theta)v(t) + 2\gamma \ln(A(\theta) + 2\eta \ln(B(\theta))}{\theta} \right]$$

where

$$\kappa = \gamma(\delta + \phi) + \eta(w + \psi)$$

$$A(\theta) = \frac{2\phi}{(\delta + \phi)(e^{\phi\theta} - 1) + 2\phi}$$

$$B(\theta) = \frac{2\psi}{(w + \psi)(e^{\psi\theta} - 1) + 2\psi}$$

$$C(\theta) = \frac{\alpha\phi(e^{\psi\theta} - 1)B(\theta) - \beta\psi(e^{\phi\theta} - 1)A(\theta)}{\phi\psi(\beta - \alpha)}$$

$$D(\theta) = \frac{\psi(e^{\phi\theta} - 1)A(\theta) - \phi(e^{\psi\theta} - 1)B(\theta)}{\phi\psi(\beta - \alpha)}$$

$$\phi = \sqrt{2\alpha + \delta^2}$$

$$\psi = \sqrt{2\beta + w^2}$$

$$w = \xi + \lambda$$

The zero-coupon rate with infinite maturity is a constant equal to $\gamma(\phi - \delta) + \eta(\psi - w)$. Note that the price of very short-term bonds is not affected by changes in the short-term volatility, since the

---

[9]It should be noted that two-factor models can also be constructed in a binomial setting, with a volatility tree superimposed on the interest tree.

[10]Their model is presented in a general equilibrium framework similar to the one in Cox, Ingersoll and Ross (1985), so that the processes for the short rate and its variance are endogenously obtained.

Fixed Income Securities

partial derivative of $B(t, T)$ with respect to $v(t)$ goes to zero as t goes to T. The zero-coupon rate curve can be flat, increasing, decreasing, or can display a hump or a U-shape. Dahlquist and Svensson (1996) show that it performs better empirically than models by Cox, Ingersoll and Ross (1985) and Nelson and Siegel (1987) in periods of high volatility.[11] This is because it allows for relatively small mispricing, as measured by a significant decrease in the squared difference of theoretical prices compared with actual market prices (see Chapter 4). On the other hand, it requires the estimation of a large number of parameters (9). This is all the more problematic since there is no clear financial interpretation for these parameters, which are also not very stable [see Dahlquist and Svensson (1996)]. The zero-coupon rate volatility function $V(t, \theta)$ is given by

$$V(t, \theta) = \frac{1}{\theta} \sqrt{\left(\frac{\alpha\beta\psi^2 y A(\theta)^2 - \alpha\beta\phi^2 z B(\theta)^2}{\phi^2 \psi^2 (\beta - \alpha)} \right) r(t) + \left(\frac{\beta\phi^2 z B(\theta)^2 - \alpha\psi^2 y A(\theta)^2}{\phi^2 \psi^2 (\beta - \alpha)} \right) v(t)}$$

where

$$y = (e^{\phi\theta} - 1)^2$$
$$z = (e^{\psi\theta} - 1)^2$$

The model allows for increasing and decreasing volatility curves, as well as curves with a U-shape and a hump shape.

The Chen (1996) and Balduzzi et al. (1996) Models   Following Fong and Vasicek (1991) and Longstaff and Schwartz (1992), Chen (1996) and Balduzzi *et al.* (1996) suggest the use of a three-factor model by adding the short-term average of the short rate $\theta(t)$. A justification for this choice may be found in the fact that these three state variables can be assimilated by the three factors that can be empirically obtained through a PCA of the term structure dynamics (see Chapter 3):

- $r(t)$ *can be interpreted as a level factor; a change in $r(t)$ implies a quasi-parallel shift of the yield curve in this model;*

- $v(t)$ *can be interpreted as a curvature factor; an increase in $v(t)$ barely affects the ends of the yield curve, while it has a more pronounced effect on the middle segment;*

- *finally, $\theta(t)$ can be interpreted as a slope factor; a change in $\theta(t)$ implies an increase or a decrease in the slope of the yield curve, depending upon the sign of the change.*

However, there is no explicit closed-form pricing formula for a discount bond. Chen (1996) derives an expression using Bessel and Kummer functions. Balduzzi *et al.* (1996) obtain the following quasi closed-form solution:

$$R^c(t, \theta) = \frac{-\ln(A(\theta)) + B(\theta)r(t) + C(\theta)\theta(t) + D(\theta)v(t)}{\theta}$$

where

$$B(\theta) = \frac{1 - e^{-k\theta}}{k}$$

$$C(\theta) = \frac{1 - e^{-k\theta} + (k/\alpha)e^{-\alpha\theta}(1 - e^{-\alpha\theta})}{\alpha - k}$$

---

[11] See equation (4.10) in Chapter 4 where we give the explicit expression for the Nelson and Siegel (1987) zero-coupon rate curve.

while $A(\theta)$ and $D(\theta)$ are solutions to a two-dimensional partial differential equation (PDE) that is solved numerically.

An advantage of these models is that they allow for the fitting of any possible shape for the yield curve. A drawback is that they require the estimation of 13 and 10 parameters, respectively, which imply a high numerical complexity and a relative loss of robustness.

Shortcomings of Multifactor Models

Multifactor models offer a more realistic description of the term structure dynamics compared to a single-factor model. In particular, they allow us to

- *account for the correlations between interest changes for different maturities more faithfully and*

- *replicate observed bond prices more faithfully.*

This comes, however, at the cost of added complexity:

- *Closed-form formulas are obtained under a very limited set of conditions; their calibration is made difficult by the fact that they imply fitting functions that contain a large number of parameters, which involves very heavy minimization algorithms.*

- *Numerical methods are needed to compute the price of standard derivatives such as bond options.*

> **Remark 12.1** Furthermore, some famous models show some theoretical inconsistency. Dybvig *et al.* (1996) and El Karoui *et al.* (1998) have actually shown that the absence of arbitrage opportunities implies that the long zero-coupon rate could never decrease. A proof for this result is provided as an exercise in the "Problem" section of this chapter. This result implies that models allowing the long zero-coupon rate to be decreasing are inconsistent with the absence of arbitrage opportunities. This is, in particular, the case for Brennan and Schwartz (1979), Nelson and Schaefer (1983) and Schaefer and Schwartz (1984).

In practice, single or multifactor models that we have just described are calibrated in such a way that the models' parameters are obtained as solutions to a minimization program of the difference (i.e., the squared spread) between market prices of reference bonds and theoretical values generated from the model. A detailed description of this procedure, which is the analog of the calibration of an interest-rate tree, has already been presented in Chapter 4.[12]

Only Longstaff and Schwartz (1992) are able to obtain an explicit closed-form solution for the price of a call option written on a pure discount bond (see the original article or Martellini and Priaulet (2000) for the exact formula). The numerical complexity involved in these models is

---

[12]A more theoretical approach would consist of using a general equilibrium framework to derive an optimal value for these parameters as part of the agents' optimization program.

a very important issue. This becomes all the more problematic since the difference between the derived yield curve and the observed curve, even though minimized, cannot be entirely eliminated.

12.3 Arbitrage Models

As we have seen, using factor models (either in discrete time or in continuous time) for valuing interest-rate options actually implies the following three-step procedure:

- *First, derive a theoretical zero-coupon rate curve using a specified factor model.*

- *Then, calibrate the model using market prices for reference bonds and obtain values for the model parameters.*

- *Finally, price the derivatives using these parameters (as will be detailed in Chapter 14).*

The problem obviously comes from the fact that, as we have just said, the spot zero-coupon rate curve is endogenously derived and may be different from the actual market curve. Since derivative pricing is relative pricing only (we aim at finding the price of an option on a bond, taking as given the price of the bond), why not use actual market prices for bonds rather than a model value? This is the purpose of arbitrage models, to which we turn now. These models feature an appealing built-in consistency with reference market prices. The formulation "arbitrage models" is related to the notion of relative pricing: the model is built to be consistent with the observed yield curve, that is, with market bond prices, and is subsequently used to price other fixed-income products, for example, interest-rate derivatives, based on that information. The approach is similar to that used by Black and Scholes (1973) for pricing an option on a common stock. The idea is to start with the currently observed yield curve, which is regarded as the underlying asset. This is in contrast to the "state variable" models described in the previous section, where a dynamic process for the short-term rate is exogenously specified.[13]

The first example of this class of so-called arbitrage models has been introduced by Ho and Lee (1986), who have assumed that pure discount bond prices, driven by a single source of uncertainty, follow dynamics that can be described by a standard binomial tree. Heath *et al.* (1990a, 1990b, 1992) have generalized this approach by allowing discount bonds prices to be driven by n-dimensional uncertainty, first in a discrete-time framework, which they later extended to a continuous-time framework with stochastic volatility. For ease of exposure, we first present discrete-time models. We then present, without proof, the main results of the Heath, Jarrow and Morton (1992) model (the HJM model), as well as some other recent extensions. We refer the interested reader to Martellini and Priaulet (2000) for a more technical and thorough treatment of these models.

12.3.1 A Discrete-Time Example: Ho and Lee's Binomial Lattice

Ho and Lee (1986) approach focuses on bond prices modeled as changing through time following a binomial process. Hence they assume

---

[13]These "state variable models" are sometimes also referred to as *equilibrium models* as one can show [see Duffie and Kan (1996)] that any "sensible" exogenously specified dynamic process for the short-term rate can, in principle, be obtained as a solution of an equilibrium model of the Cox, Ingersoll and Ross (1985) type.

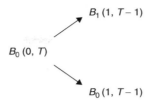

where we denote by $B_i(n, T)$, the value at date n of a zero-coupon bond with residual maturity T in the ith state of the world. In case of an up move, it goes to $B_{i+1}(n + 1, T - 1)$ and to $B_i(n + 1, T - 1)$ in case of a down move. This is similar to what we have discussed in the previous section, except that the bond prices, as opposed to short-term interest rates, are directly modeled. The method is also based upon the assumption that the tree is recombining. In other words, it is assumed that an up move followed by a down move is equivalent to a down move followed by an up move.

Perturbation Functions

In a world with certainty, if one wishes to invest at date n in order to get \$1 $T + 1$ years later, one can select either one of the two following solutions:

- *Directly buy a zero-coupon bond with maturity $T + 1$; the initial investment is then equal to $B_i(n, T + 1)$.*

- *First buy a zero-coupon bond with 1 year to maturity and then, 1 year later, another zero-coupon bond with T years to maturity; the initial investment required is*

$$B_i(n, 1)B_i(n + 1, T) = B_i(n, 1)B_{i+1}(n + 1, T)$$

Therefore, if interest rates were not to move in a stochastic way, we would have the following relationship about the forward price of a zero-coupon bond with T years to maturity at time $n + 1$:

$$B_i(n + 1, T) = B_{i+1}(n + 1, T) = \frac{B_i(n, T + 1)}{B_i(n, 1)}$$

In a world with binomial uncertainty, there are two different possible prices for the bond to be purchased at date n. If interest rates have decreased, we have an up move for the bond value

$$B_{i+1}(n + 1, T) = \frac{B_i(n, T + 1)}{B_i(n, 1)}h(T)$$

with

$$h(T) > 1$$

If interest rates have increased, then we have a down move for the bond price

$$B_i(n + 1, T) = \frac{B_i(n, T + 1)}{B_i(n, 1)}h^*(T)$$

with

$$h^*(T) < 1$$

We must have, in any case

$$h(0) = h^*(0) = 1$$

h and h^* are called *perturbation functions*. It is assumed here that they depend solely on the maturity T and not the date n. In the context of binomial option pricing, this assumption would capture a constant volatility framework.

Risk-Neutral Probability

We now form an arbitrage portfolio with two zero-coupon bonds:

$$V_i(n) = B_i(n, T) + \phi B_i(n, T')$$

One step later, two possible outcomes are possible:

- *Up state (interest rates have decreased)*

$$V_{i+1}(n + 1) = B_{i+1}(n + 1, T - 1) + \phi B_{i+1}(n + 1, T' - 1)$$
$$= \frac{1}{B_i(n, 1)}[B_i(n, T)h(T - 1) + \phi B_i(n, T')h(T' - 1)]$$

- *Down state (interest rates have increased)*

$$V_i(n + 1) = B_i(n + 1, T - 1) + \phi B_i(n + 1, T' - 1)$$
$$= \frac{1}{B_i(n, 1)}[B_i(n, T)h^*(T - 1) + \phi B_i(n, T')h^*(T' - 1)]$$

We select ϕ such that the portfolio is riskless (yields the same outcome in all states of the world)

$$V_{i+1}(n + 1) = V_i(n + 1)$$

Hence, we take

$$\phi = -\frac{B_i(n, T)[h(T - 1) - h^*(T - 1)]}{B_i(n, T')[h(T' - 1) - h^*(T' - 1)]} \tag{12.7}$$

Then, in the absence of arbitrage, the return on this portfolio must be equal to the risk-free rate, which reads

$$\frac{V_i(n)}{V_{i+1}(n + 1)} = \frac{V_i(n)}{V_i(n + 1)} = B_i(n, 1)$$

or

$$B_i(n, T) + \phi B_i(n, T') = \frac{1}{B_i(n, 1)}[B_i(n, T)h^*(T - 1) + \phi B_i(n, T')h^*(T' - 1)]B_i(n, 1)$$

Finally,

$$\phi = -\frac{B_i(n, T)[h^*(T - 1) - 1]}{B_i(n, T')[h^*(T' - 1) - 1]} \tag{12.8}$$

Comparing the two expressions for ϕ in equations (12.7) and (12.8), we get that for any T and T'

$$\frac{1 - h^*(T - 1)}{h(T - 1) - h^*(T - 1)} = \frac{1 - h^*(T' - 1)}{h(T' - 1) - h^*(T' - 1)}$$

Therefore, for all T

$$\frac{1 - h^*(T)}{h(T) - h^*(T)} = \text{constant} = \pi$$

It is easy to check that the constant π can be interpreted as a probability (less than 1, more than 0). It is the analog of the risk-neutral probabilities in binomial option pricing (see Cox *et al.* (1979) and Section 14.5.2 in Chapter 14). We indeed have

$$\pi h(T) + (1 - \pi)h^*(T) = 1$$

Substituting the definition of h and h^* in this last equation, we get

$$B_i(n, T + 1) = B_i(n, 1)[\pi B_{i+1}(n + 1, T) + (1 - \pi)B_i(n + 1, T)]$$

Hence, we have the standard interpretation that discounted prices are martingales under the risk-neutral probability. In the Cox–Ross–Rubinstein (1979) binomial model, we had

$$\pi = \frac{R - D}{U - D}$$

Here we get the same thing with

$$R = \frac{1}{B_i(n, 1)}$$

$$U = \frac{B_{i+1}(n + 1, T)}{B_i(n, T + 1)}$$

$$D = \frac{B_i(n + 1, T)}{B_i(n, T + 1)}$$

Recombining Tree Requirement

We now explicitly require a recombining tree

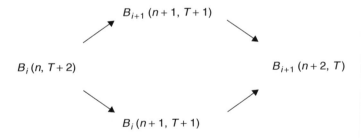

$$B_{i+1}(n + 1, T + 1)$$

$$B_i(n, T + 2) \qquad\qquad B_{i+1}(n + 2, T)$$

$$B_i(n + 1, T + 1)$$

Following an up–down move, we have

$$B_{i+1}(n + 2, T) = \frac{B_{i+1}(n + 1, T + 1)}{B_{i+1}(n + 1, 1)}h^*(T)$$

and

$$B_{i+1}(n + 1, T + 1) = \frac{B_i(n, T + 2)}{B_i(n, 1)}h(T + 1)$$

and also (the same with $T = 0$)

$$B_{i+1}(n + 1, 1) = \frac{B_i(n, 2)}{B_i(n, 1)}h(1)$$

Finally,

$$B_{i+1}(n+2, T) = \frac{B_i(n, T+2)h(T+1)h^*(T)}{B_i(n, 2)h(1)}$$

Along the same lines, following a down–up move, we get

$$B_{i+1}(n+2, T) = \frac{B_i(n, T+2)h^*(T+1)h(T)}{B_i(n, 2)h^*(1)}$$

Finally, the recombining tree requirement gives

$$\frac{h(T+1)h^*(T)}{h(1)} = \frac{h^*(T+1)h(T)}{h^*(1)}$$

Using

$$\pi h(T) + (1-\pi)h^*(T) = 1$$

we get

$$h(T+1)(1-\pi h(T))(1-\pi h(1)) = (1-\pi)h(1)h(T)(1-\pi h(T+1))$$

It can be shown (by inspection) that this last equation is equivalent to

$$h(T+1)\delta = h(T) - h(T)h(T+1)\pi(1-\delta)$$

where

$$\delta = \frac{1-\pi h(1)}{(1-\pi)h(1)}$$

One can also check that

$$\delta < 1$$

since $h(1) > 1$ and

$$1 - \delta = \frac{h(1)-1}{(1-\pi)h(1)}$$

We can use

$$h(T+1)\delta = h(T) - h(T)h(T+1)\pi(1-\delta)$$

to get

$$\frac{\delta}{h(T)} + \pi(1-\delta) = \frac{1}{h(T+1)}$$

This recursive equation in $h(T)$ can be solved (by backward recursion) to yield

$$h(T) = \frac{1}{\pi + (1-\pi)\delta^T}$$

We also had

$$h^*(T) = \frac{1 - \pi h(T)}{1 - \pi}$$

Hence,

$$h^*(T) = \frac{\delta^T}{\pi + (1-\pi)\delta^T} = \delta^T h(T)$$

Calibrating the Tree

Practical implementation of the method requires π and δ. These values are obtained through nonlinear estimation methods that consist of minimizing the squared spread between the market price of derivatives (e.g., caps) and the theoretical price given by the model.

We provide an example of application of this methodology to the pricing of bond options as an exercise in Chapter 14 and application of this methodology to the pricing of caps as an exercise in Chapter 15.

Limits of the Model

This model has four main limits:

- *Interest rates can take on negative value with positive probability.*

- *Volatility of interest rates is constant for all n (time constant) and all T (maturity constant).*

- *All possible zero-coupon yield curves at a future date are parallel.*

- *The term structure dynamics is driven by a single factor, the short-term interest rate.*

To circumvent these limitations, various authors have generalized and extended Ho and Lee's (1986) model. They have mostly done so in a continuous-time setting. We now discuss some of these extensions.

12.3.2 Arbitrage Models in Continuous Time

The general framework for continuous-time arbitrage models of the term structure has been introduced in a seminal paper by Heath *et al.* (1992). While the presentation of the model involves more sophisticated mathematical tools (introduced in a dedicated Appendix 2 to this chapter), the intuition is the same as in Ho and Lee's (1986) model.

Heath, Jarrow and Morton's General Approach

The idea is to start with the currently observed yield curve, which is regarded as the underlying asset. Then some dynamic model is specified for the dynamics of the discount bond prices, just as a binomial model was used in Ho and Lee's (1986) discrete-time setting.[14] Here, relative changes in prices $B(t, T)$ of a discount bond with maturity date T are modeled as the following continuous-time process:

$$\frac{\mathrm{d}B(t, T)}{B(t, T)} = \mu(t, T)\, \mathrm{d}t + \sigma(t, T)\, \mathrm{d}W_t \qquad (12.9)$$

where

$\mu(t, T)$ is the expected instantaneous return at date t on the discount bond $B(t, T)$;

$\sigma(t, T)$ is the instantaneous volatility at date t on the discount bond $B(t, T)$;

W is a standard Brownian motion.

---

[14]Note that Heath *et al.* (1992) specified the dynamics of the instantaneous forward rates. Hull and White (1993a) show that this is equivalent to specifying the bond price dynamics, as we do, following, for example, El Karoui *et al.* (1992).

Fixed Income Securities

It should be noted that equation (12.9) is similar to equation (12.3), except that it is written on relative bond price changes $\frac{dB(t,T)}{B(t,T)} = \frac{B(t+dt,T)-B(t,T)}{B(t,T)}$, as opposed to absolute changes in the interest-rate level. This is to prevent bond prices from taking on negative values with positive probability.

It should also be noted that the original HJM is cast in a general multidimensional framework, even though, for simplicity of exposure, we present here a one-dimensional version of the model (see Martellini and Priaulet (2000) for more details on the general formulation).

In the absence of arbitrage, Heath *et al.* (1992) rewrite the dynamics of bond prices from equation (12.9) under an *equivalent martingale measure (EMM)* as[15]

$$\frac{dB(t, T)}{B(t, T)} = r_t \, dt + \sigma(t, T) \, d\widehat{W}_t$$

where $\widehat{W}_t$ is also a Brownian motion (under the new probability measure).

The solution for this SDE can be shown to be[16]

$$B(t, T) = B(0, T) \exp\left[\int_0^t r_s \, ds + \int_0^t \sigma(s, T) \, d\widehat{W}_s - \frac{1}{2}\int_0^t \sigma^2(s, T) \, ds\right] \quad (12.10)$$

One may eliminate the short-term rate from that equation and finally get (see, for example, Martellini and Priaulet (2000) for details and proofs)

$$B(t, T) = \frac{B(0, T)}{B(0, t)} \exp\left[\int_0^t (\sigma(s, T) - \sigma(s, t)) \, d\widehat{W}_s - \frac{1}{2}\int_0^t (\sigma^2(s, T) - \sigma^2(s, t)) \, ds\right] \quad (12.11)$$

The conclusion is the following: prices only depend on the current term structure (zero-coupon bond prices $B(0, t)$ and $B(0, T)$) and the volatility structure ($\sigma(s, t)$ and $\sigma(s, T)$ for $0 \leq s \leq t$). We may also derive the future zero-coupon rate at date t for a maturity T, denoted by $R^c(t, T - t)$:

$$R^c(t, T - t) = \frac{1}{T - t}\left[\ln\left(\frac{B(0, t)}{B(0, T)}\right) - \int_0^t (\sigma(s, T) - \sigma(s, t)) \, d\widehat{W}_s \right.$$

$$\left. + \frac{1}{2}\int_0^t (\sigma^2(s, T) - \sigma^2(s, t)) \right] ds$$

and the following dynamics is obtained for the instantaneous forward rate $f(t, T)$

$$f(t, T) = f(0, T) - \int_0^t \gamma(s, T) \, d\widehat{W}_s + \int_0^t \sigma(s, T)\gamma(s, T) \, ds \quad (12.12)$$

where $\gamma(t, T)$ is the volatility of $f(t, T)$.

---

[15]See Appendix 2 of this chapter for the relation between the absence of arbitrage and the existence of an equivalent martingale measure.

[16]This can be done using Itô's lemma (see Appendix 2 of this chapter).

If we evaluate this expression at $T = t$, we also get (using $r(t) = f(t, t)$)

$$r(t) = f(0, t) - \int_0^t \gamma(s, t) \, d\widehat{W}_s + \int_0^t \sigma(s, t)\gamma(s, t) \, ds \qquad (12.13)$$

Heath, Jarrow and Morton (1992) model does not actually allow one to obtain closed-form prices for fixed-income derivatives. This can be done by resorting to numerical methods (see Appendix 2 of Chapter 16) or equivalently by considering the corresponding discrete-time tree.

There is a potential difficulty, however, because the volatility σ and its derivative γ in (12.13) may be functions of some random variables observed before t. This implies that the $(r_t)_{t \geq 0}$ process is not necessarily Markov. A process is said to enjoy the Markov property when it is memoryless or path-independent, or, more formally, when the expected value of the process, given all available information *up to* date t, is equal to the expected value, given all information *at* date t. The lack of Markov property makes the model difficult to use and computationally demanding: in a corresponding interest-rate tree, a down move followed by an up move is not equivalent to an up move followed by a down move. It is therefore impossible in this context to build a recombining tree and a "bushy" tree (lattice) needs to be built, which very significantly increases the computational burden (see the discussion on recombining versus nonrecombining trees from Section 12.1).

Some Popular Arbitrage Models

Because of this practical challenge, most applications of the HJM methodology focus on Markovian models. We now introduce three such important Markovian applications of the general Heath, Jarrow and Morton (1992) model: the continuous-time version of the Ho and Lee (1986) model, the Hull and White (1990) model and the Moraleda and Vorst (1996) model.[17]

Continuous-Time Version of the Ho and Lee (1986) Model   As recalled above, Ho and Lee (1986) have introduced their model in a discrete-time framework. This model actually has a continuous-time counterpart that fits within the HJM methodology. It can be obtained as a special case of an (one-factor) HJM model by assuming that the volatility $\gamma(t, T)$ of the instantaneous forward rates is independent of time and time-horizon:

$$\gamma(t, T) = \sigma$$

From this, and using the HJM technology, one can show the following:

- *The short-term rate is given by*

$$dr(t) = \left[\frac{\partial f(0, t)}{\partial t} + \sigma^2 t \right] dt + \sigma \, d\widehat{W}_t$$

- *Discount bond prices are given by*

$$B(t, T) = \frac{B(0, T)}{B(0, t)} \exp\left(-(T - t)[r(t) - f(0, t)] - \left(\frac{\sigma^2 (T - t)^2 t}{2} \right) \right)$$

---

[17]In all these models, spot rates and instantaneous forward rates are affine functions of the state variables. For this reason, these models are sometimes referred to as *affine* models.

Fixed Income Securities

- *Zero-coupon rates are given by*

$$R^c(t, T-t) = F(0, t, T-t) + r(t) - f(0, t) + \frac{\sigma^2(T-t)t}{2}$$

- *Instantaneous forward rates are given by*

$$f(t, T) = f(0, t) - \int_0^t \sigma \, d\widehat{W}_s + \int_0^t \sigma^2(T-s) \, ds$$

- *Volatility functions for the discount bonds and zero-coupon rates are given by*

$$\sigma(t, T) = \sigma \cdot (T-t)$$

$$V(t, T) = \sigma$$

Note that the short-term process is not a mean-reverting process. All spot rates have the same constant volatility σ, and all yield curves for different possible future dates are parallel to one another.

This model is nested in a larger family of models introduced by Hull and White (1990). As we will now see, Ho and Lee's (1986) model is actually a special case of Hull and White's (1990) model for $\lambda \to 0$, where λ is a parameter in the Hull and White (1990) model (see below).

The Hull and White (1990) Model Hull and White's model is also a special case of a (one-factor) HJM model, with the following specification for the volatility of the instantaneous forward rates[18]

$$\gamma(t, T) = \sigma \, e^{-\lambda(T-t)}$$

- *The short-term rate is given by*

$$r(t) = f(0, t) - \sigma \int_0^t e^{-\lambda(t-s)} \, d\widehat{W}_s + \frac{\sigma^2}{2\lambda^2}[1 - e^{-\lambda t}]^2$$

or equivalently

$$dr(t) = \left[\frac{\partial f(0, t)}{\partial t} + \lambda f(0, t) + \frac{\sigma^2}{2\lambda}[1 - e^{-2\lambda t}] - \lambda r(t) \right] dt - \sigma \, d\widehat{W}_t$$

which is an Ornstein–Uhlenbeck process with time-varying coefficients.

- *Discount bond prices are given by*

$$B(t, T) = \frac{B(0, T)}{B(0, t)} \exp\left(-\left(\frac{1 - e^{-\lambda(T-t)}}{\lambda} \right)[r(t) - f(0, t)] \right.$$
$$\left. - \left(\frac{\sigma^2(1 - e^{-2\lambda t})(1 - e^{-\lambda(T-t)})^2}{4\lambda^3} \right) \right)$$

---

[18] In subsequent papers, Hull and White (1994a, 1994b, 1996) introduce a discrete-time version of their model, which is a trinomial lattice (see Appendix 1 of this chapter where we present this lattice).

- *Zero-coupon rates are given by*

$$R^c(t, T - t) = F(0, t, T - t) + (r(t) - f(0, t)) \left(\frac{1 - e^{-\lambda(T-t)}}{\lambda(T-t)} \right)$$

$$+ \frac{\sigma^2 (1 - e^{-2\lambda t})(1 - e^{-\lambda(T-t)})^2}{4\lambda^3(T-t)}$$

- *Instantaneous forward rates are given by*

$$f(t, T) = f(0, t) - \int_0^t \sigma \, e^{-\lambda(T-s)} \, d\widehat{W}_s + \int_0^t \sigma \, e^{-\lambda(T-s)} \cdot \frac{\sigma}{\lambda} (1 - e^{-\lambda(T-s)}) \, ds$$

- *Volatility functions for the discount bonds and zero-coupon rates are, respectively, given by*

$$\sigma(t, T) = \frac{\sigma}{\lambda} (1 - e^{-\lambda(T-t)})$$

$$V(t, T) = \sigma \left(\frac{1 - e^{-\lambda(T-t)}}{\lambda(T-t)} \right)$$

Note that this model is consistent with the Nelson–Siegel extended family of yield curves as shown by Björk and Christensen (1999), that is, the Hull and White (1990) model produces yield curves belonging to the Nelson and Siegel extended family.[19]

The Hull and White (1990) model is arguably one of the most popular arbitrage models. Because of its importance in the industry, we present several applications of the model in the following chapters.[20] More specifically, we present pricing formulas in the Hull and White (1990) model for

- *bond options in the Appendix of Chapter 14;*

- *forward and futures options in Appendix 3 of Chapter 15;*

- *cap, floor and swaptions in Appendix 4 of Chapter 15.*

Hull and White (1990, 1994a, 1994b, 1996) introduce a trinomial lattice for a discrete-time representation of the state variable, the short rate. The construction of this trinomial lattice is discussed in Appendix 1 of this chapter.

Traders of fixed-income derivatives often calibrate the single or multifactor version of the model by taking prices of bonds and also of a set of reference standard options as given, for example, caps, floors and swaptions, and using it to price and hedge more exotic contingent claims (see Chapter 16).

It can be shown that this model is itself nested in a larger family of models discussed in Moraleda and Vorst (1996). As we will now see, Hull and White's model is actually a special case of

---

[19] With both simulated and market data, Angelini and Herzel (2002) show that the initial curve, derived either by spline methods, Nelson–Siegel (1987) or Nelson–Siegel Extended methods (see Chapter 4 for more details), has a significant impact on the estimates of the parameters of the dynamic model. In particular, it can create parameter instability in the Hull and White (1990) model, which is detrimental to the use of the model for dynamic hedging strategies.

[20] See Martellini and Priaulet (2000) for the pricing of fixed-income derivatives in a two-factor HJM model.

Moraleda and Vorst's model for $\kappa = 0$, where κ is a parameter in Moraleda and Vorst (1996) model (see below).

The Moraleda and Vorst (1996) Model This model is also a one-factor HJM model, with a volatility function for the instantaneous forward rates given by

$$\gamma(t, T) = \sigma \frac{1 + \kappa T}{1 + \kappa t} e^{-\lambda(T-t)}$$

- *The short rate can be shown to follow the process given below:*

$$dr(t) = \left\{ \left(\lambda - \frac{\kappa}{1 + \kappa t} \right) [f(0, t) - r(t)] + \frac{\partial f(0, t)}{\partial t} + \phi(t) \right\} dt + \sigma \, d\widehat{W}_t$$

with

$$\phi(t) = \int_0^t \gamma(s, t)^2 \, ds$$

- *The short rate is a state variable for the Moraleda and Vorst (1996) model. Discount bond, spot rates and instantaneous forward rates can be obtained as in the more general model introduced by Ritchken and Sankarasubramanian (1995a, 1995b, 1995c), with the restrictions on the functions $\beta(t, T)$ and $\phi(t)$ as required by the model's assumptions.*[21]

- *The volatility functions for the discount bonds and zero-coupon rates are, respectively, given by*

$$\sigma(t, T) = \sigma\beta(t, T)$$

$$V(t, T) = \frac{\sigma\beta(t, T)}{T - t}$$

The volatility functions are not stationary. The model, however, allows any possible shape for the term structure of volatility, including increasing, decreasing or hump-shaped around the 1-year maturity and decreasing beyond that point, as is frequently the case on the market.

12.4 End of Chapter Summary

A dynamic model of the term structure is needed for pricing and hedging fixed-income derivatives, that is, securities paying off random cash flows dependent upon future values of interest rates. There are two main classes of term structure models that have been discussed in the literature.

In the first class of models, some factor model for the dynamic of the short-term interest rate is exogenously defined in a discrete-time or in a continuous-time setting. One typically distinguishes between the single- and multifactor models.

The idea common to all one-factor models of the term structure is to consider the whole yield curve as a function of a single state variable, the short interest rate. Merton's (1973) and Vasicek's (1977) were the first examples of such models. The intuition for such models comes from the fact that, to a first-order approximation, prices of bonds of different maturities tend to move in a correlated way, in response to variations of the short-term interest. Single-factor models only differ in that they are based on different models for short-term rate dynamics.

---

[21] See Martellini and Priaulet (2000) for more details on that point.

A major shortcoming of single-factor models is that they imply that all possible zero-coupon rates are perfectly correlated, making bonds redundant assets. An empirical analysis of the dynamics of the interest-rate term structure shows that two or three factors account for most of the yield curve changes. This strongly suggests that a multifactor model should be used for pricing and hedging fixed-income derivatives. This comes, however, at the cost of added complexity: closed-form formulas are obtained under a very limited set of conditions. The calibration of the models is made difficult by the fact that they imply fitting functions that contain a large number of parameters, which involves very heavy minimization algorithms.

The second class of models are the arbitrage models. These models are built to be consistent with the currently observed discount rate yield curve. The first example of an arbitrage model has been proposed in a discrete-time setting by Ho and Lee (1986), who assume that discount bond prices, driven by a single source of uncertainty, follow a dynamics that can be described by a standard binomial tree. Heath, Jarrow and Morton (1990a, 1990b, 1992) have generalized this approach by allowing discount bonds prices to be driven by a multidimensional uncertainty in a continuous-time framework. The built-in consistency of arbitrage models with reference market prices explains why most practitioners tend to favor them. Markovian specific cases of the HJM model, which translate into recombining trees in discrete time, are of high practical interest because they can be implemented without too much numerical complexity.

12.5 References and Further Reading

Angelini, F., and S. Herzel, 2002, "Consistent Initial Curves for Interest Rate Models", *Journal of Derivatives*, **9**(4), 8–17.

Balduzzi, P., S.R. Das, S. Foresi, and R. Sundaram, 1996, "A Simple Approach to Three-Factor Affine Term Structure Models", *Journal of Fixed Income*, **6**(3), 43–53.

Bjerksund, P., and G. Stensland, 1996, "Implementation of the Black-Derman-Toy Interest Rate Model", *Journal of Fixed Income*, **6**(2), 67–75.

Björk, T., and B.J. Christensen, 1999, "Interest Rate Dynamics and Consistent Forward Rate Curves", *Mathematical Finance*, **9**(4), 323–348.

Black, F., "The Pricing of Commodity Contracts", 1976, *Journal of Financial Economics*, **3**(1/2), 167–179.

Black, F., E. Derman, and W. Toy, 1990, "A One-Factor Model of Interest Rates and its Application to Treasury Bond Options", *Financial Analysts Journal*, **46**, 33–39.

Black, F., and P. Karasinski, 1991, "Bond and Option Pricing when Short Rates are Lognormal", *Financial Analysts Journal*, **47**, 52–59.

Black, F., and M. Scholes, 1973, "The Pricing of Options and Corporate Liabilities", *Journal of Political Economy*, **81**, 637–659.

Brace, A., D. Gatarek, and M. Musiela, 1997, "The Market Model of Interest Rate Dynamics", *Mathematical Finance*, **7**(2), 127–155.

Brennan, M.J., and E.S. Schwartz, 1979, "A Continuous Time Approach to the Pricing of Bonds", *Journal of Banking and Finance*, **3**(2), 133–155.

Brennan, M.J., and E.S. Schwartz, 1980, "Analyzing Convertible Bonds", *Journal of Financial and Quantitative Analysis*, **15**(4), 907–929.

Brigo, D., and F. Mercurio, 2001, *Interest Rate Models: Theory and Practice*, Springer-Verlag, Heidelberg.

Brown, S.J., and P.H. Dybvig, 1986, "The Empirical Implications of the Cox, Ingersoll, Ross Theory of the Term Structure of Interest Rates", *Journal of Finance*, **41**(3), 617–632.

Brown, R.H., and S.M. Schaefer, 1994, "The Term Structure of Real Interest Rates and the Cox, Ingersoll, Ross Model", *Journal of Financial Economics*, **35**(1), 3–42.

Canabarro, E., 1995, "Where Do One-Factor Interest Rate Models Fail?", *Journal of Fixed Income*, **5**(2), 31–52.

Carverhill, A., 1994, "When is the Short Rate Markovian?", *Mathematical Finance*, **4**(4), 305–312.

Carverhill, A., 1995, "A Note on the Models of Hull and White for Pricing Options on the Term Structure", *Journal of Fixed Income*, **5**(2), 89–96.

Chan, K.C., G.A. Karolyi, F.A. Longstaff, and A.B. Sanders, 1992, "An Empirical Comparison of Alternative Models of the Short-Term Interest Rate", *Journal of Finance*, **47**(3), 1209–1227.

Chen, L., 1996, "Stochastic Mean and Stochastic Volatility—A Three Factor Model of the Term Structure of Interest Rates and its Applications in Derivatives Pricing and Risk Management", *Financial Markets, Institutions and Instruments*, **5**(1), 1–87.

Cox, J.C., J.E. Ingersoll, and S.A. Ross, 1985, "A Theory of the Term Structure of Interest Rates", *Econometrica*, **53**(2), 385–407.

Cox, J.C., S.A. Ross, and M. Rubinstein, 1979, "Option Pricing: A Simplified Approach", *Journal of Financial Economics*, **7**, 229–263.

Dahlquist, M., and L.E.O. Svensson, 1996, "Estimating the Term Structure of Interest Rates for Monetary Analysis", *Scandinavian Journal of Economics*, **98**(2), 163–183.

Dana, R.A., and M. Jeanblanc-Picqué, 1998, *Marchés Financiers en Temps Continu*, 2nd Edition, Economica, Paris.

Dothan, U., 1978, "On the Term Structure of Interest Rates", *Journal of Financial Economics*, **6**(1), 59–69.

Duffie, D., 1996, *Dynamic Asset Pricing Theory*, Princeton University Press, Princeton, NJ.

Duffie, D., and R. Kan, 1996, "A Yield-Factor Model of Interest Rates", *Mathematical Finance*, **6**(4), 379–406.

Dybvig, P.H., J.E. Ingersoll, and S.A. Ross, 1996, "Long Forward and Zero-Coupon Rates Can Never Fall", *Journal of Business*, **69**(1), 1–25.

El Karoui, N., A. Frachot, and H. Geman, 1998, "On the Behavior of Long Zero Coupon Rates in a No Arbitrage Framework", *Review of Derivatives Research*, **1**, 351–369.

El Karoui, N., and H. Geman, 1994, "A Probabilistic Approach to the Valuation of General Floating-Rate Notes with an Application to Interest Rate Swaps", *Advances in Futures and Options Research*, **7**, 47–64.

El Karoui, N., H. Geman, and J.C. Rochet, 1995, "Changes of Numeraire, Changes of Probability Measure and Option Pricing", *Journal of Applied Probability*, **32**, 443–458.

El Karoui, N., and V. Lacoste, 1992, *Multifactor Models of the Term Structure of Interest Rates*, Congrès de l'Association Française de Finance, Paris.

El Karoui, N., R. Myneni, and R. Viswanathan, 1992, *Arbitrage Pricing and Hedging of Interest Rate Claims with State Variables: I Theory—II Applications*, Working Paper, Laboratoire de Probabilités de l'Université de Paris VI et Stanford University.

El Karoui, N., and J.C. Rochet, 1989, A Pricing Formula for Options on Coupon Bonds, Working Paper No. 72, SEEDS.

Fong, H.G., and O.A. Vasicek, 1991, "Fixed-Income Volatility Management", *Journal of Portfolio Management*, **17**(4), 41–46.

Goldys, B., M. Musiela, and D. Sondermann, 1994, *Lognormality of Rates and Term Structure Models*, Working Paper, University of New South Wales.

Heath, D., R.A. Jarrow, and A. Morton, 1990, "Contingent Claim Valuation with a Random Evolution of Interest Rates", *Review of Futures Markets*, **9**(1), 23–56.

Heath, D., R.A. Jarrow, and A. Morton, 1990, "Bond Pricing and the Term Structure of Interest Rates: A Discrete Time Approximation", *Journal of Financial and Quantitative Analysis*, **25**(4), 419–440.

Heath, D., R.A. Jarrow, and A. Morton, 1992, "Bond Pricing and the Term Structure of Interest Rates: A New Methodology for Contingent Claim Valuations", *Econometrica*, **60**(1), 77–105.

Ho, T.S.Y., 1995, "Evolution of Interest Rate Models: A Comparison, *Journal of Derivatives*, **2**(4), 9–20.

Ho, T.S.Y., and S.B. Lee, 1986, "Term Structure Movements and Pricing Interest Rate Contingent Claims", *Journal of Finance*, **41**(5), 1011–1029.

Hull, J., and A. White, 1990, "Pricing Interest Rate Derivative Securities", *Review of Financial Studies*, **3**(4), 573–592.

Hull, J., and A. White, 1993a, "One Factor Interest Rate Models and the Valuation of Interest-Rate Derivative Securities, *Journal of Financial and Quantitative Analysis*, **28**(2), 235–254.

Hull, J., and A. White, 1993b, "Bond Option Pricing Based on a Model for the Evolution of Bond Prices", *Advances in Futures and Options Research*, **6**, 1–13.

Hull, J., and A. White, 1994a, "Branching Out", *Risk*, **7**(7), 34–37.

Hull, J., and A. White, 1994b, "Numerical Procedures for Implementing Term Structure Models I: Single-Factor Models", *Journal of Derivatives*, **2**(1), 7–16.

Hull, J., and A. White, 1994c, "Numerical Procedures for Implementing Term Structure Models II: Two-Factor Models", *Journal of Derivatives*, **2**(2), 37–48.

Hull, J., and A. White, 1995, "A Note on the Models of Hull and White for Pricing Options on the Term Structure: Response", *Journal of Fixed Income*, **5**(2), 97–102.

Hull, J., and A. White, 1996, "Using Hull-White Interest Rate Trees", *Journal of Derivatives*, **3**(3), 26–36.

Hull, J., and A. White, 2000, "Forward Rate Volatilities, Swap Rate Volatilities and Implementation of the Libor Market Model", *Journal of Fixed Income*, **10**(2), 46–62.

Inui, K., and M. Kijima, 1998, "A Markovian Framework in Multi-Factor Heath-Jarrow-Morton Models", *Journal of Financial and Quantitative Analysis*, **33**(3), 423–440.

James, J., and N. Webber, 2000, *Interest Rate Modeling*, John Wiley & Sons, Chichester.

Jamshidian, F., 1989, "An Exact Bond Option Formula", *Journal of Finance*, **44**(1), 205–209.

Jamshidian, F., 1991, "Forward Induction and Construction of Yield Curve Diffusion Models", *Journal of Fixed Income*, **1**(1), 62–74.

Jamshidian, F., 1997, "Libor and Swap Market Models and Measures", *Finance and Stochastics*, **1**(4), 293–330.

Karatzas, I., and S.E. Shreve, 1991, *Brownian Motion and Stochastic Calculus*, Springer-Verlag, New York.

Kerkhof, J., and A. Pelsser, 2002, "Observational Equivalence of Discrete String Models and Market Models", *Journal of Derivatives*, **10**(1), 55–61.

Klaassen, P., E. Van Leeuwen, and B. Schreurs, 1998, "One-Factor Fallacies", *Risk*, **11**(12), 56–59.

Li, A., P. Ritchken, and L. Sankarasubramanian, 1995, "Lattice Models for Pricing American Interest Rate Claims", *Journal of Finance*, **50**(2), 719–737.

Li, A., P. Ritchken, and L. Sankarasubramanian, 1995, "Lattice Works", *Risk*, **8**(11), 65–69.

Litterman, R., and J. Scheinkman, 1991, "Common Factors Affecting Bond Returns", *Journal of Fixed Income*, **1**(1), 54–61.

Longstaff, F.A., and E.S. Schwartz, 1992, "Interest Rate Volatility and the Term Structure: A Two-Factor General Equilibrium Model, *Journal of Finance*, **47**(4), 1259–1282.

Martellini, L., and P. Priaulet, 2000, *Fixed-Income Securities: Dynamic Methods for Interest Rate Risk Pricing and Hedging*, John Wiley & Sons, Chichester.

Merton, R.C., 1973, "The Theory of Rational Option Pricing", *Bell Journal of Economics and Management Science*, **4**(1), 141–183.

Miltersen, K.R., K. Sandmann, and D. Sondermann, 1997, "Closed Form Solutions for Term Structure Derivatives with Log-Normal Interest Rates", *Journal of Finance*, **52**(1), 409–430.

Moraleda, J., and T. Vorst, 1996, Pricing American Interest Rate Claims with Humped Volatility Models, Report 9607, Erasmus University Rotterdam.

Musiela, M., 1994, Nominal Annual Rates and Lognormal Volatility Structure, Working Paper, University of New South Wales.

Musiela, M., and M. Rutkowski, 1997, *Martingale Methods in Financial Modelling*, Springer Verlag, New York.

Nelson, C.R., and A.F. Siegel, 1987, "Parsimonious Modeling of Yield Curves", *Journal of Business*, **60**(4), 473–489.

Nelson, J., and S. Schaefer, 1983, The Dynamics of the Term Structure and Alternative Portfolios Immunization Strategies, *Innovations in Bond Portfolio Management: Duration Analysis and Immunization*, JAI Press, Greenwich, CT.

Pearson, N.D., and T. Sun, 1994, "Exploiting the Conditional Density in Estimating the Term Structure: An Application to the Cox, Ingersoll and Ross Model, *Journal of Finance*, **49**(4), 1279–1304.

Rebonato, R., 1998, *Interest-Rate Option Models*, John Wiley & Sons, Chichester.

Rebonato, R., 1999, "Calibrating the BGM Model", *Risk*, **12**(3), 74–79.

Revuz, D., and M. Yor, 1991, *Continuous Martingales and Brownian Motion*, Springer-Verlag, New York.

Ritchken, P., and L. Sankarasubramanian, 1995, "Volatility Structures of Forward Rates and the Dynamics of the Term Structure", *Mathematical Finance*, **5**(1), 55–72.

Ritchken, P., and L. Sankarasubramanian, 1995, "Near Nirvana", *Risk*, **8**(9), 109–111.

Ritchken, P., and L. Sankarasubramanian, 1995, "The Importance of Forward Rate Volatility Structures in Pricing Interest Rate-Sensitive Claims", *Journal of Derivatives*, **3**(1), 25–41.

Rogers, L.C.G., 1995, Which Model for Term-Structure of Interest Rates Should One Use?, *Proceedings of IMA—Workshop on Mathematical Finance*, Springer, Berlin, Heidelberg, New York, 93–115.

Rogers, L.C.G., 1996, "Gaussian Errors", *Risk*, **9**(1), 42–45.

Santa-Clara, P., and D. Sornette, 2001, "The Dynamics of the Forward Interest Rate Curve with Stochastic String Shocks", *Review of Financial Studies*, **14**, 149–185.

Schaefer, S.M., and E.S. Schwartz, 1984, "A Two-Factor Model of the Term Structure, An Approximate Analytical Solution", *Journal of Financial and Quantitative Analysis*, **19**(4), 413–424.

Strickland, C.R., 1996, "A Comparison of Diffusion Models of the Term Structure", *European Journal of Finance*, **2**(1), 103–123.

Strickland, C.R., 1996, "A Comparison of Models for Pricing Interest Rate Derivative Securities", *European Journal of Finance*, **2**(3), 261–287.

Svensson, L., 1994, Estimating and Interpreting Forward Interest Rates: Sweden 1992-94, CEPR Discussion Paper No. 1051.

Vasicek, O.A., 1977, "An Equilibrium Characterisation of the Term Structure", *Journal of Financial Economics*, **5**(2), 177–188.

12.6 Problems

Exercise 12.1 Today's term structure of par Treasury yields is assumed to have the following values:

Maturity (in years)	Par yield (%)
1	3.50
2	3.70
3	3.80

Derive the corresponding recombining binomial interest-rate tree, assuming a 1-year interest-rate volatility of 3%.

Exercise 12.2 What are the main drawbacks of the Vasicek (1977) model?

Exercise 12.3 Explain why it is better to use a multifactor model rather than a one-factor model? In which cases is it sufficient to use a one-factor model?

Exercise 12.4 We recall that Merton's (1973) model is a one-factor interest-rate model whose dynamics driven by the short rate is the following SDE under $\mathbb{Q}$, the risk-neutral probability:

$$dr_t = \mu \, dt + \sigma \, dW_t$$

Provide the zero-coupon bond price $B(0, \theta)$ using the Martingale approach. Find the zero-coupon rate $R^c(0, \theta)$.

Exercise 12.5 Compute the zero-coupon rate variance in the model of Vasicek (1977).

Exercise 12.6 Show that the correlation coefficient between zero-coupon rate changes for different maturities is equal to 1 in the model of Merton (1973).

Exercise 12.7 Show in a discrete-time framework that in the absence of arbitrage the long-term zero-coupon rate (we mean the zero-coupon rate with infinite maturity) can never decrease.

Exercise 12.8 In the continuous-time version of the Ho and Lee (1986) model, we recall that the discount bond prices under the risk-neutral probability $\mathbb{Q}$ are given by

$$\frac{dB(t, T)}{B(t, T)} = r_t \, dt + \sigma \times (T - t) \times d\widehat{W}_t$$

1. Show that discount bond prices are given by

$$B(t, T) = \frac{B(0, T)}{B(0, t)} \exp\left(-(T - t)[r(t) - f(0, t)] - \left(\frac{\sigma^2 (T - t)^2 t}{2}\right)\right)$$

where the short rate $r(t)$ is given by

$$r(t) = f(0, t) - \int_0^t \sigma \, d\widehat{W}_s + \int_0^t \sigma^2 (t - s) \, ds$$

2. Find that zero-coupon rates $R^c(t, T - t)$ are given by

$$R^c(t, T - t) = F^c(0, t, T - t) + r(t) - f(0, t) + \frac{\sigma^2 (T - t)t}{2}$$

Exercise 12.9   In the model of Ho and Lee (1986), explain

1. why interest rates can take on negative value with positive probability?
2. why volatility of interest rates is constant?
3. why all possible zero-coupon curves at a future date are parallel?

Exercise 12.10   Draw the volatility of the instantaneous forward rates

1. (a) in the Moraleda and Vorst (1996) model using the following parameter values:

σ	λ	κ
1.50%	12%	0.25

    (b) in the Hull and White (1990) model using the following parameter values:

σ	λ
1.50%	5%

    (c) in the Ho and Lee (1986) model using the value 1.50% for the parameter σ.
2. What are the different shapes that we can obtain in these three models?

Exercise 12.11   The goal of this exercise is to construct the Hull and White's trinomial tree (see Appendix 1 of Chapter 12). We consider the following parameter values

λ	σ	Δt
0.15	0.01	1 year

1. Draw the graph of the zero-coupon rate volatilities.
2. Applying the normal scheme, construct the lattice of the short-term rate r^* (with an initial value equal to 0).
3. We now assume that the spot yield curve is as follows up to the 5-year maturity:

Maturity (years)	Spot rate (%)	Discount factor
1	4.00	0.96079
2	4.15	0.92035
3	4.25	0.88029
4	4.33	0.84097
5	4.40	0.80252

Construct the lattice of the short-term rate r by using the continuous-time relationship between r and r^*

$$\alpha(t) = r(t) - r^*(t) = f(0, t) + \frac{\sigma^2}{2\lambda^2}(1 - e^{-\lambda t})^2$$

where $f(0, t)$ is the instantaneous forward rate at date 0. Here, because $\Delta t = 1$ year, it is the 1-year forward rate determined at date 0 and beginning at date t.

4. Same question as 3, but using the approach proposed by Hull and White.

5. Price the put option, which provides the following payoff at date $t = 2$:

$$Max[0; 10,000 \times (5\% - r)]$$

12.7 Appendix 1: The Hull and White Trinomial Lattice

The model has been discussed above. We simply recall that under the risk-neutral probability measure $\mathbb{Q}$, the short-term process is given by

$$dr(t) = (\theta(t) - \lambda r(t))\, dt - \sigma\, d\widehat{W}(t) \tag{12.14}$$

or equivalently

$$dr(t) = \left(\frac{\partial f(0, t)}{\partial t} + \lambda f(0, t) + \frac{\sigma^2}{2\lambda^2}(1 - e^{-2\lambda t}) - \lambda r(t)\right) dt - \sigma\, d\widehat{W}(t) \tag{12.15}$$

with $f(0, t)$ being the instantaneous forward rate calculated at date 0 and starting at date t. Hull and White (1994a, 1994b, 1996) argue that a trinomial lattice should perform better than a binomial lattice because it is likely to better capture the mean-reverting feature. Note also that using that lattice is essentially equivalent to using a finite-difference method (see Appendix 2 of Chapter 6).

12.7.1 Discretizing the Short Rate

The basic idea consists in first turning the SDE (12.14) for the short rate into an SDE for a variable r^* with initial value equal to zero. This is done by setting

$$dr^*(t) = -\lambda r^*(t)\, dt - \sigma\, d\widehat{W}(t)$$

Then, this SDE is discretized using a time step of length Δt

$$r^*(t + \Delta t) - r^*(t) = -\lambda r^*(t)\Delta t - \sigma\sqrt{\Delta t}U$$

where U is a standard Gaussian variable with mean zero and unit variance. The expected value and the variance of $r^*(t + \Delta t) - r^*(t)$ are given under $\mathbb{Q}$ by

$$\mathbb{E}_t^{\mathbb{Q}}(r^*(t + \Delta t) - r^*(t)) = -\lambda r^*(t)\Delta t \tag{12.16}$$

$$\mathbb{V}ar_t^{\mathbb{Q}}(r^*(t + \Delta t) - r^*(t)) = \sigma^2 \Delta t \tag{12.17}$$

The spread Δr between two rates on the lattice is assumed to be equal to $\sigma\sqrt{3\Delta t}$, a value which is selected to achieve a good numerical performance of the model. Define (i, j) as the node on the lattice corresponding to $t = i\Delta t$ and $r^* = j\Delta r$. Starting from an initial position $j\Delta r, r^*$ may follow the three following schemes: normal scheme, ascending scheme and descending scheme.

The Normal Scheme

It is defined by

It is based upon options of an up move, a down move and no move. Since one needs to locally match the expected value and the variance given in equations (12.16) and (12.17), we require that the probabilities p_1, p_2 and p_3, corresponding to the three possible moves, satisfy the following system:

$$\begin{cases} p_1 \Delta r - p_3 \Delta r = -\lambda j \Delta r \Delta t \\ p_1(\Delta r)^2 + p_3(\Delta r)^2 = \sigma^2 \Delta t + \lambda^2 j^2 (\Delta r)^2 (\Delta t)^2 \\ p_1 + p_2 + p_3 = 1 \end{cases}$$

which may be simplified into

$$\begin{cases} p_1 = \dfrac{1}{6} + \dfrac{(\lambda j \Delta t)(\lambda j \Delta t - 1)}{2} \\ p_2 = \dfrac{2}{3} - \lambda^2 j^2 (\Delta t)^2 \\ p_3 = \dfrac{1}{6} + \dfrac{(\lambda j \Delta t)(\lambda j \Delta t + 1)}{2} \end{cases}$$

Note that all probabilities are positive for

$$\frac{-0.816}{\lambda \Delta t} < j < \frac{0.816}{\lambda \Delta t}$$

The Ascending Scheme

It is defined by

$$
\begin{array}{ll}
& p_1 \searrow \quad (j+2)\Delta r \\
j\Delta r & \xrightarrow{\ p_2\ } (j+1)\Delta r \\
& p_3 \nwarrow \quad j\Delta r
\end{array}
$$

It is based upon two possible up moves and a possible no move. Since one needs to locally match the expected value and the variance given in equations (12.16) and (12.17), we require that the probabilities p_1, p_2 and p_3, corresponding to the three possible moves, satisfy the following system:

$$
\begin{cases}
2p_1 + p_2 = -\lambda j \Delta t \\
4p_1 + p_2 = \dfrac{1}{3} + 2\lambda^2 j^2 (\Delta t)^2 \\
p_1 + p_2 + p_3 = 1
\end{cases}
$$

which may be simplified into

$$
\begin{cases}
p_1 = \dfrac{1}{6} + \dfrac{(\lambda j \Delta t)(\lambda j \Delta t + 1)}{2} \\
p_2 = -\dfrac{1}{3} - (\lambda j \Delta t)(\lambda j \Delta t + 2) \\
p_3 = \dfrac{7}{6} + \dfrac{(\lambda j \Delta t)(\lambda j \Delta t + 3)}{2}
\end{cases}
$$

Note that all probabilities are positive for

$$
-\frac{1.816}{\lambda \Delta t} < j < -\frac{0.184}{\lambda \Delta t}
$$

The Descending Scheme

It is defined by

$$
\begin{array}{ll}
& p_1 \nearrow \quad j\Delta r \\
j\Delta r & \xrightarrow{\ p_2\ } (j-1)\Delta r \\
& p_3 \searrow \quad (j-2)\Delta r
\end{array}
$$

It is based upon two possible down moves and a possible no move. Since one needs to locally match the expected value and the variance given in equations (12.16) and (12.17), we require that the probabilities p_1, p_2 and p_3, corresponding to the three possible moves, satisfy the following system:

$$\begin{cases} p_2 + 2p_3 = -\lambda j \Delta t \\ p_2 + 4p_3 = \dfrac{1}{3} + 2\lambda^2 j^2 (\Delta t)^2 \\ p_1 + p_2 + p_3 = 1 \end{cases}$$

which may be simplified into

$$\begin{cases} p_1 = \dfrac{7}{6} + \dfrac{(\lambda j \Delta t)(\lambda j \Delta t - 3)}{2} \\ p_2 = -\dfrac{1}{3} - (\lambda j \Delta t)(\lambda j \Delta t - 2) \\ p_3 = \dfrac{1}{6} + \dfrac{(\lambda j \Delta t)(\lambda j \Delta t - 1)}{2} \end{cases}$$

Note that all probabilities are positive for

$$\frac{1.816}{\lambda \Delta t} < j < \frac{0.184}{\lambda \Delta t}$$

From One Scheme to Another

- *For* $-\dfrac{0.816}{\lambda \Delta t} < j < -\dfrac{0.184}{\lambda \Delta t}$, *one may shift from the normal scheme to the ascending scheme. This enhances the mean-reverting effect when interest rates are low.*

- *For* $\dfrac{0.184}{\lambda \Delta t} < j < \dfrac{0.816}{\lambda \Delta t}$, *one may shift from the normal scheme to the descending scheme. This enhances the mean-reverting effect when interest rates are high.*

As an illustration, we consider the following example:

λ	σ	Δt
0.12	0.0075	1 year

We now build the lattice for r^* up to $i = 2$ (see Figure 12.1) using the results discussed above.

Note that

- $\Delta r = 1.30\%$;

- *for* $j < 2$, *we apply the normal scheme;*

- *for* $j \leq -2$, *we shift to the ascending scheme;*

- *for* $j \geq 2$, *we shift to the descending scheme.*

12.7.2 Calibrating the Lattice to the Current Spot Yield Curve

Once the lattice for r^* is obtained, one needs to get a lattice for r, and that lattice should be consistent with the currently observed spot yield curve.

Rates $i=0$	Probabilities	Rates $i=1$	Probabilities	Rates $i=2$	Probabilities
					0.835
				2.60% $j=2$	0.089
					0.076
			0.114		0.114
		1.30% $j=1$	0.652	1.30% $j=1$	0.652
			0.234		0.234
	0.167		0.167		0.167
0% $j=0$	0.666	0% $j=0$	0.666	0% $j=0$	0.666
	0.167		0.167		0.167
			0.234		0.234
		-1.30% $j=-1$	0.652	-1.30% $j=-1$	0.652
			0.114		0.114
					0.076
				-2.60% $j=-2$	0.089
					0.835

Figure 12.1 Lattice for r^*.

A Tempting but Incorrect Solution

The first idea one may have in mind consists in using the continuous-time relationship between r^* and r. We define $\alpha(t)$ as

$$\alpha(t) = r(t) - r^*(t)$$

from which we obtain

$$d\alpha(t) = dr(t) - dr^*(t) = [\theta(t) - \lambda\alpha(t)]\,dt$$

or

$$\alpha(t) = e^{-\lambda t}\left(r(0) + \int_0^t e^{\lambda u}\theta(u)\,du\right)$$

or equivalently

$$\alpha(t) = f(0, t) + \frac{\sigma^2}{2\lambda^2}(1 - e^{-\lambda t})^2$$

using equations (12.14) and (12.15). Hence, we obtain an exact relationship between r^* and r, and one just needs to add to the value r^* in i the quantity $\alpha(i\,\Delta t)$ to obtain the value of r in i. The probabilities of going from one state to the other are not modified. Although that solution appears quite satisfactory, it does not allow to be fully consistent with the current spot yield curve. The reason for this is that we use a relationship based upon the continuous-time setup, and include it into a discrete lattice. For this reason, we now discuss another approach.

Fixed Income Securities

The Exact Solution

We now define $Q_{i,j}$ as the present value of an asset, which pays off \$1 if the node (i, j) is reached and 0 otherwise. Let us go back to the example above. We assume that the spot yield curve is as follows up to the 5-year maturity:

Maturity (years)	Spot rate (%)	Discount factor
1	3	0.97044
2	3.20	0.938
3	3.40	0.90303
4	3.60	0.86589
5	3.70	0.8311

Obviously, $Q_{0,0} = 1$ and α_0 takes on the value 3%, which is the 1-year spot rate. The probability to reach the node $(1, 1)$, $(1, 0)$ and $(1, -1)$ starting from $(0, 0)$ are, respectively, 0.167, 0.666 and 0.167 (see Figure 12.1). From that, we obtain the value of $Q_{1,1}$, $Q_{1,0}$, $Q_{1,-1}$:

$$Q_{1,1} = 0.167 \cdot e^{-3\%}$$

$$Q_{1,0} = 0.666 \cdot e^{-3\%}$$

$$Q_{1,-1} = 0.167 \cdot e^{-3\%}$$

α_1 is chosen so that the exact price of the 2-year discount bond $(i = 2)$ is recovered. As seen from nodes $(1, 1)$, $(1, 0)$ and $(1, -1)$, the price of that discount bond is, respectively, equal to $e^{-(\alpha_1 + \Delta r)}$, $e^{-\alpha_1}$ and $e^{-(\alpha_1 - \Delta r)}$. From that, we obtain the following relationship:

$$Q_{1,1} e^{-(\alpha_1 + 1.30\%)} + Q_{1,0} e^{-\alpha_1} + Q_{1,-1} e^{-(\alpha_1 - 1.30\%)} = e^{-3.2\%} = 0.938$$

or

$$\alpha_1 = 3.40\%$$

Hence, α_1 corresponds to the central value of the rate r at date $i = 1$, that is at the node $(1, 0)$. In the same way, we compute $Q_{2,2}$, $Q_{2,1}$, $Q_{2,0}$, $Q_{2,-1}$ and $Q_{2,-2}$:

$$Q_{2,2} = Q_{1,1} \cdot 0.114 \cdot e^{-(\alpha_1 + 1.30\%)}$$

$$Q_{2,1} = Q_{1,1} \cdot 0.652 \cdot e^{-(\alpha_1 + 1.30\%)} + Q_{1,0} \cdot 0.167 \cdot e^{-\alpha_1}$$

$$Q_{2,0} = Q_{1,1} \cdot 0.234 \cdot e^{-(\alpha_1 + 1.30\%)} + Q_{1,0} \cdot 0.666 \cdot e^{-\alpha_1} + Q_{1,-1} \cdot 0.234 \cdot e^{-(\alpha_1 - 1.30\%)}$$

$$Q_{2,-1} = Q_{1,0} \cdot 0.167 \cdot e^{-\alpha_1} + Q_{1,-1} \cdot 0.652 \cdot e^{-(\alpha_1 - 1.30\%)}$$

$$Q_{2,-2} = Q_{1,-1} \cdot 0.114 \cdot e^{-(\alpha_1 - 1.30\%)}$$

Hence,

$$Q_{2,2} e^{-(\alpha_2 + 2.60\%)} + Q_{2,1} e^{-(\alpha_2 + 1.30\%)} + Q_{2,0} e^{-\alpha_2} + Q_{2,-1} e^{-(\alpha_2 - 1.30\%)} + Q_{2,-2} e^{-(\alpha_1 - 2.60\%)}$$

$$= e^{-3.4\%} = 0.90303$$

from which we obtain

$$\alpha_2 = 3.81\%$$

Hence, we obtain the following lattice for r (see Figure 12.2).

Rates $i=0$	Probabilities	Rates $i=1$	Probabilities	Rates $i=2$	Probabilities
					0.835
				6.41%	0.089
					0.076
			0.114		0.114
		4.70%	0.652	5.11%	0.652
			0.234		0.234
	0.167		0.167		0.167
3%	0.666	3.40%	0.666	3.81%	0.666
	0.167		0.167		0.167
			0.234		0.234
		2.10%	0.652	2.51%	0.652
			0.114		0.114
					0.076
				1.21%	0.089
					0.835

Figure 12.2 Lattice for r.

Hull and White (1994a, 1994b, 1996) have extended that approach and have obtained formulas for the coefficients α_i and $Q_{i,j}$. We denote by $B(0, (m+1)\Delta t)$ the price of a discount bond that pays \$1 at date $(m+1)\Delta t$. We have

$$B(0, (m+1)\Delta t) = \sum_{j=-n_m}^{j=n_m} Q_{m,j} \cdot e^{-(\alpha_m + j\Delta r)\Delta t} \qquad (12.18)$$

where n_m is the number of nodes above and below the central node at date $m\Delta t$. The solution to equation (12.18) is

$$\alpha_m = \frac{\ln\left(\sum_{j=-n_m}^{j=n_m} Q_{m,j} \cdot e^{-j\Delta r\Delta t}\right) - \ln[B(0, (m+1)\Delta t)]}{\Delta t}$$

Having obtained α_m, one may then compute $Q_{i,j}$ for $i = m+1$ using

$$Q_{m+1,j} = \sum_k Q_{m,k} \cdot p(k,j) \cdot e^{-(\alpha_m + k\Delta r)\Delta t}$$

where $p(k,j)$ is the probability to move from node (m,k) to node $(m+1,j)$.

12.7.3 Option Pricing

Option pricing can be done with Hull and White (1994a, 1994b, 1996) trinomial lattice as with any other lattice. We use the example above, and try to price a call option that pays at date $i = 2$:

$$\max[100(r - 3.5\%); 0]$$

From the lattice derived above, we may obtain the cash flow for each of the possible terminal nodes. For example, 2.91 corresponds to $100(6.41\% - 3.5\%)$. The rate 6.41% below is the rate with 1-year maturity and with starting date $i = 2$, which corresponds to that node of the lattice (see lattice below):

$$
\begin{array}{ccccc}
 & & & & \begin{matrix} 2.91 \\ 6.41\% \end{matrix} \\
 & & & \begin{matrix} 1.387 \\ 4.70\% \end{matrix} & \begin{matrix} 1.61 \\ 5.11\% \end{matrix} \\
 & & \begin{matrix} 0.533 \\ 3\% \end{matrix} & \begin{matrix} 0.459 \\ 3.40\% \end{matrix} & \begin{matrix} 0.31 \\ 3.81\% \end{matrix} \\
 & & & \begin{matrix} 0.071 \\ 2.10\% \end{matrix} & \begin{matrix} 0 \\ 2.51\% \end{matrix} \\
 & & & & \begin{matrix} 0 \\ 1.21\% \end{matrix}
\end{array}
$$

Cash flows at date $i = 1$ are obtained in a classic way by discounting back to present the cash flows to be received at date $i = 2$ under the risk-neutral probability, which actually is the probability under which the lattice has been built. For example, we obtain

$$(0.114 \times 2.91 + 0.652 \times 1.61 + 0.234 \times 0.31)\, e^{-4.70\%} = 1.387$$

Working backward through the lattice up to date $i = 0$, we finally obtain as value for the option $0.533. Note that the lattice has been developed in the presence of a single state variable. We refer the reader to Hull and White (1994c) for the same method with two state variables.

12.8 Appendix 2: An Introduction to Stochastic Processes in Continuous Time

We provide below a rather informal introduction to the theory of stochastic processes in continuous time and its application to finance in general and interest rates models in particular. We state all results without a proof. We refer the interested reader to standard texts such as Karatzas and Shreve (1991) or Revuz and Yor (1991) for a more detailed and formal treatment of the mathematical tools, and to Duffie (1996) and Dana and Jeanblanc-Picqué (1998) for an introduction to the applications in asset pricing theory.

12.8.1 Brownian Motion

A Gaussian (or normal) random variable with mean 0 and variance 1 has a density given by (for $x \in \mathbb{R}$)

$$f(x) = \frac{1}{\sqrt{2\pi}} \exp\left(-\frac{x^2}{2}\right)$$

with

$$\int_{-\infty}^{+\infty} f(x)\, dx = 1$$

If $\mathcal{E}$ is normally distributed with mean 0 and variance 1, then we denote this by $\mathcal{E} \hookrightarrow \mathcal{N}(0, 1)$. If a and b are two real numbers with $b \neq 0$, then $a + b\mathcal{E}$ is normally distributed with mean a and variance b^2. We express this using the following notation:

$$a + b\mathcal{E} \hookrightarrow \mathcal{N}(a, b^2)$$

Standard Brownian Motion

Definition 12.1   A standard Brownian motion $(W_t, t \geq 0)$ defined on a standard probability space $(\Omega, \mathcal{F}, (\mathcal{F}_t), \mathbb{P})$ is a stochastic process in continuous time. For a given state of the world ω, the path $t \longmapsto W(t, \omega)$, with $t \in \mathbb{R}_+$, is a function of time. A standard Brownian motion is defined by the following properties:

1. $W_0 = 0$.

2. Independent increments: for all $t \geq 0$ and all $h \geq 0$, $W_{t+h} - W_t$ is independent of the σ−field generated by past values of the process, that is, $\sigma\{W_s, s \leq t\}$.

3. For all $t \geq 0$ and all $h \geq 0$, $W_{t+h} - W_t \hookrightarrow \mathcal{N}(0, h)$.

4. Stationarity: the distribution of W_h is identical to the distribution of $W_{t+h} - W_t$ (a Gaussian variable with zero mean and variance equal to h).

Remark 12.2   Note that points 2 and 3 are consistent: if $t_1 \geq 0$ and $t_2 \geq 0$, then

$$\mathbb{V}ar(W_{t_1+t_2}) = \mathbb{V}ar(W_{t_1+t_2} - W_{t_1} + W_{t_1})$$
$$= \mathbb{V}ar(W_{t_1+t_2} - W_{t_1}) + \mathbb{V}ar(W_{t_1}) + 2\mathbb{C}ov(W_{t_1+t_2} - W_{t_1}, W_{t_1})$$
$$= (t_1 + t_2 - t_1) + t_1 + 0$$

since $W_{t_1+t_2}$ and W_{t_1} are independent. Thus

$$\mathbb{V}ar(W_{t_1+t_2}) = t_1 + t_2$$

which is consistent with $W_{t_1+t_2} \hookrightarrow \mathcal{N}(0, t_1 + t_2)$.

Remark 12.3   Note finally that the property of independent increments can be formulated in the following way: $\forall n \in N, \forall t_i, 0 \leq t_0 \leq t_1 \leq \cdots \leq t_n$, the variables $(W_{t_n} - W_{t_{n-1}}, \ldots, W_{t_1} - W_{t_0}, W_{t_0})$ are independent. Equivalently, we have that $W_{t+h} - W_t$ is independent of $W_s, \forall s \leq t$. In words, it means that the past values of the processes before time t do not convey any information concerning the future values of the processes after t.

Remark 12.4   Random Walk

If $(W_t, t \geq 0)$ is a standard Brownian motion and $T > 0$, then W_T can be regarded as an infinite sum of infinitely small independent Gaussian increments. Let $N > 0$ and $\Delta t = \frac{T}{N}$. We divide the interval $[0, T]$ into N subintervals with length Δt. We have

$$W_T \sim \sum_{i=1}^{N} \mathcal{E}_i \sqrt{\Delta t} \text{ where } \mathcal{E}_i \hookrightarrow \mathcal{N}(0, 1)$$

and $\mathcal{E}_i$ are independent. Then

$$\mathbb{E}(W_T) = \sum_{i=1}^{N} \mathbb{E}(\mathcal{E}_i)\sqrt{\Delta t} = 0$$

and

$$\mathbb{V}ar(W_T) = \sum_{i=1}^{N} \mathbb{V}ar(\mathcal{E}_i\sqrt{\Delta t}) + 2\sum_{i<j} \mathbb{C}ov(\mathcal{E}_i\sqrt{\Delta t}, \mathcal{E}_j\sqrt{\Delta t})$$

$$= \sum_{i=1}^{N} \Delta t + 0 = N\Delta t = T$$

Therefore

$$W_T \hookrightarrow \mathcal{N}(0, T)$$

The Brownian motion is obtained in the limit of N going to infinity (that is, as the length of each subinterval decreases to zero). W is also called a *Wiener process*. For small Δt, $\Delta W = W_{t+\Delta t} - W_t \sim \mathcal{E}\sqrt{\Delta t}$ where $\mathcal{E} \hookrightarrow \mathcal{N}(0, 1)$.

Proposition 12.1   Brownian Motion Paths

Brownian motion paths are continuous and nowhere differentiable almost surely (a.s.).

Proposition 12.2   Properties of the Standard Brownian Motion

The Brownian motion is a Gaussian process such that

1. $\mathbb{E}(W_t W_s) = \inf(s, t) = s \wedge t$

2. $(W_t, t \geq 0)$ is a martingale with respect to its canonical filtration $\mathcal{F}_t = \sigma\{W_s, s \leq t\}$

Proposition 12.3   Martingale Property

1. The process $(W_t^2 - t)$ is a martingale. Conversely, if (W_t) is a continuous process such that (W_t) and $(W_t^2 - t)$ are martingales, then (W_t) is a Brownian motion.

2. The process $(\exp\{\lambda W_t - \frac{1}{2}\lambda^2 t\})$ is a martingale for any real number λ. Conversely, if (W_t) is a process such that $(\exp\{\lambda W_t - \frac{1}{2}\lambda^2 t\})$ is a continuous martingale for any real number λ, then (W_t) is a Brownian motion.

Generalization

Starting from a standard Brownian motion (W_t), we define a process X by

$$\forall t \geq 0, \; X_t = X_0 + bt + \sigma W_t$$

We have

$$X_t \hookrightarrow \mathcal{N}(X_0 + bt, \sigma^2 t)$$

and

$$X_{t+h}/\mathcal{F}_t \hookrightarrow \mathcal{N}(X_t + bh, \sigma^2 h)$$

X_0 is the value of X at $t = 0$. The drift term is b, the volatility term is σ^2. We introduce the informal definition (see the stochastic integral for a formal definition of that expression)

$$dX_t = b\,dt + \sigma\,dW_t$$

X is a *generalized* Brownian motion.

Remark 12.5

1. *If $\sigma = 0$, then $dX_t = b\,dt$ or $X_t = X_0 + bt$. X is then a deterministic process.*

2. *For $X_0 = 0$, $b = 0$ and $\sigma = 1$, we recover the standard Brownian motion.*

Proposition 12.4 Let $(\Omega, \mathcal{F}, (\mathcal{F}_t), \mathbb{P})$ be a standard probability space and W_t a Brownian motion defined on that probability space. If $X_t = bt + \sigma W_t$, then, for all real number β, $(\exp\{\beta X_t - (b\beta + \frac{1}{2}\sigma^2\beta^2)t\})$ is an $\mathcal{F}_t$-martingale. Conversely, if (X_t) is a continuous process such that $(\exp\{\beta X_t - (a\beta + \frac{1}{2}b^2\beta^2)t\})$ is an $\mathcal{F}_t$-martingale, then there is an $\mathcal{F}_t$ Brownian motion (W_t) such that $X_t = bt + \sigma W_t$.

12.8.2 Stochastic Integral

Construction and Properties

Let X be a generalized Brownian motion with

$$X_t = X_0 + bt + \sigma W_t$$

For $t_0 = 0 < t_1 < t_2 < \cdots < t_{N-1} < t_N = t$, we have

$$X_t = X_0 + \sum_{i=1}^{N} [b(t_i - t_{i-1}) + \sigma(W_{ti} - W_{ti-1})]$$

Taking the limit as N goes to infinity, we obtain

$$X_t = X_0 + \int_0^T (b\,dt + \sigma\,dW_t) = X_0 + \int_0^T dX_t$$

with

$$dX_t = b\,dt + \sigma\,dW_t$$

More generally, if b and σ are not constant numbers but functions of t and X_t

$$\begin{cases} b(t, X_t) \\ \sigma(t, X_t) \end{cases}$$

then we define

$$X_t = X_0 + \int_0^T [b(t, X_t)\, dt + \sigma(t, X_t)\, dW_t]$$

which is the limit of

$$X_t = X_0 + \sum_{i=1}^N [b(t_{i-1}, X_{ti-1})(t_i - t_{i-1}) + \sigma(t_{i-1}, X_{ti-1})(W_{ti} - W_{ti-1})]$$

when N goes to infinity. Then,

$$dX_t = b(t, X_t)\, dt + \sigma(t, X_t)\, dW_t$$

X is then a *diffusion process* such that

1. X_0 is the value of the process at $t = 0$;

2. $b(t, X_t)$ is the instantaneous drift of the process at date t;

3. $\sigma^2(t, X_t)$ is the instantaneous variance of the process at date t.

The integral

$$\int_0^T \sigma(t, X_t)\, dW_t$$

is a stochastic integral.

Proposition 12.5   Properties of Stochastic Integral

Let $M(T) = \int_0^T \sigma(t, X_t)\, dW_t$.

1. Linearity: $\int_0^T (\sigma(t, X_t) + \psi(t, X_t))\, dW_t = \int_0^T \sigma(t, X_t)\, dW_t + \int_0^T \psi(t, X_t)\, dW_t$;

2. Martingale: the process $M(T)$ is a continuous martingale

$$\mathbb{E}\left\{\int_0^T \sigma(s, X_s)\, dW_s / \mathcal{F}_t\right\} = \int_0^t \sigma(s, X_s)\, dW_s$$

and

$$\mathbb{E}(M_T) = 0.$$

3. The process $\{\int_0^t \sigma(s, X_s)\, dW_s\}^2 - \int_0^t \sigma^2(s, X_s)\, ds$ is a martingale.

4. The variance of $M(t)$ is $\int_0^t \mathbb{E}[\sigma^2(s, X_s)]\, ds$.

5. $\mathbb{E}\{\int_0^T \sigma(s, X_s)\, dW_s \int_0^T \psi(s, X_s)\, dW_s\} = \mathbb{E}\{\int_0^T \sigma(s, X_s)\psi(s, X_s)\, ds\}$.

Itô Process

Definition 12.2   A process $(X_t, t \geq 0)$ is an Itô process if

$$X_t = x + \int_0^t b_s\, ds + \int_0^t \sigma_s\, dW_s$$

where b is an adapted process such that $\int_0^t |b_s|\,\mathrm{d}s$ is finite a.s. for all t and σ is a process in Λ, the set of adapted process θ which are càdlàg (right-continuous and left-limited, from the French "continu à droite et limité à gauche) and satisfy $\mathbb{E}\{\int_0^t \theta^2(s,\omega)\,\mathrm{d}s\} < \infty$, a.s.

We recall the following notation:

$$\begin{cases} \mathrm{d}X_t = b_t\,\mathrm{d}t + \sigma_t\,\mathrm{d}W_t \\ \qquad X_0 = x \end{cases}$$

where b is a drift term and σ is a diffusion term.

Proposition 12.6   Properties of Itô Processes

1. If $b_t = 0$ and $\sigma \in \Lambda$, the process $(X_t, t \geq 0)$ is a continuous martingale.

2. If $\sigma \in \Lambda$, then $\mathbb{E}(X_t) = \mathbb{E}(X_0) + \int_0^t \mathbb{E}(b_s)\,\mathrm{d}s$ and $\forall t \geq s$

$$\mathbb{E}(X_t/\mathcal{F}_s) = \mathbb{E}(X_0) + \mathbb{E}\left(\int_0^t b_s\,\mathrm{d}s/\mathcal{F}_s \right) + \int_0^s \sigma_u\,\mathrm{d}W_u$$

$$= X_s + \mathbb{E}\left(\int_s^t b_u\,\mathrm{d}u/\mathcal{F}_s \right)$$

3. Starting from a well-defined stochastic integral with respect to an Itô process X, we have

$$\int_0^t \theta_s\,\mathrm{d}X_s = \int_0^t \theta_s b_s\,\mathrm{d}s + \int_0^t \theta_s \sigma_s\,\mathrm{d}W_s$$

12.8.3   Stochastic Differential Equations (SDE)

Definition 12.3   A stochastic differential equation is an equation of the following type:

$$X_t = x + \int_0^t b(s, X_s)\,\mathrm{d}s + \int_0^t \sigma(s, X_s)\,\mathrm{d}W_s$$

or, in a differential form:

$$\begin{cases} X_t = b(t, X_t)\,\mathrm{d}t + \sigma(t, X_t)\,\mathrm{d}W_t \\ \qquad X_0 = x \end{cases} \tag{12.19}$$

We want to investigate under which conditions on b and σ, the SDE admits a unique solution.

Theorem 12.1   Existence and Uniqueness of the Solution to a SDE

Let us assume that

1. $b(t, x)$ and $\sigma(t, x)$ are continuous functions;

2. there is a positive real number K such that for all $t \in [0, T]$, $x \in \mathbb{R}$, $y \in \mathbb{R}$
   (a) $|b(t, x) - b(t, y)| + |\sigma(t, x) - \sigma(t, y)| \leq K|x - y|$ (Lipschitz condition),
   (b) $|b(t, x)|^2 + |\sigma(t, x)|^2 \leq K^2(1 + |x|^2)$ (growth condition);

3. the initial condition X_0 is independent of $(W_t, t \geq 0)$ and squared-integrable.

Then there is a unique solution with continuous paths to the above SDE, and that solution satisfies

$$\mathbb{E}\left(\sup_{0 \le t \le T} |X_t|^2\right) < \infty$$

Proposition 12.7   Markov Property

We denote by $X_s^{t,x}$ the solution to the SDE with initial condition x at date t, so that

$$X_s^{t,x} = x + \int_t^s b(u, X_u^{t,x})\, du + \int_t^s \sigma(u, X_u^{t,x})\, dW_u$$

The process X_t solution to the SDE is a Markov process with respect to the filtration $(\mathcal{F}_t)$ and we have

$$\mathbb{E}(f(X_s)/\mathcal{F}_t) = \Phi(X_t)$$

where $\Phi(x) = \mathbb{E}(f(X_s^{t,x}))$.

This result is important because it allows an easy calculation of the conditional expectations.

12.8.4   Asset Price Process

A standard continuous-time model for asset price P dynamics is

$$\frac{dP_t}{P_t} = \mu\, dt + \sigma\, dW_t$$

where W is a standard Brownian motion. An equivalent formulation is

$$dP_t = \mu P_t\, dt + \sigma P_t\, dW_t$$

This is a specific case of a diffusion process

$$b(t, P_t) = \mu P_t$$

$$\sigma(t, P_t) = \sigma P_t$$

For a small Δt

$$\frac{\Delta P_t}{P_t} = \mu \Delta t + \sigma \Delta W_t = \mu \Delta t + \sigma \mathcal{E}\sqrt{\Delta t} \text{ with } \mathcal{E} \hookrightarrow \mathcal{N}(0, 1)$$

and therefore

$$\frac{\Delta P_t}{P_t} \hookrightarrow \mathcal{N}(\mu \Delta t, \sigma^2 \Delta t)$$

where $\Delta P_t / P_t$ is the rate of return on the asset between dates t and $t + \Delta t$.

12.8.5   Representation of Brownian Martingales

Let $(W_t)_{0 \le t \le T}$ be a standard Brownian motion defined on a probability space $(\Omega, \mathcal{F}, \mathbb{P})$ and let $(\mathcal{F}_t)_{0 \le t \le T}$ be its canonical filtration. If $(H_t)_{0 \le t \le T}$ is an adapted and *predictable* process with $\mathbb{E}(\int_0^T H_s^2\, ds) < \infty$, the process $(\int_0^T H_s\, dW_s)$ is a squared-integrable martingale, with initial condition equal to zero. The following theorem shows that all Brownian martingales can be represented with a stochastic integral.

Theorem 12.2 Let $(M_t)_{0 \leq t \leq T}$ be a squared-integrable martingale with respect to the filtration $(\mathcal{F}_t)_{0 \leq t \leq T}$. Then there is an adapted and predictable process $(H_t)_{0 \leq t \leq T}$ such that $\mathbb{E}(\int_0^T H_s^2 \, ds) < +\infty$ and

$$\forall t \in [0, T], M_t = M_0 + \int_0^t H_s \, dB_s \text{ a.s.}$$

Note that the above representation holds only for martingales with respect to the canonical Brownian filtration. One can also show that if $(M_t)_{0 \leq t \leq T}$ is a non-squared-integrable martingale, there is a representation similar to the representation above, with a process merely satisfying $\int_0^T H_s^2 \, ds < \infty$.

12.8.6 Continuous-Time Asset Pricing

Unidimensional Itô's Lemma

Let X be a continuous-time process satisfying

1. $dX_t = b_X(t, X_t) \, dt + \sigma_X(t, X_t) \, dW_t$;

2. X starts with initial condition X_0 at $t = 0$;

3. $b_X(t, X_t)$ and $\sigma_X(t, X_t)$ are, respectively, the instantaneous drift and volatility terms of X;

4. W is a standard Brownian process.

We consider the continuous-time process Y such that

$$\forall t \geq 0, Y_t = f(t, X_t)$$

where f is a real-valued function defined on $\mathbb{R}_+ \times \mathbb{R}$, continuous and, respectively, once and twice continuously differentiable with respect to t and X_t. The following is a very useful result for asset pricing theory.

Proposition 12.8 Itô's Lemma

Y given by $\forall t \geq 0, Y_t = f(t, X_t)$ is a diffusion process such that

$$dY_t = b_Y(t, X_t) \, dt + \sigma_Y(t, X_t) \, dW_t, \forall t \geq 0$$

$$Y_0 = f(0, X_0)$$

with

$$b_Y(t, X_t) = \frac{\partial f}{\partial t}(t, X_t) + \frac{\partial f}{\partial x}(t, X_t) b_X(t, X_t) + \frac{1}{2} \frac{\partial^2 f}{\partial x^2}(t, X_t) \sigma_X^2(t, X_t)$$

and

$$\sigma_Y(t, X_t) = \frac{\partial f}{\partial x}(t, X_t) \sigma_X(t, X_t)$$

Before turning to an informal proof of Itô's lemma, let us specify the case with

$$dX_t = \sigma_X(t, X_t) \, dW_t$$

$$f(t, X_t) = f(X_t) \text{ with } \frac{\partial^2 f}{\partial x^2} > 0$$

that is a case such that X is a martingale and f is a convex function of a single variable X_t. Using Itô's lemma, $Y_t = f(t, X_t)$ is the diffusion process

$$dY_t = \frac{1}{2}\frac{\partial^2 f}{\partial x^2}(t, X_t)\sigma_X^2(t, X_t)\,dt + \frac{\partial f}{\partial x}(t, X_t)\sigma_X(t, X_t)\,dW_t, \ \forall t \geq 0$$

$$Y_0 = f(0, X_0)$$

or, equivalently,

$$Y_t = Y_0 + \int_0^t \frac{1}{2}\frac{\partial^2 f}{\partial x^2}(s, X_s)\sigma_X^2(s, X_s)\,ds + \int_0^t \frac{\partial f}{\partial x}(s, X_s)\sigma_X(s, X_s)\,dW_s$$

and

$$X_t = X_0 + \int_0^t \sigma_X(s, X_s)\,dW_s$$

Since

$$\mathbb{E}\left(\int_0^t \frac{\partial f}{\partial x}(s, X_s)\sigma_X(s, X_s)\,dW_s\right) = \mathbb{E}\left(\int_0^t \sigma_X(s, X_s)\,dW_s\right) = 0$$

because any integral with respect to Brownian motion is a martingale, and hence has an expected value equal to zero at $t = 0$ (to see that, use $\int_0^0(\_) = 0$), then

$$\mathbb{E}(X_t) = X_0$$

$$\mathbb{E}(Y_t) = Y_0 + \mathbb{E}\left(\int_0^t \frac{1}{2}\frac{\partial^2 f}{\partial x^2}(s, X_s)\sigma_X^2(s, X_s)\,ds\right)$$

or, equivalently,

$$\mathbb{E}[f(X_t)] = f\mathbb{E}(X_t) + \mathbb{E}\left(\int_0^t \frac{1}{2}\frac{\partial^2 f}{\partial x^2}(s, X_s)\sigma_X^2(s, X_s)\,ds\right)$$

Also, since f is a convex function, we know that (Jensen's inequality)

$$\mathbb{E}[f(X_t)] \geq f[\mathbb{E}(X_t)]$$

The term

$$\mathbb{E}\left(\int_0^t \frac{1}{2}\frac{\partial^2 f}{\partial x^2}(s, X_s)\sigma_X^2(s, X_s)\,ds\right)$$

is a positive term since $\frac{\partial^2 f}{\partial x^2} > 0$ and $b_X^2(s, X_s) \geq 0$. This term measures the difference between $\mathbb{E}[f(X_t)]$ and $f\mathbb{E}(X_t)$ in Jensen's inequality. Therefore, the standard

$$dY_t = \frac{\partial f}{\partial t}(t, X_t)\,dt + \frac{\partial f}{\partial x}(t, X_t)\,dX_t$$

cannot hold because it would imply omitting the term $\frac{1}{2}\frac{\partial^2 f}{\partial x^2}(t, X_t)\sigma_X^2(t, X_t)\,dt$. In the example above, with $Y_t = f(X_t)$ and $dX_t = \sigma_X(t, X_t)\,dW_t$, that would contradict $dY_t = \frac{\partial f}{\partial x}(t, X_t)\,dX_t = \frac{\partial f}{\partial x}(t, X_t)\sigma_X(t, X_t)\,dW_t$, so that we would have $\mathbb{E}[f(X_t)] = f[\mathbb{E}(X_t)]$, which is wrong in general by Jensen's inequality for a nonaffine function.

In differential notation, Itô's lemma is written as

$$dY_t = \frac{\partial f}{\partial x}(t, X_t)\, dt + \frac{\partial f}{\partial x}(t, X_t)\, dX_t + \frac{1}{2}\frac{\partial^2 f}{\partial x^2}(t, X_t)\sigma_X^2(t, X_t)\, dt$$

The first two terms are standard terms: the response of $Y_t = f(X_t)$ to some infinitesimal variation dt and dX_t is proportional to the partial derivatives of f with respect to t and X_t. The new term $\frac{1}{2}\frac{\partial^2 f}{\partial x^2}(t, X_t)\sigma_X^2(t, X_t)\, dt$ is related to the fact that X_t and Y_t are stochastic, nondeterministic functions of time.

Some intuitive understanding of Itô's lemma can be obtained through a second-order Taylor expansion $\Delta Y_t = f(t + \Delta t, X_t + \Delta X) - f(t, X_t)$. The result is obtained by noting that $\Delta W_t = \sqrt{\Delta t}\mathcal{E}$ and assuming that $\mathcal{E}^2 = 1$ in the limit of a vanishing Δt. We first have

$$\Delta Y = \left(\frac{\partial f}{\partial x} + \frac{\partial f}{\partial x}b_X(t, X_t) + \frac{1}{2}\frac{\partial^2 f}{\partial x^2}\sigma_X^2(t, X_t)\right)\Delta t + \frac{\partial f}{\partial x}\sigma_X(t, X_t)\Delta W$$

so that

$$dY_t = b_Y(t, X_t)\, dt + \sigma_Y(t, X_t)\, dW_t, \forall t \geq 0$$

with

$$b_Y(t, X_t) = \frac{\partial f}{\partial t}(t, X_t) + \frac{\partial f}{\partial x}(t, X_t)b_X(t, X_t) + \frac{1}{2}\frac{\partial^2 f}{\partial x^2}(t, X_t)\sigma_X^2(t, X_t)$$

$$\sigma_Y(t, X_t) = \frac{\partial f}{\partial x}(t, X_t)\sigma_X(t, X_t)$$

A Multidimensional Version of Itô's Lemma

Proposition 12.9 Let $(X_i, i = 1, 2)$ be two Itô processes such that

$$dX_i = b_i(t)\, dt + \sigma_i(t)\, dW_t$$

Let f be a twice continuously differentiable function defined on $\mathbb{R}^2$ and taking values in $\mathbb{R}$. We have

$$df(X_1(t), X_2(t)) = f_1(X_1(t), X_2(t))\, dX_1(t) + f_2(X_1(t), X_2(t))\, dX_2(t)$$
$$+ \frac{1}{2}(f_{11}\sigma_1^2(t) + 2f_{12}\sigma_1(t)\sigma_2(t) + f_{22}\sigma_2^2(t))(X_1(t), X_2(t))\, dt$$

where f_i is the partial derivative of f with respect to $x_i, i = 1, 2$ and f_{ij} the second partial derivative of f with respect to x_i and x_j.

We have the following equivalent formulation:

$$df(X_1(t), X_2(t)) = \sum_i f_i\, dX_i(t) + \frac{1}{2}\sum_{i,j} f_{ij}\sigma_i\sigma_j\, dt$$

Example:

$$d(X_1(t)X_2(t)) = X_1(t)\, dX_2(t) + X_2(t)\, dX_1(t) + \sigma_1(t)\sigma_2(t)\, dt.$$

Fixed Income Securities

Proposition 12.10   The General Case

Let $(X_t, t \geq 0)$ be a multidimensional Itô process with components $X_i, i = 1, \ldots, n$, such that

$$dX_i = b_i(t)\,dt + \sigma_i(t)\,dW_i(t)$$

Let f be a twice continuously differentiable function defined on $\mathbb{R}^n$ and taking values in $\mathbb{R}$. We have

$$df(t, X_t) = f_t\,dt + \sum_{i=1}^{n} f_i\,dX_i(t) + \frac{1}{2}\sum_{i,j=1}^{n} f_{ij}\,dX_i\,dX_j$$

We use the following useful convention $dW_i\,dW_j = \rho_{ij}\,dt$, $dW_i\,dt = 0$, $dt\,dt = 0$.

Integration by Parts

Proposition 12.11   Let X_t and Y_t be two Itô processes such that $X_t = X_0 + \int_0^t K_s\,ds + \int_0^t H_s\,dW_s$ and $Y_t = Y_0 + \int_0^t K_s'\,ds + \int_0^t H_s'\,dW_s$. Then

$$X_t Y_t = X_0 Y_0 + \int_0^t X_s\,dY_s + \int_0^t Y_s\,dX_s + \langle X, Y \rangle_t$$

with the convention

$$\langle X, Y \rangle_t = \int_0^t H_s H_s'\,ds$$

Girsanov Theorem

Proposition 12.12   Change of Measure

Let $\mathbb{P}$ and $\mathbb{Q}$ be two equivalent probability measures on $(\Omega, \mathcal{F}_T)$, such that $\mathbb{P}$ and $\mathbb{Q}$ are equivalent. Then there is a positive $\mathcal{F}_t$−martingale L_t such that $\mathbb{Q} = L_T \mathbb{P}$ on $\mathcal{F}_T$ and $\mathbb{Q}_{/\mathcal{F}_t} = L_t \mathbb{P}_{/\mathcal{F}_t}$, that is, such that $\mathbb{E}^{\mathbb{Q}}(X) = \mathbb{E}^{\mathbb{P}}(L_t X)$ for all integrable and $\mathcal{F}_t$−measurable random variable X.

Proposition 12.13 M_t is a $\mathbb{Q}$-martingale if and only if $L_t M_t$ is a $\mathbb{P}$-martingale.

Theorem 12.3   Girsanov's Theorem

Let W_t be a Brownian motion defined on a space $(\Omega, \mathcal{F}, \mathbb{P})$ and $\mathcal{F}_t$ its canonical filtration. Let

$$L_t = \exp\left\{\int_0^t \theta(s)\,dW_s - \frac{1}{2}\int_0^t \theta^2(s)\,ds\right\}, t \leq T$$

where θ is an adapted predictable process such that $\mathbb{E}^{\mathbb{P}}[\exp(\int_0^t \theta^2(s)\,ds)] < \infty$. Then L_T is a positive variable with expected value under $\mathbb{P}$ equal to 1 and L_t is a $\mathbb{P}$-martingale. If $\mathbb{Q} = L_T \mathbb{P}$, that is, if $\mathbb{E}^{\mathbb{Q}}(X) = \mathbb{E}^{\mathbb{P}}(L_T X)$, for all integrable and $\mathcal{F}_T$−measurable variables X, then W_t can be written as $W_t = \widehat{W}_t + \int_0^t \theta(s)\,ds$ where $\widehat{W}_t$ is a $\mathbb{Q}$-Brownian motion.

Remark 12.6 Let

$$L_T^t = \exp\left\{\int_t^T \theta(s)\,dW_s - \frac{1}{2}\int_t^T \theta^2(s)\,ds\right\} \quad t \leq T$$

then

$$\mathbb{E}^{\mathbb{Q}}(X/\mathcal{F}_t) = \frac{\mathbb{E}^{\mathbb{P}}(L_T X/\mathcal{F}_t)}{\mathbb{E}^{\mathbb{P}}(L_T/\mathcal{F}_t)} = \frac{\mathbb{E}^{\mathbb{P}}(L_T X/\mathcal{F}_t)}{L_t} = \mathbb{E}^{\mathbb{P}}(L_T^t X/\mathcal{F}_t)$$

Application to Finance

Let $(S_t, t \geq 0)$ satisfy

$$dS_t = S_t(b(t)\,dt + \sigma(t)\,dW_t)$$

By Girsanov's theorem, one can obtain a probability measure $\mathbb{Q}$ such that under $\mathbb{Q}$

$$dS_t = S_t(r(t)\,dt + \sigma(t)\,d\widehat{W}_t)$$

where $\widehat{W}_t$ is a Brownian motion under $\mathbb{Q}$ and r is the risk-free rate. For that, just take

$$\theta(t) = -\sigma^{-1}[b(t) - r(t)]$$

provided that θ is an integrable process.

The probability measure $\mathbb{Q}$ is called *risk-neutral probability*. Let $R_t = \int_0^t r(s)\,ds$ be the discount factor. Under $\mathbb{Q}$, the process of discounted prices $S_t R_t$ is such that $d(S_t R_t) = S_t R_t \sigma_t\,d\widehat{W}_t$, and hence is a martingale.

That result is important; one can show that the absence of arbitrage opportunity is essentially equivalent to the existence of a probability measure $\mathbb{Q}$ such that discounted prices are martingales under $\mathbb{Q}$.[22]

12.8.7 Feynman–Kac Formula

Let X_t be the following diffusion process:

$$X_s^{t,x} = x + \int_t^s b(X_u^{t,x}, u)\,du + \int_t^s \sigma(X_u^{t,x}, u)\,dW_u$$

Proposition 12.14 Feynman–Kac Formula

If b and σ satisfy the Lipschitz condition, if the real-valued functions f, g and ρ satisfy the Lipschitz condition on $\mathbb{R}^K \times [0, T]$ for a scalar $T > 0$, and if the functions $b, \sigma, f, g, \rho, b_x, \sigma_x, u_x, f_x, \rho_x, b_{xx}, \sigma_{xx}, u_{xx}, f_{xx}$ and ρ_{xx} are continuous and satisfy the growth condition, then the

---

[22]No arbitrage and existence of an EMM (equivalent martingale measure) are equivalent in the finite-dimensional case. Further technical conditions need to be imposed in the infinite-dimensional case to ensure that the absence of arbitrage implies the existence of an EMM [see, for example, Duffie (1996)].

(twice continuously differentiable) function $V : \mathbb{R}^K \times [0, T] \to \mathbb{R}$ defined by

$$V(x, t) = \mathbb{E}\left[\int_t^T e^{-\phi(u)} f(X_u^{t,x}, u) \, du + e^{-\phi(T)} g(X_T^{t,x}, T)\right]$$

where ϕ is the discount factor and

$$\phi(s) = \int_t^s \rho(X_u^{t,x}, u) \, du$$

is the unique solution to the following PDE:

$$\mathcal{D}V(x, t) - \rho(x, t)V(x, t) + f(x, t) = 0 \quad (x, t) \in \mathbb{R}^K \times [0, T]$$

with limit condition

$$V(x, T) = g(x, T) \quad x \in \mathbb{R}^K$$

where

$$\mathcal{D}V(x, t) = V_t(x, t) + V_x(x, t)b(x, t) + \frac{1}{2}tr[\sigma^T(x, t)V_{xx}(x, t)\sigma(x, t)]$$

12.8.8 Application to Equilibrium Models of the Term Structure

General Methodology

The price at date t of a zero-coupon bond $B(t, T)$ maturing at date $T > t$ is a function of the short-term interest rate:

$$B(t, T) = B(t, T, r)$$

Finally, the prices of zero-coupon bonds are derived using one of the two equivalent approaches discussed next. The first approach consists in deriving a parabolic PDE, which can sometimes be solved analytically and can always be solved numerically. The second approach is based on an explicit computation of the conditional expectations under the risk-neutral measure. Using Feynman–Kac (see above) representation for the solutions of PDEs, these approaches can be shown to be equivalent.

The PDE approach

Applying Itô's lemma to $B(t, T, r)$ and using

$$dr_t = \mu(t, r_t) \, dt + \sigma(t, r_t) \, dW_t$$

one gets

$$dB = \left[\frac{\partial B}{\partial t} + \frac{\partial B}{\partial r}\mu + \frac{1}{2}\sigma^2\frac{\partial^2 B}{\partial r^2}\right] dt + \frac{\partial B}{\partial r}\sigma \, dW_t$$

$$= \mu_B B \, dt + \sigma_B B \, dW_t \tag{12.20}$$

where the last equality implicitly defines the expected return μ_B and the volatility[23] σ_B of the zero-coupon bond.

---

[23] Asset "volatility" is defined as the standard deviation of the return on that asset.

We now set up a riskless portfolio $P = B_1 + \phi B_2$ involving two zero-coupon bonds:

$$B_1 = B(t, T_1, r)$$

$$B_2 = B(t, T_2, r)$$

Selecting the position ϕ in the second bond, which renders the portfolio riskless, we find the following condition:

$$\frac{\partial B_1}{\partial r} + \phi \frac{\partial B_2}{\partial r} = 0$$

or, equivalently,

$$\phi = -\frac{\partial B_1}{\partial r} \Big/ \frac{\partial B_2}{\partial r} \tag{12.21}$$

which can be interpreted as the ratio of sensitivities to the risk variable.[24]

We obtain

$$dP = \left[\frac{\partial B_1}{\partial t} + \frac{\partial B_1}{\partial r}\mu + \frac{1}{2}\sigma^2 \frac{\partial^2 B_1}{\partial r^2} \right] dt$$

$$+ \phi \left[\frac{\partial B_2}{\partial t} + \frac{\partial B_2}{\partial r}\mu + \frac{1}{2}\sigma^2 \frac{\partial^2 B_2}{\partial r^2} \right] dt$$

Since the portfolio is riskless, it should have a return equal to the risk-free rate[25]

$$\frac{dP}{P} = r \, dt$$

or equivalently,

$$\left[\frac{\partial B_1}{\partial t} + \frac{\partial B_1}{\partial r}\mu + \frac{1}{2}\sigma^2 \frac{\partial^2 B_1}{\partial r^2} \right] + \phi \left[\frac{\partial B_2}{\partial t} + \frac{\partial B_2}{\partial r}\mu + \frac{1}{2}\sigma^2 \frac{\partial^2 B_2}{\partial r^2} \right] = r(B_1 + \phi B_2)$$

Finally, using (12.21)

$$\frac{\frac{\partial B_1}{\partial t} + \frac{\partial B_1}{\partial r}\mu + \frac{1}{2}\sigma^2 \frac{\partial^2 B_1}{\partial r^2} - rB_1}{\frac{\partial B_1}{\partial r}} = \frac{\frac{\partial B_2}{\partial t} + \frac{\partial B_2}{\partial r}\mu + \frac{1}{2}\sigma^2 \frac{\partial^2 B_2}{\partial r^2} - rB_2}{\frac{\partial B_2}{\partial r}}$$

Hence, the quantity (the same as the above except that we have divided by σ)

$$\lambda = \lambda(t, r_t) = \frac{\frac{\partial B}{\partial t} + \frac{\partial B}{\partial r}\mu + \frac{1}{2}\sigma^2 \frac{\partial^2 B}{\partial r^2} - rB}{\frac{\partial B}{\partial r}\sigma} \tag{12.22}$$

is a constant across all bonds at a given date. That is to say, the price of risk is constant.

---

[24]Note that this is quite similar to what was done in Chapters 5 and 6 when we addressed the question of hedging a bond portfolio.

[25]Between dates t and $t+dt$, the short-term rate is actually risk-free because it is known with certainty; there is no random component in its dynamics.

Fixed Income Securities

Dividing the numerator and denominator by B in equation (12.22), we get

$$\lambda = \frac{\mu_B - r}{\dfrac{1}{B}\dfrac{\partial B}{\partial r}\sigma}$$

or, equivalently (using the definition of σ_B in equation (12.20)),

$$\mu_B - r = \lambda \sigma_B$$

We give the following interpretation: the excess return (return on the bond above the risk-free rate) is equal to λ times a factor measuring the risk (volatility) of the bond. Hence, λ can be interpreted naturally as the market price of (interest rate) risk.

We finally arrive at the following *PDE* for B:

$$\frac{\partial B}{\partial t} + \frac{\partial B}{\partial r}\mu + \frac{1}{2}\sigma^2\frac{\partial^2 B}{\partial r^2} - rB = \frac{\partial B}{\partial r}\sigma\lambda$$

or

$$\frac{\partial B}{\partial t} + \frac{\partial B}{\partial r}(\mu - \lambda\sigma) + \frac{1}{2}\sigma^2\frac{\partial^2 B}{\partial r^2} - rB = 0$$

with the boundary condition

$$B(T, T, r) = 1$$

This equation can be solved explicitly in some simple cases [see the Vasicek (1977) model] or numerically in general, using either finite-difference methods or Monte Carlo simulations (see Appendix 2 of Chapter 16). Note that, in any case, one first needs to estimate μ, λ and σ, which are not yet specified. The trickiest input to obtain is probably the market price for interest risk λ. It may be derived as part of the solution of an optimization program by the agents (the equilibrium approach), or extracted from the price of traded securities and then used to price redundant assets (the arbitrage approach). For convenience, it is sometimes assumed that $\lambda = 0$ (Merton, 1973) or λ is a constant (Vasicek, 1977). Note also that both the explicit derivation and numerical computations based on Monte Carlo simulations require a Feynman–Kac representation of the solution to the PDE as the following expectation:

$$B(t, T) = \mathbb{E}_t^{\mathbb{Q}}\left[\exp\left(-\int_t^T r_s\,\mathrm{d}s\right)\right]$$

where the $\mathbb{Q}$-dynamics for the short rate is given by

$$\begin{aligned}
\mathrm{d}r_t &= (\mu - \lambda\sigma)\,\mathrm{d}t + \sigma\,\mathrm{d}\widehat{W}_t \\
&= (\mu - \lambda\sigma)\,\mathrm{d}t + \sigma(\mathrm{d}W_t + \lambda\,\mathrm{d}t) \\
&= \mu\,\mathrm{d}t + \sigma\,\mathrm{d}W_t
\end{aligned}$$

This establishes the connection (and the equivalence) with the martingale approach, which we develop now. Note that neither λ nor $\mathbb{Q}$ are specified by the model. The agents trading in the actual markets define prices, and thus, implicitly define these quantities.

The Martingale Approach

Recall that under the original probability $\mathbb{P}$ we had

$$\mathrm{d}r_t = \mu \, \mathrm{d}t + \sigma \, \mathrm{d}W_t$$

and

$$\frac{\mathrm{d}B}{B} = \mu_B \, \mathrm{d}t + \sigma_B \, \mathrm{d}W_t$$

We know that there exists some $\lambda = \lambda(t, r)$ such that, dropping the indices, for any asset whose price depends on r_t (including r_t itself)

$$\lambda = \frac{\mu_B - r}{\sigma_B} = \frac{\mu - r}{\sigma}$$

Thus, we get

$$\frac{\mathrm{d}B}{B} = r \, \mathrm{d}t + \sigma_B(\lambda \, \mathrm{d}t + \mathrm{d}W_t) = r \, \mathrm{d}t + \sigma_B \, \mathrm{d}\widehat{W}_t$$

and

$$\mathrm{d}r = (\mu - \lambda\sigma) \, \mathrm{d}t + \sigma \, \mathrm{d}\widehat{W}_t$$

where we know, by Girsanov's theorem, that $(\widehat{W}_t)_{t \geq 0} = (W_t + \int_0^t \lambda_s \, \mathrm{d}s)_{t \geq 0}$ is a $\mathbb{Q}$-Brownian motion, where $\mathbb{Q}$ is the (equivalent) measure defined through its Radon–Nikodym derivative with respect to $\mathbb{P}$

$$\frac{\mathrm{d}\mathbb{Q}}{\mathrm{d}\mathbb{P}}(T) = \exp\left[-\int_0^T \lambda_t \, \mathrm{d}W_t - \frac{1}{2}\int_0^T \lambda_t^2 \, \mathrm{d}t\right]$$

Next, we introduce discounted prices

$$B^*(t, T) = \exp\left(-\int_0^t r_s \, \mathrm{d}s\right) B(t, T)$$

Using Itô's lemma, we get

$$\frac{\mathrm{d}B^*(t, T)}{B^*(t, T)} = \frac{\mathrm{d}B(t, T)}{B(t, T)} - r_t \, \mathrm{d}t = \sigma_B \, \mathrm{d}\widehat{W}_t$$

Hence, discounted bond prices are martingales under $\mathbb{Q}$, which implies

$$B^*(t, T) = \mathbb{E}_t^{\mathbb{Q}}[B^*(T, T)]$$

or, equivalently,

$$\exp\left(-\int_0^t r_s \, \mathrm{d}s\right) B(t, T) = \mathbb{E}_t^{\mathbb{Q}}\left[\exp\left(-\int_0^T r_s \, \mathrm{d}s\right) B(T, T)\right]$$

Finally, (using $B(T, T) = 1$)

$$B(t, T) = \mathbb{E}_t^{\mathbb{Q}} \left[\exp \left(- \int_t^T r_s \, ds \right) \right]$$

which is the general pricing equation applied to the zero-coupon bond case. Again, this equation can be solved numerically or explicitly in the most simple cases, such as the Vasicek (1977) framework.

13

Modeling the Credit Spreads Dynamics

Default is defined as the failure of a debtor to meet a contractual obligation to a creditor. Consequently, claims on a debtor who is likely to default are subject to default risk.[1] In principle, this risk concerns a broad range of economic agents (individuals, businesses and governments) and debt securities. In this chapter, we shall focus on credit risk of bonds issued by corporate borrowers.

Broadly speaking, there are two situations in which a firm might default. On one hand, the shareholders may decide to break the debt contract, knowing that if they default on a payment, they enjoy limited liability. On the other hand, default may stem from the possibility (sometimes written in the loan agreement) of creditors forcing the company into bankruptcy if certain conditions are not satisfied. We shall return to these protective clauses (or covenants) later on.

The consequences for a company in default can vary. First, it may file immediately for bankruptcy: following the breach of the debt contract, the creditors take possession of the company and, in theory, divide its assets on the basis of the legal rank (seniority) and nominal value of their securities. Second, the company may be forced into some form of legal reorganization. In the United States, for example, Chapter 11 of the Bankruptcy Act grants defaulting companies a period of time during which they can overcome their financial difficulties. Bankruptcy laws vary considerably from one country to another. Lastly, a default may lead to informal negotiations between a company's shareholders and creditors, culminating in a proposal that creditors swap their existing debt securities for a combination of newly issued paper and cash.

A consequence of default risk is that the promised yield is the maximum possible yield to maturity of the bond, not necessarily the actual yield to maturity. The expected yield to maturity can be computed as the weighted average of all possible yields, weighted by their probabilities.

The risk of individual bonds depends on various factors, such as

- *sales,*

- *profitability (earnings before interest and taxes),*

- *cash reserves (retained earnings),*

- *liquidity (working capital),*

- *leverage (ratio of total debt to market value of equity).*

To compensate investors for the possibility of bankruptcy, a corporate bond must offer a default premium or credit spread. It reflects market perception of a counterparty's creditworthiness.

---

[1] In this chapter, we use the terms "default risk" and "credit risk" somewhat interchangeably. A distinction should however be made as credit risk may refer to a change in the credit rating of a given company, without necessarily leading to default.

Intuitively, the default premium depends on two main factors:

- *the probability of default;*

- *the likely financial loss of the bondholder in the event of default.*

This credit spread is the main focus of investors in corporate bonds. In what follows, we will discuss different approaches used to analyze and model the economic content of credit spreads. In Chapter 16, we present a new class of securities, credit derivatives, which are a very useful tool for credit risk management.

13.1 Analyzing Credit Spreads

The first piece of normative data available to market practitioners for assessing credit risk is the rating published by specialized agencies. For this reason, it is vital to understand the concept of ratings, to know their structure and limitations and, more importantly, to be aware of the corresponding level of risk, which should be reflected in an appropriate interest-rate spread.

13.1.1 Ratings

A credit rating is a judgement on a company's ability to honor its obligations. According to Moody's, a rating measures the probability that an issuer will default; for long-term securities, it also aims to anticipate the recovery rate once the issuer has defaulted. By extension, it measures investors' expected economic loss. Expected loss is defined as the product of the likelihood and the severity of default.

In 1859, Robert Dun published the first ratings guide (an analysis of the trading firms operating out of the port of New York). Dun's competitor, John Bradstreet, published his first ratings in 1857. The credit rating industry flourished: the two firms merged in 1933, and the product of that merger, Dun and Bradstreet, bought Moody's in 1962.

John Moody first published his ratings in 1909, concentrating initially on the bonds issued by railway companies and later moving on to those of municipal authorities and local contractors. The acid test of the ratings industry came with the crash of 1929, when companies whose paper was rated "investment grade" were three times less likely to default than those with a "speculative grade" rating.

Moody's Investors Service and Standard & Poor's Corporation, formed in 1941, provide ratings of the default risk of corporate bonds.[2] Moody's designates the highest-grade bonds by the letters Aaa (S&P uses AAA), followed by Aa (AA), A (A), Baa (BBB), Ba (BB) and B, and so on. These ratings are measures of relative risk, rather than of absolute risk. Consequently, the yields on bonds with different ratings move up and down together, but the spreads between them are not constant over time. Bonds in the categories Aaa (AAA), Aa (AA), A (A), and Baa (BBB) are known as *Investment Grade Bonds*, while bonds in the categories Ba (BB), B (B), Caa (CCC), Ca (CC), or C (C) are known as *Speculative Grade Bonds*, or *junk bonds*.

---

[2]See Table 1.1 in Chapter 1 where we provide Moody's and S&P's rating scales.

Table 13.1   Moody's Rating Transition Matrices in the US Market as of End 1999.

	Moody's	Aaa (%)	Aa (%)	A (%)	Baa (%)	Ba (%)	B (%)	Caa (%)	D (%)
					TO				
	Aaa	88.66	10.29	1.02	0.00	0.03	0.00	0.00	0.00
	Aa	1.08	88.70	9.55	0.34	0.15	0.15	0.00	0.03
F	**A**	0.06	2.88	90.21	5.92	0.74	0.18	0.01	0.01
R	**Baa**	0.05	0.34	7.07	85.24	6.05	1.01	0.08	0.16
O	**Ba**	0.03	0.08	0.56	5.68	83.57	8.08	0.54	1.46
M	**B**	0.01	0.04	0.17	0.65	6.59	82.70	2.76	7.06
	Caa	0.00	0.00	0.66	1.05	3.05	6.11	62.97	26.16
	D	0.00	0.00	0.00	0.00	0.00	0.00	0.00	100.00

Table 13.2   Standard & Poor's Rating Transition Matrices in the US Market as of End 1999.

	S&P	AAA (%)	AA (%)	A (%)	BBB (%)	BB (%)	B (%)	CCC (%)	D (%)
					TO				
	AAA	91.94	7.46	0.48	0.08	0.04	0.00	0.00	0.00
	AA	0.64	91.80	6.75	0.60	0.06	0.12	0.03	0.00
	A	0.07	2.27	91.69	5.11	0.56	0.25	0.01	0.04
F	**BBB**	0.04	0.27	5.56	87.87	4.83	1.02	0.17	0.24
R	**BB**	0.04	0.10	0.61	7.75	81.49	7.89	1.11	1.01
O	**B**	0.00	0.10	0.28	0.46	6.95	82.80	3.96	5.45
M	**CCC**	0.19	0.00	0.37	0.75	2.43	12.13	60.44	23.69
	D	0.00	0.00	0.00	0.00	0.00	0.00	0.00	100.00

The ratings issued by Moody's (M) and Standard & Poor (S&P) are detailed in Tables 13.1 and 13.2, representing rating transition matrices, which show for each rating category the 1-year likelihood of upgrade, downgrade and/or default, derived from historical data in the US market, as of end 1999.

The ratings in the first column are the current ratings, the ratings in the first row are the ratings at the risk horizon. For example, the likelihood of a migration from B to D in one year is equal to 7.06% according to Moody's and 5.45% according to S&P. Furthermore, each row of the matrices sums to 100%.

Moody's uses a 26-year data set of rating changes over the issuers they cover. Most of these issuers are US-based companies, but the participation of international firms is increasing more and more. Moody's only considers issuers that are still rated at the end of the year. In contrast, S&P happens to include no longer rated companies, that is, companies whose outstanding issue is paid off or whose debt issuance program matures.

Rating changes cannot be considered rare events since they occur in more than 10% of the cases. Note that the vast majority of rating changes seldom exceeds one grade, except for B. Greater jumps are relatively rare. When they are positive, they are typically linked to the purchase of a company by another one having a far better rating. The bonds issued by the company that has been taken over receive the rating of the buyer.

13.1.2   Default Probability

Complementary to the knowledge of the rating change likelihood over an annual horizon is the knowledge of default probabilities for various maturity sets. The charts below show the term structure of annual default probabilities for different rating categories (see Figures 13.1 and 13.2).

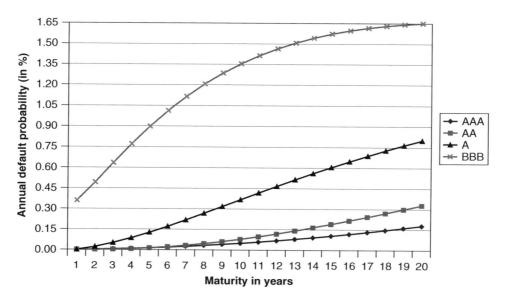

Figure 13.1   Term structure of annual default probabilities—ratings AAA, AA, A and BBB.

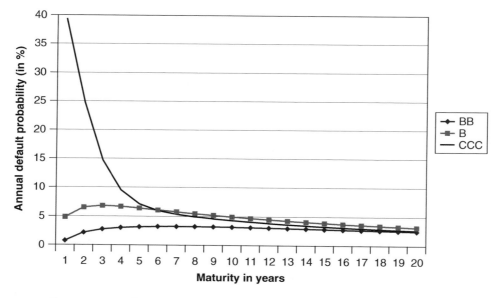

Figure 13.2   Term structure of annual default probabilities—ratings BB, B and CCC.

Table 13.3 Recovery Rate Statistics by Seniority Class.

Seniority class	Recovery rate (%)	Standard deviation (%)
Senior secured	54	27
Senior unsecured	51	25
Senior subordinated	39	24
Subordinated	33	20
Junior subordinated	17	11

You can see that term structures are rising for all investment grade rating categories and humped with decreasing trend or are decreasing for all speculative grade rating categories. Indeed, the longer the maturity of an investment-grade bond, the higher the likelihood that its rating deteriorates and hence that the bond defaults. Conversely, the longer the maturity of a speculative grade bond the higher the likelihood that its rating improves and hence the lower the likelihood that the bond defaults.

13.1.3 The Severity of Default

Once the likelihood of default for a bond is known, it is important to consider its seniority, that is, its priority rank over other debt and equity in the event of default, in order to estimate its credit risk. The higher the seniority of a bond the lower the loss incurred, that is, the higher its recovery rate. Table 13.3 represents recovery statistics by seniority class.

According to the bond indenture, a bond may be a senior or a junior claim. This means that in case of default, senior bonds come before junior bonds in the pecking order. Senior debt can be secured or unsecured. "Secured" means backed by a specific asset. In case of default, the lender the asset is pledged to may repossess it, and recover his due through selling it. No bankruptcy proceeding is needed. In contrast, "unsecured" means backed only by the general assets of the borrower. In case of default, the lender must force bankruptcy and the liquidation of the assets in order to recover his due. Subordinated is a rank that is lower in priority than the two previous ones when assets are distributed in liquidation.

Regarding the subordinated classes, recovery rates are very different from one another. In contrast, secured and unsecured senior debts have nearly similar recovery rates. This can be attributable to the fact that in case of default the lower the seniority the more questionable the value to salvage from the remaining assets.

The two main problems facing the practitioner are to link a rating with a market value and to compare securities that have different characteristics and ratings. For this purpose, a model of the credit spread is needed. In other words, we need a benchmark to tell us what *should be* the spread on a given bond, so that we can understand whether the *observed spread* represents an investment opportunity or not.

13.2 Modeling Credit Spreads

Roughly speaking, credit risk models can be divided into two categories: models based on the value of the firm (also known as *structural models*) and intensity-based models (also known as *reduced-form models*). We will see that the latter approach conveniently allows to deal with the question of credit risky fixed-income securities within the framework of term structure modeling we have previously discussed in this book (see Chapter 12). On the other hand, structural models contain more economic information on how default is triggered, and have therefore an appealing element of interpretability. More generally, this distinction between structural and reduced-form models raises the question of whether default is considered from the viewpoint of the investor or the issuer.

13.2.1 Structural Models

These are models based on the value of the firm, where the firm value is measured in terms of market value, as opposed to book value. In these models, a corporate bond is essentially regarded as a contingent contract written on the company's real assets, and contingent claim analysis, initiated by the seminal work by Black and Scholes (1973) and Merton (1973), is used to derive the fair value of the bond. One advantage of this approach is that it is based on the arbitrage valuation technique, which requires a minimum set of assumptions regarding investors' expectations and preferences.[3]

The first example of such value-based models goes back to seminal papers by Black and Scholes (1973) and Merton (1974). In these early models, default can only occur upon the maturity date of the debt. We recall here the main points of the argument. More sophisticated models will also be exposed.

Merton's Model

Merton (1974) considers a company whose assets have a market value that is subject to operating risk, and thus changes randomly, and whose capital structure consists of equity and a zero-coupon bond.

General Principles   Merton (1974) makes two further assumptions: first, the company cannot issue securities that are senior to the zero-coupon bond during its life and, second, default cannot occur before the debt matures. As we can see, Merton's (1974) interpretation of default is extremely narrow. At maturity, there are two possible outcomes:

- *In the first case, the firm's asset value is sufficient to repay all creditors in full. The creditors receive the face value of the zero-coupon bond while the shareholders pocket the difference between the current value of the assets and the face value of the redeemed bond.*

- *By contrast, in the second case, firm asset value is lower than the face value of the zero-coupon bond. The shareholders, invoking their limited liability, will exercise their option to default and receive nothing. As a result, the creditors get the full asset value.*

---

[3]On the other hand, it does entail heroic assumptions about the market for the firm value. This market must satisfy two conditions: it must be arbitrage-free and complete. Absence of arbitrage assumes that sure returns cannot be generated without an initial cost, while completeness implies the possibility of duplicating any derivative by means of dynamic strategies based on the underlying securities. For this reason, extreme caution should be exercised when using arbitrage arguments to value securities.

The payoff the creditors receive when the zero-coupon bond matures is the minimum between the firm's asset value on the maturity date and the face value of the bond. This is equivalent to the payoff obtained by buying the risk-less zero-coupon bond with a face value and maturity identical to those of a risky zero-coupon bond, and writing a put option on the company's assets with a strike price equal to the bond face value and the same maturity. Accordingly, equity capital is equivalent to a call option written on the company's assets, with a strike price equivalent to the face value of the zero-coupon bond and with the same maturity as the bond.

The Model   More formally, the equity of a firm E can be considered as a *call* option on the value of the firm. Indeed, if debt has face value equal to F, and the value V of the assets of the firm at maturity is less than F, then, in principle, the firm goes bankrupt and bondholders take over. In other words, on maturity date T, stockholders get $E_T = \max(V_T - F, 0)$. On the other hand, the payoff for bondholders is $\min(V_T, F)$, which can be rewritten as $F - \max(F - V_T, 0)$.

In Merton's (1974) model, the dynamics of the value of the firm is modeled as a geometric Brownian motion under the so-called risk-neutral probability measure (see Appendix 2 of Chapter 12)

$$dV_t = r V_t \, dt + \sigma_V V_t \, dW_t$$

where r is the interest rate, assumed to be deterministic in Merton's (1974) model. The value of the equity can then be obtained through the Black–Scholes–Merton (1973) formula for call option pricing (case with constant interest rate r), which is

$$E_t = V_t \Phi(d_1) - e^{-r(T-t)} F \Phi(d_2) \tag{13.1}$$

with

$$d_1 = \frac{\ln \frac{V_t}{F} + \left(r + \frac{1}{2}\sigma_V^2\right)(T-t)}{\sigma_V \sqrt{T-t}}$$

$$d_2 = d_1 - \sigma_V \sqrt{T-t}$$

and where $\Phi(x)$ is the distribution function of a standardized Gaussian, that is, it is the probability that a normally distributed variable with a mean of zero and a standard deviation of 1 is less than x. The value of the risky debt is then simply obtained as: $D_t = V_t - E_t$.

Implementation of Merton's Approach   This approach is intuitively appealing and seems to be easy to use in practice. If one wishes to use Merton's (1974) model in practice, one, however, has to face the following problem: the firm's asset value and the volatility of its dynamics are not directly observable. At least, equity market value and equity volatility are easily observable if the equity and options on that equity are traded. One just gets the total market value of equity by multiplying the number of shares outstanding by the price of a share, and the (implied) volatility can be inferred from option prices using, for example, Black–Scholes–Merton (1973) option pricing model. The problem lies actually in the fact that the market value of liabilities is not usually observed (even though book value is easy to know). Indeed, the total value of liabilities includes current liabilities, short- and long-term debt, as well as some less easy liabilities to categorize such as preferred stocks. And some of these are not traded. However, approximations can be performed, using traded debt of comparable maturity and risk. Also, we know that an upper bound to the volatility of the firm's assets is given by the volatility of the firm's equities.

More specifically, the common practical procedure to implement Merton's (1974) model is as follows. It is actually possible to show that the volatility of equity and the volatility of assets are related through the following equation[4]

$$\sigma_E E_0 = \Phi(d_1)\sigma_V V_0 \tag{13.2}$$

From equations (13.1) and (13.2) as well as estimates for E and σ_E, one may obtain V and σ_V. For a publicly traded company with traded options, E and σ_E may easily be obtained from the market prices of the stock and option on the stock. It is now time to turn to an example.

> **Example 13.1** We would like to know the theoretical value of a corporate bond with face value \$8 million and 1 year maturity, issued by a company with equity value $E_0 = \$4$ million and equity volatility $\sigma_E = 60\%$. We know that the risk-free rate is $r = 5\%$. We solve (13.1) and (13.2) to obtain $V_0 = \$11.59$ million and $\sigma_V = 21.08\%$. This can be done using the Solver function in Excel. You first need to set up the computation of the Black–Scholes (1973) formula for a call option, and then impose that the value of the Black–Scholes (1973) formula is equal to the value of equity $E_0 = 4$, subject to the constraint that $\Phi(d_1)\sigma_V V_0 = 4 \times 60\% = 2.4$. Finally, $D_0 = V_0 - E_0 = 11.59 - 4 = \$7.59$ million.

Term Structure of Credit Spreads in Merton's Model Merton's (1974) model can not only be used to generate an explicit formula for the value of the risky zero-coupon bond but also for its spread. By definition, the yield Y of the zero-coupon bond is such that

$$D_t = F e^{-Y^c(t,T)(T-t)}$$

Since the risk-less rate is constant at r, the credit spread S of the risky zero-coupon bond is given by

$$S(t,T) \equiv Y^c(t,T) - r = \frac{1}{T-t} \ln\left(\frac{F}{D_t}\right) - r$$

The relationship between the spread and the maturity of the debt is the term structure of the credit spreads. Figures 13.3 and 13.4 below show the two kinds of curve generated by the model, decreasing and increasing.

In the first case, the present value of the company's commitments exceeds the current value of its assets. The company is therefore in financial distress because it would default if its debt became callable immediately. In these circumstances, the debt's spread is a decreasing function of its maturity: the more distant the maturity, the greater the probability that the asset value at maturity will be sufficient to repay creditors in full.

Conversely, in the second case, the current value exceeds the present value of the company's commitments. Accordingly, if the debt were to become callable immediately, the creditors would be repaid in full and the default risk would be nonexistent. In these circumstances, by extending the life of the debt, we increase the probability that the asset value will be insufficient at maturity

---

[4]This is an application of Itô's lemma (see Appendix 2 of Chapter 12).

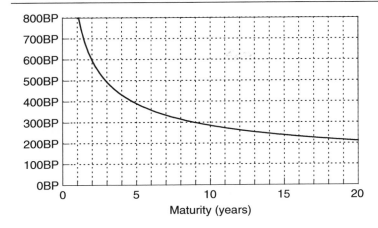

Figure 13.3

Decreasing term structure of credit spreads (case 1).

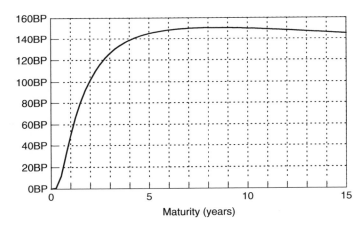

Figure 13.4

Increasing term structure of credit spreads (case 2).

to allow the zero-coupon bond to be redeemed in full at face value. Consequently, the first part of the spread curve increases with the maturity. We observe a slight downturn on the second part of the curve, but this is merely an artifact of the modeling process because it is impossible to default on a zero-coupon bond with infinite maturity.

If we classify debts by rating and maturity, and plot the observed term structure of credit spreads,[5] we actually obtain curves that are very similar to those produced by the Merton's (1974) model: the term structures of credit spreads are often upward-sloping in the case of investment grades and downward-sloping in the case of speculative grades. As we will see, most of the extensions of Merton's (1974) model, even the most complex, produce similar kinds of term structures. Consequently, despite its assumptions and narrow interpretation of default, Merton's (1974) model is extremely robust.

---

[5]See Chapter 4 for details on how to derive the current credit spread term structure.

13.2.2 Subsequent Models

The most direct extension of Merton's (1974) model concerns coupon bonds (Geske, 1977, 1979). Regarding the Merton's (1974) model, note that a risky coupon bond cannot be analyzed as the weighted sum of risky zero-coupon bonds because any default on a midterm coupon payment entails a default on all subsequent payments. Consequently, defaults on different payments are not independent, and it is not possible to price a bond by summing a sequence of individually valued risky flows. By contrast, as Geske (1979) points out, a risky coupon bond can be considered as a compound option. In other words, shareholders have an option to default at each coupon date: they will pay interest only if the value of the equity capital after such a payment is greater than the coupon amount.

The second set of extensions calls into question Merton's (1974) restrictive interpretation of default. In reality, a company can go bankrupt at any time, regardless of whether the default coincides with a payment date. Challenging Merton's (1974) discrete concept of default, the authors propose a continuous concept, where default can occur at any time during the life of the debt.

This new concept was initiated by Black and Cox (1976), who extended Merton's (1974) model to cases in which creditors can force the firm into bankruptcy at any time during the life of the zero-coupon bond if its asset value falls below an exogenous threshold defined in the indenture. This situation corresponds to the existence of a protective clause (or covenant) that allows creditors to assume control of a firm that is mismanaged by its shareholder-managers. More formally, they assume that the bondholder can file for bankruptcy when the value of the assets of the firm goes below a critical value $h_t = he^{-r(T-t)}$. Hence the cash flow received by the bondholders is $\min(V_T, F)$ (where we recall that F is the face value of the bond) at date T if default has not occurred at that date, and some amount h_τ at date τ otherwise, where $\tau = \inf\{t : V_t < h_t\}$ is the default date. In this setup, Black and Cox (1976) derive an explicit valuation formula for a risky zero-coupon bond and for its credit spread.[6] The resulting term structures are very similar to those obtained with the Merton's (1974) model.

In turn, the Black and Cox (1976) model has served as a basis for numerous extensions, most of which take interest-rate risk into consideration. For example, Kim *et al.* (1993) use numerical methods to value all types of risky bonds. Briys and de Varenne (1997) extend the Black and Cox (1976) model in the presence of stochastic interest rates, while maintaining an explicit formula. More restrictive assumptions in Merton's (1974) model have been relaxed in some subsequent models, such as the Longstaff and Schwartz (1995) model. In their model, interest rates are not constant and are assumed to follow a mean-reverting process [such as in the Vasiceck (1977) model], with a potentially nonzero correlation with the uncertainty driving the value of the firm's assets. They also allow for complex capital structure and priority rule (with various class of claimants to which assets are allocated when financial distress occurs). Longstaff and Schwartz (1995) define default

---

[6]They proceed as follows. They first note that the payoff to the bondholder writes $\min(V_T, D)\mathbf{1}_{\{\tau \geq T\}} + h_\tau \mathbf{1}_{\{\tau < T\}}$, where $\mathbf{1}_{\{A\}} = 1$ if A is true, and 0 otherwise. Then they note that the value of the first term is directly given by Merton's (1974) model, while the second term can be priced as a barrier option.

solely in relation to an exogenous barrier without solvency conditions at payment dates. This singular (and debatable) definition of default allows the authors not only to produce a straightforward model but also to value coupon bonds as the weighted sum of zero-coupon bonds. While most structural models of default risk assume that the default boundary remains constant over time, in practice there is evidence that firms typically adjust their capital structure in response to changes in asset value, creating time-varying default thresholds, and mean-reverting (stationary) leverage ratios. Collin-Dufresne and Goldstein (2001) relax the simplifying assumption of a constant default boundary, that they blame for implying the counterfactual prediction of a downward-sloping term structure of credit spreads for speculative grade debt, and introduce a framework where the leverage ratio is modeled as a stationary process.

In all the models derived from Black and Cox (1976), the bankruptcy barrier is exogenous. It is either defined explicitly in the indenture or induced implicitly by a flow condition [as in the case of Kim *et al.* (1993)]. Challenging this type of bankruptcy, Leland (1994a) has returned to the notion of the shareholders' option to default. If there is no protective covenant in the indenture, the shareholders can elect to default as soon as their limited liability is brought into play. In this case, the default option is not European-style, as in Merton (1974), but American-style (i.e., exercisable at any time), while bankruptcy is no longer exogenous but endogenous. The models developed by Leland (1994b) and Leland and Toft (1996) extend this approach to stationary debt structures that are more realistic.

Despite their complexity, continuous-concept models of default (with exogenous or endogenous barriers) are not noticeably more effective than Merton's (1974) model. For example, the results of an empirical study by Guoming, Wei and Guo (1997) comparing the performance of the Merton's (1974) model with that of Longstaff and Schwartz (1995) are not sufficient to prove the latter's superiority, despite its higher degree of complexity. In a recent paper ("Structural Models of Corporate Bond Pricing: An Empirical Analysis"), Eom *et al.* (2002) empirically test five structural models of corporate bond pricing: those of Merton (1974), Geske (1977), Leland and Toft (1996), Longstaff and Schwartz (1995), and Collin-Dufresne and Goldstein (2001). They implement the models using a sample of 182 bond prices from firms with simple capital structures during the period 1986 to 1997. They find that the predicted spreads in their implementation of the Merton's (1974) model are too low. The compound option approach of Geske (1979) comes much closer to the spreads observed in the market, on average, but still underpredicts spreads. In contrast, the Leland and Toft (1996) model substantially overestimates credit risk on most bonds, and especially so for high-coupon bonds. The Longstaff and Schwartz (1995) model modifies Merton to incorporate a stochastic interest rate and a correlation between interest rates and firm value. While the correlation and the level of interest rates have little effect, higher interest-rate volatility leads to higher predicted spreads. However, this and other features of this model result in spreads that are often too high for risky bonds and too low for safe bonds. The target leverage ratio model of Collin-Dufresne and Goldstein (2001) helps to raise the spreads on the bonds that were considered very safe by the Longstaff and Schwartz (1995) model, but overall tends toward overestimation of credit risk. The conclusion perhaps is that structural models do not systematically underpredict spreads, as often believed, but accuracy is a problem. Moreover, some of the simplifications made to date lead to overestimation of credit risk on the riskier bonds while scarcely affecting the spreads of the safest bonds.

A distinctive feature in most structural models is that default does not come as a surprise to an agent who observes asset prices. For example, if default is triggered by a barrier stipulated in the indenture, it is possible at any time to gauge the "proximity" of the asset value to that barrier. This necessarily implies that investors have complete information regarding changes in the firm's value and financial situation. Accordingly, risky bond prices do not move suddenly when default occurs but converge continually toward their recovery value. But in practice, securities' prices generally jump down on news of an impending default, thus undermining the tacit assumption that investors are fully informed. This criticism forms the basis for an alternative avenue of research, which considers default to be unpredictable.

The realities of the risky debt market are doubtless somewhere in between these two extremes, fully predictable default assumption implicit for structural models, and fully unpredictable default assumption for reduced-form models. This is the view of Duffie and Lando (1997), who have developed a model based on contingent claims theory in which investors receive only partial information about the characteristics of the company, due to imperfect accounting reports.

13.2.3 Reduced-Form Models

The advantage of the concept of default as an unpredictable event is that it boils down credit risk to just two parameters: probability of default and recovery rate. Jarrow and Turnbull (1992, 1995), Madan and Unal (1995) and Duffie and Singleton (1999) are important examples of reduced-form models.

General Setup

The essence of such models is as follows. A firm is supposed to default on its obligation at some unpredictable random date.[7] The firm's instantaneous probability of default at date t is denoted by p_t.[8] In case of a constant instantaneous probability of default p, this translates into a chance of default over some small time interval Δt equal to $e^{-p\Delta t} \simeq 1 - p\Delta t$.

Consider now a zero-coupon bond that pays nothing in the event of default. The bond matures in Δt years. At maturity, its payoff is either one, with probability $e^{-p\Delta t} \simeq 1 - p\Delta t$, or zero, with probability $1 - e^{-p\Delta t} \simeq p\Delta t$. The default-free interest rate is r, so that the price of a default-free zero-coupon bond is $P = e^{-r\Delta t}$. One can show that the zero-coupon default-risky bonds are priced using a formula similar to that for zero-coupon default-free bond prices. The only difference is that the discount rate is adjusted to account for p. Indeed, the price at date 0 of a corporate default-risky bond maturing at date Δt is given by

$$P(0, \Delta t) = (e^{-p\Delta t} \times e^{-r\Delta t} \times 1) + ((1 - e^{-p\Delta t}) \times e^{-r\Delta t} \times 0) = e^{-(r+p)\Delta t}$$

This is a remarkable result, since it states that the framework we have presented so far still applies for defaultable bonds provided that we use a generalized short-term interest rate given by $\tilde{r} = r + p$.

---

[7] That date is usually modeled as the date of the first jump of a Poisson process.

[8] In principle, one should make a distinction between the actual probability of default and the risk-adjusted probability of default (see Section 13.2.4).

More generally, one can show in a context with stochastic interest rates and time-varying probability of default that the value at date t of the defaultable claim with maturity T generalizes to

$$P(0, T) = \mathbb{E} \left[\exp \left(- \int_0^T (r_t + p_t) \, ds \right) \right]$$

where the expectation is taken under an equivalent martingale measure (see Appendix 2 of Chapter 12).

One can also allow for partial recovery in the event of default. Hence, if we denote by L the fractional loss in market value in the event of a default at time t, Duffie and Singleton (1999) show that the value at date t of the defaultable claim with maturity T is now

$$P(0, T) = \mathbb{E} \left[\exp \left(- \int_0^T (r_t + p_t L_t) \, ds \right) \right] \tag{13.3}$$

These techniques allow to account both for time value of money, and also for risk value of money related to the uncertainty induced by the possibility of default, in a parsimonious manner.

A Simple Model

There is a simple reduced-form model proposed by Fons (1994), which allows investors to relate ratings with bond prices [see Gauthier *et al.* (1998) for an application to credit risk reporting]. The model consists in valuing the flow sequence engendered by the risky bond, assuming that investors are risk-neutral. In this setting, the value of the risky bond is equal to its certain equivalent, expressed as the expected value of the sum of the flows discounted at the risk-less interest rate. The expected value of each flow is expressed as the sum of the flow received if the firm does not default (equal to the flow specified in the indenture), weighted by the probability of survival, and the flow received in the event of default (equal to the sum of the nominal value and the contractual flow, multiplied by the recovery rate), weighted by the probability of default.

Consider a risky bond with face value 1, coupon C and maturity T. Again, we denote by p_t the probability of default in year t given that the bond has not defaulted before that date (this probability can be read in a bond "mortality table" because the annual probabilities of default are computed in relation to the number of surviving securities at the start of the year). Seen from date $t = 0$, the probability of survival at date t (i.e., the absence of default until t) is given by

$$S_t = \prod_{s=1}^{t} (1 - p_s)$$

Similarly, seen from $t = 0$, the probability D that the bond will default in year t is given by

$$D_t = S_{t-1} p_t$$

Denoting by μ the recovery rate, the expected value of the random flow $\widetilde{F}_t$ received in t is such that

$$\mathbb{E}(\widetilde{F}_t) = S_t C + D_t \mu (1 + C)$$

Fixed Income Securities

Assuming risk-neutral investors, the price P of the risky bond at date t is

$$P = \sum_{t=1}^{T} \frac{S_t C + D_t \mu (1 + C)}{(1 + r)^t} + \frac{S_T}{(1 + r)^T}$$

where r is the yield to maturity of a risk-less bond with the same characteristics. With this formula, we can compute the spread s of the risky bond, defined by the following equation:

$$P = \sum_{t=1}^{T} \frac{C}{(1 + r + s)^t} + \frac{1}{(1 + r + s)^T}$$

where P results from the above valuation formula.

In this setup, the investor is not concerned with the causes of the default but with its probability and consequences (in terms of recovery rate). The expected probabilities of default can be computed from the Moody's rating histories in the previous section. Each security is assigned a probability of default and survival corresponding to its Moody's rating. The use of Fons (1994) model also requires to know the recovery rate, which does not depend on the rating but can be estimated from the seniority of the bond and from the bankruptcy laws of the issuer's home country (see previous section).

One key problem with that model is that it assumes risk-neutral investors. We argue below that such an assumption is not consistent with empirical evidence. As a result, a risk-adjusted probability of default, and not an actual probability of default, should be used in the implementation of Fons (1994) model.

13.2.4   Historical versus Risk-Adjusted Probability of Default

From bond prices and estimates of recovery rates, it is possible to infer an implied probability of default. To see this just consider equation (13.3) in a simple context with constant parameter. The spread over the Treasury rate can be computed as $s = pL = p(1 - R)$, where p is the probability of default and L is the percentage loss in case of default, and R the recovery rate. For example, A rated bonds typically yield at least 50 bps over Treasuries. Using the assumption of $s = 0.5\%$ and various assumptions for the recovery rate, we use the equation $p = \frac{s}{1-R}$ to generate implied probabilities of default that we report in Table 13.4.

From Standard & Poor's rating transition matrix in the US Market as of end 1999, we indeed report that the actual probability of default within a year for a grade A bond is around 0.04%, which is at least 10 times lower than the implicit probability of default, assuming a very low 10% recovery rate!

Table 13.4   Implied Probability of Default Extracted from Credit Spreads.

Recovery rate (%)	10	20	30	40	50	60	70	80	90
Implied probability of default (%)	0.56	0.63	0.71	0.83	1.00	1.25	1.67	2.50	5.00

Note: This table reports the implied probabilities of default consistent with a credit spread of 50 basis points for various levels of recovery rate (from 10 to 90%).

That implied probabilities of default are consistently and significantly higher than the observed probabilities of default is a puzzling fact. It is somewhat similar to the fact that implied volatility from option prices tends to be consistently higher than historical volatility.

Possible explanations of this puzzle are a liquidity effect (the liquidity of corporate bonds is less than that of Treasury bonds) and/or a so-called peso problem effect (bond traders may be factoring into their pricing depression scenarios much worse than anything seen in the last 20 years, in the same way as option traders understand that out-of-the-money options might be exercised in case of a not-so-unlikely large price change). A deeper explanation follows. The default probabilities estimated from bond prices are "risk-neutral" (i.e., risk-adjusted) default probabilities, while the default probabilities estimated from historical data are real-world default probabilities.

The original, as well as risk-adjusted, probability of default may actually be computed in a simple structural model [see, for example, Bohn (1999)]. In a simple structural model such as Merton's (1974), the default probability is given by the actual probability, p, that the value of the firm's assets will be less than the face value of the debt at maturity

$$p = \mathbb{P}(V_T < F)$$

where V_T is the value of the firm assets at date T, maturity date of the debt, and F is the face value of debt. We assume that the value of the firm assets follows a geometric Brownian motion

$$\frac{dV_t}{V_t} = \mu_V \, dt + \sigma_V \, dW_t^V$$

Using Itô's lemma (see Appendix 2 of Chapter 12) and integrating from time t to time T, we obtain the solution for the actual probability as of time t that default may occur before date T is

$$p_{t,T} = \Phi\left(\frac{\log F - \log V_0 - \mu_V(T - t) + \frac{1}{2}\sigma_V^2(T - t)}{\sigma\sqrt{T - t}}\right) \tag{13.4}$$

where $\Phi(\cdot)$ is the cumulative normal distribution function. Then, the formula for the risk-neutral probability will be similar to equation 13.4 except that μ_V will be replaced by r, the risk-free rate. Using, for example, Sharpe's Capital Asset Pricing Model (CAPM), we can formulate the relationship between the expected return on the firm assets and the overall expected return on the market portfolio

$$\mu_V - r = \frac{\text{cov}(r_V, r_M)}{\sigma_M^2}(\mu_M - r) = \sigma_V \times \rho_{M,V} \times \beta$$

where $\beta = \frac{\mu_M - r}{\sigma_M}$ is interpreted as the market price of risk, μ_M is the expected return of the market, σ_M is the market volatility, and $\rho_{M,V}$ the correlation between the market return and the return on the value of the firm assets. Returning to the formulation for the risk-neutral probability, after rearranging terms, we obtain the following formula for the risk-neutral probability of default $q_{t,T}$:

$$q_{t,T} = \Phi(\Phi^{-1}(p_{t,T}) + \rho_{M,V}\beta\sqrt{T - t})$$

Note that this formulation for $q_{t,T}$ relies on the assumption that default can occur only at maturity. One may actually easily modify the analysis to calculate the (cumulative) risk-neutral probability of default given that a firm hitting the default barrier will not recover. Bohn (1999) shows that, at a first-order approximation, this implies the following small modification[9]

$$q_{t,T} = 2\Phi\left(\Phi^{-1}\left(\frac{1}{2}p_{t,T}\right) + \rho_{M,V}\beta\sqrt{T-t}\right)$$

First note that when $\rho_{M,V} = 0$, there is no adjustment to the actual probability of default, and $q = p$. Besides, when $\rho_{M,V} > 0$ (assets of the company have a positive beta), then the risk-adjusted probability of default is greater than the actual probability of default. This corresponds to a situation such that instantaneous probability of default increases on average when the value of the firm assets decreases, which also happens on average when the value of the market portfolio decreases if the firm is a positive beta firm. Hence, the intuition is that default risk is priced (i.e., the risk-adjusted probability of default is higher than the actual probability of default) in such a situation because it is not diversifiable: default hurts more because it occurs more frequently in those states of the world where the market return tends to be low.

13.3 End of Chapter Summary

Default is defined as the failure of a debtor to meet a contractual obligation to a creditor. Consequently, claims on a debtor who is likely to default are subject to default risk. Investors in corporate bond markets focus on credit spreads and credit ratings.

A credit rating is a judgement on a company's ability to honor its obligations. A rating measures the probability that an issuer will default; for long-term securities, it also aims to anticipate the recovery rate once the issuer has defaulted. By extension, it measures investors' expected economic loss, defined as the product of the likelihood and the severity of default. Two main problems facing the practitioner are to link a rating with a market value and to compare securities that have different characteristics and ratings. For that, a model of the credit spread is needed.

Roughly speaking, credit risk models can be divided into two categories: models based on the value of the firm (also known as *structural models*) and intensity-based models (also known as *reduced-form models*). While the latter approach conveniently allows to deal with the question of credit risky fixed-income securities within the framework of term structure modeling we have previously discussed in this book, structural models contain more economic information on how default is triggered, and have therefore an appealing element of interpretability.

In structural models, a corporate bond is essentially regarded as a contingent contract written on the company's real assets, and contingent claim analysis is used to derive the fair value of the bond. It is based upon the remark that equity can be regarded as a call option written on

---

[9]This formula can also be extended to account for the presence of a term structure for the market price for risk [see Bohn (1999)].

the company's assets, with a strike price equivalent to the face value of debt. From this model, implicit probabilities of default can be obtained when corporate bond prices are given.

A puzzling fact is that implied probabilities of default are consistently and significantly higher than observed probabilities of default. It is somewhat similar to the fact that implied volatility from option prices tends to be consistently higher than historical volatility. A possible explanation of this puzzle is a liquidity effect. Another explanation is that default probabilities estimated from bond prices are risk-adjusted default probabilities, while the default probabilities estimated from historical data are real-world default probabilities. Since the instantaneous probability of default is likely to increase on average when the economy is slowing down and investors' overall portfolio values are decreasing, we expect default risk to be rewarded in equilibrium.

13.4 References and Further Reading

13.4.1 Books and Papers

Ammer, J., and F. Packer, 2000, "How Consistent are Credit Ratings? A Geographic and Sectoral Analysis of Default Risk", *Journal of Fixed Income*, **10**(3), 24–30.

Black, F., and J.C. Cox, 1976, "Valuing Corporate Securities: Some Effects of Bond Indenture Provisions", *Journal of Finance*, **31**, 351–367.

Black, F., and M. Scholes, 1973, "The Pricing of Options and Corporate Liabilities", *Journal of Political Economy*, **81**, 637–659.

Bohn, J., 1999, A Survey of Contingent-Claims Approaches to Risky Debt Valuation, Working Paper, KMV Corporation.

Briys, E., and F. de Varenne, 1997, "Valuing Risky Fixed Rate Debt: An Extension, *Journal of Financial and Quantitative Analysis*, **32**, 239–248.

Brown, D.T., 2001, "An Empirical Analysis of Credit Spread Innovations", *Journal of Fixed Income*, **11**(2), 9–27.

Cantor, R., and E. Falkenstein, 2001, "Testing for Rating Consistency in Annual Default Rates", *Journal of Fixed Income*, **11**(2), 36–51.

Collin-Dufresne, P., and B. Goldstein, 2001, "Do Credit Spreads Reflect Stationary Leverage Ratios?", *Journal of Finance*, **56**, 1926–1957.

Das, S.R., G. Fong, and G. Geng, 2001, "Impact of Correlated Default Risk on Credit Portfolios", *Journal of Fixed Income*, **11**(3), 9–19.

Duffie, D., and D. Lando, 1997, Term Structures of Credit Spreads with Incomplete Accounting Information, Working Paper, Stanford University.

Duffie, D., M. Schroder, and C. Skiadas, 1996, "Recursive Valuation of Defaultable Securities and the Timing of Resolution of Uncertainty", *Annals of Applied Probability*, **6**, 1075–1090.

Duffie, D., and K. Singleton, 1999, "Modeling Term Structures of Defaultable Bonds", *Review of Financial Studies*, **12**, 687–720.

Eom, Y., J. Helwege, and J.Z. Huang, 2002, Structural Models of Corporate Bond Pricing: An Empirical Analysis, Working Paper, Ohio State University.

Fons, J., 1994, "Using Default Rates to Model the Term Structure of Credit Risk", *Financial Analysts Journal*, **Sep/Oct**, 57–64.

Gauthier, C., P. De La Noue, and E. Rouzeau, 1998, Analyzing Corporate Credit Risk: A Quantitative Approach, Quants Review, HSBC-CCF, No. 29.

Geske, R., 1977, "The Valuation of Corporate Liabilities as Compound Options", *Journal of Financial and Quantitative Analysis*, **12**(4), 541–552.

Geske, R., 1979, "The Valuation of Compound Options", *Journal of Financial Economics*, **7**, 63–81.

Guoming, W.D., and D. Guo, 1997, "Pricing Risky Debt: An Empirical Comparison of the Longstaff and Schwartz and Merton Models, *Journal of Fixed Income*, **7**, 8–28.

Jarrow, R., and S. Turnbull, 1992, "Drawing the Analogy", *Risk*, **5**(9), 63–71.

Jarrow, R., and S. Turnbull, 1995, "Pricing Derivatives on Financial Securities Subject to Credit Risk", *Journal of Finance*, **50**, 53–85.

Kim, I.J., K. Ramaswamy, and S. Sundaresan, 1993, "Does Default Risk affect the Valuation of Corporate Bonds? A Contingent Claims Model", *Financial Management*, **22**, 117–131.

Lando, D., 1996, Modeling Bonds and Derivatives with Default Risk, Working Paper, University of Copenhagen.

Leland, H.E., 1994a, "Corporate Debt Value, Bond Covenants, and Optimal Capital Structure", *Journal of Finance*, **49**(4), 1213–1252.

Leland, H.E., 1994b, Bond Prices, Yield Spreads and Optimal Capital Structure with Default Risk, Working Paper, Haas School of Business, University of California at Berkeley.

Leland, H.E., and K. Toft, 1996, "Optimal Capital Structure, Endogenous Bankruptcy and the Term Structure of Credit Spreads", *Journal of Finance*, **51**, 987–1019.

Longstaff, F.A., and E.S. Schwartz, 1995, "A Simple Approach to Valuing Risky Fixed and Floating Rate Debt", *Journal of Finance*, **50**(3), 789–819.

Madan, D., and H. Unal, 1995, Pricing the Risks of Default, Working Paper, College of Business and Management, University of Maryland.

Merton, R.C., 1973, "The Theory of Rational Option Pricing", *Bell Journal of Economics and Management Science*, **4**(1), 141–183.

Merton, R.C., 1974, "On the Pricing of Corporate Debt: The Risk Structure of Interest Rates", *Journal of Finance*, **29**, 449–470.

Scholtens, B., 1999, "On the Comovement of Bond Yield Spreads and Country Risk Ratings", *Journal of Fixed Income*, **8**(4), 99–103.

Vasicek, O.A., 1977, "An Equilibrium Characterisation of the Term Structure", *Journal of Financial Economics*, **5**(2), 177–188.

Wei, D.G., and D. Guo, 1997, "Pricing Risky Debt: An Empirical Comparison of the Longstaff and Schwartz and Merton Models", *Journal of Fixed Income*, **7**(2), 8–28.

Zhou, C., 2001, "Credit Rating and Corporate Defaults", *Journal of Fixed Income*, **11**(3), 30–40.

13.4.2 Websites

www.moodys.com.

www.standardandpoors.com.

www.fitchratings.com.

www.defaultrisk.com.

13.5 Problems

Exercise 13.1   Order the following securities from the lowest yield to the highest yield and explain your choice:

>   *A rated callable bonds*
>
>   *AAA rated callable bonds*
>
>   *Junk bonds*
>
>   *BBB rated option-free bonds*
>
>   *AAA rated option-free bonds*
>
>   *BBB rated putable bonds*
>
>   *A rated convertible bonds*

Exercise 13.2   Order the following securities from the lowest to the highest recovery rate:

>   *Subordinated*
>
>   *Senior unsecured*
>
>   *Junior subordinated*
>
>   *Senior secured*
>
>   *Senior subordinated*

Exercise 13.3   To which of the S&P credit categories does the Moody's category Baa correspond?

Exercise 13.4   Consider the following credit transition matrix from S&P:

	S&P	AAA (%)	AA (%)	A (%)	*TO* BBB (%)	BB (%)	B (%)	CCC (%)	D (%)
	AAA	91.94	7.46	0.48	0.08	0.04	0.00	0.00	0.00
	AA	0.64	91.80	6.75	0.60	0.06	0.12	0.03	0.00
F	**A**	0.07	2.27	91.69	5.11	0.56	0.25	0.01	0.04
R	**BBB**	0.04	0.27	5.56	87.87	4.83	1.02	0.17	0.24
O	**BB**	0.04	0.10	0.61	7.75	81.49	7.89	1.11	1.01
M	**B**	0.00	0.10	0.28	0.46	6.95	82.80	3.96	5.45
	CCC	0.19	0.00	0.37	0.75	2.43	12.13	60.44	23.69
	D	0.00	0.00	0.00	0.00	0.00	0.00	0.00	100.00

1. What is the probability of going from category AAA to CCC and from CCC to AAA?
2. What is the probability of a bond rated AAA being downgraded?

Exercise 13.5   On September 1, these spot rates on US treasury and industrial corporates were reported by Bloomberg (type CURV [GO]):

Maturity	Treasuries (%)	Aaa Corporates (%)	Baa Corporates (%)
0.5	4.98	5.46	5.86
1	5.00	5.44	5.84
1.5	4.93	5.42	5.82
2	4.87	5.40	5.79

Exercise 13.6   1. Compute the implied prices of 2-year 6.5% Treasury, Aaa and Baa bonds.
2. Compute the yield to maturity (YTM) on these 3 bonds. Analyze the spreads.
3. Which factors account for them?

Exercise 13.7   Using the same data as in the previous exercise,

1. Compute the implied probabilities of default on the Aaa and Baa bonds, assuming a recovery rate equal to 5% (very low recovery rate assumption).
2. Comment on the numbers you find.

Exercise 13.8   Consider a corporate bond with face value $20 million and 1-year maturity, issued by a company with equity value $E_0 = \$5$ million and equity volatility $\sigma_E = 50\%$. We know that the risk-free rate is $r = 5\%$. What is the theoretical value of this corporate bond using Merton's (1974) model?

Exercise 13.9   Test of the impact of maturity on the value of the corporate debt. Assume the same conditions as in the previous example (bond with face value $20 million, equity value $E_0 = \$5$ million, equity volatility $\sigma_E = 50\%$, risk-free rate $r = 5\%$), except that we now let the debt maturity vary from 1 to 5 years.

1. Compute the debt value for maturities ranging from 1 to 5 years, and comment.
2. Compute the YTM of the corporate bond as a function of time-to-maturity? Compute also the term structure of corporate spreads, and comment.
3. What is the limit of the spread for vanishing time-to-maturity? What do you think of the result you obtain?

Exercise 13.10   Reverse engineering. Consider a corporate bond with face value $10 million and 1-year maturity, issued by a company with equity value $E_0 = \$3$ million, equity volatility $\sigma_E = 50\%$. We know that the risk-free rate is $r = 5\%$. You believe that corporate debt is fairly priced by the market at $8 million. Under these conditions, would you conclude that equity is under or overvalued?

Plain Vanilla Options and More Exotic Derivatives

PART VII

14

Bonds with Embedded Options and Options on Bonds

Most traded bonds issued by corporations are not straight bonds; they contain all kinds of embedded options. In this chapter, we first discuss callable and putable bonds, and then move on to studying convertible bonds. Not only do some bonds contain embedded options but standard options are also written on bonds just as they are written on stocks. We discuss these standard options in Section 14.3.

14.1 Callable and Putable Bonds

14.1.1 Institutional Aspects

Definition and Characteristics

Callable and putable bonds contain an embedded call option and an embedded put option, respectively. A callable bond is a bond that can be redeemed by the issuer before its maturity date. A putable bond is a bond that can be sold by the bond holder before its maturity date. Hence, buying a callable bond comes down to buying an option-free bond and selling a call option to the issuer of the bond. Similarly, buying a putable bond comes down to buying an option-free bond as well as a put option. The embedded call or put option can be exercised from a specified date on or on a specified date(s), depending on the bond, and at a specified price. Let us give some examples.

> **Example 14.1** The UK Treasury bond with coupon 5.5% and maturity date 09/10/2012 can be called in full or part from 09/10/2008 on, at a price of £ 100.

> **Example 14.2** The US Treasury bond with coupon 7.625% and maturity date 02/15/2007 can be called on coupon dates only, at a price of $100, from 02/15/2002 on. Such a bond is said to be discretely callable.

> **Example 14.3** The Bayerische Landesbank bond with coupon 6% and maturity date 03/10/2020 can be put on 03/10/2010 only, at a price of Eur100.

Uses

Let us now discuss the respective advantages and drawbacks of this bond category from an investor's and an issuer's viewpoints.

A callable bond allows its issuer to buy back his debt at par value prior to maturity in case interest rates fall below the coupon rate of the issue. So, he will have the opportunity to issue a new bond at a lower coupon rate. On the other hand, a callable bond has two disadvantages for an investor. First, if it is effectively called, the investor will have to invest in another bond yielding a lower rate than the coupon rate of the callable issue; hence, he incurs a loss in interests. Second, a callable has the unpleasant property for an investor to appreciate less than a normal similar bond when interest rates fall. This property is called *negative convexity*.[1] In order to be compensated for these drawbacks, an investor will be willing to buy such a bond at a lower price than a comparable option-free bond. A putable bond allows its holder to sell the bond at par value prior to maturity in case interest rates exceed the coupon rate of the issue. So, he will have the opportunity to buy a new bond at a higher coupon rate. On the other hand, the issuer of this bond will have to issue another bond at a higher coupon rate if the put option is exercised. Hence, a putable bond trades at a higher price than a comparable option-free bond.

14.1.2 Pricing

Unlike an option-free fixed coupon bond, a bond with an embedded option is a contingent claim, that is, its future cash flows are not known with certainty, because they are dependent on the future values of interest rates. As recalled in Chapter 12, to price such a bond, we need to use a model that accounts for the fact that future interest rates are uncertain. This uncertainty is described by volatility (the annualized standard deviation of the relative changes in interest rate). Given an initial interest rate, the volatility measures the range within which it is expected to be at the end of the year. The most commonly used method is binomial interest-rate tree model, introduced in Chapter 12. We also discuss a numerical Monte Carlo methodology. Before presenting them, we also review the traditional yield-to-worst approach that is fairly popular amongst investors, because it gives a quick measure of the potential return that can be earned on a bond with an embedded option.

Yield-to-Worst

Let us consider a bond with an embedded call option trading over its par value. This bond can be redeemed by its issuer prior to maturity from its first call date on. Apart from yield-to-maturity (YTM), we can compute a yield-to-call on all possible call dates.[2] The yield-to-worst is the lowest of the yield-to-maturity and all yields-to-call. Let us consider an example.

> **Example 14.4** An investor wants to assess the potential return he can earn on a 10-year bond bearing an interest coupon of 5%, discretely callable after 5 years and trading at

---

[1] See Chapter 6 for a definition of convexity.

[2] The yield-to-call is the internal rate of return that equalizes the sum of all discounted cash flows of a bond until the call date to its trading gross price. For example, the cash flows until the first call date of a bond with coupon 5%, maturity 10 years and callable at 100 after 5 years are $F_1 = 5$, $F_2 = 5$, $F_3 = 5$, $F_4 = 5$ and $F_5 = 105$.

102. There are five possible call dates before maturity. Let us compute the corresponding yields-to-call and the yield-to-maturity of the bond. The table below summarizes the results.

	Yield-to-call (%)
Year 5	4.54
Year 6	4.61
Year 7	4.66
Year 8	4.69
Year 9	4.72
	Yield-to-maturity (%)
Year 10	4.74

So, the yield-to-worst of this bond is equal to 4.54%.

Hence, the yield-to-worst is the worst yield that an investor can achieve on a callable bond at the current market price, given that the issuer of the callable bond has the choice to call or not to call the bond. For a putable bond, the yield-to-worst concept is meaningless since the put option is exercised by the investor. The yield-to-worst measure has the following limits. Like the YTM measure, it is based upon the following assumptions:

- *An investor will hold the bond until its call exercise date;*
- *The coupons of the bond will be reinvested at one single rate: the yield-to-worst.*

These assumptions are of course unrealistic.

Indeed, the yield-to-worst measure neither takes into account price risk (in case the investor sells the bond before the call exercise date), nor reinvestment risk (in case the bond is called by the issuer during the investment period).

Furthermore, it assumes that the issuer will call the bond on the call date, which of course depends on the level of interest rates on that date. If the issuer redeems the bond on another date, the yield-to-worst measure will be of course irrelevant.

Because it is a static and simplistic return measure, the yield-to-worst cannot be reasonably used for accurate valuation of bonds with embedded options. For this purpose, one needs to use a methodology taking into account the uncertain nature of future interest rates. Such methodologies have at least the following common features:

- *Interest rates are assumed to be lognormal (see equation (12.2) from Chapter 12), so that changes in interest rates are proportional to the level of interest rates. Moreover, this property ensures that interest rates are never negative.*
- *The models are built so as to be free of arbitrage opportunities: they must perfectly reflect today's market prices of risk-free bonds (this is a matter of calibration).*

So as to understand the nature of the valuation methodologies, one must first remark that a bond can be priced in two different ways leading to exactly the same results: by using spot interest rates or by using forward interest rates. Let us illustrate this through the following example.

Example 14.5   Consider a bond with maturity 3 years and annual coupon 5%. We denote by $R(0, t)$ the zero-coupon rate with maturity t years and by $F(0, s, t - s)$ the forward rate currently determined, starting on year s, with maturity $(t - s)$ years. Today's price P of the bond is equal to

$$P = \frac{5}{(1 + R(0, 1))} + \frac{5}{(1 + R(0, 2))^2} + \frac{105}{(1 + R(0, 3))^3}$$

or alternatively

$$P = \frac{5}{(1 + R(0, 1))} + \frac{5}{(1 + R(0, 1))(1 + F(0, 1, 1))}$$
$$+ \frac{105}{(1 + R(0, 1))(1 + F(0, 1, 1))(1 + F(0, 2, 1))}$$

$$P = \frac{\dfrac{\left(\dfrac{105}{(1 + F(0, 2, 1))} + 5\right)}{(1 + F(0, 1, 1))} + 5}{(1 + R(0, 1))}$$

That is, the price discovery process of the bond can be viewed as a backward process. First, the price of the bond 2 years from now is equal to the sum of its cash flows on year 3 (principal plus coupon) discounted at the forward rate starting in 2 years and with maturity 1 year. Then, the price of the bond 1 year from now is equal to the sum of its cash flows on year 2 (price on year 2 previously computed + coupon) discounted at the forward rate starting in 1 year and with maturity 1 year. Finally, the current price of the bond is equal to the sum of its cash flows on year 1 (price on year 1 previously computed + coupon) discounted at the 1-year spot rate.

The latter pricing method is the one used in the two methodologies we are going to develop, except that forward interest rates are replaced by assumed future short-term interest rates derived from a volatility assumption about these rates.

The Binomial Interest-Rate Tree Methodology

Presentation   Let us assume here that a binomial tree has been already built and calibrated as explained in Chapter 12 from which we borrow the notation. The valuation method consists in recursively pricing the bond. Knowing its redemption value V, its call date(s) and price(s) T_k and CP_k, its annual coupon rate C and its maturity T, we infer its price by beginning with the last cash flows and going back step by step to the first ones. Formally, we can visualize that through the chart below:

| Period 0 | Period 1 | Period 2 | ... | Period $n-1$ | Period n | Maturity of the bond |

On period n, we have

$$P_{nu} = \frac{V + C}{1 + r_{nu}}$$

and

$$P_{(n-k)u,kl} = \frac{V + C}{1 + r_{(n-k)u,kl}}$$

On period $n - 1$, we have

$$P_{(n-1)u} = \frac{1}{2}\left(\frac{\min(P_{nu}, CP_n) + C}{1 + r_{(n-1)u}} + \frac{\min(P_{(n-1)u,l}, CP_n) + C}{1 + r_{(n-1)u}}\right)$$

and

$$P_{(n-1-k)u,kl} = \frac{1}{2}\left(\frac{\min(P_{(n-k)u,kl}, CP_n) + C}{1 + r_{(n-1-k)u,kl}} + \frac{\min(P_{(n-1-k)u,(k+1)l}, CP_n) + C}{1 + r_{(n-1-k)u,kl}}\right)$$

Indeed, the price cash flow to be discounted on period $n - 1$ is the minimum value of the price computed on period n and the call price on period n and so on, until we get the price P of the callable bond.

On period 1, we have

$$P_u = \frac{1}{2}\left(\frac{\min(P_{uu}, CP_2) + C}{1 + r_u} + \frac{\min(P_{ul}, CP_2) + C}{1 + r_u}\right)$$

Fixed Income Securities

and

$$P_l = \frac{1}{2} \left(\frac{\min(P_{ul}, CP_2) + C}{1 + r_l} + \frac{\min(P_{ll}, CP_2) + C}{1 + r_l} \right)$$

Hence, the price P of the callable bond on period 0 is

$$P = \frac{1}{2} \left(\frac{\min(P_u, CP_1) + C}{1 + y_1} + \frac{\min(P_l, CP_1) + C}{1 + y_1} \right)$$

For a putable bond, the formulas are exactly the same except that instead of taking at each node the minimum value of the computed price of the bond and its call price(CP), we take the maximum value of the computed price of the bond and its put price.

Example 14.6 We consider a callable bond with maturity 2 years, annual coupon 5%, callable in 1 year at 100. The interest-rate tree is the same as the one determined in the previous example.

We have

$$P_u = \frac{100 + 5}{1 + 4.66\%} = 100.32$$

$$P_l = \frac{100 + 5}{1 + 4.57\%} = 100.41$$

Hence, the price of the callable bond is

$$P = \frac{1}{2} \left(\frac{\min(100, 100.32) + 5}{(1 + 4\%)} + \frac{\min(100, 100.41) + 5}{(1 + 4\%)} \right) = 100.96$$

In practice, implementing the interest-rate tree methodology raises the following issues.

- *The period frequency must be greater than 1 year: at least semiannual. This is of course due to the fact that bond maturities are very rarely multiples of 1 year. The higher the period frequency, the more accurate the valuation method, but also the more demanding its implementation. There is clearly a trade-off between complexity and efficiency. For the purpose of pricing a very long-term bond, you need not choose as high a period frequency as for pricing a short-term bond, because the number of computation steps is significantly higher.*

- *Many bonds with embedded options contain American options that can be exercised at any time after the first exercise date, which requires a fine node spacing and significantly complicates the model's implementation.*

- *Very often, cash flows fall between two nodes, which does not make the computation easy.*

- *The volatility parameter is fixed arbitrarily. One can take an estimate of the historical volatility of the short-term interest rate over a given period—to be chosen—or consider the implied volatility of an option on an interest rate with similar maturity and behavior. Anyway, the higher the volatility parameter, the higher the value of the embedded call option (put option, respectively) and the lower the price of the callable bond (the higher the price of the putable bond, respectively).*

- *In the presentation of the methodology, we have assumed a single interest-rate volatility for all periods. This may seem rather simplistic. It is in fact possible to incorporate a term structure of volatility.*

The Monte Carlo Methodology

This methodology is much less used than the interest-rate tree methodology because it is mostly dedicated to the pricing of path-dependent securities like mortgage-backed securities. The future cash flows of these securities do not depend only on the future level of interest rates, like bonds with embedded options, but also on the path taken by the short-term interest rate over time. We will briefly review the methodology and describe its application to the pricing of bonds with embedded options, a detailed analysis being beyond the scope of this chapter. The methodology can be divided into several steps:

Step 1 Given the current value of the short-term interest rate r, a large number of future short-term interest-rate paths are generated using the discrete-time version of the general model for the dynamics of the short-term rate (see equation (12.3) from Chapter 12)

$$\Delta r_t = r_{t+\Delta t} - r_t = \mu(r, t)\Delta t + \sigma(r, t)\varepsilon_t \sqrt{\Delta t}$$

where

Δr designates the change in the short-term interest rate over one period;

Δt designates the change in time from one period to another;

$\mu(.,.)$ designates the expected absolute return on the short-term interest rate per time unit: it is potentially a function of both the short-term interest rate r and time t;

$\sigma(.,.)$ designates the standard deviation of the absolute change in the short-term interest rate per time unit: it is potentially a function of both the short-term interest rate r and time t;

ε_t designate independent normally distributed random variables with zero mean and a standard deviation of 1.

Here, we choose for simplicity

$$\mu(r, t) = \mu r$$

$$\sigma(r, t) = \sigma r$$

or

$$\Delta r = \mu r \Delta t + \sigma r \varepsilon \sqrt{\Delta t}$$

where

μ designates the expected relative return on the short-term interest rate per time unit;

σ designates the volatility of the short-term interest rate per time unit (i.e., the standard deviation of the relative change unit).

Example 14.7 Let us assume a current 1-year interest rate of 4%. μ is assumed to be equal to 4.5% per annum and σ 5% per annum. The period frequency is supposed to be annual, so

$\Delta t = 1$. Then, the future 1-year interest rates are generated from 1 year to another according to the following formula:

$$\Delta r = 0.045r + 0.05r\varepsilon$$

If r_k stands for the 1-year interest rate starting on year k (year 0 meaning currently), we have

$$r_0 = 4\%$$

$$r_n = 0.045r_{n-1} + 0.05r_{n-1}\varepsilon$$

In order to simulate ε you can use the Box–Müller method, which is briefly described hereafter.

If x_1 and x_2 are two random variables uniformly distributed on]0,1[, the following random variables y_1 and y_2 defined as

$$y_1 = \sqrt{-2 \ln x_1} \cos 2\pi x_2$$

$$y_2 = \sqrt{-2 \ln x_1} \sin 2\pi x_2$$

follow the centered and reduced normal law. This is practically very easy to implement on an Excel spreadsheet since x_1 and x_2 can be generated by the function RANDOM().

We present hereafter the simulation of 6 short-term interest-rate paths with a 10-year length using the Box–Müller method and the above formula for r_n. As r is a 1-year interest rate and the interest-rate paths' length equals 10 years, n is equal to 10.

Period	Path 1 (%)	Path 2 (%)	Path 3 (%)	Path 4 (%)	Path 5 (%)	Path 6 (%)
1	4.00	4.00	4.00	4.00	4.00	4.00
2	4.08	4.14	4.29	4.24	4.28	4.28
3	3.83	4.02	4.35	4.27	4.24	4.23
4	4.15	3.88	4.25	3.87	4.17	4.30
5	4.27	4.26	4.68	4.58	4.29	3.99
6	4.69	4.49	4.33	4.29	4.47	4.32
7	4.88	5.10	5.24	5.08	5.27	4.70
8	5.14	4.94	4.75	5.54	5.25	5.08
9	5.24	5.47	5.15	5.26	5.43	5.64
10	5.59	5.04	5.29	5.58	5.38	5.02

In practice, the model is calibrated to the current term structure of interest rates by adding the same drift term to each simulated short-term interest rate maturing on the same period, so that the average present value of a par coupon bond, discounted on all paths, is exactly equal to 100 (see the "Problems" section where we consider an exercise on this subject).

Step 2 Along each interest-rate path, the price P of the bond with embedded options is recursively determined. Let us consider a callable bond, with maturity n years ($n > 5$), annual coupon C, redemption value V and call price CP exercisable after 5 years. P_k denoting the price of the bond on year k and r_k the 1-year interest rate starting on year k, we have

$$P_{n-1} = \frac{V + C}{1 + r_{n-1}}$$

$$P_{n-2} = \frac{\min(CP, P_{n-1}) + C}{1 + r_{n-2}}$$

$$\ldots$$

$$P_4 = \frac{\min(CP, P_5) + C}{1 + r_4}$$

$$P_3 = \frac{P_4 + C}{1 + r_3}$$

$$\ldots$$

$$P = P_0 = \frac{P_1 + C}{1 + r_0} = \frac{P_1 + C}{1 + r}$$

Example 14.8 The table below shows the prices of a callable bond with annual coupon 4.57%, maturity 10 years, redemption value 100 and callable at 100 after 5 years, along the 6 interest-rate paths presented in the previous example.

	Path 1	Path 2	Path 3	Path 4	Path 5	Path 6
Price of the callable bond	100.43	100.55	99.90	99.76	99.68	100.55

Step 3 The price of the bond is computed as the average of its prices along all interest-rate paths.

Example 14.9 The price of the above presented callable bond is equal to

$$P = \frac{1}{6}(100.43 + 100.55 + 99.90 + 99.76 + 99.68 + 100.55) = 100.14$$

The larger the number of interest-rate paths simulated, the more accurate the pricing of a bond. Generally speaking, you need to simulate at least about 300 interest-rate paths in order to get a reasonable valuation.

14.1.3 OAS Analysis

The direct application of the two methodologies presented above lies in comparing the computed theoretical price of a bond with embedded options with its market price. As market participants are more familiar with yield spreads than with price spreads, a market habit has developed, which consists in determining the yield spread that, when added to all short-term interest rates derived from either valuation model, equalizes the theoretical price of the bond to its market price. It is the so-called option-adjusted spread (OAS). The denomination "option adjusted" refers to the fact that the cash flows of the bond to be priced are adjusted for the option exercise price(s). In other words, unlike the traditional yield spread, the OAS takes the optional feature of the bond into account. The Option-Adjusted Spread depends on the volatility parameter assumed in the valuation model. The higher the volatility of the short-term interest rate, the lower (respectively, the higher) the theoretical price of a callable (respectively, putable) bond, and hence, the lower (respectively, the higher) the OAS of the callable (respectively, putable) bond. As the valuation models are mostly calibrated to the term structure of government interest rates, the OAS of a bond with an embedded option mainly represents the liquidity premium and/or the credit premium attached to it.

Example 14.10 Let us take up our former callable bond valuation example in the binomial interest-rate tree framework. The market price of the bond is assumed to be 100.5. Its theoretical price is 100.96. So the OAS of this bond is such that

$$P = \frac{1}{2} \left(\frac{\min\left(100, \dfrac{100+5}{1+4.66\%+OAS}\right)+5}{(1+4\%+OAS)} + \frac{\min\left(100, \dfrac{100+5}{1+4.57\%+OAS}\right)+5}{(1+4\%+OAS)} \right) = 100.5$$

We find

$$OAS = +43 \text{ bp}$$

Example 14.11 Let us now move on to our former callable bond valuation example in the Monte Carlo framework. The market price of the bond is assumed to be 99.5. Its theoretical price is 100.14. So the OAS of this bond is such that the average of the callable bond's present values along each option-adjusted interest-rate path equals 99.5.[3] Hence, we find

$$OAS = +9 \text{ bp}$$

14.1.4 Effective Duration and Convexity

The cash-flow structure of a bond with an embedded option being directly impacted by the level of interest rates, the traditional modified duration and convexity measures are not relevant for such a bond. Market participants use instead what is known as *effective duration* and *effective convexity*, which are calculated in the following manner.

Let us denote by P the current price of the bond, by Δy the absolute change in the Treasury bond yield curve, by P_+ the price of the bond after shifting upwards the yield curve by Δy and by P_- the price of the bond after shifting downwards the yield curve by Δy. The formulas of effective

---

[3] By option-adjusted interest-rate path, we mean that we add the OAS to all short-term interest rates of all paths.

duration and convexity for the bond are given by

$$Effective\ Duration = \frac{1}{2}\left(\frac{P_- - P}{P \times \Delta y} + \frac{P - P_+}{P \times \Delta y}\right) = \frac{1}{2}\left(\frac{P_- - P_+}{P \times \Delta y}\right)$$

$$Effective\ Convexity = \frac{1}{2}\left(\frac{P_+ + P_- - 2P}{2 \times P \times (\Delta y)^2}\right)$$

Now, let us focus on the determination of P_+ and P_-.

In the binomial interest-rate tree framework,

- *First, compute the OAS of the bond;*

- *Second, shift the Treasury yield curve upwards (respectively, downwards) by a small number of basis points;*

- *Third, calculate the resulting two new interest-rate trees;*

- *Fourth, add the OAS to each of the two interest-rate trees;*

- *Finally, price the bond backwards along each option-adjusted interest-rate tree so as to get P_+ and P_-.*

In the Monte Carlo framework,

- *First, compute the OAS of the bond along each interest-rate path;*

- *Second, shift the Treasury yield curve upwards (respectively, downwards) by a small number of basis points along each interest-rate path;*

- *Third, find the new short-term interest rates along each path;*

- *Fourth, add the corresponding OAS to the short-term interest rates along each path;*

- *Fifth, price the bond backwards along each option-adjusted interest-rate path;*

- *Finally, compute P_+ (respectively, P_-) as the average of the bond prices calculated along all upwards (respectively, downwards) shifted option-adjusted paths.*

Example 14.12 Let us follow our previous example in the binomial interest-rate tree framework.

Step 1: The OAS of the callable bond is equal to 43 bp.

Step 2: Let us shift upwards and downwards the initial yield curve by 10 bp. We get

Maturity (in years)	Par yield shifted upwards by 10 bp (%)	Par yield shifted downwards by 10 bp (%)
1	4.10	3.90
2	4.40	4.20
3	4.60	4.40

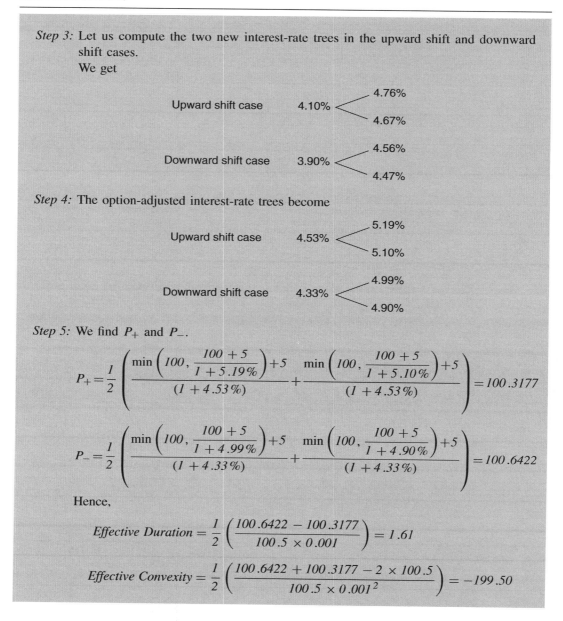

Step 3: Let us compute the two new interest-rate trees in the upward shift and downward shift cases.
We get

Upward shift case   4.10% $<$ 4.76% / 4.67%

Downward shift case   3.90% $<$ 4.56% / 4.47%

Step 4: The option-adjusted interest-rate trees become

Upward shift case   4.53% $<$ 5.19% / 5.10%

Downward shift case   4.33% $<$ 4.99% / 4.90%

Step 5: We find P_+ and P_-.

$$P_+ = \frac{1}{2}\left(\frac{\min\left(100, \frac{100+5}{1+5.19\%}\right)+5}{(1+4.53\%)} + \frac{\min\left(100, \frac{100+5}{1+5.10\%}\right)+5}{(1+4.53\%)} \right) = 100.3177$$

$$P_- = \frac{1}{2}\left(\frac{\min\left(100, \frac{100+5}{1+4.99\%}\right)+5}{(1+4.33\%)} + \frac{\min\left(100, \frac{100+5}{1+4.90\%}\right)+5}{(1+4.33\%)} \right) = 100.6422$$

Hence,

$$\textit{Effective Duration} = \frac{1}{2}\left(\frac{100.6422 - 100.3177}{100.5 \times 0.001} \right) = 1.61$$

$$\textit{Effective Convexity} = \frac{1}{2}\left(\frac{100.6422 + 100.3177 - 2 \times 100.5}{100.5 \times 0.001^2} \right) = -199.50$$

14.2 Convertible Bonds

14.2.1 Institutional Aspects

Definition

A convertible bond is a security that gives a bondholder the right to exchange the par amount of a bond for common shares of the issuer at some fixed ratio during a particular period. Convertible securities are usually either convertible bonds or convertible preferred shares, which are most often exchangeable into the common stock of the company issuing the convertible security. Being debt or preferred instruments, they have an advantage over the common stock in case of distress or bankruptcy. If the securities are debt, they have a termination value that must be paid at maturity. If preferred, they have a liquidation value. There is less risk in holding the convertible because it has seniority in payment. Convertible bonds offer the investor the safety of a fixed-income instrument coupled with participation in the upside of the equity markets.

Sometimes convertible bonds are issued with call or put options allowing prepayment before the maturity date.

- *A call exercisable by the issuer can force the convertible bondholder to sell him the bond when the underlying equity exceeds a given value.*

- *A put exercisable by the bondholder can force the issuer to buy the bond at a determined price when the underlying equity falls below a given value.*

Terminology

We now define some terms that are essential to understanding what a convertible bond is.

- *The convertible price is the price of the convertible bond.*

- *The bond floor (or investment value) is the price of the bond if there is no conversion option.*

- *The conversion ratio is the number of shares a bond is exchanged for.*

- *The conversion price is the share price at which the face value of the bond may be exchanged for shares; it is the strike price of the embedded equity option, and it is given by the following formula*

$$Conversion\ Price = Par\ Value\ of\ Convertible\ Bond/Conversion\ Ratio$$

- *The conversion value is equal to*

$$Conversion\ Value = Current\ Share\ Price \times Conversion\ Ratio$$

- *The conversion premium is equal to*

$$Conversion\ Premium = \frac{(Convertible\ Price - Conversion\ Value)}{Conversion\ Value}$$

- *The income pickup is the amount by which the yield-to-maturity of the convertible bond exceeds the dividend yield of the share.*

Example 14.13   AXA $2^{1/2}$ 01/14 Convertible Bond Description on Bloomberg

AXA has issued in the Euro zone a convertible bond paying a 2.5% coupon rate and maturing on 01/01/2014 (Figure 14.1). The amount issued initially was Eur 1.698 billion. The coupon frequency is annual and the day-count basis is Actual/Actual. The conversion ratio is 4.04. On 12/13/2001, the current share price was Eur 24.12 and the bid–ask convertible price was

```
1                                                    DL19 Corp   DES
SECURITY DESCRIPTION                      Page 1/ 1
AXA SA            AXASA 2 ½ 01/14    156.5971/157.5971(FLAT TRAD)BGN  @12/12
CONVERTIBLE INFORMATION      IDENTIFIERS        1) Additional Sec Info
CONV TO         4.0400 SHARES  Common  009458468  2) Softcall Schedule
PER        165.00 NOMINAL      ISIN   FR0000492076 3) Convertible Info.
CS   (FP )  €24.12 (  0.55)    French 049207      4) Identifiers
CONVERTIBLE UNTIL  1/ 1/14     RATINGS           5) Ratings
PARITY   97.44 PREMIUM    61.73%  Moody's    A2   6) Fees/Restrictions
ISSUER INFORMATION           S&P        A-       7) Sec. Specific News
Name AXA                     Composite  A3       8) Involved Parties
Market of Issue EURO-ZONE    ISSUE SIZE          9) Custom Notes
SECURITY INFORMATION         Amt Issued          10) Issuer Information
Coupon 2 ½       FLAT TRADING EUR  1,698,000  (M) 11) ALLQ
ANNUAL      ACT/ACT           Amt Outstanding     12) Pricing Sources
Maturity   1/ 1/2014 Series   EUR  1,517,978  (M) 13) Prospectus Request
CONVERTIB Redeems @   139.930 Min Piece/Increment 14) Related Securities
Country FR      Currency EUR      165.00/    165.00 15) Issuer Web Page
1st Coupon Date  1/ 1/00      Par Amount     165.00
Price @ Issue  100.0000       BOOK RUNNER/EXCHANGE
Calc Typ ( 89)FRANCE:COMPND METH DLJSEC,GS,PAR    65) Old DES
HAVE PROSPECTUS              EURONEXT-PARIS       66) Send as Attachment
PROVISIONAL CALL. PRX/SHR=€40.8415. 10% CLEAN-UP CALL. SHORT 1ST CPN.  NOTES
CEASE TO ACCRUE INT FROM 1/PRECEDING HLDRS CONVERSION.
Australia 61 2 9777 8600      Brazil 5511 3048 4500       Europe 44 20 7330 7500      Germany 49 69 92041210
Hong Kong 852 2977 6000 Japan 81 3 3201 8900 Singapore 65 212 1000 U.S. 1 212 318 2000 Copyright 2001 Bloomberg L.P.
                                                                    I356-711-1 13-Dec-01 13:22:25
```

Figure 14.1 © 2003 Bloomberg L.P. All rights reserved. Reprinted with permission.

156.5971/157.5971. The conversion value called *parity* was equal to 97.44. The conversion premium calculated with the ask price 157.5971 was 61.73%. The redemption value on 01/01/2014 is equal to Eur 230.8845 (139.93% × 165). The conversion of the bond into 4.04 shares can be executed on any date before the maturity date.

Uses

For the Issuer   Issuing convertible bonds enables a firm to obtain better financial conditions. In fact, the coupon rate of such a bond is always inferior to that of a bullet bond with the same characteristics in terms of maturity and coupon frequency. This comes directly from the conversion advantage that is attached to this product. Besides, the exchange of bonds for shares diminishes the liabilities of the firm issuer and increases its equity in the same time so that its debt capacity is improved.

For the Bondholder   A convertible bond is a defensive security, very sensitive to a rise in the share price and protective when the share price decreases. If the share price increases, the convertible price will react in the same manner and it will not be inferior to the bond floor if the share price decreases. Recall that the bond floor is the price of the bullet bond with no conversion option.

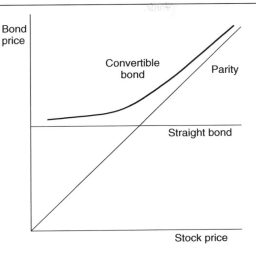

Figure 14.2

Price of a convertible bond as a function of the price of the underlying stock.

14.2.2 Valuation of Convertible Bonds

A convertible bond is similar to a normal coupon bond plus a call option on the underlying stock, with an important difference: the effective strike price of the call option will vary with the price of the bond, which itself varies with interest rates. Because of this characteristic, it is difficult to price the conversion option using a Black–Scholes (1973) formula or other similar models that assume constant interest rates.

The conversion value is a floor below which the price of the bond cannot fall. Figure 14.2 illustrates how the price of a convertible bond varies with the price of the underlying stock, assuming all other factors remain constant.

In practice, a popular method for pricing convertible bonds is the component model, also called the *synthetic model*. The convertible bond is divided into a straight bond component and a call option on the conversion price, with strike price equal to the value of the straight bond component. The fair value of the two components can be calculated with standard formulas, such as the famous Black–Scholes (1973) valuation formula.

This pricing approach, however, has several drawbacks [see, for example, Ammann *et al.* (2001)]. First, separating the convertible into a bond component and an option component relies on restrictive assumptions, such as the absence of embedded options. Callability and putability, for instance, are convertible bond features that cannot be considered in the above separation. Second, as recalled above, convertible bonds contain an option component with a stochastic strike price. This is in contrast to standard call options, where the strike price is known in advance. It is stochastic because the value of the bond to be delivered in exchange for the shares is usually not known in advance unless conversion is certain not to occur until maturity. In effect, the future strike price depends on the future development of interest rates and the future credit spread.

Theoretical research on convertible bond pricing was initiated by Ingersoll (1977) and Brennan and Schwartz (1977), who both applied the contingent claims approach to the valuation of convertible bonds. In their valuation models, the convertible bond price depends on the firm value as the underlying variable. Brennan and Schwartz (1980) extend their model by including stochastic interest rates. However, they conclude that the effect of a stochastic term structure on convertible bond prices is so small that it can be neglected for empirical purposes. These models rely heavily on the theory of stochastic processes and require a relatively high level of mathematical sophistication [see, for example, Martellini and Priaulet (2000) for an introduction to stochastic models applied to the valuation of fixed-income securities].

In this section, we use again a binomial setup to the problem of pricing convertible securities in the presence of embedded options. Since the problem involves the dynamics of the stock price, we actually need to also model the stochastic evolution of stock returns.

The Binomial Model

We first provide a brief overview of the binomial model in the context of pricing options on stocks.[4] It is similar in spirit to the model of the dynamics of the short-term rate introduced in Chapter 12.

The binomial model for option pricing was introduced by Cox, Ross and Rubinstein in 1979. It is based on an arbitrage argument stating that the option can be replicated with the underlying stock and bonds. The objective is both to find the price of the option and derive the replicating portfolio. In this setup, we first assume that the price of the stock can only go up to a given value or down to a given value (see Figure 14.3).

Besides, there is a bond (bank account) that will pay an interest of r. We assume u (up) $> d$ (down). For consistency, so as to preclude arbitrage opportunities, we also need $u > (1+r) > d$. In Figure 14.4, we assume, for example, that $u = 1.25; d = 0.80; r = 10\%$.

It is a basic model that describes a simple world. As the number of steps increases, it becomes more realistic. We introduce a European call option with exercise price $K = 110$ that matures at the end of the period (see Figure 14.5).

We can replicate the option with the stock and the bond. For that, one may construct a portfolio that pays C_u in state u and C_u in state d. The price of that portfolio has to be the same as the

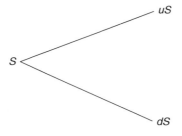

Figure 14.3

Binomial model: 2-period case.

---

[4]We refer the reader to a specialized textbook on option pricing, for example, Hull (1998) for more details.

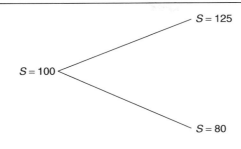

Figure 14.4

Binomial model: an example.

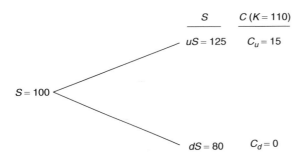

Figure 14.5

Binomial model: option pay-offs.

option price. Otherwise there will be an arbitrage opportunity. We buy Δ shares and invest B in the bank. These numbers can be positive (buy or deposit) or negative (shortsell or borrow). We want then

$$\begin{cases} \Delta u S + B(1+r) = C_u \\ \Delta d S + B(1+r) = C_d \end{cases}$$

The solution is

$$\begin{cases} \Delta = \dfrac{C_u - C_d}{S(u - d)} \\ B = \dfrac{u C_d - d C_u}{(u - d)(1 + r)} \end{cases}$$

In our example, we get

$$\begin{cases} \Delta = \dfrac{C_u - C_d}{S(u - d)} = \dfrac{15 - 0}{100 \times (1.25 - 0.8)} = \dfrac{1}{3} \\ B = \dfrac{u C_d - d C_u}{(u - d)(1 + r)} = \dfrac{1.25 \times 0 - 0.8 \times 15}{(1.25 - 0.8) \times 1.1} = -24.24 \end{cases}$$

The cost of the portfolio is $\Delta S + B = \frac{1}{3} \times 100 - 24,24 = 9.09$. The price of the European call must be 9.09, otherwise, there is an arbitrage opportunity. If the price was lower than 9.09, we would buy the call and shortsell the portfolio. If it was higher, we would do the opposite.

We can reformulate the expression for the call price in the following way:

$$C = \Delta S + B = \dfrac{C_u - C_d}{S(u - d)} \times S + \dfrac{u C_d - d C_u}{(u - d)(1 + r)}$$

or, after some algebra

$$C = \frac{1}{1+r} \times \left[\frac{1+r-d}{u-d} C_u + \frac{u-(1+r)}{u-d} C_d \right]$$

The coefficients $\frac{1+r-d}{u-d}$ and $\frac{u-(1+r)}{u-d}$ are positive and smaller than 1 (remember that $u > (1+r) > d$). Furthermore, they obviously add up to 1. Therefore, they can be regarded as probabilities. We rewrite

$$C = \frac{1}{1+r} \times [pC_u + (1-p)C_d]$$

with $p = \frac{1+r-d}{u-d}$. Note that this pricing equation corresponds to the valuation of a risk-neutral investor with subjective probabilities p and $1-p$. This is the reason these probabilities are known as *risk-neutral probabilities*.

This setup can easily be generalized to a multiperiod case. Suppose, for example, 2-period setup as in Figure 14.6.

The price of the option will be

$$C = \frac{1}{(1+r)^2} \times [p^2 \max(u^2 S - K, 0) + 2p(1-p) \max(udS - K, 0)$$
$$+ (1-p)^2 \max(d^2 S - K, 0)]$$

More generally, the valuation approach consists in computing the value of the option at the end of the tree, and then working the valuation rule backward to the first node. What remains to be estimated is the value for u and d. One can show that u is related to the underlying stock volatility through the following formula $u = \exp\left(\sigma\sqrt{\frac{T}{n}}\right)$, where T is the maturity date and n the number of periods.

Application to the Valuation of Convertible Securities

Given that a convertible bond is nothing but an option on the underlying stock, we expect to be able to use the binomial model to price it. At each node, we test
1. *whether conversion is optimal;*

2. *whether the position of the issuer can be improved by calling the bonds.*
It is a dynamic programming procedure:

max(min(Q1,Q2),Q3)

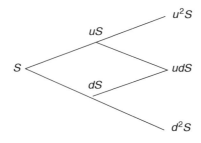

Figure 14.6

Binomial model: 2-period case.

where

Q1 = value given by the rollback (neither converted nor called back)

Q2 = call price

Q3 = value of stocks if conversion takes place

The methodology is perhaps best understood in the context of a simple illustration. We assume that the underlying stock price trades at $50.00 with a 30% annual volatility. We consider a convertible bond with a 9-month maturity and a conversion ratio of 20. The convertible bond has a $1,000.00 face value, a 4% annual coupon. We further assume that the risk-free rate is a continuously compounded 10%, while the yield-to-maturity on straight bonds issued by the same company is a continuously compounded 15%. We also assume that the call price is $1,100.00.

We use a 3-period binomial tree for stock price dynamics to value that convertible bond. On the other hand, we assume a constant interest rate (see remark below). Using $u = \exp\left(\sigma\sqrt{\frac{T}{n}}\right)$, where the elementary time step is $\frac{T}{n} = \frac{9}{3} = 3$ months, or 1/4 year, and $\sigma = 30\%$, we obtain that $u = \exp\left(0.3 \times \sqrt{\frac{1}{4}}\right) = 1.1618$, while $d = 1/u = 0.8607$. The risk-neutral probability $p = \frac{\exp\left(\frac{10\%}{4}\right) - d}{u - d} = 0.547.$[5]

Figure 14.7 provides the value of the convertible bond at each node of the tree, as well as information on the relevant interest rate to be used.

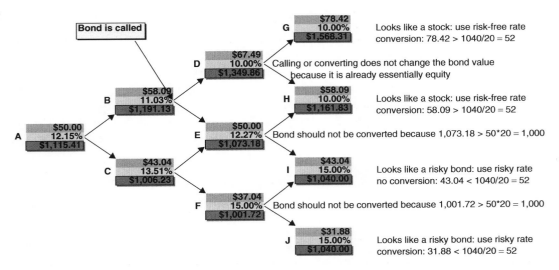

Figure 14.7 Valuation of convertible bonds in the presence of a call option and default risk.

---

[5]We use $\exp\left(\frac{10\%}{4}\right)$, as opposed to $1 + \frac{10\%}{4}$, to reflect that the 10% rate is a continuously compounded annual rate.

As usual, we start with the terminal nodes. At node G, the bondholder optimally chooses to convert, since what is obtained under conversion ($1,568.31) is higher than the payoff under the assumption of no conversion ($1,040.00). The same applies to node H. On the other hand, at nodes I and J, the value under the assumption of conversion is lower than if the bond is not converted to equity. Therefore, bondholders optimally choose not to convert, and the payoff is simply the nominal value of the bond, plus the interest payments, that is $1,040.00.

Working our way backward through the tree, we obtain at node D the value of the convertible bond as the discounted expected value, using risk-neutral probabilities of the payoffs at nodes G and H. Hence the value is

$$\$1,349.86 = e^{-\frac{3}{12} \times 10\%} \times [p \times 1,568.31 + (1 - p) \times 1,161.83]$$

At node F, the same principle applies, except for one difference. Because the bond will not be converted at subsequent nodes I and J, it can be regarded at node F as a standard bond. The valuation of a standard bond cannot be made by discounting the cash flows at the risk-free rate of 10% because that would assume away default risk. We therefore use the rate of return on a comparable, nonconvertible bond issued by the same company as a discount rate. We have assumed that the defaultable rate is 15% and therefore, the value is

$$\$1,001.72 = e^{-\frac{3}{12} \times 15\%} \times [p \times 1,040.00 + (1 - p) \times 1,040.00] = e^{-\frac{3}{12} \times 15\%} \times 1,040.00$$

At node E, the situation is more interesting because the convertible bond will end up as a stock in case of an up move (conversion), and as a bond in case of a down move (no conversion). As an approximate rule of thumb, one may use a weighted average of the risk-free and risky interest rate in the computation, where the weighting is performed according to the (risk-neutral) probability of an up versus a down move $p \times 10\% + (1 - p) \times 15\% = 12.27\%$

$$\$1,073.18 = e^{-\frac{3}{12} \times 12.27\%} \times [p \times 1,161.83 + (1 - p) \times 1,040.00]$$

Note that at nodes D, E and F, calling or converting is not relevant because it does not change the bond value since the bond is already essentially equity.

At node B, it can be shown that the issuer finds it optimal to call the bond. If the bond is indeed called by the issuer, bondholders are left with the choice between not converting and getting the CP ($1,100), or converting and getting $20 \times 58.09 = 1,161.8$, which is what they optimally choose. Now, this is less than $1,191.13, the value of the convertible bond if it were not called, and this is precisely why it is called by the issuer.

Eventually, the value at node A, that is, the present fair value of the convertible bond, is computed as $1,115.41.

Remark 14.1 This valuation model is based upon the assumption of optimal conversion from the bondholder. If the bondholder fails to convert optimally, then the theoretical value computed by the model is higher than the actual value of the security. Similarly, there is ample evidence that issuers call back their bond late. This would tend to increase the value of convertible bonds compared to the model predictions.

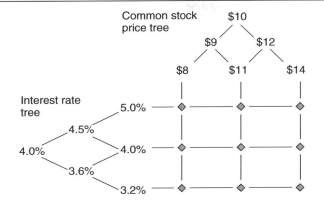

Figure 14.8

Valuation of convertible bonds in the presence of interest-rate risk.

Remark 14.2 The previous approach for valuing convertible bonds has a shortcoming, however. It is based on the assumption of a constant interest-rate process. Such a simplistic assumption might prove to be problematic, especially in the valuation of long-term convertible bonds. One may actually easily generalize the previous model by allowing for the presence of two intersecting recombining binary trees, an interest-rate tree and a stock price tree, as illustrated in Figure 14.8.

Both trees terminate at the maturity date of the bond. This model assumes that the bond yield and the stock price are the two most important factors in valuation and that these factors are independent of each other.[6] This formula is applied at each maturity node of the tree. Working backwards through the tree the intrinsic value of the conversion option is compared with the wait value of the conversion option, that is, the option value from subsequent nodes discounted at the appropriate interest rate.

14.2.3 Convertible Arbitrage

Convertible securities are priced as a function of the price of the underlying stock, expected future volatility of equity returns, risk-free interest rates, call provisions, supply and demand for specific issues, issue-specific corporate/Treasury yield spread and expected volatility of interest rates and spreads. Thus, there is large room for relative misvaluations.

Convertible arbitrage strategies attempt to exploit anomalies in prices of corporate securities that are convertible into common stocks such as convertible bonds, warrants or convertible preferred stocks. Roughly speaking, if the issuer does well, the convertible bond behaves like a stock, and if the issuer does poorly, the convertible bond behaves like a distressed debt. Convertible bonds tend to be underpriced because of market segmentation: investors discount securities that are likely to change types.

---

[6]One may also allow for a nontrivial correlation between the process for interest rate and the process for stock return.

The CSFB (Credit Swiss First Boston)/Tremont Convertible Arbitrage Index (an asset-weighted benchmark of convertible hedge funds) produced a return of 25.1% in the first 11 months of 2000, beating the convertible bond indexes by more than 35%. There are currently over 120 hedge funds focused on convertible arbitrage. Collectively, they represent about US$10 billion in net assets. The managers of these funds exploit arbitrage opportunities not only in convertible bonds but also in other convertible securities including convertible preferreds, zeros and mandatory convertibles. Many pension funds and other institutions have invested in convertible arbitrage hedge funds over the years no doubt, in part, because of their ability to perform well even in a down market. In the recent past, however, a formidable increase in the demand for convertible bonds emanating from hedge funds following strategies similar to the ones we describe below may have caused prices to get back to normal. Some actually now speak of a hedge-fund driven convertible bond bubble.

The Mechanism

Convertible arbitrage hedge-fund managers typically buy (or sometimes sell) these securities and then hedge part or all of the associated risks by shorting the stock.

Take, for example, Internet company AOL's (America online) zero coupon converts due December 6, 2019. These bonds are convertible into 5.8338 shares of AOL stock. With AOL common stock trading at $34.80 on December 31, 2000, the conversion value was $203 (5.8338 × 34.80). As the conversion value is significantly below the investment value (calculated at $450.20), the investment value dominated and the convertible traded at $474.10. When, or if, the stock trades above $77.15, the conversion value will dominate the pricing of the convertible because it will be in excess of the investment value.

In a typical convertible bond arbitrage position, the hedge fund is not only long the convertible bond position but also short an appropriate amount of the underlying common stock. The number of shares shorted by the hedge-fund manager is designed to match or offset the sensitivity of the convertible bond to common stock price changes. The price of a convertible bond will decline less rapidly than the underlying stock in a falling equity market and will mirror the price of stock more closely in a rising equity market. In other words, as the stock price decreases, the amount lost on the long convertible position is countered by the amount gained on the short stock position, theoretically creating a stable net position value. As the stock price increases, the amount gained on the long convertible position is countered by the amount lost on the short stock position, theoretically creating a stable net position value. This is known as *delta hedging* (see Figure 14.9). Different variables affect the price of convertible changes after the initial position has been set, so one may have to adjust the hedge ratio to maintain delta neutrality by selling more shares or covering some of the initial short position (see Figure 14.8). Delta neutrality is often targeted and overhedging is sometimes appropriate when there is concern about default, as the excess short position may partially hedge against a reduction in credit quality.

In the AOL example, the delta for the convertible is approximately 50%. This means that for every $1 change in the conversion value, the convertible bond price changes by $0.5. To delta hedge the equity exposure in this bond we need to short half the number of shares that the bond converts into, for example, 2.9 shares (5.8338/2).

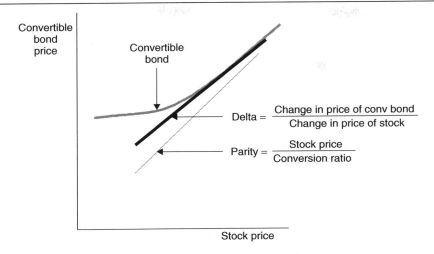

Figure 14.9 Convertible arbitrage—delta hedging.

The combined long convertible bond/short stock position should be relatively insensitive to small changes in the price of AOL's stock. As the price of AOL rises, the profit in the convertible bond should be offset by the loss on the short AOL stock position. Conversely, as the price of AOL declines, the loss on the convertible bond should be offset by the gain on the short equity position. This relatively simple adjustment allows convertible arbitrage hedge-fund managers to create portfolios that are less dependent on market direction.

The primary source of return is the current income generated by the arbitrage position. The convertible security pays a coupon and the short equity position generates interest income on the proceeds of the short sale if strategy is unleveraged. Because both of these return components are stable income, a lower volatility asset class is created. In addition, capital gains can be realized by managing the hedge ratios of these positions. A convertible arbitrage return objective might range from 2 to 6% above the risk-free rate (90-day Treasury bills rate).

Convertible arbitrage is considered to be a relatively conservative strategy with moderate expected volatility. Generally, the strategy offers a compelling alternative to traditional fixed-income port-folios. However, this form of investing is far from riskless and requires constant monitoring.

The Risks Involved

Essentially, a convertible bond is a bond plus an option to switch. As a result, it is the combination of a short position in the stock (makes money when stock price goes down), long position in the embedded option (loses money when stock price goes down) and long position in the embedded bond (loses money when credit quality deteriorates).

The risks involved relate to changes in the price of the underlying stock (equity market risk), changes in the interest-rate level (fixed-income market risk), changes in the expected volatility of the stock (volatility risk) and changes in the credit standing of the issuer (credit risk). As a result, these strategies will typically make money if expected volatility increases (long vega), make money if the stock price increases rapidly (long gamma), pay time-decay (short theta) and make money if the credit quality of the issuer improves (short the credit differential).

The convertible bond market as a whole is also prone to liquidity risk as demand can dry up periodically, and bid–ask spreads on bonds can widen significantly. Because convertible bond arbitrage also involves the short sale of underlying common stock, the strategy is also subject to stock-borrow risk. This is the risk that the hedge-fund manager will be unable to sustain the short position in the underlying common shares.

In addition, convertible arbitrage hedge funds use varying degrees of leverage, which can magnify both risks and returns. While some conservative convertible arbitrage hedge funds may use only one-time leverage, most are leveraged four to seven times the capital.

Irrespective of the strategy, hedge-fund investors are perhaps most vulnerable to manager risk. The majority of hedge-fund portfolios are critically dependent on the performance of a star manager, so manager risk is always present. The fortunes of a convertible arbitrage portfolio or any other hedge-fund strategy depend largely on the skill of the manager. If the manager gets it wrong, it does not matter if the market environment for arbitrage is favorable.

14.3 Options on Bonds

Not only do some bonds contain embedded option features but standard options are also written on bonds just as they are written on stocks.

14.3.1 Definition

An option is a contract in which the seller (writer) of the option grants the buyer of the option the right to purchase from, or sell to, the seller a designated instrument at a specified price within a specified period of time. The seller grants this right to the buyer in exchange for a certain sum of money called the *option price* or *option premium*.

The price at which the instrument may be bought or sold is called the *exercise* or *strike price*. The date after which an option is void is called the *expiration date*. An American option may be exercised any time up to and including the expiration date. A European option may be exercised only on the expiration date.

When an option seller grants the buyer the right to purchase the designated instrument, it is called a *call option*. When the option buyer has the right to sell the designated instrument to the seller, the option is called a *put option*. The buyer of any option is said to be long the option; the seller is said to be short the option.

It can be shown that there exists a specific relationship between the price of a call option and the price of a put option on the same underlying debt instrument, with the same strike price and the same expiration date. This is known as *put–call parity relationship*.

- *Put–call parity relationship for European options on zero-coupon bonds:*

  Under the assumption of no coupon payments and no premature exercise, consider a portfolio where we purchase one zero-coupon bond, one put European option, and sell (write) one

European call option. Both options are written on the zero-coupon bond; they have the same time to maturity T and the same strike price X. At maturity, all states can be divided into those where the bond price is less than the exercise price and those where it is greater than or equal to the exercise price. Let B_T denote the bond price at the expiration date. The payoffs from the portfolio in either state at the expiration date are listed as follows:

$B_T < X:$

You hold the bond: B_T
The call option is worthless: 0
The put option is worth: $X - B_T$
Thus, your net position is: X

$B_T \geq X:$

You hold the bond: B_T
The call option is worth: $-(B_T - X)$
The put option is worthless: 0
Thus, your net position is: X

No matter what state of the world obtained at the expiration date, the portfolio will be worth X. Thus, the payoff from the portfolio is risk-free, and we can discount its value at the risk-free rate r_f. Using continuous discounting, this is

Current value of the portfolio $(= B_0 + C_0 - P_0) = Xe^{-r_f T}$

where B_0 is the current price of the underlying bond, P_0 is the current put price, C_0 is the current call price and $Xe^{-r_f T}$ is the present value of the strike price. From this equation, we obtain

$$C_0 = B_0 + P_0 - Xe^{-r_f T}$$

This equation is known as the put–call parity relationship for European options on zero-coupon bonds.

Put–call parity relationship for European options on coupon bonds:

Current value of the portfolio $(= B_0 + C_0 - P_0) = Xe^{-r_f T} + PV(coupons)$

where $PV(coupons)$ is the present value of coupon payments. From this we obtain that

$$C_0 = B_0 + P_0 - Xe^{-r_f T} - PV(coupons)$$

This equation is known as the put–call parity relationship for European options on coupon bonds.

14.3.2 Uses

Naked Strategies

There are four basic option strategies that financial intermediaries might employ to hedge movement in interest rates. These four strategies are referred to as *naked* strategies because neither the buyer nor the writer owns the underlying asset, the bond. Next, we will review *covered* strategies including covered calls and covered puts.

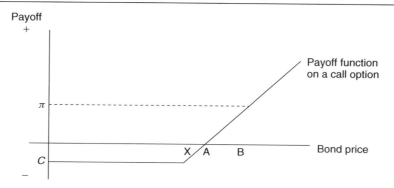

Figure 14.10

- *Buying a Call Option on a Bond provides the buyer with the right, but not the obligation, to purchase the underlying bond from the writer of the option at the exercise or strike price on or before the expiration date. The payoff diagram is shown in Figure 14.10 for the call option:*

  Above the horizontal line the payoff is positive; below the horizontal line the payoff is negative. The call premium, C, is the cost that the buyer of the option pays to the writer of the option. Until the underlying bond reaches the strike or exercise price, X, the call option is "out-of-the-money." Notice that the payoff function is linked at the strike price. At point X, the call option is said to be "at-the-money" and as the value of the underlying bond rises above the strike price, the call option is said to be "in-the-money." At point A, the buyer of the call option breaks even (net of transaction costs). If the option buyer exercises the call at point B, he realizes profit, π.

  Since the underlying asset is a bond, there are two important points to remember: (1) as interest rates fall, bond prices rise and the potential for a positive payoff for the buyer of the call option increases and (2) as interest rates rise, bond prices fall and the potential for a negative payoff for the buyer of the call option increases. However, the losses of the buyer are limited to the amount of the call premium, C, paid up front to the writer of the option. Thus, unlike interest-rate futures whose prices and payoffs move symmetrically with changes in the level or rates, the payoffs on bond call options are asymmetrical.

- *Writing a Call Option on a Bond occurs when a writer sells the right, but not the obligation, to the buyer to purchase the underlying bond at the strike price on or before the expiration date. The writer, unlike the buyer, is obligated to perform (i.e., sell the underlying bond) if the buyer exercises the call option. The payoff diagram is shown in Figure 14.11.*

  The two payoff diagrams above demonstrate that the payoff functions to the buyer and the writer of the call are mirror images of one another. This may be viewed as a "zero-sum" game where one party wins at the expense of the other. If the call option is in-the-money and exercised by the buyer, the seller loses and the buyer wins. If the call option expires out-of-the-money, then the seller wins and the buyer loses the call premium. It is important to note that the downside potential for loss by the buyer is limited to the call premium that is also the maximum upside potential for gain by the writer. The upside (downside) potential for gain (loss) of the buyer (writer) is unlimited!

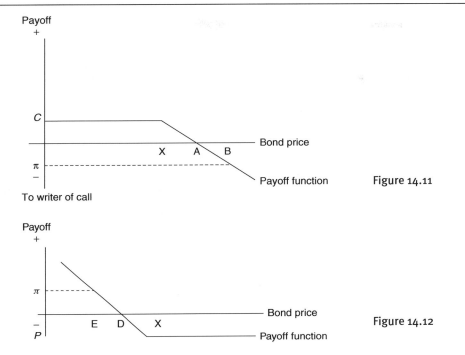

Figure 14.11

Figure 14.12

- *Buying a Put Option on a Bond provides the buyer the right, but not the obligation, to sell the underlying bond to the writer of the put option at the strike or exercise price on or before the expiration date. The payoff diagram is shown in Figure 14.12.*

  The buyer of the put option on the bond pays the put premium, P, to the writer of the put option. Until point X, the option is out-of-the-money. At the link, point X or the strike price, the option is at-the-money. At point D the buyer breaks even and beyond this point, the buyer makes a profit. The two points to consider when viewing this diagram are (1) when interest rates and bond prices fall, the probability of making a profit increases for the buyer of the put option on the bond and (2) when interest rates fall and bond prices rise, the probability of a loss to the buyer (limited to the put premium) increases.

- *Writing a Put Option on a Bond, the writer receives the put premium, P, in return for standing ready to buy the underlying bond at the strike or exercise price should the buyer of the put option choose to exercise the option. The payoff diagram is shown in Figure 14.13.*

  Again, it should be noted that the payoff functions to the buyer and writer of a put option are mirror images of one another. The writer (buyer) makes (loses) money, the put premium, as long as the option expires out-of-the-money and the buyer (writer) makes (loses) money, an unlimited amount potentially, if the put ends up in-the-money.

Covered Strategies

The four strategies defined above are referred to as *naked* strategies because neither the buyer nor the writer owns the underlying asset, the bond. Next, we will review *covered* strategies including covered calls and covered puts.

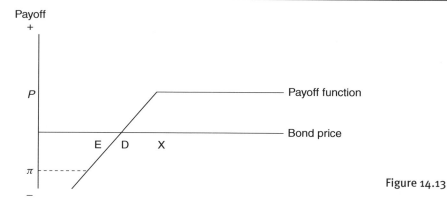

Figure 14.13

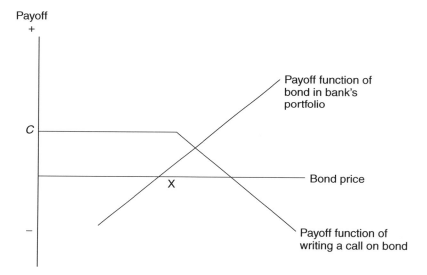

Figure 14.14

Writing a Call Option to Hedge Interest-Rate Risk on a Bond Writing the call option may hedge the financial intermediary when rates fall and bond prices rise (i.e., the increase in value of the bonds is offset by the loss on the written call), but the reverse is also true. When rates increase, the intermediary's profit from the written call may be sufficient to offset the loss on the bond due to the income from the call premium that is received. The payoff diagram is shown in Figure 14.14.

Buying a Put Option to Hedge the Interest-Rate Risk on a Bond With this strategy, the intermediary is "long the bond" in its portfolio and seeks to hedge the interest-rate risk on that bond by purchasing a put option on a bond. The payoff diagram is shown in Figure 14.15.

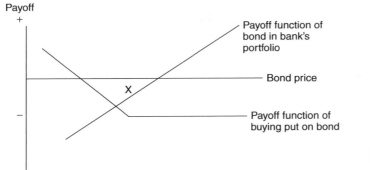

Figure 14.15

14.3.3   Pricing

Factors that Influence the Option Price

The Current Price of the Underlying Security   As the price of the underlying bond increases, the value of a call option rises and the value of a put option falls. This is because the holder of a call option tends to benefit from high prices for the underlying security, but the put holder tends to benefit from low prices for the underlying security.

The Strike Price   Call options become more valuable as the exercise price decreases because the holder stands to gain more on exercise of the option. Put options become more valuable as the exercise price increases, for the same reason.

Time to Expiration   For American options (both calls and puts), the longer the time to expiration, the higher the option price. This is because all the exercise opportunities open to the holder of the short-life option are also open to the holder of the long-life option. For European call options, the longer the time to expiration, the higher the call option price. As the call option maturity is increased, there is an increasing probability of a large change in the price of the underlying instrument. This is desirable, since the option buyer exhibits a large profit potential with a limited loss potential. In contrast, the effect of the time to expiration on the put option price is ambiguous. An increase in maturity lowers a European put value by lowering the present value of the exercise price when it is received if it is exercised; however, it also increases the put value by increasing the total uncertainty about the terminal stock price.

Short-Term Risk-Free Interest Rate over the Life of the Option   The price of a call option on a bond will increase and the price of a put option on a bond will decrease as the short-term risk-free interest rate rises. As the short-term interest rate increases, the financing cost of purchasing (i.e., the cost of carrying) the underlying bond is higher. Thus, the forward price of the bond increases and the net effect is very much like a higher current price—the call becomes more valuable. However, when the bond prices increase, the value of a put option falls. For options on futures, an increase in the short-term interest rate decreases the value of the call option, as well as the put option. The short-term risk-free rate represents the opportunity cost of funds invested in the underlying asset; however, no investment is required to assume a futures option.

Coupon Rate   For options on bonds, coupons tend to reduce the price of a call option because the coupons make it more attractive to hold the bond than the option. Thus, call options on coupon-bearing bonds will tend to be priced lower than similar call options on noncoupon-bearing bonds. Conversely, coupons tend to increase the price of put options since higher coupons usually mean less price appreciation.

Expected Volatility of Yields (or Prices) over the Life of the Option   As the expected volatility of yields over the life of the option increases, the price of the option will also increase. This is because the greater the expected volatility (as measured by the standard deviation or variance of yields), the greater the probability that the price of the underlying bond or futures contract will move in the direction that will benefit the option buyer. For the call owner, there is no limit to the amount he can gain from high prices, but there is a limit to his losses from low prices (i.e., call premium). For the put owner, high prices can at worst cost the option holder his premium, but low prices are not so limited in their benefit.

Option Pricing Models

There are two types of models for pricing options: the Black–Scholes model [Black and Scholes (1973), introduced in Chapter 13] and the binomial option-pricing model [Cox *et al.* (1979), introduced in Chapters 12 and 14]. For equities, the usual model is the Black–Scholes model, suitably adapted to account for various features of potential importance. For bond options, on the other hand, there are a series of problems that eliminate the Black–Scholes model from consideration.

- *The probability distribution for the prices assumed by the Black–Scholes model is a lognormal distribution, which permits some probability that the price can take any positive value. However, in the case of a zero-coupon bond, the price cannot take on a value above the maturity value. In the case of a coupon bond, the price cannot exceed the sum of the coupon payments plus the maturity value. Thus, unlike stock prices, bond prices have a maximum value. The only way that a bond price can exceed the maximum value is if negative interest rates are permitted. This is not likely to occur.*

- *The short-term interest rate is constant over the life of the option. Yet the price of an interest-rate option will change as interest rates change. A change in the short-term interest rate changes the rates along the yield curve. Thus, to assume that the short-term rate will be constant is inappropriate for interest-rate options.*

- *The variance of prices is constant over the life of the option. However, as a bond moves closer to maturity, its price volatility declines. Thus, to assume that price variance will be constant is inappropriate.*[7]

Obviously, a binomial option-pricing model based on the price distribution of the underlying bond suffers from the same problems. A solution to the problem is to consider an interest-rate model, as described in Chapter 12. One may cast the interest-rate model in a discrete-time binomial setting or continuous-time setting.[8]

---

[7]In the case of a short-term option on a long instrument, the duration will not change very much over the life of the option, and Black–Scholes model provides a relatively good approximation of the option value.

[8]One may also use arbitrage models to price options on bonds. In an exercise, we consider an application of Ho and Lee's model to the problem of bond option pricing. In the Appendix of this chapter, we discuss the pricing of bond options in

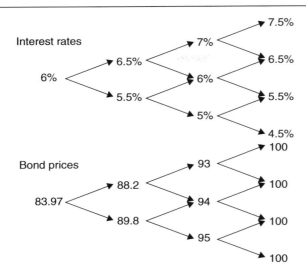

Figure 14.16

Binomial Model Figure 14.16 shows a tree for the 1-year rate of interest. As explained in Chapter 12, the interest-rate tree should be calibrated to the current zero-coupon fitted term structure of Treasury bonds. For simplicity, we use the 1-year rate as if it were the very short-term rate of interest. Interest rates can move up or down with equal probability. The figure also shows the values for a discount bond (par = 100) at each node in the tree.

Consider a 2-year European call on this 3-year bond struck at 93.5. If by the end of the second year the short-term rate has risen to 7% and the bond is trading at 93, the option will expire worthless. If the bond is trading at 94 (corresponding to a short-term rate of 6%), the call option is worth 0.5; and if the bond is trading at 95 (short-term rate = 5%), the call is worth 1.5. To derive the value of the call today, we start by filling in these values for the option at expiration. Let us denote the values of the call corresponding to an up and a down move as C_u and C_l, respectively. The unknown value is calculated as:

$$C_0 = \frac{1}{1+6\%}[0.5C_u + 0.5C_d]$$

with

$$C_u = \frac{1}{1+6.5\%}[0.5 \times 0 + 0.5 \times 0.5] = 0.2347$$

$$C_l = \frac{1}{1+5.5\%}[0.5 \times 0.5 + 0.5 \times 1.5] = 0.9479$$

Thus, the value of the option at any point in time is the discounted expectation of its value 1 period hence. The value today turns out to be

$$C_0 = \frac{1}{1+6\%}[0.5 \times 0.2347 + 0.5 \times 0.9479] = 0.5573$$

a special case of an HJM-type of model, the Hull and White model introduced in Chapter 12.

Fixed Income Securities

Continuous-Time Models   We now discuss the pricing of bond options within the framework of factor models for the short-rate cast in continuous time. We provide below a summary of the results concerning the pricing formula for a call option on discount bonds in various continuous-time models.

A consistent method for pricing discount bonds is actually a key ingredient for the pricing of all kinds of fixed-income derivatives. For example, Jamshidian (1989) argues that holding a call option on a coupon bond is equivalent to holding a portfolio of call options on discount bonds with suitably defined maturity dates and strike prices.[9] Besides, it can be shown that a cap can be regarded as a portfolio of put options on discount bonds, a floor as a portfolio of call option on discount bond and a swaption as a bond put option. In Chapter 15, we discuss the decomposition of other fixed-income derivatives in some detail.

Table 14.1 summarizes the results concerning the pricing formula for a call option C with strike E and maturity T on a discount bond with maturity T_B in the context of some popular one-factor models.

In the case of Cox, Ingersoll and Ross (1985) formula, $\chi^2(.; p, q)$ is the distribution function for the chi-squared law with p degrees of freedom and with noncentered parameter q. Functions A, D and γ have been defined previously in the zero-coupon rate formula (see equations (12.4) to (12.6)). Other single-factor models do not provide closed-form solutions for the pricing of options on discount bonds.

In the Appendix of this chapter, we also present the pricing formulas for a call on a zero-coupon bond and on a coupon bond in the 1-factor Hull and White (1990) model (see Chapter 12 for an

Table 14.1   Various Pricing Formulas for a Call Option on a Discount Bond.

Author	Call option formula
Merton (1973)	$C_t = B(t, T_B)\Phi(h) - EB(t, T)\Phi(h - \sigma_C)$ with $h = \dfrac{\ln\left[\dfrac{B(t, T_B)}{EB(t, T)}\right]}{\sigma_C} + \dfrac{\sigma_C}{2}$ and $\sigma_C^2 = \sigma_1{}^2(T_B - T)^2(T - t)$
Vasicek (1977)	same formula with $\sigma_C = \dfrac{v(t, T)(\exp[\mu_2(T_B - T)] - 1)}{\mu_2}$ and $v(t, T)^2 = \dfrac{\sigma_1{}^2(\exp[2\mu_2(T - t)] - 1)}{2\mu_2}$
Cox, Ingersoll and Ross (1985)	$C_t = B(t, T_B)\chi^2\left(2r^*[\phi + \psi + D(T - t)]; \dfrac{4\mu_1}{\sigma_2^2}, \dfrac{2\phi^2 r_t \exp[\gamma(T - t)]}{\phi + \psi + D(T - t)}\right)$ $- EB(t, T)\chi^2\left(2r^*[\phi + \psi]; \dfrac{4\mu_1}{\sigma_2^2}, \dfrac{2\phi^2 r_t \exp[\gamma(T - t)]}{\phi + \psi}\right)$ with $\phi = \dfrac{2\gamma}{\sigma_2^2(\exp[\gamma(T - t)] - 1)}$ $\psi = \dfrac{(-\mu_2 + \lambda + \gamma)}{\sigma_2^2}$ $r^* = \dfrac{\ln\left(\dfrac{A(T_B - T)}{E}\right)}{D(T_B - T)}$

[9]This decomposition only applies to European contingent claims, that is, contingent claims that may be exercised at maturity only.

overview of this model). We refer to Martellini and Priaulet (2000) for more details about the pricing of interest-rate derivatives in multifactor continuous-time models.

14.4 End of Chapter Summary

Most traded bonds issued by corporations are not straight bonds; they contain all kinds of embedded options. In this chapter, we first discuss callable and putable bonds, and then move on to studying convertible bonds. Not only do some bonds contain embedded options but also standard options are written on bonds just as they are written on stocks.

A callable bond is a bond that can be redeemed by the issuer before its maturity date. A putable bond is a bond that can be sold by the bond holder before its maturity date. Hence, buying a callable bond comes down to buying an option-free bond and selling a call option to the issuer of the bond. Similarly, buying a putable bond comes down to buying an option-free bond as well as a put option. These options can be priced using standard interest-rate models, such as a binomial model.

A convertible bond is a security that gives the bondholder the right to exchange the par amount of the bond for common shares of the issuer at some fixed ratio during a particular period. Being debt or preferred instruments, they have an advantage over the common stock in case of distress or bankruptcy.

A convertible bond is similar to a normal coupon bond plus a call option on the underlying stock. Convertible securities are therefore priced as a function of the price of the underlying stock, expected future volatility of equity returns, risk-free interest rates, call provisions, supply and demand for specific issues, issue-specific corporate/Treasury yield spread and expected volatility of interest rates and spreads.

Convertible arbitrage strategies are pursued by many hedge-fund managers who attempt to exploit anomalies in prices of corporate securities that are convertible into common stocks. Convertible arbitrage hedge-fund managers typically buy (or sometimes sell) these securities and then hedge part or all of the associated risks by shorting the stock.

An option is a contract in which the seller (writer) of the option grants the buyer of the option the right to purchase from, or sell to, the seller a designated instrument at a specified price within a specified period of time. The seller grants this right to the buyer in exchange for a certain sum of money called the *option price* or *option premium*. The price at which the instrument may be bought or sold is called the *exercise* or *strike price*. The date after which an option is void is called the *expiration date*. An American option may be exercised any time up to and including the expiration date. A European option may be exercised only on the expiration date.

When an option seller grants the buyer the right to purchase the designated instrument, it is called a *call option*. When the option buyer has the right to sell the designated instrument to the seller, the option is called a *put option*. The buyer of any option is said to be long the option; the seller is said to be short the option.

Pricing options on bonds requires the use of a model for the short-term rate dynamics. These models can be cast either in a discrete-time (binomial or trinomial) setting or in a continuous-time (single or multifactor) setting. There exists a specific relationship, known as the *put–call parity relationship*, between the price of a call option and the price of a put option on the same underlying debt instrument, with the same strike price and the same expiration date.

14.5 References and Further Reading

14.5.1 On Callable and Putable Bonds

Buetow, G.W., B. Hanke, and F.J. Fabozzi, 2001, "Impact of Different Interest Rate Models on Bond Value Measures", *Journal of Fixed Income*, **11**(3), 41–53.

Jordan, B.D., S.D. Jordan, and R.D. Jorgensen, 1995, "A Reexamination of Option Values Implicit in Callable Treasury Bonds", *Journal of Financial Economics*, **38**, 141–162.

Jordan, B.D., S.D. Jordan, and R.D. Jorgensen, 1998, The Mispricing of Callable US Treasury Bonds: A Closer Look, *Journal of Futures Markets*, **18**(1), 35–51.

Kalotay, A.J., and L.A. Abreo, 1999, "Putable/Callable/Rest Bonds: Intermarket Arbitrage with Unpleasant Side Effects", *Journal of Derivatives*, **6**(4), 1–6.

Leland, E.C., and P. Nikoulis, 1997, "The Putable Bond Market: Structure, Historical Experience, and Strategies", *Journal of Fixed Income*, **7**(3), 47–60.

Longstaff, F.A., 1992, "Are Negative Option Prices Possible? The Callable US Treasury-Bond Puzzle", *Journal of Business*, **65**, 571–592.

14.5.2 On Convertible Bonds

Ammann, A., A. Kind, and C. Wilde, 2003, "Are Convertible Bonds Underpriced? An Analysis of the French Market", *Journal of Banking and Finance*, **27**(4), pp. 635–653.

Black, F., and M. Scholes, 1973, "The Pricing of Options and Corporate Liabilities", *Journal of Political Economy*, **81**, 637–659.

Brennan, M.J., and E.S. Schwartz, 1977, "Convertible Bonds: Valuation and Optimal Strategies for Call and Conversion", *Journal of Finance*, **32**(3), 1699–1715.

Brennan, M.J., and E.S. Schwartz, 1980, "Analyzing Convertible Bonds", *Journal of Financial and Quantitative Analysis*, **15**(4), 907–929.

Burke, J., and J.M. Pagli Jr., 1999, "Convertible Arbitrage: A Manager's Perspective", *Journal of Alternative Investments*, **2**(1), 72–78.

Cox, J., S. Ross, and M. Rubinstein, 1979, "Option Pricing: A Simplified Approach", *Journal of Financial Economics*, **7**, 229–263.

Ferguson, R., R., Butman, H. Erickson, and S. Rossiello, 1995, "An Intuitive Procedure to Approximate Convertible Bond Hedge Ratios and Durations", *Journal of Portfolio Management*, 103–111.

Hull, J.C., 1998, *Futures and Options Markets*, 3rd Edition, Prentice Hall, New York.

Hull, J., 2002, *Options, Futures and Other Derivatives*, 5th Edition, Prentice Hall, New York.

Ingersoll, J., 1977, "A Contingent Claims Valuation of Convertible Securities", *Journal of Financial Economics*, **4**, 289–322.

Jung, J., 2000, "Valuation and Performance of Convertible Bonds with Hedge Funds", *Journal of Alternative Investments*, **2**(4), 24–34.

Lee, I., and T. Loughran, 1998, "Performance Following Convertible Bond Issuance", *Journal of Corporate Finance*, **4**, 185–207.

Martellini, L., and P. Priaulet, 2000, *Fixed-Income Securities: Dynamic Methods for Interest Rate Risk Pricing and Hedging*, John Wiley & Sons.

McConnell, J., and E. Schwartz, 1986, "LYON Taming", *Journal of Finance*, **41**(3), 561–577.

Pagli Jr., J.M., 2000, "Convertible Arbitrage: A Manager's Perspective", *Journal of Alternative Investments*, **2**(4), 42–49.

Takahashi, A., T. Kobayashi, and N. Nakagawa, 2001, "Pricing Convertible Bonds with Default Risk", *Journal of Fixed Income*, **11**(3), 20–29.

Tsiveriotis, K., and C. Fernandes, 1998, "Valuing Convertible Bonds with Credit Risk", *Journal of Fixed Income*, **8**(2), 95–102.

Wolfe, S., S. Dliakopoulos, and O.A. Gwilym, 1999, "Equity Valuation Effects of the Issuance of Convertible Bonds: U.K. Evidence", *Journal of Fixed Income*, **9**(3), 7–18.

14.5.3 On Options on Bonds

Black, F., and M. Scholes, 1973, "The Pricing of Options and Corporate Liabilities", *Journal of Political Economy*, **81**, 637–659.

El Karoui, N., and J.C. Rochet, 1989, A Pricing Formula for Options on Coupon Bonds, Working Paper No. 72, SEEDS.

Heath, D., R.A. Jarrow, and A. Morton, 1990, "Contingent Claim Valuation with a Random Evolution of Interest Rates", *Review of Futures Markets*, **9**(1), 23–56.

Heath, D., R.A. Jarrow, and A. Morton, 1990, "Bond Pricing and the Term Structure of Interest Rates: a Discrete Time Approximation", *Journal of Financial and Quantitative Analysis*, **25**(4), 419–440.

Heath, D., R.A. Jarrow, and A. Morton, 1992, "Bond Pricing and the Term Structure of Interest Rates: a New Methodology for Contingent Claim Valuations", *Econometrica*, **60**(1), 77–105.

Ho, T.S.Y., 1995, "Evolution of Interest Rate Models: A Comparison", *Journal of Derivatives*, **2**(4), 9–20.

Ho, T.S.Y., and S.B. Lee, 1986, "Term Structure Movements and Pricing Interest Rate Contingent Claims", *Journal of Finance*, **41**(5), 1011–1029.

Hull, J., and A. White, 1990, "Pricing Interest Rate Derivative Securities", *Review of Financial Studies*, **3**(4), 573–592.

Hull, J., and A. White, 1993, "One Factor Interest Rate Models and the Valuation of Interest-Rate Derivative Securities", *Journal of Financial and Quantitative Analysis*, **28**(2), 235–254.

Hull, J., and A. White, 1993, "Bond Option Pricing Based on a Model for the Evolution of Bond Prices", *Advances in Futures and Options Research*, **6**, 1–13.

Hull, J., and A. White, 1994, "Branching Out", *Risk*, **7**(7), 34–37.

Hull, J., and A. White, 1994, "Numerical Procedures for Implementing Term Structure Models I: Single-Factor Models", *Journal of Derivatives*, **2**(1), 7–16.

Hull, J., and A. White, 1994, "Numerical Procedures for Implementing Term Structure Models II: Two-Factor Models", *Journal of Derivatives*, **2**(2), 37–48.

Hull, J., and A. White, 1996, "Using Hull-White Interest Rate Trees", *Journal of Derivatives*, **3**(3), 26–36.

Jamshidian, F., 1989, "An Exact Bond Option Formula", *Journal of Finance*, **44**(1), 205–209.

Martellini, L., and P. Priaulet, 2000, *Fixed-Income Securities: Dynamic Methods for Interest Rate Risk Pricing and Hedging*, John Wiley & Sons, Chichester.

Merton, R.C., 1973, "The Theory of Rational Option Pricing", *Bell Journal of Economics and Management Science*, **4**(1), 141–183.

14.6 Problems

Exercise 14.1 Let us consider an option-free bond, a callable bond and a putable bond with the same maturity and coupon.

1. Compare their prices with each other.
2. In what market interest-rate situation is the price of the callable bond similar to the price of the option-free bond? Same question for the putable bond.

Exercise 14.2 What is effective duration? Why is the modified duration measure generally inappropriate to bonds with embedded options? In what particular context is it all the same a good proxy for effective duration?

Exercise 14.3 What does the yield-to-worst concept refer to? What is its value equal to under a low interest-rate environment? Under a high interest-rate environment? Why can't it be reasonably used for pricing bonds with embedded options?

Exercise 14.4 Consider a callable bond with semiannual coupon 4%, maturity 5 years and market price 100.5.

1. Compute its yield-to-worst if it is callable at 104 at the end of year 1, at 103 at the end of year 2, at 102 at the end of year 3 and at 101 at the end of year 4.
2. Same question if it is callable at 100 after 1 year.

Exercise 14.5 Today's term structure of par Treasury yields is assumed to have the following values:

Maturity (in years)	Par yield (%)
1	3.50
2	3.70
3	3.80

1. Derive the corresponding recombining binomial interest-rate tree, assuming a 1-year interest-rate volatility of 3%.
2. Determine the theoretical price of a 3-year callable bond with annual coupon 5%, callable at the end of year 1 at 102 and at the end of year 2 at 101. Its market price being equal to 102.5, determine its OAS.
3. Determine the theoretical price of a 3-year putable bond with annual coupon 4%, putable at 100 after 1 year. Its market price being equal to 100.2, determine its OAS.

Exercise 14.6 1. Determine the effective duration and convexity of the callable bond presented in the previous exercise.
2. Determine the effective duration and convexity of the putable bond presented in the previous exercise.

Exercise 14.7   We use the same assumptions as in the previous exercise.

1. Simulate 10 arbitrage-free 1-year interest-rate paths based on the Monte Carlo method, assuming a 1-year interest-rate return of 4% and a 1-year interest-rate volatility of 3%.
2. Determine the theoretical price of a 3-year callable bond with annual coupon 5%, callable at the end of year 1 at 102 and at the end of year 2 at 101. Its market price being equal to 102.5, determine its OAS.
3. Determine the theoretical price of a 3-year putable bond with annual coupon 4%, putable at 100 after 1 year. Its market price being equal to 100.2, determine its OAS.

Exercise 14.8   1. Determine the effective duration and convexity of the callable bond presented in the previous exercise.
2. Determine the effective duration and convexity of the putable bond presented in the previous exercise.

Exercise 14.9   Consider a 5%, 10-year bond that is callable at par in 5 years. Consider also a 5%, 5-year option-free bond and a 5%, 10-year option-free bond. How does the price of the callable bond evolve compared to that of the 5-year option-free bond? of the 10-year option-free bond? Explain why.

Exercise 14.10   We consider the following interest-rate tree:

$$0.055$$
$$0.04$$
$$0.035$$

Consider a 2-year bond with coupon rate 4.25 and 100 face value.

1. Calculate the bond price at the 3 nodes of the tree.
2. Now assume that the bond can be called at par at dates 0 and 1. Calculate the price of the call at the 3 nodes of the tree.
3. Assume the issue is long the call option. Calculate the price of the callable bond at the 3 nodes of the tree.
4. Redo questions 2 and 3 in the case of a put option struck at par and for a putable bond.

Exercise 14.11   If a bond can be converted into 40.57 shares of the company's common stock, and that common stock is currently selling for $30, then calculate the conversion value.

Exercise 14.12   A 9-month discount bond issued XYZ company with a face value of $100. Assume that it can be exchanged for 2 shares of company's stock at any time during the 9 months. It is callable for $115 at any time. Assume that the initial stock price = $50, volatility = 30% per annum and no dividend; risk-free yield curve to be flat at 10% per annum. Yield curve corresponding to bonds issued by the company is assumed to be flat at 15%. Find the fair price of the convertible bond using a binomial tree with a 3-months time step. Calculate the value of the conversion option.

Exercise 14.13   Consider the following callable convertible debt: zero coupon, $1000 face value per bond, conversion ratio: 50 shares, maturity at $t = 2$, callable (by firm) at face value at $t = 1$, convertible (by bondholders) any time before or on maturity, 500,000 bonds outstanding. Common stock: 40 million shares outstanding. The risk-free rate is 10%. The market value of equity is 1,000 million dollars at $t = 0$ and follows a binomial process.

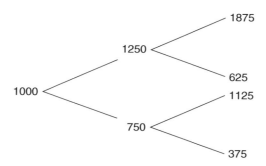

Here $u1 = 1.25$, $d1 = 0.75$ and $p1 = 0.7$, while $u2 = 1.5$, $d2 = 0.5$ and $p2 = 0.6$. Compute the value of the convertible debt, assuming away default risk. (Note: here you should take into account dilution).

Exercise 14.14   Consider the following interest-rate process. The current short rate is $r_0 = 0.05$, and $r_{t+1} = r_t + \begin{pmatrix} \sigma \\ -\sigma \end{pmatrix}$ with probability $(.5, .5)$, where $\sigma = 0.01$.

Calculate the tree process for the interest rate for dates 0 to 4. What do you think of such a process?

Exercise 14.15   Consider the following interest-rate tree:

				0.053074
			0.052287	
		0.051513		0.051505
	0.05075		0.050742	
0.05		0.04999		0.049983
	0.049251		0.049242	
		0.048513		0.048506
			0.047787	
				0.047072

We consider a bond, callable at 100, with 5 years maturity, redemption value equal to 100 and a 5% annual coupon rate. What is the value of that bond?

Exercise 14.16 Consider the following interest-rate tree (4 1-year periods):

				0.338464
			0.262012	
		0.196941		0.245776
	0.14318		0.186493	
0.1		0.137401		0.17847
	0.097916		0.13274	
		0.095862		0.129596
			0.09448	
				0.094106

1. Calculate the value at each node of the tree of a 5-year pure discount bond with face value 100. What is the YTM on that bond?
2. Calculate the price of an identical bond that would be callable at $75. Calculate the YTM on that bond and the spread over the straight bond. What is the value of the embedded call option according to the model?
3. Assume that the market price of the callable bond is $44. What is the OAS of the bond, that is, what is the constant spread that must be added to all rates in the tree to make the model price equal to the market price?
4. Redo question 2 for a call price equal to 80.
5. Assuming that the market price is 50, calculate the OAS for that bond.

Exercise 14.17 Consider a 2-year binomial model. The short riskless interest rate starts at 50% and moves up or down by 25% each year (i.e., up to 75% or down to 25% at the first change). The probability of each of the 2 states at any node is .5. What is the price at each node, of a discount bond with face value of $100 maturing two periods from the start? What is the value at each node of a call option on the discount bond (with face of $100 maturing two periods from now) with a strike price of $60 and maturity 1 year from now?

Exercise 14.18 Consider an option to purchase a 1 period zero-coupon bond with face value $1,000, in a year from now, at a strike price $K = \$960$. Assume the short-term rate today is at 4%, and it can take on 2 possible values at date 1, 2 and 6%, respectively. Construct a portfolio of a 1-period and 2-period zero-coupon bond that replicates the payoff of the option. Calculate the price of the replicating portfolio. Finally, calculate the price of the option using risk-neutral pricing.

Exercise 14.19 You are given below current prices of financial securities. You are to determine if any arbitrage possibilities exist, and you are to explain why. If arbitrage is possible, describe a simple portfolio strategy, which will earn arbitrage profits and compute the minimum profit. The option is a European option and the underlying bond is a zero-coupon instrument.

	Current Price ($)
Underlying bond	40
European call option that has an exercise price of $40 and that matures in 4 months	3
European put option that has an exercise price of $40 and that matures in 4 months	2
Annualized interest rate for 4 month loans is 5%	—
Part b	—
Underlying bond	60
European call option that has an exercise price of $40 and that matures in 1 year	22
Annualized interest rate for 1 year loans is 11.111%	—

Hint: You need to think of the range of possible current values for put.

Exercise 14.20 Option Pricing in Ho and Lee's Lattice. We want to price a put option, with maturity of 1 year and strike price $980 on a 3-month T-bill with face value equal to $1,000. This option gives the right to the owner to buy at date $t = 1$ a T-bond paying $1,000 at date $t = 1.25$. We consider $\Delta t = 0.25$ (3 months). Therefore, there will be four subperiods during the life of the option ($T = 1, 2, 3, 4$). We first start from the initial term structure, which we derive, as usual, from prices

$$B(0, 1) = 0.98260$$

$$B(0, 2) = 0.9651$$

$$B(0, 3) = 0.9474$$

$$B(0, 4) = 0.9296$$

$$B(0, 5) = 0.9119$$

Find the price of the option, if you take as given the values of π and δ (see Chapter 12 for more information about Ho and Lee's (1986) model and notation)

$$\pi = \frac{1}{2}$$
$$\delta = 0.997$$

14.7 Appendix: Bond Option Prices in the Hull and White (1990) Model

We use the same notations as in Chapter 12. We refer the reader to Martellini and Priaulet (2000) for the description of a more general 2-factor model. We provide the formulas for call options. Proofs of these formulas are available in Priaulet (1997). Put option prices are obtained by using the call–put parity. In the Hull and White (1990) model, we simply recall that the volatility function for discount bonds, denoted by $\sigma(t, T)$, is equal to

$$\sigma(t, T) = \frac{\sigma}{\lambda}\left[1 - e^{-\lambda(T-t)}\right]$$

14.7.1 Call on Zero-Coupon Bond

The price at date t of a European call C_t with

- *maturity date T,*
- *strike price K and*
- *as underlying asset a discount bond $B(t, T_B)$ with $T < T_B$*

is given by

$$C_t = B(t, T_B)\Phi(-s_0 + v) - KB(t, T)\Phi(-s_0) \tag{14.1}$$

where Φ is the cumulative distribution function of the standard Gaussian distribution, and with s_0 and v given by

$$s_0 = \frac{1}{v}\ln\left[\frac{B(t, T)K}{B(t, T_B)}\right] + \frac{1}{2}v$$

$$v = \sqrt{\int_t^T (\sigma(s, T_B) - \sigma(s, T))^2\, ds}$$

14.7.2 Call on Coupon Bond

The price at date t of a European call C_t with

- *maturity date T,*
- *strike price K and*
- *as underlying asset a bond paying deterministic $F_1, F_2, \ldots, F_n$ at dates $T_1, T_2, \ldots, T_n$*

is given by

$$C_t = \sum_{j=1}^{n} F_j B(t, T_j)\Phi(-s_0 + v_j) - KB(t, T)\Phi(-s_0) \tag{14.2}$$

with s_0 and v_j given by

$$\sum_{j=1}^{n} F_j B(t, T_j)\exp\left[v_j s_0 - \frac{1}{2}v_j^2\right] = B(t, T)K$$

and

$$v_j = \sqrt{\int_t^T (\sigma(s, T_j) - \sigma(s, T))^2\, ds}$$

15

Options on Futures, Caps, Floors and Swaptions

In this chapter, we introduce options on futures, caps, floors and swaptions, which are known as *plain-vanilla* (or standard) interest-rate options. Exchange-traded futures options (commonly called *futures options*) are standardized options, while caps, floors and swaptions are over-the-counter contracts. We show how we can price and hedge these products against the different sources of risk and focus on their uses in practice.

The rapid rise of the fixed-income option markets was prior to the development of complex interest rates models.[1] Therefore, practitioners have started using Black (1976) model to price and hedge standard fixed-income derivatives. This model, which is particularly tractable and simple to use, remains currently the reference for the market in terms of pricing and hedging standard assets such as options on futures, caps, floors and swaptions, despite on the one hand, a strong simplifying assumption related to a stationary interest rate and a unique underlying asset with constant volatility, and, on the other hand, the absence of a real model for the term structure dynamics.[2]

15.1 Options on Futures

15.1.1 Definition and Terminology

An option on a futures contract gives the buyer the right to buy from or sell to the seller

- *one unit of a designated futures, called the trading unit,*

- *at a determined price, called the strike price,*

- *on the maturity date of the option (in this case we speak of a European option) or at any time during the option life (in this case we speak of an American option).*

> **Example 15.1** The trading unit of the CBOT (Chicago Board of Trade) 10-year US Treasury Note futures option is one CBOT 10-year US T-Note futures (of a specified delivery month) having a face value at maturity of $100,000. There are both American and European calls and puts.

---

[1] See Chapter 12. Note that the first real model for the term structure dynamics was provided in Vasicek (1977). Arbitrage models consistent with the current term structure were developed, roughly, 10 years later with Ho and Lee (1986), Hull and White (1990) and Heath, Jarrow and Morton (HJM) (1990a, 1990b, 1992).
[2] The Black (1976) model is all the more the reference for such products than new market models such as Brace, Gatarek and Musiela (BGM)/Jamshidian models are built to recover exactly the prices of caps, floors and swaptions as obtained in the Black (1976) model. Appendix 5 of this chapter is devoted to a presentation of these market models whose final goal is to price and hedge more exotic options (see Chapter 16).

The strike price is expressed in the same basis as the futures price, and there are usually strike price intervals.

> **Example 15.2** Strike price intervals for the Long Gilt Futures option quoted on Liffe are 0.50%, for example, 102%, 102.50%...

Expiry months depend on each futures option.

> **Example 15.3** Expiry months for the 3-month Sterling futures option quoted on Liffe are March, June, September and December.

- *A call enables the buyer to acquire a long position in the underlying futures if he exercises the option. Conversely and if exercised, the seller has a short position in the futures.*

- *A put enables the buyer to acquire a short position in the underlying futures if he exercises the option. Conversely and if exercised, the seller has a long position in the futures.*

The option buyer has no margin to deposit after having paid the option premium because his maximum loss is equal to this premium. On the contrary, if the buyer exercises the option, the seller is in position, short or long, depending on the callable or putable nature of the option. Then when he sells the option, he is required to deposit the margin pertaining to the underlying futures (see Chapter 11), plus the option premium.

> **Example 15.4** Consider a firm that buys a T-bond futures call with a 110 strike price, which matures in 3 months. One month later, the futures price is 115 and the buyer decides to exercise his option. The futures positions of the two counterparts are immediately marked to market. It means that the futures exchange obtains 5 from the seller and gives 5 to the buyer. The buyer now has a long position at 115, while the seller has the opposite short position. Finally, the buyer has two alternatives. Either he liquidates the futures position at 115 and definitely makes a profit of 5 (minus the option premium), or he prefers to stay exposed by maintaining the long position.

Options on futures are traded all over the world on the same markets as futures contracts. There are standardized options. We give in Tables 15.1 and 15.2 the list of options on futures traded on 09/03/01 in the CME (Chicago Mercantile Exchange), CBOT (Chicago Board of Trade), LIFFE (London International Financial Futures and Options), EUREX (the European Derivatives Market) and MATIF (Marché à Terme International de France). Most of them are options written on Treasury bond futures (T-bill, T-note, T-bond, Gilt, OAT, Bund, Bobl or Schatz etc.) or assimilated (agency notes, municipal bond index), interest rate futures (Libor, Euribor etc.) and swapnote futures.

Fixed Income Securities

Table 15.1   CME, CBOT and LIFFE Options on Futures.

CME	CBOT	LIFFE
Eurodollar Options	30-Year US T-Bond Options	Long Gilt Options
5-Year Eurodollar Bundle Options	10-Year US T-Note Options	German Government Bond Options
13 Week T-Bill Options	5-Year US T-Note Options	3-Month Sterling Options
1-Month Libor Options	2-Year US T-Note Options	3-Month Euribor Options
Euro Yen Options	10-Year Agency Note Options	3-Month Euro Swiss Options
	5-Year Agency Note Options	2-Year Euro Swapnote Options
	Long-Term Municipal Bond Index Options	5-Year Euro Swapnote Options
	Mortgage Options	10-Year Euro Swapnote Options

Table 15.2   EUREX and MATIF Options on Futures.

EUREX	MATIF
3-Month Euribor Futures Options	Euro Notional Futures Options
Euro-Schatz Futures Options	5-Year Euro Futures Options
Euro-Bobl Futures Options	3-Month Euribor Futures Options
Euro Bund Futures Options	

The whole description of these options on futures as well as those of bond and interest-rate options on futures on other markets may be obtained on Bloomberg (OTM and OEM functions), on Reuters or on the websites of futures markets.

15.1.2   Pricing and Hedging Options on Futures

We give below the price formula for European options on futures in the Black (1976) model. Note that the price of forward options is equivalent to that of options on futures because we assume that interest rates are deterministic in the Black (1976) model.[3] As options on futures may be American options, one can also use the Barone-Adesi and Whaley (1987) model to price them. In Appendix 3 of this chapter, we also give the pricing formula for four different futures and forward European options in the Hull and White (1990) model introduced in Chapter 12:

- *A call option on a T-bond forward contract*

- *A call option on a Libor forward contract*

- *A call option on a T-bond futures contract*

- *A call option on a Libor futures contract.*

Futures Call and Put Formulas in the Black Model

Futures Call Formula   Let us consider at date t a futures option that expires at date T, with nominal amount N, strike price E, based upon a futures asset denoted by F.

---

[3]In the Appendix of Chapter 11 on Forwards and Futures, we have shown that forward price and futures price of two similar contracts are equivalent when rates are deterministic.

The futures call price at date t, denoted by C_t, in Black (1976) model is given by

$$C_t = N \times B(t, T) \times [F_t \Phi(d_f) - E \Phi(d_f - \sigma \sqrt{T - t})] \qquad (15.1)$$

where

Φ is the cumulative distribution function of the standard Gaussian distribution;

F_t is the price of the futures asset at date t;

d_f is given by

$$d_f = \frac{\ln\left(\dfrac{F_t}{E}\right) + 0.5\sigma^2(T - t)}{\sigma \sqrt{T - t}}$$

σ is the volatility of the futures asset F.

Futures Put Formula   Using the standard put–call parity formula

$$\frac{P_t - C_t}{N} = E \times B(t, T) - F_t$$

we obtain the futures put price, denoted by P_t, with the same notations as before

$$P_t = N \times B(t, T) \times [-F_t \Phi(-d_f) + E \Phi(-d_f + \sigma \sqrt{T - t})]$$

Futures Call and Put Greeks in the Black Model

Greeks of futures call and put with respect to the different variables can be obtained in closed-form formulas. They allow the seller of these products to easily implement dynamic hedging strategies.

Futures Call Greeks   For a futures call, we obtain the following results:

- *Delta* (Δ), *which is the first derivative of the futures call price with respect to the underlying rate F_t, is given by*

$$\Delta = N \times B(t, T)\Phi(d_f)$$

- *Gamma* (γ), *which is the second derivative of the futures call price with respect to the underlying rate F_t, is given by*

$$\gamma = N \times \left(\frac{B(t, T)}{\sigma \sqrt{T - t} F_t} \Phi'(d_f)\right)$$

- *Vega* (ν), *which is the first derivative of the futures call price with respect to the volatility parameter σ, is given by*

$$\nu = N \times B(t, T)\sqrt{T - t} F_t \Phi'(d_f)$$

- *Rho* (ρ), *which is the first derivative of the futures call price with respect to the interest rate $R^c(t, T - t)$, is given by*

$$\rho = -(T - t) \times C_t$$

where $R^c(t, T - t) = -\frac{1}{T-t} \ln[B(t, T)]$ is at date t the continuously compounded zero-coupon rate with maturity $T - t$.

- *Theta* (θ), *which is the first derivative of the futures call price with respect to time, is given by*

$$\theta = R^c(t, T - t)C_t - N \times \frac{B(t, T)\sigma F_t}{2\sqrt{T - t}} \Phi'(d_f)$$

Fixed Income Securities

Futures Put Greeks For a futures put, we obtain the following results:

- *Delta* (Δ), *which is the first derivative of the futures put price with respect to the underlying rate* F_t, *is given by*

$$\Delta = -N \times B(t, T)\Phi(-d_f)$$

- *Gamma* (γ), *which is the second derivative of the futures put price with respect to the underlying rate* F_t, *is given by*

$$\gamma = N \times \left(\frac{B(t, T)}{\sigma \sqrt{T - t} F_t} \Phi'(-d_f) \right)$$

- *Vega* (ν), *which is the first derivative of the futures put price with respect to the volatility parameter* σ, *is given by*

$$\nu = N \times B(t, T)\sqrt{T - t} F_t \Phi'(-d_f)$$

- *Rho* (ρ), *which is the first derivative of the futures put price with respect to the interest rate* $R^c(t, T - t)$, *is given by*

$$\rho = -(T - t) \times P_t$$

  where $R^c(t, T - t) = -\frac{1}{T-t} \ln[B(t, T)]$ *is at date t the continuously compounded zero-coupon rate with maturity* $T - t$.

- *Theta* (θ), *which is the first derivative of the futures put price with respect to time, is given by*

$$\theta = R^c(t, T - t)P_t - N \times \frac{B(t, T)\sigma F_t}{2\sqrt{T - t}} \Phi'(-d_f)$$

Example 15.5 Consider a firm which contracts a call on a T-bond futures at date $t = 05/04/02$ whose features are the following:

- *Nominal amount: $10,000,000*

- *Maturity date:* $T = 06/04/02$

- *Strike rate:* $E = 103.50\%$.

Assuming that the T-bond futures price is 102.99% at date t, its volatility is 5% and that the zero-coupon rate $R^c(t, T - t)$ is equal to 5%, the price at date t of this call using the Black model is

$$C_t = \$37,773$$

We obtain the following Greeks:

$$\Delta = 3,684,851$$

$$\gamma = 250,537,596$$

$$v = 1,128,501$$

$$\rho = -3,208$$

$$\theta = -330,291$$

When the futures price goes up to 103.09%, the price variation is approximately the delta value multiplied by the price change

$$Price\ Variation \simeq \Delta \times 0.1\% = \$3,685$$

For a best approximation of the price variation, we must take into account the convexity of the option price with the gamma value so that

$$Price\ Variation = \$3,811 \simeq \Delta \times 0.1\% + \gamma \times \frac{(0.1\%)^2}{2} = \$3,810$$

This is closer to the true price variation, which is equal to

$$Price\ Variation = C_t(F_t = 103.09\%) - C_t(F_t = 102.99\%) = \$3,811$$

When the volatility goes up to 6%, the price variation is approximately the vega value multiplied by the volatility change

$$Price\ Variation \simeq v \times 1\% = \$11,285$$

The true price variation is

$$Price\ Variation = C_t(\sigma = 6\%) - C_t(\sigma = 5\%) = \$11,394$$

When the zero-coupon rate $R^c(t, T - t)$ goes up to 6%, the price variation is approximately the rho value multiplied by the zero-coupon rate change

$$Price\ Variation = -\$32 \simeq \rho \times 1\%$$

which is equal to the true price variation $C_t(R^c(t, T - t) = 6\%) - C_t(R^c(t, T - t) = 5\%)$.

One day later when we reprice the futures call, the price variation due to time is approximately the theta value multiplied by $\frac{1}{365}$

$$Price\ Variation \simeq \theta \times \frac{1}{365} = -\$905$$

while the true price variation is $-\$912$.

15.1.3 Market Quotes

Quotation of interest-rate options on futures depends on the nature of the futures underlying asset, a T-bond futures or an interest-rate (typically, Libor or Euribor) futures.

Options on T-bond futures are usually quoted in percentage of the T-bond futures face value, up to the second decimal, or to the nearest $\frac{1}{64}$ of 1% in the United States. We show below two examples of T-bond options on futures quoted on Bloomberg.

Fixed Income Securities

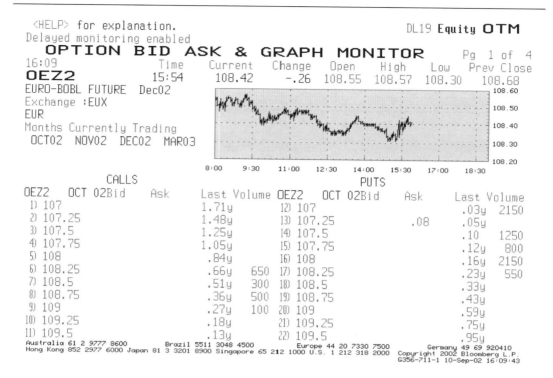

Example 15.6 Euro-Bobl Futures Option

On 09/10/02, we see in Figure 15.1 the quotation of calls and puts with maturity on October 2002 written on the Euro-Bobl futures with maturity on December 2002. The current futures price is 108.42% as strike prices range from 107 to 109.5%. For example, the last quotation for the call with strike price 107.50% is 1.25% of the futures face value.

Example 15.7 US 5-Year Note Futures Option

On 09/10/02, we see in Figure 15.2 the quotation of calls and puts with maturity on November 2002 written on the US 5-year note futures with maturity on December 2002. The current futures price is 111-17% $\left(= 111 + \frac{17}{64}\right)$ as strike prices range from 109 to 114.5%. For example, the last quotation for the put with strike price 111.50% is $\frac{61}{64}$% of the futures face value as the present bid–ask is $\left[1 + \frac{5}{64}; 1 + \frac{7}{64}\right]$.

Options on interest-rate futures are usually quoted in percentage of the futures contract size, up to the third decimal. We show below an example of a Libor futures option quoted on Bloomberg.

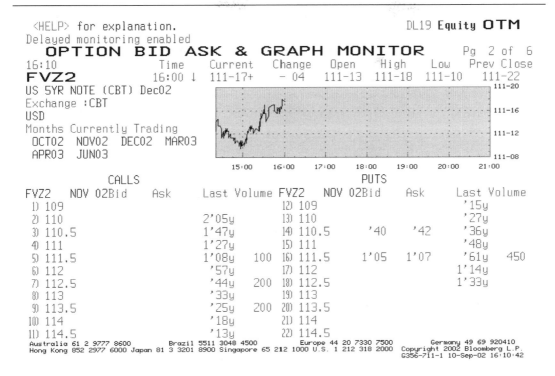

Figure 15.2 Quotations of US 5-Year Note Futures Options. © 2003 Bloomberg L.P. All rights reserved. Reprinted with permission.

Example 15.8   Sterling 3-Month Libor Futures Option

On 09/09/02, we see in Figure 15.3 the quotation of calls and puts with maturity on March 2003 written on the £ 3-month Libor futures with maturity on March 2003. The current futures price is 96.040% as strike prices range from 95.375 to 96.625%. For example, the last quotation for the call with strike price 96.50% is 0.125% of the futures face value as the present bid−ask is [0.100; 0.115].

Note finally that options on futures have minimum price movement, called *tick size*, which depends on each option.

Example 15.9   The tick size of the £ 3-month Libor futures option quoted on Liffe is 0.005% of the futures contract size, which amounts to £6.25 (0.005%/4 of £500,000).

The tick size of the CBOT 10-year US T-Note futures option is 1/64 of a basis point, which amounts to $15.625 ($100,000/6,400).

Fixed Income Securities

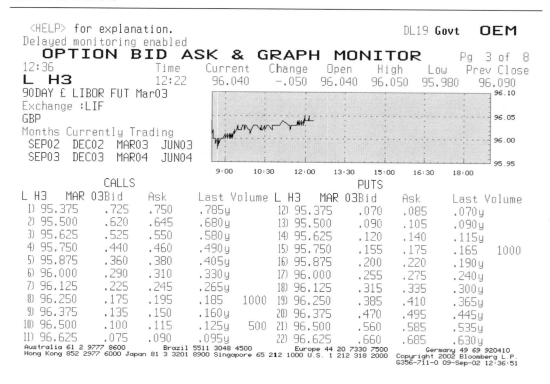

Figure 15.3 Quotations of the £ 3-Month Libor Futures Options. © 2003 Bloomberg L.P. All rights reserved. Reprinted with permission.

15.1.4 Uses of Futures Options

We have seen in Chapter 11 that firms can use futures to reduce their interest-rate risk. One drawback of such hedging strategies is that they do not allow firms to profit from favorable movement in prices or rates. One alternative to futures is to use options on futures because they allow firms to be hedged against defavorable movements of prices or rates while still benefiting from favorable movements. Because T-bond futures prices are highly correlated with T-bond prices, T-bond options are usually used to hedge T-bonds. Besides, buyers of calls on interest-rate futures make profit when rates go up and buyers of puts on the same products make profit when rates go down. Then firms with liabilities or assets whose values are exposed to a rise or fall in short-term interest rates use interest-rate options on futures to hedge their exposure.[4]

15.2 Caps, Floors and Collars

15.2.1 Definition and Terminology

A *cap* is an over-the-counter contract by which the seller agrees to payoff a positive amount to the buyer of the contract if the *reference rate* exceeds a prespecified level called the *exercise rate*

---

[4]See also Chapters 5 and 6 to see in detail how to hedge the interest-rate risk, and Chapter 11 to see how to use futures contracts as hedging assets.

of the cap on given future dates. Conversely, the seller of a *floor* agrees to pay a positive amount to the buyer of the contract if the reference rate falls below the exercise rate on some future dates. We first define some terms:

- *The notional or nominal amount is fixed in general.*

- *The reference rate is an interest-rate index based, for example, on Libor, T-bill and T-bond yield to maturity, swap rates from which the contractual payments are determined. The most usual ones are the 1-month, 3-month, 6-month and 1-year Libor rates, the Constant Maturity Swap (CMS) and Constant Maturity Treasury (CMT) rates.*

- *The exercise rate or strike rate is a fixed rate determined at the origin of the contract.*

- *The settlement frequency refers to the frequency with which the reference rate is compared to the exercise rate. The time between two payments is known as the tenor. It is expressed in years. The most common frequencies are monthly, quarterly, semiannually and annually.*

- *The starting date is the date when the protection of caps, floors and collars begins.*

- *The maturity of caps, floors and collars can range from several months to 30 years.*

- *The premium of caps, floors and collars is expressed as a percentage of the notional amount.*

We give below an example of caps and floors.

Example 15.10   Let us consider a cap with a nominal amount of $1,000,000, an exercise rate E, based upon a Libor rate with a δ-month maturity denoted by $R^L(t, \delta)$ at date t and with the following schedule

t	—	T_0	—	T_1	—	T_2	—	—	—	$\ldots$	—	—	—	T_n
—	—	—	—	C_1	—	C_2	—	—	—	—	—	—	—	C_n

T_0 is the starting date of the cap as the difference between $T_n - T_0$ expressed in years is the maturity of the cap. For all $j = 1, \ldots, n$, we assume a constant tenor $T_j - T_{j-1} = \delta$. On each date T_j, the cap holder receives a cash flow C_j

$$C_j = \$1,000,000 \times \delta \times [R^L(T_{j-1}, \delta) - E]^+$$

C_j is a call option on the Libor rate $R^L(t, \delta)$ observed on date T_{j-1} with a payoff occurring on date T_j. The cap is a portfolio of n such options. The n call options of the cap are known as the *caplets*.

Let us now consider a floor with the same characteristics. The floor holder gets on each date T_j (for $j = 1, \ldots, n$) a cash flow F_j

$$F_j = \$1,000,000 \times \delta \times [E - R^L(T_{j-1}, \delta)]^+$$

F_j is a put option on the Libor rate $R^L(t, \delta)$ observed on date T_{j-1} with a payoff occurring on date T_j. The floor is a portfolio of n such options. The n put options of the floor are known as the *floorlets*.

A *collar* is a combination of a cap and a floor. There are two kinds of collars, the collar that consists in buying a cap and selling a floor at the same time and conversely, the collar that consists in buying a floor and selling a cap at the same time. In the first case, the idea is that the premium of the floor reduces the cost of the cap, whereas the premium of the cap reduces the cost of the floor in the second case. We will see concrete examples of these two products in Section 15.2.4.

15.2.2 Pricing and Hedging Caps, Floors and Collars

Cap and Floor Formula in the Black Model

Cap Formula Let us consider a cap with nominal amount N, exercise rate E, based upon a reference linear rate denoted as $R^L(t, \delta)$ at date t and with the following schedule:

t	—	T_0	—	T_1	—	T_2	—	—	—	...	—	—	—	T_n
—	—	—	—			C_1	—	C_2	—	—	—	—	—	C_n

For all $j = 1, \ldots, n$, we assume a constant $T_j - T_{j-1} = \delta$. At each date T_j, the cap holder receives a cash flow C_j

$$C_j = N \times [\delta \cdot (R^L(T_{j-1}, \delta) - E)]^+$$

The cap price at date t in the Black (1976) model is given by

$$CAP_t = \sum_{j=1}^{n} Caplet_t^j = \sum_{j=1}^{n} N \times \delta \times B(t, T_j) \times [F(t, T_{j-1}, T_j)\Phi(d_j) - E\Phi(d_j - \sigma_j\sqrt{T_{j-1} - t})]$$

where (15.2)

Φ is the cumulative distribution function of the standard Gaussian distribution.

$F(t, T_{j-1}, T_j)$ is the underlying rate of the caplet relative to the cash flow C_j received at date T_j. It is the forward linear rate as seen from date t, beginning at date T_{j-1}, and finishing at date T_j. Note in particular that

$$F(T_{j-1}, T_{j-1}, T_j) = R^L(T_{j-1}, \delta)$$

d_j is given by

$$d_j = \frac{\ln\left(\dfrac{F(t, T_{j-1}, T_j)}{E}\right) + 0.5\sigma_j^2(T_{j-1} - t)}{\sigma_j\sqrt{T_{j-1} - t}}$$

σ_j is the volatility of the underlying rate $F(t, T_{j-1}, T_j)$, which is usually referred to as the *caplet volatility*.

Note that the first caplet yielding the cash flow C_1 is not taken into account in the cap price once the cap is initiated at date T_0, since, at that date, $R^L(T_0, \delta)$ is already known.

Floor Formula Let us now consider a floor with nominal amount N, exercise rate E, based upon a reference linear rate denoted as $R^L(t, \delta)$ at date t and with the following schedule:

$$
\begin{array}{ccccccccccc}
t & - & T_0 & - & T_1 & - & T_2 & - & - & - & \cdots & - & - & - & T_n \\
- & - & - & - & F_1 & - & F_2 & - & - & - & - & - & - & - & F_n
\end{array}
$$

For all $j = 1, \ldots, n$, we assume a constant $T_j - T_{j-1} = \delta$. At each date T_j, the floor holder receives a cash flow F_j

$$
F_j = N \times [\delta \times (E - R^L(T_{j-1}, \delta))]^+
$$

The price at date t of a floor with the same parameters as those used for the cap is given by

$$
FLOOR_t = \sum_{j=1}^{n} Floorlet_t^j = \sum_{j=1}^{n} N \times \delta \times B(t, T_j) \times [-F(t, T_{j-1}, T_j)\Phi(-d_j)
$$
$$
+ E\Phi(-d_j + \sigma_j\sqrt{T_{j-1} - t})] \tag{15.3}
$$

The price at date t of a collar is simply the difference between the cap price and the floor price if we buy the cap and sell the floor. We obtain an opposite formula when we sell the cap and buy the floor.

A proof of the cap and floor formulas is given in Appendix 1 of this chapter. Note also that Appendix 4 of this chapter provides the cap and floor prices in the Hull and White (1990) model introduced in Chapter 12.

Cap and Floor Greeks in the Black Model

Greeks of caplets and floorlets with respect to the different variables can be obtained in closed-form formulas. They allow the seller of the cap or floor to easily implement dynamic hedging strategies.

Cap Greeks   The caplet corresponding to the cash flow C_j received at date T_j has the following Greeks:

- *Delta[5] (Δ), which is the first derivative of the caplet price with respect to the underlying rate $F(t, T_{j-1}, T_j)$, is given by*

$$
\Delta = N \times \delta \times B(t, T_j)\Phi(d_j)
$$

- *Gamma (γ), which is the second derivative of the caplet price with respect to the underlying rate $F(t, T_{j-1}, T_j)$, is given by*

$$
\gamma = N \times \delta \times \left(\frac{B(t, T_j)}{\sigma_j\sqrt{T_{j-1} - t}F(t, T_{j-1}, T_j)}\Phi'(d_j) \right)
$$

---

[5]Usually, that number is multiplied by a factor of 10 basis points (0.10%) to define the sensitivity of the caplet price with respect to a change of 10 basis points in the underlying rate

$$
dCaplet = \Delta dF = \Delta/1{,}000
$$

In terms of hedging and as shown in Chapters 5 and 6, the idea is to create a global portfolio (caplet + hedging asset) that has a zero sensitivity to changes in the underlying rate. The same principle applies for all other Greek parameters.

- *Vega (ν), which is the first derivative of the caplet price with respect to the volatility parameter σ_j, is given by*

$$\nu = N \times \delta \times B(t, T_j)\sqrt{T_{j-1} - t}\, F(t, T_{j-1}, T_j)\Phi'(d_j)$$

- *Rho (ρ), which is the first derivative of the caplet price with respect to the interest rate $R^c(t, T_j - t)$, is given by*

$$\rho = -(T_j - t) \times Caplet$$

where $R^c(t, T_j - t) = -\frac{1}{T_j - t}\ln[B(t, T_j)]$ is the continuously compounded zero-coupon rate at date t with maturity $T_j - t$.

- *Theta (θ), which is the first derivative of the caplet price with respect to time, is given by*

$$\theta = R^c(t, T_j - t)Caplet_t^j - N \times \delta \times \frac{B(t, T_j)\sigma_j F(t, T_{j-1}, T_j)}{2\sqrt{T_{j-1} - t}}\Phi'(d_j)$$

Floor Greeks The floorlet corresponding to the cash flow F_j received at date T_j has the following Greeks:

- *Delta (Δ), which is the first derivative of the floorlet price with respect to the underlying rate $F(t, T_{j-1}, T_j)$, is given by*

$$\Delta = -N \times \delta \times B(t, T_j)\Phi(-d_j)$$

- *Gamma (γ), which is the second derivative of the floorlet price with respect to the underlying rate $F(t, T_{j-1}, T_j)$, is given by*

$$\gamma = N \times \delta \times \left(\frac{B(t, T_j)}{\sigma_j\sqrt{T_{j-1} - t}\, F(t, T_{j-1}, T_j)}\Phi'(-d_j)\right)$$

- *Vega (ν), which is the first derivative of the floorlet price with respect to the volatility parameter σ_j, is given by*

$$\nu = N \times \delta \times B(t, T_j)\sqrt{T_{j-1} - t}\, F(t, T_{j-1}, T_j)\Phi'(-d_j)$$

- *Rho (ρ), which is the first derivative of the floorlet price with respect to the interest rate $R^c(t, T_j - t)$, is given by*

$$\rho = -(T_j - t) \times Floorlet$$

- *Theta (θ), which is the first derivative of the floorlet price with respect to time, is given by*

$$\theta = R^c(t, T_j - t)Floorlet_t^j - N \times \delta \times \frac{B(t, T_j)\sigma_j F(t, T_{j-1}, T_j)}{2\sqrt{T_{j-1} - t}}\Phi'(-d_j)$$

Example 15.11 Consider a firm which contracts a floorlet at date $t = 04/19/02$ whose features are the following:

- *nominal amount: $10,000,000*
- *reference rate: the 6-month Libor $R^L\left(t, \frac{1}{2}\right)$*

- *strike rate $E = 4.70\%$*

- *the schedule of the floorlet is the following:*

$t = 04/19/02$	$T_0 = 05/27/02$	$T_1 = 11/27/02$
When the floorlet is contracted	*When the floorlet starts*	*Payoff payment*

Assuming that the 6-month Libor forward is 4.73% at date t, the floorlet volatility 15% and that the zero-coupon rate $R^c(t, T_1 - t)$ is equal to 4.80%, the price at date t of this floorlet using the Black model is

$$Floorlet_t = \$3,844$$

We obtain the following Greeks:

$$\Delta = -2,176,437$$

$$\gamma = 848,870,402$$

$$\upsilon = 30,070$$

$$\rho = -2,371$$

$$\theta = -21,181$$

When the 6-month Libor forward changes for 4.74%, the price variation is approximately the delta value multiplied by the interest-rate change

$$Price\ Variation = -213.41 \simeq \Delta \times 0.01\% = -217.64$$

For a best approximation of the price variation, we must take into account the convexity of the option price with the gamma value so that

$$Price\ Variation = -213.41 \simeq \Delta \times 0.01\% + \gamma \times \frac{(0.01\%)^2}{2} = -213.40$$

When the volatility changes for 16%, the price variation is approximately the vega value multiplied by the volatility change

$$Price\ Variation = 300.86 \simeq \upsilon \times 1\% = 300.70$$

When the zero-coupon rate $R^c(t, T_1 - t)$ changes for 5.80%, the price variation is approximately the rho value multiplied by the zero-coupon rate change

$$Price\ Variation = -23.31 \simeq \rho \times 1\% = -23.71$$

One day later when we reprice the floorlet, the price variation due to time is approximately the theta value multiplied by $\frac{1}{365}$

$$Price\ Variation = -59.24 \simeq \theta \times \frac{1}{365} = -58.03$$

Cap and Floor as Portfolios of Zero-Coupon Bond Options

Let us consider a cap with nominal amount $1, with exercise rate E, based on a linear rate (for example Libor) with maturity δ denoted $R^L(t, \delta)$ and with the following schedule:

t	—	T_0	—	T_1	—	T_2	—	—	—	—	$\ldots$	—	—	—	T_n
—	—	—	—	C_1	—	C_2	—	—	—	—	—	—	—	—	C_n

For $j = 1, \ldots, n$, we have $T_j - T_{j-1} = \delta$.

In terms of discount bond prices, we have

$$B(T_{j-1}, T_j) = \frac{1}{1 + \delta R^L(T_{j-1}, \delta)}$$

or, equivalently,

$$\delta R^L(T_{j-1}, \delta) = \frac{1}{B(T_{j-1}, T_j)} - 1$$

The cap holder gets (for $j = 1, \ldots, n$) a cash flow C_j at each date T_j

$$C_j = [\delta(R^L(T_{j-1}, \delta) - E)]^+$$

We denote by ξ_j the exercise set of the flow C_j

$$\xi_j = \left\{ \frac{1}{B(T_{j-1}, T_j)} - 1 \geq \delta E \right\}$$

$$\xi_j = \left\{ B(T_{j-1}, T_j) \leq \frac{1}{1 + \delta E} \right\}$$

ξ_j is the exercise set of a European put with maturity date T_{j-1}, exercise price $\frac{1}{1+\delta E}$, written on a discount bond with maturity T_j. Hence, the cap price is given by the sum of n European puts with same exercise price $\frac{1}{1+\delta E}$.

Let us now consider a *floor* with same characteristics. The floor holder gets at each date T_j (for $j = 1, \ldots, n$) a cash flow F_j

$$F_j = [\delta(E - R^L(T_{j-1}, \delta))]^+$$

We again denote by χ_j the exercise set of the cash flow F_j

$$\chi_j = \left\{ \frac{1}{B(T_{j-1}, T_j)} - 1 \leq \delta E \right\}$$

$$= \left\{ B(T_{j-1}, T_j) \geq \frac{1}{1 + \delta E} \right\}$$

χ_j is the exercise set of a European call with maturity date T_{j-1}, exercise price $\frac{1}{1+\delta E}$, written on a discount bond with maturity T_j. Hence, the floor price is given by the sum of n European calls with the same exercise price $\frac{1}{1+\delta E}$.

15.2.3 Market Quotes

Caps, floors and collars are priced using the Black (1976) model. This is why caplet and floorlet prices are usually quoted in terms of implied volatility.

Table 15.3   Volatility Curve for 3-Month Euribor Caplets and Floorlets—08/12/02.

```
<HELP> for explanation.                              DL19 Govt  SWYV
Enter 1 <Go> to save setting
                    Euro Volatility
                     Cap/Floor

                        ▌ (B-Bid /A-Ask /M-Mid )            Page 1/3
       1 wk    1 mo    2 mo    3 mo    4 Mo    5 mo    6 mo    9 mo    1 yr
Cap :                                                           23.300
Flr :                                                           23.900
Time:                                                           12:18
Src :                                                           CMPN
       18 mo   2 yr    30 mo   3 yr    4 yr    5 yr    6 yr    7 yr    8 yr
Cap :          23.400          21.200  19.700  18.500          16.900
Flr :          23.400          21.000  20.000  18.200          16.800
Time:          16:24           12:18   12:18   12:18           12:18
Src :          CMPN            CMPN    CMPN    CMPN            CMPN
       9 yr   10 yr    11 yr   12 yr   15 yr   20 yr   25 yr   30 yr
Cap :          15.500
Flr :          15.600
Time:          12:18
Src :          CMPN

Source: CMPN 16:24               <Menu> to select another ccy
                                 1 <Go> to save Bid/Ask/Mid
                                 2 <Go> to modify sources
Australia 61 2 9777 8600       Brazil 5511 3048 4500    Europe 44 20 7330 7500      Germany 49 69 920410
Hong Kong 852 2977 6000 Japan 81 3 3201 8900 Singapore 65 212 1000 U.S. 1 212 318 2000 Copyright 2002 Bloomberg L.P.
                                                                    G356-711-0 12-Aug-02 23:13:51
```

Remark 15.1   Given the price of the caplet or floorlet, one obtains the implied volatility by inversion of the Black (1976) formula. The implied volatility is then the volatility introduced in the Black (1976) formula that enables us to recover exactly the option price.

Note in particular that the market reference is the implied volatility curve as a function of the maturity of the option.[6] As an illustration, we display hereafter the volatility curve for 3-month Euribor caplets and floorlets, extracted from Bloomberg on 08/12/02 (see Table 15.3). Maturities of caplets and floorlets[7] range from 1 to 10 years. The implied volatility quoted here is the mean of the bid and ask quotations. For example, the caplet with 5-year maturity has an 18.5% volatility as the floorlet with 10-year maturity has a 15.6% volatility.

---

[6]Note that two caplets with same option maturity and underlying rate but different strikes do not have, in general, the same implied volatility. For a given option maturity (strike), we can draw the implied volatility curve depending on the strike level (option maturity), which is called the caplet smile. The same holds for the floorlet smile.

[7]Knowing the volatility curve for 3-month Euribor caplets and floorlets, we can deduce the volatility curve for 3-month Euribor caps and floors. The cap (floor) volatility is defined as the flat volatility used in each caplet (floorlet) so as to recover the cap (floor) price.

15.2.4 Uses of Caps, Floors and Collars

Caps, floors and collars are fixed-income securities designed to hedge the interest-rate risk. More precisely, a cap enables the buyer to cap the reference rate associated to a liability as a floor enables the buyer to protect the total return of assets. The buyer of a cap is hedged against an increase in interest rates (e.g., for hedging a floating-rate loan), while the buyer of a floor is hedged against a decrease in interest rates (e.g., for a floating-rate asset).

Limiting the Financial Cost of Floating-Rate Liabilities

Caps, and collars consisting in buying a cap and selling at the same time a floor, are options used to limit the financial cost of floating-rate liabilities.

Example 15.12 On 12/04/00, a firm that pays semiannually the 6-month Libor to a bank for the next 2 years with a $1,000,000 notional amount wants to be hedged against a rise in this index. This firm decides to buy a cap with the following features:

- *notional amount: $1,000,000*

- *reference rate: 6-month Libor*

- *strike rate: 5.5%*

- *starting date: 12/11/00*

- *maturity: 2 years*

- *tenor: 6 months*

- *day-count: Actual/360*

The premium due by the buyer of the cap, which is paid on 06/11/01, 12/11/01, 06/11/02 and 12/11/02, is equal to 0.2% of the notional amount prorated to the period. Taking the point of view of the firm, the schedule of the cap is the following:

12/04/00	**12/11/00**
Date when the cap contract is concluded	Starting date of the cap
06/11/01	**12/11/01**
$10^6 \cdot \frac{182}{360} \cdot ([L_{12/11/00} - 5.5\%]^+ - 0.2\%)$	$10^6 \cdot \frac{183}{360} \cdot ([L_{06/11/01} - 5.5\%]^+ - 0.2\%)$
06/11/02	**12/11/02**
$10^6 \cdot \frac{182}{360} \cdot ([L_{12/11/01} - 5.5\%]^+ - 0.2\%)$	$10^6 \cdot \frac{183}{360} \cdot ([L_{06/11/02} - 5.5\%]^+ - 0.2\%)$

where L_j is the value of the 6-month Libor on date j.

If the 6-month Libor is higher than 5.5%, the firm will receive the difference between the 6-month Libor and 5.5%, and zero otherwise. By buying this cap, the firm has limited its financing cost to $5.5\% + 0.2\% = 5.7\%$ while benefiting from a lower cost of financing if the 6-month Libor falls below 5.5%. In this case and if the 6-month Libor remains stable at 3.5% during the life of the cap, the financing cost for the firm is equal to 3.7% (3.5% plus the premium).

The second example is about a collar (buy a cap and sell a floor) that limits the financing cost of floating-rate liabilities for a firm while reducing the cost of the hedge, that is, the premium paid for the protection. But the drawback is that the firm will not benefit from a lower financing cost if the reference rate falls below the strike rate of the floor.

Example 15.13 We consider the same assumptions as in the previous example. But the firm wants to reduce the hedge cost, and, for that purpose, sells at the same time a floor with the following features:

- *notional amount: $1,000,000*

- *reference rate: 6-month Libor*

- *strike rate: 4.5%*

- *starting date: 12/11/00*

- *maturity: 2 years*

- *tenor: 6 months*

- *day-count: Actual/360*

The premium due by the buyer of the floor, which is paid on 06/11/01, 12/11/01, 06/11/02 and 12/11/02, is equal to 0.1% of the notional amount prorated to the period. Taking the point of view of the firm, the schedule of the collar is the following

12/04/00
Date when the cap and floor contracts are concluded
12/11/00
Starting date of the cap and the floor
06/11/01
$10^6 \cdot \frac{182}{360} \cdot ([L_{12/11/00} - 5.5\%]^+ - [4.5\% - L_{12/11/00}]^+ - 0.1\%)$
12/11/01
$10^6 \cdot \frac{183}{360} \cdot ([L_{06/11/01} - 5.5\%]^+ - [4.5\% - L_{06/11/01}]^+ - 0.1\%)$
06/11/02
$10^6 \cdot \frac{182}{360} \cdot ([L_{12/11/01} - 5.5\%]^+ - [4.5\% - L_{12/11/01}]^+ - 0.1\%)$
12/11/02
$10^6 \cdot \frac{183}{360} \cdot ([L_{06/11/02} - 5.5\%]^+ - [4.5\% - L_{06/11/02}]^+ - 0.1\%)$

There are three different situations for the firm:

- *If the 6-month Libor is higher than 5.5%, the firm will receive the difference between the 6-month Libor and 5.5%.*

- *If the 6-month Libor is lower than 4.5%, the firm will pay the difference between 4.5% and the 6-month Libor.*

- *If the 6-month Libor is between 4.5 and 5.5%, no cash flow is exchanged.*

By contracting this collar, the firm has limited its cost of hedge to 0.2% − 0.1% = 0.1%, 0.2% being the premium paid for buying the cap and 0.1% is the premium received for selling the floor. This collar enables the firm to limit its financing cost to $5.5\% + 0.1\% = 5.6\%$ while benefiting from a lower financing cost if the 6-month Libor is between 4.5 and 5.5%. In this case and if the 6-month Libor remains stable, for example, at 5% during the life of the collar, the financing cost for the firm is equal to 5.1% (5% plus the premium). But if the 6-month Libor falls below 4.5%, the firm will not benefit from a lower financing cost. For example, if the 6-month Libor remains stable, for example, at 3% during the life of the collar, the financing cost for the firm will be 4.6% (4.5% plus the premium).

Protecting the Rate of Return of a Floating-Rate Asset

Floors, and collars consisting in buying a floor and selling at the same time a cap, are options used to protect the rate of return of a floating-rate asset.

Example 15.14 On 01/02/01, a firm which has invested $10,000,000 in the 3-month Libor for the next year wants to be hedged against a decrease in this index. This firm decides to buy a floor with the following features:

- *notional amount: $10,000,000*

- *reference rate: 3-month Libor*

- *strike rate: 4%*

- *starting date: 01/08/01*

- *maturity: 1 year*

- *tenor: 3 months*

- *day-count: Actual/360*

The premium due by the buyer of the floor, which is paid on 04/08/01, 07/08/01, 10/08/01 and 01/08/02, is equal to 0.2% of the notional amount prorated to the period. Taking the point of view of the firm, the schedule of the floor is the following:

01/02/01	**01/08/01**
Date when the floor contract is concluded	Starting date of the floor
04/08/01	**07/08/01**
$10^7 \cdot \frac{90}{360} \cdot ([4\% - L_{01/08/01}]^+ - 0.2\%)$	$10^7 \cdot \frac{91}{360} \cdot ([4\% - L_{04/08/01}]^+ - 0.2\%)$
10/08/01	**01/08/02**
$10^7 \cdot \frac{92}{360} \cdot ([4\% - L_{07/08/01}]^+ - 0.2\%)$	$10^7 \cdot \frac{92}{360} \cdot ([4\% - L_{10/08/01}]^+ - 0.2\%)$

where L_j is the value of the 3-month Libor at date j.

If the 3-month Libor is lower than 4%, the firm will receive the difference between 4% and the 3-month Libor, and zero otherwise. By buying this floor, the firm has guaranteed a minimum rate of return of $4\% - 0.2\% = 3.8\%$ while benefiting from a better rate on his investment if the 3-month Libor exceeds 4%. In this case, and if the 3-month Libor remains stable at 6% during the life of the floor, the firm has guaranteed a rate of 5.8%.

The second example is about a collar (buy a floor and sell a cap) that protects the rate of return of a floating-rate asset while reducing the cost of the hedge, that is, the premium paid for the protection. But the inconvenience is that the firm will not benefit of better conditions on its investment if the reference rate goes up above the strike rate of the cap.

Example 15.15 We consider the same assumptions as in the previous example. But the firm wants to reduce the cost of the hedge, and, for that purpose, sells at the same time a cap with the following features:

- *notional amount: $10,000,000*

- *reference rate: 3-month Libor*

- *strike rate: 6.5%*

- *starting date: 01/08/01*

- *maturity: 1 year*

- *tenor: 3 months*

- *day-count: Actual/360*

The premium due by the buyer of the cap, which is paid on 04/08/01, 07/08/01, 10/08/01 and 01/08/02, is equal to 0.05% of the notional amount prorated to the period. Taking the point of view of the firm, the schedule of the collar is the following:

01/02/01
Date when the cap and floor contracts are concluded
01/08/01
Starting date of the cap and the floor
04/08/01
$$10^7 \cdot \frac{90}{360} \cdot ([4\% - L_{01/08/01}]^+ - [L_{01/08/01} - 6.5\%]^+ - 0.15\%)$$
07/08/01
$$10^7 \cdot \frac{91}{360} \cdot ([4\% - L_{04/08/01}]^+ - [L_{04/08/01} - 6.5\%]^+ - 0.15\%)$$
10/08/01
$$10^7 \cdot \frac{92}{360} \cdot ([4\% - L_{07/08/01}]^+ - [L_{07/08/01} - 6.5\%]^+ - 0.15\%)$$
01/08/02
$$10^7 \cdot \frac{92}{360} \cdot ([4\% - L_{10/08/01}]^+ - [L_{10/08/01} - 6.5\%]^+ - 0.15\%)$$

There are three different situations for the firm:

- *If the 3-month Libor is lower than 4%, the firm will receive the difference between 4% and the 3-month Libor.*

- *If the 3-month Libor is higher than 6.5%, the firm will pay the difference between the 3-month Libor and 6.5%.*

- *If the 3-month Libor is between 4 and 6.5%, no cash flows are exchanged.*

By contracting this collar, the firm has limited its hedging cost to $0.2\% - 0.05\% = 0.15\%$, 0.2% being the premium paid for buying the floor and 0.05% is the premium received for selling the cap. This collar enables the firm to guarantee a rate of return to $4\% - 0.15\% = 3.85\%$ while benefiting from a better rate of return if the 3-month Libor is between 4 and 6.5%. In this case and if the 3-month Libor remains stable, for example, at 5.5% during the life of the collar, the rate of return on the firm's investment is equal to 5.35%. But if the 3-month Libor exceeds 6.5%, the firm will not benefit from a better rate of return. For example, if the 3-month Libor remains stable at 8% during the life of the collar, the rate of return on the firm's investment will be 6.35%.

15.3   Swaptions

15.3.1   Definition and Terminology

Swaptions are over-the-counter contracts. A European swaption is an option allowing the holder to enter some prespecified underlying swap contract on a prespecified date, which is the expiration date of the swaption. There are two kinds of European swaptions:

- *The receiver swaption is an option that gives the buyer the right to receive the fixed leg of the swap.*

- *The payer swaption is an option that gives the buyer the right to pay the fixed leg of the swap.*

We now introduce some terminology:

- *The exercise rate or strike rate is the specified fixed rate at which the buyer can enter into the swap.*

- *The maturity or expiry date is the date when the option can be exercised. The maturity of swaptions can range from several months to 10 years.*

- *The premium of swaptions is expressed as a percentage of the principal amount of the swap.*

Note that the underlying asset of the swaption is most commonly a plain-vanilla swap whose maturity can range from 1 to 30 years.

We give below an example of a European swaption.

Example 15.16   We consider a standard 1-year Libor swap contract with \$10,000,000 nominal amount. The swaption with expiration date T_0 is defined by the following schedule:

Fixed Leg					$-F_1$		$-F_2$								$-F_n$
—	t	—	T_0	—	T_1	—	T_2	—	—	—	...	—	—	—	T_n
Variable Leg	—	—	—	—	V_1	—	V_2	—	—	—	—	—	—	—	V_n

We assume that the buyer of the swaption has the right on date T_0 to enter a swap where he receives the variable leg and pays the fixed leg. In other words, this is a payer swaption.

For all $j = 1, \ldots, n$, we have $T_j - T_{j-1} = 1$ year.

Cash flows for the fixed leg are on dates T_j for $j = 1, \ldots, n$

$$-F_j = -10,000,000 \times F$$

where F is the swap fixed rate.

Cash flows for the floating leg are on dates T_j for $j = 1, \ldots, n$

$$V_j = 10,000,000 \times R^L(T_{j-1}, 1)$$

where $R^L(T_{j-1}, 1)$ is the 1-year Libor at date T_{j-1}.

Note that Bermudan and American swaptions give the buyer the opportunity to enter a swap on several specified dates in the future and at any time before the maturity date of the option, respectively.

15.3.2 Pricing and Hedging Swaptions

Swaption Formula in the Black Model

We consider a standard underlying swap contract. The swaption with maturity date T_0 is defined by the following schedule:

Fixed Leg	—	—	—	—	$-F_1$	—	$-F_2$	—	—	—	—	—	—	—	$-F_n$
—		t	—	T_0	—	T_1	—	T_2	—	—	—	$\ldots$	—	—	—	T_n
Variable Leg	—	—	—	—	V_1	—	V_2	—	—	—	—	—	—	—	V_n

The swaption is a payer swaption. For all $j = 1, \ldots, n$, we have $T_j - T_{j-1} = \delta$.

- *Cash flows for the fixed leg are at dates T_j for $j = 1, \ldots, n$*

$$-F_j = -\delta \times N \times F$$

  where F is the swap fixed rate, and N the nominal amount of the swap.

- *Cash flows for the floating leg are at dates T_j for $j = 1, \ldots, n$*

$$V_j = \delta \times N \times R^L(T_{j-1}, \delta)$$

  where $R^L(T_{j-1}, \delta)$ is the Libor rate at date T_{j-1} finishing at date $T_j = T_{j-1} + \delta$.

Recall from Chapter 10 that the swap pricing formula is given by

$$SWAP_t = N \times \left(\sum_{j=1}^{n} (V_j - F_j) B(t, T_j) \right)$$

Fixed Income Securities

We now define the swap rate $S(t)$ which is such that the value at date t of the swap contract be zero. $S(t) = F$ and the swap price is given by

$$SWAP_t = N \times \left[(S(t) - F) \sum_{j=1}^{n} \delta \cdot B(t, T_j) \right]$$

The swaption pricing formula is then given by

$$SWAPTION_t = N \times \left(\sum_{j=1}^{n} \delta \times B(t, T_j) \times [F_S(t)\Phi(d) - F\Phi(d - \sigma_S\sqrt{T_0 - t})] \right) \tag{15.4}$$

where

$F_S(t)$, the swap forward rate computed at date t, is the swaption underlying rate. We have in particular

$$F_S(T_0) = S(T_0)$$

d is such that

$$d = \frac{\ln\left(\dfrac{F_S(t)}{F}\right) + 0.5\sigma_S^2(T_0 - t)}{\sigma_S\sqrt{T_0 - t}}$$

σ_S is the volatility of the underlying rate $F_S(t)$.

Note that the following pricing formula applies in the case of a receiver swaption:

$$SWAPTION_t = N \times \left(\sum_{j=1}^{n} \delta \times B(t, T_j) \times [-F_S(t)\Phi(-d) + F\Phi(-d + \sigma_S\sqrt{T_0 - t})] \right) \tag{15.5}$$

A proof of the swaption formula is given in Appendix 2 of this chapter. Note also that Appendix 4 of this chapter provides the swaption price in the Hull and White (1990) model, introduced in Chapter 12.

Swaption Greeks in the Black Model

Swaption Greeks with respect to the different variables can be obtained in closed-form formulas.

Greeks of a Payer Swaption For a payer swaption, Greeks are as follows:

- *Delta* (Δ), *which is the first derivative of the swaption price with respect to the underlying rate* $F_S(t)$, *is given by*

$$\Delta = N \times \left(\sum_{j=1}^{n} \delta B(t, T_j)\Phi(d) \right)$$

- *Gamma* (γ), *which is the second derivative of the swaption price with respect to the underlying rate* $F_S(t)$, *is given by*

$$\gamma = N \times \left(\frac{\displaystyle\sum_{j=1}^{n} \delta B(t, T_j)}{\sigma_S\sqrt{T_0 - t}F_S(t)}\Phi'(d) \right)$$

- *Vega (υ), which is the first derivative of the swaption price with respect to the volatility parameter σ_S, is given by*

$$\upsilon = N \times \left(\sum_{j=1}^{n} \delta B(t, T_j) \sqrt{T_0 - t} F_S(t) \Phi'(d) \right)$$

- *Rho (ρ), which is the first derivative of the swaption price with respect to the interest rate R^c, is given by*

$$\rho = -N \times \delta \times \left(\sum_{j=1}^{n} (T_j - t) \times B(t, T_j) \times [F_S(t) \Phi(d) - F \Phi(d - \sigma_S \sqrt{T_0 - t})] \right)$$

where R^c is the unique continuously compounded rate (we assume a flat yield curve) such that $B(t, T_j) = e^{-R^c \times (T_j - t)}, \ \forall j = 1, \ldots, n.$

- *Theta (θ), which is the first derivative of the swaption price with respect to time, is given by*

$$\theta = R^c \cdot SWAPTION_t - N \cdot \left(\frac{\sum_{j=1}^{n} \delta B(t, T_j) \sigma_S F_S(t)}{2\sqrt{T_0 - t}} \Phi'(d) \right)$$

Example 15.17 Consider a firm that contracts a European payer swaption on 04/19/02 whose features are the following:

- *Nominal amount: \$1,000,000;*

- *Underlying swap: a 4-year 6-month Libor swap with semiannual payments on two legs;*

- *Strike rate $F = 5.36\%$;*

- *The schedule of the swaption is the following:*

$t = 04/19/02$	$T_0 = 05/27/02$
When the swaption is contracted	When the swaption matures and the swap begins

Assuming that the swap forward rate $F_S(t)$ is 5.36% at date t, the swaption volatility 20% and that the continuously compounded zero-coupon rate R^c is equal to 5%, the price at date t of this swaption using the Black (1976) model is

$$SWAPTION_t = \$2,876$$

We obtain the following Greeks:

$$\Delta = 1,270,216$$

$$\gamma = 383,927,229$$

$$\upsilon = 22{,}967$$

$$\rho = -6{,}593$$

$$\theta = -21{,}916$$

When the swap forward rate $F_S(t)$ changes for 5.37%, the price variation is approximately the delta value multiplied by the interest-rate change

$$\textit{Price Variation} = 128.94 \simeq \Delta \times 0.01\% = 127.02$$

For a best approximation of the price variation, we must take into account the convexity of the option price with the gamma value so that

$$\textit{Price Variation} = 128.94 \simeq \Delta \times 0.01\% + \gamma \times \frac{(0.01\%)^2}{2} = 128.95$$

When the volatility changes for 21%, the price variation is approximately the vega value multiplied by the volatility change

$$\textit{Price Variation} = 230.54 \simeq \upsilon \times 1\% = 229.67$$

When the zero-coupon rate R^c changes for 6%, the price variation is approximately the rho value multiplied by the zero-coupon rate change

$$\textit{Price Variation} = -65 \simeq \rho \times 1\% = -65.93$$

One day later when we reprice the swaption, the price variation due to time is approximately the theta value multiplied by $\frac{1}{365}$

$$\textit{Price Variation} = -60.04 \simeq \theta \times \frac{1}{365} = -60.39$$

Greeks of a Receiver Swaption For a receiver swaption, Greeks are as follows:

- *Delta (Δ), which is the first derivative of the swaption price with respect to the underlying rate $F_S(t)$, is given by*

$$\Delta = -N \times \left(\sum_{j=1}^{n} \delta B(t, T_j) \Phi(-d) \right)$$

- *Gamma (γ), which is the second derivative of the swaption price with respect to the underlying rate $F_S(t)$, is given by*

$$\gamma = N \times \left(\frac{\displaystyle\sum_{j=1}^{n} \delta B(t, T_j)}{\sigma_S \sqrt{T_0 - t} F_S(t)} \Phi'(-d) \right)$$

- *Vega* (v), *which is the first derivative of the swaption price with respect to the volatility parameter* σ_S, *is given by*

$$v = N \times \left(\sum_{j=1}^{n} \delta B(t, T_j) \sqrt{T_0 - t} F_S(t) \Phi'(-d) \right)$$

- *Rho* (ρ), *which is the first derivative of the swaption price with respect to the interest rate* R^c, *is given by*

$$\rho = N \times \delta \times \left(\sum_{j=1}^{n} (T_j - t) \times B(t, T_j) \times [F_S(t) \Phi(-d) - F \Phi(-d + \sigma_S \sqrt{T_0 - t})] \right)$$

where R^c *is the unique continuously compounded rate (we assume a flat yield curve) such that* $B(t, T_j) = e^{-R^c \times (T_j - t)}$, $\forall j = 1, \ldots, n$.

- *Theta* (θ), *which is the first derivative of the swaption price with respect to time, is given by*

$$\theta = R^c \times SWAPTION_t - N \times \left(\frac{\sum_{j=1}^{n} \delta B(t, T_j) \sigma_S F_S(t)}{2\sqrt{T_0 - t}} \Phi'(-d) \right)$$

A Swaption as a Coupon Bond Option

Let us consider a receiver swaption with maturity date T_0, with the following schedule:

Fixed Leg	—	—	—	—	F_1	—	F_2	—	—	—	—	—	—	—	F_n
—	t	—	T_0	—	T_1	—	T_2	—	—	—	$\ldots$	—	—	—	T_n
Floating Leg	—	—	—	—	$-V_1$	—	$-V_2$	—	—	—	—	—	—	—	$-V_n$

For all $j = 1, \ldots, n$, we have $T_j - T_{j-1} = \delta$.

- *Cash flows for the fixed leg are at dates* T_j *for* $j = 1, \ldots, n$

$$F_j = \delta \times N \times F$$

where F *is the swap fixed rate, and* N *the nominal amount of the swap.*

- *Cash flows for the floating leg are at dates* T_j *for* $j = 1, \ldots, n$

$$V_j = \delta \times N \times R^L(T_{j-1}, \delta)$$

Using the zero-coupon pricing method as described in Chapter 10, we obtain the price at date T_0 of that swaption as given by

$$SWAPTION_{T_0} = [N \left(\sum_{j=1}^{n} \delta F B(T_0, T_j) + B(T_0, T_n) \right) - N]^+$$

It is equal to the value of a European call with exercise price N, written on a bond with a fixed-coupon rate F and nominal amount N. Alternatively, the payer option on the same plain-vanilla

Table 15.4   Volatility Matrix for Swaptions Written on 1 to 10-Year 3-Month Euribor Swaps—08/12/02.

```
<HELP> for explanation.                              DL19 Govt  SWYV
Enter 1 <Go> to save setting
                      Euro Volatility
                      Swaption Implied
                              (Bid/Ask/Mid)                    Page 2/3
Option                    Term
Expiry    1 yr    2 yr    3 yr    4 yr    5 yr    7 yr    10 yr  ->
  1 mo    29.60 C  27.60 C  24.70 C  22.50 C  20.90 C  18.10 C  15.00 C
  3 mo    25.85 C  24.70 C  22.60 C  20.90 C  18.65 C  16.95 C  14.10 C
  6 mo    24.75 C  23.40 C  21.10 C  19.25 C  17.85 C  16.00 C  14.00 C
  9 mo
  1 yr    22.65 C  20.60 C  18.80 C  17.40 C  16.30 C  14.25 C  13.35 C

  2 yr    18.15 C  16.55 C  15.45 C  15.35 C  14.75 C  13.90 C  12.85 C
  3 yr    16.90 C  15.30 C  14.60 C  14.10 C  13.70 C  13.20 C  12.50 C
  4 yr    15.30 C  14.10 C  13.50 C  13.10 C  12.90 C  12.50 C  12.00 C
  5 yr    14.20 C  13.40 C  12.80 C  12.40 C  12.30 C  12.00 C  11.60 C
  7 yr    12.90 C  12.40 C  12.00 C  11.70 C  11.50 C  11.30 C  11.00 C

 10 yr    12.00 C  11.60 C  11.30 C  11.10 C  10.90 C  10.80 C  10.60 C

Source:  CMPN 20:59              <Menu> to select another ccy
                                 1 <Go> to save Bid/Ask/Mid
                                 2 <Go> to modify sources
Australia 61 2 9777 8600      Brazil 5511 3048 4500   Europe 44 20 7330 7500   Germany 49 69 920410
Hong Kong 852 2977 6000 Japan 81 3 3201 8900 Singapore 65 212 1000 U.S. 1 212 318 2000 Copyright 2002 Bloomberg L.P.
                                                                          G356-711-0 12-Aug-02 23:14:39
```

swap is equivalent to a European put with exercise price N, written on a bond with a fixed-coupon rate F and nominal amount N.

15.3.3   Market Quotes

Swaption prices are expressed in terms of the implied volatility of the Black (1976) model. As for the cap/floor market, the market reference is the implied volatility curve as a function of the maturity of the option.[8] As an illustration, we display here the volatility matrix for swaptions written on 1 to 10-year 3-month Euribor swaps, as measured on a particular date t (see Table 15.4). Maturity options range from 1 month to 10 years. The implied volatility quoted here is the mean of the bid and ask quotations. For example, the volatility of the 1-year swaption written on the 10-year swap is 13.35%.

15.3.4   Uses of Swaptions

Like caps, floors and collars, swaptions are fixed-income securities designed to hedge the interest-rate risk.

---

[8]Note that two similar swaptions except that they have different strike rates do not have, in general, the same implied volatility. For a given option maturity (strike), we can draw the implied volatility curve depending on the strike level (option maturity), which is called the swaption smile.

More precisely, a payer swaption can be used in two ways:
- *It enables a firm to fix a maximum limit to its floating-rate debt.*

- *It enables an investor to transform its fixed-rate assets into floating-rate assets to benefit from a rise in interest rates.*

> **Example 15.18** Consider a firm with a 3-month Libor debt for the next 5 years and $10 million principal amount. The swap rate for a 3-month Libor swap with 5-year maturity is 6%. The treasurer of this firm fears a rise in interest rates. Instead of entering a 3-month Libor swap where he pays the fixed leg and receives the floating leg during 5 years, he prefers to wait for the effective rise in rates. He contracts now a payer swaption maturing in 6 months with a 6% strike rate and whose underlying swap has a 4.5-year maturity.
>
> In 6 months, if the swap rate of the 3-month Libor swap with a 4.5-year maturity is superior to 6%, the treasurer will exercise the swaption. On the contrary, if the swap rate is inferior to 6%, he will give up the option, and if he wishes to modify the nature of its debt, he will enter a swap at the better conditions of the moment.

Symmetrically, a receiver option on swap can be used in two ways:
- *It enables a firm to transform its fixed-rate debt into a floating-rate debt in a context of a decrease in interest rates.*

- *It enables an investor to protect its floating-rate investment.*

> **Example 15.19** A portfolio manager who has invested in a 5-year maturity bond that delivers annually the 1-year Libor, and expects a decrease in rates in 3 months, will typically contract a receiver swaption maturing in 3 months whose underlying swap has a 4.75-year maturity.

15.4 End of Chapter Summary

In this chapter, we introduce options on futures, caps, floors and swaptions, which are known as *plain vanilla* (or standard) interest-rate options. Futures options are standardized options, while caps, floors and swaptions are over-the-counter contracts.

A *cap* is an over-the-counter contract by which the seller agrees to payoff a positive amount to the buyer of the contract if the *reference rate* exceeds a prespecified level called the *exercise rate* of the cap on given future dates. Conversely, the seller of a *floor* agrees to pay a positive amount to the buyer of the contract if the reference rate falls below the exercise rate on some future dates. A *collar* is a combination of a cap and a floor.

Caps, floors and collars are fixed-income securities designed to hedge the interest-rate risk. The buyer of a cap is hedged against an increase in interest rates while the buyer of a floor is hedged against a decrease in interest rates.

Swaptions are over-the-counter contracts, allowing the holder to enter some prespecified underlying swap contract on or up to a prespecified date that is the expiration date of the swaption. Like caps, floors and collars, swaptions are fixed-income securities designed to hedge the interest-rate risk.

Practitioners actually heavily use Black's (1976) model, although it is not an interest-rate model.

The rapid rise of the fixed-income option markets was prior to the development of complex interest-rate models. Therefore, practitioners have started using Black (1976) model to price and hedge standard fixed-income derivatives. This model, which is particularly tractable and simple to use, remains currently the reference for the market in terms of pricing and hedging standard assets such as options on futures, caps, floors and swaptions, despite the set of simplifying assumptions it is based upon. This model has become a benchmark and is currently used in the calibration of other interest-rate models, the so-called "market models."

15.5 References and Further Reading

15.5.1 Books and Papers

Andersen, L., 1999, "A Simple Approach to the Pricing of Bermudan Swaptions in the Multi-Factor Libor Market Model", *Journal of Computational Finance*, **3**, 5–32.

Barone-Adesi, G., and R.E. Whaley, 1987, "Efficient Analytic Approximation of American Option Values", *Journal of Finance*, **42**, 301–320.

Black, F., 1976, "The Pricing of Commodity Contracts", *Journal of Financial Economics*, **3**(1/2), 167–179.

Brace, A., D. Gatarek, and M. Musiela, 1997, "The Market Model of Interest Rate Dynamics", *Mathematical Finance*, **7**(2), 127–155.

Cherif, T., 1994, Les Contrats de FRA et les Options sur FRA: Application à l'Option sur le Contrat Pibor, *Cahiers de la Caisse Autonome de Refinancement*, no. 8, Paris.

Collin-Dufresne, P., and R.S. Goldstein, 2002, "Pricing Swaptions within an Affine Framework", *Journal of Derivatives*, **10**(1), 9–26.

El Karoui, N., and T. Chérif, 1992, Pricing d'Options de Taux: Application aux Options sur le Contrat Notionnel, *Cahiers de la Caisse Autonome de Refinancement*, no. 2, Paris.

Fabozzi, F.J., (Editor), 2000, *The Handbook of Fixed Income Securities*, 6th Edition, McGraw-Hill, New York.

Heath, D., R.A. Jarrow, and A. Morton, 1992, "Bond Pricing and the Term Structure of Interest Rates: A New Methodology for Contingent Claim Valuations", *Econometrica*, **60**(1), 77–105.

Hull, J., 2002, *Options, Futures and Other Derivatives*, 5th Edition, Prentice Hall, New York.

Hull, J., and A. White, 1990, "Pricing Interest Rate Derivative Securities", *Review of Financial Studies*, **3**(4), 573–592.

Jamshidian, F., 1997, "Libor and Swap Market Models and Measures", *Finance and Stochastics*, **1**(4), 293–330.

Longstaff, F.A., P. Santa-Clara, and E. Schwartz, 2001, "The Relative Valuation of Caps and Swaptions: Theory and Empirical Evidence", *Journal of Finance*, **56**(6), 2067–2109.

Martellini, L., and P. Priaulet, 2000, *Fixed-Income Securities: Dynamic Methods for Interest Rate Risk Pricing and Hedging*, John Wiley & Sons, Chichester.

Priaulet, P., 1997, Structure par Terme des Taux d'Intérêt: Reconstitution, Modélisation et Couverture, Thèse de doctorat en sciences économiques, Université Paris IX-Dauphine.

Siegel, D.R., and D.F. Siegel, 1990, *Futures Markets*, Dryden Press, Chicago.

15.5.2 Websites

www.cme.com.

www.cbot.com.

www.sfe.com.

www.tiffe.org.jp.

www.hkfe.com.

www.me.org.

www.eurexchange.com.

www.liffe.com.

www.matif.fr.

www.futuresindustry.org.

www.bloomberg.com.

www.reuters.com.

15.6 Problems

Exercise 15.1 1. You have invested in long-term T-bonds. You expect a decrease in interest rates and a corresponding increase in bond prices. You want to profit from this move while limiting your potential loss if interest rates increase. What is your strategy?

2. You hold a bond portfolio and expect rates to be stable. You want to increase your return. What is your strategy?

Exercise 15.2 Suppose that you buy a call on the CBOT 10-year T-Note futures whose strike price is 105-48 (in % of the futures contract size). The call price is 1-16 (in % of the futures contract size) and the futures contract size is $100,000. Draw the $P\&L$ graph of this call.

Exercise 15.3 Let us consider a put on a T-bond futures contracted at date $t = 10/24/02$ with nominal amount $10,000,000, strike price $E = 116\%$, which expires on $T = 12/13/02$.

1. What is the price formula of this put using the Black (1976) model?

2. Assuming that the T-bond futures price is 115.47% at date t, its volatility 8% and that the zero-coupon rate $R^c(t, T - t)$ is equal to 5%, give the price of this put.

3. Compute the put greeks.

4. We consider that the futures price increases by 0.10%. Compute the actual put price variation. Compare it with the price variation estimated by using the delta, and by using the delta and the gamma.

5. We consider that the volatility increases by 1%. Compute the actual put price variation. Compare it with the price variation estimated by using the vega.

6. We consider that the interest rate increases by 1%. Compute the actual put price variation. Compare it with the price variation estimated by using the rho.

7. We reprice the put one day later. Compute the actual put price variation. Compare it with the price variation estimated by using the theta.

Exercise 15.4   Same exercise as the previous one, but we now consider a call on a Libor futures contracted at date $t = 07/18/02$ with nominal amount \$1,000,000, strike price $E = 96.50\%$, which expires on $T = 09/14/02$. We further assume that the Libor futures price is 96.40% at date t, its volatility 30% and that the zero-coupon rate $R^c(t, T - t)$ is equal to 4%.

Exercise 15.5   Show the following put–call parity relationship:

$$Cap\ Price - Floor\ Price = Swap\ Price$$

when the cap and the floor are based on the same reference (we will take, for example, the 3-month Libor denoted by $R^L\left(t, \frac{1}{4}\right)$) and have the same strike rate E, starting date and settlement frequency.

Exercise 15.6   On 12/16/02, a firm that pays quarterly the 3-month Libor to a bank for the next year with a \$10,000,000 notional amount wants to be hedged against a rise in this index. This firm decides to buy a cap with the following features:

- notional amount: \$10,000,000
- reference rate: 3-month Libor
- strike rate: 4%
- starting date: 12/20/02
- maturity: 1 year
- tenor: 3 months
- day-count: Actual/360

We assume that the premium, which is paid quarterly, is equal to 0.15% of the notional amount prorated to the period.

What is the cap schedule for the firm? Provide in particular all the caplet cash flows.

Exercise 15.7   Let us consider a caplet contracted at date $t = 05/13/02$ with nominal amount \$10,000,000, exercise rate $E = 5\%$, based upon the 6-month Libor $R^L\left(t, \frac{1}{2}\right)$ and with the following schedule

$t = 05/13/02$	$T_0 = 06/03/02$	$T_1 = 12/03/02$
When the caplet is contracted	When the caplet starts	Payoff payment

At date $T_1 = 12/03/02$, the cap holder receives the cash flow C

$$C = \$10,000,000 \times Max\left[0; \delta \cdot \left(R^L\left(T_0, \frac{1}{2}\right) - 5\%\right)\right]$$

where $\delta = T_1 - T_0$ (expressed in fraction of years using the Actual/360 day-count basis).

1. Draw the *P&L* of this caplet considering that the premium paid by the buyer is equal to 0.1% of the nominal amount.
2. What is the price formula of this caplet using the Black (1976) model?
3. Assuming that the 6-month Libor forward is 5.17% at date t, its volatility 15% and that the zero-coupon rate $R(t, T_1 - t)$ is equal to 5.25%, give the price of this caplet.
4. Find the margin taken by the seller of this caplet.
5. Compute the caplet greeks.
6. Assuming that the 6-month forward goes from 5.17 to 5.18%, compute the actual caplet price variation and compare it with the approximated price variation using first the delta, and then the delta and the gamma.
7. Assuming that the volatility goes from 15 to 16%, compute the actual caplet price variation and compare it with the approximated price variation using the vega.
8. Assuming that the interest rate $R^c(t, T_1 - t)$ goes from 5.25 to 5.35%, compute the actual caplet price variation and compare it with the approximated price variation using the rho.
9. Compute the caplet price one day later. Compare the actual caplet price variation with the approximated price variation using the theta.

Exercise 15.8   On 11/18/02, a firm which has invested $100,000,000 in the 6-month Libor for the next 3 years wants to be hedged against a decrease in this index. This firm decides to buy a floor with the following features:

- notional amount: $100,000,000
- reference rate: 6-month Libor
- strike rate: 3.5%
- starting date: 11/25/02
- maturity: 3 years
- tenor: 6 months
- day-count: Actual/360

The premium due by the floor buyer, which is paid semiannually, is equal to 0.30% of the notional amount prorated to the period.

But the firm, which wants to reduce the hedge cost, sells at the same time a cap with the following features:

- notional amount: $100,000,000
- reference rate: 6-month Libor
- strike rate: 5.5%
- starting date: 11/25/02
- maturity: 3 years
- tenor: 6 months
- day-count: Actual/360

The premium due by the cap buyer, which is paid semiannually, is equal to 0.10% of the notional amount prorated to the period.

1. What is the collar schedule for the firm? Provide in particular all the collar cash flows.
2. Summarize the three different situations for the firm. What are the advantages and drawbacks of this collar compared to the floor?

Exercise 15.9   Consider a firm that contracts a collar at date $t = 04/12/02$ by buying a caplet and selling a floorlet. The features of the two products are the following:

- nominal amount: $10,000,000
- reference rate: the 6-month Libor $R^L\left(t, \frac{1}{2}\right)$
- strike rate of the caplet: $E_1 = 4.60\%$
- strike rate of the floorlet: $E_2 = 4.20\%$
- the schedule of the collar is the following:

$t = 04/12/02$	$T_0 = 05/20/02$	$T_1 = 11/20/02$
When the collar is contracted	When the collar starts	Payoff payment

1. What is the collar payoff?
2. Draw the $P\&L$ of this collar considering that the caplet premium is equal to 0.04% of the nominal amount as the floorlet premium is 0.002%.
3. Assuming that the 6-month Libor forward is 4.59% at date t, the caplet volatility 14%, the floorlet volatility 17% and that the zero-coupon rate $R^c(t, T_1 - t)$ is equal to 4.5%, give the price of this collar using the Black (1976) model.
4. Conclude.

Exercise 15.10   1. Consider a firm with a 6-month Libor debt for the next 10 years and $100-million principal amount. The swap rate for a 6-month Libor swap with 10-year maturity is 5.5%. The firm treasurer fears a rise in interest rates in 3 months. What is the treasurer strategy?
2. A portfolio manager has invested in a 10-year bond that delivers annually the 1-year Libor. He expects a decrease in rates very shortly. What is his strategy?

Exercise 15.11   Let us consider a firm that contracts a European receiver swaption on 04/19/02 whose features are the following:

- nominal amount: $1,000,000
- underlying swap: a 5-year 6-month Libor swap with semiannual payments on two legs.
- strike rate $F = 5.36\%$
- the swaption schedule is the following:

$t = 04/19/02$	$T_0 = 05/27/02$
When the swaption is contracted	When the swaption matures and the swap begins

1. What is the price formula of this swaption using the Black (1976) model?
2. Assuming that the swap forward rate $F_S(t)$ is 5.42% at date t, the swaption volatility 25% and that the continuously compounded zero-coupon rate R^c is equal to 5%, give the price at date t of this swaption.
3. Compute the swaption greeks.
4. Assuming that the swap forward rate goes from 5.42 to 5.43%, compute the actual swaption price variation and compare it with the approximated price variation using first the delta and then the delta and the gamma.
5. Assuming that the volatility goes from 25 to 26%, compute the actual swaption price variation and compare it with the approximated price variation using the vega.
6. Assuming that the interest rate R^c goes from 5 to 6%, compute the actual swaption price variation and compare it with the approximated price variation using the rho.
7. Calculate the swaption price one day later on 04/20/02. Compare the swaption price variation with the approximated price variation using the theta.

Exercise 15.12 Cap Pricing in Ho and Lee's Lattice
We want to price a cap with the following features in the Ho and Lee lattice (see Chapter 12 for details about Ho and Lee's lattice):

- maturity: 1 year
- reference rate: 3-month Libor
- nominal amount: $100,000,000
- strike rate: 5%
- tenor: 3 months

Each caplet is prepaid so that the payoff at date t is as follows:

$$\text{Payoff} = \frac{\text{Max}\left[0; \dfrac{100,000,000}{4} \times (L_t - 5\%)\right]}{(1 + L_t/4)}$$

where L_t is the 3-month Libor at date t. We consider that the time interval Δt to construct the lattice is equal to 0.25 (3 months). The initial term structure that we derive from zero-coupon bond prices is given by

$$B(0, 0.25) = 0.99128817$$

$$B(0, 0.5) = 0.98019867$$

$$B(0, 0.75) = 0.96826449$$

$$B(0, 1) = 0.9555196$$

$$B(0, 1.25) = 0.94235332$$

We take as given the values of π and δ

$$\pi = \frac{1}{2}$$

$$\delta = 0.996$$

1. Compute the values of the perturbation functions for $T = 1$ to 5.
2. Compute the lattice of the 3-month discount factor.
3. Find the lattice for the 3-month Libor.
4. Compute the value of each caplet and find the total cap price.
5. Compute the total cap price for the following values of δ

Parameter δ	0.994	0.995	0.996	0.997	0.998

and conclude.

Exercise 15.13 What are the main differences between the HJM model and the BGM model?

15.7 Appendix 1: Proof of the Cap and Floor Formulas in the Black (1976) Model

First recall that the jth caplet pays at date T_j the cash flow

$$C_j = N \times [\delta \cdot (R^L(T_{j-1}, \delta) - E)]^+ = N \times [\delta \cdot (F(T_{j-1}, T_{j-1}, T_j) - E)]^+$$

Under the risk-neutral probability measure $\mathbb{Q}$, discounted prices are martingales (see Appendix 2 of Chapter 12). Hence, we obtain

$$Caplet_t^j = N \times \mathbb{E}_t^{\mathbb{Q}}(e^{-\int_t^{T_j} r(s)\, ds} C_j)$$

Introducing a new probability measure $\mathbb{Q}_{T_j}$ defined by its Radon–Nikodym derivative with respect to $\mathbb{Q}$ (see Appendix 2 of Chapter 12)

$$\frac{d\mathbb{Q}_{T_j}^t}{d\mathbb{Q}^t} = \frac{1}{B(t, T_j)} e^{-\int_t^{T_j} r(s)\, ds}$$

we have (see Appendix 2 of Chapter 12)

$$Caplet_t^j = N \times B(t, T_j) \mathbb{E}_t^{\mathbb{Q}_{T_j}}(C_j) \tag{15.6}$$

We now show that $F(t, T_{j-1}, T_j)$ is a martingale under $\mathbb{Q}_{T_j}$.

In the absence of arbitrage opportunity, it is equivalent to receiving $\$1 + \delta \cdot F(T_{j-1}, T_{j-1}, T_j)$ at date T_j or $\$1$ at date T_{j-1}, or $\$B(t, T_{j-1})$ at date t. Hence, we have

$$B(t, T_{j-1}) = \mathbb{E}_t^{\mathbb{Q}}(e^{-\int_t^{T_j} r(s)\, ds}[1 + \delta \cdot F(T_{j-1}, T_{j-1}, T_j)])$$

or

$$\frac{B(t, T_{j-1})}{B(t, T_j)} = \mathbb{E}_t^{\mathbb{Q}_{T_j}}(1 + \delta \cdot F(T_{j-1}, T_{j-1}, T_j))$$

or finally

$$1 + \delta \cdot F(t, T_{j-1}, T_j) = \mathbb{E}_t^{\mathbb{Q}_{T_j}}(1 + \delta \cdot F(T_{j-1}, T_{j-1}, T_j))$$

Hence, we obtain that $F(t, T_{j-1}, T_j)$ is a martingale under $\mathbb{Q}_{T_j}$. It is then implicitly assumed that the dynamics of $F(t, T_{j-1}, T_j)$ under $\mathbb{Q}_{T_j}$ is given by

$$dF(t, T_{j-1}, T_j) = \sigma_j F(t, T_{j-1}, T_j) d\widehat{W}^{T_j}(t) \tag{15.7}$$

where $\widehat{W}^{T_j}(t)$ is a standard Brownian motion under $\mathbb{Q}_{T_j}$.

Using standard techniques and equations (15.6) and (15.7), we obtain a pricing formula for the jth caplet. Adding up all caplets prices, we obtain the cap pricing formula (15.2)

$$CAP_t = \sum_{j=1}^{n} Caplet_t^j = \sum_{j=1}^{n} N \cdot \delta \cdot B(t, T_j) \cdot [F(t, T_{j-1}, T_j)\Phi(d_j) - E\Phi(d_j - \sigma_j\sqrt{T_{j-1} - t})]$$

The floor pricing formula (15.3) may be obtained in the same way

$$FLOOR_t = \sum_{j=1}^{n} Floorlet_t^j = \sum_{j=1}^{n} N \cdot \delta \cdot B(t, T_j) \cdot [-F(t, T_{j-1}, T_j)\Phi(-d_j)$$
$$+ E\Phi(-d_j + \sigma_j\sqrt{T_{j-1} - t})]$$

15.8   Appendix 2: Proof of the Swaption Formula in the Black (1976) Model

We consider a standard underlying swap contract. The swaption with maturity date T_0 is defined by the following schedule:

Fixed leg	—	—	—	—	$-F_1$	—	$-F_2$	—	—	—	—	—	—	—	$-F_n$
—		t	—	T_0	—	T_1	—	T_2	—	—	—	...	—	—	—	T_n
Variable leg	—	—	—	—	V_1	—	V_2	—	—	—	—	—	—	—	V_n

We assume that the buyer of the swaption wishes to receive the variable leg and pay the fixed rate. In other words, it is a payer swaption.

For all $j = 1, \ldots, n$, we have $T_j - T_{j-1} = \delta$.

Cash flows for the fixed leg are at dates T_j for $j = 1, \ldots, n$

$$-F_j = -N \cdot \delta \cdot F$$

where F is the swap fixed rate and N the nominal amount of the swap.

Cash flows for the floating leg are at dates T_j for $j = 1, \ldots, n$

$$V_j = N \cdot \delta \cdot R^L(T_{j-1}, \delta)$$

where $R^L(T_{j-1}, \delta)$ is the Libor rate at date T_{j-1} finishing at date $T_j = T_{j-1} + \delta$.

Recall that the swap pricing formula is given by

$$SWAP_t = N \cdot \left(\sum_{j=1}^{n} (V_j - F_j) B(t, T_j) \right)$$

We now define the swap rate $S(t)$, which is such that the value at date t of the swap contract be zero. $S(t) = F$ and the swap price is given by

$$SWAP_t = N \cdot (S(t) - F) \sum_{j=1}^{n} \delta \cdot B(t, T_j)$$

Hence, the swaption price at date t is given by

$$SWAPTION_t = N \times \mathbb{E}_t^{\mathbb{Q}} \left(e^{-\int_t^{T_0} r(s)\,ds} \left[(S(T_0) - F) \sum_{j=1}^n \delta \cdot B(T_0, T_j) \right]^+ \right)$$

where $F_S(t)$, the swap forward rate computed at date t, is the swaption underlying rate. We have in particular

$$F_S(T_0) = S(T_0)$$

Jamshidian (1997) shows that there is a probability measure $\mathbb{Q}_F$ under which the swap rate $F_S(t)$ is a martingale (see Appendix 2 of Chapter 12). Under that probability measure $\mathbb{Q}_F$, he gets in particular

$$SWAPTION_t = N \times \sum_{j=1}^n \delta \cdot B(t, T_j) \cdot \mathbb{E}_t^{\mathbb{Q}_F} ([F_S(T_0) - F]^+) \tag{15.8}$$

It is then implicitly assumed that the dynamics of $F_S(t)$ under $\mathbb{Q}_F$ is given by

$$dF_S(t) = \sigma_S F_S(t) \, d\widehat{W}^F(t) \tag{15.9}$$

where $\widehat{W}^F(t)$ is a standard Brownian motion under $\mathbb{Q}_F$.

Using standard techniques and equations (15.8) and (15.9), we obtain the swaption pricing formula (15.4)

$$SWAPTION_t = N \times \sum_{j=1}^n \delta \cdot B(t, T_j) \cdot [F_S(t)\Phi(d) - F\Phi(d - \sigma_S\sqrt{T_0 - t})]$$

Using the same method, the swaption pricing formula (15.5) is obtained for a receiver swaption

$$SWAPTION_t = \sum_{j=1}^n \delta \cdot B(t, T_j) \cdot [-F_S(t)\Phi(-d) + F\Phi(-d + \sigma_S\sqrt{T_0 - t})]$$

15.9   Appendix 3: Forward and Futures Option Prices Written on T-Bond and Libor in the Hull and White (1990) Model

We use the same notations as in Chapter 12. We refer the reader to Martellini and Priaulet (2000) for the description of a more general 2-factor model. We provide the formulas for call options. Proofs of these formulas are available in Priaulet (1997). Put option prices are obtained by using the call–put parity. In the Hull and White (1990) model, we simply recall that the volatility function for discount bonds, denoted by $\sigma(t, T)$, is equal to

$$\sigma(t, T) = \frac{\sigma}{\lambda}[1 - e^{-\lambda(T-t)}]$$

15.9.1   Options on Forward Contracts

Call Option on a T-Bond Forward Contract

The price C_t of a call option with

- *maturity date T,*

- *strike price K and*

- *as underlying asset, a forward contract with maturity date $T_F(T_1 > T_F > T)$ on a T-bond paying deterministic coupons $F_1, F_2, \ldots, F_n$ at dates $T_1, T_2, \ldots, T_n$*

is given by

$$C_t = \sum_{i=1}^{n} F_i B(t, T_i) \Phi(-u_0 + w_i) - KB(t, T_F)\Phi(-u_0)$$

with

$$\sum_{i=1}^{n} F_i B(t, T_i) \exp\left[w_i u_0 - \frac{1}{2} w_i^2 \right] = B(t, T_F)K$$

and

$$w_i = \sqrt{\int_t^T (\sigma(s, T_i) - \sigma(s, T_F))^2 \, ds}$$

Call Option on a Libor Rate Forward Contract

The price C_t of a call option with

- *maturity date T,*

- *exercise price K and*

- *as underlying asset, a forward contract with maturity date T_F on a Libor rate, denoted by FRA_t, with guarantee period from date T_F to $T_F + \theta$*

is given by

$$C_t = B(t, T_F) \left(\left(e^{\frac{v_\theta^2}{2} + m} \right) \Phi(-d_\theta) - \left(K + \frac{1}{\theta} \right) \Phi(-d_\theta + v_\theta) \right)$$

with

$$d_\theta = \frac{\ln\left(K + \frac{1}{\theta} \right) - m - v_\theta^2}{v_\theta}$$

and

$$v_\theta = \sqrt{\int_t^T (\sigma(s, T_F + \theta) - \sigma(s, T_F))^2 \, ds}$$

and

$$m = \frac{v_\theta^2}{2} + \ln\left[\frac{B(t, T_F)}{\theta B(t, T_F + \theta)} \right]$$

15.9.2 Options on Futures Contracts

Call Option on a T-Bond Futures Contract

The price C_t of a call option with

- *maturity date T,*

Fixed Income Securities

- *exercise price K and*

- *as underlying asset, a futures contract with maturity date T_F ($T_1 > T_F > T$) on a T-bond paying deterministic coupons $F_1, F_2, \ldots, F_n$ at dates $T_1, T_2, \ldots, T_n$*

is given by

$$C_t = \sum_{i=1}^{n} F_i \Psi_1(T, T_F, T_i) \Psi_2(T, T_F, T_i) \frac{B(t, T)B(t, T_i)}{B(t, T_F)} \Phi(-f_i) - KB(t, T_F) \Phi(-f_0)$$

with

$$\Psi_1(T, T_F, T_i) = \exp\left[\int_t^{T_F} \sigma(s, T_F) \cdot (\sigma(s, T_F) - \sigma(s, T_i)) \, ds \right]$$

$$\Psi_2(T, T_F, T_i) = \exp\left[\int_t^{T} (\sigma(s, T_F) - \sigma(s, T_i)) \cdot (\sigma(s, T_F) - \sigma(s, T)) \, ds \right]$$

f_0 is the unique solution of the following equation:

$$\sum_{i=1}^{n} F_i \Psi_1(T, T_F, T_i) B(t, T_i) \exp[w_i f_0 - m_i] = B(t, T_F) K$$

with

$$f_i = f_0 + w_i$$

and

$$m_i = \frac{1}{2} \int_t^{T} (\sigma^2(s, T_i) - \sigma^2(s, T_F)) \, ds - \int_t^{T} \sigma(s, T)(\sigma(s, T_i) - \sigma(s, T_F)) \, ds$$

and

$$w_i = \sqrt{\int_t^{T} (\sigma(s, T_i) - \sigma(s, T_F))^2 \, ds}$$

Call Option on a Libor Rate Futures Contract

The price C_t of a call option with

- *maturity date T,*

- *exercise price K and*

- *as underlying asset, a futures contract with maturity date T_F on a Libor rate, denoted by FU_t, with guarantee period from date T_F to $T_F + \theta$*

is given by

$$C_t = \frac{1}{\theta} \Gamma_1(T, T_F, T_F + \theta) \Gamma_2(T, T_F, T_F + \theta) \left(\frac{B(t, T)B(t, T_F)}{B(t, T_F + \theta)} \right) \Phi(-f_\theta - v_\theta)$$

$$- \left(K + \frac{1}{\theta} \right) B(t, T) \Phi(-f_\theta)$$

with

$$\Gamma_1(T, T_F, T_F + \theta) = \exp\left[\int_t^{T_F} \sigma(s, T_F + \theta) \cdot (\sigma(s, T_F + \theta) - \sigma(s, T_F))\, ds\right]$$

$$\Gamma_2(T, T_F, T_F + \theta) = \exp\left[\int_t^{T} (\sigma(s, T_F + \theta) - \sigma(s, T_F)) \cdot (\sigma(s, T_F + \theta) - \sigma(s, T))\, ds\right]$$

$$\frac{1}{\theta}\Gamma_1(T, T_F, T_F + \theta) B(t, T_F) \exp[v_\theta f_\theta - m_\theta] = \left(K + \frac{1}{\theta}\right) B(t, T_F + \theta)$$

$$m_\theta = \frac{1}{2}\int_t^{T} (\sigma^2(s, T_F) - \sigma^2(s, T_F + \theta))\, ds - \int_t^{T} (\sigma(s, T)(\sigma(s, T_F) - \sigma(s, T_F + \theta))\, ds$$

$$v_\theta = \sqrt{\int_t^{T} (\sigma(s, T_F + \theta) - \sigma(s, T_F))^2\, ds}$$

15.10   Appendix 4: Cap, Floor and Swaption Prices in the Hull and White (1990) Model

We use the same notations as in Chapter 12. We refer the reader to Martellini and Priaulet (2000) for the description of a more general 2-factor model. We only provide formulas for cap, floor and swaption. Proofs of these formulas are available in Priaulet (1997).

15.10.1   Cap and Floor

Let us consider a cap with nominal amount \$1, with exercise rate E, based on a Libor rate with maturity δ denoted $R^L(t, \delta)$ and with the following schedule:

t	—	T_0	—	T_1	—	T_2	—	—	—	$\ldots$	—	—	—	T_n
—	—	—	—	C_1	—	C_2	—	—	—	—	—	—	—	C_n

For $j = 1, \ldots, n$, we have $T_j - T_{j-1} = \delta$.

The cap holder gets (for $j = 1, \ldots, n$) a cash flow C_j at each date T_j

$$C_j = [\delta(R^L(T_{j-1}, \delta) - E)]^+$$

The price at date t of this cap is given by

$$CAP_t = \sum_{j=1}^{n}\left[-B(t, T_j)\Phi(s_{j-1} - v_{j-1}) + \frac{1}{1 + \delta E} B(t, T_{j-1})\Phi(s_{j-1})\right]$$

where s_{j-1} and v_{j-1} are given by

$$s_{j-1} = \frac{1}{v_{j-1}} \ln\left[\frac{B(t, T_{j-1})}{B(t, T_j)(1 + \delta E)}\right] + \frac{1}{2}v_{j-1}$$

Fixed Income Securities

and

$$v_{j-1} = \sqrt{\int_t^{T_{j-1}} (\sigma(s, T_j) - \sigma(s, T_{j-1}))^2 \, ds}$$

Let us now consider a *floor* with the same characteristics. The floor holder gets at each date T_j (for $j = 1, \ldots, n$) a cash flow F_j

$$F_j = [\delta(E - R^L(T_{j-1}, \delta))]^+$$

The price of this floor is given by

$$FLOOR_t = \sum_{j=1}^{n} \left[B(t, T_j)\Phi(-s_{j-1} + v_{j-1}) - \frac{1}{1 + \delta E} B(t, T_{j-1})\Phi(-s_{j-1}) \right]$$

with s_{j-1} and v_{j-1} defined as in the case of the cap.

15.10.2 Swaption

Let us consider a payer swaption with maturity date T_0, with the following schedule:

Fixed Leg	—	—	—	—	$-F_1$	—	$-F_2$	—	—	—	—	—	—	—	$-F_n$
—	t	—	T_0	—	T_1	—	T_2	—	—	—	$\ldots$	—	—	—	T_n
Floating Leg	—	—	—	—	V_1	—	V_2	—	—	—	—	—	—	—	V_n

For $j = 1, \ldots, n$, we have $T_j - T_{j-1} = \delta$.

The cash flows for the fixed leg are at date T_j for $j = 1, \ldots, n$

$$-F_j = -\delta S$$

where S is the swap rate.

The cash flows for the floating leg are at date T_j for $j = 1, \ldots, n$

$$V_j = \delta R^L(T_{j-1}, \delta) = \frac{1}{B(T_{j-1}, T_j)} - 1$$

where $R^L(T_{j-1}, \delta)$ is the Libor rate at date T_{j-1} finishing at date $T_j = T_{j-1} + \delta$.

The price at date t of this payer swaption is given by

$$SWAPTION_t = -\sum_{j=1}^{n} \delta S B(t, T_j)\Phi(s_0 - v_j) - B(t, T_n)\Phi(s_0 - v_n) + B(t, T_0)\Phi(s_0)$$

where s_0 and v_j are given by

$$\sum_{j=1}^{n} \delta S B(t, T_j) \exp\left(v_j s_0 - \frac{1}{2}v_j^2 \right) + B(t, T_n) \exp\left(v_n s_0 - \frac{1}{2}v_n^2 \right) = B(t, T_0)$$

and

$$v_j = \sqrt{\int_t^{T_0} (\sigma(s, T_j) - \sigma(s, T))^2 \, ds}$$

Similarly, the price at date t of a receiver swaption is given by

$$SWAPTION_t = \sum_{j=1}^{n} \delta S B(t, T_j) \Phi(-s_0 + v_j) + B(t, T_n) \Phi(-s_0 + v_n) - B(t, T_0) \Phi(-s_0)$$

where s_0 and v_j are given as above.

15.11 Appendix 5: Market Models (BGM/Jamshidian Approach)

Brace *et al.* (1997) and Jamshidian (1997) have recently introduced a new class of models, which are known as *market models*. The characteristic feature is that these models are built to be consistent with the market prices of standard derivatives that are obtained through the Black (1976) model. More precisely, the model of Brace *et al.* (1997) is consistent with the market prices of caps and floors, while the Jamshidian (1997) model is consistent with swaption prices. These models are now heavily used by the market.

Starting with the Heath, Jarrow and Morton (1992) model, the authors define new variables that are called *market variables*. These variables are short-term forward contract rates and forward swap rates. These variables follow the lognormal processes built so that they display the same volatilities as in the Black (1976) model. We now discuss the broad steps in the derivation of the Brace, Gatarek and Musiela (1997) model, also known as the *caps market model*.

15.11.1 Why Define New Variables?

Forward rates and forward swap rates are lognormally distributed in the Black (1976) model, which insures that they may not take on negative values. It is therefore tempting to check whether one may get lognormally distributed instantaneous forward rates $f(t, T)$ in the Heath, Jarrow and Morton (1992) model. Unfortunately, this is not possible. Using equation (12.12) in the case of a 1-dimensional Brownian motion, we obtain

$$f(t, T) = f(0, T) - \int_0^t \gamma(s, T) \, d\widehat{W}(s) + \int_0^t \gamma(s, T)\sigma(s, T) \, ds \qquad (15.10)$$

Then, setting, for example, $\gamma(t, T) = \sigma f(t, T)$, equation (15.10) turns into

$$f(t, T) = f(0, T) \exp\left[\int_0^t \int_u^T f(u, s) \, ds \, du \right] \exp\left(-\frac{\sigma^2 t}{2} + \sigma \widehat{W}(t) \right) \qquad (15.11)$$

However, Heath *et al.* (1992) have shown that there is no finite solution to equation (15.11). Hence, instantaneous forward rates go to infinity with a positive probability, which implies a zero price for discount bonds, and therefore arbitrage opportunities.

Various authors have tried to use new variables that would be lognormally distributed. Goldys *et al.* (1994) have introduced a variable, the rate $j(t, T)$, defined as

$$1 + j(t, T) = e^{f(t,T)}$$

Then, Musiela (1994) generalized this approach[9] by defining the rate $q(t, T)$

$$(1 + \delta q(t, T))^{\frac{1}{\delta}} = e^{f(t,T)}$$

These models have not been very successful because they do not allow closed-form solutions for the prices of standard derivatives, such as options on discount bonds, to be obtained. Finally, Brace *et al.* (1997) have chosen to start with forward rates.[10] We now discuss their model.

15.11.2 Building New Variables

We recall the notation used in the Heath, Jarrow and Morton (1992) model:

- $B(t, T)$ *is the price at date t of a discount bond paying off $1 at date T;*

- $f(t, T)$ *is the short forward rate as seen from date t and starting at date T.*

Under the risk-neutral probability $\mathbb{Q}$, these two variable dynamics are defined as follows:

$$\frac{\mathrm{d}B(t, T)}{B(t, T)} = r(t)\,\mathrm{d}t + \sigma(t, T)\,\mathrm{d}\widehat{W}(t)$$

$$\mathrm{d}f(t, T) = \gamma(t, T)\sigma(t, T)\,\mathrm{d}t + \gamma(t, T)\,\mathrm{d}\widehat{W}(t)$$

Note that these variables have fixed maturity T. We now define new variables with moving maturity θ:

- $D(t, \theta)$ *is the price at date t of a discount bond with maturity $T = t + \theta$. More precisely, at date $t + \Delta t$, $D(t, \theta)$ turns into $D(t + \Delta t, \theta)$ with maturity $t + \Delta t + \theta$, while $B(t, t + \theta)$ turns into $B(t + \Delta t, t + \theta)$ with maturity $t + \theta$.*

- $r(t, \theta)$ *is the forward short rate as seen from date t and with starting date $T = t + \theta$. Hence, at date $t + \Delta t$, $r(t, \theta)$ turns into $r(t + \Delta t, \theta)$ starting at date $t + \Delta t + \theta$, while $f(t, t + \theta)$ turns into $f(t + \Delta t, t + \theta)$ starting at date $t + \theta$.*

We note that at date t

$$D(t, \theta) = B(t, t + \theta)$$

$$r(t, \theta) = f(t, t + \theta)$$

But one instant later at date $t + \Delta t$, these variables are not equal.

Differentiating $D(t, \theta)$ and $r(t, \theta)$, we obtain

$$\mathrm{d}D(t, \theta) = \mathrm{d}B(t, t + \theta) + \frac{\partial B(t, t + \theta)}{\partial T}\,\mathrm{d}t$$

$$\mathrm{d}r(t, \theta) = \mathrm{d}f(t, t + \theta) + \frac{\partial f(t, t + \theta)}{\partial T}\,\mathrm{d}t$$

---

[9]Taking $\delta = 1$, one recovers the variable $j(t, T)$ from Goldys *et al.* (1994).

[10]Note that Miltersen *et al.* (1997) have developed a similar idea. Also, in a "swaptions market model," Jamshidian (1997) offers a model for the forward swap rates.

or, equivalently,

$$dD(t, \theta) = [r(t, 0) - r(t, \theta)]D(t, \theta)\, dt + \sigma(t, t + \theta)D(t, \theta)\, d\widehat{W}(t) \tag{15.12}$$

$$dr(t, \theta) = \frac{\partial}{\partial \theta}\left[r(t, \theta) + \frac{1}{2}(\sigma(t, t + \theta))^2\right] dt + \gamma(t, t + \theta)\, d\widehat{W}(t) \tag{15.13}$$

Using the same notation as in the Brace, Gatarek and Musiela (1997) model, we now transform the volatility functions as follows:

$$\sigma(t, t + \theta) = \sigma(t, \theta)$$

$$\gamma(t, t + \theta) = \gamma(t, \theta)$$

Equations (15.12) and (15.13) may then be rewritten as

$$dD(t, \theta) = [r(t, 0) - r(t, \theta)]D(t, \theta)\, dt + \sigma(t, \theta)D(t, \theta)\, d\widehat{W}(t)$$

$$dr(t, \theta) = \frac{\partial}{\partial \theta}\left[r(t, \theta) + \frac{1}{2}(\sigma(t, \theta))^2\right] dt + \gamma(t, \theta)\, d\widehat{W}(t) \tag{15.14}$$

Using the variables $r(t, \theta)$[11] and $D(t, \theta)$, the market variable is $L(t, \theta)$, which is the forward rate as seen from date t, starting at date $t + \theta$ with maturity $t + \theta + \delta$.

We have

$$1 + \delta L(t, \theta) = \frac{D(t, \theta)}{D(t, \theta + \delta)} = \frac{\exp(-\int_0^\theta r(t, s)\, ds)}{\exp(-\int_0^{\theta+\delta} r(t, s)\, ds)}$$

from which we obtain

$$L(t, \theta) = \frac{\exp(\int_\theta^{\theta+\delta} r(t, s)\, ds) - 1}{\delta}$$

Going back to Heath *et al.* (1992), we now define at a date t the variable $K(t, t + \theta)$ by

$$K(t, t + \theta) = L(t, \theta)$$

and

$$dK(t, t + \theta) = dL(t, \theta) - \frac{\partial K(t, t + \theta)}{\partial T}\, dt \tag{15.15}$$

We now derive stochastic differential equations followed by $L(t, \theta)$ and $K(t, t + \theta)$.[12]

15.11.3 The Dynamics of $L(t, \theta)$ and $K(t, t + \theta)$

Under $\mathbb{Q}$, we have

$$dL(t, \theta) = \delta^{-1} d \exp\left(\int_\theta^{\theta+\delta} r(t, s)\, ds\right)$$

---

[11] Note that the short rate $r(t, 0)$ dynamics are given by

$$dr(t, 0) = \frac{\partial}{\partial \theta}(r(t, \theta)\, dt + \langle \gamma(t, \theta), d\widehat{W}(t)\rangle)\, |_{\theta=0}$$

which is not Markov in general.

[12] Note that $K(t, t + \theta)$ is a fixed maturity variable, while $L(t, \theta)$ is a floating maturity variable. At a given date t, these two variables are identical but they differ when one calculates $dK(t, t + \theta)$ and $dL(t, \theta)$.

Fixed Income Securities

Using Itô's lemma and equation (15.14), we obtain

$$dL(t, \theta) = \delta^{-1} \exp\left(\int_\theta^{\theta+\delta} r(t, s)\, ds\right) d\left(\int_\theta^{\theta+\delta} r(t, s)\, ds\right)$$

$$+ \frac{\delta^{-1}}{2} \exp\left(\int_\theta^{\theta+\delta} r(t, s)\, ds\right) (\gamma(t, \theta + \delta) - \gamma(t, \theta))^2\, dt$$

or

$$dL(t, \theta) = \delta^{-1} \exp\left(\int_\theta^{\theta+\delta} r(t, s)\, ds\right) \cdot \left\{ \left[r(t, \theta + \delta) - r(t, \theta) + \frac{1}{2}\sigma^2(t, \theta + \delta) - \frac{1}{2}\sigma^2(t, \theta) \right] dt \right.$$

$$+ (\sigma(t, \theta + \delta) - \sigma(t, \theta))\, d\widehat{W}(t) + \frac{1}{2}(\sigma(t, \theta + \delta) - \sigma(t, \theta))^2\, dt \Big\}$$

$$dL(t, \theta) = \delta^{-1}[1 + \delta L(t, \theta)] \cdot \{[r(t, \theta + \delta) - r(t, \theta) + \sigma(t, \theta + \delta)\sigma(t, \theta + \delta) - \sigma(t, \theta)]\, dt$$

$$+ (\sigma(t, \theta + \delta) - \sigma(t, \theta))\, d\widehat{W}(t)\}$$

Finally,

$$dL(t, \theta) = \left[\frac{\partial L(t, \theta)}{\partial \theta} + \delta^{-1}[1 + \delta L(t, \theta)]\sigma(t, \theta + \delta)[\sigma(t, \theta + \delta) - \sigma(t, \theta)] \right] dt$$

$$+ \delta^{-1}[1 + \delta L(t, \theta)][\sigma(t, \theta + \delta) - \sigma(t, \theta)]\, d\widehat{W}(t)$$

We get a lognormal volatility structure for $L(t, \theta)$ by specifying

$$dL(t, \theta) = (\ldots)\, dt + \sigma_L(t, \theta) L(t, \theta)\, d\widehat{W}(t)$$

which implies that

$$\delta^{-1}[1 + \delta L(t, \theta)][\sigma(t, \theta + \delta) - \sigma(t, \theta)] = \sigma_L(t, \theta) L(t, \theta)$$

or, equivalently,

$$\sigma(t, \theta + \delta) = \sigma(t, \theta) + \frac{\delta \sigma_L(t, \theta) L(t, \theta)}{1 + \delta L(t, \theta)} \tag{15.16}$$

From this equation, we find that

$$\sigma(t, \theta) = \sum_{k=1}^{[\delta^{-1}\theta]} \frac{\delta \sigma_L(t, \theta - k\delta) L(t, \theta - k\delta)}{[1 + \delta L(t, \theta - k\delta)]}$$

Finally, the dynamics of $L(t, \theta)$ is

$$dL(t, \theta) = \left[\frac{\partial L(t, \theta)}{\partial \theta} + \sigma_L(t, \theta) L(t, \theta)\sigma(t, \theta) + \frac{\delta L^2(t, \theta)}{1 + \delta L(t, \theta)}\sigma_L^2(t, \theta) \right] dt$$

$$+ \sigma_L(t, \theta) L(t, \theta),\ d\widehat{W}(t)$$

We now provide a similar analysis for $K(t, t + \theta)$. Using equation (15.15), we obtain

$$dK(t, t + \theta) = \sigma_L(t, \theta) K(t, t + \theta)\sigma(t, \theta)\, dt + \frac{\delta \sigma_L(t, \theta) L(t, \theta)}{1 + \delta L(t, \theta)}\, dt + d\widehat{W}(t)$$

or, using equation (15.16)

$$dK(t, t + \theta) = \sigma_L(t, \theta) K(t, t + \theta)\sigma(t, \theta + \delta)\, dt + d\widehat{W}(t)$$

We define

$$d\widehat{W}^{t+\theta+\delta}(t) = d\widehat{W}(t) + \sigma(t,\theta+\delta)\,dt$$

which is a Brownian motion under the *forward neutral probability* $\mathbb{Q}^{t+\theta+\delta}$ (see Appendix 2 of Chapter 12). We finally obtain

$$dK(t,t+\theta) = \sigma_L(t,\theta)K(t,t+\theta)\,d\widehat{W}^{t+\theta+\delta}(t)$$

Hence, $K(t,t+\theta)$ is a lognormal process (with zero drift) under the probability measure $\mathbb{Q}^{t+\theta+\delta}$. Hence, it is a martingale under this probability measure.

Note, finally, that the variable $f(t,t+\theta)$ from the Heath, Jarrow and Morton (1992) model is the limit of $K(t,t+\theta)$ as δ goes to zero. The Brace, Gatarek and Musiela model may actually be regarded as a specific case of the Heath, Jarrow and Morton (1992) model with a discount bond volatility function $\sigma(t,\theta+\delta)$ given in (15.16). We note, in particular, that the volatility function $\sigma_L(t,\theta)$ is deterministic, but such is not the case for $\sigma(t,\theta+\delta)$.

We now discuss the pricing of caps in this framework.

15.11.4 Pricing of Caps

Let us consider a cap with nominal amount \$1, strike rate E, based on a reference rate that is a Libor rate $R^L(t,\delta)$ with the following schedule:

t	—	T_0	—	T_1	—	T_2	—	—	—	...	—	—	—	T_n
—	—	—	—	C_1	—	C_2	—	—	—	—	—	—	—	C_n

For all $j = 1,\ldots,n$, we have $T_j - T_{j-1} = \delta$.

At each date T_j, the holder of the cap receives a cash flow C_j

$$C_j = [\delta \cdot (R^L(T_{j-1},\delta) - E)]^+ = [\delta \cdot (K(T_{j-1},T_{j-1}) - E)]^+$$

We denote by $Caplet_t^j$ the value at date t of the cash flow C_j received at date T_j. One may easily show that[13]

$$Caplet_t^j = B(t,T_j)\mathbb{E}_t^{\mathbb{Q}^{T_j}}(C_j)$$

Given that $K(t,T_{j-1})$ is lognormally distributed under $\mathbb{Q}_{T_j}$, we obtain

$$Caplet_t^j = \delta B(t,T_j)[K(t,T_{j-1})\Phi(d_j) - E\Phi(d_j - h_j(t,T_{j-1}))]$$

where d_j and h_j are given by

$$\begin{cases} d_j = \dfrac{\ln\left(\dfrac{K(t,T_{j-1})}{E}\right) + 0.5h_j^2(t,T_{j-1})}{h_j(t,T_{j-1})} \\[2em] h_j^2(t,T_{j-1}) = \int\limits_t^{T_{j-1}} \sigma_L^2(s,T_{j-1}-s)\,ds \end{cases}$$

---

[13] See Appendix 1 in Chapter 15.

The price CAP_t at date t of the cap is given by the sum of the $Caplet_t^j$

$$CAP_t = \sum_{j=1}^{n} \delta B(t, T_j)[K(t, T_{j-1})\Phi(d_j) - E\Phi(d_j - h_j(t, T_{j-1}))]$$

Note that Brace *et al.* (1997) recover the Black (1976) pricing formula for swaptions subject to an approximation.

15.11.5   Calibration of the Model

The Brace, Gatarek and Musiela (1997) model is calibrated so that it matches the price of caps obtained using the Black (1976) model

$$CAP_t = \sum_{j=1}^{j=n} \delta B(t, T_j)[K(t, T_{j-1})\Phi(d_j) - E\Phi(d_j - \sigma_j\sqrt{T_{j-1} - t})]$$

where

$$d_j = \frac{\ln\left(\dfrac{K(t, T_{j-1})}{E}\right) + 0.5\sigma_j^2(T_{j-1} - t)}{\sigma_j\sqrt{T_{j-1} - t}}$$

Assuming that at date t we have $\forall j \in \{1, \dots, n\}$,

$$\sigma_j^2(T_{j-1} - t) = h_j^2(t, T_{j-1}) = \int_t^{T_{j-1}} \sigma_L^2(s, T_{j-1} - s)\, ds \qquad (15.17)$$

there is a full consistency between the two models. The function σ_L is actually defined so that the model is consistent with both market prices and historic forward rate correlations, as is now discussed.

In fact, the Brace, Gatarek and Musiela (1997) model may be calibrated in a variety of ways. To be consistent with market prices, the model must satisfy the following equation (15.17) for each caplet C_j.

The procedure we present is a two-stage process:

- *Defining the function σ_L*

  We assume that the vector function $\sigma_L(t, T - t)$ with dimension N is a deterministic function in maturity

  $$\sigma_L(t, T - t) = \sigma_L \times (T - t)$$

  which may be written for $j \in \{1, \dots, n\}$ as

  $$\sigma_L(T_{j-1} - t) = \alpha_j(g_1(T_{j-1} - t), \dots, g_N(T_{j-1} - t)) = \alpha_j g_L(T_{j-1} - t)$$

  Using equation (15.17), the parameters α_j are given by

  $$\alpha_j^2 = \frac{\sigma_j^2 \times (T_{j-1} - t)}{\displaystyle\int_t^{T_{j-1}} g_L^2(T_{j-1} - s)\, ds}$$

  which allows to ensure that the model is calibrated automatically with respect to the caplet's market prices. Note that the result applies whatever be the choice for g_L.

- *Computing the correlations of the forward rates changes*

  The second step consists in computing the correlations of the forward rates changes. Hence $\forall j \in \{1, \ldots, n\}$ and $\forall k \in \{1, \ldots, n\}$ with $j \neq k$, we compute $corr(dK(t, T_{j-1}), dK(t, T_{k-1}))$ and try to best match the correlation surface implied at date t. For that, one first needs to make explicit the vector function g_L, that is, provide its dimensionality and detail the different components in terms of the chosen parameters. Note that the calibration to the correlation surface is done through these parameters. For more details about the calibration of this model, we refer the reader to Brace et al. (1997) and Rebonato (1999).

This model is particularly useful for the pricing and hedging of structured products such as barrier caps, flexicaps, choosercaps and other similar derivatives.[14] However, no closed-form solution can be obtained for these derivatives, and one has to use numerical methods to get prices.[15]

Jamshidian (1997) has developed a similar approach on the basis of the swaptions prices obtained through the Black (1976) model. The variables that are modelled are the swap rates. They are lognormally distributed with no drift under a suitably defined risk-neutral probability measure referred to as *the forward swap probability measure*. Jamshidian (1997) also shows that his model is not compatible with the caps market model. Indeed, if the forward rates are lognormally distributed, then swap rates cannot be lognormally distributed themselves, since they can be expressed as a weighted average of these forward rates. Hence, it is better to select the appropriate model depending upon which contingent claim one is trying to price even if the differences in terms of prices are not large.

---

[14] See Chapter 16 for a detailed description of exotic options.

[15] See Appendix 2 of Chapter 16 for a quick overview of these methods.

16

Exotic Options and Credit Derivatives

This chapter is devoted to exotic options and credit derivatives. These are very important because they expand the available range of risk-management opportunities and provide insights into previously little-considered risk dimensions. Exotic options and credit derivatives are mainly used

- *by firms to create more appropriate hedge structures for their risk exposures, exotic options offering even cost reductions when compared to plain-vanilla options such as caps, floors and swaptions;*

- *by portfolio managers to enhance their assets yield and*

- *by financial institutions to deal with their asset and liability mismatches.*

16.1 Interest-Rate Exotic Options

Interest-rate exotic options usually are path-dependent (PD), correlation-dependent (CD), time-dependent (TD) or a mix of these features:

- *Path-dependent (PD) options:* *option payoffs are a function of the path that interest rates follow over the option life;*

- *Correlation-dependent (CD) options:* *option payoffs are based on the relationship between several interest rates;*

- *Time-dependent (TD) options:* *the buyer has the right to choose an option characteristic as a function of time.*

Note also that options differ in the way they can be exercised. Sometimes, Bermudan and American interest-rate options are referred to as *exotic options* as opposed to European options because they are difficult to price and require sophisticated models of the yield curve. Recall that a European option is an option that can be exercised at maturity. A Bermudan option can be exercised on several specified dates until maturity, and an American option can be exercised at any time during its life.

16.1.1 Barrier Caps and Floors

A barrier cap or floor provides a payoff depending on whether the reference rate has reached a prespecified level called a *barrier* during a certain period of time (American style) or at expiration date (European style). We distinguish four different types of barrier caps and floors:

- *Up-and-In barrier cap:* *this cap is activated when the reference rate reaches or goes above the barrier during a certain period of time (American style) or is equal or above the barrier at expiration date (European style).*

- *Up-and-Out barrier cap:* this cap is desactivated when the reference rate reaches or goes above the barrier during a certain period of time (American style) or is equal or above the barrier at expiration date (European style).

  Note that the barrier is necessary above the strike for these two barrier caps.

- *Down-and-In barrier floor:* this floor is activated when the reference rate reaches or falls below the barrier (American style) or is equal or below the barrier at expiration date (European style).

- *Down-and-Out barrier floor:* this floor is desactivated when the reference rate reaches or falls below the barrier (American style) or is equal or below the barrier at expiration date (European style).

Note that the barrier is necessary below the strike for these two barrier floors.

Barrier caps and floors have the advantage of offering a hedging cost lower than caps and floors but have the drawback of offering a lower protection.

Example 16.1   Up-and-Out Barrier Cap

On 01/02/01, a firm with a 2-year maturity loan indexed on the 3-month Libor expects a small rise in rates. Instead of contracting a 2-year maturity cap with a 5% strike rate, this firm contracts a 2-year maturity Up-and-Out barrier cap with the following features:

- *Notional amount: $10,000,000*

- *Reference rate: 3-month Libor*

- *Strike rate: 5%*

- *Starting date: 01/08/01*

- *Maturity: 2 years*

- *Tenor: 3 months*

- *Day-count: Actual/360*

- *Barrier: 6%*

- *European style*

This barrier cap operates as the standard cap if the reference rate is below the 6% barrier. If the reference rate goes above the barrier, the corresponding barrier caplet is desactivated and no cash flow is exchanged between the seller and the buyer. In this case, the protection disappears for the buyer of the barrier cap.

The payoff of this option for the buyer on 04/08/01 is

$$\text{Payoff} = \$10,000,000 \times \frac{90}{360} \times \text{Max}\left[0; R\left(01/08/01, \frac{1}{4}\right) - 5\%\right] \times \mathbf{1}_{R\left(01/08/01, \frac{1}{4}\right) < 6\%}$$

Fixed Income Securities

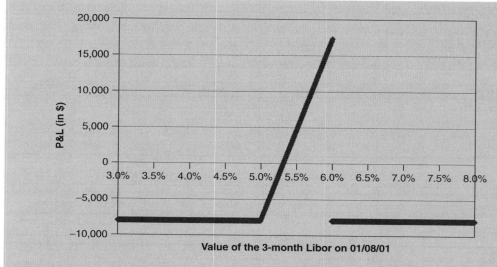

Figure 16.1

where $R\left(01/08/01, \frac{1}{4}\right)$ is the 3-month Libor rate observed on 01/08/01, 90 is the number of days between 01/08/01 and 04/08/01, and $\mathbf{1}_A = 1$ if event A occurs and 0 otherwise.

If we assume that the premium of the option is 0.08% of the nominal amount, the P&L is given by the following formula:

$$P\&L = Payoff - \$10,000,000 \times 0.08\%$$

and appears in the following graph (Figure 16.1):

The advantage of this option compared to a classical caplet is that the buyer will pay a lower premium. The drawback is that he will gain only if the reference rate is above the 5% strike rate but below the 6% barrier.

Note that the sum of the value of the European Up-and-In caplet and of the European Up-and-Out caplet is equal to the value of the caplet. Besides the sum of the value of the European Down-and-In floorlet and of the European Down-and-Out floorlet is equal to the value of the floorlet.

In Appendix 1 of this chapter, we provide pricing formulas and Greeks for European barrier caps and floors in the Black (1976) model.

16.1.2 Bounded Caps, Floors, Barrier Caps and Floors

Bounded caps and floors (sometimes called *B-caps and B-floors*) are caps and floors whose payout is limited to a particular amount of money. Similarly, bounded barriers caps and floors are barrier caps and floors whose payout is limited to a particular amount of money. These exotic products offer a reduced cost compared with caps, floors, barriers caps and floors, but of course, a lower protection. The lower the bound, the cheaper the premium and vice versa.

> **Example 16.2** A firm buys a bounded cap with a maximum payout equal to $10,000,000. It means that cash flows from this cap are paid as long as they do not exceed $10,000,000. Above this sum, the cap is desactivated.

16.1.3 Cancelable Swaps

There are two kinds of cancelable swaps—callable and putable swaps. A callable (putable) swap is a structure where the fixed-rate payer (receiver) of a swap buys a receiver (payer) swaption, so that it has the right to cancel the swap at maturity (European style) or at some specified dates during the swap life (Bermudan style).

16.1.4 Captions and Floortions

Captions and floortions are compound options. A caption is an option that gives the buyer the right to buy or sell a cap at the maturity date and for a specified premium. As for any option, there are four different caption profiles, which are:

- *buy the right to buy a cap in the future;*

- *buy the right to sell a cap in the future;*

- *sell the right to buy a cap in the future;*

- *sell the right to sell a cap in the future.*

The strike price is represented here by the cap premium.

Caption and floortion pricing depends on the evolution of cap and floor premiums that depends on the level, volatility and correlation of the underlying forward rates.

16.1.5 Choosercaps and Flexicaps-and-Floors

Choosercaps (floors) and flexicaps (floors) offer the buyer a maximum (minimum) interest rate for a limited number n of caplets (floorlets) and not for all the caplets (floorlets) that constitute the cap (floor). With a flexicap (floor), the guaranteed maximum (minimum) rate applies to the first n number of fixings that are greater than the strike rate. Thereafter, the buyer of a flexicap (floor) is not protected and must pay (receives) interest at an uncapped (unfloored) rate. With a choosercap (floor), the protection does not apply to the first n number of fixings greater than the strike rate. In fact, the buyer of a choosercap (floor) decides to exercise n caplets (floorlets) in the money amongst all the caplets (floorlets) in the money.

> **Example 16.3** On 01/02/01, we consider a choosercap and a flexicap with the following features:
>
> - *Notional amount: $10,000,000*
>
> - *Reference rate: 3-month Libor*

Fixed Income Securities

- *Strike rate: 6%*
- *Starting date: 01/08/01*
- *Maturity: 5 years*
- *Tenor: 3 months*
- *Day-count: Actual/360*
- *Choosercap: 8/20*
- *Flexicap: 12/20*

8/20 choosercap is a choosercap that allows the buyer to exercise any 8 of the 20 caplets of the cap. 12/20 flexicap is a flexicap that allows the buyer to exercise the first 12 of the 20 caplets of the cap that are in the money.

The advantage of these two products is that a firm can be hedged against a rise in interest rates at a lower cost than a traditional cap. Besides, they enable a firm to use a hedging strategy adapted to how they anticipate the market will move. Consider, for example, a firm with a 3-year maturity loan indexed on the 3-month Libor that expects a large rise in interest rates for the next months but that does not know when it will happen. It buys a 3-year maturity choosercap with the 3-month Libor as reference rate. If rates increase rapidly by a large proportion, the firm will choose to exercise the first caplets. But if rates remain stable or increase by a small proportion, the firm will choose not to exercise the first caplets and to wait for the large rise it anticipates. We see, in particular, that choosercaps have greater flexibility than flexicaps. Consequently, for the same number of caplets, the premium paid is higher for choosercaps than for flexicaps.

The drawback of these two products is that they do not offer a perfect protection over the life of the cap. Besides, the buyer of a choosercap is exposed to the risk of not exercising optimally the product, which is similar to the risk to which a holder of an American-style option is exposed. Conversely, chooserfloors and flexifloors are used by investors who invest in floating-rate assets in the same spirit as choosercaps and flexicaps operate.

Note that super choosercaps (floors) are a modified version of choosercaps (floors). Consider a super choosercap (floor) with a notional amount N. When he exercises a caplet (floorlet), the buyer has the right to choose its notional amount as long as the sum of the notional amounts of the exercised caplets do not exceed N. Super choosercaps and floors are well suited when the buyer wants to be much more involved in the risk-management decision making. Of course, the optimal way to use these products is to choose the maximum notional amount at the time caplets and floorlets are the deepest in the money.

Example 16.4 Consider the following super choosercap:

- *Notional amount: $100,000,000*
- *Reference rate: 6-month Libor*

- *Strike rate: 6%*

- *Starting date: 01/08/01*

- *Maturity: 2 years*

- *Tenor: 6 months*

- *Day-count: Actual/360*

- *Super choosercap: 3/4*

The buyer of this option has exercised the first two caplets for a notional amount of $30,000,000, and $20,000,000, respectively. If any, he will exercise the third last caplet for a notional amount of $50,000,000.

16.1.6 Contingent Premium Caps and Floors

A contingent premium cap (floor) is a standard cap (floor) where the buyer pays a smaller premium than for a cap (floor), but may have to pay an additional premium if the reference rate goes above (below) a specified contingent level on any one reset date. The contingent premium cap (floor) is cheaper than the standard cap (floor) when the contingent level is not reached. If it is reached, the premium is more expensive than for a standard cap or floor. The contingent premium cap (floor) is an adequate protection when the buyer expects rates to stay below (above) the contingent level.

Example 16.5 Consider a floor with the following characteristics:

- *Notional amount: $10,000,000*

- *Reference rate: 6-month Libor*

- *Strike rate: 6%*

- *Starting date: 01/08/01*

- *Maturity: 4 years*

- *Tenor: 6 months*

- *Day-count: Actual/360*

- *Contingent level: 5%*

The premium of the standard floor is equal to 2% of the notional amount as it is 1.4% of the nominal amount for the contingent premium floor if the reference rate stays above 5% on any reset date. If it goes below, the buyer pays an additional premium of 1.2%. In this case, the premium is equal to 2.6% of the notional amount.

16.1.7 Extendible Swaps

An extendible swap is a plain-vanilla swap in which one party has the right at a determined date, or at several future dates, to extend the swap maturity for a specified period.

> **Example 16.6** A firm enters a 5-year extendible swap where it pays the fixed rate. Each year, the treasurer of this firm has the right to add 2 years to the maturity of his plain-vanilla swap.

16.1.8 Incremental Fixed Swaps

An incremental fixed swap is a swap in which the fixed leg may be transformed into the combination of a fixed leg and a floating leg, depending on the level of the floating rate. When the floating rate increases, the fixed component increases in proportion. A firm with a floating-rate debt and the payer of the fixed leg will benefit from an efficient hedge when rates increase, while profiting from a reduced financing cost when rates are low. Note that the incremental fixed swap rate is higher than the standard swap rate.

> **Example 16.7** We consider a 3-month Libor incremental fixed swap with \$10,000,000 nominal amount in which the fixed portion is determined as follows:
>
> | Libor level | Fixed portion (%) |
> | --- | --- |
> | $5.5\% <$ Libor | 100 |
> | $4.5\% <$ Libor $\leq 5.5\%$ | 75 |
> | $3.5\% <$ Libor $\leq 4.5\%$ | 50 |
> | Libor $\leq 3.5\%$ | 0 |
>
> The fixed leg is paid annually, while the floating leg is received quarterly. The incremental fixed swap rate is equal to 6.3%.
>
> The swap is as follows:
>
> $$\text{fixed leg} = -\$10,000,000 \times [(y \times 6.3\%) + (1-y) \times \text{Libor}]$$
>
> $$\text{floating leg} = \frac{\$10,000,000}{4} \times \text{Libor}$$
>
> where y is the fixed portion depending on the Libor level.
>
> If the Libor is equal to 4.8%, the fixed leg is then equal to
>
> $$\text{fixed leg} = -\$10,000,000 \times [(75\% \times 6.3\%) + (25\% \times 4.8\%] = -\$592,500$$
>
> We consider that the standard swap rate is equal to 6%, and we calculate the financing cost of a firm with a 3-month Libor debt in three different situations: when it does nothing, when it contracts a standard swap and when it contracts an incremental fixed swap. The results are summarized in the following table:

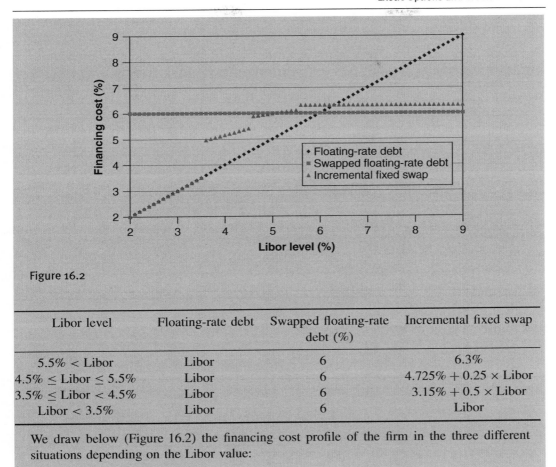

Figure 16.2

Libor level	Floating-rate debt	Swapped floating-rate debt (%)	Incremental fixed swap
5.5% < Libor	Libor	6	6.3%
4.5% ≤ Libor ≤ 5.5%	Libor	6	4.725% + 0.25 × Libor
3.5% ≤ Libor < 4.5%	Libor	6	3.15% + 0.5 × Libor
Libor < 3.5%	Libor	6	Libor

We draw below (Figure 16.2) the financing cost profile of the firm in the three different situations depending on the Libor value:

16.1.9   Index Amortizing Bonds and Swaps

An Index Amortizing Bond (IAB) and an Index Amortizing Swap (IAS) are, respectively, a fixed-rate bond and an interest-rate swap, whose nominal amounts are amortized according to the level of an interest-rate index, on the basis of preset rules. These products are mainly used by insurance companies and banks. In fact, risks encountered by insurance companies and banks result from options embedded in life insurance contracts and loans that are given free of charge to customers. The risk is clearly a prepayment risk. By buying assets such as IAB and IAS, insurance companies and banks can manage to replicate their liability profile.[1]

We give below an example of IAB (see Table 16.1).

---

[1] See Hull and White (1993) and Boisseau *et al.* (1998) for details about the prepayment risks encountered by insurance companies and banks.

Table 16.1   The CADES 12-Year IAB.

Issue date	07/15/98
Redemption date	07/15/10
Issue price	100%
Redemption price	100%
Maximum maturity	12 years
Coupon	4.60%
Benchmark	Tec 10
Base case	7.50%
Grace period	1 year
Number of amortization payments	11
Cleanup call	5%

Source: Quants Review—HSBC-CCF.

Example 16.8   The amortization schedule (see Table 16.2) depends on the future levels of an interest-rate index (called the *benchmark*). The base case is the benchmark level when amortization is triggered. The grace period is the period during which no amortization is made. The cleanup call is the percentage of the outstanding nominal amount below which the IAB is fully redeemed. Note that the amortization rate applies to the outstanding nominal amount.

Complexity of IAB and IAS in terms of pricing stems from two of their basic characteristics: their path-dependent nature and the fact that their price depends on the entire interest-rate spectrum. The IAB's price is clearly dependent on the evolution of the Tec 10 index (in the example above), that is, the contractual determinant of future levels of redemption. Since each amortization payment is applied to the outstanding nominal amount, it is not only the level of the Tec 10 at, say, $t+4$ years, that will indicate the nominal amount to be amortized, but its previous values at $t+1$ year, $t+2$ years and $t+3$ years. This link to the path covered by the index makes the IAB path-dependent. This property stems from the IAB's intrinsic purpose, which is to replicate the prepayment option, itself path-dependent. The second difficulty in valuing the IAB is due to the fact that it is a "yield-curve product." An IAB with a 12-year maturity is basically a 12-year bond configured with a number of call features indexed to future movements of the Tec 10 index. Consequently, to value the IAB at any given date, we need to consider both its straight bond component and the expected evolution of the Tec 10. This means that the value of the IAB depends on the complete term structure.

Table 16.2   The Amortization Schedule of the CADES 12-Year IAB.

Tec 10 (%)	Amortization rate (%)
<7.50	0
7.50	25
8.00	50
8.50	100

Source: Quants Review—HSBC-CCF.

16.1.10 Marked-to-Market Caps

A marked-to-market cap is a defensive product that offers a protection against the deterioration of a swap portfolio by capping the loss. Concretely, the buyer who holds the swap portfolio has the right at any reset date over a given period to enter new swaps that enables him to limit his loss to a specified amount.

> **Example 16.9** Consider a firm that holds a swap portfolio with a 7-year maturity. The marked-to-market value of this portfolio is $500,000, and the firm treasurer fears a deterioration of the position. Then he buys a marked-to-market cap that ensures him a loss limited to $500,000.

16.1.11 Moving Average Caps and Floors

A moving average cap (floor) is a cap (floor) whose payoff depends on the maximum of reference rate averages calculated over several periods, called *window periods*. There is only one payment at maturity because of the averaging characteristics of the product.

> **Example 16.10** Consider the following moving average cap on 01/08/02:
>
> - *Notional amount: $10,000,000*
>
> - *Reference rate: 3-month Libor*
>
> - *Strike rate: 6%*
>
> - *Starting date: 03/08/02*
>
> - *Maturity: 1 year*
>
> - *Day-count: Actual/360*
>
> - *Window period: 6-months*
>
> We simulate one path for the 3-month Libor. Values are the following, and we find the average as well as the maximum of averages over each window period:
>
> | Date | 3-month Libor (%) |
> | --- | --- |
> | 03/08/02 | 6.85 |
> | 06/08/02 | 5.99 |
> | 09/08/02 | 5.13 |
> | 12/08/02 | 5.42 |
>
> As the window to calculate the average is 6 months, the average rate for the first window is 6.42% (mean of 6.85% and 5.99%), 5.56% for the second window period (mean of 5.99%

and 5.13%) and 5.275% for the third period. The maximum of these averages, denoted by M, is then equal to 6.42%, and the payoff is equal to

$$\text{Payoff} = \$10,000,000 \times \text{Max}[0; 6.42\% - 6\%] = \$42,000$$

16.1.12 N-Caps and Floors

An N-cap (also called *Double Strike Cap*) is a modified version of the Up-and-Out cap. Recall that the Up-and-Out cap is desactivated when the reference rate reaches or goes above the barrier. When the barrier is reached in an N-cap, the original cap is replaced by another one with a higher strike.

An N-floor is a modified version of the Down-and-Out floor. Recall that the Down-and-Out floor is desactivated when the reference rate reaches or falls below the barrier. When the barrier is reached in an N-floor, the original floor is replaced by another one with a lower strike.

The price of an N-cap (N-floor) is higher than the price of an Up-and-Out cap (Down-and-Out floor) but lower than that of a cap (floor). And logically, the protection provided by an N-cap (N-floor) is between that of an Up-and-Out cap (Down-and-Out floor) and that of a cap (floor). An N-cap (N-floor) is the sum of an Up-and-Out cap (Down-and-Out floor) and an Up-and-In cap (Down-and-In floor) with different strike rates but the same barrier.

Example 16.11 A firm holds a bond portfolio indexed on the 1-year Euribor with a 5-year maturity. The portfolio manager of this firm anticipates that rates will decrease in the future. He buys a 5-year N-floor with a 5% strike, a 4% barrier and a second floor with a 3.5% strike. We assume that the nominal amount and the tenor are, respectively, equal to Eur 10,000,000 and 1 year. The payoff of each N-floorlet is given by

$$10,000,000 \times [(5\% - L_1)^+ \cdot \mathbf{1}_{L_1 > 4\%} + (3.5\% - L_1)^+ \cdot \mathbf{1}_{L_1 \leq 4\%}]$$

where L_1 is the 1-year Euribor.

We draw below the graph of this payoff (Figure 16.3):

16.1.13 Q-Caps and Floors

A Q-cap (also called *Quantity Cap*) gives a protection against a loan cost over a period. While purchasing a Q-cap, the loan borrower receives the guarantee that its interest cost will not exceed a certain amount (here the strike price) over a given period.

A Q-floor enables an investor to have a guarantee of interest income over a period. While buying a Q-floor, the investor receives the guarantee that its interest income will not be less than a certain amount over a given period.

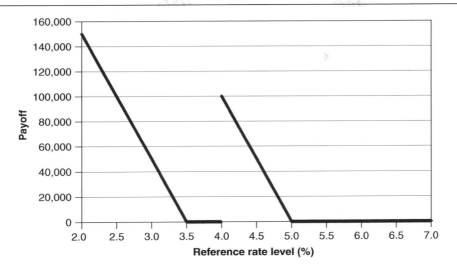

Figure 16.3

Q-caps (floors) enable borrowers (investors) to profit from a decrease (increase) in rates while fixing a maximum interest cost (a minimum interest income).

Example 16.12 A firm has a floating debt indexed on the 3-month Libor for the next 3 years. The nominal amount of this debt is equal to $100,000,000. The firm treasurer, who anticipates an increase in rates and wants to limit the annual debt cost to $3,500,000, now buys a 3-year Q-cap with a strike at $3,500,000. Once the annual cost exceeds $3,500,000, the Q-cap is activated and the firm receives the difference between its actual cost and $3,500,000.

16.1.14 Range Accrual Swap

A range accrual swap, sometimes called *corridor*, is a swap in which the interest on the fixed leg accrues only when a floating reference rate is in a certain range. The range can be fixed or moves during the product life. This product is used by investors who anticipate that rates will remain stable into a range (when they receive the range accrual fixed leg), or, on the contrary, anticipate that rates will be affected by a large volatility (when they pay the range accrual fixed leg).

Example 16.13 Consider on 09/30/02 a range accrual swap that starts on 10/14/02 and matures on 10/14/07. The floating reference rate is the 6-month Libor. It is also the floating rate used on the floating leg. The nominal amount is $10,000,000. The range is [4%; 5%] . Then, the fixed rate accrues only on days when the 6-month Libor is in the range. A firm wants to pay the fixed leg and receive the floating leg. The cash flow received on the floating leg is as in a plain-vanilla swap and the cash flow paid every six months on the fixed leg is

$$\text{Cash flow} = \frac{1}{2} \times \$10,000,000 \times F \times \frac{n}{N}$$

where F is the fixed rate, N the number of days of the period and n the number of days of the period when the 6-month Libor is in the range $[4\%; 5\%]$.

The range accrual swap can be callable, which provides one counterpart the right to terminate the transaction.

16.1.15 Ratchet Caps and Floors

A ratchet cap (floor), also known as *adjustable strike cap* (floor), or sometimes called *momentum cap* (floor), is a cap (floor) whose strike depends on the last fixing of the reference rate. We consider below some of the most popular ratchet caps and floors and their extensions.

- *A ratchet cap is a cap whose strike rate is determined by the following relationship:*

  Strike of the ith caplet = Fixing of the $(i-1)$th caplet

- *A ratchet floor is a floor whose strike rate is determined by the following relationship:*

  Strike of the ith floorlet = Fixing of the $(i-1)$th floorlet

- *A ratchet cap with margin is a cap whose strike rate is determined by the following relationship:*

  Strike of the ith caplet = Min{Fixing of the $(i-1)$th caplet;

  Strike of the $(i-1)$th caplet + margin}

- *A variomax is a particular ratchet floor whose strike rate is determined by the following relationship:*

  Strike of the ith floorlet = Max{Fixing of the $(i-1)$th floorlet; Strike of the $(i-1)$th floorlet}

- *A momentum cap is a cap whose strike rate is determined by the conditional following relationship. If the reference rate of the $(i-1)$th caplet increases by more than $x\%$*

  Strike of the ith caplet = Strike of the $(i-1)$th caplet + $y\%$

  otherwise, the strike is unchanged. Note that there is an upper limit for the strike rate.

- *A momentum floor is a floor whose strike rate is determined by the conditional following relationship. If the reference rate of the $(i-1)$th caplet decreases by more than $x\%$*

  Strike of the ith floorplet = Strike of the $(i-1)$th floorlet − $y\%$

  otherwise, the strike is unchanged. Note that there is a lower limit for the strike rate.

Example 16.14 A momentum floor has a 5% strike rate and a 5-year maturity. The reference rate is the 6-month Libor and the tenor is equal to 6 months. If the last fixing of the reference rate decreases by more than 30 bps, the strike moves down by 20 bps. Otherwise, the strike remains at the same level. The strike cannot be less than 3.5%.

Ratchetcaps and floors are structured so that they may better incorporate anticipations of the buyer and/or the next future evolution of the yield curve while keeping a complete hedging strategy. Note that these products are path-dependent. A buyer of such products typically expects to obtain the same protection for a lower premium, or a better protection for the same premium.

Example 16.15 We consider a momentum cap with a 6% strike and a 2-year maturity. The reference rate is the 3-month Libor and the tenor is equal to 3 months. If the last fixing of the reference rate increases by more than 30 bps, the strike increases by 20 bps. Otherwise, the strike remains at the same level. The strike cannot be more than 7.5%. We simulate a scenario of evolution for the 3-month Libor, and compare the financing cost of a firm in three different cases: when it contracts a 3-month Libor loan, when it contracts a 2-year cap with a 6% strike based on the 3-month Libor and when it contracts the momentum cap. The cap premium is equivalent to a 0.24% premium paid for each caplet as the momentum cap premium, necessarily lower than the cap premium, is equivalent to a 0.18% premium paid for each caplet. We obtain the following results in terms of financing cost on each period:

Period	Scenario (%)	3-month Libor loan (%)	Cap (%)	Momentum cap (%)
1	5.88	5.88	6.12	6.06
2	6.18	6.18	6.24	6.18
3	5.99	5.99	6.23	6.17
4	6.24	6.24	6.24	6.18
5	6.20	6.20	6.24	6.18
6	6.49	6.49	6.24	6.18
7	6.75	6.75	6.24	6.18
8	7.04	7.04	6.24	6.18

We see clearly that the momentum cap gives better results than the cap (for any period) and the 3-month Libor loan (for any period except periods 1 and 3).

16.1.16 Reflex Caps and Floors

A reflex cap (floor) is a standard cap (floor) with two distinguishing features:

- *First, the premium is paid periodically.*

- *Second, each premium is paid if the reference rate goes above (below) a specified barrier.*

Buyers of these products benefit from a protection against the interest-rate risk, while taking some bets on the yield-curve level in order to diminish the hedging cost. The reflex cap is expensive when the cap is deep in the money, and cheap when the reference rate is marginally above the strike.

> **Example 16.16** Consider a firm with a 2-year loan indexed on the 3-month Euribor. The firm treasurer fears a rates increase, but does not expect the 3-month to go above 6%. He then buys a reflex cap with a 5.5% strike and a 6% barrier.

16.1.17 Rental Caps and Floors

Rental caps and floors are standard caps and floors with two distinguishing features:

- *First, the premium is paid periodically.*
- *Second, the buyer has the right to terminate the option at specified dates in the future.*

16.1.18 Rolling Caps and Floors

Rolling caps and floors are a modified version of caps and floors. As opposed to caps and floors, in which the notional amount is the same on each payment date, the notional amount of rolling caps and floors can increase over their life. More precisely, each time a caplet or floorlet is not exercised, its nominal amount is added to the nominal amount of the next one. Note that a rolling cap (floor) in which the buyer chooses the nominal amount he affects to the different caplets (floorlets) is a super choosercap (floor), already described in Section 16.1.5. In terms of pricing, note that a rolling cap (floor) is always more expensive than the corresponding standard cap with the same notional amount.

> **Example 16.17** On 06/25/02, a firm buys a rolling cap with the following features:
>
> - *Notional amount: $10,000,000*
> - *Reference rate: 6-month Libor*
> - *Strike rate: 6%*
> - *Starting date: 08/01/02*
> - *Maturity: 3 years*
> - *Tenor: 6 months*
> - *Day-count: Actual/360.*
>
> We assume a scenario in which the 6-month Libor at date t, denoted by L_t, takes the following values: $L_{08/01/02} = 5.74\%$, $L_{02/01/03} = 6.15\%$, $L_{08/01/03} = 5.89\%$, $L_{02/01/04} = 5.66\%$, $L_{08/01/04} = 5.98\%$ and $L_{02/01/05} = 6.35\%$. The first, third, fourth and fifth caplets are not exercised because they are out of the money. Their nominal amount have been added to the next caplet so that the two cash flows paid on 08/01/03 and 08/01/05 are
>
> $$\text{Cash flow}_{08/01/03} = \$20,000,000 \times \frac{181}{360} \times (6.15\% - 6\%)$$
>
> $$\text{Cash flow}_{08/01/05} = \$40,000,000 \times \frac{181}{360} \times (6.35\% - 6\%)$$

16.1.19 Spread Options

A spread option is an option whose payoff depends on the difference between two rates. These two rates can either be extracted or not from the same yield curve.

> **Example 16.18** A call option whose underlying reference spread is the difference between the 30-year Constant Measured Treasury (CMT) and the 10-year CMT is an example of spread option with two rates from the same curve.
>
> A put option whose underlying reference spread is the difference between the 10-year CMT and the 3-month Libor is an example of spread option with two rates from two different curves.

Spread options are typically used to semihedge some active positions like butterfly trades whose aim is to bet on flattening or steepening move of the yield curve. When you bet on a steepening (flattening) move, you want to be hedged against a flattening (steepening) move, so you buy a spread option. We now illustrate that point through a concrete example.

> **Example 16.19** Consider a trader who anticipates a flattening of the yield curve around the 5-year maturity and then structures a regression butterfly by selling the body and buying the wings (see Chapter 8 for details about the butterfly strategy). The body is a 5-year bond with a 5.5% YTM (yield to maturity) as the wings are a 2-year bond with a 4.5% YTM and a 10-year bond with a 6% YTM. The total return of his position is positive in case the yield curve flattens but is negative in case the yield curve steepens. He then decides to buy a spread option with a maturity corresponding to his investment horizon, and whose payoff is given by
>
> $$\text{Payoff} = N \times \text{Max}[\text{10-year YTM} - \text{2-year YTM} - 1.5\%; 0]$$
>
> where N is the nominal amount and the strike of 1.5% is simply the difference between the 10-year YTM and the 2-year YTM.
>
> So the trader's position is hedged in case the yield curve steepens, while being exposed in case the yield curve flattens.

16.1.20 Subsidized Swaps

A subsidized swap is the combination of a plain-vanilla swap where the firm pays the fixed rate with the sale of a cap. This product is interesting for a firm that wants to lock in the floating rate of its debt. If the floating rate stays below the cap strike, the firm pays the fixed rate minus the prorated cap premium. If the floating rate goes above the cap strike, the firm pays the floating rate minus the difference between the cap strike plus the prorated premium minus the swap fixed rate.

Example 16.20 Consider a firm with a 2-year debt of $10,000,000 nominal amount indexed on the 3-month Libor. The treasurer of this firm wants to lock in the floating rate of its debt. He contracts a subsidized swap:

- *he enters a standard 3-month Libor swap with a $10,000,000 nominal amount, where he pays the 5% fixed rate and receives the 3-month Libor and*

- *sells a 2-year cap with a $10,000,000 nominal amount, the 3-month Libor as reference rate, and 6.5% as strike. The cap premium, which is paid quarterly, is equal to 0.2% of the nominal amount.*

We now calculate the financing cost for the firm in the three different situations, when the treasurer contracts a 3-month Libor debt, when he swaps its debt and when he contracts a subsidized swap. The results depend on the value of the floating rate on each reset date, superior or inferior to 6.5%. We summarize them in the following table:

	Floating-rate debt	Swapped floating-rate debt (%)	Subsidized swap (%)
Libor ≤ 6.50%	Libor	5	4.80
Libor > 6.50%	Libor	5	Libor − 1.70

When the 3-month Libor stays below 6.5%, the financing cost of the subsidized swap is equal to $5\% - 0.2\% = 4.8\%$. When the 3-month Libor goes above 6.5%, the firm has to pay (prorated to the period) Libor − 6.50% to the cap buyer. Its financing cost is then equal to $4.80\% + \text{Libor} - 6.50\% = \text{Libor} - 1.70\%$, which is still below that of Libor. We draw below (Figure 16.4) the financing cost profile of the firm in the three different situations depending on the Libor value:

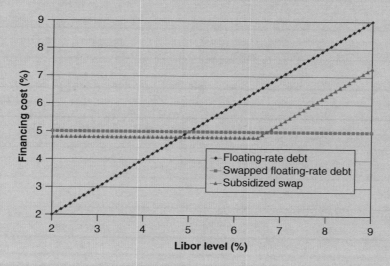

Figure 16.4

16.1.21 Pricing and Hedging Interest-Rate Exotic Options

Pricing and hedging interest-rate exotic options are usually performed in Markovian-specific cases of the HJM model or in the BGM and Libor market models (see Chapter 12 and Appendix 5 of Chapter 15 for a description of these models). However, since most exotic products have complex random payoffs, they may not be easily priced in closed-form. To obtain a price for these instruments, one first has to precisely derive the payoff structure, and then use numerical methods such as

- *Monte Carlo (MC) methods (see Appendix 2 of this chapter), which consist of generating a very large number of paths for the variables of interest under the risk-neutral measure, and then taking an average of the payoffs over these paths;*

- *finite-difference (FD) methods (see Appendix 2 of this chapter), consisting in a discretization of the partial differential equation associated with the price of the contingent claim of interest;*

- *binomial and trinomial trees, consisting in a discretization of the stochastic process followed by the factors, with respect to which the dynamics of the yield curve is Markov (see Chapter 12 where we detail them).*

The first method is particularly suited to the pricing of path-dependent (PD) derivatives, while the second and third approach are usually used for pricing options when an Optimal Exercise Policy (OEP) must be derived (American and Bermudan options). Note, nevertheless, that trees are now less used than finite-difference (FD) methods.

In Table 16.3 below, we give the characteristics of each exotic option in terms of path dependency, correlation dependency and time dependency. We also provide the adequate numerical method to price each of them.

16.2 Credit Derivatives

A credit derivative contract intends to transfer the risk of the total return in a credit transaction falling below a stipulated rate, without transferring the underlying asset. For example, if bank A enters into a credit derivative with bank B relating to the former's portfolio, bank B bears the risk, of course for a fee, inherent in the portfolio held by bank A, while bank A continues to hold the portfolio. A more formal definition of credit derivatives can be: "Credit derivatives can be defined as arrangements that allow one party (protection buyer or originator) to transfer credit risk of a reference asset, which it may or may not own, to one or more other parties (the protection sellers)."

The motivation to enter into credit derivative transactions are well appreciable. In part, it is a design by a credit institution, say a bank, to diversify its portfolio risks without diversifying the inherent portfolio itself. In part, the trend toward credit derivatives has been motivated by the bankers' need to meet their capital adequacy requirements.

16.2.1 The Significance of Credit Derivatives

Recent awareness of the need to manage credit risks has spurred the development of credit derivatives. These products allow financial institutions to reduce or eliminate their credit risk. Credit derivatives have emerged as a major risk-management tool in recent years. The total volume outstanding of credit derivatives is estimated in the hundreds of millions of dollars. Once largely

Fixed Income Securities

Table 16.3 Characteristics of the Different Interest-Rate Exotic Options and the Adequate Numerical Method to Price Them.

Exotic option	PD	CD	TD	OEP	NPM
Barrier cap and floor*	•			•	MC
Bounded cap, floor, Barrier cap and floor	•				MC
Callable range accrual swap				•	FD
Cancelable swap				•	FD
Captions, floortions					MC or FD
Choosercap and floor	•		•	•	FD
Contingent premium cap and floor	•				MC
Extendible swap				•	FD
Flexicap and floor	•				MC
Incremental fixed swap	•				MC
Index amortizing swap	•				MC
Marked-to-market cap				•	FD
Moving average cap and floor	•				MC
N-Cap and floor	•				MC
Q-Cap and floor	•				MC
Ratchet cap and floor	•				MC
Reflex cap and floor	•				MC
Rental cap and floor				•	FD
Rolling cap and floor	•			•	MC or FD
Spread option		•			MC or FD
Subsidized swap					CFS
Superchoosercap and floor	•		•	•	MC or FD

Note: PD stands for path-dependent, CD for correlation-dependent, TD for time-dependent, OEP for optimal exercise policy, NPM for numerical pricing method, MC for Monte Carlo, FD for finite difference and CFS for closed-form solution.
*Note that there also exist European-style barrier caps (floors), and American-style bounded barrier caps (floors).

confined to banks, the market participants have expanded to include insurance companies, hedge funds, mutual funds, pension funds, corporate treasuries and other investors looking for yield enhancement or credit risk transference. The market has evolved from the financial institutions' needs to manage their illiquid credit concentrations and their use of default puts to hedge their credit exposure. Existing derivative techniques have been used for emerging market debt and have further been applied to corporate bonds and syndicated bank loans. Total Return Swaps (TRSs) (see below), for example, were developed to sell customized exposures to investors looking for a pickup in yields on their portfolios. These structures enable investors to obtain exposure to portfolios that were not available to them previously and provides them with new diversification opportunities.

Several factors have contributed to the development of the credit derivative market. The key driving factors for the growth of the market initially were the commercial bank loan books and the desire to transfer credit risk without selling assets themselves and impairing client relationships. Investors have subsequently shown interest in these products for yield enhancement given the increasingly narrow credit margins on conventional corporate and emerging market sovereign issues. As investors have come to understand these products more fully, trading volumes have increased. Now dealers are more frequently warehousing trades in the same way they warehouse and manage interest-rate risk. Over-the-counter brokers have entered the market and the International Swaps and Derivatives Association (ISDA) is responding to the call for standardized documentation.

16.2.2 Types of Credit Derivatives

The easiest and the most traditional form of a credit derivative is a guarantee. Financial guarantees have existed for hundreds of years. However, the present day concept of credit derivatives has traveled much further than a simple bank guarantee.

Credit derivatives can be divided into three main categories, depending on their mechanisms and on the aims of their users:

- *credit derivatives designed as hedging vehicles for default risk;*
- *credit spread derivatives, based on differences in credit worthiness;*
- *products that synthetically replicate the performance of the underlying.*

The first category includes credit default swaps (CDSs) and credit-linked notes (CLNs). The second includes credit spread options (CSOs) and spread forwards. And the third group comprises total return swaps (TRSs) and total return linked notes. We will now take a detailed look at CDSs, CLNs, CSOs and TRSs. Many other hybrid products exist.

Credit Default Swap

Credit default swap (CDS) is a refined form of a traditional financial guarantee, with the difference that a credit swap need not be limited to compensation upon an actual default but might even cover events such as downgrading, apprehended default and so on. In a CDS, the protection seller agrees, for an upfront or continuing premium or fee, to compensate the protection buyer upon the happening of a specified event, such as a default, downgrading of the obligor, apprehended default and so on. Credit default swap (CDS) covers only the credit risk inherent in the asset, while risks on account of other factors such as interest-rate movements remains with the originator. To better understand how a CDS works, consider the following examples.

Example 16.21 Company C wants to borrow $100 million from Bank A and can afford to pay a spread of 25 bp over a benchmark rate, say Euribor. The deal interests Bank A, which can fund at a spread of −10 bp but it can lend only $50 million because of its line of credit on C. However, it wants to do the whole deal with Company C so as to maintain its commercial relationship. Bank B could take on one-half of the transaction, but its cost of funds, that is, 10 bp, would yield a margin of just 15 bp, which it considers inadequate. For A and B, the solution consists in negotiating a CDS on Company C. Bank A lends Company C $100 million but transfers the credit risk on one-half of the transaction to Bank B via the fixed leg of the CDS with a 25 bp-spread. In return, Bank B offers Bank A a guarantee on a nominal amount of $50 million in the event that Company C defaults. The outcome of

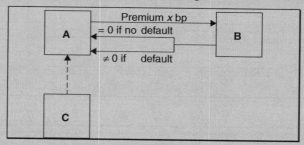

EXHIBIT A – CREDIT DEFAULT SWAP
Bank A is a protection buyer. It pays spread x, known as a premium, at regular intervals. Bank B is a protection seller: if a credit event occurs on reference issuer C, Bank B pays prearranged cashflows to Bank A.

Figure 16.5 *Source*: Quants Review–HSBC-CCF.

the deal is as follows. Bank A earns a margin of 35 bp on a nominal amount of $50 million and 10 bp on a nominal amount of $50 million. Also, it strengthens its relationship with Company C by taking on the entire deal. Bank B generates a 25 bp margin on a nominal amount of $50 million and is able to diversify its loan portfolio. Moreover, thanks to the deal, it also has an opportunity for regulatory capital arbitrage. The diagram in Exhibit A (Figure 16.5) shows the cash flows generated by a CDS.

Example 16.22   The protection buyer (X company) is agreeing to pay the protection seller (Y company) a fee (of 25 bps) and in return the seller of the credit default swap (CDS) agrees to pay the buyer the default payment if the bond issuer fails to pay his coupon when due (known as the *credit event* or the *default event*). The default payment in this example is the value of the bond below par at the time of the credit event multiplied by the notional amount of the bond that is held. If the bond issuer continues to ensure that all coupon payments are made when due then the seller of the default swap will not have to make any payment. Unless all conditions of the credit default event are satisfied the buyer will not receive any part of the default payment. An example of such a contract follows.

- *Default protection buyer: X company.*

- *Default protection seller: Y company.*

- *Trade date: 01/01/99.*

- *Effective date: 2 working days after trade date.*

- *Maturity: 5 years.*

- *Early termination date: With three business days notice following a credit event with a termination payment being made.*

- *Calculation amount: $45 million.*

- *Payment amount and dates: 125 bps on semiannual Actual/360 basis calculated from the effective date.*

- *Credit default event: When the calculation agent is aware of publicly available information as to the existence of a credit condition and at the same time materiality exists.*

- *Credit condition: Either payment default (Either issuer fails to pay any amount due of the reference amount when due; or any other future indebtedness of the issuer in aggregate of not less than $45 million that is not paid when due, or within any applicable grace period as the case may be) or bankruptcy event (the declaration of issuer of a general moratorium in or rescheduling of payments on any external indebtedness in an aggregate amount of not less than $45 million) in respect of the issuer.*

- *Coupon: 8% paid semiannually.*

- *Termination Payment: Calculation amount × par value − market value + accrued interest on the reference obligation where a dealer panel using the market bid price will determine market value.*

In these simple examples, the terms of the swap are relatively clear and concise. In practice, however, there is no standardized format and each counterparty to the agreement will attempt to negotiate an agreement that satisfies them. A reference credit must be nominated whose default will trigger the credit payment and a reference credit asset issued by this body must also be nominated. It is important that the price of this reference asset has been agreed to especially where the default payment is based on the postdefault price of the security.

In addition to the default event, some CDSs may require another trigger in order to activate the default payment. Typically, this may be the occurrence of another specified event in relation to another referenced entity such as a movement in equity prices, commodity prices or interest rates. The resulting protection under a contingent credit swap such as this is weaker, and therefore cheaper, which is even more so when the correlation between the two events is low.

Credit Spread Options

Credit spread products enable hedgers to acquire protection from unfavorable movements of an asset as measured by a widening of the asset's credit spread. A credit spread option transfers the credit spread risk from the credit spread hedger to the investor in return for a premium.

Example 16.23 For example, the current credit spread of a bond that Company X is holding is 75 bps in relation to the risk-free equivalent (which is usually a government bond). This company believes that the spread will widen in the short term; therefore, it will pay a premium to Company Y to protect them against any widening in the spread. The two companies will agree on a spread (called the *strike spread*) and at agreed intervals (annually, semiannually) Company Y will pay any increase above the strike spread to Company X.

> A buyer and seller of a credit spread option will never reference a default event, only a widening in credit spreads.

Buying or selling an option on a borrower's credit spread provides an opportunity to gain exposure on the borrower's future credit risk. One can lock in the current spread or earn premium for the risk of adverse movement of credit spreads. It also presents a method of buying securities on a forward basis at favorable prices. Credit Spread Options are normally associated with bonds, which are priced and traded at a spread over a benchmark instrument of comparable maturity. The yield spread represents the risk premium the market demands for holding the issuer's bonds relative to holding riskless assets like US Treasuries. Options can refer to the borrower's spread over US Treasury Bonds, Libor or any other relevant benchmark.

Example 16.24 An investor might sell an option on the credit spread of a BBB-rated corporate bond with 5-year maturity to a bank in exchange for a premium up front. The option gives the bank the right to sell the bond to the investor at a certain strike price (assume 150 basis points). The strike price here is expressed in terms of credit spread over the 5-year Treasury note. On the option's exercise date, if the actual spread of the corporate bond is less than 150 basis points, the option expires worthless. If it is higher than 150 basis points, then the investor delivers the underlying bond and the investor pays the price whose yield spread over the benchmark equals 150 basis points.

This structure allows investors to buy the bonds at attractive terms. If the option expires worthless, the total cost of the bond is reduced by the amount of the premium. Otherwise the investor pays for the bond at the chosen strike price. There could be different strategic variations of this, such as (1) using options on credit spreads to take position on the relative performance of two different bonds and (2) locking in the current spread by buying calls and selling puts on the spread with the possibility of earning a premium in the transaction. Again, this derivative structure allows investors to take a position in the underlying assets synthetically rather than buying assets in the cash market.

Credit spread options also give end users protection in the event of a large, unfavorable credit shift, which falls short of default. Spreads should move to reflect any downgrading in the credit rating. End users who purchased spread options will be able to cash in even though the referenced credit has not defaulted.

One particular type of credit option is a put option where the buyer of the option has the right to sell the spread to the seller of the option. Thus, if the spread increases above the particular strike spread then the buyer of the option benefits from the sale of the spread. Under a call option, the buyer of the option has the right to buy the spread if it decreases below a certain spread and thus benefit from the fall in spread.

Example 16.25   Assume that an investor believes that the credit on bonds issued by Company X are going to narrow in the short term. The investor can realize these expectations by selling the following put option on credit spreads. An example of such a contract follows.

- *Notional amount: $10 million*

- *Maturity: 1 year*

- *Premium: 0.75% flat*

- *Offer spread: 75 bps*

- *Strike spread: 95 bps*

- *Reference bond: Company X's 7.5% 5-year bonds*

- *Reference treasury: US Treasury benchmark 5-year bond*

- *Reference spread: Yield of the reference bond minus the yield of the reference treasury*

- *Option payoff: The purchaser of the option can either reflect cash settlement or put the reference bonds to the seller at the strike price over the yield on the reference treasury at the expiratory date. The investor will receive the premium and because he believes that the spread will narrow in the short term he is happy to offer protection against the spread widening. However, if the reference spread does increase to 95 bps, then he is under an obligation to pay the buyer of the option the payoff sum.*

In the above example the buyer has a choice of payoff. He can either receive a cash settlement for the difference between the strike spread and the actual spread, or deliver the reference asset (i.e., X company bonds of the notional amount) to the seller. Like CDSs, the terms of the agreement are negotiable and it is up to the counterparties involved to agree to these terms at the commencement of the agreement.

Credit spread products can have many variations. The reference security may be a floating- or a fixed-rate security; they can take the form of puts or calls. They can be either American or European-style options, they can take the form of knock-in structures, knock out structures, levered structures and so on. An example of a knock out structure is where a credit spread option appears to have disappeared because it would appear that the credit quality of the asset has improved. A knock in structure does not become active until the spread widens to a certain level. At that point the investor will take delivery of the asset at a much wider spread.

An investor who wants to hedge a long position can do so by electing to receive periodic payments based on the credit spread to the risk-free benchmark reference yield. In return for this payment the investor pays an ongoing premium. This can be structured as a simple forward with periodic net payments.

Credit-Linked Notes

From a historical perspective, the CLN was the first-ever credit derivative. Credit-Linked Notes (CLN) are a securitized form of credit derivatives. The technology of securitization here has been

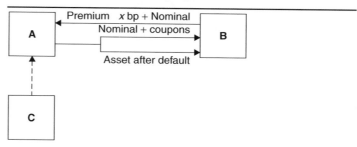

EXHIBIT B – CREDIT LINKED NOTE
Entity A issues a CLN on reference issuer C. Investor B buys the CLN as if it were buying a risky bond with embedded options on the default risk of Company C.

Figure 16.6   *Source*: Quants Review–HSBC-CCF.

borrowed from the catastrophe bonds or risk securitization instruments. Here, the protection buyer issues notes. The investor who buys the notes has to suffer either a delay in repayment or has to forego interest, if a specified credit event, say, default or bankruptcy, takes place. This device also transfers merely the credit risk and not other risks involved with the credit asset. In short, a CLN is a synthetic defaultable bond (see Exhibit B, Figure 16.6).

The Credit-Linked Note market is one of the fastest growing areas in the credit derivatives sector. Under this structure, the coupon or price of the note is linked to the performance of a reference asset. It offers borrowers a hedge against credit risk and investors a higher yield for buying a credit exposure synthetically rather than buying it in the publicly traded debt.

CLNs are created through a Special Purpose Company (SPC), or trust, which is collateralized with AAA-rated securities. Investors buy the securities from the trust that pays a fixed or floating coupon during the life of the note. At maturity, the investors receive par unless the referenced credit defaults or declares bankruptcy, in which case they receive an amount equal to the recovery rate. Here the investor is, in fact, selling the credit protection in exchange for higher yield on the note.

The trust on the one hand enters into a default swap with a deal arranger. In the case of default, the trust pays the dealer par minus the recovery rate in exchange for an annual fee. This annual fee is passed on to the investors in the form of a higher yield on the notes. In this structure, the investors can obtain higher yield for taking the same risk as the holder of the underlying reference credit. The investor does, however, take the additional risk, albeit limited, of its exposure to the AAA-rated trust. The Credit-Linked Note allows a bank to lay off its credit exposure to a range of credits to other parties. J.P. Morgan has completed one of the more noted CLN transactions, which was based on the credit of Wal-Mart.

As well as the main variant described, CLNs are also used in funded or partially funded (synthetic) securitizations, where the return is floating libor + spread, so that there is no upside linkage to reference portfolio of assets, but downside linkage if there is default in reference portfolio.

Total Return Swap

As the name suggests, a total return swap (TRS) is a swap of the total return out of a credit asset against a contracted prefixed return. The total return out of a credit asset can be affected by various factors, some of which may be quite extraneous to the asset in question, such as interest-rate movements, exchange rate fluctuations and so on. Nevertheless, the protection seller here guarantees a prefixed return to the originator, who in turn, agrees to pass on the entire collections from the credit asset to the protection seller. That is to say, the protection buyer swaps the total return from a credit asset for a predetermined, prefixed return.

A TRS is a derivative instrument that allows an investor to receive the total economic return of an asset (income plus or minus any change in capital value) without actually buying the asset. One party pays the total economic return on a notional amount of principal to another party in return for periodic fixed- or floating-rate payment (plus some spread). The underlying reference credit (e.g., Libor) can be any financial asset, basket of assets or an index. There can be many variations on the basic TRS structure. For instance, one can use a basket of assets instead of a single credit. Maximum and minimum levels for the floating-rate leg of the structure can be set via embedded caps on a reference credit. One other definition of a TRS is where the purchase price of the reference asset is paid, in exchange for total return (of principal and interest). On occurrence of credit event, the total return payer delivers the reference asset to total return receiver, and TRS is terminated.

Maturity of these swaps generally runs from 1 to 3 years (see exhibit C (Figure 16.7)).

Although the cash flows of the underlying reference security are effectively transferred under a TRS, there may be certain aspects of control over the reference security that remain with the total return payer such as voting rights; for example, if the reference obligation was a 10-year 12% coupon Eurobond whose terms provided the bondholders with voting rights where they may vary the terms of the bond. If a bondholder entered into a TRS and swapped out the returns of the bond

EXHIBIT C – TOTAL RETURN SWAPS
Entity A buys protection from Entity B, transferring to it all the cashflows on bond C, together with any value-changes. In return, B pays A a reference rate (Euribor) plus a margin, together with any net depreciation in value of bond C.

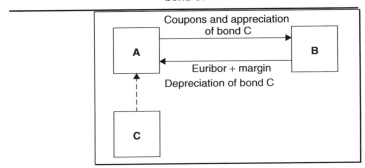

Figure 16.7 *Source*: Quants Review–HSBC-CCF.

in return for a premium, he will remain the bondholder even though he is no longer receiving the returns of the bond. If the bond issuer was to get into financial difficulty, he could call a meeting of the bondholders and ask their consent to reduce the coupon by 4% and extend the maturity to 25 years. All the adverse financial consequences of agreeing to this have been passed on to the receiver; therefore, the swap payer would have no objection to the terms of the bond being changed. The receiver is not the bondholder although he receives all the cash returns from the bond, and therefore he does not have any voting rights unless the provisions of the TRS provide for this.

The above example shows a TRS linked to a single security, but it is also possible to have TRSs linked to baskets of securities or to a specified index.

One of the main benefits from using TRSs is the ability to change the maturity of the credit exposure to suit the parties to the agreement. For example, a TRS could reference a 5-years fixed-coupon bond yet the maturity of the swap could be only 1 year. This allows a degree of flexibility in the exposure that the investor will have to the market. The returns for TRSs are generally greater than for CDSs with the same maturity. The main reason for this is that the TRS, unlike the default swap, incorporates compensation to the seller for both default risk and price risk. Price risk becomes increasingly important where the maturity of the reference asset is substantially different from the TRS.

For TRSs with maturities shorter than the reference assets, the benefit to the investor is that they are getting an asset with a shorter maturity than may currently be available on the market. However, he is now subject to more market risk than what was previously present. This means that the price of the reference asset will fluctuate because of movements in the market rate of interest. If interest rates rise, the price of the reference asset may decline and vice versa. This means that the price of the reference asset may fall (or rise) despite the fact that the creditworthiness of the reference asset has not changed, it may even have improved.

Banks use this product as a way of transferring the risk exposure of an asset to another interested party. Investors seeking exposure to a bank portfolio use TRSs to enhance their yield. For example, a bank might agree to pay total return on a $50 million loan portfolio to an insurance company in exchange for semiannual payments of Libor plus 100 basis points. This allows the bank to reduce its exposure to the credit risk portion of the portfolio without selling the loans. The insurance company, on the other hand, obtains exposure to the portfolio without bearing the expense of originating and administering these loans, except via the bank's margin on the swap. The swap enables banks to keep the entire asset on their books, but maintain only the desired amount of credit exposure. Why is this of value to the banks in an era when return on assets is so carefully scrutinized by equity analysts? It seems on the surface that they would look to move as much off their balance sheet as possible. In many cases, banks want to keep the loans on their books to avoid jeopardizing their relationship with a customer or breaching client confidentiality.

Investors can leverage and diversify their portfolios to achieve higher yields by taking on this credit exposure. A TRS enables the investor to make loans synthetically without the administrative burden of documenting the loan agreement and periodically resetting the interest rate. TRSs can provide an extremely economic way of using leverage to maximize return on capital. The investors do not have to put up $50 million to gain exposure to a $50 million bank portfolio. The exposure on an interest rate is not as large as its notional principal amount since only the respective interest payments are made. Only the total return of the portfolio is exchanged with the fixed or floating semiannual payments.

16.3 End of Chapter Summary

Exotic options and credit derivatives allow investors to expand the available range of risk-management opportunities, and provide insights into previously little-considered risk dimensions. Exotic options and credit derivatives are mainly used by firms to create more appropriate hedge structures for their risk exposures, by portfolio managers to enhance their assets yield, and by financial institutions to deal with their asset and liability mismatches.

Interest-rate exotic options usually are path-dependent (PD) (option payoffs are a function of the path that interest rates follow over the option life), correlation-dependent (CD) (option payoffs are based on the relationship between several interest rates), time-dependent (TD) (the buyer has the right to choose an option characteristic as a function of time) or a mix of these features. These options also differ in the way they can be exercised.

Credit derivatives can be defined as arrangements that allow one party (protection buyer or originator) to transfer credit risk of a reference asset, which it may or may not own, to one or more other parties (the protection sellers). The motivation to enter into credit derivatives transactions are well appreciable. In part, it is a design by a credit institution, say a bank, to diversify its portfolio risks without diversifying the inherent portfolio itself. In part, the trend toward credit derivatives has been motivated by the bankers' need to meet their capital adequacy requirements. There are three kinds of credit derivatives: (1) credit derivatives designed as hedging vehicles for default risk (e.g., CDSs and CLNs); (2) credit spread derivatives, based on differences in creditworthiness (e.g., credit spread options) and (3) products that synthetically replicate the performance of the underlying (e.g., total return swaps and total return linked notes).

One main characteristic of all these products is that they are difficult to price and hedge owing to the complex nature of their payoff. The pricing and hedging of interest-rate exotic options and credit derivatives is typically performed using a suitably adapted version of interest-rate models presented previously in this book. Explicit solutions are not available in general, and numerical methods are heavily used.

16.4 References and Further Reading

16.4.1 On Interest-Rate Exotic Options

Assoun, L., C. Chaussade, and D. Khougazian, 1994, Structured Bonds: Taking the Exotic Option, Quants 14, HSBC-CCF.

Bellalah, M., E. Briys, H.M Mai, and F. de Varenne, 1998, *Options, Futures and Exotic Derivatives*, John Wiley & Sons.

Boisseau, X., I. Florent, C. Pochart, P. Priaulet, and C. Rosa, 1998, The Index Amortizing Bond: An Effective ALM Tool for Insurance Companies, Quants 1, HSBC-CCF.

Chang, C.C., and S.L. Chung, 2002, "Pricing Asian-Style Interest Rate Swaps", **9**(4), 45–55.

Das, S., 2001, *Structured Products and Hybrid Securities*, 2nd Edition, John Wiley & Sons, New York.

Flavell, R., 2002, *Swaps and Other Instruments*, John Wiley & Sons, New York.

Hull, J., 2000, *Options, Futures and Other Derivatives*, Prentice Hall, New York.

Hull, J., and A. White, 1993, "Finding the Keys", *Risk*, **September**, 109–112.

Poncet, P., and F. Quittard-Pinon, 2000, 'Pricing and Hedging Asian Options on Interest Rates", *Banque & Marchés*, **48**(48), 5–14.

16.4.2 On Credit Derivatives

Brunel, V., and P. de la Noue, 2001, Using Credit Derivatives? Quants 40, HSBC-CCF.

Cheng, W., 2001, "Recent Advances in Default Swap Valuation", *Journal of Derivatives*, **1**, 18–27.

Choudhry, M., 2000, Credit Derivatives: An Introduction for Portfolio Managers, Working Paper, Department of Management, Birkbeck College, University of London.

Choudhry, M., 2001, *Bond Market Securities*, Prentice Hall, New York.

Choudhry, M., 2001, *Capital Market Instruments: Analysis and Valuation*, Prentice Hall, New York.

Choudhry, M., 2003, Some Issues in the Asset-Swap Pricing of Credit Default Swaps, to appear in Fabozzi, F.J., (Editor), *Professional Perspectives on Fixed-Income Portfolio Management—Volume 4*, John Wiley & Sons.

Duffie, D., 1999, "Credit Swap Valuation", *Financial Analysts Journal*, **January/February**, 73–87.

Hull, J., and A. White, 2000, "Valuing Credit Default Swaps 1: No Counterparty Default Risk", *Journal of Derivatives*, **1**, 29–40.

Hull, J., and A. White, 2001, "Valuing Credit Default Swaps 2: Modeling Default Correlations", *Journal of Derivatives*, **3**, 12–22.

Jarrow, R., 2001, "Default Parameter Estimation using Market Prices", *Financial Analysts Journal*, **5**, 75–92.

Jarrow, R., and S. Turnbull, 1995, "Pricing Derivatives on Financial Securities Subject to Credit Risk", *Journal of Finance*, **50**, 53–85.

Jarrow, R., and Y. Yildirim, 2002, "Valuing Default Swaps Under Market and Credit Risk Correlation", *Journal of Fixed Income*, **11**(4), 7–19.

Risk Books, 1998, *Credit Derivatives: Applications for Risk Management, Investment and Portfolio Optimisation*, Risk Books, London.

Wei, J.Z., 2001, "Rating and Firm Value-Based Valuation of Credit Swaps", *Journal of Fixed Income*, **11**(3), 52–64.

16.4.3 On Numerical Methods (See the Appendix 2)

Dupire, B., (editor), 1998, *Monte Carlo: Methodologies and Applications for Pricing and Risk Management*, Risk Books, London.

Karatzas, I., and Shreve, S.E., 1991, *Brownian Motion and Stochastic Calculus*, Springer-Verlag, New York.

Mitchell, A., and Griffiths, D., 1980, *The Finite Difference Method in Partial Differential Equations*, John Wiley & Sons, New York.

Smith, G., 1985, *Numerical Solution of Partial Differential Equations: Finite Difference Methods*, Clarendon Press, Oxford.

Wilmott, P., 1998, *Derivatives : The Theory and Practice of Financial Engineering*, John Wiley & Sons, Chichester.

16.4.4 Websites and Others

www.creditgrades.com/intro/intro.

www.ciberconta.unizar.es/bolsa/ini73.htm.

www.defaultrisk.com.

see HSBV the Bloomberg site of the global fixed-income strategy of HSBC.

16.5 Problems

Exercise 16.1 What is the difference between a flexicap and a choosercap?

Exercise 16.2 1. Prove that the value of a European Caplet Up-and-In is equal to the value of a European Caplet minus the European Caplet Up-and-Out.
2. In the same spirit, prove that the value of a European Floorlet Down-and-In is equal to the value of a European Floorlet minus the European Floorlet Down-and-Out.

Exercise 16.3 The idea of this exercise is to show that the payoff $Min(X, Y)$, where X and Y are two interest rates, may be decomposed into an equivalent payoff including a spread option.

Show that the payoff $Min(X, Y)$ is equal to $X - \text{Max}(0; X - Y)$ or $Y - \text{Max}(0; Y - X)$.

Exercise 16.4 On 05/13/02, a firm buys a barrier caplet Up-and-In whose features are the following:
- Notional amount: $10,000,000
- Reference rate: 3-month Libor
- Strike rate: 5%
- Starting date: 06/03/02
- Barrier: 6%
- Day-count: Actual/360

1. What is the payoff of this option for the buyer on 09/03/02?
2. Draw the P&L of this caplet considering that the premium paid by the buyer is equal to 0.08% of the nominal amount.
3. What is the advantage and the drawback of this option compared to a classical caplet?

Exercise 16.5 On 05/13/02, a firm buys a barrier floorlet Down-and-In whose features are the following:
- Notional amount: $10,000,000
- Reference rate: 3-month Libor

- Strike rate: 5%
- Starting date: 06/03/02
- Barrier: 4%
- Day-count: Actual/360

1. What is the payoff of this option for the buyer on 09/03/02?
2. Draw the P&L of this floorlet considering that the premium paid by the buyer is equal to 0.07% of the nominal amount.
3. What is the advantage and the drawback of this option compared to a classical floorlet?

Exercise 16.6   Same questions as in the previous exercise but now the firm buys a barrier floorlet Down-and-Out.

Exercise 16.7   A firm has a floating-rate debt of $100,000,000 indexed on the 6-month Libor with a 4-year maturity. The treasurer of this firm anticipates that rates will increase in the future. He buys a 4-year N-cap with a 5% strike, a 6% barrier and a second cap with a 6.5% strike. We assume that the nominal amount and the tenor are respectively equal to $100,000,000 and 6 months. What is the payoff of each N-caplet? Draw it on a graph.

Exercise 16.8   A firm holds a bond portfolio of $100,000,000 indexed on the 6-month Libor with a 10-year maturity. The portfolio manager of this firm anticipates that rates will decrease in the future. He buys a 10-year N-floor with a 7% strike, a 6% barrier and a second floor with a 5% strike. We assume that the nominal amount and the tenor are respectively equal to $100,000,000 and 6 months.

What is the payoff of each N-floorlet? Draw the graph of this payoff.

Exercise 16.9   We consider a 6-month Libor incremental fixed swap with $100,000,000 nominal amount where the fixed portion is determined as follows:

Libor level	Fixed portion (%)
7% < Libor	100
6% < Libor ≤ 7%	80
5% < Libor ≤ 6%	60
4% < Libor ≤ 5%	40
Libor ≤ 4%	0

The fixed leg is paid annually as the floating leg is received semiannually. The incremental fixed swap rate is equal to 7.2% as the plain-vanilla swap rate is 6.8%.

1. What is the value of the fixed leg if the 6-month Libor is equal to 6.5%?
2. Calculate the financing cost for a firm with a 6-month Libor debt in three different situations: when it does nothing, when it contracts a standard swap and when it contracts an incremental fixed swap.

3. We suppose that the firm contracts an incremental fixed swap. What is its financing cost when the 6-month Libor is, respectively, 8%, 6.8%, 5.7%, 4.8% and 3.5%?

Exercise 16.10 Consider a firm with a 5-year debt of $100,000,000 nominal amount indexed on the 6-month Libor. The treasurer of this firm wants to lock in the floating rate of its debt. He contracts a subsidized swap:

- He enters a standard 6-month Libor swap with a $100,000,000 nominal amount, where he pays the 6.5% fixed rate and receives the 3-month Libor.
- Sells a 5-year cap with a $100,000,000 nominal amount, the 6-month Libor as reference rate, and 8% as strike. The cap premium, which is paid semiannually, is equal to 0.5% of the nominal amount.

Calculate the financing cost for the firm in the three different situations, when the treasurer contracts a 6-month Libor debt, when he swaps its debt and when he contracts a subsidized swap.

Exercise 16.11 1. We consider the following payoff:

$$\text{Payoff} = \text{Max}(0; X - K) \times \mathbf{1}_{H_1 \leq X < H_2}$$

where X is the underlying asset, K is the strike and H_1 and H_2 are two barriers with $H_1 < H_2$.
Show that this payoff is equal to the difference between two Up-and-In barrier options, in particular:

$$\text{Max}(0; X - K) \times \mathbf{1}_{H_1 \leq X < H_2} = \text{Max}(0; X - K) \times \mathbf{1}_{X \geq H_1}$$
$$- \text{Max}(0; X - K) \times \mathbf{1}_{X \geq H_2}$$

2. We now consider the following payoff:

$$\text{Payoff} = \text{Max}(0; K - X) \times \mathbf{1}_{H_1 < X \leq H_2}$$

Show that this payoff is equal to the difference between two Down-and-In barrier options, in particular:

$$\text{Max}(0; K - X) \times \mathbf{1}_{H_1 < X \leq H_2} = \text{Max}(0; K - X) \times \mathbf{1}_{X \leq H_1}$$
$$- \text{Max}(0; K - X) \times \mathbf{1}_{X \leq H_2}$$

Exercise 16.12 A portfolio manager has determined that the bank has too much exposure to XYZ Inc. and that exposure to the company should be reduced by $20 million. Please suggest how to use a certain kind of credit derivatives that can be used to achieve this goal.

Exercise 16.13 Give at least 3 reasons why a bank may use credit derivatives.

Exercise 16.14 Consider a $100 million, 5-year swap executed at the prevailing market condition in which one party pays a fixed rate of 6% and the other party pays a floating rate at Libor. Suppose that in 6 months the prevailing swap rate for a 4.5-year swap

580

is 5.50%. What is the cost incurred by the nondefaulting counterparty receiving the fixed rate if the counterparty is paying the fixed rate of 6% defaults.

Exercise 16.15 (Borrowed from Moorad Choudhry's "Credit derivatives: an introduction for portfolio managers") XYZ plc is a Baa2-rated corporate. The 7-year asset swap for this entity is currently trading at 93 basis points; the underlying 7-year bond is hedged by an interest-rate swap with an Aa2-rated bank. The risk-free rate for floating-rate bonds is Libid minus 12.5 basis points (assume the bid-offer spread is 6 basis points). Compute the credit swap price.

16.6 Appendix 1: Pricing and Hedging Barrier Caps and Floors in the Black Model

We consider hereafter the pricing and hedging of European barrier caps and floors in the Black (1976) model.

16.6.1 Barrier Cap Formulas

We consider a cap Up-and-In with nominal amount N, exercise rate E, barrier H, based upon a reference rate (e.g., δ-month Libor) denoted by $R^L(t, \delta)$ at date t and with the following schedule:

t	—	T_0	—	T_1	—	T_2	—	—	—	$\ldots$	—	—	—	T_n
—	—	—	—	C_1	—	C_2	—	—	—	—	—	—	—	C_n

For all $j = 1, \ldots, n$, we assume a constant $T_j - T_{j-1} = \delta$. At each date T_j, the cap holder receives a cash flow C_j

$$C_j = N \times [\delta \times (R^L(T_{j-1}, \delta) - E)]^+ \times \mathbf{1}_{R^L(T_{j-1}, \delta) \geq H}$$

where $R^L(T_{j-1}, \delta)$ is the δ-month Libor at date T_{j-1}.

The price of the cap Up-and-In at date t is given by

$$CAP\ Up\ \&\ In_t = \sum_{j=1}^{j=n} N \times \delta \times B(t, T_j) \times [F(t, T_{j-1}, T_j)\Phi(y_j) - E\Phi(y_j - \sigma_j\sqrt{T_{j-1} - t})]$$

where:

Φ is the cumulative distribution function of the standard Gaussian distribution.

$F(t, T_{j-1}, T_j)$ is the underlying of the caplet relative to the cash flow C_j received at date T_j. Note in particular, that

$$F(T_{j-1}, T_{j-1}, T_j) = R^L(T_{j-1}, \delta)$$

y_j is given by

$$y_j = \frac{\ln\left(\frac{F(t, T_{j-1}, T_j)}{H}\right) + 0.5\sigma_j^2(T_{j-1} - t)}{\sigma_j\sqrt{T_{j-1} - t}}$$

σ_j is the volatility of the underlying rate $F(t, T_{j-1}, T_j)$, which is usually referred to as the caplet volatility.

The price of the cap Up-and-Out at date t is simply the price of the cap minus the price of the cap Up-and-In.

16.6.2 Barrier Floor Formulas

We now consider a floor Down-and-In with nominal amount N, exercise rate E, barrier H, based upon a reference rate (e.g., δ-month Libor) denoted by $R^L(t, \delta)$ at date t and with the following schedule:

t	—	T_0	—	T_1	—	T_2	—	—	—	$\ldots$	—	—	—	T_n
—	—	—	—	F_1	—	F_2	—	—	—	—	—	—	—	F_n

For all $j = 1, \ldots, n$, we assume a constant $T_j - T_{j-1} = \delta$. At each date T_j, the floor holder receives a cash flow F_j

$$F_j = N \times [\delta \times (E - R^L(T_{j-1}, \delta))]^+ \times \mathbf{1}_{R^L(T_{j-1}, \delta) \leq H}$$

The price of the floor Down-and-In at date t is given by

$$FLOOR\ Down\ \&\ In_t = \sum_{j=1}^{j=n} N \times \delta \times B(t, T_j) \times [-F(t, T_{j-1}, T_j)\Phi(-y_j)$$
$$+ E\Phi(-y_j + \sigma_j\sqrt{T_{j-1} - t})] \tag{16.1}$$

The price of the floor Down-and-Out at date t is simply the price of the floor minus the price of the floor Down-and-In.

16.6.3 Barrier Cap and Floor Greeks

Greeks of barrier caplets and floorlets with respect to the different variables are obtained in Closed-Form Solutions (CFSs).

Barrier Cap Greeks

For a caplet Up-and-In, we obtain the following Greeks:

- *Delta* (Δ), *which is the first derivative of the caplet Up-and-In price with respect to the underlying rate* $F(t, T_{j-1}, T_j)$, *is given by*

$$\Delta = N \times \delta \times B(t, T_j)\left[\Phi(y_j) + \frac{\Phi'(y_j)}{\sigma_j\sqrt{T_{j-1} - t}}\left(1 - \frac{E}{H}\right)\right]$$

- *Gamma* (γ), *which is the second derivative of the caplet Up-and-In price with respect to the underlying rate* $F(t, T_{j-1}, T_j)$, *is given by*

$$\gamma = N \times \delta \times \frac{B(t, T_j).\Phi'(y_j)}{\sigma_j^2(T_{j-1} - t)F(t, T_{j-1}, T_j)}\left[\sigma_j\sqrt{T_{j-1} - t} - y_j\left(1 - \frac{E}{H}\right)\right]$$

- *Vega (ν), which is the first derivative of the caplet Up-and-In price with respect to the volatility parameter σ_j, is given by*

$$\nu = N \times \delta \times B(t, T_j) F(t, T_{j-1}, T_j) \Phi'(y_j) \left[\sqrt{T_{j-1} - t} - \frac{y_j}{\sigma_j} \left(1 - \frac{E}{H} \right) \right]$$

- *Rho (ρ), which is the first derivative of the caplet Up-and-In price with respect to the interest rate $R^c(t, T_j - t)$, is given by*

$$\rho = -(T_j - t) \times (Caplet\ Up\ \&\ In)_t^j$$

  where $R^c(t, T_j - t) = -\frac{1}{T_j - t} \ln[B(t, T_j)]$ is the continuously compounded zero-coupon rate at date t with maturity $T_j - t$.

- *Theta (θ), which is the first derivative of the caplet Up-and-In price with respect to time, is given by*

$$\theta = R^c(t, T_j - t)(Caplet\ Up\ \&\ In)_t^j$$
$$-N \times \delta \times \frac{B(t, T_j) F(t, T_{j-1}, T_j) \Phi'(y_j)}{2(T_{j-1} - t)} \left[\sigma_j \sqrt{T_{j-1} - t} - y_j \left(1 - \frac{E}{H} \right) \right]$$

As a caplet Up-and-Out is the difference between a caplet and a caplet Up-and-In, we find very simply the Greeks for that product.

Barrier Floor Greeks

For a floorlet Down-and-In, we obtain the following Greeks:

- *Delta (Δ), which is the first derivative of the floorlet Down-and-In price with respect to the underlying rate $F(t, T_{j-1}, T_j)$, is given by*

$$\Delta = -N \times \delta \times B(t, T_j) \left[\Phi(-y_j) + \frac{\Phi'(-y_j)}{\sigma_j \sqrt{T_{j-1} - t}} \left(1 - \frac{E}{H} \right) \right]$$

- *Gamma (γ), which is the second derivative of the floorlet Down-and-In price with respect to the underlying rate $F(t, T_{j-1}, T_j)$, is given by*

$$\gamma = N \times \delta \times \frac{B(t, T_j) \cdot \Phi'(-y_j)}{\sigma_j^2 (T_{j-1} - t) F(t, T_{j-1}, T_j)} \left[\sigma_j \sqrt{T_{j-1} - t} - y_j \left(1 - \frac{E}{H} \right) \right]$$

- *Vega (ν), which is the first derivative of the floorlet Down-and-In price with respect to the volatility parameter σ_j, is given by*

$$\nu = N \times \delta \times B(t, T_j) F(t, T_{j-1}, T_j) \Phi'(-y_j) \left[\sqrt{T_{j-1} - t} - \frac{y_j}{\sigma_j} \left(1 - \frac{E}{H} \right) \right]$$

- *Rho (ρ), which is the first derivative of the floorlet Down-and-In price with respect to the interest rate $R^c(t, T_j - t)$, is given by*

$$\rho = -(T_j - t) \times (Floorlet\ Down\ \&\ In)_t^j$$

- *Theta (θ), which is the first derivative of the floorlet Down-and-In price with respect to time, is given by*

$$\theta = R^c(t, T_j - t)(\text{Floorlet Down \& In})_t^j$$

$$-N \times \delta \times \frac{B(t, T_j)F(t, T_{j-1}, T_j)\Phi'(-y_j)}{2(T_{j-1} - t)}\left[\sigma_j\sqrt{T_{j-1} - t} - y_j\left(1 - \frac{E}{H}\right)\right]$$

As a floorlet Down-and-Out is the difference between a floorlet and a floorlet Down-and-In, we find very simply the Greeks for that product.

16.7 Appendix 2: Numerical Methods

There are two possible ways to look at a pricing problem. One way is to consider the value of the contingent claim as the solution to a PDE subject to appropriate boundary conditions. The other way is to consider the value of the contingent claim as an expectation, under a risk-neutral probability measure, of a discounted payoff. These two approaches are equivalent by the Feynman–Kac representation (see Appendix 2 of Chapter 12). This appendix deals with numerical approximations for computing expectations, and also addresses the question of finite-difference methods for solving a PDE. We provide here a brief overview of these topics, and refer the interested reader to the book edited by Dupire (1998) for more details about the theory behind numerical techniques and their applications to finance.

16.7.1 Monte Carlo Simulations

Principle

Summarizing the above presentation using a simple formula, the value V_0 of some contingent claim paying at date T a function Φ of an underlying asset price S_T is

$$V_0 = e^{-rT}\mathbb{E}^{\mathbb{Q}}[\Phi(S_T)]$$

where the underlying asset price is assumed to follow a diffusion process under the risk-neutral probability measure

$$\frac{dS_t}{S_t} = r\,dt + \sigma d\widehat{W}_t$$

Note that we first assume constant interest rates for simplicity; the case of a stochastic interest rate is discussed below.

The scheme for computing an approximation of the value V_0 is as follows:

1. *Simulate the risk-neutral geometric Brownian motion as discussed below, starting at today's value of the asset S_0, over the time-horizon T. This gives one realization of the asset path $S_T(\omega_1)$, where ω_1 is a possible state.*

2. *For this realization, compute the contingent claim payoff $\Phi[S_T(\omega_1)]$.*

3. *Perform the first two steps a large number N of times, and get $\Phi[S_T(\omega_i)]$ for $i = 1, \ldots, N$.*

4. *Calculate the average payoff over all realizations* $\frac{1}{N} \sum\limits_{i=1}^{N} \Phi[S_T(\omega_i)]$.

5. *Take the discounted value of this average* $e^{-rT} \frac{1}{N} \sum\limits_{i=1}^{N} \Phi[S_T(\omega_i)]$; *this is an approximation of the contingent claim value.*

Generating Asset Paths

Generating asset paths first requires the generation of random numbers from a standardized Normal distribution (mean zero and unit variance). Then, the N paths are generated using the following recursive equation:

$$S_{t+\delta t} = S_t (1 + r\delta t + \sigma \sqrt{\delta t} \xi)$$

where ξ is a standardized Normally distributed variable.[2]

This discretization method is called the *Euler method*. It can easily be applied to any stochastic differential equation, and has a discretization error of $O(\delta t)$.

Application to Fixed-Income Securities

When the interest rate is not constant but is stochastically time-varying, the procedure is slightly more involved, because an appropriate discount rate must be selected. The method of computing approximate values for contingent claims with stochastic interest rates is as follows:

1. *Simulate the risk-neutral diffusion process for the interest rate, starting at today's value r_0, over the time-horizon T. This gives one realization of the interest-rate path $r_T(\omega_1)$.*

2. *For this realization, compute two quantities, the payoff and the average interest rate realized up until the payoff is received.*

3. *Perform the first two steps a large number N of times.*

4. *For each realization, calculate the present value of the payoff for this realization using the average rate as the discount rate.*

5. *Compute the average present value of the payoffs over all realizations; this is an approximation of the contingent claim value.*

Generating Multidimensional Processes

Some pricing problems involve a number $n > 1$ of state variables following diffusion processes (in the example above, one had to generate a joint path for the underlying asset and the short-term interest rate). Monte Carlo (MC) simulation can be extended to address this issue. First, run simulations for each of the n state variables S_t^i as explained above

$$S_{t+\delta t}^i = S_t^i (1 + r\delta t + \sigma_i \sqrt{\delta t} \xi_i)$$

---

[2] A simulation method using Normal variables such as the Box and Müller method (see Chapter 14 for a description of that method), is assumed.

One needs to account for correlations between the random perturbation terms $\mathbb{E}(\xi_i \xi_j) = \rho_{ij}$. A method known as *Cholesky factorization* can be used to generate correlated random variables, starting from uncorrelated ones.

Let us denote by $\gamma = (\gamma_1, \ldots, \gamma_n)^{\mathsf{T}}$ the column vector of uncorrelated random variables generated in a standard way. One can obtain a vector $\xi = (\xi_1, \ldots, \xi_n)^{\mathsf{T}}$ of correlated variables with a correlation matrix Σ by applying the following transformation

$$\xi = M\gamma$$

where M satisfies $MM^{\mathsf{T}} = \Sigma$.

It is easy to check that

$$\mathbb{E}(\xi \xi^{\mathsf{T}}) = \Sigma$$

To see this, first consider

$$\xi \xi^{\mathsf{T}} = M\gamma \gamma^{\mathsf{T}} M^{\mathsf{T}}$$

Taking expectations:

$$\mathbb{E}(\xi \xi^{\mathsf{T}}) = M\mathbb{E}(\gamma \gamma^{\mathsf{T}})M^{\mathsf{T}} = MM^{\mathsf{T}} = \Sigma$$

which concludes the proof.

Note that the decomposition of the correlation matrix into the product MM^{T} is not unique. The Cholesky factorization gives a method for selecting such a decomposition so that one obtains a lower triangular matrix for M.

16.7.2 Finite-Difference Methods

In this section, we give a brief introduction to finite-difference methods. These methods are used to calculate prices of fixed-income securities whenever no explicit CFS can be derived. The price is obtained as a solution to some partial differential equation, which we consider here to have a general formulation. For more details on both the theoretical and practical subtleties involved, we refer the reader to Mitchell and Griffiths (1980), Smith (1985) and Wilmott (1998).

General Presentation

We first consider a basic asset, for example, a bond with price A_t that follows a general Itô process under the original measure $\mathbb{P}$:

$$\frac{\mathrm{d}A_t}{A_t} = b(A_t, t)\,\mathrm{d}t + \sigma(A_t, t)\,\mathrm{d}W_t$$

or under an equivalent martingale measure $\mathbb{Q}$:

$$\frac{\mathrm{d}A_t}{A_t} = r(A_t, t)\,\mathrm{d}t + \sigma(A_t, t)\,\mathrm{d}\widehat{W}_t$$

We recall that the price at date t of a contingent claim on that asset with payoff $g(A_T)$ at date T is given by

$$V(A_t, t) = \mathbb{E}^{\mathbb{Q}}\left(\exp\left(-\int_t^T r(A_t, t)\,\mathrm{d}s\right) g(A_T)\right)$$

Using the Feynman–Kac representation, we know that this price is a solution to the following partial differential equation:

$$\mathcal{D}V(x,t) - r(x,t)V(x,t) = 0 \qquad (x,t) \in \mathbb{R}^K \times [0,T]$$

with limit condition

$$V(x,T) = g(x,T) \qquad x \in \mathbb{R}^K$$

where

$$\mathcal{D}V(x,t) = V_t(x,t) + xr(x,t)V_x(x,t) + \tfrac{1}{2}\sigma^2(x,t)x^2 V_{xx}(x,t)$$

Finally, we rewrite that equation as

$$V_t(x,t) + \alpha(x,t)x^2 V_{xx}(x,t) + \beta(x,t)V_x(x,t) + \gamma(x,t)V(x,t) = 0$$

to emphasize the generality of the method we discuss below.

Furthermore, subject to appropriate regularity conditions [see Karatzas and Shreve (1991)], the solution to this partial differential equation is unique. We now explain how to derive an approximation for the solution.

The first difficulty lies in the fact that the domain is unbounded in space. For this reason we first solve the equation on a finite domain $[-K, K] \times [0, T]$. Then, further boundary conditions are needed to specify what happens for $x = -K$ or K. For example, in the case of a European call option on a stock in a standard Black–Scholes model, it is easy to show that for any t in $[0, T]$

$$V_x(S_t, t) \xrightarrow[x \to \infty]{} 1$$

in which case a natural boundary condition is[3]

$$V_x(K, t) = V_x(-K, t) = 1$$

We consider a discretization scheme for the set $[-K, K] \times [0, T]$. Here, we use a grid with constant time and price step:[4]

$$x_i = -K + i\frac{2K}{I+1} \text{ for } 0 \le i \le I+1$$

$$t_j = j\varepsilon \text{ for } 0 \le j \le J \text{ with } J = \frac{T}{\varepsilon}$$

The goal is to obtain a series $(V_{i,j})_{\substack{i=0,\dots,I+1 \\ j=0,\dots,J}}$ such that for vanishing space step size $h = \frac{2}{I+1}$ and time step size ε

$$V_{i,j} \simeq V(x_i, t_j)$$

Two types of approximation schemes may then be defined: explicit schemes and implicit schemes.

---

[3] A condition on the first derivative of the price function is referred to as a *Neumann* condition, while a condition on the price function, such as $V(K, t) = V(-K, t) = a$ for some real number a, is referred to as a *Dirichlet* condition.

[4] Note, however, that nonequally spaced nodes may be used instead (see Wilmott (1998) for a discussion of the advantages and disadvantages).

Explicit Schemes

An explicit scheme is defined by

$$V_t(x_i, t_j) = \frac{\partial V(x_i, t_j)}{\partial t} \simeq \frac{V_{i,j} - V_{i,j-1}}{\varepsilon}$$

$$V_x(x_i, t_j) = \frac{\partial V(x_i, t_j)}{\partial x} \simeq \frac{V_{i+1,j} - V_{i-1,j}}{2h}$$

$$V_{xx}(x_i, t_j) = \frac{\partial^2 V(x_i, t_j)}{\partial t^2} \simeq \frac{V_{i,j+1} - 2V_{i,j} + V_{i-1,j}}{h^2}$$

Plugging these values into the partial differential equation

$$V_t(x, t) + \alpha(x, t)V_{xx}(x, t) + \beta(x, t)V_x(x, t) + \gamma(x, t)V(x, t) = 0$$

we obtain

$$\frac{V_{i,j} - V_{i,j-1}}{\varepsilon} + \alpha_{i,j}\frac{V_{i,j+1} - 2V_{i,j} + V_{i-1,j}}{h^2} + \beta_{i,j}\frac{V_{i+1,j} - V_{i-1,j}}{2h} + \gamma_{i,j}V_{i,j} = 0$$

This equation may be rearranged to put the j term on the left-hand side:

$$V_{i,j-1} = A_{i,j}V_{i-1,j} + (1 + B_{i,j})V_{i,j} + C_{i,j}V_{i+1,j}$$

with suitably defined $A_{i,j}$, $B_{i,j}$ and $C_{i,j}$ so that the equivalence between the two formulations is ensured. If we know $V_{i,j}$ for all i, then we obtain directly the value $V_{i,j-1}$ by that equation. That is why that scheme is referred to as an "explicit" scheme. Starting from the boundary condition given by the payoff function, one may then work one's way backward into the grid to finally obtain the present value for the contingent claim.

Implicit Schemes

An implicit scheme, on the other hand, is defined by

$$V_t(x_i, t_j) = \frac{\partial V(x_i, t_j)}{\partial t} \simeq \frac{V_{i,j+1} - V_{i,j}}{\varepsilon}$$

$$V_x(x_i, t_j) = \frac{\partial V(x_i, t_j)}{\partial x} \simeq \frac{V_{i+1,j} - V_{i-1,j}}{2h}$$

$$V_{xx}(x_i, t_j) = \frac{\partial^2 V(x_i, t_j)}{\partial t^2} \simeq \frac{V_{i,j+1} - 2V_{i,j} + V_{i-1,j}}{h^2}$$

In this case, the following equation holds:

$$\frac{V_{i,j+1} - V_{i,j}}{\varepsilon} + \alpha_{i,j}\frac{V_{i,j+1} - 2V_{i,j} + V_{i-1,j}}{h^2} + \beta_{i,j}\frac{V_{i+1,j} - V_{i-1,j}}{2h} + \gamma_{i,j}V_{i,j} = 0$$

The solution of the above equation is no longer straightforward. To get $V_{i,j}$ from $V_{i,j+1}$ now involves solving a set of linear equations. This is why this method is referred to as an "implicit" scheme. Standard methods, such as the Crank–Nicolson method, may be used to solve such a system [see, for example, Wilmott (1998)].

Overall, it appears that implicit methods are more demanding from a computational standpoint. However, implicit methods are much more stable than explicit methods, and are therefore usually preferred.

Securitization

PART VIII

Mortgage-backed securities (MBSs) and asset-backed securities (ABSs) make up what is called the securitized debt market. The MBS and ABS creation process, called securitization, consists in transforming the illiquid assets of a lending entity (financial institution or corporation) into tradable securities, backed by these assets. More precisely, MBSs and ABSs are collateralized by a pool of loans, whose cash flow payments are used to pay the cash flows on the securities. Basically, three participants are involved in the securitization process:

- *The originator, that is, the original lender.*

- *The issuer, also called the conduit, that is, the investor who buys loans from the originator, gathers them into a pool and issues securities guaranteed by the pool. Typically, the issuer creates a bankruptcy remote trust, also known as a Special Purpose Vehicle (SPV), designed for holding the pool of loans separately from the other assets of the originator, and so ensuring that the cash flows from the pool are entirely dedicated to servicing the securities backed by this pool. In case the originator goes bankrupt, the SPV continues to pay the proceeds from the loans to security holders.*

- *The trustee, that is, the entity that protects the rights of the security holders.*

Although MBSs and ABSs are complex in nature, they are very popular amongst issuers and investors in the United States as well as in the United Kingdom and in the Euro area. Actually, over the last 20 years, the securitized debt market has not stopped growing and has become a major means of financing for corporations and an alternative to both the Treasury debt market and the high investment-grade corporate debt market. Indeed, MBSs and ABSs present several advantages for investors as well as for borrowers:

- *They generally have a high credit quality (AA–AAA).*

- *They produce higher yields than bonds with comparable quality and maturity.*

- *They are more liquid than corporate securities.*

- *They historically exhibit far less rating downgrades than corporate securities.*

- *They represent an attractive source of financing.*

Asset securitization was originally developed by banks for the purpose of generating value from the assets on their balance sheet. Indeed, it allows a lending institution to

- *improve the liquidity of its balance sheet, since the original loan, which is held until maturity, is replaced by a bond security that can be sold before maturity;*

- *reduce the size of its balance sheet by transferring a part of its assets, and so to improve its equity/asset ratio, which in turn allows it to release funds and reallocate them to more profitable business;*

- *refinance at an attractive cost, since the interest payable on ABSs and MBSs is lower than the interest payable on the underlying loans.*

The chart below summarizes the securitization process.

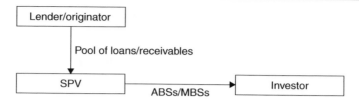

MBSs and ABSs have different uses, both from an issuer's and an investor's standpoints.

- ***From an issuer's standpoint*** MBSs and ABSs are used by issuers to reduce the size of their balance sheet and release capital that can be put back to work. In other words, MBSs and ABSs give them the opportunity to leverage off part of their capital so as to generate higher revenues. For example, they can acquire new loans or receivables from the sale of MBSs or ABSs, that is, they will replace their securitized assets with new loans or receivables. For issuers belonging to regulated industries, the resulting capital reallocation allows them to achieve capital adequacy levels required by regulatory entities.

- ***From an investor's standpoint*** MBSs and ABSs are used by investors to capture spread over Treasury bonds and enhance the yield on their portfolios without giving up credit quality and liquidity. In particular, when structured as multiclass securities, they are designed for asset–liability management. Indeed, the duration of a given liability can be matched by choosing the appropriate MBS or ABS maturity class.

17

Mortgage-Backed Securities

17.1 Description of MBSs

17.1.1 Definition

Mortgage-backed securities (MBSs) are securities that are backed by the cash flows of a mortgage or a pool of mortgages. They can be divided into three types, which will be examined later on:

- *Mortgage pass-through securities*
- *Collateralized mortgage obligations (CMOs)*
- *Stripped mortgage-backed securities.*

Let us begin with the description of a mortgage. A mortgage is a loan secured by the collateral of some specified real estate property. In case the borrower, also called *the mortgagor*, fails to make the contracted payments, the lender, also called *the mortgagee*, has the right to seize the property so as to be paid back. There basically exist two categories of property: commercial property and residential property. Commercial mortgages are backed by income-yielding properties such as office buildings, multifamily apartments, hotels, industrial properties and retail shopping centers, whereas residential mortgages are backed by single-family residential properties. Some residential MBSs, called *agency residential* MBSs, benefit from a built-in government guarantee, which is not the case for their commercial counterparts. Typically, commercial mortgages have shorter maturities than residential mortgages. They are either nonamortizing or partially amortizing, as opposed to residential mortgages, which are fully amortizing. Besides, residential mortgages can be prepaid without penalty, unlike commercial mortgages, which bear a prepayment penalty. Let us now look in detail at the amortization mechanism and the prepayment feature.

17.1.2 The Amortization Mechanism

Mortgage loans differ from one another as regards their amortization pattern. In this respect, the most simple and common mortgage type is the fixed-rate, level-payment mortgage. Actually, the borrower makes equal monthly payments (MPs) at the beginning of every month until the loan is fully amortized. Each MP consists of an interest part, equal to one-twelfth of the mortgage rate times the principal outstanding amount at the beginning of the previous month, and a principal part, corresponding to the repayment of a fraction of the principal outstanding. Let us denote by P the initial principal amount of the mortgage loan, by r the interest rate of the mortgage, by n the maturity of the mortgage, as expressed in number of months and by M the constant MP on the mortgage. The monthly periodic interest rate, equal to $\frac{r}{12}$, is the internal rate of return of the cash-flow series $(-P, M, M, \ldots, M)$.

Hence

$$-P + \sum_{k=1}^{n} \frac{M}{\left(1 + \dfrac{r}{12}\right)^k} = 0$$

That is,

$$M = \frac{\dfrac{r}{12}P}{1 - \dfrac{1}{\left(1 + \dfrac{r}{12}\right)^n}}$$

Let us now compute on month j, the interest component i_j and the principal component p_j of the MP. After $j-1$ months, the principal outstanding amount P_{j-1} is equal to the present value of the remaining monthly cash flows. So,

$$P_{j-1} = \sum_{k=1}^{n-j+1} \frac{M}{\left(1 + \dfrac{r}{12}\right)^k}$$

That is

$$P_{j-1} = \frac{M}{\dfrac{r}{12}}\left(1 - \frac{1}{\left(1 + \dfrac{r}{12}\right)^{n-j+1}}\right)$$

$$P_{j-1} = P\frac{\left(1 + \dfrac{r}{12}\right)^n - \left(1 + \dfrac{r}{12}\right)^{j-1}}{\left(1 + \dfrac{r}{12}\right)^n - 1}$$

We can deduce

$$i_j = \frac{r}{12}P_{j-1}$$

$$i_j = \frac{r}{12}P\frac{\left(1 + \dfrac{r}{12}\right)^n - \left(1 + \dfrac{r}{12}\right)^{j-1}}{\left(1 + \dfrac{r}{12}\right)^n - 1}$$

and

$$p_j = M - i_j$$

$$p_j = \frac{r}{12}P\frac{\left(1 + \dfrac{r}{12}\right)^{j-1}}{\left(1 + \dfrac{r}{12}\right)^n - 1}$$

Example 17.1 Consider a \$1-million level-payment mortgage loan with a 15-year maturity and a 12% interest rate. Let us compute its amortization schedule. Each of the 180-monthly payments M amounts to

$$M = \frac{\dfrac{12\%}{12} \times 10^6}{1 - \dfrac{1}{\left(1 + \dfrac{12\%}{12}\right)^{180}}}$$

$$M = \$12{,}001.68$$

The table hereafter summarizes the amortization schedule.

Month	Interest payment	Principal payment	Residual principal amount	Monthly payment
0			1,000,000.00	
1	10,000.00	2,001.68	997,998.32	12,001.68
2	9,979.98	2,021.70	995,976.62	12,001.68
3	9,959.77	2,041.91	993,934.71	12,001.68
4	9,939.35	2,062.33	991,872.37	12,001.68
...	...	...	...	...
90	7,148.83	4,852.85	710,030.00	12,001.68
91	7,100.30	4,901.38	705,128.62	12,001.68
92	7,051.29	4,950.39	700,178.23	12,001.68
93	7,001.78	4,999.90	695,178.33	12,001.68
...	...	...	...	...
177	468.30	11,533.38	35,296.77	12,001.68
178	352.97	11,648.71	23,648.05	12,001.68
179	236.48	11,765.20	11,882.85	12,001.68
180	118.83	11,882.85	0.00	12,001.68

Other amortization types include the following:

- **Graduated payment mortgages:** Monthly payments grow over time according to a preset schedule. The initial payments are lower than the mortgage interest, so that the principal amount increases at the beginning of the loan (this is called negative amortization).

- **Growing equity mortgages:** Monthly payments grow over time, the initial payment being the same as that on a level-payment mortgage. Hence, amortization is faster.

- **Tiered-payment mortgages:** They are similar to graduated payment mortgages, except that the initial payments are completed by withdrawals from a buydown account, so that amortization is not negative.

- **Adjustable-rate mortgages:** The mortgage rate is equal to a reference rate index plus a spread. Monthly payments are periodically reset. Usually, the mortgage rate is bounded by a cap limit and a floor limit that protect the borrower against a dramatic increase (respectively, decrease) in interest rates.

- **Balloon mortgages:** *They are partially amortizing and so mature with a significant principal outstanding amount called balloon.*

17.1.3 The Prepayment Feature

Prepayment potentially affects all mortgage loans, especially residential mortgages. It designates any early principal payment made in excess of the regular amortization schedule. Broadly speaking, there are five sources of prepayment. We list them below in decreasing order of importance:

- **Home sales** *A mortgagor may sell his home, following a job change compelling him to move, or because he wants to buy a larger house.*

- **Refinancings** *A mortgagor may have the opportunity to refinance at a lower cost, if interest rates fall below the interest rate of the mortgage.*

- **Defaults** *A mortgagor may be unable to honor his obligations, in which case the mortgage is foreclosed and liquidated. For a residential mortgage, this means that the home is seized and sold.*

- **Extra payments** *A mortgagor may wish to pay more than the scheduled payment each month so as to build up equity in his home faster.*

- **Accidents** *A mortgagor may have his home destroyed by an accident or a natural disaster.*

In the first and third cases, the mortgage loan is paid off with the proceeds from home sale; in the last case, the mortgage loan is paid off with the insurance proceeds.

As MBSs are backed by mortgages, they are also subject to prepayment. This feature makes them equivalent to callable bonds. For an investor, prepayment risk is a serious issue as prepayments tend to take place when interest rates are going down (refinancing motive), that is, at times when reinvestment opportunities in similar securities are not particularly attractive. More specifically, for an investor, prepayment risk translates into

- *cash-flow uncertainty because an MBS may be prepaid at any time before maturity;*

- *reinvestment risk because the actual maturity of an MBS may be lower than the investment horizon;*

- *negative convexity because an MBS has an embedded prepayment option.*

Projecting prepayment is critical for the analysis and valuation of an MBS. A good prepayment model should be

- *flexible so as to capture the time-varying nature of the factors affecting prepayments (costs of refinancing, borrower demographic characteristics, etc.);*

- *robust over time and apply to any case, whatever may be the borrower and mortgage types.*

We review in the next section various prepayment approaches used by market practitioners.

17.1.4 Typology of MBS

Mortgage Pass-Throughs

Mortgage pass-throughs are the simplest form of MBSs. Actually, a pass-through unit represents a share of the underlying mortgage pool. The cash flows generated by the pool are passed on to the security holders on a pro-rata basis. They are delivered monthly and consist of three components: interest payments, scheduled principal payments and prepayments.

> **Example 17.2**   Consider 100 mortgage loans, each amounting to $1 million, gathered into a pool. Therefore, the value of the pool is $100 million. Let us assume that 200 units of a pass-through backed by that pool are issued. So, each unit amounts to $500,000 and is entitled to 0.5% of the cash flows.

In the United States, there exist two types of pass-throughs: agency pass-throughs and nonagency (or simply conventional) pass-throughs. Agency pass-throughs are mainly issued by three organizations: the Government National Mortgage Association (Ginnie Mae), the Federal Home Loan Mortgage Corporation (Freddie Mac) and the Federal National Mortgage Association (Fannie Mae). As Ginnie Mae is a federally related institution, its pass-through securities are backed by the full faith and credit of the US government. As such, they are free of default risk, like Treasury securities. In contrast, Freddie Mac and Fannie Mae being government-sponsored entities, their pass-through securities are not guaranteed by the US government but only by the agencies themselves.

Collateralized Mortgage Obligations (CMOs)

CMOs differ from mortgage pass-throughs in that they distribute cash flows to security holders on a priority basis. Indeed, they are structured in maturity classes, called *tranches*. All principal payments (regular principal payments as well as prepayments) are allocated to the first tranche until it is fully paid off; then, it is the turn of the second tranche and so on. In this way, prepayment risk is redistributed among the different tranches, the first tranche absorbing prepayment first, then the second tranche and so on. As a result, the first tranche has the shortest maturity, while the last tranche has the longest maturity. Note that all tranches still receive interest payments on a pro rata basis. Compared to mortgage pass-throughs, the maturity of each CMO class is less uncertain.

> **Example 17.3**   Getting back to our previous example, we assume a CMO structured in three classes: A, B and C. Class A amounts to $60 million, Class B $25 million and Class C $15 million. Class A will receive all principal payments until $60 million are paid off; then Class B will receive all principal payments until $25 million are paid off. Class C is the last to receive principal payments. Note that each unit of a given class is entitled to receive a proportion of the payments on that class. If 100 units are issued on Class A, each unit will be entitled to 1% of the cash flows on Class A.

Stripped MBSs

Stripped MBSs are structured in two classes: an Interest Only class (IO) and a Principal Only class (PO). The IO class receives all interest payments, while the PO class receives all principal payments. Stripped MBSs are highly sensitive to prepayment rates, and hence riskier than mortgage pass-throughs. The higher the prepayment rate on the mortgage pool, the faster the POs are paid off, that is, the higher the price of the POs, and the lower the total cash flows received on the IOs, that is, the lower the price of the IOs; and conversely.

Fixed Income Securities

17.2 Market Quotes and Pricing

MBSs are traded in a highly active secondary market. They are generally considered as liquid as high investment-grade corporate bonds. In particular, the major agency mortgage pass-throughs are as liquid as Treasury bonds. MBSs are quoted in basis points above the on-the-run Treasury yield curve or above the swap yield curve. For this purpose, market makers compute what is called the weighted average life (WAL) of an MBS, based on some prepayment rate assumption. WAL is nothing but the average time for receiving future principal payments, weighted by the amount of each principal cash flow. Then the yield of the MBS is compared against either the interpolated on-the-run Treasury-bond yield with maturity equal to the WAL of the MBS or the interpolated swap yield with maturity equal to the WAL of the MBS.

The coupon of an MBS is typically inferior to the weighted average coupon[1] on the underlying mortgage pool by an amount equal to the fee paid to the servicer[2] of the mortgage loans.

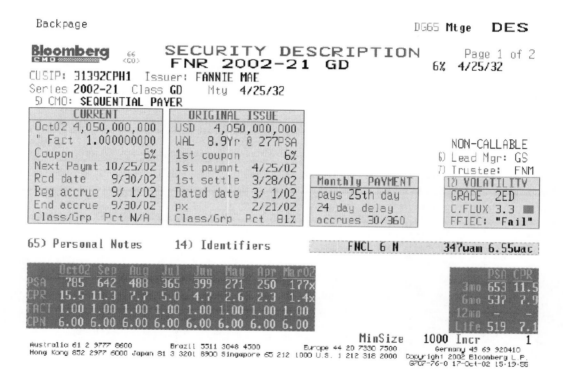

Figure 17.1 © 2003 Bloomberg L.P. All rights reserved. Reprinted with permission.

---

[1] The weighted average coupon on a mortgage pool is calculated by weighting the coupon of each mortgage loan by the ratio of the mortgage loan balance over the total balance of the mortgage pool.

[2] The servicer of a mortgage loan is responsible for collecting interest payments, sending regular statements to borrowers and chasing overdue payments.

```
Page                                        DG65 Mtge    DES
    50<Go> for alternate group.
Bloomberg        GROUP DESCRIPTION          Page 2 of 2
CMO           FNR 2002-21  Group-2: 30YR/8.5/FNMA/G2   last 10/1/02
                 Issuer: FANNIE MAE
Series 2002-21                          375 Pools:    FNCL 6 N

  GROUP - CURRENT        GROUP - ORIGINAL    Oct02 PSA-GROUP-CPR        FNCL 6 N
Oct02 4,757,782,196   USD   4,999,999,999   1mo    785   15.5    881   16.6
Net             6%    Net             6%    3mo    653   11.5    714   15.1
WAC         6.545%    WAC         6.548%    6mo    537    7.9    570   11.1
WAM  28:11   347 mo   WAM  29:8   356 mo    12mo     -      -    539   12.6
AGE   0:10    10 mo   AGE   0:4     4 mo    Life   519    7.1    513    5.8
Next Paymt 10/25/02   1st paymt  4/25/02
Rcd date    9/30/02   1st settle 3/28/02    Monthly PAYMENT        NON-CALLABLE
B.Median        PSA   px 277 PSA  2/21/02   pays 25th day
PAC 2.5%   SUP 1.6%   PAC 2.4%   SUP 1.7%   MIXED Delay          6) Lead Mgr: GS
Beg Accrue    MIXED   Dated         MIXED   accrues 30/360       7) Trustee:  FNM

      Oct02 Sep  Aug  Jul  Jun  May  Apr Mar02
PSA    785  642  488  365  399  271  250  177x
CPR   15.5 11.3  7.7  5.0  4.7  2.6  2.3  1.4x
WAM    347  349  350  351  352  353  355  356
WAC   6.55 6.55 6.55 6.55 6.55 6.55 6.55 6.55
```

Figure 17.2 © 2003 Bloomberg L.P. All rights reserved. Reprinted with permission.

17.2.1 Market Quotes

We give hereafter the description of an MBS as it appears on a Bloomberg screen (Figures 17.1 and 17.2).

The Bloomberg identifying code of the MBS is FNR 2002-21 GD. It was issued by Fannie Mae in March 2002. It bears an annual interest coupon of 6% and matures on 04/25/32. It is a class GD bond, belonging to a sequential-pay class CMO issue, for which the different classes are fully paid off in order of priority. The class that is considered here has not been paid off at all for the time being. Indeed, its current outstanding amount is equal to $4,050,000,000 as of September 2002, which corresponds to 100% of the original principal balance. Its original weighted average life (WAL) is equal to 8.9 years for a prepayment rate assumption of 277% PSA (Public Securities Association). Cash flows are paid monthly, on the 25th day of each month.

The current outstanding amount of the underlying mortgage loan pool is equal to $4,757,782,196 as of July 2002; the original outstanding amount was equal to $5,000,000,000. The current weighted average coupon[3] rate of the underlying collateral pool amounts to 6.545%, which is, as expected, higher than the coupon rate of the CMO. The current weighted average remaining maturity[4] of

---

[3]The weighted average coupon of the loan pool is equal to the average coupon of all the loans in the pool, weighted by the principal balance of each loan.

[4]Same type of definition as for the weighted average coupon of a loan pool.

the loan pool is equal to 347 months (28 years and 11 months), its current weighted average age[5] to 10 months. At the bottom of the screen appears a history of PSA and constant prepayment rate (CPR), weighted average maturity and coupon of the loan pool.

17.2.2 Pricing of MBSs

The valuation of an MBS comes down to the valuation of a callable bond. From the two pricing methods that have been presented in Chapter 14, only one is valid, the Monte Carlo simulation method.[6] Indeed, MBSs are path-dependent securities, which means that their price is dependent on the past evolution of interest rates. Let us explain why. As we have seen in Section 17.1.3, the cash flows of an MBS are directly influenced by the level of prepayment rates. On a given month, this level is dependent on whether there have been refinancing opportunities in the past.[7] More precisely, a mortgage pool that has experienced refinancing opportunities in the past will have, other things being equal, lower refinancing rates than a pool that had no such experience. This phenomenon is due to the fact that refinancings change the composition of the pool, removing fast and capable refinancers from the pool at a faster rate than slow and less capable refinancers.[8] In other words, the pool will include a higher and higher proportion of slow refinancers over time, resulting in a decrease in the refinancing rate over time. As an illustration, let us have a look at the following example.

Example 17.4 We consider a pool of 100 mortgage loans with two categories of mortgagors: fast refinancers (50% of the pool) and slow refinancers (50% of the pool). The "fast" category has a refinancing rate equal to 70% per period, the "slow" one a refinancing rate of 30% per period.

At the end of the first period, the refinancing rate R_1 of the pool is equal to

$$R_1 = \frac{50 \times 70\% + 50 \times 30\%}{100} = 50\%$$

There remain 50 mortgages in the pool: 15 in the "fast" category and 35 in the "slow" category.

At the end of the second period, the refinancing rate R_2 of the pool is equal to

$$R_2 = \frac{15 \times 70\% + 35 \times 30\%}{50} = 42\%$$

and so on. The refinancing rate of the pool decreases gradually to the refinancing level of the "slow" category of the pool.

---

[5]Same type of definition as for the weighted average coupon of a loan pool.

[6]Actually, the nonrecombining binomial tree method works also, but not the recombining one.

[7]Refinancing opportunities depend on the level of interest rates. Broadly speaking, refinancings tend to increase (respectively, decrease) as the interest rate on new mortgage loans falls below (respectively, rises above) that on existing mortgage loans.

[8]This partition of borrowers into fast and slow refinancers corresponds to the fact that the likelihood of refinancing varies from one borrower to the other, because of differences in financial capability and knowledge as well as the opportunity to move in a near future, among other reasons.

Using the Monte Carlo simulation method, the valuation of an MBS is a five-step process:

- *[Step 1:]*   *simulation of interest-rate paths;*

- *[Step 2:]*   *simulation of prepayment rate paths based on a dynamic prepayment model;*

- *[Step 3:]*   *computation of the expected cash flows along each path;*

- *[Step 4:]*   *computation of the MBS price along each path;*

- *[Step 5:]*   *computation of the MBS price as the average of its prices along each path.*

As for bonds with embedded options, market practitioners often compute Option Adjusted Spreads (OAS) on mortgage-backed securities (MBSs).

From this discussion, it can be seen that the valuation of an MBS is fairly complex because of the prepayment feature. We provide hereafter a brief introduction to a few static prepayment models that are popular among practitioners, and we refer the reader to specialized literature for more sophisticated (dynamic) prepayment models.

- **The 12-year prepaid life model**   *This approach, based on historical data, assumes that a mortgage loan is fully prepaid at the end of its twelfth anniversary. It is seldom used because it is too simplistic, arbitrary and not dynamic.*

- **The constant prepayment rate (CPR) model**   *The prepayment rate is assumed to be constant. It is expressed on an annual basis and computed as follows. Let us consider a mortgage pool and denote by π the constant proportion of the outstanding mortgages that are prepaid within a month. $1 - \pi$ is the constant proportion of the outstanding mortgages that are still remaining after a month. After 1 year, the constant proportion of the outstanding mortgages that are still remaining is equal to $(1-\pi)^{12}$ or $1 - CPR$. Hence the CPR is equal to: $CPR = 1 - (1-\pi)^{12}$.*

- **The Federal Home Administration (FHA) experience-based model**   *It is based on the data collected by the Federal Home Administration, which are periodically updated. Prepayment rates are assumed to change with both the age and the default likelihood of the mortgage loans.*

- **The PSA experience-based model**   *This is the most commonly used model. It combines the information provided by the Federal Home Administration and the CPR method. It is based on the empirical observation that prepayment rates tend to be stable after 30 months. A mortgage is said to be 100% PSA when its initial annualized prepayment rate is 0.2% and increases linearly by 0.2% each month until reaching 6% at the end of the 30th month. In that case, the CPR for month n is equal to*

$$CPR_n = 6\% \times \min\left(1, \frac{n}{30}\right)$$

More generally, a mortgage is said to be $x\%$ PSA when it has an initial prepayment rate and increase equal to $x\%$ the 100% PSA. In that case, the CPR for month n is equal to

$$CPR_n = 6\% \times \min\left(1, \frac{n}{30}\right) \times \frac{x}{100}$$

When computing the expected cash flows of a mortgage loan, prepayment rate is applied to the end-of-month remaining principal balance.

We now present a simple static pricing framework.

Considering the PSA experience based model, let us compute the expected cash flows of a mortgage loan. The regular MPs in the absence of prepayment (scheduled MP) are denoted by MP, the remaining principal balance in the absence of prepayment at the end of month n by P_n, the expected cash flow on month n by $\mathbb{E}(CF_n)$ and the CPR on month n by CPR_n. First, let us convert the annualized prepayment rate on month n into a monthly prepayment rate π_n on month n.

$$CPR_n = 1 - (1 - \pi_n)^{12}$$

Hence,

$$\pi_n = 1 - (1 - CPR_n)^{\frac{1}{12}}$$

The expected cash flows are as follows:

$$\mathbb{E}(CF_1) = MP + \pi_1 \times P_1$$

$$\mathbb{E}(CF_2) = (1 - \pi_1) \times (MP + \pi_2 \times P_2)$$

$$\mathbb{E}(CF_3) = (1 - \pi_1) \times (1 - \pi_2) \times (MP + \pi_3 \times P_3)$$

More generally, on month n

$$\mathbb{E}(CF_n) = \prod_{k=1}^{n}(1 - \pi_k) \times (MP + \pi_n \times P_n)$$

Example 17.5 Considering our previous example in Section 17.1.2 and assuming a mortgage prepayment function of 100% PSA, we show below the expected cash flow table of the mortgage loan.

Month	Residual principal amount	Scheduled monthly payment	Monthly prepayment rate (%)	Scheduled and unscheduled monthly payments
0	1,000,000.00			
1	997,998.32	12,001.68	0.02	12,168.17
2	995,976.62	12,001.68	0.03	12,332.23
3	993,934.71	12,001.68	0.05	12,493.76
4	991,872.37	12,001.68	0.07	12,652.68
. . .	. . .	. . .	. . .	. . .
90	710,030.00	12,001.68	0.51	10,668.98
91	705,128.62	12,001.68	0.51	10,597.01
92	700,178.23	12,001.68	0.51	10,525.34
93	695,178.33	12,001.68	0.51	10,453.95
. . .	. . .	. . .	. . .	. . .
177	35,296.77	12,001.68	0.51	5,302.17
178	23,648.05	12,001.68	0.51	5,248.96
179	11,882.85	12,001.68	0.51	5,195.90
180	0.00	12,001.68	0.51	5,142.99

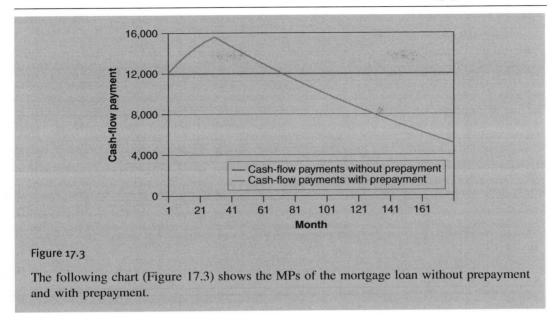

Figure 17.3

The following chart (Figure 17.3) shows the MPs of the mortgage loan without prepayment and with prepayment.

We consider a mortgage pass-through security that has the same characteristics as the above mortgage loan. Applying the PSA static prepayment function, it is easy to compute the price of that MBS. This price P is equal to

$$P = \sum_{k=1}^{6} \frac{\mathbb{E}(CF_k)}{\left(1 + \frac{r_k}{12} \times k\right)} + \sum_{k=7}^{n} \frac{\mathbb{E}(CF_k)}{\left(1 + \frac{r_k}{12} \times 6\right)^{\frac{k}{6}}}$$

where r_k denotes the zero-coupon rate with maturity k months, $\mathbb{E}(CF_k)$ the expected cash flow of the MBS on month k and n the maturity, expressed in months, of the MBS.

17.3   End of Chapter Summary

Mortgage-backed Securities (or MBSs) are securities that are backed by the cash flows of a mortgage or a pool of mortgages, which are loans secured by the collateral of some specified commercial or residential real estate property.

There exist three main types of MBS: Mortgage pass-throughs, Collateralized Mortgage Obligations and Stripped MBSs. Mortgage pass-throughs are the simplest form of MBSs; they represent shares of the underlying mortgage pool, which entitle the security holder to monthly cash flows generated by the pool on a pro-rata basis. Collateralized Mortgage Obligations (CMOs) differ from mortgage pass-throughs in that they are structured in maturity classes, called *tranches*. All principal payments (regular principal payments as well as prepayments) are allocated to the first tranche until it is fully paid off; then, it is the turn of the second tranche and so on. Hence, prepayment risk is redistributed among the different tranches, the first tranche absorbing prepayment first. Stripped MBSs are structured in two classes: an Interest Only class (IO) and a Principal Only class (PO). The IO class receives all interest payments, while the PO class receives all principal payments.

Stripped MBSs are highly sensitive to prepayment rates, and hence riskier than mortgage pass-throughs. The higher the prepayment rate on the mortgage pool, the faster POs are paid off, that is the higher the price of POs, and the lower the total cash flows received on IOs, that is the lower the price of IOs.

As MBSs are backed by mortgages, they are also subject to prepayment which potentially affects all mortgage loans, and especially residential mortgages. It designates any early principal payment made in excess of the regular amortization schedule. Prepayment can be triggered mainly by home sales, refinancings and defaults. For an investor, prepayment risk is a serious issue as prepayment tends to occur when interest rates go down, that is, at times when reinvestment opportunities in similar securities are not particularly attractive.

Projecting prepayment is critical for the analysis and valuation of an MBS. Pricing of MBS is performed using the Monte Carlo simulation method to generate interest-rate paths and prepayment rate paths. Because refinancings change the composition of the pool, removing fast and capable refinancers from the pool at a faster rate than slow and less capable refinancers, the pool will include a higher and higher proportion of slow refinancers over time, resulting in a decrease in the refinancing rate over time. This feature makes MBSs path-dependent securities, as their price is dependent on the past evolution of interest rates.

17.4 References and Further Reading

17.4.1 Books and Papers

Anderson, G.A., J.R. Barber, and C.H. Chang, 1993, "Prepayment Risk and the Duration of Default Free Mortgage Backed Securities", *Journal of Financial Research*, **16**(1), 1–9.

Arora, A., D.K. Heike, and R.K. Mattu, 2000, "Risk and Return in the Mortgage Market: Review and Outlook", *Journal of Fixed Income*, **10**(1), 5–18.

Breeden, D.T., 1991, "Risk, Return and Hedging of Fixed-Rate Mortgages", *Journal of Fixed Income*, **1**(2), 85–107.

Breeden, D.T., 1994, "Complexities of Hedging Mortgages", *Journal of Fixed Income*, **4**(3), 6–41.

Chaudhary, S., L.S. Hayre, and R. Young, 2000, "Anatomy of Prepayments", *Journal of Fixed Income*, **10**(1), 19–49.

Choudhry, M., 2001, *Bond Market Securities*, Prentice Hall, New York.

Fabozzi, F.J., (Editor), 2000, *The Handbook of Fixed Income Securities*, 6th Edition, McGraw-Hill, New York.

Fabozzi, F.J., (Editor), 2001, *Handbook of Mortgage Backed Securities*, 5th Edition, McGraw-Hill, New York.

Florent, I., and P. Priaulet, 2001, Focus on Interest Rates: Comparing the Approaches of Portfolio Managers and Option Writers, Quants, HSBC-CCF, No. 39.

Goodman, L.S., and J. Ho, 1997, "Mortgage Hedge Ratios: Which one Works Best?", *Journal of Fixed Income*, **7**(3), 23–34.

Hayre, L.S., 1994, "A Simple Statistical Framework for Modeling Burnout and Refinancing Behavior", *Journal of Fixed Income*, **4**(3), 69–74.

Hayre, L.S., and H. Chang, 1997, "Effective and Empirical Durations of Mortgage Securities", *Journal of Fixed Income*, **6**(4), 17–33.

Hayre, L.S., S. Chaudhary, and R. Young, 2000, *Anatomy of Prepayments: The Salomon Smith Barney Prepayment Model*, Salomon Smith Barney Mortgage Research.

Huang, C., S. Wong, D. Tang, and M. Liu, 1999, "Hong Kong Residential Mortgage Prepayment Analysis and Modeling", *Journal of Fixed Income*, **8**(4), 55–66.

Jegadeesh, N., and X. Ju, 2000, "A Non-Parametric Prepayment Model and Valuation of Mortgage-Backed Securities", *Journal of Fixed Income*, **10**(1), 50–67.

Kariya, T., and M. Kobayashi, 2000, "Pricing Mortgage-Backed Securities (MBS): A Model Describing the Burnout Effect", *Asia Pacific Financial Markets*, **7**, 189–204.

Kupiec, P., and A. Kah, 1999, "On the Origin and Interpretation of OAS", *Journal of Fixed Income*, **9**(3), 82–92.

Schwartz, E.S., and W.N. Torous, 1989, "Prepayment and the Valuation of Mortgage-Backed Securities", *Journal of Finance*, **44**, 375–392.

Stanton, R., 1995, "Rational Prepayment and the Valuation of Mortgage-Backed Securities", *Review of Financial Studies*, **8**, 677–708.

Wise, M.B., and V. Bhansali, 2001, *Universal Asymptotic Behavior of Mortgage Prepayments*, California Institute of Technology, CALT 68–2307, CA.

17.4.2 Websites

www.ginniemae.gov.

www.fanniemae.com/markets/mbssecurities.

www.freddiemac.com/mbs.

17.5 Problems

Exercise 17.1   What does debt securitization consist in?

Exercise 17.2   Consider an MBS collateralized by a pool of fixed-rate level-payment mortgages with the following characteristics:

- Weighted average maturity: 15 years
- Borrowed amount: $1 million
- Weighted average coupon: 10%

For the sake of simplicity, we assume that there is no servicing fee, that is, the interest-rate coupon of the MBS is equal to the weighted average coupon of the mortgage pool. Furthermore, the maturity of the MBS is supposed to be equal to the weighted average maturity of the mortgage pool.

1. Compute the constant monthly payment of the MBS.
2. Determine the amortization schedule of the MBS. Compute the value of the MBS assuming no prepayment and a flat yield curve at 9%.
3. Assuming a prepayment function equal to 150% PSA and again a flat yield curve at 9%, compute the value of the MBS. Draw on a chart the monthly payments of the MBS with and without prepayment.

Exercise 17.3   To what extent can an MBS be considered a callable bond?

Exercise 17.4   What are the three main types of MBSs? Describe each of them.

Exercise 17.5   What are the four main sources of prepayment on a residential mortgage?

Exercise 17.6   What are the differences between a commercial mortgage and a residential mortgage?

Exercise 17.7   1. Why are stripped MBSs riskier than mortgage pass-throughs?
    2. What is the effect of a prepayment increase on the price of a PO security and an IO security? Explain why.

Exercise 17.8   Why is a recombining binomial tree not appropriate for pricing an MBS?

Exercise 17.9   Explain why the maturity of a residential MBS is not a correct measure of its life. What is an appropriate measure?

Exercise 17.10   Why is it necessary to use a prepayment forecasting model when pricing an MBS?

Exercise 17.11   Why is the coupon interest rate of an MBS higher than that of the underlying mortgage pool?

18

Asset-Backed Securities

In this chapter, we provide the reader with an introduction to asset-backed securities (ABSs). We also present CAT bonds and CAT derivatives.

18.1 Description of ABSs

18.1.1 Definition

ABSs are securities exclusively collateralized by the cash flows of a package of financial assets. There basically exist two categories of collaterals: consumer financial assets and commercial financial assets. To the former belong, for example, automobile loans, recreational vehicle loans, boat loans, home equity loans, student loans and credit card receivables. The latter category contains among others computer leases, manufactured housing loans, small business administration loans, agricultural machinery loans and trade receivables. The three major collateral types are automobile loans, home equity loans and credit card receivables.

In comparison to typical corporate bonds, which hold a general claim on the business assets of a corporation, ABSs have the highest priority claim on a pool of specific assets, isolated by the issuer from the whole assets of the company. This gives ABSs their secured status.

Typically, a trust issues ABSs with different credit ratings. These credit ratings correspond to priority ranks in receiving cash flow payments from the trust in case of default. The ranks are referred to as *seniority classes*. An ABS may have two or more such classes. For instance, it may be structured in three classes: a senior class, rated AAA, a middle or "mezzanine" class, rated A and a subordinated class, rated BBB or BB. The higher-rated senior class holds the highest rank in priority to receive cash flow payments from the trust, whereas the lower-rated subordinated classes hold successively lower priority to receive cash flows.

18.1.2 Credit Enhancement

In order to provide bondholders with a protection against adverse credit events like defaults, the credit quality of ABSs is improved in comparison to that of the underlying loans or receivables through what is known as the *credit enhancement mechanism*. Credit enhancement can take several forms:

- *Excess spread protection* *The interest rate on the underlying assets is generally much higher than that of the ABSs. The difference between the two, adjusted for servicing fees, trust costs and default provisions, is equal to the excess spread. It is usually payable to the issuer. However, it can be distributed to bondholders in case losses are greater than provisioned.*

- *Subordination* *The ABS is structured in two portions: a senior tranche and a junior tranche, that is subordinated to the senior tranche. The senior tranche holds priority in receiving cash flow payments from the trust. In other words, in case of a cash flow shortfall from the collateral, the obligations of the senior tranche are the first ones to be honored. The junior tranche serves as a buffer that absorbs losses fully or partly until it is completely exhausted. This form of credit enhancement is widely used in the ABS market.*

- **Early amortization** *An early amortization of the collateral cash flows is triggered as soon as certain features of the collateral pool deteriorate to a predetermined threshold. The features that are most frequently taken into account are the yield level and the loss rate on the collateral portfolio. A decrease in the collateral portfolio's yield below a specified rate would reduce the money available for the coupon payments on the ABS. An increase in the collateral portfolio's loss rate above a specified rate would increase the credit risk of the ABS.*

- **Letter of credit** *Letters of credit, which are put up by highly rated banks, guarantee a specified amount of cash to the trust in case the collateral pool is affected by losses.*

- **Cash reserve account** *A cash reserve account is created, when the ABS is originated, to reimburse the trust for losses affecting the collateral pool up to the cash amount of the reserve account.*

- **Insurance** *A third-party insurance company agrees to reimburse the trust for losses on the collateral pool up to a stated amount of cash.*

- **Overcollateralization** *When the face amount of the collateral portfolio exceeds that of the ABS, the ABS is said to be overcollateralized. The excess cash flows generated by the larger collateral pool are available to absorb losses.*

18.1.3   Cash-Flow Structure

The cash-flow structure of an ABS is determined by the cash flow structure of its underlying collateral. There basically exist two categories of cash flows for a collateral:

- *Regular cash flows based on a precise amortization schedule until a stated maturity date; they are borne by installment loans such as automobile loans, recreational vehicle loans, home equity loans, manufactured housing loans and agricultural machinery loans.*

- *Irregular cash flows with neither a determined amortization schedule nor a precise maturity date; they are borne by revolving loans such as credit card receivables and trade receivables. These loans may be extended at any time.*

Consequently, the cash flows of installment loans are less uncertain than those of revolving loans. As is the case for mortgage loans, the uncertainty that affects the cash flows of either collateral category is due to prepayments, that is, early principal repayments made partially or fully out of an amortization schedule. For example, prepayments on automobile loans may come from the sale of the vehicle, requiring complete reimbursement of the loan, the loss or destruction of the vehicle, the full reimbursement of the loan with cash so as to save interest cost or a loan refinancing opportunity at a lower interest rate.

ABSs backed by installment loans are usually structured either as pass-through securities or multiclass securities. Let us take the example of ABSs backed by automobile loans. The pass-through structure is referred to as a *grantor trust*, while the multiclass structure is referred to as an *owner trust*.

Grantor trusts were the original ABS structures in the market. They simply reflect the cash flow structure of the underlying automobile loans, that is, they pay monthly over a period of 36 to 72 months. The cash flows (interest, scheduled principal repayment and prepayment) are distributed to all security holders at the same time, whatever the tranche they have invested in. The interest rate on the automobile loans exceeds the interest rate on the pass-through security, providing a protection against default. The average life of the pass-through security depends on the prepayment rate on the underlying loans. The faster the prepayment speed, the shorter the average life of the security.

Owner trusts are the most commonly used structures today. Like Collateralized Mortgage Obligations (CMOs), they were created to meet asset–liability management (ALM) needs. Indeed, from an ALM viewpoint, traditional grantor trusts are not particularly attractive since they equally expose all investors to prepayment risk. This risk is reduced by owner trusts through reallocating the cash flows from the underlying automobile loan pool to the different security classes ordered by maturity. There are typically a short-term money-market class, a 1-year class, a 2-year class and a 3-year class. The owner trust makes sequential cash-flow payments and repays investors in order of maturity. First, it usually pays interest to all classes. Then, it pays principal to each class in order of maturity. It distributes all principal payments to the money-market class until it is reimbursed, then makes the principal payments to the 1-year class until it is repaid and so on. Consequently, the prepayment risk of the collateral has been redistributed among the different classes of the ABS. The short-term money-market class absorbs prepayments first, then the 1-year class and so on. The result of this process is that the short-term money-market class is effectively a shorter-term security than the other classes, the last class having the longest maturity. Given the duration of their liability, institutional investors choose the most appropriate class to their needs. Note that in the event of a default on the collateral pool, the priority to receive cash flows is reestablished in seniority order.

ABSs backed by revolving loans are characterized by a so-called revolving period, during which they do not amortize principal. In other words, the principal repayment from the underlying collateral is not distributed to the security holders during the revolving period. It is instead retained by the trust and reinvested in additional revolving loans.

In what follows, we take the example of the famous credit card ABSs. Typically, credit cardholders are assigned a credit limit, up to which they can generally borrow cash. They may reimburse their debt fully or partly at any time, and can borrow additional cash as long as the total amount of their debt does not exceed the credit limit. Since cardholders can reimburse each month as much or as little principal as they want, provided it is higher than a small minimum payment, a credit card has no real maturity and the amount of principal on receivables may vary over time. Credit card ABSs can bear fixed or floating interest coupons, which they usually pay monthly, quarterly or semiannually. During the revolving period, they pay only interest; afterwards, the principal can be repaid according to either of the three following methods:

- **Controlled amortization**   *It consists in repaying the principal according to a stated amortization schedule. A usual controlled amortization schedule is made of 12 equal monthly payments. This implies a principal payment rate of $100/12 = 8.33\%$ per month. If the principal payment rate of the credit card pool is lower than 8.33%, the principal payment on the ABS is extended. If the principal payment rate of the pool is higher than 8.33%, repayments exceeding the amortization schedule are used to invest in new receivables. The controlled amortization feature ceases when an early amortization[1] event occurs, that is, an event that, if further repeated, may deteriorate*

---

[1] An early amortization event may be
- *the increase in the loss rate of the underlying collateral pool, which may generate losses for investors;*
- *the decrease in the yield on the underlying collateral pool, which may reduce the funds available to pay interests on the ABS.*

the credit of the ABSs and expose investors to losses. As soon as it is detected by the trust, such an event triggers immediate amortization of the ABS.

- **Soft bullet** *Soft bullet credit card ABSs distribute a single bullet principal payment on the last scheduled interest payment date. The revolving period is followed by an accumulation period, during which repayments from the credit card pool are stored in a principal funding account and reinvested in short-term highly rated instruments, rather than in new receivables. Usually, the accumulation period amounts to 12 months. So, the principal payment rate needed to avoid an extension of the principal payment is equal to 100/12 = 8.33%. Soft bullet credit card ABSs are subject to early amortization events.*

- **Unscheduled amortization** *A credit card ABS with unscheduled amortization repays principal after the revolving period as repayments from the credit card pool are made, until it is retired.*

18.2 Market Quotes and Pricing

ABSs are traded in a highly active secondary market. Like Mortgage-Backed Securities (MBSs), they are quoted in yield spread over the Treasury-bond yield curve or the swap yield curve, using the weighted average life (WAL) measure. The bid/ask spread generally varies between 2 and 15 bps. The liquidity of ABSs is considered as good as that of investment-grade corporate bonds.

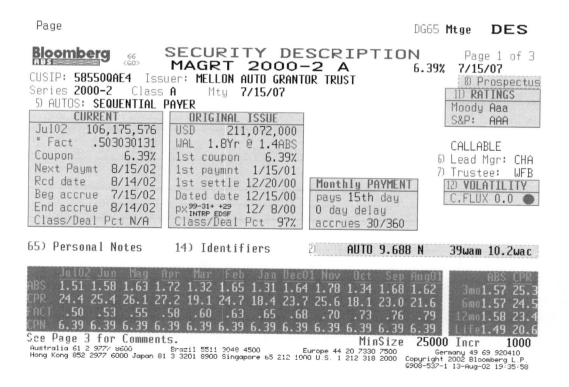

Figure 18.1 © 2003 Bloomberg L.P. All rights reserved. Reprinted with permission.

Page   DG65 Mtge   **DES**

Bloomberg   DEAL DESCRIPTION   Page 2 of 3
ABS   MAGRT 2000-2   last 7/ 1/02
              Issuer: MELLON AUTO GRANTOR TRUST   8) Prospectus
Series **2000-2**   Aggregate: AUTO 9.69 N

DEAL - CURRENT			DEAL - ORIGINAL			Jul02	ABS-DEAL-CPR		AUTO 9.5 N	
Jul02		109,459,874	USD		217,601,029	1mo	1.51	24.4	–	–
Net		9.688%	Net		9.649%	3mo	1.57	25.3	–	–
WAC		10.188%	WAC		10.149%	6mo	1.57	24.5	–	–
WAM	3:3	39 mo	WAM	4:8	56 mo	12mo	1.58	23.4	–	–
AGE	2:0	24 mo	AGE	0:5	5 mo	Life	1.49	20.6	–	–
Next Paymt		8/15/02	1st paymt		1/15/01					
Rcd date		8/14/02	1st settle		12/20/00	Monthly PAYMENT				
B.Median		PSA	px1.40 ABS		12/ 8/00	pays 15th day				
PAC	0% SUP	0%	PAC	0% SUP	0%	0 day delay			6) Lead Mgr:	CHA
Beg Accrue		7/15/02	Dated		12/15/00	accrues 30/360			7) Trustee:	WFB

	Jul02	Jun	May	Apr	Mar	Feb	Jan	Dec01	Nov	Oct	Sep	Aug01
ABS	1.51	1.58	1.63	1.72	1.32	1.65	1.31	1.64	1.78	1.34	1.68	1.62
CPR	24.4	25.4	26.1	27.2	19.1	24.7	18.4	23.7	25.6	18.1	23.0	21.6
WAM	39	40	41	42	43	44	44	45	46	47	48	49
WAC	10.2	10.2	10.2	10.2	10.2	10.2	10.2	10.2	10.2	10.2	10.2	10.2

See Page 3 For Comments.
Australia 61 2 9777 8600   Brazil 5511 3048 4500   Europe 44 20 7330 7500   Germany 49 69 920410
Hong Kong 852 2977 6000 Japan 81 3 3201 8900 Singapore 65 212 1000 U.S. 1 212 318 2000 Copyright 2002 Bloomberg L.P.
                                                                        G908-537-1 13-Aug-02 19:36:59

Figure 18.2   © 2003 Bloomberg L.P. All rights reserved. Reprinted with permission.

We give hereafter the description of an automobile ABS as it appears on a Bloomberg screen (Figures 18.1, 18.2, and 18.3).

The Bloomberg identifying code of the ABS is MAGRT 2000-2 A. It bears an annual interest coupon of 6.39% and matures on 07/15/07. It has been issued by the Mellon Auto Grantor Trust in December 2000. It is a class A bond belonging to a sequential-pay class ABS issue. As such, it has the shortest maturity of the issue and is entitled to receive all principal payments (coming from scheduled amortization and prepayments) until it is fully paid off, before all other classes. Its current outstanding amount is equal to $106,175,576 as of July 2002, which corresponds to 50.3% of the original principal amount ($211,072,000). Its original weighted average life is equal to 1.8 years for an absolute prepayment rate[2] assumption of 1.4%. It is rated AAA by S&P and Moody's. Cash flows are paid monthly, on the 15th day of each month. The ABS trustee is Wells Fargo Bank. At the bottom of the screen appears a history of absolute and conditional prepayment rates,[3] factor rates[4] and coupon level. The ABS was originally quoted 29 bps over the Treasury yield curve.

---

[2]The absolute prepayment rate measures the monthly rate of loan prepayments as a percentage of the original pool size.
[3]The conditional prepayment rate measures the annualized monthly rate of loan prepayments as a percentage of the current pool size.
[4]The factor rate represents the percentage of the original principal amount still outstanding.

Fixed Income Securities

Page   DG65 Mtge   **DES**

Bloomberg   COMMENTS: MAGRT 2000-2   Page 3 of 3
ABS

CALL FEATURE: 10% Deal Cleanup.
CO-MANAGER: Mellon Financial Markets,LLC.
SERVICER: Mellon Bank, N.A.
CREDIT ENHANCEMENTS: Reserve Account, Excess Spread, Subordination.
ORIGINAL COLLATERAL CHARACTERISTICS:
 TYPE: Retail installment sale contracts.
 NEW VEHICLES: 53%
 GEO DIST (>5%): PA 73.0%; NJ 12.1%; DE 9.2%.

Australia 61 2 9777 8600   Brazil 5511 3048 4500   Europe 44 20 7330 7500   Germany 49 69 920410
Hong Kong 852 2977 6000 Japan 81 3 3201 8900 Singapore 65 212 1000 U.S. 1 212 318 2000 Copyright 2002 Bloomberg L.P.
G908-537-1 13-Aug-02 19:37:18

Figure 18.3 © 2003 Bloomberg L.P. All rights reserved. Reprinted with permission.

The current outstanding amount of the underlying automobile loan pool is equal to $109,459,874 as of July 2002; the original outstanding amount was equal to $217,601,029. The current weighted average coupon[5] of the pool amounts to 10.188%. Its current weighted average remaining maturity[6] is equal to 39 months (3.25 years), its current weighted average age[7] to 24 months (2 years). At the bottom of the screen appears a history of absolute and conditional prepayment rates, weighted average maturity and coupon of the loan pool.

Three types of credit enhancement have been combined in the structure: cash reserve account, excess spread protection and subordination.

The valuation of ABSs is very similar to that of MBSs, except that they are far less exposed to prepayment risk than MBSs.

18.3 CAT Bonds and CAT Derivatives

A last class of somewhat related instruments are catastrophe bonds. For reasons detailed below, securitization has also been developed to help solve the mismatch between the size of annual

---

[5] See definition in Chapter 17.
[6] See definition in Chapter 17.
[7] See definition in Chapter 17.

insurance premia and the much larger size of catastrophe losses. These alternative sources of funds allow insurance and reinsurance companies to rely upon additional capital to back up ever-increasing commitments. Instruments such as *catastrophe bonds* (also known as *CAT bonds* or *Act of God* bonds), as well as various forms of catastrophe-based futures and options, have recently been offered at the Chicago Board of Trade (CBOT) and the Bermuda Commodities Exchange.

Because of the inability of reinsurance to provide fully efficient risk transfer of catastrophe risk, it has been suggested that capital markets could provide some more capital to the catastrophe insurance business. Consequently, a variety of catastrophe-related financial instruments have been recently introduced. They can roughly be divided into two categories: (1) insurer-specific catastrophe bonds and (2) index-linked catastrophe derivatives. An important difference between these two types of contracts is that index-linked derivatives typically pay off on an industry-wide loss index based on a variety of possible catastrophic events, while the payoff on CAT bond is based upon insurer-specific and usually event-specific loss experience. The fact that CAT derivatives are based upon an aggregated index, capturing events occurring in more than one area, makes these assets relatively inconvenient to work with for pricing and hedging purposes. Since the loss pattern on a given contract or portfolio of contracts is imperfectly correlated to the loss pattern on the index, these instruments involve, in particular, a significant amount of *cross-hedge* risk.

Catastrophe bonds are actually corporate bonds with a special language that requires the bond-holders to forgive or defer some or all payments of interest or principal if actual catastrophe losses surpass a specified amount, or trigger. When that happens, an insurer or reinsurer who issued catastrophe bonds can pay claims with the funds that would otherwise have gone to the bondholders. And, to the extent that bondholders forgive repayment of principal, the insurer or reinsurer can write down its liability for the bonds, boosting surplus and potentially staving off insolvency.

At least 10 insurers have used catastrophe bonds to obtain protection against losses caused by hurricanes, earthquakes or other perils. For example, in 1997, a special-purpose reinsurer, Residential Re, sold $477 million in catastrophe bonds and used the proceeds to provide reinsurance protection to the United Services Automobile Association (USAA). The same year, another special-purpose reinsurer, SR Earthquake Fund, Ltd., issued $137 million in catastrophe bonds and provided reinsurance for California earthquake losses to the Swiss Reinsurance Company. In 1998, the special-purpose reinsurer Trinity Re, Ltd., issued $83.6 million in catastrophe bonds and sold reinsurance to Centre Solutions (Bermuda) Ltd. Later that year, Residential Re sold another $450 million in catastrophe bonds and again used the proceeds to provide reinsurance to USAA.

The insurance industry defines a catastrophe as "an event that causes in excess of $5 million in insured property damage and affects a significant number of insured and insurers." Natural hazards that are potential candidates for triggering catastrophic losses cover a large spectrum including earthquakes, floods and hurricanes. Catastrophe insurance has recently attracted much attention because of a dramatic increase in the severity and frequency of losses. In the 9 years and 10 months from January 1989 to October 1998, the US property/casualty industry suffered an

Table 18.1   Costliest Insurance Losses from 1970 to 1998.

Disaster	Year	Country	Victims	Losses
Hurricane Andrew	1992	US	38	18.6
Northridge earthquake	1994	US	60	13.8
Typhoon Mireille	1991	Japan	51	6.7
Hurricane Diara	1990	Europe	95	5.7
Hurricane Hugo	1989	US, Porto Rico	61	5.5
Autumn storm	1987	Europe	19	4.3
Hurricane Vivian	1990	Europe	64	4.0
Hurricane Georges	1998	US, Caribbean	600	3.5
Piper Alpha oil rig	1988	UK	167	2.8
Kobe earthquake	1995	Japan	6,000	2.6

inflation-adjusted $98 billion in catastrophe losses, that is, 101.2% more than the inflation-adjusted $48.7 billion in catastrophe losses during the 39 years from January 1949 to December 1988 (ISO, 1999)![8] Partly responsible for this is the 1992 hurricane Andrew, which caused $15 billion in insured losses, the largest ever single-event loss, a number that would have been much higher if Andrew had hit Miami. A few years later, in 1994, the Northridge earthquake, with $12.5 billion in insured losses, had also forced some insurers into insolvency and seriously impaired the financial health of others. Other recent severe catastrophes are listed in Table 18.1 [borrowed from Swiss Re Sigma (1999)[9]], with insured losses expressed in billion dollars.[10] To this list, the recent hurricane Floyd (September 1999) shall be added, for which loss estimates are not yet available.[11]

While the origins of such increase in catastrophe risk are not fully understood and are still objects of debate,[12] it is clear that private insurers and reinsurers have experienced major difficulties in providing coverage for catastrophe losses. In particular, the reinsurance industry's international capital capacity severely limits the amount of risk that can be internationally diversified. For example, the reinsurance brokerage firm Guy Carpenter estimates that the capacity of the reinsurance market to reinsure any one primary insurer was about $500 million in 1997 and 1998. This is the main reason securitization has been developed to help solve the mismatch between the size of a potential catastrophe and the size of the reinsurance industry.

---

[8] Insurance Services Office, 1999, "Financing catastrophe risk: capital market solutions," ISO publication.

[9] Swiss Re, sigma publication, 1999, "Natural catastrophes and man-made disasters 1998: storms, hail and ice cause billion-dollar losses."

[10] These numbers are the amount of *insured loss*, which is of course different from the *total loss*. For example, for the 1995 Kobe earthquake, the cost of insured loss was roughly $1 billion, while the cost of uninsured repairs was estimated at $100 billion.

[11] In 1992, when hurricanes Andrew and Iniki struck, a record 63 property/casualty insurers became insolvent. Fifteen of those insolvencies were directly attributable to the losses that these storms caused in Florida, Louisiana and Hawaii. In the 9 years and 10 months from January 1989 to October 1998, the US property/casualty industry suffered an inflation-adjusted $98.0 billion in catastrophe losses, 101.2% more than the inflation-adjusted $48.7 billion in catastrophe losses during the 39 years from January 1950 to December 1988.

[12] An obvious factor is the increase in insurance coverage in most countries. Global warming is also often blamed for the increasing number of hurricanes and floods. Given the low frequency of the events, it is, however, extremely difficult to test this claim against the null hypothesis of a pure random climatic variability.

18.4 End of Chapter Summary

ABSs are securities exclusively collateralized by the cash flows of a package of financial assets. There basically exist two categories of collaterals: consumer financial assets (e.g., automobile loans, recreational vehicle loans, boat loans, home equity loans, student loans and credit card receivables) and commercial financial assets (e.g., computer leases, manufactured housing loans, small business administration loans, agricultural machinery loans and trade receivables).

In comparison to typical corporate bonds, ABSs have the highest priority claim on a pool of specific assets, isolated by the issuer from the whole assets of the company. This gives ABSs their secured status. Typically, a trust issues ABSs with different credit ratings. These credit ratings correspond to priority ranks, referred to as *seniority classes*, in receiving cash flow payments from the trust in case of default.

In order to provide bondholders with a protection against adverse credit events like defaults, the credit quality of ABSs is improved in comparison to that of the underlying loans or receivables through what is known as the *credit enhancement mechanism*. The cash flow structure of an ABS is determined by the cash flow structure of its underlying collateral, which can be regular or irregular cash flows.

ABSs are traded in a highly active secondary market. Like MBSs, they are quoted in yield spread over the Treasury-bond yield curve or the swap yield curve, using the weighted average life (WAL) measure. The bid/ask spread generally varies between 2 and 15 bps. The liquidity of ABSs is considered as good as that of investment-grade corporate bonds.

The valuation of ABSs is very similar to that of MBSs, except that they are far less exposed to prepayment risk than MBSs.

A last class of somewhat related instruments are catastrophe bonds. Because of the inability of reinsurance to provide fully efficient risk transfer of catastrophe risk, securitization has been developed to help solve the mismatch between the size of annual insurance premia and the much larger size of catastrophe losses. Instruments such as *catastrophe bonds*, as well as various forms of catastrophe-based futures and options, have recently been introduced at the Chicago Board of Trade and the Bermuda Commodities Exchange.

18.5 References and Further Reading

Fabozzi, F.J., (Editor), 2000, *The Handbook of Fixed Income Securities*, 6th Edition, McGraw-Hill, New York.

Ganapati, S., and B. Starr, 1997, *Student Loan ABS*, Lehman Brothers.

Jablansky, P., 1997, *The Student Loan ABS Market: Programs, Players and Valuation*, Salomon Smith Barney Mortgage Research.

Kane, M.E., and P. Dimartino, 2001, "*A Primer on Autos and Credit Cards*", Salomon Smith Barney Mortgage Research.

Lehman Brothers Document, 1994, *Introduction to Asset-Backed Securities*, Lehman Brothers.

18.6 Problems

Exercise 18.1   Show that ABSs can be categorized in two different ways.

Exercise 18.2   What is credit enhancement?

Exercise 18.3   What is the counterpart of a mortgage pass-through for an ABS? of a CMO?

Exercise 18.4   Why is prepayment risk lower on an automobile loan than on a mortgage loan?

Exercise 18.5   What are the three most frequent types of ABSs?

Exercise 18.6   What is the most suitable form of ABS for asset–liability management purposes? Explain why.

Exercise 18.7   To what extent are the cash flows of a credit card receivable more uncertain than those of an automobile loan?

Exercise 18.8   What is a sequential-pay ABS class?

Exercise 18.9   Explain why the issuer of an ABS must be independent from the seller of the underlying assets from a legal perspective.

Exercise 18.10   Recall the definition of a catastrophe bond. Elaborate on the similarities with defaultable bonds. Do you expect to be able to apply pricing formulas for defaultable bonds to the case of catastrophe bonds?

Subject Index

Author Index

Printed and bound by CPI Group (UK) Ltd, Croydon, CR0 4YY